History of the

4th (British) Infantry

Division

1914-1919

G P KINGSTON

The London Press

London British Library Cataloguing in Publication Data:

Kingston, G. P.
History of the 4th (British) Infantry Division, 1914-1919
1. Great Britain. Army. Infantry Division, 4th - History
2. World War, 1914-1918 - Regimental histories
3. World War, 1914-1918 - Campaigns - Great Britain
I.Title
940.4'1241
ISBN-10: 1905006152

Plate 1
*Lieutenant-General Thomas D'Oyly Snow who, as a Major-General was the Com-
mander of the 4th Division upon its' departure for France on the 22nd August, 1914.*

Dedication

To those who fought, never to return.
To those who fought and returned without hope.
To the families of those who fought.

Table of Contents

Acknowledgments

I owe a debt of gratitude to:

The staff of the National Archives, Kew, for their unfailingly friendly and professional support. The details catalogued in this history have been drawn largely from the Division, Brigade and Battalion diaries held by that fine establishment.

Mr. Richard Snow, grandson of Lieutenant-General Snow, General Officer Commanding the 4th Division when it first travelled to France, for his kind consent to contribute the introduction, which has added the personal touch.

Mr. Peter Snow, brother of Richard and grandson of Lieutenant-General Snow, for his kind consent to use the portrait of Lieutenant-General Snow as the introductory plate.

Mr. Lloyd Clarke, MA, Senior Historian at the Royal Military Academy, Sandhurst, who acted as the catalyst in my decision to undertake the writing of this history. I am eternally grateful for his time in escorting me over the battlefields of France and Belgium.

Dr. P. J. Thwaites, MA, MSc, DMS, AMA, MCMI, Curator at the Royal Military Academy, Sandhurst, for his permission to use maps and diagrams from the archive and his friendly and professional approach in smoothing the way through some rather difficult problems.

Mr. Andrew Orgill, Senior Librarian, Central Library, the Royal Military Academy, Sandhurst, for making available the extensive resources of the Academy Library.

My wife, Lesley, who encouraged me when I was little inclined to concentrate, supplied her computing experience in printing drafts and editing. She offered suggestions and corrections to my rather 'unique' keyboard skills, undertook the editing of the graphics contained herein and accompanied me over many miles through the scenes of battle. Thanks Les.

The Commonwealth War Graves Commission, for its kind permission to quote details of deaths and burials from the CWGC web site.
Mrs. J. Elkington for her kind permission to reproduce details of Lieutenant-Colonel Elkington from the Elkington Family website.

Foreword

The participation of so many of the Allied nations in the Great War was largely in consequence of the 1839 Treaty of London between Great Britain, Austria, Prussia, Russia, and France, which guaranteed the freedom of the recently formed sovereign state of Belgium. Additional to that rather extensive agreement the equally loose Franco-British Entente Cordiale of 1904, whilst not obliging Britain or France to a binding alliance, acted as a catalyst in the combined military efforts of both nations against the common foe. On the 2nd August 1914, Germany declared war on France and its' armies immediately crossed the Belgian border en-route to French territory. Under the terms of the Treaty of London, Britain issued an ultimatum to Germany and, as no response was received by the prescribed time, Britain declared war on Germany at 11:00pm on the 4th August 1914. So began the trial that was to engulf much of the world for the ensuing four and a half years.

Following Britain's declaration of war on Germany, there existed an urgency to get the British army to the Western Front. Without affecting her ability to defend herself at home, Britain possessed six infantry divisions on which she could call but responded initially by sending four of those formations at the shortest possible notice. The 1st and 2nd Divisions constituted I Corps while the 3rd and 5th Divisions formed II Corps, all of which was accompanied by the Cavalry Division and the independent 19th Infantry Brigade. The British Expeditionary Force, as it was then known, landed in France and made its way to Belgium to assist the Belgian and French Armies. Having deployed in the area between Binche and Tournai, it was followed a week later, by the 4th Infantry Division, having landed on French soil in the early hours of the 23rd August 1914. Those divisions, with the later addition of the 6th Infantry Division, were to become the famous 'Old Contemptibles'.

Since the end of that conflict, the histories of many divisions that served in the Great War, have been written, each cataloguing the events in which the lives of millions of young men were interrupted by the greatest conflict the civilised world had seen. Of the 'Old Contemptible' divisions, the histories of the 2nd, 3rd and 5th Divisions were written between 1918 and 1939. Of the total seventy-nine British division, there remains the history of some forty or more yet to be documented. Consequently, it is without doubt that a large gap remains in the library of knowledge of one of Britain's greatest trials in military and civil history. The history of the 4th Infantry Division is an attempt to contribute to the filling of that gap and, of all of the 'Old Contemptible' divisions, there now only remain the histories of the 1ˢᵗ Infantry and 1ˢᵗ Cavalry Divisions yet to be completed. It is hoped that publication of those will be achieved in the near future.

In recent decades, interest in the Great War has increased and witnessed the contribution of some excellent writings based on the wisdom of hindsight and the availability of the many original records. In committing to pen the history of the 4ᵗʰ Division, so long after the cessation of hostilities, the author has relied on those extensive collections, which exist in the safekeeping of the Public Records Office, Imperial War Museum, Royal Military Academy, Sandhurst, and the various Regimental Museums. Unit diaries, official histories, maps, and personal diaries have all been drawn upon. In using these sources, particularly the primary sources, an effort has been made to use the words of the contemporary authors as regularly as possible in an effort to embody the views of the participants.

When reading the diaries and translating the pencil lines drawn on maps, many written ninety years ago, there is a sense of urgency, yet they demonstrate the formal, organised thinking of the diarist and planners. The diaries of the 4ᵗʰ Division exist almost complete and, when read in date order, transmit the moods and feelings of the day quite clearly and never fail to take the reader into the emotions of the time. To assure accuracy, direct quotes have been used as regularly as possible. Where conflicting statements were found within the diaries, the author has used discretion as to the accuracy of each but has endeavoured to impart the salient points of both views. Sadly, few of the original campaigners remain and the memory of those who returned, after so many years, cannot be relied upon for the accuracy that this record demands.

The 4ᵗʰ Division was one of the regular army divisions then in service and began mobilisation on the 4ᵗʰ August 1914, fought throughout, and undertook demobilisation in 1919, when it passed out of one of the most difficult and controversial periods of world history. Such were the losses in the period between the commencement of the Battle of Mons on the 22ⁿᵈ August 1914 and the conclusion of the Second Battle of Ypres on the 27ᵗʰ May 1915, the British divisions mentioned above virtually ceased to exist as the British Regular Army.

I desire that this history should also stand as testimony to the sacrifices made by the families of those men, where many were to lose sons, fathers and brothers and to those who returned with lifetime injuries and sufferings that only they knew. The maps embodied in this volume are an attempt to translate, visually, the topography and difficulties through which those men fought and should be consulted in conjunction with the description of events as they occurred. Only then can we appreciate the contribution made by those who participated.

In writing this history, the process of a division growing from a young and inexperienced formation to a thoroughly professional fighting force is examined. From the early days after landing in France, where it participated in the retreat from Mons, the division entered combat with its' three infantry brigades and only part of its' artillery strength. From the moment of initial engagement, with no signals, field ambulances, or engineers, to the last great battles of November 1918, which finished in 1918 almost exactly where it had started in 1914. The division grew in skill and achievement to become one of the great stories of human achievement. Whilst the history focuses on the activities of the 4th Division the reader should be aware of the larger environment represented by Western Front.

Introduction

By
Richard Snow
Grandson of Lieutenant-General T. D'O. Snow

I was delighted when the author contacted me about writing an introduction to this book. My grandfather, Lieutenant–General Sir Thomas D'Oyly Snow, was the General Officer Commanding the 4th Division from 1911 to 1914, a crucial time in its history, and so led it to war. His career was interspersed with some of the most recognised military actions undertaken by the British Army in modern times, and it is fitting that the author has chosen to write the history of the 4th Division during the period of his command and for the subsequent period thereafter.

General Snow was born in Newton Valence, Hampshire, on the 5th May 1858 and was educated at Eton and Cambridge. Upon graduation, he enlisted in the 1st Battalion, 13th Regiment of Foot (Prince Albert's Somerset Light Infantry) as a 2nd Lieutenant and joined the battalion in Zululand in 1879 as a part of the British Relief Force where he participated in the deciding actions against the Zulu nation. In 1884-85, he was an officer in the Egyptian Expedition, which engaged in the unsuccessful effort to relieve Khartoum, in the Sudan, and save General Gordon. During that campaign he fought at Abu Klea and El Gubat, where he was seriously wounded. In 1885, he was promoted to the rank of Captain, followed in 1887 by the appointment to the position of Adjutant of the 1st Battalion, Somerset Light Infantry, while based at Colchester.

In 1893, after serving with the 1st Battalion on Gibraltar, where he transferred to the 2nd Battalion, which was returning from Egypt, and attended the Staff College, Sandhurst, as a student. Upon graduation, he was posted to the Headquarters Staff of the Somerset Light Infantry. On the 1st May 1897, he was promoted to the rank of Major and transferred to the staff of the Inniskilling Fusiliers in Omagh, Ireland. By July 1898, he was a Brigade-Major on the staff of the Egypt Expeditionary Force, under General Kitchener, during which he fought at Athara, on the way to Khartoum. Following the Egyptian Expedition, he was promoted, in November 1898, to the rank of Lieutenant Colonel of the Royal Inniskilling Fusiliers.

From 1910-11, he commanded the 11th Infantry Brigade, 4th Division, with the rank of Brigadier-General and then assumed full command, as

Major General, of the 4th Division from late 1911 to September 1914. It was under his command that the division went France, fought its first battle at Le Cateau, undertook the retreat from Mons, and participated in the advance of September 1914 over the river Marne. It was during the crossing of the Marne that Major-General Snow suffered a serious pelvic injury after being thrown from his horse. Following his recovery, he assumed command of the 27th Division in November of 1914, a command he retained until June 1915, and during which he was awarded the KCB. He led the 27th Division in some of the most violent fighting in the Second Battle of Ypres during April and May 1915 during which gas was introduced as an offensive weapon.

Following his departure from the 27th Division, he assumed command of VII Corps and was responsible for the attack on the northern end of the British line in the 1st July 1916 offensive, in front of Gommecourt. The VII Corps also participated in the Battle of Arras in April 1917 and the German counter attack at Cambrai in December 1917. It was during the tumultuous times of late 1917 that he received the KCMG for service rendered to the nation. He was promoted to Lieutenant General and assumed command of Western Command in the United Kingdom. From 1919–29 he held the post of Colonel of the Somerset Light Infantry regiment.

During the war, Lieutenant-General Snow was affectionately known by two nicknames – 'slush' and the more familiar 'snowball', much favoured by his friend, Sir Henry Wilson. Like many wartime leaders, he was the subject of considerable criticism, some of which may not be justified. However, as the commander of troops during some of the largest and most intense battles of the Great War, criticism was unavoidable. He died on the 30th August 1940, during a later world crisis, and was buried in the Brookwood Cemetery, Surrey, in the United Kingdom. He played a major role in the history of the 4th Division until September 1914, as described in the early part of this book.

I am sure you will enjoy reading of a fascinating and history-making time.

Richard Snow.

Composition of the Division

(As at departure for France 22nd August 1914)

Division Troops

General Officer Commanding
G.O.C., Division Artillery
O.C. Division Engineers
"B" Squadron, 19th Hussars
Division Cyclist Company
14th Brigade, Royal Field Artillery
29th Brigade, Royal Field Artillery
32nd Brigade, Royal Field Artillery
37th Brigade, Royal Field Artillery
Division Ammunition Column
7th Field Company
9th Field Company
1/1st West Lancashire Field Company
Division Signal Company
10th Field Ambulance
12th Field Ambulance
11th Field Ambulance
Mobile Veterinary Section
Division Train (18th, 25th, 32nd, 38[th]Coy, ASC)

10th Brigade

2nd Royal Dublin Fusiliers
1st Royal Irish Fusiliers
2nd Seaforth Highlanders Regiment
1st Royal Warwickshire Regiment

11th Brigade

1st Hampshire Regiment
1st Rifle Brigade
1st East Lancashire Regiment
1st Somerset Light Infantry

12th Brigade

2nd Essex Regiment
2nd Royal Inniskilling Fusiliers
1st King's Own Royal Lancaster Regiment
2nd Lancashire Fusiliers

Officers List (August – 1914)

General Headquarters

G.O.C.	Maj. General T. D'O. Snow, C.B.
G.S.O.I	Col. J. E. Edwards, C.B.
G.S.O.II	Lt.-Colonel A. A. Montgomery
G.S.O.III	Capt. E. T. Humphreys

Adjutant & Quartermaster-General s Branch

A. Adj. & Q.M.G.	Lt.-Colonel F. P. S. Taylor
D.A. Adj. & Q.M.G.	Capt. B. F. Burnett-Hitchcock
D.A.Q.M.G.	Capt. H. J. Elles

Administrative Services and Departments

A.D.M.S	Col. C. E. Faunce
D.A.D.M.S	Major H. Ensor, D.S.O.
A.D.V.S	Major R. H. Holmes
D.A.D.O.S.	Major O.B. Harter
Field Cashier	Major C. V. Isacke

Special Appointment

A.P.M.	Lt. F. A. Atchison

H.Q. Division Artillery

D.A. Commander	Brig.-General G. F. Milne, C.B., D.S.O.
Brigade-Major	Capt. E. H. G. Leggett
Staff Captain	Capt. C. A. L. Graham

H.Q. Division Engineers

Commander	Lt.-Colonel H. B. Jones
Adjutant	Capt. W.G.S. Dobbie

H.Q. 10th Brigade

Commander	Brig.-General J.A.L. Haldane, C.B., D.S.O
Brigade-Major	Major A. A. H. Wilson
Staff Captain	Capt. T. H. C. Frankland

H.Q. 11th Brigade

Commander	Brig.-General A.G. Hunter-Weston, C.B., D.S.O.
Brigade-Major	Capt. G.F. Boyd, D.S.O
Staff Captain	Capt. W. H. M. Freestun

H.Q. 12th Brigade

Commander	Brig.-General H.F.M. Wilson, C.B.
Brigade-Major	Capt. C. M. Davies
Staff Captain	Capt. O.H. North

1914 - Home by Christmas

August - 1914

At 11:00pm on the 4th August 1914, the probability of war turned to certainty as the British Prime Minister announced the declaration of war on Germany. Instructions to mobilize had been distributed before the declaration was published and, accordingly, 4th Division Headquarters received the order to mobilize at 7:00pm on that day, some four hours before the official declaration. At the moment of receipt of those orders, the various units of the 4th Division, then a part of Eastern Command, were located in towns either side of the Thames Estuary, guarding the eastward approaches to London, being distributed thus:

Woolwich:
Division HQ with the Headquarters of the Artillery and the Engineers.
4th Signals Company (HQ and No.1 Section)
One battery of the 32nd Brigade R.F.A. with Brigade HQ.
9th Field Company
37th Howitzer Brigade R.F.A.
31st Heavy Battery and ammunition Column.

West Croydon:
HQ and HQ Company, 4th Division Train.

Shorncliffe:
7th Field Company R.E.
29th Brigade R.F.A (less one battery)
No.2 Section, Division Ammunition Column.
Part of the four battalions of the 10th Brigade (about 600 men).

Gravesend:
Part of the Royal Dublin Fusiliers, 10th Brigade (about 300 men).

Warley:
No.3 Company, Division Train.

Dover:
Part of the four battalions of the 12th Brigade (about 800 men).
No.4 Company, Division Train.
Maidstone:
10th Field Ambulance.

Colchester:
11th Brigade.
4th Brigade R.F.A.
One section of the 4th Division Ammunition Column.
11th Field Ambulance.

Hounslow:
"B" Squadron, 19th Hussars.

Although there had existed a previous expectation of war and basic preparations had been made, some troops were on leave and events focused very much upon the calling of all officers and men to their units and equipping them for immediate service.

The following five days were spent in an emotionally charged atmosphere, promulgating orders to brigade and battalion headquarters, the issuing of weapons and ammunition, and receiving supplies. At 7:17pm on the 7th August Colonel A. Elles, General Staff, Eastern Command, placed a telephone call to the G.O.C. 4th Division, Major-General Snow, instructing him to prepare the division for movement to defensive stations and confirmed those instructions in writing that same day.

The mobilisation orders included instructions that the division was a part of the home defence scheme and was responsible for the East Coast of England, under the command of Eastern Command. *"In confirmation of my telephone message 7:17pm, 7th August, under instructions from the war Office, you are to make the following arrangements forthwith: -11th Brigade)*

1st Brigade R.F.A.)
20th Hussars) To be held ready at Colchester to meet any raid on the coast

12th Brigade)   To be held ready to move as soon as possible.
(from Dover and Chatham) by rail to Cromer and 1 Battery R.F.A. from Woolwich.
10th Brigade)   (from Shorncliffe and Gravesend).
1 Battery R.F.A.) (from Shorncliffe) To be held ready to move by rail to York as soon   as possible
1 Battery R.F.A.) (from Woolwich) To be railed to Edinburgh as soon as possible".

As the division had been largely located in the area south of the Wash, the move was relatively simple although a considerable amount of rail transport was required for such a large body of troops and its' associated equipment. Departure commenced in the early hours of the 8th, when the 10th and 12th Brigades entrained for Cromer and York, while the 11th Brigade, already located at Colchester, stood fast. Upon arrival, the division was become a part of Northern Command[9]

The move of the two brigades was fraught with difficulties. Two companies of the 2nd Seaforth Highlanders and two companies of the 1st Royal Warwickshire Regiment were, through error in rail traffic control, incorrectly sent to Cromer, where the Warwickshire's had detrained before realising that they were in the wrong location. No sooner had they arrived back in York than a part of the 10th Brigade headquarters, the 2nd Seaforth Highlanders and the 1st Royal Irish Fusiliers departed to take up stations at Darlington. While those units moved to their new stations, Lieutenant-Colonel Elkington, O.C. Royal Warwickshire Regiment, remained at York with the remainder of the brigade, the 2nd Royal Dublin Fusiliers and 1st Royal Irish Fusiliers, having been temporarily classified as a flying column.

On the 9th, General Snow, accompanied by his GSO1[10], visited Eastern Command headquarters to receive final instructions which had the division assume responsibility for the defence of No. 2 section, covering the eastern coastline from a position north of the Thames Estuary to Yorkshire. The days were filled with matters of logistics, securing accommodation for large bodies of troops, establishing reporting structures in the event of an enemy landing and a multitude of procedures meant to establish the division as a fighting force.

As the 10th Brigade was detraining in York and Darlington, the 12th Brigade arrived in Cromer and by the 10th August, 4th Division headquarters had re-located to Bury St. Edwards. Problems soon arose when it was found that several of the buildings and factories, allocated for the purpose of billeting the troops, were unsuitable and forced changes of accommodation were made at short notice. Further dissatisfaction with the billeting arrangements continued and most of the troops were transferred to tents in nearby fields and parks.

Upon arrival, the battalions assumed their posts. The fear of spies and saboteurs was rife and the York police advised the division that they felt it necessary to maintain surveillance of the remaining German popula-

---

[9] *Then under the command of Lieutenant-General Sir Herbert Plumer.*

[10] *General Staff Officer, Grade 1.*

tion, the majority of which had departed in the previous fortnight for Germany. One of the first acts of securing the area was to ask the York police to take responsibility for four German subjects who had been detained by troops of the 12th Brigade.

Moving from a peacetime formation to a fighting force revealed inherent difficulties. An indication of the lack of preparedness of the troops of the division was displayed in the daily report of the 11th of August in which several concerns were expressed:

"(1) That a number of medical officers were wearing arm brassards which had been supplied by them without authority and did not carry an authorisation number on them.
(2) The telephone communications at Ipswich were unsatisfactory, in fact, the public telephone system was being used, and calls were taking hours to get through to the various Headquarters.
(3) No method of distinguishing between friendly naval aircraft and German aircraft had been established.
(4) No description of German uniforms had been received.
(5) A serious shortage of maps existed.
(6) Civilian road traffic was holding up the progress of military traffic.
(7) The only ammunition available to the troops was that which the carried with them when moving from their peacetime station to their wartime station (approx. 200-300 rounds)."

The nature of the report indicated that the troops did not know what a German soldier should look like[11], did not possess sufficient ammunition to fight a sustained battle and did not know whether an aircraft was friend or foe. Barely had the troops arrived and information was received to the effect that the division was to prepare to move overseas. With that prospect in mind, a flurry of activity commenced which was to persist until the day of departure. Inoculation of the troops commenced on the 12th, continuing until the 19th when the division was in its final stages of preparation and the veterinary officer isolated nine animals of the 1st Irish Horse after it was discovered that were suffering from strangles. Notwithstanding these inconveniences, the troops remained cheerful and eager to get to France.

---

[11] *The problem associated with identifying German troops manifested itself on the occasion of the Division's first major contact, on the 26th August, when troops of the 2 Essex Regiment mistook German Cavalry as French Cavalry. That error allowed several enemy machine guns to be brought forward, which resulted in many casualties.*

At 11:30am on the 15th, orders were received for the brigades to proceed to Harrow, Kenton and North Wembley, near London, on the 18th of the month. Preparations proceeded apace and the next few days were occupied with arrangements for accommodation for the troops in Harrow, train transport for troops and bicycles of the Cycle Company and arranging for the hand over of maps and instructions to the relieving force. In order to facilitate the return of those manning outlying posts, Northern Command was asked to relieve those troops guarding the railway with incoming units and, once relieved, they were instructed to rejoin their battalions immediately. By the 17th, the duties of coastal defence had been taken over by the Special Reserve and the division was ready to move.

The 10th Brigade departed York on the morning of the 18th, followed closely by the 11th and 12th Brigades and associated artillery. On arrival in Middlesex, Weald Park, near Harrow Station became the temporary home for the 10th Brigade where they established a tent camp. Similarly, the 11th Brigade camped on the Harrow School football field near Kenton Lane Station, and the 12th Brigade was accommodated in various locations around Brent Reservoir, close to North Wembley station. On arrival, warning orders were issued for the division to be ready to turn out at short notice, either for dispatch overseas or in the event of a German landing on home soil. The few days spent in and around Harrow were occupied with route marching, completing inoculations and in final preparations of equipment and animals. The division was also paid a visit by Lieutenant-General Pulteney[12], G.O.C., III Corps, of which the 4th Division, at this early stage, was the only unit[13].

Whilst the 4th Division had been manning the coastal defences, the Cavalry Corps and four infantry divisions, constituting the British Expeditionary Force, had crossed to France and advanced into Belgium. The 4th Division was destined to join them and final instructions were issued on the 21st for the division to entrain for Southampton, where it would embark for France the following day. The receipt of those instructions had the immediate effect of transforming every unit into a hive of activity, handing over maps, preparing equipment and loading vehicles. During the afternoon, the division commenced the move for overseas service. The 10th Brigade proceeded to Harrow station from

---

[12] *Lieutenant-General Sir William Pulteney (1861-1941) commanded III Corps from September 1914 until February 1918.*

[13] *III Corps was finally constituted when the 6 Division joined the 4 near Paris on the 5 September, upon completion of the retreat from Le Cateau.*

which it departed at 11:05pm, the 12th Brigade similarly entrained at North Wembley and the 11th Brigade at Kenton Lane.

On arrival at Southampton, at 3:00am on the 22nd August[14], the 10th Brigade headquarters, accompanied by the 1st Royal Warwickshire Regiment, 2nd Royal Dublin Fusiliers and 29th Field Artillery Brigade, embarked on the S.S. *Caledonia*. The remaining two battalions, the 2nd Seaforth Highlanders and 1st Royal Irish Fusiliers, embarked upon the S.S. *Michigan*. Both vessels sailed at 10:30am and arrived at Boulogne at 8:00pm, where the troops, due to traffic congestion, remained on board overnight and commenced disembarkation early in the morning of the 23rd. After disembarking, the 10th Brigade marched to Rest Camp No.1 (Marlborough), about three-quarters of a mile south of the Napoleon Column and settled down amidst steady rain.

While the 1st Somerset Light Infantry and a half battalion of the 1st Hampshire Regiment embarked on the S.S. *Braemer Castle*[15], the remainder of the 11th Brigade boarded the S.S. *Cestrian* and sailed, before noon, for Le Havre, where they arrived before midnight. They too, remained on board until the next morning. At 5:30am, the 2nd Essex Regiment and 2nd Royal Inniskilling Fusiliers of the 12th Brigade embarked on the S. S. *Corsican* and sailed for Le Havre. The 1st King's Own Royal Lancashire Regiment and 2nd Lancashire Fusiliers, of the same brigade, aboard the S.S. *Saturnia*, sailed for Boulogne and arrived at 11:00pm. These last two battalions, the King's Own and Lancashire Fusiliers, entrained almost immediately, and travelled to St. Leonards, about thirty kilometres north of Le Havre where they arrived in the early evening, detrained and marched to Rest Camps No.3 and No.4.

Time was not to be wasted and the process of moving to the front began in the early hours of the 24th August. The advanced party, representing 4th Division headquarters, consisting of Lieutenant-Colonels Taylor and Montgomery and Captain Elles proceeded by motor to Amiens to confirm instructions for the arrival of the division. There they spoke to the Line of Communications headquarters and proceeded to Valenciennes where they discovered that no orders existed for the reception of the division. The advanced party then travelled to G.H.Q.,

---

[14] *It was only several hours later on the same day that the 4 Dragoon Guards made the first contact with German Uhlans north of Mons.*

[15] *The S.S. Braemer Castle was used extensively as a troop ship during the war. It was later converted to a hospital ship and struck a mine in the Aegean Sea. After repairs she continued service until 1924 when it was sold for scrap.*

the headquarters of Field Marshall Sir John French at Le Cateau, where instructions were received to detrain at Busigny. The party continued its journey to Busigny where they made all appropriate arrangements for the arrival of the division. While the advanced guard was en-route to Le Cateau, the main body of the division was occupied with en-training the various units[16].

While the 4th Division was in transit to Le Cateau, I and II Corps had been heavily engaged at Mons and had begun withdrawing to the south and south-east. It was deemed necessary that the 4th Division should place itself to the left of II Corps and act as flank guard to that Corps as it withdrew. On arrival at Le Cateau[17] the 10th Brigade immediately marched to bivouacs at Inchy, three miles east of Le Cateau while the 12th Brigade, having arrived at Bertry, marched into billets at Montigny and Ligny[18]. While the 10th and 12th Brigades moved to their positions, two battalions of the 11th Brigade, the 1st Somerset Light Infantry and 1st East Lancashire Regiment, marched immediately for advanced positions south-west and south-east of Solesmes. Shortly after, the 1st Rifle Brigade marched to Bévillers to join the Somerset's and East Lancashire's while the Hampshire's moved west to Briastre, on outpost duty. All 2nd line transport was ordered to Ligny while the division headquarters established at Inchy.

Major-General Snow proceeded to G.H.Q. for a conference with the Commander-in-Chief, Sir John French. His instructions required the 4th Division to advance and assume positions about Briastre to protect the left flank of the rearguard of the retiring 3rd Division and 19th Brigade. Once the rearguard had passed through the division, it was to retire, in line with the remainder of II Corps, to the defensive line of Caudry – Wambaix, from which the entire B.E.F. was then to continue the retirement. While that meeting was taking place, Brigadier-General Haldane, O.C., 10th Brigade, reconnoitred the ground west of Le Cateau, where he established secure rear positions on the line of La Soliers - Audencourt - Le Coquelet F[e] – Carriers, as the line of retirement for the division. Whilst Haldane was thus engaged, the O.C., 12th

---

[16] *During the trip to Le Cateau the Division was to suffer its first casualty when the groom to the adjutant of the 11· Brigade was trying to calm a horse after it panicked while passing through a tunnel. The groom was kicked out of the train and killed.*

[17] *See map 1: France, Valenciennes, Edition 2, sheet 12, 1:100,000*

[18] *Ligny was to be long remembered by the Division after their action in the area two days later.*

Brigade, Brigadier-General Wilson, was also conducting a reconnaissance in the direction of Solesmes, to the north.

The advance of the 4th Division commenced in the small hours of the morning of the 25th. The 10th Brigade marched to St. Python, on the River Selle, the 12th Brigade to Point 129[19], about 400 yards south-west of Viesly, and the 11th Brigade proceeded to Briastre. By 5:30am, the 2nd Essex was across the River Erclin and half a mile north-east of Prayelle, close to Viesly where they observed shells landing on the ridge west of the village. By dawn the division had taken up the general position with the 10th Brigade extending south-west of Solesmes, 11th Brigade on it's right and 12th in reserve.[20]

Some elements of the division were still detraining from at Le Cateau and, while the infantry were taking up their positions, some of the batteries of the division artillery were hurried forward to give the infantry support. Four batteries were immediately sent to Montigny, where they arrived at 9:00am. By mid-morning, a company of the 1st King's Own and one of the 2nd Essex had entrenched on high ground, a mile to the west of Viesly and extended a mile to the south, following the route of the Béthencourt – Quievy railway. While the Battalions taking up their positions, division headquarters established at Solesmes, accompanied by two squadrons of Irish Horse. Accurate information was difficult to obtain and, to establish the whereabouts of the approaching enemy, Lieutenant-Colonel Montgomery reconnoitred in a north-easterly direction reaching Famars, on the outskirts of Valenciennes[21], without coming into contact with the enemy.

Enemy fire was first heard at 6:45am and two hours later, the troops of the division saw their first hostile plane as it flew over, observing for the advancing enemy columns. Information was also received that strong enemy forces were advancing along the Sauleir-Hastings road. As the dispositions of the German formations became clearer, so the need for a readjustment of the line was recognised and, at 11:00am, a proposal

---

[19] *It was common practice in the British army to use the height of a hill, indicated on a map, as a reference point for that location. This was regularly referred to as Point (number).*

[20] *One of the difficulties at this very early stage of the war was the fact that neither the French nor British High Commands new in what strength the Germans were advancing nor from which direction they should be expected.*

[21] *It was in this area that the 4 Division was to see the cessation of fighting in November 1918.*

was forwarded to G.H.Q. to shorten the line in the expectation of enemy action. As the Signal Company had not yet arrived, representations had been made to G.H.Q. to the effect that the division had no communications, so six motorcyclists were sent to assist. By mid-morning, the 10th Brigade made changes in the dispositions of its front line by bringing the Royal Warwickshire Regiment forward from reserve, in order to extend the right flank. One brigade of the Field Artillery arrived in position at Viesly at 12:30pm just as signs of the approaching enemy from the north was noted, mainly cavalry and horse artillery.

The situation confronting the 4th Division on the 25th was somewhat daunting. The division was acting as left flank guard to II Corps (3rd and 5th Divisions). It was defending the Corps from expected attacks from the 8th German Division, IV Corps, which was descending directly from the north. Unknown to the 4th Division was the existence of the German 2nd Cavalry Division of the II Cavalry Corps, supported by the 4th and 7th Jaeger Regiments and associated artillery, approaching from the north-west[22]. G.H.Q. had been making preparations for the withdrawal of the neighbouring 1st Cavalry Division and the 19th Brigade[23], which were about to leave Solesmes and retire to Le Cateau. Many attempts had been made by the 4th Division to establish contact with the 19th Brigade and the 3rd Division, but with little success. When contact was finally established, at 4:30pm, the 19th Brigade fell under the orders of the 4th Division.

As daylight progressed into evening, the battle arrived directly on the division front. At 6:30pm, shots were exchanged with German cavalry near Bévillers and Quievy by troops of the 12th Brigade and the German artillery shelled those Seaforth Highlanders, who were digging a trench in a beet paddock, resulting in the wounding of three men. During the evening Lieutenant-General Smith-Dorrien, G.O.C., II Corps, had asked Major-General Snow, G.O.C., 4th Division, to place the division under the orders of II Corps[24]. The neighbouring 3rd Division, on the

---

[22] *It was that Division that the 4 Division was to meet on the morning of the next day with such effect.*

[23] *The 19 Brigade was an independent brigade, not permanently attached to any particular Division and, on several occasions, was attached to the 4 Division to provide additional troops.*

[24] *The 4 Division was, officially, a part of III Corps. However, as it was the first Division of that Corps to arrive in France, it was sent into action to support of II Corps, where it continued to fight as a part of that Corps until the 5 September, at the completion of the retreat, whereupon it rejoined III Corps with the newly arrived 6 Division.*

right of the 4th and the French Cavalry, on the left, were both under pressure. In order to conform to the movement of the 3rd Division the 4th Division commenced its retirement during the night to take up positions on the left of II Corps between Caudry and Wambaix, a front of 5 miles, with reserves at Haucourt[25].

The onset of dusk and the close proximity of the German forces complicated the withdrawal. The 12th Brigade, having arrived from Ligny during the morning, now had to continue the march to positions north-west of Haucourt, nearly two miles to the west of Ligny. After nightfall, the brigade commenced its retirement led by the Essex Battalion. The 11th Brigade followed, albeit via a more westerly route, through Béthencourt – Beauvois – Fontaine-Aux-Pire where it arrived at 2:45am on the 26th. Arrangements had also been made during the night to send the 10th Brigade to Haucourt, via Beauvois, a distance of some eight miles. Whilst en-route to Viesly, the Seaforth Highlanders, the rearguard battalion, were approached by a German Uhlan[26] patrol. The patrol was fired upon and a wounded trooper of the 11th Uhlans was recovered, along with two loose horses[27].

The 10th Brigade continued on its way but soon came upon the rear of the 11th Brigade at Viesly, which was blocked by the horse transport. Due to the delays, the rearguards of the two brigades formed a common rearguard to the division, allowing the transport and artillery to negotiate the village ahead of them, thus allowing the 11th Brigade to move on. Such was the urgent nature of the general withdrawal that, at about midnight, the 10th Brigade marched out of Viesly, with the scattered remains of the 7th Brigade and other elements of I and II Corps, and again acted as rearguard. Due to the proximity of the German cavalry, the retirement was conducted very quietly.

As the rearguard continued towards Haucourt, the troops had to march on pavé roads in intense heat and endured a heavy rainstorm, without having had a meal for nearly eighteen hours. The night of the 25th had been a strenuous time for all in the division. On arrival on the Beauvois – Fontaine au Pire line, at 3:30am on the 26th, the exhausted troops, having been attacked several times by German cavalry patrols, were

---

[25] *This move represented the first day of the retreat for the Division, which was to last until the 5 September.*

[26] *German Cavalry. Approximately equivalent to the British Lancer.*

[27] *He later died of his injuries.*

forced to sleep in the streets of the village. The two companies of the 2nd Essex Regiment, which had remained at Béthencourt acting as rearguard to the 12th Brigade, also arrived at Ligny at 3:00am, after having withdrawn through Caudry.

On arrival at Ligny, delays were experienced, caused by a column of artillery that had stopped on the road to cook breakfast, forcing the infantry to move in single file through the village. Once clear, the rearguard marched into Esnes, at 4:30am, where they acted in reserve for the 12th Brigade. The move by the Essex to Esnes, on the extreme left flank of the British line, was supported by French cavalry, which had been reconnoitring to the north. Upon arrival in the streets of that village, they found the French cavalry having coffee, which was readily shared with the infantry.

The expectation of continuing the retreat was taken for granted and, in the early hours of the 26th, orders were received to retire to Le Catelet. However, circumstances that were to have a lasting effect on the British Expeditionary Force occurred at 5am on the 26th when Lieutenant-General Smith-Dorrien, commander of II Corps, decided to stand and fight. At 5:30am, instructions were sent to Major-General Snow and the brigades were notified to stand fast, although some elements of the division were still en-route to Harcourt and Esnes.

We take a brief pause here to appreciate the overall positions of the division and the nature of the ground over which it was to fight for the remainder of the day[28]. The situation confronting the British Army on the morning of the 26th August was largely one of unequal numbers in troops and artillery. The British Expeditionary Force of 55,000 faced 140,000 German infantry and cavalry, which had been advancing with the intention of enveloping both flanks of the British Army. II Corps, consisting of the 3rd, 4th and 5th Divisions and 19th Brigade attached, was retiring with I Corps on its right.

The 4th Division had acted as the rearguard to II corps and had retired in sympathy with the movements of the 3rd Division until it had reached positions south of the Cambrai – Le Cateau Road. Here the decision was made to stand against the pursuing German army, with the intention of slowing it advance long enough to permit an organised withdrawal[29]. The 4th Division assumed a position on the extreme left of

---

[28] See map Belgium, Valenciennes, Edition 2, sheet 12 for details, 1:100,000.

[29] Controversy continues today over the decision taken by Smith-Dorrien to make a stand while I Corps continued the retirement.

the British line, facing north from a ridge on the northern side of a valley, referred to as the Warnelle Ravine, through which meandered a small river of the same name.

Forward of the ridge and situated on the right of the division boundary lay Caudry, one of the larger towns in the area. To the left and forward of the line, stood the village of Wambaix. Almost mid-way between these two towns and some distance forward of the ridge lay the village of Fontaine-au-Pire. Beyond this line of villages, to the north, lay several smaller villages, in particular, Cattenières, which sat astride the Cambrai-Le Cateau railway. A little further again, lay the main Cambrai – Le Cateau Road.

The 11th and 12th Brigades held the division front. The right, held by the 11th Brigade, occupied a line from Le Coquelet F[m30], 300 yards to the south of Caudry, and extended to the railway line near Fontaine, a distance of 3000 yards. That line placed the 11th Brigade entirely on the northern ridge of the ravine, facing north-east from which the ground sloped away gently towards the Cambrai road. The 12th Brigade continued the line to the left, which bent back slightly, in a south-easterly direction, to cross the Warnelle River and extend to Mont D'Esnes, just north-west of Esnes, a further 6,000 yards. The valley slopes were quite steep on the right half of the line and slowly dropped away as the Warnelle river approached the village of Esnes. Wambaix, being slightly higher, overlooked Esnes.

Behind the front line, the northern side of the ravine descended to the river. Half way down the slope, and about halfway between the two flanks, lay the farm known as Longsart Farm. The whole line represented a large, but shallow, 'V' with the apex pointing to the north, near Fontaine. To the south of the river lay Esnes on the far left, Haucourt in the centre but some 1,500 yards behind the front line, where the 10th Brigade was kept in reserve, and Ligny, near the right flank. The crests of both ridges gave an excellent view of the other and it was imperative that the enemy should be kept as far as possible from the crest of the northern ridge, to prevent tactical observation.

At 4:00am officers patrols from the 1st King's Own Royal Lancashire Regiment and 2nd Lancashire Fusiliers, 12th Brigade, extended out as far as Wambaix railway station[31] without detecting any presence of the en-

---

12

emy. By 4:30am, the battalions of the 12th Brigade had arrived and occupied temporary bivouacs in a cornfield on the southern slope of the valley. During the move to Haucourt, the 1st line transport of the 10th Brigade, travelling at the head of the line with brigade headquarters, became separated from the infantry battalions and reached Cattenières at dawn[32]. Finding itself in front of the outpost line of the division, the columns marched south for Haucourt, where it arrived at 6:00am.

No sooner had they arrived, then suddenly and without warning, the positions of the King's Own Royal Lancashire Regiment and Lancashire Fusiliers (12th Brigade) were subjected to intense artillery and machine-gun fire from the direction of Cattenières and north-west of Haucourt. The Lancashire Fusiliers had dug in, but the King's Own, their arrival having been delayed at Ligny, was still in the process of deploying and suffered heavily. The two battalions replied with accurate rifle fire but the concentrated fire of the German machine guns, supplemented by that of field guns located between Wambaix and Cattenières railway station, was too intense to be beaten down by rifle fire alone.

Immediately, two companies of the 2nd Royal Dublin Fusiliers lined the Haucourt - Ligny road while the remaining two companies remained in reserve. To assist, two companies of the 1st Royal Warwickshire Regiment assumed position on the right of the Dublin's as well as holding two companies in reserve behind Haucourt. Of the four companies lining the road, the senior officer present, Colonel Elkington of the 1st Warwickshire Regiment, decided that, under the circumstances, the best manner with which to meet the situation was to attack across the Warnave Ravine in the direction of Wambaix.

At about 6:30am the entire Royal Warwickshire Regiment, supported by some of the forward troops of the King's Own Royal Lancashire Regiment of the 12th Brigade, under Major Christie, attacked over the

---

[31] *The route that these patrols followed was over the high ground to the north-west of the front line. It was from this position that the Germans launched their attack on the Division only one hour later.*

[32] *The confusion at the time was such that Lieutenant-General Sir Aylmer Haldane K.C.B., then Brigadier-General and commander of the 10 Brigade, wrote in his book, A brigade of the Old Army 1914, p8, when speaking of the retreat from Viesly "At length, about 3:40am., we arrived at a village, the name of which could not be ascertained, as not a soul was to be seen. The divisional general, who had shared my road-hunting operations, and who had no more idea than I had where we were, now rode off, no doubt to try and find his other troops, and at daylight the problem was solved when the name of the village, Cattenières, was discovered on a board inside the railway station."*

ridge, in the direction of Wambaix. The Dublin Fusiliers immediately followed, with dire consequences later in the day.

They were immediately absorbed into heavy fighting but, by 7:30am, the ridge had been secured. However, an enemy counter-attack of artillery and machine-gun fire caused heavy losses and forced them to retire. The Dublin Fusiliers took cover in a lane on the reverse slope of the northern ridge. The Warwickshire's, leaving a company in position on the Haucourt – Cattenières road, also withdrew, in good order, to the lane, having suffered losses of seven officers wounded and forty men killed, wounded, or missing. They held this position for the rest of the day, suffering further casualties of one officer and fourteen men wounded.

Haucourt village, housing the balance of the 10th Brigade, was subjected to intense artillery and long-range rifle fire just as some of the stragglers from the front line were arriving. Captain D'Esterre, A.D.C. to the division commander, was wounded, along with several other men. A part of the 10th Brigade, marching up the southern ridge, was caught in column of route and suffered heavily. When the firing commenced, the 10th Brigade Commander, Brigadier-General Haldane, who had just arrived with the transport column from Cattenières, was on a reconnaissance with the division commander, reconnoitring the ground behind Haucourt.

General Snow attempted to get to Cattenières by motor, not realising that the village was occupied by the enemy, but was held up by the shellfire. Consequently, he went to the positions of the 14th Field Artillery Brigade, southwest of Haucourt, from where he issued orders, as no other means of communications were available.

On returning to his brigade, Brigadier-General Haldane could not establish contact with the Dublin Fusiliers or the Warwicks, due to their involvement in the fighting on the ridge, but found the remaining two battalions, the Seaforth Highlanders and the Royal Irish Fusiliers in reserve behind Haucourt village. He recognised the possibility of a German attempt to work around the left flank of the division, through Serenvillers – Crèvecoeur-sur-l'Escaut and Esnes. To prevent this he placed the two reserve battalions on a line stretching from 800 yards east of Point 137, the artillery positions, to a point just west of Maison De Haucourt, to resist any approach by the enemy from the west.

When the attack had commenced, the 11th Brigade was in the process of taking up positions facing north-east towards Beauvois and astride the light St. Quentin – Cambrai railway. A wide gap existed between the left flank of the 11th Brigade and the right flank of the 12th Brigade and the only way to prevent enemy penetration was by concentrating the fire of the machine guns of both brigades onto the intervening ground. This ground offered a good field of fire, particularly to 'D' Company of the Essex Regiment which, from a position north of the railway line, drove off the German cavalry and, later in the day, the reinforcements of the IV Reserve Corps.

Penetrating that field of fire presented great difficulties for the oncoming German cavalry and they relied heavily on long distance machine-gun and artillery fire. As a result, the crest and northern face of the ridge was very heavily shelled, a position which required considerable effort to maintain.

"The noise of firing at 6:00am aroused C and D companies, of the Essex, who were having coffee with French. The French Cavalry moved off into action and the companies immediately fell in. At this time a French cavalry trooper gave Lieut. -Colonel Anley a message stating that the 12th Brigade was being driven back. He at once ordered both companies to advance to the sugar factory on the slope of Longsart ridge to cover the retirement of the other units. D Company entrenched on the south side of the Esnes - Haucourt road with their right opposite the factory[33] and C Company on their left flank. The remains of A Company slowly formed up on the right of D Company and B Company on the left of C. Shortly after this movement was complete C and D Companies opened fire on the Germans at a range of 1300 yards, checking their advance[34]".

As the 12th Brigade took up its positions, the covering parties of the Hampshire's and Rifle Brigade were able to withdraw. In doing so, B Company, which had been constantly engaged, inflicted heavy casualties on a platoon of Jaeger, which had emerged in pursuit, from Fontaine au Pire.

---

[33] *The factory referred to in the report was a sugar factory located on the southern slope of the Longsart Ridge in front of Haucourt and north of the Warnelle River.*

[34] *Extracted from Essex Units in the War 1914-1919, 2 Battalion the Essex Regiment Vol. 2, John Wm. Burrows, F.S.A.*

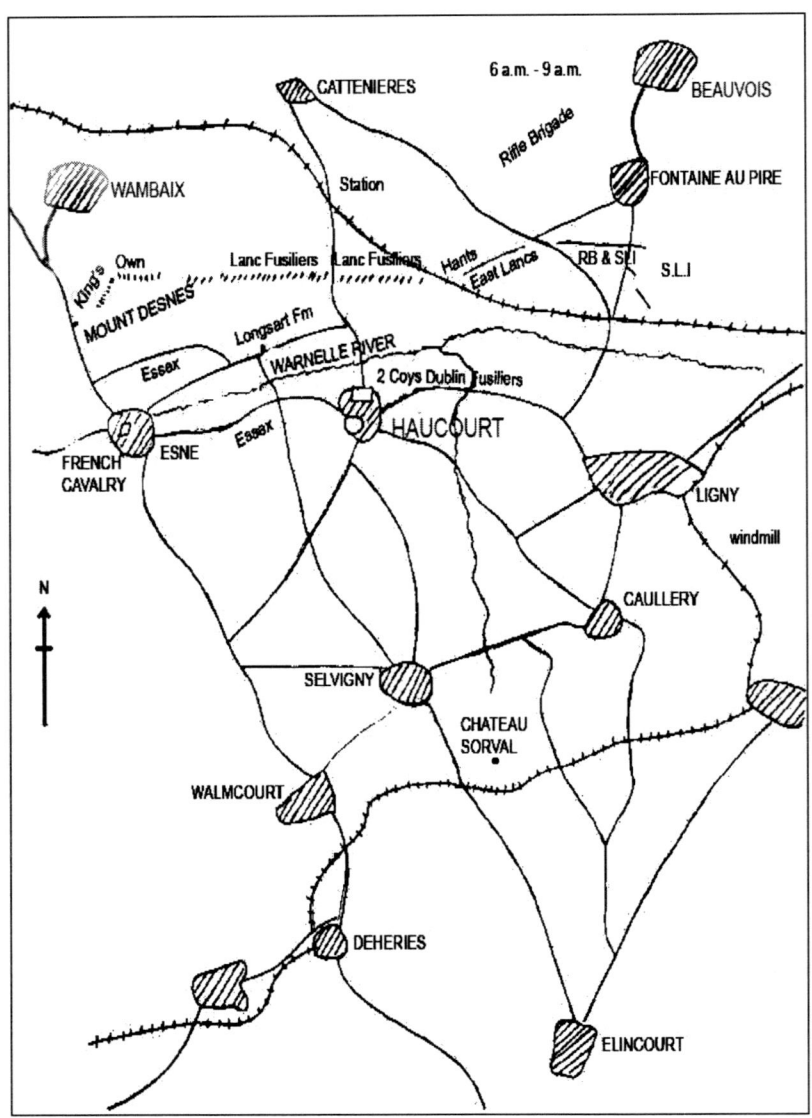

Plate 2
Position of the 4th Division between 6.00 am and 9:00am on the 26th August 1914

The horse transport, being restricted to the roads, had not been able to follow the infantry brigades across country and the additional distance resulted in much longer journeys for horse and driver. However, some of the SAA[35] carts had managed to reach Ligny and deliver their loads. As they were leaving, they came under artillery fire, which destroyed one cart and caused damage to several others. Further to the left the Lancashire Fusiliers of the 12th Brigade, being in entrenched positions, held on, but suffered severely as the Germans filtered around on the left and fired in enfilade. This fire also caused casualties amongst two companies of Essex and two of the Inniskilling Fusiliers. The remaining two companies of Inniskilling Fusiliers, situated west of Esnes, rendered valuable assistance by holding up the outflanking movement.

At about 9:00am, the troops of 'D' Company, 2nd Essex, observed Germans advancing in large masses over the northern ridge. The company commander, Captain Palk, reserved the fire of the left half of his company until the enemy was quite close. As the enemy descended the slope, the company opened fire with great effect, forcing the surviving attackers to retreat to the crest of the ridge, some 500 yards away. No further attempt at attack was made and the German dismounted cavalry 'maintained a desultory fire from a respectful distance'. As expected, the enemy made efforts to creep around the left flank but was met by 'A' Company. Some got close enough to call out 'retire' but the attempts at deception were ignored.

The pressure on the left of the division, that is, the line held by the 12th Brigade, was beginning to tell. Under heavy artillery and machine-gun fire, the left of the brigade was forced to retire from the line on the ridge, just north of Longsart. The new line extended from the railway line on the northern ridge south-west through Harcourt to Point 137 in order to offer a defensive flank for the remainder of the British line[36]. While the 12th Brigade retired, the 1st Hampshire's of the 11th Brigade offered support by creeping forward a little and firing on a German battery, which had unlimbered near Cattenières, at a range of 1200 yards and forced it to withdraw. Sharpshooters of the Hampshire's also took opportunities to shoot down the occasional machine-gun crew and artillery officers, who marked themselves by their drawn swords.

---

[35] *Military acronym for Small Arms Ammunition. Each brigade had its own ammunition column, which was responsible for the supply o ammunition, of all description, to the fighting troops. At the time of the action many of the horse transport wagons were still en-route to the division after detraining.*

[36] *The 4 Division occupied the left flank of the British line. A large gap existed between the 4 Division and the French lines many miles to the north-east and this gap was held by a thin line of French Cavalry while they waited for the French Cavalry Corps to arrive.*

The King's Own moved to the south side of the Warnelle Ravine and covered the retirement of the Warwicks on the ridge north of Haucourt. The Lancashire Fusiliers also withdrew to the southern ridge, midway between Haucourt and Esnes, covered by the fire of A and B Companies of the Essex[37]. While this withdrawal was being affected, B Company of the Essex was subjected to enfilade fire from enemy machine guns and suffered many casualties[38]. The withdrawal of the Lancashire Fusiliers and the King's Own carried them through the 2nd Essex, which was lining the Haucourt-Esnes Road. Two companies of the 2nd Essex and the 2nd Royal Inniskilling Fusiliers remained in their positions on the road until 3:00pm, when the brigade again advanced to their old positions on the ridge.

At 11:00am, the 12th Brigade was reinforced by the 1st Royal Irish Fusiliers of the 10th Brigade, and the 14th Field Artillery Brigade, located on Point 137, which turned its guns upon the opposing artillery about Wambaix. Those elements of the Dublin Fusiliers and Royal Warwickshire Regiment, which were available near Haucourt, were ordered to advance and take positions on either side of the Warnelle River and act in support of the 12th Brigade. Communications between the brigades and division headquarters were never good, but at this time all communications were temporarily lost. Instructions had been given for the division to continue the withdrawal; however, in many instances the poor communications and intense shelling prevented orders from getting through. In preparation for the continuation of the withdrawal, division headquarters moved, at about noon, to a point near Le Chemin Vert, close to the guns on Point 137.

The risk of a breakthrough was real and, at about midday, the decision was taken to move troops to Ligny, close to the junction with the 3rd Division, which was considered to be the point of greatest risk. In order to support the strengthening of Ligny, the 135th Battery was placed close in front of the village to cover a stretch of flat ground over which the enemy would have to advance, should they choose to follow up the retirement of the 11th Brigade. In turn about two hundred men of the 1st Somerset Light Infantry and a Cavalry machine-gun section, which had come to the assistance of the division, supported the guns.

---

[37] *That fire was responsible for the severe handling of a battalion of German dismounted cavalry, which appeared along their front in close formation.*

[38] *Machine guns had been brought forward by German cavalry, which had been mistaken for French cavalry covering the left flank.*

To this point, the division had managed to hold the line of the northern ridge against far greater numbers. Early in the afternoon reinforcements from the German IV Reserve Corps began to arrive and, although the impact of the additional troops was not immediately felt, it signalled a change in the tempo of the German attack, yet undetected by III Corps. The various units of the 12th Brigade had become mixed up but, although the 2nd Essex was some 500 yards to the rear of their original positions, they were able to maintain a better field of fire and keep reasonable communications. Next to them, the 11th Brigade had been holding its positions on the northern ridge under constant artillery and machine-gun fire and, by 1:00pm, the right flank of the brigade had still not established contact with the left flank of the 3rd Division.

An attempt to establish contact was made by a staff officer of the 4th Division who was sent to find the left flank of the 3rd Division and to explain the situation. The guns were unable to suppress the increasing enemy shellfire, and little chance existed of supplying additional infantry, as the reserves of the division had all been absorbed in the conflict. None remained to offer support, should a breakthrough occur.

The objective of the division had always been to continue the retirement and, in preparation for the breaking of contact with the Germans, the 12th Brigade was ordered to place Selvigny, to the south of Harcourt, in a state of defence. The intention being to preserve troops who were sent to the headquarters, as a reserve. However, due to the failure in communications, this order was not received and Selvigny remained open and undefended.

The weight of the additional enemy troops began to have an effect on the far left of the line. Germans infantry vigorously attacked the Esnes - Sucrerie[39] line, still held by the companies of the Essex and Inniskilling Fusiliers, but were beaten back as the artillery, located on Point 137, opened fire. The tactical importance of Ligny was now evident, and the 10th Brigade was asked to send as many men as they could spare to reinforce the garrison, but none were available so the garrison of 200 men, six guns and two machine remained until the 11th Brigade retired.

---

[39] *Sucrerie is the French title for a sugar factory. The particular sucrerie here referred to lies midway along the Haucourt – Esnes Road and should not be confused with the previously mentioned sugar factory on the Longsart Ridge. These two factories stood opposite each other on opposing ridges, separated by the Warnave River. The author visited the building in May 2003 and discovered it little changed.*

At 1:20pm two battalions of the 19th Brigade, 2nd Royal Welsh Fusiliers and 1st Scottish Rifles were made available to the 4th Division and orders were prepared for their placement in the line. The orders required them to take up positions on the eastern end of Ligny and to the southeast through the woods to a mill. Again, communications played a part in the events of the day and the two battalions were withdrawn to assist the 5th Division before having received those orders from the 4th Division[40]. The intense pressure of the German attack was felt all along the line and through the adjoining divisions, as the German IV Reserve Corps, which had been following the advanced guard, joined battle.

As the afternoon progressed the situation became a little clearer. The 11th Brigade continued to hold its ground and the attackers made no serious attempt to outflank the 12th Brigade from the west. As there was no apparent need to retire, what appeared to be an improved situation was reported to the 3rd Division, which was urged to hold on[41]. Attempts were then made to collect the scattered troops of the 12th Brigade. Twelve hundred men were collected from the locality of Haucourt. Those men were reorganised and advanced across the Warnelle to Longsart Farm and regained the original line on the northern ridge. This was done with surprisingly little opposition as the enemy had evacuated the ridge, due to the heavy rifle and machine-gun fire, especially that of the 11th Brigade. During this advance many dead and wounded of the 12th Brigade and those of the enemy[42] were found and recovered along with some horse transport, which had been abandoned during the initial attack.

That opportunity was short lived, as the Germans guns again concentrated fire on the newly occupied positions and again forced the troops

---

[40] *The 5 Division had taken the larger part of the attack. By early afternoon the 5the Division had pushed back and commenced to withdraw. The poor communications that prevailed during the afternoon of the 26 prevented the news of the withdrawal from reaching the headquarters of the 4 Division and it was only when it was realised that the neighbouring 3 Division was in the process of withdrawing, that orders were issued for the 4 Division to do likewise.*

[41] *Unbeknown to Major-General Snow the 3 Division had already commenced to withdraw, in sympathy with the 5 Division on its right.*

[42] *Ironically, among the German dead were troops of a Jaeger Regiment who were wearing the Gibraltar badge, the same as worn by the Essex. The Hanoverian Regiment had assisted the 2 Essex (then known as the 56 Regiment of Foot) in the defence of Gibraltar, 150 years before.*

to retire[43]. At 3.00pm orders to continue the retirement were issued but failed to reach several of the foremost units. After holding the positions for a short time, the 12th Brigade began to withdraw behind the 10th Brigade, having been designated as rearguard. While doing so, the retiring troops were shelled severely as they re-crossed the valley of the Warnave. While the withdrawal on Ligny and Haucourt was taking place the Hampshire's attempted to take the pursuing Germans in flank but the intense artillery barrage forced the Hampshire's to return to their trenches, having suffered many casualties.

"At 3pm a number of German guns appeared on the ridge north-east of the farm and shelled the Essex and Haucourt heavily with shrapnel. At this time the German 2nd Cavalry Division, who had been confronting the 4th Division, was being reinforced with the IV Reserve Corps. This fire caught the right of the 12th Brigade and then swept along the line. There was no effective artillery reply and the centre and right of the line and the men were ordered to withdraw, they were to walk and not run. Not a man ran. Most of the shrapnel burst too high to be effective but put a terrible strain on men who had never been under fire before. As the troops retired they passed two of the division guns, the subaltern in charge saying that he only had time for few more rounds.[44] "

The staff officer previously sent to establish contact with the 3rd Division, returned at about 3:00pm to report that the division had retired out of Caudry, to positions around Montigny, to the south-east[45]. With the 12th Brigade in the process of withdrawing and the 3rd Division having already commenced retiring, the 11th Brigade was vulnerable to attack from either flank and left the contingent around Ligny dangerously exposed. At 3:30pm the formal order for a general retirement was given. The message, received by the 12th Brigade at 4:30pm, instructed the brigade to retire to Selvigny, prepare its defences, and hold it at all costs.

That instruction represented the initial movement to disengage from the enemy and have the whole division continue its retirement. When

---

[43] *Heavy fire prevented many of the dead and wounded of the Division being recovered and these fell into the hands of the Germans during the night and following morning as the retreat continued.*

[44] *Extraction from Essex Units in the War 1914-1919, 2 Battalion the Essex Regiment Vol. 2, John Wm. Burrows, F.S.A., John H. Burrows & Sons, Ltd., Southend-on-Sea (1927)*

[45] *The 3 Division had retired in sympathy with the 5 Division, on its right, which had taken the brunt of the German attack.*

the order was received, the right flank of the 12th Brigade was in the process of falling back on Ligny while the left flank was falling back on Haucourt. Because of the order to retire, the 12th Brigade continued on its course to Selvigny, without stopping.

Verbal instructions were passed to the 11th Brigade that, should the position of the brigade become too difficult, it was to retire onto the prepared position at Ligny. Brigadier-General Hunter-Weston, C.O. of the 11th Brigade, being aware of the danger to his brigade, needed no further encouragement and ordered the 11th Brigade to withdraw. Covered by the guns of the 32nd Field Artillery Brigade the retirement was carried out successfully with few casualties, given the shellfire to which they were subjected. The enemy followed and attacked Ligny, but was repulsed.

With the 11th Brigade in Ligny and the 12th on its way to Selvigny, the remains of the two battalions of the 10th Brigade, the 1st Royal Warwickshire Regiment and the 2nd Royal Dublin Fusiliers, had become the front line troops. The remaining two battalions, the Royal Irish Fusiliers and Seaforth Highlanders had retired to Selvigny, to which Brigade Headquarters had relocated.

At about 4:00pm the division headquarters received information that the neighbouring 3rd Division had continued through Montigny and was heading south, to Clary, three miles south of Caudry. This exposed not only the right flank of Ligny where the 11th Brigade was now gathering, but also Haucourt and it was now considered that the 4th Division should conform to the withdrawal of the 3rd Division or risk the loss of the 11th and 10th Brigades.

It was intended that the most advanced units should pass through the support lines, which had been established on the high ground east of Caullery and Selvigny, the former being held by the artillery, the latter by the 12th Brigade. It was also intended that the infantry of the 11th Brigade should withdraw from Ligny under the cover of the artillery and retire on the line of Walincourt – Malincourt to La Catelet. The troops of the 11th Brigade in Ligny were to move first, to the high ground three-quarters of a mile north of Deheries.

It was to be followed by the 10th Brigade, to the high ground between Soval Chateau and Hurlemont Fm[46]. The 12th Brigade was to remain holding Selvigny while the artillery withdrew from one covering posi-

---

[46] *Commonly used abbreviation for 'farm'.*

tion to another. The batteries were to pass through each other in turn, to the high ground three-quarters of a mile north of Deheries, with the 11th Brigade and the division was then to assemble at Deheries and continue the withdrawal.

It was mistakenly believed that those elements of the 10th Brigade, which were fighting in the front line, had withdrawn at the same time as the 11th Brigade. At about 4:00pm orders were sent to the 10th Brigade, which was thought to be located between Caullery and Haucourt, to retire up the valley between these two villages to the high ground, south of the Sorval Chateau. That order was not received until 5:00pm. A similar order was sent to the 2nd Royal Dublin Fusiliers of the 10th Brigade in their advanced position north of Caullery.

The confusion as to the exact whereabouts of the various units of the 10th Brigade was a direct result of the isolation of the brigade commander, Brigadier-General Haldane, whose Brigade Headquarters was located near Selvigny[47]. The two reserve battalions, the Royal Irish Fusiliers and the Seaforth Highlanders were also in the area. Haldane was ordered, verbally, through the G.O.C., 12th Brigade, to act as rearguard to the whole division when the retirement started. He received this message just after having received the previous message; that he was to retire up the valley between Haucourt and Caullery and understood that it was the same message being repeated and not, as it really was, a new set of instructions.

Brigadier-General Haldane interpreted the instructions as an order to retire through Walincourt and Malincourt, instead of proceeding to the high ground south of Sorval Chateau. That resulted in he, accompanied by the Royal Irish Fusiliers and the Seaforth Highlanders, initially moving southeast instead of southwest with the rest of the division.

When he halted to establish whether the retirement had begun, he had lost touch with the main body of the division, then some two miles to the west. From inhabitants and stragglers he established the direction that the division had taken and followed it up some five or six hours in

---

[47] "I had, before leaving the vicinity of my two battalions on the right, observed what appeared to be them conforming to a rearward movement of the 11[·] Infantry Brigade, and as I had not succeeded in getting into communication with them nor received any reports during the day, I trusted that their commanders would succeed in withdrawing them in safety. The time had now come for me to retire, as the troops were assembled and ready to carry out the movement ordered, so sending for my horse, which I had left close by in Selvigny, in a building which guaranteed safety from German shrapnel, I mounted and rode to join my two battalions". Quoted from A Brigade of the Old Army 1914, pp25-26, Lieutenant-General Haldane.

rear, along the same route, through Malincourt and Vendhuille, eventually rejoining the division at Roisel.

As the withdrawal proceeded, the two front line battalions of the 10th Brigade, the Warwickshire's and Dublin Fusiliers were, in fact, still fighting near Ligny and Caullery. Elements of the Warwicks and Dublin's were arriving, still under fire, in the area of Ligny, fragmented and out of touch with brigade headquarters. Both battalions had been involved in some of the heaviest fighting, north and north-west of Haucourt, with the Germans directing heavy artillery fire on those positions for most of the day, and communication with the C.O.'s had been almost impossible.

Neither the Warwickshire's nor the Dublin Fusiliers realised that the rest of the division had withdrawn until it was noticed that the firing of the supporting artillery had died away during the late afternoon. Captain Watson, the adjutant to the Royal Dublin Fusiliers, whilst searching for the remainder of the division, was given instructions by a staff officer to retire as best they could, given that the other two brigades were already well on their way.

Those instructions were then reported to Lieutenant-Colonel Mainwaring of the Royal Dublin Fusiliers. Out of touch with his two forward companies of the Dublin Fusiliers fighting in front of Caullery, Lieutenant-Colonel Mainwaring, accompanied by his adjutant and about forty men of the reserve companies, withdrew from Ligny, and marched to Malincourt. That small group rejoined the division on the 28th, two days later.

A second body of troops, those of the Dublin Fusiliers, under the command of Major Shewan, waited until dark and left Haucourt as the Germans filtered into the northern end of the village. The group then moved east, to Ligny, which had also been occupied by Germans troops, where they got involved in close fighting and many were killed or captured. A small remnant of that group, under Captain Clarke, managed to escape and travelled for several days and nights with the advancing Germans until they reached the coast where they were sent back to England to rejoin the battalion in October.

The 1st Royal Warwickshire Regiment was in a similar position. 'A' and 'B' Companies, reserve companies of the Warwickshire's had retired as escort for the guns from Ligny[48]. Those of the fragmented front line companies, 'C' and 'D', were in small groups in and around Haucourt. Not knowing the location of the division, a group under Lieutenant-Colonel Elkington withdrew from Haucourt towards Ligny. Realising that Ligny was also in the process of being evacuated, the group marched south for St. Quentin and during the march, were augmented by other isolated groups, finally rejoining the brigade on the 28th.

Those still gathering around Haucourt disengaged as best they could and withdrew in small groups throughout the night. On realising that the division was retiring, Major Poole, with a further mixed group of about three hundred and fifty men of the Warwickshire's, Dublin Fusiliers and Irish Fusiliers managed to leave Haucourt at about 10:00pm whilst surrounded on three sides by German troops. They withdrew, at great risk, in the dark and rejoined the brigade on the 28th.

At 6:30pm the 12th Brigade, holding covering positions in Selvigny, was ordered to act as advanced guard and was sent ahead of the main body to Vendhuille, fifteen kilometres to the south. Marching via Walincourt, Malincourt, Villers-Outrèaux and Aubencheul the brigade arrived at Vendhuille at 9:30pm where it was established that the brigade had suffered casualties of one thousand and twelve officers and men in the day's action. At about 8:00pm, the remainder of the division moved off, with the objective of passing through the advanced guard and reaching Le Catelet. The journey continued through the night until Vendhuille was reached at 1:00am on the 27th. Here they stopped for a short rest.

With the 10th Brigade already fragmented and dispersed, the 11th Brigade was soon to follow suit, albeit, temporarily. The brigade left Vendhuille at 2:30am on the 28th and travelled across country under local guidance, skirted the north of Beaurevoir to escape the congested roads and marched north of Estrées to Nauroy, where they arrived at 8:30am and stopped for three hours. Here a report was received at 10:45am stating that Uhlans had been sighted in the next village, Bellicourt, and the brigade quickly retired, somewhat disorganised. The 1st East Lancashire Regiment, accompanied by fragments of other battalions, withdrew to the south-west across the Canal D'Escaut, under

---

[48] *During the withdrawal, two guns, which had been dug in at Ligny, were abandoned, as there was no way of getting the gun teams up to the front, due to the heavy shellfire. It was suspected that they may have been used later by the Germans to shell British positions during the battle of Chateau Thierry.*

cover of a large wood, and marched via Pontru, Vermand, Étreillers, and Aubigny to Ham[49].

A second portion of the brigade, chiefly the 1st Rifle Brigade, portions of the East Lancashire's and the 1st Hampshire Regiment retired west through Villeret, turning south and eventually joining the main body of the 4th Division at Tertry during their night march to Voyenne. A third section of the brigade left Villers-Outrèaux and marched to Le Catelet, where the 4th Division headquarters was found.

The deviation from the prescribed route had placed the 11th Brigade five miles to the east of the main body of the division. As a united fighting force, the division now consisted of the battle damaged 12th Brigade, two battalions of the 10th Brigade, the 1st and 2nd Line transport and some artillery. The 12th Brigade again led the march to Lempire where it stopped just south of the village, and assumed the role of rearguard as the remainder of the troops passed through. Major-General Snow had sent a message to Major-General Allenby, G.O.C., Cavalry Division, requesting that the Cavalry Division cover the 4th Division during the next stage of the withdrawal, as they did not possess mounted troops.

With the 12th Brigade and Cavalry holding the high ground above and to the south of Lempire, the division reached Ronssoy at about 7:00am where it halted for a short rest. An hour later the retirement resumed and, with about 18 kilometres to cover, the division marched through Tempeleaux-le-Guérard and took up a position about two kilometres south of the village, on Point 144. The troops were in a state of exhaustion and the pack animals in constant need of water. During the break, the French cavalry engaged the oncoming Germans at Villers-Faucon, about three kilometres to the north-east of the division. Notwithstanding the condition of the troops, the march was immediately resumed in the direction of Roisel, where the division stopped and rested until the evening.

A portion of the Rifle Brigade, under the command of Colonel Bidulph, remained at Le Catelet to act as a communications centre and to gather up stragglers as they passed through. Meanwhile, the group of Warwicks under Major Poole, which had retired separately from Haucourt, was trying to rejoin the division, but had no definite information

---

[49] *Unbeknown to either group the 11· Brigade, while located in Nauroy, was not far from that portion of the 10· Brigade, led by Lieutenant-Colonel Elkington, which was making its way towards St. Quentin.*

as to its whereabouts. The party under Lieutenant-Colonel Elkington had reached St. Quentin during the day of the 27th. Upon arrival, the Mayor of that city informed Colonel Elkington that the Germans had threatened to bombard the city if the British troops did not surrender. With the imminent threat to the city, Lieutenant-Colonel Elkington agreed and drew up a document of surrender[50]. This he later withdrew and left the town alone.

The mixed group of troops, with the 1st Line Transport, then found its way to Ham under the command of Lieutenant Cowper where they met Lieutenant Walker and Captain Bannerman, who had been disassociated from the brigade during the fighting at Haucourt. Lieutenant Cowper's party was sent by rail that night to Compiègne under the direct orders of G.H.Q. As the division approached Hancourt, a defensive line was occupied about Bernes and Hervilly, on the high ground overlooking Roisel, as protection against the approaching German cavalry. The infantry entrenched the positions and manned them with all available troops, although many managed to obtain some rest. At dusk, the division once again concentrated around Hancourt and continued the march with orders to get across the Canal de la Somme at Voyennes, where it was to take up positions covering the crossings.

The 10th Brigade led the way. All available carts in the area were pressed into service while the artillery and baggage vehicles were used to carry those troops who, through exhaustion, were incapable of marching. At 11pm, II Corps ordered that all ammunition wagons and any impedimenta not absolutely required should be off-loaded and officers and men were to be carried to full capacity of all transport, both horse drawn and mechanical. The division war diary for that date states *"This order was carried to the letter with the result that officers were without any kit except what they stood up in and a great many men were without waterproof sheets for the next month, which inflicted unnecessary hardships on all ranks.....everything that could be done was being done and a great many carts had been impressed, so the order was quite unnecessary."*

To this point the weather had remained fine but that was not to last. The march continued throughout the night, and arrived at Voyennes between 4:00am and 5:30am on the 28th August without incident and the troops were distributed throughout the village, with defensive outposts north of the canal. German Cavalry was in close pursuit and their proximity was such on the 28th that, early in the morning, the 12th Bri-

---

[50] *Lieutenant-Colonels Elkington and Mainwaring were later arrested and court-martialled for the part in the agreement to surrender.*

gade was ordered to find outposts covering Voyennes and Offoy from the north.

By 8:00am, the brigades were concentrated, ready to march. The 11th Brigade was situated to the north of the bridge at Offoy while the 10th Brigade stood north of the bridge at Voyennes, all covered by the 12th Brigade and the 32nd Brigade, R.F.A., at Sancourt. The brigade Commanders of the 10th and 11th Brigades met the division commander at the bridge near Offoy where it was explained that the division was now to act as rearguard to II Corps. The brigades were to remain where they were and maintain strong positions protecting the canal to allow the remainder of the Corps to continue the retirement. As II Corps continued on its southerly journey, the division began moving into its allocated positions along the banks of the Canal De Somme. Here the troops remained in position for four and half-hours.

From the moment of its arrival in France the 4th Division had advanced, fought and retreated without the assistance of the medical, signal or engineering services. Those units had been the last to disembark and, by the time they were ready to entrain at the ports of disembarkation, the division had engaged the enemy and commenced the retirement. While the brigades assumed defensive positions around Offoy, news was received from the C.R.E (Commander, Royal Engineers) that the 7th and 9th Field Companies, Signal Company, Cyclist Company and Field Ambulances were waiting in the Cavalry Barracks at Noyon. The Ammunition Column, with the Bridging Train of the Field Companies was also at Compiègne. Initially theses units were requested to join the division, however, G.H.Q. would not allow them to move forward, and they finally joined the division south of the River Oise.

It was intended that the retirement should continue during the evening, however, the 3rd Division had departed from its position and continued the retirement at 12:00 noon. There was little point in delaying the withdrawal any longer. Orders were issued, at 1:30pm, for the brigades to continue in the direction of Caisnes, approximately 50 kilometres away. II Corps was notified that it was impossible to reach Caisnes that night, after crossing the Oise River at Pont l'Évêque and it was proposed to halt at Sempigny just south of the Oise. The 12th Brigade led the way south, through Offoy and Hombleux to Campagne, each alternately passing through the other to act as advanced guard, main body, and rearguard. The 12th Brigade halted at Campagne while the 11th Brigade continued to Fréniches, near Libermont, and bivouacked along the road until dawn. The 10th Brigade continued through Muirancourt to Bussy.

Still fifteen kilometres from Sempigny, exhaustion had overcome the troops and it was necessary to stop where they were, while the artillery was withdrawn to Muirancourt with division headquarters. During the day, orders were received to hold all crossings over the River Oise from Bregny to Pont Oise. It was during this pause that Lieutenant-Colonel Elkington and two hundred and eighty men, who had joined him, re-joined the 10th Brigade, along with Major Christie, all being sent to a rest camp. Major Poole's party rejoined at 8:00pm with ninety men and fifteen officers. These troops were sent by rail to Rouen, arriving the following day, in order to rest and refit.

Good news arrived at 9:20am on the 29th, in the form of an order from II Corps, stating that the division could remain in their present positions in order to rest and, if they wished, to find billets for the men in Sempigny. Shortly after 10:30am headquarters received information that the 2nd Cavalry Brigade, located at Le Plessis, nearly 10 kilometres north east of the division, was being attacked and was falling back on Noyen, with the intention of making a stand at Guiscard only a few kilometres from the division.

We should pause for a brief description of the situation that faced the 4th Division at that moment. The division was located to the west of the Ham-Noyon Road with its left flank, held by the recently joined Cyclist Company, opposite and about 3,500 yards from Guiscard, where the Cavalry were expected. The dispositions of the three brigades, the 10th at Bussy, 12th at Chevilly and the 11th at Sermaize, represented a triangle with the apex pointing towards the Ham-Noyon road, from the west. Guiscard was located about halfway between Ham and Noyon, to the north-east of the divisions' positions. This meant that the Cavalry, and the pursuing Germans, would pass directly across the division front.

All brigades were warned for possible action. The Cyclist Company, being closest to the enemy positions, was warned of the German advance and instructed to call upon the 12th Brigade for support if required. The 10th and 12th Brigades were requested to reconnoitre outposts on the right of the 11th Brigade in preparation for possible contact. At 12:40pm, a warning was issued to be prepared to move and support the 2nd Cavalry Brigade and division headquarters notified II Corps that they were ready and anxious to move forward if necessary. However, early in the afternoon the 3rd Division reported that it was already covering the 2nd Cavalry Brigade with one infantry and one field artillery brigade, with a second brigade in support, until 2:00pm.

Officer's patrols were sent from 11th Brigade to Point 89, near Cendrieres, in front of Bussy. Those patrols, which had penetrated beyond Guiscard, stated that all firing had ceased. The 4th Cavalry Brigade, from their positions near Esmery-Hallon, also reported the firing having ceased. However, the 12th Brigade noted that firing was continuing in the direction of Muirancourt. As the hour was late, all brigades were informed that there was no intention of moving during the remainder of the day and the field ambulances were ordered to proceed to the road junction just north of Perquericourt, on the Noyon - Roye Road, to assist with stragglers. As the division was no longer required to support the cavalry, the engineers, who had just arrived, prepared the bridges across the canal and river at Sempigny for destruction.

Final adjustments of the line were made in the late afternoon as the 10th Brigade and the Cyclist Company covered the retirement of the 11th and 12th Brigades as they crossed the River Oise, above Beaurains. In order to effect the crossing, the 10th Brigade marched via Pont l'Évêque to the high ground about Le Cloyes and Carlepont, a distance of about five kilometres, where outposts were placed on the River Oise. It also provided support for the withdrawal of the 2nd Cavalry Brigade. At 6:00pm, the 11th Brigade marched through the western suburbs of Noyon, followed by the 12th Brigade, to the road junction at Le Cloyes, where they were joined by division engineers and the 10th and 12th Field Ambulances.

At 1:00am on the 30th, the division continued the retirement, in company with II Corps headquarters and the 2nd Cavalry Brigade during which all proceeded to the line of the River Aisne, twelve kilometres to the south. The main body was to clear the Carlepont line before 5:30am and demolish all bridges, with the exception of those at Pont l'Évêque, which were to be destroyed on the orders of the rearguard. In accordance with those orders, the 12th Brigade withdrew the outpost line in time to join the 10th Brigade rearguard at Les Cloyes and then marched via Bailly and Tracy-le-Mont to within two and a half miles of Breuil. Here it halted for a meal. The conditions were very trying for the troops. The day was hot and dry, there was no water or shade for the troops, and the road was flat and open. Consequently, exhaustion caused many to straggle well behind the main body of troops.

The route took the division through the Foret de Laigue, across the River Aisne and through the Foret de Compiègne. In order that the bridges over the River Aisne were available for the Cavalry, following behind the division, they were to be prepared for demolition but were to be held until ordered. The bridges at Pimprez and Bailly, which were being guarded by the Cyclist Company, had to remain intact until the 10th Brigade was clear of Carlepont, in the middle of the Foret de Laigue. However, the 10th Brigade had been notified that the baggage transport would not be clear of Carlepont until 6:45am and therefore, had to wait for their arrival. Aggravating that situation was the fact that a company of the 1st Royal Irish Fusiliers had lost its way and the bridges could not be blown until they were found. The tail of the main body passed through Bailly at 8:30am and, at 9:10am, the 10th Brigade was still waiting for the Irish Fusiliers.

The 10th Brigade, with the Cyclist Company, a squadron of Irish Horse and the 10th Field Ambulance finally crossed the River Oise at about 10:00am, demolished the bridge at Bailly, and marched for Tracy Le Mont where it rejoined the rest of the division. While the 10th Brigade was on the move, the 12th Brigade had established a bridgehead on the high ground north of the Aisne between Berneuil-sur-Aisne and Bethordes where it established contact with 5th Division. The situation eased a little when, at about 10:00am, II Corps reported that the overall situation had very much improved and the columns could halt when convenient, for water and food and to await orders, all previous orders being cancelled.

During this brief pause, arrangements were made for the demolition of the bridges in the area and the 9th Field Company travelled to Compiègne to prepare the bridge there for demolition. In the early afternoon permission was granted for the march to continue according to the wishes of the G.O.C., 4th Division. The retirement continued at a more leisurely pace, with the 11th Brigade passing through the 12th Brigade outpost line at 4:45pm, followed by the 10th Brigade at 6:30pm. Although the pressure on the exhausted troops had eased, serious problems remained. On arrival at the billeting area, the 11th Brigade experienced great difficulty securing bivouacs, due to the number of troops in the area. The problem was compounded by a reported outbreak of smallpox, so the troops spent a wretched night in the streets of Pierrefords.

During the evening, an unfortunate incident befell the division. The 11th Brigade had been instructed to supply an escort for a party of Royal Engineers, which was being sent to the Bailly Bridge for special duty. As the escort arrived, it was discovered that Major Barstow[51], commanding the engineers, had already proceeded with the party. He was not seen

---

[51] *Major John Baillie Barstow was killed during the action at the bridge and is now buried in the Noyon New British Cemetery, France.*

again and few of the party returned. It was later learnt that he had been hit when the advancing Germans fired the group on.

The division continued its retirement, took it through the Foret De Compiègne, in the direction of Senlis[52]. Because of the nature of the terrain, the division had to negotiate the roads through the forest without the support of the other divisions of II Corps and had to protect itself against attack from the north. The passage was negotiated without incident and, upon exiting from the forest; it met the 19th Brigade, which was then placed under the orders of the 4th Division. Up to this point, the 4th Division had been attached to II Corps but, as the 6th Division had arrived in France, it was informed that, on its arrival at Verberie, it was to rejoin III Corps.

The events of the previous six days had been particularly trying and the troops were in a state of exhaustion. It was intended that the division would commence the march at 7:00am on the 31st and, before departure, all sick were evacuated to the refilling point at Villeneuve. The division was to travel in two columns on two converging roads, the 10th and 19th Brigades marching on the right and the 11th and 12th Brigades on the left. Once again, faulty communications played a part, as the 10th and 19th Brigades, having failed to receive the order to march, were forced to delay their departure for a further hour. Due to this delay, the left column was instructed to halt for one hour at midday, to allow the right-hand column to catch up.

As the journey proceeded, communications between the two columns continually broke down and it was found necessary to implement special arrangements, using mounted troops, to maintain a connection between the two columns and the rearguard. By 12:30pm, the left column had passed through Fontenoy and the right hand column had made up some of the lost ground.

On arrival at Verberie, the G.O.C., was informed that German formations were advancing south from Compiègne. The baggage train presented a problem, as it was still at St. Jean Au Bois, more than ten kilometres behind, due to state of the roads[53]. It was decided to concen-

---

[52] *Although Senlis was not to be a destination for the division, the location of the town was used to indicate the direction of travel, that is, to the south-west. Senlis is located about twenty three kilometres north of the modern day Charles De Gaulle International Airport.*

[53] *The condition of the roads and the proximity of the German cavalry caused several trucks of the baggage train to be abandoned. The exact reason is not known, but the 1*

trate the division on the line Santines - Verberie - Rhuis, that is, astride the Compiègne - Senlis road, in the path of the oncoming enemy cavalry and push north to La Croix St. Ouen in order to allow the delayed transport to arrive behind the front line.

The right hand column continued to experience delays. The 19th Brigade was late and it was not expected to arrive at St. Sauveur, the village it was to defend, before dark. The defence of that village was allotted to a battalion of the 11th Brigade. As the baggage train arrived safely at about 7:00pm, the 19th Brigade was redirected into billets at Santines. The 10th Brigade, having acted acting as the rearguard, had also experienced delays. Having taken the wrong road the artillery had became blocked in the streets of Santines, at midnight, by other transport.

 At that time, the transfer of the 4th Division to III Corps became effective. Late in the evening, the baggage train was instructed to retire to the south to Baron via Raray and Rully. Train and transport were ordered to move as early as possible and reach the St. Vaast Plateau a few kilometres away, at which time the fighting troops would follow.

Cavalry Brigade, acting as rearguard to the 4 Division, found the vehicles and supplied drivers. They were eventually returned to the 4 Division on the 5 September.

September - 1914

Early in the morning of the 1st September, the division prepared to move to Baron, following the path of the transport. The move began on two separate roads, one leading from Nery and the other from St. Vaast, both of which joined near Raray, from where the brigades would then continue as a single column. The ammunition column started early, at 4:00am, followed immediately by the Division Train.

Such was the proximity of the enemy that the 19th, 12th, and 10th Brigades were under instruction that, in the event of being attacked, they were to form a line on a stream, a tributary of the Oise, which ran just north of Santines and Verberie. As expected, at about 4:30am, the outposts of the 1st East Lancashire Regiment of the 11th Brigade were attacked at the eastern end of St. Saveur with machine-gun and rifle fire. To assist the East Lancashires the 1st Somerset Light Infantry took up positions about Fey Fm, and the Rifle Brigade on high ground south of Vaucelle, to cover the retirement of the Lancashires and the Hampshire's. Those positions were assumed just in time for the 19th Brigade to become involved in action elsewhere.

At about 5:30am three artillery batteries of the German 4th Cavalry Division, drawn up during the night close to the lines of the 1st Cavalry Brigade at Nery, opened fire on the six guns of "L" Battery from high ground 800 - 1000 yards distant. Those guns were they moved further south, a distance of 500 – 600 yards from which a clear field of fire could be gained. That fire immediately knocked out three of the six guns and killed many horses and gunners of the Queens Battery, with only three guns of the battery able to reply. Whilst under devastating fire, many acts of bravery were performed and, finally, a single gun, manned by two of the crew, remained to answer the enemy fire. The 10th, 11th and 12th Brigades were warned to expect an attack and it was suggested that the 11th Brigade, about St. Saveur, might get into the rear of the German Cavalry via Betsey St. Pierre.

Although it was pointed out that the intention of the division was to continue the withdrawal, it was to punish the German cavalry first. The 19th Brigade, Royal Warwickshire Regiment and the Royal Dublin Fusiliers, being close to the scene, assisted the cavalry troopers of the 1st Cavalry Brigade, by attacking the enemy guns and driving back the enemy infantry and cavalry. The Cavalry Brigade managed to capture eight of the enemy guns and take seventy prisoners. By 9:45am, the Cavalry Brigade, with the assistance of the Dublin Fusiliers and the Warwickshire's, had driven the Germans out of the area around Nery and the Ambulances were brought forward to evacuate the wounded, while the artillery removed the captured guns.

While the Dublin Fusiliers and Warwickshire's were engaged at Nery, the remainder of the 10th Brigade was preparing to leave Verberie and, upon hearing the heavy artillery and rifle fire to the east, the Seaforth Highlanders and Royal Irish Fusiliers, immediately marched via St. Vaast towards Fey F[m]. On reaching the top of the hill, they discovered that the Dublin Fusiliers and Warwickshire Regiment had already attacked. The two battalions immediately launched and a second, supporting, attack. However, on reaching Nery it was established that the enemy position had previously been occupied[54].

Immediately following the events at Nery a large concentration of German cavalry advanced from Pierrepont towards Rocquemont[55]. These were engaged by artillery and riflefire and forced them to retire to the east. Once reorganised the division continued the withdrawal in two columns, the first travelling to Chamizy and the second to Montepillot. The Inniskilling Fusiliers, who had been holding the defensive positions on the stream near Verberie, then free from German attacks, made for St. Vaast. The enemy pressed the retiring Fusiliers closely so a second battalion was sent to prevent the risk of the Fusiliers being overrun. By mid-morning, the 12th Brigade had taken up positions at Heleux in company with the 4th Cavalry Brigade.

During the retirement, communications with 11th Brigade had been temporarily lost. The Rifle Brigade and Somerset Light Infantry, still in St. Saveur, were again subjected to attack, but managed to repulse the enemy and inflicted considerable losses. Whilst those two battalions were fighting off the perpetual attacks, the 1st East Lancashire Regiment and 1st Hampshire Regiment, neither of which was engaged, managed to retire up the Nery Valley with only a few casualties. When contact had been re-established with the 11th Brigade, it was directed to assume the role of rearguard once the evacuation of the wounded from Nery was complete. Having seen the ambulance units out of Nery and the captured guns removed, the 11th Brigade retired across the open St. Vaast plateau, finally billeting in Rozières.

---

[54] *It was determined that the enemy was in fact the 4 (German) Cavalry Brigade accompanied by twelve guns, eight of which were left on the field and captured. One of the damaged guns of 'L' Battery is currently displayed in the Imperial War Museum, London.*

[55] *These villages are all located in a very small area, which simplified the amount of marching undertaken by the troops as they made their attacks, and moved in support.*

Due to the delay at Nery, it was seen necessary for the whole division to conduct a night march to Dammartin, a distance of 28 kilometres, in order to disengage from the enemy. The late arrival of the orders placed a great strain on the already exhausted troops. However, led by the transport column and ammunition train, the march commenced at 10:00pm, protected by the 10th Brigade and 29th Field Artillery Brigade[56]. Minor delays were experienced in the darkness but, by 3:00am, the division was again on the move. The journey was carried out without interference from the enemy and by 6:30pm in the evening of the 3rd, the 11th Brigade had reached Rozières while the 10th Brigade remained at Baron with perimeter guards against the pursuing Uhlans. The division war diary stated *"This was Sedan Day and the Division was quite proud of the fact the Germans had achieved little to celebrate."*

The halt by the brigades during the evening was only temporary and, by 1:30am on the 3rd September, the 10th Brigade had marched for Nanteuil and the 12th Brigade for Eve. Once again, delays were caused, as the orders for the night march did not reach the 11th Brigade until 3:00am, well after the other brigades had departed. Finally, at 4:00am, the 11th Brigade followed in the path of the 12th Brigade. The journey continued all night without incident and by daylight, the division was well on its way. During the course of this journey one infantry and an artillery brigade remained at Eve while the remainder of the division stopped on the Dammartin - St. Mard line for the night. The 10th Brigade had reached Dammartin at about midday and bivouacked in the town, with outpost guards outstretched on a five-mile radius.

At 2:00pm the 11th Brigade reported that two German cavalry brigades were being driven across its front by the 1st Cavalry Brigade and asked if they should assist but was advised, an hour later, that they should not get involved as it might delay the withdrawal of the division. During the day the remains of "L" Battery was temporarily attached to the 4th Division for the purposes of transport of the damaged guns.

Exhausted as they were, the retirement continued. At 6:00pm on the evening of the 4th, the division received instructions to continue the retirement, in two columns, during the night. The right hand column, under the command of Brigadier-General Wilson, consisting of the Division Ammunition Column, 19th and 12th Infantry Brigades, Division Train, 3rd Field Ambulance and the 7th and 9th Field Companies

---

[56] *The march on the night of the 3 and 4 September proved to be one of the most gruelling tests of endurance undertaken by the retiring troops.*

marched at 10:00pm to Gournay[57], via St. Mard. Before departure, the 12th Brigade had reported German Cavalry and machine-gun fire near Le Sec and a little later, refugees were reported to be digging trenches across the road, on the line of advance. Officers of the brigade were forced to remove the refugees and repair the damage

The main body, under the command of Brigadier-General Hunter-Weston, consisting of the 37th Field Artillery Brigade, 32nd Field Artillery Brigade, 14th Field Artillery Brigade, and the Northern Irish Horse, followed the same route. The 11th Brigade departed from Eve at 11:35pm and marched to the Chateau Fontinville, via Dammartin, where it arrived at about noon the next day, the 5th September.

The 10th Brigade, the 29th Field Artillery Brigade and the Cyclist Company marched as the left-hand column, under the command of Brigadier-General Haldane. The 10th Brigade cleared St. Mard early in the morning of the 4th and, as there was no enemy activity in the area, six ambulances were sent to meet the brigade at Annet-sur-Marne to pick up the sick. As if the trials already faced by the troops was not enough. Their passage along the roads, like that of the 12th Brigade, was made increasingly difficult by the discovery of French Territorials tearing up the roads and again, the officers of the 4th Division had to stop the destruction as they passed through.

The condition of troops defies accurate description, but the level of exhaustion was exacerbated, on the 5th, by the hot and dusty conditions. The columns of marching troops were visibly at the end of their endurance and, as the march progressed, the number of stragglers increased as men simply reached the end of their ability to take another step. It was under these conditions that, at 10:15pm, after a very trying day, the 12th Brigade, marching as escort to the Ammunition Column, finally crossed the River Marne at Lagny, a distance of some 20 kilometres.

During the afternoon sixty-nine of the German prisoners, which had been captured at Nery and had been marching with the division, were sent to the railhead at Tournon for dispatch to a prisoner of war camp. During the march, the news that the British Army was to return to the offensive was promulgated to the troops. That news produced an immediate lift in morale. Although they had enjoyed little rest, their spirits were high as they looked forward to the opportunity of taking the fight

---

[57] *Gournay, at the time of writing, is located 20 kilometres due west of the centre and well within the western suburbs of modern Paris.*

to the enemy[58]. The 12th Brigade, accompanied by French troops, continued to Serris, south-east of Lagny and nearly one thousand stragglers, who had been collected along the way, were sent by rail to Coulonnies for rest and reorganisation, thereafter rejoining their units at Ozoir two days later.

The 10th Brigade completed the crossing of the Marne behind the 12th Brigade, at 6.30pm. It had marched and fought for nearly thirty-one hours with little or no sleep, except what little rest that could be achieved after a brief stop at Dammartin. Except for those movements required for readjustment of the line, the division had finally completed the retirement, having lasted for nearly two weeks[59].

The billeting area for the 19th Brigade and the 4th Division was on the line of Chevry – Brie Comte Robert. The rearguard remained on the line of Gretz – Ozoir – La-Ferrière, fifteen kilometres south of the Marne and set up outposts, after destroying all bridges, as protection in the event of an attempt by the enemy to cross the river. The division was ordered to stop where it stood and all troops were to have a complete rest, with no digging or other operations. During this final day of retreat, information was received that the Germans were moving in a south-easterly direction and represented no immediate threat[60]. Congratulations were sent from II Corps for their performance since landing in France twelve days before.

Minor tasks were still required and the units, which had rejoined the division in recent days, performed most of that work. The Cyclist Company provided an escort to the 7th Field Company who was to demolish a bridge across the Marne. The 10th, 11th and 12th Brigades and the division artillery supplied special reconnaissance parties consisting of one officer and four men[61]. The Cyclist Company was sent, with a

---

[58] *During the 5 September, the 32 Royal Artillery Brigade was detached from the 4 Division to replace 'L' Battery, of the 1 Cavalry Division, which had suffered so severely at the hands of the German artillery at Nery.*

[59] *The war diary of the 4 Division on the 4 September; "This was to be the last day of retirement, much to the relief of all ranks."*

[60] *It was the south-easterly movement of the German First Army (von Kluck) that decided Joffre to attack the right flank of that army as it passed across the front of the French and British Armies.*

[61] *Two of these groups were later used by III Corps headquarters; one led by Lieutenant Brinstead, of the 2 Essex Regiment, 12 Brigade, and the other by 2 Lieutenant Lane of the 1 Somerset Light Infantry, 11 Brigade.*

French officer, to destroy the Chalifert Railway Bridge and to reconnoitre in the direction of Isle de Villenois Bridge. The remainder of the day was spent in reorganising and refitting in preparation for an early advance.

During the course of the preceding few days, it had been noted that the German 1st Army, instead of approaching Paris from the east, had swung to the south-east and joined the pursuit of the French 5th Army. The change in direction drew the German 1st Army across the front of the French 6th Army and the British Expeditionary Force. On the 3rd September, General Joffre, French Commander-in-Chief, took the decision to attack the exposed German left flank. The advance was to take place with the B.E.F. situated between the French 6th Army, on the left, and the French 5th Army, on the right. The general direction of the advance, being to the north-east, required the B.E.F. to cross several rivers, the Grand Morin, Petit Morin, Marne, and ultimately the River Aisne.

The various units of the division were spread over a wide area and the 5th of September consisted of considerable movements within each brigade, as they concentrated in preparation for the advance. To achieve rapid reorganisation, III Corps had ordered the 4th Division to retire to the south-west, out of the main line of defence and, as far as possible, to remain concealed. The troops were to have precious little time to prepare for the advance, as the attack against the German right flank was to commence early the next morning, the 6th September. This placed great demands upon the officers and men who had just completed a most gruelling journey of one hundred and forty miles. Fortunately, distances to new billeting areas were short and every officer and man made great efforts and, by evening, order prevailed. Men rested whenever possible, medical attention was given to those in need and hot meals were provided for all.

On the 5th, whilst the division was resting, nearly all of the officers and four hundred men of the 1st Royal Warwickshire Regiment, accompanied by one hundred and four men of the 2nd Royal Dublin Fusiliers, having become separated from the division on the 26th August, rejoined the 10th Brigade. These were further supplemented, late in the morning, by a batch of newly arrived reinforcements, which also joined the 10th Brigade. An incident also took place, which had its roots in the battle at Haucourt on the 26th August. Lieutenant-Colonel Elkington, the Commanding Officer of the 1st Royal Warwickshire Regiment, was placed under arrest for his conduct at St. Quentin on the 28th of August[62].

At 7:58pm operation orders were received from III Corps stating: *"British forces are about to assume the offensive north-eastward against the German right flank in conjunction with the French 6th Army, the Germans having moved south-east against the left flank of the French 5th Army about St. Barthelemy. III Corps is to advance towards Serris acting with II Corps on its right. The 4th Division is to furnish the advanced guard of one Brigade and attached troops, and a left flank guard of two Battalions and a battery on reaching Les Fermieres Fe. The 19th Brigade to follow the 4th Division."*

The Commander-in-Chief of the British Expeditionary Force, Field-Marshall Sir John French, wisely saw the need to nurture the troops and to provide rest and sustenance, which was still very much needed. Although the retirement had finished on the 5th, the time spent in the following 24 hours was very busy and rest remained a luxury. The orders of the day required that the troops should halt, every hour, in the course of the advance[63].

Because the brigades would commence from different locations, III Corps had ordered that the 4th Division should concentrate about Jossigny – Conches as the advance progressed, with advanced troops at Magny Le Hongre and Coupray, while the 19th Brigade would meet the main body of the division at Conches. At 10:30pm on the 5th, instructions were issued to the effect that the advance was to commence at

---

[62] *Lieutenant-Colonel Elkington was tried by Courts-Martial on a charge of shameful conduct. He was found guilty and dishonourably discharged from the army. He was not however, without influence in some quarters and was a dedicated officer. He immediately joined the French Foreign Legion with which he fought with distinction, being badly wounded at Navarin Farm, east of Rheims. In 1916, he was forgiven for his actions and awarded the Distinguished Service Order in private investiture at Buckingham Palace. His colleague, Lieutenant-Colonel Mainwaring, Commanding Officer of the 2⁰ Dublin Fusiliers, who also partook of the proposed surrender at St. Quentin was not so fortunate. He was also tried and found guilty. He was very ill and did not receive the same forgiveness. He was never accepted back into the army.*

[63] *As well intentioned as this may have been, the next few days were to show that the German withdrawal was so rapid that the mobile field kitchens experienced great difficulty in keeping food supplies up to the forward troops. The speed of the pursuit created large scale traffic congestion, and as the weather worsened, the tactical demands of rapid movement often meant that the troops enjoyed conditions that were only little better than those suffered in the recently completed retreat.*

3:00am on the 6th and the division was to follow a general course through Pontcarré, Ferrières Fe, and Jossigny to Serris.

The 10th Brigade, accompanied by the 29th Field Artillery Brigade, was to act as the advanced guard for the division. As the brigade would be passing through the Forêt d'Armainviliers and the Forêt de Cracey special defensive instructions were issued, in view of the fact that a German division was at Guerard, to protect the right flank of the brigade, as it advanced on the western edge of the forest. The 12th Brigade, North Irish Horse and the Cyclist Company were to act as the flank guard from Les Fermieres Fe.

As instructed, the 10th Brigade commenced the advance at 3:00am on the 6th September, one hour before the main body of the division and halted at 3:50am halfway between the main road and the railway crossing, south of Pontcarré, on its first scheduled break. The G.O.C. informed all of the brigades that he did not intend going beyond Serris and, that on arrival they should place outposts and reconnoitre as far as possible. Shortly after receiving those instructions, the 10th Brigade cleared the railway crossing, having been held up by train traffic and reached Pontcarré at 5:20am, a distance of approximately one and a half kilometres. Once through the village, the Cyclist Company, which had been scouting ahead of the 10th Brigade, reported all roads clear into Jossigny, so instructions were issued to push on as fast as possible without tiring the men or 'scamping' on reconnaissance.

As the 10th Brigade was making its way northward to Jossigny, the 11th Brigade had also marched north, on the right of the 10th Brigade, to Villeneuve-Le-Comte where it became the reserve to the 10th Brigade, should it find itself in difficulties. By 7:30am, the 10th Brigade had reached Jossigny, a distance of 10 kilometres from the start line, and halted in the town for their hourly break. Here they were informed by local inhabitants that Germans had been in St. Germain, 8 kilometres away, at 8:00am that morning. The Cyclist Company also reported that inhabitants had told them that one thousand German troops were still in Guerard, so patrols were sent out to place a guard around the village. While the brigade was resting Brigadier-General Haldane carried out a reconnaissance and, on returning at about 11:00am, ordered the 1st Royal Irish Fusiliers to Billy - Romainvilliers, south-east of Serris.

The 4th Division had received instructions to move at once to support I Corps, which had been attacked. At 2:00pm, the 10th Brigade moved to Voulangis, leaving a flank guard at Villiers-Sur-Morin, on the river Le

G^d. Morin[64]. On arrival at Voulangis, the 2nd Seaforth Highlanders were sent to Pt 138[65], south-west of Crécy, with instructions to conduct a reconnaissance of the Le G^d Morin, while the artillery assembled in the area about one mile west, and to the rear, of the 10th Brigade. The remainder of the division moved to Villeneuve Le Compte.

By 4:30pm, the situation of I Corps had improved substantially and the division was ordered to remain where it was, that is, with the 10th and 12th Brigades over looking the valley of the Le G^d Morin while the 11th Brigade remained behind the 10th Brigade. The 19th Brigade remained at Villeneuve St. Denis, some 10 kilometres behind the advanced guard, as division reserve. Most of the night was spent in reconnaissance, securing bridges and preparing for the next day.

In the early hours of the 7th the Cyclist Company, which had been scouting in advance of the division, had reported all roads clear as far as St. Fiacre, 5 miles ahead of the division. The Royal Warwickshire Regiment (10th Brigade), was immediately instructed to occupy Férrolles, on the opposite bank of the Gd Morin and cover the crossing of the remainder of the division at Crécy. After Férrolles had been occupied, the division continued its advance in two columns. The right hand column, consisting of the 10th Brigade, advanced through Crécy to Maisoncelles-en-Brie, while the 11th Brigade followed a similar route through Voulangis and joined the 10th Brigade at Maisoncelles-en-Brie at about 2:40pm where water for men and horses was made available.

The 12th Brigade, accompanied by the 14th Field Artillery, led the left-hand column further to the north, via Montarbin Bridge, where it crossed Le G^d Morin, passed through Bouleurs and advanced towards La Haute Maison, where it halted, and awaited further orders. The 12th Brigade, now 2,500 yards ahead of the 10th, had assumed the role of advanced guard. As the 2nd Essex Regiment, the advanced guard of the 12th Brigade, approached La Haute Maison it came under rifle and machine-gun fire. The opposition was overcome with little trouble and resulted in the capture of several prisoners, one of which informed the battalion of the existence of a company of Germans in the woods northeast of La Haute Maison.

---

[64] *The English translation would be the Grand Morin. Le Gd Morin is a substantial river, which flows from the east through the Vallee du Grd. Morin, in which lies Crécy. Le Gd Morin enters the Marne near Esbly.*

[65] *Point 138 was a piece of high ground, 138 meters above sea level, overlooking Le Gd Morin.*

During the halt the 2nd Seaforth Highlanders, 2nd Royal Dublin Fusiliers and Cyclist Company, had formed an outpost line on the left of the division at Calabres. Here they reported that a German rearguard of 3000 of all arms had passed Bisset, at 2:00pm and were "stone cold"[66], however, the pursuit of the enemy column was not deemed necessary and, at 3:30pm, the 10th Brigade departed from Maisoncelles-en-Brie for Douve. While the North Irish Horse and Cyclists were gathered in, they observed German machine guns, mounted on motor lorries, retiring along the main road towards Bouleurs[67].

Upon arrival at Les Fermieres, at 6:15pm, bivouacs were taken for the night. No food supplies had been issued to the field kitchens the previous night so the troops had to eat the field rations that they carried with them. The left column moved without incident until about 6:20pm when a German battery shelled the advanced guard of the 12th Brigade, the 2nd Royal Inniskilling Fusiliers. During that shelling the Fusiliers encountered and "turned out" five Uhlans and, having done so, came under concentrated rifle fire, suffering several casualties. The 2nd Essex Regiment also met a Uhlan patrol near a wood north of La Grande Rue, drove it back, and also came under rifle fire from the edge of the wood to the north of the village. Two officers and nineteen men were killed or wounded in this single action.

During the night hot food arrived as the transport had managed to catch up with the infantry. After dark, the 2nd Essex Regiment sent patrols north and north-east and engaged German patrols. They also heard Germans talking in the village of Pierre Levée, three quarters of a mile north of La Haute Maison and noted that there was considerable movement of enemy travelling north.

The pursuit was to continue at 6:00am the next morning and if, as expected, the enemy had evacuated Pierre Levée, the division was to move on Jouarre[68] in two columns. The right column was to consist of the 10th and 12th Brigades under the command of Major-General Snow, and was to march via Petit Courrois and Le Grande Glairet. The left column, under Brigadier-General Hunter-Weston, was to consist of the 19th and 11th Brigades and the 14th Field Artillery Brigade, and was to

---

[66] *The expression 'stone cold' inferred that the German rearguard was exhausted.*

[67] *Such was the uncertainty of the German positions that the German vehicles were retiring behind the advancing 4 Division. The 12 Brigade had passed through Bouleurs only hours before in its advance to la Haute Maison.*

[68] *Jouarre lies about 1 mile to the south of the River Marne.*

march via Pierre Levée, through Signy Signets to Les Corbiers, to the east of Jouarre.

So as to arrive at its assembly positions at the prescribed time the various units of the 10th Brigade set out at 3:45am and assembled at Les Fermieres Fe. The leading units commenced the advance as early as 4:45am as it had been established that Pierre Levée was apparently unoccupied. The leading battalion of the 12th Brigade moved through the village without any sign of the enemy, however, as the patrols reached the northern exit, the scouts were fired on from a small farm 300 yards beyond.

As the 12th Brigade had made good progress on the right, so too had the 10th Brigade. Acting as the left flank guard it had advanced towards Gd Loge Fe and reconnoitred towards Petit Courrois[69]. The 19th Brigade had also secured the corner of the Forêt du Man's by 6:00am and, as soon as it was established that there were no enemy troops in the vicinity, the brigade stopped and cooked breakfast.

The 11th Brigade, following behind the advanced brigades, moved off at 8:00am from La Barde to La Haute Maison where it halted to wait for the 19th Brigade to move through Pierre Levée. As the 19th Brigade exited from Pierre Levée, it was subjected to heavy and accurate shellfire from the high ground about Morintru-Le-Haute. The supporting artillery came up as quickly as possible but was held up by the 1st line transport of the 19th Brigade. On getting past the transport, the enemy fire was soon silenced and few casualties were suffered.

Good progress was made and the leading troops of the 12th Brigade had reached Les Savants Fe by 7.55am and advanced patrols had ventured along the north-east edge of the wood near Montebise Chateau, while two battalions were sent to Petit Courrois and reconnaissance patrols to L'Isle Jourdain. French cavalry units informed the division that the enemy had retired in two columns on La Ferté[70] and Trilport the previous night, but a German rearguard remained in the woods south of Signy Signets. Both of these towns were located on the Marne River and were important crossing points. Aircraft reconnaissance showed no significant strength of the enemy south of the line of the River Marne but

---

[69] *The villages mentioned here were very small, sometimes only numbering several homes and small acreages. They were all located in a small area just north of Pierre Levée and were only a matter of two to three hundred yards apart.*

[70] *La Ferté is located astride the River Marne and had been designated as the preferred crossing point for the division.*

reported large bodies of the enemy crossing at La Ferté, just ahead of the 4th Division.

The German withdrawal had been carried out in some haste and the need to establish contact with the main body of the enemy was paramount. To that end, III Corps had stated that the objective for both columns was to seize the high ground north of the line Jouarre – Signy Signets as quickly as possible. The 11th and 12th Brigades were informed that it was essential that they close with the enemy at once, and the right column was told to push on to La Grande Glairet. It was also deemed that an additional advanced guard, under Colonel Anley, should seize the high ground about Perreuse Chateau, which would enable the artillery to shell the bridge at La Ferté.

In response to the urgency of the moment, the 12th Brigade cleared the woods north-east of Petit Courrois late in the morning and reached La Grande Glairet by midday. The existence of Germans in Romeny, two kilometres to the east, required two companies to be detached from the advanced guard to clear the village as the brigades moved towards Jouarre and Les Corbiers. A further company of the 12th Brigade was sent to secure the high ground about Les Corbiers

It is necessary that we pause in the narrative at this point to understand the geography over which the division fought in this early stage of the offensive. The Battle of the Marne, as it is commonly referred to in English speaking histories, was fought along an extensive length of the river of that name. The river acted as the first line of enemy resistance, and the German rearguards held the northern banks of the river to allow tome for the main body of the German army to retire to the intended final line of resistance, the River Aisne, some 40 miles to the north.

La Ferté stood almost mid-way along the strategically important Coulommiers – Château Thierry Road and provided the major crossing of the river along that route. The river flowed in a westerly direction through a valley in which lay several smaller villages. To the east of La Ferté the river wound in several large loops between two and five kilometres deep where it flowed north-west, past Château Thierry. To the west, the river travelled in a comparatively straight line to the west for a distance of approximately seven kilometres where it turned north for some distance and looped once again to the south, past Meaux.

La Ferté, through the middle of which flowed the river, lay at the base of the last of several large curves to the east, at the point were the river straightened out in its westerly meandering. A tributary, the Petit Morin, joined the Marne from the south, just to the west of La Ferté, thus placing the village in the 'V' of the junction and straddling the River Marne. To the north of La Ferté lay Reuil-en-Brie, Chamigny, Vaux, and St. Aulde, all located on the southern arm of the last loop.

Within the southern confines of the loop lay the villages of Courtaron, Messy and Luzancy, forming a triangle, with Messy at the northern apex. To the west of La Ferté lay Sammeron, Sept Sorts and Les Corbiers, located on high ground and slightly to the south of the river. The division had approached from the south and it was intended to cross at La Ferté and advance along the Château Thierry Road, which followed the loop of the river in a northerly direction, through Chamigny and Coulombs-en Valois.

By 1:00pm on the 7th, the advanced units of the division were only a mile from the River Marne, on a line Le Grande Glairet – Pereus Chateau, but had no view over the river or of the enemy activity near La Ferté. The 12th Brigade, as advanced guard, was pushing for La Ferté but had halted temporarily at the southern entrance to Jouarre in order to allow the Cyclists to clear the village. The brigade advanced to the high ground south of La Ferté, about Les Corbiers and, from these vantage points, the troops had a clear view of what lay ahead.

From the heights above the river, German cavalry and a column of transport were seen retiring from Les Maneaux in the direction of Rougeville far to the north. It was discovered that the enemy had largely evacuated the southern half of La Ferté although they had located a field gun on the southern side of the river. They still defended the northern half of the village and continued to hold control over the river and the crossings.

The 12th Brigade was ordered to seize the bridge at Courcelles, near La Ferté, cross the river, eject the Germans and to establish on the high ground north of that village. At 3:30pm, the right column, principally the 12th Brigade, with the 10th Brigade in support, set out with these instructions in mind. Although the troops were tired, rapid progress was made and at 5:05pm, the 12th Brigade reported that the Courcelles Bridge was intact and that advanced troops were making good the high ground about Le Bondows and Les Abymes. In preparation for the river crossing, the 10th Brigade requested that the two battalions, being held as Corps reserve, be permitted to move to Fringale, however, only two companies were authorised to rejoin.

The left column, consisting of the 11th and 19th Brigades, was shelled by German artillery while waiting near Signy Signets for orders. Having received orders to secure the spur to the north-east of Signy Signets and the high ground around Les Corbiers, the column had achieved the objectives by 1:40pm and were in touch with the right-hand column. By mid-afternoon the advanced guard of the 11th Brigade had reached Condetz, overlooking La Ferté, secured roads east and west of the village, and reported the bridge at La Ferté as clear.

Two battalions of the 19th Brigade had remained about Signy Signets, to hold the high ground in support of the remainder of the division. While the 19th Brigade was thus employed, the 9th Field Company of Royal Engineers proceeded to Jouarre to put those houses on the north-eastern side of the village, which were facing Courcelles, into a defensive condition, as Courcelles was still, temporarily, in enemy hands. On completion, the engineers remained to hold the village throughout the night, until reinforced before daybreak by a battalion of the 10th Brigade.

During the afternoon, the 3rd Cavalry Brigade had placed, at the disposal of the division, a squadron of the 16th Lancers, which remained with the division until the 15th, doing excellent work. With the arrival of the Lancers, "A" Squadron of the North Irish Horse, which had been attached to the division since mobilisation, returned to rejoin G.H.Q. at Coulommiers. As this manoeuvring took place news arrived that fourteen officers and one thousand, three hundred and thirty three men were reported as being in transit to Coulommiers, several miles behind the front, as replacements for the losses suffered by the division. During the day the division had made an advance of six and three quarter miles in fine weather and experienced considerable fighting, but few casualties.

While the initial efforts to secure Le Ferté were underway, the 12th Brigade crossed the Petite Morin River at Jouarre and occupied the heights above Courcelles. That secured the high ground about Chateau Les Bondon where, despite the advantage of height and observation, the 12th Brigade could not dislodge a party of German troops in the main street of Le Ferté, because of the heavy sniping and machine-gun fire. The 19th Brigade had also established strong detachments at La Ferté, Signy Signets and Jouarre. Although the sniping in the streets of La Ferté had ceased by 9:00pm, it was not possible to get right through the southern part of the village without coming under fire from the northern side of the river. For the moment, both brigades were impaled upon the only known major crossing of the River Marne by heavy resistance from a well concealed and determined rearguard, while the main body of the German army, the very objective of the pursuit, continued to slip the net.

Although the division had made great efforts to reach the river in sufficient numbers to force a crossing, it was not to be. The 11th Brigade, having been seriously delayed in its attempts to cross the Petite Morin behind the 12th and 19th Brigades, relieved the 12th Brigade during the night and assumed responsibility affecting a crossing, but the resistance of the enemy rearguard prevented all attempts. During the evening, aviators had reported that the bridges at Changis, Sammeron and La Ferté had been destroyed, although the railway bridges at Courtoron Le Jardinets and Nanteuil were intact[71]. However, despite the difficulties, the intention was to continue the offensive at daybreak with the view of capturing the high ground about Tartarel, to the north.

As preparations for the advance continued, the remaining German rearguard crossed to the north bank of the Marne early in the morning of the 8th, destroying the bridges at La Ferté and Luzancy as they passed. It was the final demolition of the bridges that had caused both field companies to concentrate at Le Ferté and they were under instructions to repair the bridge as quickly as possible.

While waiting for the 11th Brigade to come into line, units of the 12th Brigade, accompanied by the first two battalions of the 11th Brigade, the Somerset Light Infantry and the Rifle Brigade, had occupied Tartarel and the surrounding high ground by 7:00am. From those positions six motor lorries on the La Ferté – Montreuil road could be seen, apparently waiting to pick up the German rearguard.

While Tartarel was being secured, the East Lancashires of the 11th Brigade occupied the houses, formerly those occupied by the enemy rearguard, on the southern bank of the River Marne in La Ferté, from which the damaged bridge could be watched. The fact that German machine guns and snipers had occupied houses on the northern bank of the Marne made any movement on the southern bank impossible and the enemy artillery kept the ridge north of Signy Signet under constant fire to obstruct observation from the heights.

By 9:00pm, the engineers had still not been able to get near the bridge due to the machine-gun fire. Division headquarters impressed upon the

---

[71] *These latter named bridges were several miles from the current position of the 4 Division and could not be used for crossing the Marne.*

11th Brigade the importance of getting the bridge at La Ferté repaired and that any advance towards Chamigny and Luzancy, which had also been allotted to that brigade, was of secondary importance.

The machine guns and snipers of the 11th Brigade had taken a heavy toll of the enemy on the other side of the river, about seven hundred, according to the local inhabitants, however, the position remained heavily defended and could not be overcome by machine guns and rifles alone. In an effort to subdue the resistance the artillery was called upon and the howitzers were moved into position, authorised to use Lydite[72] shells. In preparation for the shelling all troops of the 11th Brigade were withdrawn from the southern half of the town, in order to give the artillery a free hand. During the shelling, the field companies waited in readiness.

Although the gunfire was heavy, there had been difficulties from the outset. Determining the location of the enemy machine guns was by observation through smoke and shellfire. To exacerbate the problem of observation, the artillery brigades were under the orders of division headquarters and communicating requests and the indication of targets took a considerable time. By 2:30pm, it was reported that the enemy on the northern bank had remained uninjured by the howitzer fire and the sniping and machine-gun fire continued throughout the afternoon.

During the night of the 8th, the French 45th Division, on the right of the 4th Division, and the British 5th Division, on the left, had slowly pushed across the river. The movement of divisions on both sides of the 4th Division intensified the need to sweep the resistance from La Ferté and the decision was taken to circumvent Le Ferté. Patrols were sent in both directions along the river to discover other locations suitable for fording.

In the early hours of the 9th, patrols of 12th Brigade had moved along the riverbank to the west and, as they approached Reuil-en-Brie, 1000 yards upstream, they encountered heavy shellfire from an enemy howitzer. The gun was directed upon the Le Ferté – Montreuil road, along which the approach was made and forced the advancing troops to retire. To subdue that fire, field guns were sent to Tartarel from where they could fire on the enemy positions. Supported now by artillery, the 12th Brigade attempted a crossing of the river Reuil-en-Brie using boats.

---

[72] *Lydite was a high explosive used in early British and German shells. Because of the shortage of shells available to the British army in the first two years of the war, Lydite shells could only be used with authorisation.*

Progress was slow but the numbers gradually grew as the day progressed.

At about 9:30am, patrols of the 12th Brigade had also discovered that the railway bridge at Le Saussoy was intact but held by a party of about twenty of the enemy. Two hours later the defending party was seen to retire across the bridge towards Nanteuil, partially destroying the Railway Bridge as they went.

Even further to the west, the 2nd Essex Regiment and 2nd Lancashire Fusiliers, of the same brigade, moved through the woods to the Barrage, south of Chamigny[73]. Although they took with them machine guns, which were brought to bear on the enemy holding the crossing, they had to cross open fields, which extended down to the riverbanks. Each time they exposed themselves in the fields the same howitzer that was harassing the King's Own and Royal Inniskilling Fusiliers also fired upon the Essex and further attempts to cross at that point were cancelled. The local inhabitants had reported, however, that it was possible to cross by the Barrage itself. Taking advantage of that advice patrols reconnoitred a covered approach and found that it could be crossed with minimum resistance and by 3:45pm, some troops had managed to cross over the Barrage with only light casualties. A bridgehead was soon established on the northern bank to cover the crossing of additional troops.

While the 12th Brigade was thus engaged, the 1st Rifle Brigade, of the 11th Brigade, had pressed down to the southern bank of the Marne, to ascertain whether the enemy was still holding the houses on the opposite bank. Finding no enemy in sight, they attempted to cross by using small boats. Twenty minutes later those still on the southern bank saw several of the Rifle Brigade holding positions on the opposite side and witnessed German infantry retiring from the lower western bridge.

While the division struggled with the difficulties of getting across the river, the 3rd Cavalry Brigade reported large bodies of Germans retiring west to east within range of the heavy guns and that the French were shelling the rear of the columns from the direction of Ourcq. The close proximity of the enemy in such large numbers prompted the suspension of the orders for the battalions to cross the Marne. *"These orders to the 10th and 12th Brigades were issued as it was thought that the two Bat-*

---

[73] *The Barrage was a construction across the river, which controlled water flow in times of flood. It lay several hundred yards north of the position at Reuil-en-Brie, where the 12. Brigade was also attempting to cross the river by boat.*

talions that had crossed at Chamigny would be dangerously exposed in view of the German movement reported by the 3rd Cavalry Brigade and also in view of the apparent isolated position of II Corps, across the river, that it might be necessary to for the 4th Division to move at short notice across the Marne at Méry to go to its assistance[74]." The 10th Brigade was then ordered to move to Les Poupelains via Jouarre.

The 5th Division was still looking for assistance and appealed to the 4th Division to deal with German artillery near Chamoust. The 12th Brigade immediately sent troops in that direction and successfully ejected the German guns and cyclists off the Saussoy Ridge. In response to the large numbers of German infantry in front of the division and the calls from the 5th Division for assistance, the 12th Brigade established a strong bridgehead on the northern bank of the Marne to cover the Barrage and the Railway Bridge at Chamigny.

Anxious to commence the work on the La Ferté Bridge, the division engineers had gathered the material for bridging and the piers were under construction, with the view of beginning work on the bridge at the first possible moment. Communications with division headquarters continued to be difficult because of the distances involved and to mitigate the delays the division headquarters moved to Tartarel. On the way the G.O.C., Major-General Snow suffered a bad fall from his horse and Brigadier-General Wilson, G.O.C., 12th Brigade, assumed temporary command[75].

By 6:00pm the 2nd Royal Inniskilling Fusiliers, 12th Brigade, had begun to cross by the damaged Saussoy Railway Bridge and continued throughout the night while the 1st King's Own Royal Lancashire Regiment held the high ground at Venteuil, overlooking the bridge. While the Fusiliers were crossing at the Saussoy Bridge, the Essex Regiment was also crossing at the Barrage, followed by the Lancashire Fusiliers and the remainder of the Rifle Brigade (11th Brigade). The artillery of the 12th Brigade then crossed, by using the Railway Bridge and, after joining the infantry, moved as the advanced guard to the division.

On completion the entire infantry of the 12th Brigade was situated on the high ground on the northern bank where it picqueted the crossings. The appearance of the 12th Brigade behind Le Ferté forced the last of

[74] Extract from the Divisional war diary WO95/1439

[75] Major-General Snow was seriously injured in the fall, as his horse had rolled over him, damaging his pelvis. He was repatriated to England for recuperation and returned to France in November 1914 as the General Officer Commanding the 27 Division.

the German rearguard to withdraw and the engineers commenced work on the main bridge immediately. With hard work a pontoon and a barrel bridge was thrown across the river during the night, whilst continuing to work on the main bridge.

While the construction of the bridges was under way the 1st Hampshire and the 1st East Lancashire Regiments, of the 11th Brigade, had crossed during the night by using rowing boats, and secured the high ground on the line from Beogete to Morintru[76]. Now that the crossing had been affected, the 12th Brigade, 14th Field Artillery Brigade, 37th Field Artillery Brigade, 16th Lancers and the Cyclist Company assembled at the road junction west of St. Aulde[77], at 6:00am on the 10th. They formed the advanced guard and, soon after, the 2nd Royal Inniskilling Fusiliers captured three German prisoners and a spy.

The 19th Brigade and one battery of the 14th Field Artillery Brigade, which were still on the southern bank of the river, were due to cross at La Ferté at 5:00am, ahead of all other troops and form the left flank guard. It was intended that the main body of the division, the 10th Brigade, 19th Field Artillery Brigade and 31st Heavy Battery was to cross over the Marne through the south-east of La Ferté and follow the rear of the 19th Brigade. The rearguard, consisting of the 11th Brigade, accompanied by the 7th and 9th Field Companies and one battery of the 37th Field Artillery Brigade was to remain at the bridge to cover the rear of the division.

Ongoing delays and heavy rain bedevilled the engineers and they reported, at 1:40am, that they expected to have the bridge at Le Ferté open to traffic by 5:30am. As work progressed slowly, the estimated time for completion was changed to 6:00am[78]. However, frustration at further delay was evident when, at 5:25am, the engineers reported that supplies of bridging material were in short supply and it was hoped that the bridge would be completed by 6:30am. Yet again, at 6:45am, further delays were experienced and the expected completion time was

---

[76] *A report from an aircraft, which landed in the 4th Division area at 9:00pm in the evening, indicated that the area south of Soissons was clear and that all roads running north and north-east from Rocourt were full of German units on the march.*

[77] *St. Aulde was 5,000 yards north of La Ferté and located on the eastern loop of the River Marne*

[78] *Although the engineers had reported that the bridge at Luzancy was suitable for mechanical traffic the decision was taken to affect the crossing at La Ferté, as the bridge was nearing completion.*

extended to 7:00am and movement warning orders were issued to the 19th, 11th, 10th Brigades.

In the expectation that the bridge would be ready at 5:30am, the 10th Brigade had set out from its positions at Gd Mt. Bernard at 5:15am with the intentions of crossing the bridge after the 19th Brigade. On discovering that the bridge was not ready, the brigade was ordered to cross the Marne by the Saussoy Railway Bridge and it was with considerable difficulty that the troops and artillery doubled back to Le Saussoy Chateau and marched northward. The crossing was a slow process with the carts having to bump over the railway sleepers. To assist the remaining artillery and ambulances to negotiate the difficulties, the 2nd Royal Dublin Fusiliers remained at the bridge while rest of the fighting troops continued to advance. The 10th Brigade halted near Le Davids between 1:30pm to 2:00pm to allow the tail end units to catch up.

Meanwhile the 11th Brigade Headquarters and the Somerset Light Infantry had managed to cross using the pontoon bridge at Le Ferté and had left a company to guard the bridge and engineers. By 7:00am, the main bridge had been completed sufficiently to allow infantry and artillery to cross, and slowly the 19th Brigade began the process of passing to the northern bank.

With the 19th and 10th Brigades still struggling across the river, the advanced guard, the 12th Brigade, had made steady progress. Patrols had reached Rouget where the local inhabitants had stated that German cavalry, infantry and artillery had left the village at 5:30pm the previous day in the direction of Jaignes. The delays at the two bridges had caused the deployment of the division to stretch out over a considerable distance and, in order to allow the rear units to close up the 12th Brigade was ordered to halt at 2:00pm for half an hour.

During that halt, the 10th Brigade assembled, in column of route, on the main La Ferté – Chateau-Thierry road about a mile north of La Ferté behind the advanced guard. That allowed the 11th Brigade to move forward and close up to the main body. After three days of enemy resistance and delays with the engineering works, the fighting units of the division were now fully assembled on the northern side of the river in readiness to continue the pursuit.

As the advance progressed throughout the afternoon, the 11th Field Ambulance moved forward and picked up forty wounded German prisoners at Cocherel while the 12th Brigade engaged and drove off several German cyclists. By 5:00pm, the advance had reached Montigny. As the division marched forward, the Royal engineers, still at Le Ferté, had completed the main bridge and now had to disassemble the temporary pontoon bridge, which was expected to take all night.

The advance was to resume early in the morning of the 11th, advancing north by St. Quentin[79], Marizy St. Genevieve and Chouy to Le Loge Fe. Minor delays were experienced as the artillery brigades relocated from the overnight defensive positions to travel with the infantry brigades but, with the 10th Brigade leading the way, the division had cleared Montigny by 4:30am.

Following behind the 10th Brigade, the 11th Brigade had advanced at 4:00am. The East Lancashires and the Rifle Brigade marched from Ocquerre, on the west bank of the River Ourcq, through Vendrest, where they were joined by the Somerset Light Infantry and Hampshire's at Coulombs. The brigade, as a whole, then marched to Hervilliers where a staff officer then led the way along a track from Cerfroid F[m] to St. Quentin, where it arrived at about 11:30am. That route, having saved a march of some two miles, had brought the 11th Brigade onto the main road behind the advance guard, the 10th Brigade, but ahead of the remainder of the column. There it had a two-hour wait while the 12th and 19th Brigades that had travelled by the main road to the west of the Bois de Montigny, passed.

All went well until the 10th Brigade approached the rear of French transport between Montigny and St. Quentin. Although an officer went forward to see the French Commandant about sharing the road, little could be done to relieve the traffic congestion. The brigade finally reached St. Quentin at 8:15am but further progress was then blocked by the 14th and 15th Brigades of the 5th Division, which were passing through. It was discovered that the 15th Brigade was following the same route as the 4th Division as far as Chouy.

The resulting traffic congestion brought the division to a halt until 10:00am. Brigadier-General Wilson rode to St. Quentin to speak to the 5th Division headquarters about them using roads that had been allocated to the 4th Division. In that conversation it was determined that the head of the 5th Division column had been blocked by bad roads and would not be clear of St. Quentin until 1:00pm. As the 5th Division had found itself on the 4th Division roads accidentally, the only way to sort

---

[79] *The village of St. Quentin, north of the Bois de Montigny, should not to be confused for the much larger city, situated south of Cambrai, through which elements of the 1ʳ Royal Warwickshire Regiment passed during the retreat a week before.*

it out was to let the 5th Division through and have the 4th Division follow.

By mid-afternoon heavy rain was falling and under the weight of traffic the roads fell into disrepair and prevented further progress. Ahead lay a second river crossing, that of the River Ourcq, besides which the division had advanced for the previous twelve hours. The river flowed from the east between Marizy St. Genevieve and Chouy and the crossing point had to be reached and secured as a matter of urgency. To assist with the crossing the pontoons were ordered forward, escorted by the Seaforth Highlanders, to follow behind the fighting troops.

The division had advanced nearly eight miles to St. Quentin in wet and muddy conditions and had suffered major hold ups caused by deteriorating roads. As the troops passed along the roads the consequences of the German retreat were evident. Dead horses lay strewn along the roadside, the wrecks of two aeroplanes lay near the road, bicycles thrown aside, a motor car and two motor lorries, artillery ammunition and supplies were all strewn at random, all reminiscent of the British retreat, finished only seven days before.

The 16th Lancers had also captured a German ammunition wagon full of small arms ammunition. There was little to be gained by continuing the advance, so the division retired to billets around Passy-en-Valois, where it remained for the night. While the troops were settling into their billets, three Germans of the 48th Regiment surrendered to the headquarters of the 10th Brigade when the officers occupied the building in which they were hiding.

On the morning of the 12th, the division was instructed to cross the River Ourcq at Marizy St-Mard and proceed to Chouy, 2000 yards to the north. The 10th Brigade again assumed the role of advanced guard and cleared St. Quentin at 4:30am, allowing the remainder of the division to follow. The advance proceeded smoothly with the entire division reaching Chouy by mid-morning. The problem of supply was ever-present and hot food had not reached the 10th Brigade during the night, leaving the men the worse for wear. To remedy the situation the cook's carts were ordered back to La Loge Fe to draw supplies.

Having received the supplies, the constant rain had seriously damaged the roads, which resulted in a one-hour delay. Having completed the meal, progress continued and the 10th Brigade discovered, when speaking to the local inhabitants of Villiers-Hélon, that the Germans had left two days before. Progress continued and the division was now approaching Soissons, at the time heavily defended, although it was in the process of being evacuated. The 10th Brigade was closing with the enemy rearguard, protecting the main body of the German army as it crossed the River Aisne.

The Aisne, not unlike the Marne, was a substantial waterway, which flowed from east to west through the centre of Soissons. To the east of the city the river meandered in large loops through a valley that, in many places, sloped to the waters edge and crossings were located at regular intervals along its length. It was not intended that the division should enter Soissons, but to pass to the east and cross the River Aisne at Venizel, a village located about 5 kilometres to the east.

The act of bypassing such a heavily defended city exposed the division to possible attacks from two different directions; by the enemy rearguard from the north, and by those forces in Soissons to the west. Warnings arrived late in the morning, which indicated that strong German forces were covering Soissons from the east, near the village of Villet Culteret. Notwithstanding that threat, the Corps Commander clearly stated his intention of reaching the Aisne and seizing the crossings that same day.

For the twelve-kilometre journey to Venizel, the 12th Brigade was to follow the most direct route, through Villers-Hélon, Rozières sur Crise and Septmonts, to Venizel. The start line for the advance lay between the two villages of Tigny, to the right of the line of advance and Vierzy to the west of the Villers-Hélon - Venizel road, a frontage of 4,000 yards. The 10th Brigade was to advance through Villemontoire, Buzancy, Rozières, Septmonts, Billy and Venizel, as the French and division cavalry had indicated that there were no Germans between Septmonts and the river, the passage appeared clear.

The 10th Brigade objective was to take the high ground north of Septmonts and then press on to secure the crossing at Venizel and report the condition of the bridge as early as possible. Because of the late hour of the receipt of the orders and the pressing need to secure the crossing the division moved off the start line before assembly was complete. While the 11th Brigade was taking a short break at Montramboeuf F^{m,} it received orders to draw up the brigade in lines, behind the ridge about Point 132, half a mile south-west of Raperie. From there they were to act as reserve for the 12th Brigade, which was drawn up in the same formation immediately to the east. The 19th Brigade remained in Corps reserve.

Assisted by British cavalry, steady progress was made during the late morning. The arrival of the cavalry allowed the artillery of the advanced guard to move forward and the 10th Brigade to advance towards the town under the cover of the guns, while the cavalry reconnoitred a passage at Venizel. During the course of the reconnaissance, the 16th Lancers discovered that the Railway Bridge at Venizel was being held by a party of about 40 Germans, with several lines of German infantry entrenched south of that village. Several hours later those same observers noted that the bridge had been destroyed and the defending party had retired to a line of trenches several hundred yards north of the river. It was suggested that guns situated at a point half a mile south of Billy Sur Aisne would be very effective against the trenches.

To ensure that the artillery was in position as quickly as possible, the 31st Howitzer Battery was pushed to the head of the main column. Following a short halt, the 11th Brigade continued, in pouring rain, its advance via Villemontoire to Septmonts, where it arrived at 6:30pm. The 12th Brigade had been drawn up in formation on the road to the south-west of Buzancy and had been instructed not to move until the bridge had been secured. Apart from a small body of Germans in Venizel, the area was seen to be clear, so the 12th Brigade moved forward immediately and relieved the 10th Brigade, to assume the role of advanced guard.

Not wishing to repeat the difficulties of Le Ferté, the task of capturing the bridge at Venizel fell to the 11th Brigade. In preparation for the advance, the brigade moved to Septmonts during the night of the 12th and deployed to seize the crossing. At 3:30am on the 13th, the 12th Brigade moved up in support of the 11th Brigade and the division artillery took up positions south of Billy Sur Aisne. At 5:00am, amid heavy rain, the 11th Brigade commenced its march on Venizel. The bridge was seriously damaged, but undefended and was crossed by the advanced guard, which immediately established a bridgehead. After securing the crossing, the infantry battalions of the 11th Brigade crossed and continued north towards Bucy Le Long under the cover of the division artillery and by 5:47am, three of those battalions had occupied spurs on the high ground, north-west, north, and north-east of the village.

Following the 11th Brigade, the 12th Brigade had set out at 5:30am, marched through Billy-sur-Aisne to Venizel, and managed to get one battalion across, which followed in the footsteps of the 11th Brigade. On schedule, the 10th Brigade moved down by covered positions to Billy-Sur-Aisne where the head of the column came under heavy artillery fire at the northern exit to the town. This forced the brigade to divert by a sidetrack, leaving its first line transport at Neul.

The damaged bridge would not support the weight of loaded wagons, so each had to be unloaded and the contents passed across man-to-man. The empty wagons then crossed, were reloaded, and followed on behind the infantry. The process was slow and caused traffic congestion for a considerable time.

The priorities were to get artillery support to the 11th Brigade and get the bridge repaired. The responsibility of the bridge fell to the 7th and 9th field companies and, in preparation, both companies moved to Venizel, in order to commence work at daybreak. To assist the neighbouring 5th Division, the Cyclist Company was directed to secure the bridge at Missy-sur-Aisne, approximately four kilometres to the east and, if found unoccupied, to hold it until the 5th Division arrived to take over[80]. The Cyclists managed to take possession of the bridge but the Germans played a searchlight on it and kept it under regular rifle and machine-gun fire.

In conversations with local inhabitants, it was established that the bridge was only suitable for infantry to cross and division headquarters advised III Corps that, if the bridge needed to be held at all, it would send a company of infantry to support the Cyclists. No clear response was received to this inquiry and the Cyclists remained holding the position for the rest of the night, under constant fire. In the morning, 2nd Lieutenant Lane and his troops were driven off the bridge by superior numbers and were forced to fall back on the approaching 5th Division. He and three men were wounded but were recovered without further loss.

Just before 9:00am, a body of German troops, estimated at about four hundred, were observed entrenching on the heights at Chivres-Val, east of Bucy Le Long, and another, of about a battalion in strength, entrenching at Richobour, half a mile further east again[81]. Between Bucy le Long and Chivres lies the two small villages of Moncel and Sainte Marguerite and the Rifle Brigade was sent with the view of taking the latter.

---

[80] *The 5 Division was advancing on the right of the 4 but was a little behind the line of that reached by the 4 Division.*

[81] *Chivres-Val is located high in the hills to the north of the river Aisne and was located in the 5 Division area. A visit to the area immediately demonstrates the difficulties confront an attacking force.*

A considerable volume of shellfire came from the German batteries located on the high ground about Chivres and the 5th Division was asked to occupy Chivres and the high ground to the east, in an attempt to overcome the increasing fire.

The need for artillery support was urgent and the C.R.A.[82] was ordered to get a brigade of artillery across the river to support the 11th Brigade and, if necessary, to ferry them across or manhandle the guns over the bridge. The transport problems at Venizel were compounded by the fact that, during the evening, the transport of the 12th Brigade was trying to cross the same damaged bridge. In an effort to alleviate the difficulties, the division engineers were instructed to complete a pontoon bridge, as soon as possible, for use by the transport. Such was the urgency for the new bridge that all transport was ordered off the roads to free up access for the engineers. By 8:30am, an artillery brigade had managed to get across the river and began firing in support the 11th Brigade.

The northern heights of the River Aisne represented the line on which the retreating German army was to stand. The Allied armies had driven the enemy onto the edge of the plateau, which was formed by the northern edge of the valley, through which flowed the River Aisne and the southern edge of the valley of the River l'Ailette, further to the north. Here the enemy was to stand and prevent any further Allied advance. It was on this approximate line that it stood for the next two years. Chivres, Moncel, and Sainte Marguerite are located on the heights north of the River Aisne and observation over the Allied line of advance was extensive. Because of the steep and rugged nature of the hills, the German artillery could conceal itself with ease and, though held lightly, presented a particularly difficult objective to capture.

The 4th Division was facing the German 3rd Division. Resistance grew rapidly and III Corps ordered that the northern edge of the plateau should be occupied as soon as sufficient forces had crossed the river. At this time, the 11th Brigade had occupied the high ground around Bucy Le Long and St. Marguerite with three battalions, and was engaged by the Germans on both flanks.

Many of the difficulties experienced in the attempts to repair the bridge were caused by the German artillery fire, which had been brought to bear on the area. Such was the effect of the shelling that aeroplanes were requested in order to locate the German heavy howitzers responsible for

---

[82] *Commander, Royal Artillery.*

the fire. At 10:15am, III Corps stated that the 4th Division was not making enough effort to get its guns across the river and that rafting was to be discontinued. The rest was to be manhandled across. By 10:45am, the permanent bridge at Venizel had been made somewhat safer and the three remaining battalions of the 12th Brigade crossed.

The 11th Brigade was getting the worst of things during the early part of the afternoon. It had been under heavy fire since its assault on St. Marguerite. The Rifle Brigade, located in that village, had lost thirty men killed and it was realised that some of the guns of the 5th Division were also contributing to that fire. When the 5th Division had been advised of the error, much of the shelling stopped.

In an attempt to silence the German guns, the 2nd Essex Regiment and 2nd Lancashire Fusiliers (12th Brigade) attacked the Chivres heights but were met with galling machine-gun and rifle fire. The Lancashire Fusiliers in particular had suffered heavily, although a company of Inniskilling Fusiliers had under very difficult circumstances, reinforced them.

Having been in action since leaving the bridge at Venizel, the battalions of the 12th Brigade, subjected to vigorous German counter-attacks, was running short of small arms ammunition. Although the enemy was repulsed, each attack compounded the ammunition problem. While the 12th Brigade was thus engaged, the 11th Brigade had continued to the line La Quiney – Le Pont Rouge – Braye, as sufficient infantry and artillery became available. Initially the advance was successful but, having proceeded nearly 3,000 yards, the attack was met by German counter attacks and pushed back. The advance of 12th Brigade was also held up, not only by enemy attacks on its own front but also by those on the 11th Brigade.

Due to oncoming darkness, all further attempts to advance were postponed and outposts placed on the foremost line of advance. As the engineers had finished the bridge at Venizel by early evening, the vital ammunition supplies were got across and delivered to the sorely pressed 12th Brigade. In an effort to relieve the pressure on the 12th Brigade, the 5th Division sent the 2nd Manchester Regiment (14th Brigade), as reinforcements. Encouragement was also given to the 5th Division to press on with their attempts to take the heights near Chivres.

Corresponding with the attack of the 5th Division, the 10th Brigade, which had played no active part in the previous days advance, was also to cross the river at Venizel and attack through the 11th and 12th Brigades at 5:00am, with the objective of driving the enemy back. It was thought that if the 5th Division could hold the attention of the Germans on the front from Vregny to Perriere F[e] the 4th Division could possibly break out[83].

The number of troops facing the 4th Division was thought to be small but the superiority of the enemy artillery prevented any movement by day. Although the enemy appeared to be a well posted rearguard, their positions, though not held in strength, were naturally strong and for the brigade to do this alone would have been costly.

During the night, the 10th Brigade managed to cross via the damaged main bridge and marched for Bucy Le Long, with the object of gaining the northern edge of the Vregny – Braye Plateau. In preparation, two battalions of the 10th Brigade, the 2nd Seaforth Highlanders and the 2nd Royal Dublin Fusiliers, took up positions on the high ground north of Bucy-Le-Long while the remaining two battalions remained in bivouac to the south of the village. To assist in the attack the 2nd Seaforth Highlanders received six additional machine guns.

The neighbouring French 45th Division was also planning an attack on the left of the 4th Division and III Corps intended to use the French artillery bombardment to assist the 10th Brigade. That information was communicated to the Brigade Headquarters with the request that they be prepared to cooperate with the 45th Division[84]. Confusion existed as to the French artillery arrangements. III Corps was under the impression that the French artillery was going to support their attack, northwest of the Maubeuge Road, by firing from positions on a hill northeast of Crouy at daybreak. However, division headquarters knew that the hill in question was in German hands.

---

[83] *On the 14, the British III Corps lay to the right of the 6 French Army. The 4 Division was on the extreme left and in touch with the French. The line was continued to the right by II Corps and then I Corps, which was in touch with the French 18 Corps.*

[84] *The French 45 Division was part of the French 6 Corps, which had been advancing, with the British III Corps since the 6 September.*

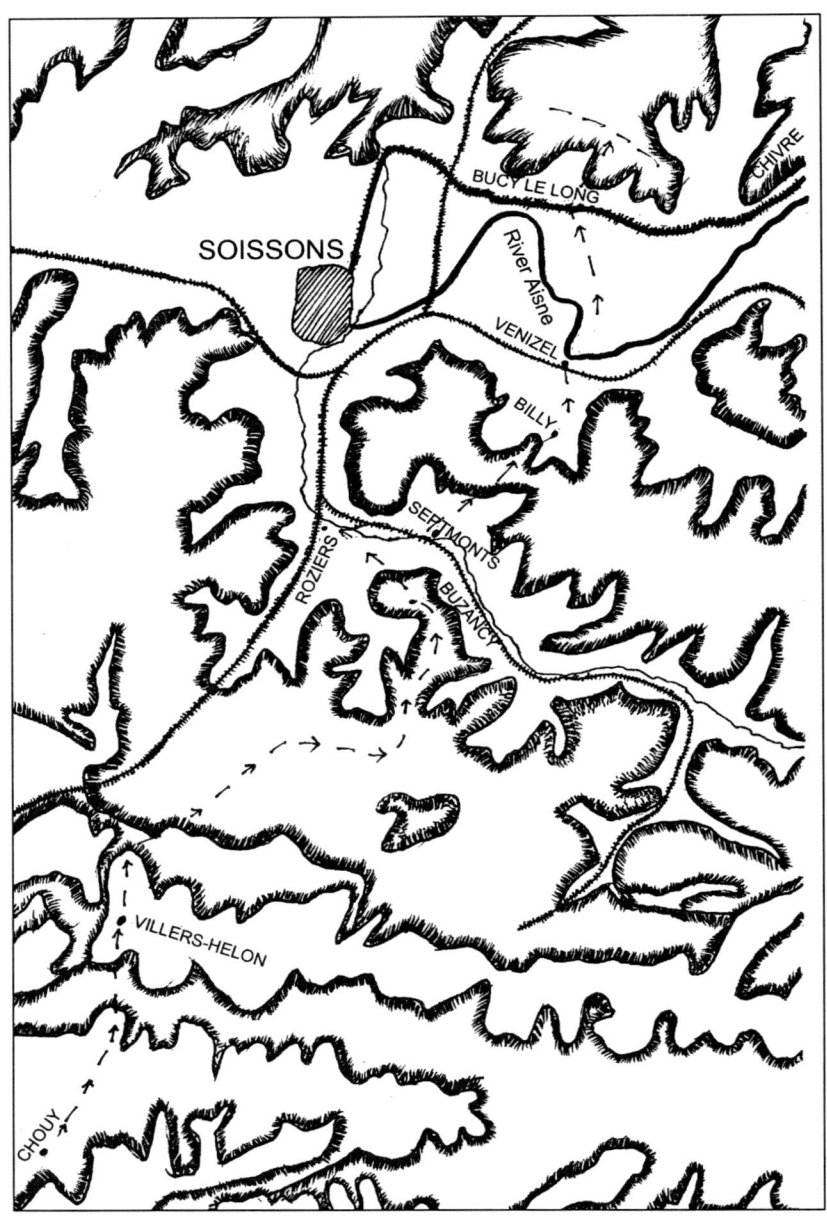

By 9:00pm, the 12th Brigade had stabilised its position. It held a strong outpost line from Moncel to just north of St. Marguerite, where the 5th Division continued the line to the right. To the left, the 11th Brigade

extended the line as far as Crouy. The attack on Chivres had reached Point 142[85], taking the foremost trenches but, in the face of determined resistance, had failed to get any further. During the night, the Essex Regiment remained in their forward positions about Braye but the 1st Duke of Cornwall Light Infantry (14th Brigade) had to relieve the Lancashire Fusiliers, which had suffered badly under the German fire. The artillery had also experienced its own problems, as suitable gun positions could not be found from which they could support a further advance. The days heavy fighting concluded with doctors being urgently despatched to the churches at St. Marguerite and Bucy Le Long to attend the wounded.

By midnight on the 13th, the 6th French Army had completed its crossing of the River Aisne while I and III Corps still struggled with damaged and destroyed bridges. On the 14th, III Corps clearly indicated that it was necessary to take the heights west of Chivres, as it would ensure that the Germans artillery positions would be enfiladed, thus forcing a withdrawal. It was thought that such a withdrawal from Chivres would force the enemy, opposite III Corps and the French division, also to withdraw. To that end, the 5th Division was instructed to attack the heights about Chivres on the morning of the 14th.

The preparation for the attack involved much effort in relocating the artillery, but the lack of clarification of the French positions complicated the barrage plan. Because of the lack of clarity, the two brigades holding the front line, the 11th and 12th, were instructed not to initiate any action until the French attack had commenced. To cooperate with the 5th Division against Chivres the 19th Brigade sent two heavy batteries and two batteries of the 29th Field Artillery Brigade to the high ground a mile north-east of Le Mesnils.

Originally planned for dawn, the attack was delayed until mid-morning due to a heavy mist obscuring the objectives but, at 9:30am, the French advance commenced. The 10th Brigade passed through the other two brigades and advanced under heavy artillery fire while 4th Division artillery provided considerable support for the attack of the neighbouring 5th Division.

The resistance was such that the 10th Brigade found that the plateau, north-east of Crouy, untenable because of the artillery and machine-

---

[85] *Point 142 was a hill before Chivres. The terrain on which Chivres stands is quite steep and provides an easily defended position. The River Aisne is clearly visible from those heights.*

gun fire. Any movements by the 10th, 11th, or 12th Brigade attracted immediate and heavy fire of all calibres. It was shortly after the attack commenced that Colonel Bradford, O.C. of the 2nd Seaforth Highlanders[86], 10th Brigade, was killed by shellfire in a trench while, conferring with the O.C. of the Rifle Brigade.

Some nervousness was evident. An officer of the 1st Rifle Brigade reported that the battalion was being attacked from the north-west and requested reinforcements. Two companies of the 1st Royal Warwickshire Regiment, 10th Brigade, were sent immediately to act in support. However, a little later, the same officer reported that the enemy was retiring and the Warwicks were recalled. Later still, the same officer reported a further attack and requested support but was promptly ignored. A third report, from the same officer, at 9:00pm, stated that an attack by one thousand, five hundred Germans, from the north-west, was underway and again support was sent, only to have him contradict his statement ten minutes later. When the Officer Commanding the Rifle Brigade learnt of these series of reports, he immediately informed the Brigade Headquarters that, in fact, there was no attack. Such was strain of the moment.

Several factors had combined to produce difficulties. The brigades had been involved in intense fighting and had faced several counter-attacks along the front and the inconsistent supply of ammunition had caused serious concern, particularly for the 12th Brigade. Although the flow of ammunition had improved, the problem of the traffic congestion at Venizel had not been completely resolved and had resulted in ongoing difficulties of supply. To exacerbate the situation, the lack of hand tools had caused delays with the preparation of trenches and dugouts. To help alleviate that situation, tools were gathered from the local villages and utilised by the troops.

Medical assistance was also wrought with difficulties. The wounded, largely those of the 12th Brigade, could not be evacuated to Chateau Thierry because to transport difficulties. The only chance of removing them to hospitals was to evacuate them in the hours of darkness to an ambulance train waiting at the railhead.

The War Diary of the 12th Brigade notes for this day: *"the outstanding fact of this days fighting has been that the 11th and 12th Brigades have*

---

[86] *Sir Evelyn Ridley Bradford, son of Colonel Sir Edward Bradford, 1st Bart., and of Lady Bradford (nee Knight). He was married to Elsie Clifton, Lady Bradford (nee Brown) of Medstead Manor, Alton, Hampshire. Details by kind permission of the Commonwealth War Graves Commission.*

been passively holding on to the positions held by them near the southern crest of the Plateau Crouy – St. Marguerite awaiting the capture of the heights east of Chivres by the 5th Division. This capture by the three Brigades of the 5th Division have not yet been able to effect. The line held by the 12th Brigade was from about 200 yards north of the _L_ of Moncel, north-eastwards to the edge of the plateau near the _M_ of Malvoisine with the right (flank) back to the area of St. Marguerite, the stream here marking the dividing line between the 12th Brigade and the 5th Division. From near Point 146 at the edge of the woods on the eastern edge of the plateau the machine guns of the Essex Regt. were able to enfilade part of the enemy's position on the western slope of Chivres Heights. The enemy's attempted to draw in the forward line of the 11th and 12th Brigades but without success. 12th Brigade was not seriously engaged. Throughout the fighting on the plateau it appeared that we were opposed chiefly by guns supported by a comparatively small number of infantry (estimated from one source - 100)."

During the night, in spite of continued fighting, there was no change to the situation for the 4th Division. At days end it was realised that further offensive action was not going to achieve an advance on the scale required. Instructions were issued that all offensive action was to cease and existing positions were to be strengthened, which necessitated some changes in the dispositions of the artillery. In an attempt to reorganise the troops the front, above Bucy Le Long – St. Marguerite, was divided into brigade sections and the 19th Brigade was placed under the orders of the 12th Brigade.

In the early hours of the morning of the 15th, the 9th Field Company had completed a second pontoon bridge across the River Aisne at Le Roches with materials supplied by the Bridging Train and the supply situation eased rapidly. The consolidation of the front line held high priority and all available resources were directed to that end. Materials for the construction of head cover were gathered and assembled during the night and the 7th Field Company assisted by constructing wire entanglements after dark.

Further attempts were made by the 5th Division to take the high ground near Chivres. The 31st Heavy Battery, 29th Field Artillery Brigade, a battery of the 14th Field Artillery Brigade, and a battery of the 37th Field Artillery Brigade supported an attack throughout the day but, by 3:00pm, this too, had failed. The War Diary for the 12th Brigade stated: "5th Division failed in their attack on the Chivres Heights and withdrew from Missy. (III Corps) Suspected that the Germans intended to use great force to push back the Allied line, thus isolating I Corps, however *the hopelessness of attempting to retire from this position with the river Aisne behind us, sufficiently defines for us the absolute necessity of holding on to our ground. This we feel fairly confident in being able to do."*

While the guns bombarded the Chivres heights, two German aircraft flew above the advanced positions of the 4th Division and it was noticed that a flash signal from the planes was soon followed by accurate artillery fire. That fire inflicted several losses to the howitzers of the 37th Battery, which was withdrawn, with several casualties in men and horses. To discourage further observation by enemy aircraft, an anti-aircraft battery was obtained and two aircraft of the Royal Flying Corps were secured to assist with artillery observation.

The wounded were finally evacuated throughout the day and two battalions of the 5th Division were placed at the disposal of the 4th Division, if they should be required. German guns were also seen to move to the high ground, east of Chivres, where they could enfilade the trenches of the 10th Brigade. Consequently, transverses were added to the trenches to minimise casualties and the artillery were directed upon the enemy guns. When the enemy batteries were engaged a heavy artillery dual lasted throughout the night, in heavy rain and the trenches of the 10th Brigade suffered considerable damage. Unfortunately, the previous nervousness shown by an officer of the Rifle Brigade resulted in a further report, made at 12:30pm on the 16th, being ignored. An extract from the war diary states; *"Reports of a similar nature from this unit have proved uniformly unreliable".*

Considerable activity had taken place behind the German lines at Chivres during the night. Bonfires and a searchlight were seen and a little later, the 12th Brigade reported that the enemy on their front was retiring. Cavalry patrols were sent out to ascertain the true situation and it was determined that the enemy still held their positions in strength and that those that were seen were just a few retiring, possibly after having been relieved.

As the opposing lines were strengthened, artillery and machine-gun fire acted as the main form of defence for both sides and patrol engagements were regular. Bucy-Le-Long was shelled with heavy guns of various calibres for most of the 17th until about 6:00pm and almost completely destroyed the village, one house being set on fire, five men and several horses killed and a further thirty men wounded. The headquarters and bivouacs of the 10th and 11th Brigades, all located in the vicinity, were relocated and the hospital evacuated as it was considered that the area was no longer tenable.

The rain had continued for several days, without any sign of abatement and the ground held by both sides was quickly converted to a field of mud with *"the streets running like rivers"*. Working parties spent much time the following day in Bucy-Le-Long, burying the dead and collecting equipment from the village.

Because the troops of various units were mixed together, considerable difficulty was experienced in issuing orders and carrying out daily administration. In the rain, the opportunity was taken to reorganise the 10th and 11th Brigades and, owing to the prospect of a prolonged stay in the area, extra measures were taken to clean up the neighbourhood, the transport, horse lines and to regulate sanitation. The 12th Brigade was using the church at St. Marguerite as a hospital but it suffered considerably whenever the village was shelled and the wounded had to be evacuated each night

It was a depressing time for the troops, largely because of the weather conditions and the mud. Those who had abandoned their kit at Voyenne during the retreat suffered considerably in the rain and cold, as little of the equipment had been replaced. Much effort, with the assistance of the engineers, was applied to making the trenches more habitable. Hot food reached the front line every night but the ordinance stores did not reach the trenches in the quantities required, resulting in the troops having to conserve what ammunition and bombs they possessed.

Until the 13th of September, the 4th Division had fought a mobile war. However, in this sector the belligerents had settled into a form of trench warfare that was to continue, largely for the next four years. The daily routine continued, with casualties incurred by the thrust and parry of trench warfare as each side measured the strengths and weaknesses of the opposition. Small incidents occurred regularly. On the 20th September, the 10th Brigade suffered three men killed and nine wounded when German patrols approached the brigade front and opened fire on those manning the trenches. The resulting counter fire, taken up all along the line, caused confusion with the German transports travelling along the Maubeuge road. The following day the Rifle Brigade lost one man killed, as a result of a trench being rushed by the enemy. A sniper of the Somerset Light Infantry shot a German artillery officer, he being the eleventh man to be killed in this way since the arrival of the division at Bucy.

The prolonged stay by the division had resulted in the straw, hay and provisions, owned by the local inhabitants, having been consumed rapidly by the troops and, after several, arrangement were made to ensure adequate compensation to the owners[87]. The position of the 4th Division was deemed vulnerable and to consolidate, communication trenches were dug, all machine guns were placed in the front line, and orders were issued to the effect that the line should be held to the last.

On the 27th, the French, on the left of the division, attempted to break through the German lines with a concerted attack, supported by the artillery of the 4th Division. The furthest advance took the French line forward early 150 yards. That movement required the 11th Brigade to extend its trenches forward to connect with the new French positions. Many men, who had been separated from the division during the fighting of the 26th August at Haucourt, continued to rejoin the division and, on the 29th, a party of 45 men of the 10th Brigade, returned to the 2nd Royal Dublin Fusiliers.

---

[87] *At 11:00am on the 23 September Brigadier-General Wilson temporarily relinquished command of the 4 Division to Major-General Sir Henry Rawlinson while Wilson awaited his promotion to Major-General. Brigadier-General Wilson had commanded the Division from the 9th September 1914, when Major-General Snow was injured by a fall from his horse while travelling to Tartarel.*

October - 1914

By late September the decision to withdraw the British divisions and concentrate them on the left of the French forces had been taken and the moves commenced on the 1st October. On the morning of the 1st the 4th Division received instructions to relieve the 5th Division during the course of the following day. Accordingly, arrangements were made with its neighbour to take over the line by extending the brigades to the right. This was done in thick mist, which obscured the troops movements and the relief was completed in the early hours of the 2nd.

While the relief of the 5th Division was underway, so too was the neighbouring 45th French Division relieved by the French 55th Division. Shortly after the relief had been completed, the German artillery, supported two attacks by the opposing 1st Pomeranian Regiment, subjected the 11th Brigade, on the left of the line, to severe shelling and heavy machine-gun fire. Each attack was successfully repelled without the brigade suffering any casualties, although seven enemy dead were later recovered.

On the morning of the 3rd, the G.O.C. inspected the trenches and the artillery positions of the 6th Division, which had been attached to the 4th Division. During the inspection, he issued instructions for the howitzer battery to register on various woods and the Conde - Chivres Plateau while the 18-pounders registered on the plateau behind the woods. Those locations were to be bombarded the next day, in support of an expected attack by the French[88]. The Germans response to this artillery fire was the slow, but constant shelling of Missy and St. Marguerite for several hours. Later in the week information from French sources indicated that the German 3rd Division had withdrawn during the night but patrols of the 11th Brigade confirmed that all was being held securely.

The French 55th Division was planning further attacks in an attempt to drive the enemy out of Crouy and requested that the division heavy artillery should shell Point 132, as the attack developed. The night passed quietly, covered by a slight mist. The attack commenced at 1:20pm in the afternoon of the 4th but took little ground against such heavy defences and failed to break into the German line. On the even-

---

[88] *At 5:30am, 5 October Major-General H. Wilson again assumed command of the 4 Division from Major-General Sir Henry Rawlinson. He remained in this command until the 29 September 1915. Brigadier-Generals Haldane, commanding the 10 Brigade and Hunter-Weston, 11 Brigade, were also recommended for immediate promotion on this date.*

ing of the 4th the division was notified that the entire Corps (4th and 6th Divisions) was to leave the line during the night of the 5th, after being relieved by the 45th (French) Division. In preparation for the withdrawal, all attached units were returned to their own divisions with the exception of the 16th Brigade, which had been attached, from the 6th Division, in the event of need[89].

The efforts of the French continued into the next day and, to assist the attack, the division artillery was given warning to commence the bombardment of the Missy-Chivres-Vregny and Conde Plateau areas at 4:00pm, for an hour. While the attack was underway, the 2nd Lancashire Fusiliers (12th Brigade) were subjected to considerable German sniper fire, originating from the eastern side of the railway. The dense and accurate fire was emanated from houses in Carreaux, several hundred yards to the north. In an effort to suppress the sniping, the artillery attached to the Durham Light Infantry, 6th Division, located near Ciry, fired in enfilade and slowly subdued the fire.

While the French were still engaged in their attack, notification was received, indicating that the 45th Division would not be available until the 6th to carry out the relief. As a result of that communication, all units were instructed to stand fast in their current positions for the night, with the exception of the 1st East Lancashire Regiment (11th Brigade), which was relieved due to the high casualty rate. The withdrawal of all non-essential troops and transport began immediately. The 4th Siege Battery was ordered to be at the head of the Nampteul Valley at 6:00pm.

The 10th, 11th and 12th Brigades were warned to prepare for the move and the pontoon bridge west of Venizel was dismantled and replaced with a barge bridge. Following the relief, the division was to retire through Villers Cotterets and Bonneuil to entrain at Béthencourt[90]. It was a night of little enemy activity and, on the 6th, the troops awoke to a day of light rain and fog patches. Because of the British shelling of the German positions on the Conde Plateau Woods and Chivres, the amount of sniping from the German positions increased, it was thought, through fear of an attack. French staff officers from the 45th

---

[89] *The withdrawal of the 4 Division from the line was a part of the concentration of the BEF on the northern flank of the line.*

[90] *Béthencourt-en-Valois is approximately 5 kilometres from Nery, where the 10 Brigade was involved in repelling the attack upon 'L' Battery of the 1 Cavalry Brigade on the 1 of September. The journey to entrain involved what was ultimately a march of about 90 kilometres, some of it in areas through which the division has marched during the retreat, six weeks before.*

Division arrived in the early hours and were passed to the headquarters of the 11th and 12th Brigades to commence the hand over.

The process of relief began at 6:30pm in the evening of the 6th and the units gathered throughout the night. The Lancashire Fusiliers (12th Brigade), having been relieved during the night of 5th, had waited near the Missy Bridge to be joined by the Essex, King's Own Royal Lancashires, and the Royal Inniskilling Fusiliers. Once gathered together, the 12th Brigade marched to Septmonts and went into billets where it remained in support of the 45th Division for twenty-four hours. At 1:00am the 10th Brigade also marched to the collection point at Septmonts, via Bucy-Le-long. The 11th Brigade largely withdrew but left the 1st East Lancashire Regiment and the Cyclist Company to hand over to the French during the early evening of the 7th. Once completed, the Cyclists, "H" Battery, and the 9th Field Company rejoined the 11th Brigade at Plessier-Huleu.

After weeks in the trenches, the men needed exercise and a change of environment. While arrangements for further transport and billeting were made, the troops undertook a programme of drill and route marching to achieve a level of fitness. The division was under instruction to march on the night of the 8/9th and in order to be well clear of any enemy observation, the 10th and 11th Brigades departed at midnight from Septmonts for Betz. After a short rest at Rozet-St. Albin, they turned east and marched via Chouy to Villers–Cotterêts where the battalions went into billets for another short rest. Those two brigades, along with the associated artillery, field ambulance and signals, then marched to Betz, a total of nearly sixty miles however, on arrival, entraining was delayed for 15 hours.

While the 10th and 11th Brigades were on the march, the 12th Brigade, 37th Brigade R.F.A., 10th Field Ambulance, 4th Company Field Engineer, and the division train had remained in Septmonts under the orders of III Corps. The brigade finally departed at 2:30pm on the 8th and marched a short distance to Chacrise for a brief respite. At 9:15pm, they continued in the path of the other brigades and arrived at Coyolles, near Betz, at 2:00am on the 9th.

It is appropriate, at this point, to appreciate those tasks that the division had undertaken since its arrival in France and what was expected of it for the immediate future. By the 9th October the division had been in France for seven weeks in which time it had fought an intense battle against overwhelming numbers, undertaken eleven days of arduous retreat while fighting off an approaching enemy, then immediately turned around and undertook six weeks of advance and punishing fighting. During those seven weeks the troops had marched and fought nearly five hundred kilometres. The division was now to move north and partake in the defence of the left flank of the battlefront that was rapidly extending to the Belgian coast.

The initial thrust by the Germans had required the French, Belgian and British forces to be used wherever the emergency was greatest, which resulted in the left of the line being defended by a conglomeration of the Belgian and French armies. The Battle of the Aisne had done something to stem the German thrust in the south and had forced the German Command to seek other ways of defeating the Allies. The strategy was to take the coastal cities of Calais and Boulogne, thus isolating Paris and dividing the French and British armies. By October of 1914, every effort had been made by the French and Germans to outflank the other on the northern end of the line, in a process that was later termed in British histories as "the race to the sea". Strategically, to achieve the outflanking movement by either side could well have brought defeat upon its opponent.

The fact that the British Expeditionary Force was located many miles from its supply bases on the coast had led to serious problems of logistics. The decision was taken to re-organise the Armies and allocate the extreme left of the defences, on the coast, to the Belgian Army, with the British continuing the line to the right, or south. As the outflanking manoeuvres continued and the line became longer, it was necessary to move many divisions to the northern sector as soon as possible. The move was made with the offensive spirit in mind and it was considered essential that the German army should be pushed back as far as possible, the objective being to force a German evacuation from the coastal cities of Belgium.

Thus, it was to fall to the lot of III Corps to be called north, to the French-Belgian border and it was advised that it would be required for an attack on German positions in the area of Ypres. Due to the delays with travel arrangements, the 10th and 11th Brigades were ordered to stand and not move before 3:00pm. At that hour the 10th Brigade marched and reached Rully, where they stayed overnight[91]. The next morning the journey was continued to Longueil where the 1st Royal Warwickshire Regiment and 1st Royal Irish Fusiliers entrained. The 2nd Seaforth Highlanders and the 2nd Royal Dublin Fusiliers entrained at

---

[91] *For a second time elements of the Division passed through the area in which they had fought during the retreat.*

Pont-St-Mance. The 12th Brigade transport and horses continued via Vez and Verberie[92] to Le Meux, south of Compiègne, a distance of some fifty kilometres. The transport was then followed by the infantry, which arrived in the evening of the 10th.

While the brigades were moving to their respective departure points, the advanced party for the division had arrived at St. Omer, Belgium, and completed arrangements for accommodation for the brigades. Throughout the 10th and 11th, the brigades arrived at St. Omer, Arques, Blendecques and Wizern. On arrival it was discovered that several towns in which the various units detrained were on different railway lines, separated by a canal, the bridge over which had been demolished earlier in the war by the French. Detraining of the 4th Division commenced immediately after the 6th Division, which had arrived earlier in the afternoon, had completed its disembarkation.

On completion, the 10th Brigade marched for St. Omer to meet with the other brigades. An interesting note in the war diary of the 4th Division headquarters on this date states, " *the detrainment of the 19th Brigade and the 6th Division, ahead of the 4th Division, was covered on the left flank by the French Cavalry at Horsbrouch. These bolted without being attacked at all during the night of the 10/11th, the strength of which were 2 regiments and 5 Battalions of French T (Territorial) infantry. These would have liked to bolt, but we prevented it.*" The process of detraining continued throughout the day and into the night, finally being completed at 5:00pm on the 12th October.

The fighting troops were followed immediately by the artillery brigades, field ambulance, and engineers, as each became available. The whole process of detraining and assembly was carried out under the protection of the division Mounted Troops, which were sent to locations northwest of Watten to act as forward warning in the event of an enemy attack. It had been arranged for the 10th and 11th Brigades, on the opposite side of the canal, to leave at 1:00pm in buses provided by the French, however the delayed arrival of that transport resulted in the two brigades not departing until at 5:00pm.

The 12th Brigade and two batteries of the 37th (Howitzer) Brigade detrained at Hazebrouck station at 5:00am on the 13th. Here staff officers who were deploying the brigades as they arrived. Much time was spent

---

[92] *At Verberie, the 4 Division crossed the path that it had followed in August, during the retreat. On this occasion, they were travelling west instead of south, although the troops were just as tired.*

between midnight of the 12th and 6:00am on the 13th in coordinating times of departure with the neighbouring 6th Division, reconnoitring traffic conditions on the roads and experiencing delays in the arrival of the various battalions. While these preparations were underway, information from the Cyclist Company confirmed the existence of enemy troops defending entrenched positions on the line of Les-Quartre-Fils – Météren – Les-Trois-Tilleuls.

II Corps was to advance in an easterly direction, with the intention of engaging and driving back the enemy wherever met. The direction of march was to take the division through Météren, Bailleul, Armentières, and further towards Lille. Early in the morning, orders were issued for the advance on Météren[93]. A part of the order read "*4th Division to make Bailleul its first objective and then, covered by cavalry about Berthen and a strong flank guard at Bailleul, to conform to the operations of the 6th Division.*"

It had been intended that the 4th Division assume a starting line from St. Sylvestre to Ceastre from which the advance was to commence[94]. Due to the delays in getting the brigades to start line, the 19th Brigade, which was providing cover for the unloading point, was asked to hold the start line until the division could take over. Due to other obligations, it was necessary to relieve the 19th Brigade immediately upon arrival. In cold and heavy rain, 10th Brigade, accompanied by its 1st line transport, set out via Arques for St. Sylvestre, where the 1st Royal Irish Fusiliers and 2nd Royal Dublin Fusiliers remained as the 10th Brigade reserve. The 1st Royal Warwickshire Regiment and 2nd Seaforth Highlanders continued to Ceastre.

By 10:00am, the 10th Brigade, acting as the advanced guard, had commenced the advance and proceeded unhindered until the leading battalion, the Royal Warwickshire Regiment, approached Flêtre at about 11:30am, where it was necessary to engage small groups of defending enemy. However, on emerging from the eastern end of the village the Royal Warwickshire's encountered a barricade barring the road. To deal with the obstacle the guns of the 88th Battery, which accompanied the advanced guard, took up positions south of Flêtre and fired on the de-

---

[93] *Météren lies on high ground west of Armentières.*

[94] *St. Sylvestre and Ceastre are located on the Cassel – Armentières Road with Météren lying about midway along the route, two miles to the west of Bailleul. The 12 Brigade took up position at St. Sylvestre, behind the leading 10 Brigade, which commenced the advance from Ceastre.*

fenders. To assist in the attack the Seaforth Highlanders moved along the northern side of the road until level with the Warwicks. The barrier and covering trenches were taken with few casualties and the Warwicks occupied several houses around Pine Boom. At this point, the 10th Brigade was ordered to stand fast.

The enemy was known to be holding the area, about Fontaine Houck and Météren in strength and a combined attack of the 4th and 6th Divisions was proposed and agreed to by III Corps shortly after midday[95]. The assault on Météren was to commence at 3:30pm with the 1st Cavalry Division on the left, 4th Division in the centre and the 6th Division on the right[96]. The 4th division was to capture the enemy line from Point 62[97], through Fontaine Houck to a point approximately 1,000 yards south of Météren. The 10th Brigade, on the left, was to advance with the 1st Royal Warwickshire Regiment and Seaforth Highlanders and take that part of the line from Point 62 to Fontaine Houck. The 12th Brigade, on the right, was to extend the line with the 2nd Essex Regiment and 1st King's Own Royal Lancashire Regiment and attack from Fontaine Houck to the southern end of the line. The Cavalry Corps cooperated by attacking Berthen, north of Fontaine Houck.

After having experienced delays in gathering in the outposts of the 11th Brigade, the division advanced at 3:30pm on the 13th. From the outset, the 10th Brigade experienced difficulties keeping up with the 12th Brigade, due largely to poor visibility caused by heavy mist. The two leading battalions of the 12th Brigade, the Essex Regiment and the King's Own, reached a line of road west of Le Ormes unopposed and by 3:35pm had progressed to the Métérenbecque[98], but could not establish contact with the 6th Division.

The 10th Brigade advanced with little difficulty and soon drew level with the adjoining 12th Brigade, which allow the Essex Regiment and the Royal Warwickshire's to advance in line. In doing so, the Warwick-

---

[95] *The British Official History quotes the combined attack of the 4' and 6' Divisions as being the first formal attack of the war. Military Operations, France and Belgium, 1914, volume 2, page 96.*

[96] *The troops holding Météren and Fontaine Houck were those of the 3' and 6' Bavarian Cavalry Divisions*

[97] *Point 62 was a hill on the extreme left of the division line where the Warwickshire Regiment was in touch with units of the Cavalry Division.*

[98] *The Métérenbecque is a small river, with its source north of Ceastre, which flows into the Canal de Lys 4 miles west of Merville.*

shire's, due to mist, moved increasingly to the right, across the front of the Essex Regiment, and became mixed up with troops of the King's Own on the extreme right of the division. The King's Own and the Essex then came under heavy rifle, machine gun, and artillery fire, which brought their advance temporarily to a halt. The division artillery, which had been shelling Météren, ceased firing at 3:45pm as the attacking troops, many of them of the Warwickshire Regiment, had entered the village. Reports from the Cavalry Corps, at 1:00pm, stated that the 1st Royal Warwickshire Regiment, acting on their right, had "*got almost, if not entirely, into Météren at a very early period and that the part that did so, under Major Christie, were all killed or captured.*" [99] [100]

The gap between the 12th Brigade and the 6th Division, which, due to enemy resistance, had fallen well behind, had continued to grow. In the midst of the fighting about Météren the 12th Brigade was ordered to cover the flanks of the 6th Division, by closing the gap between the two divisions. Later in the afternoon, the Cavalry confirmed that the enemy in front of the 12th brigade had retired and established that the gap between the 12th Brigade and the left of the 6th Division was about 1000 yards wide. That gap had caused considerable concern and it was not finally closed until after nightfall.

In an effort to close the gap the 12th Brigade swung to the right, which then opened a gap between itself and the 10th Brigade, on the left. The 2nd Lancashire Fusiliers, acting in support, saw the difficulty and worked its way round the right flank of the King's Own Royal Lancashires. This extended the line further to the south but only reduced the gap to about 800 yards. In an effort to achieve temporary protection the

---

[99] *Whilst this report somewhat exaggerates the reality of the event, it indicates that the fighting in the village was intense. The losses to the 10 Brigade on that day was 3 officers and 65 men killed with 9 officers and 169 men wounded. Météren was still in German hands and this action was the preliminary step in securing the starting point for the main attack on Bailleul. Major Charles William Christie, aged 41 years, who had played such an important role in the retirement of the Warwickshires at Haucourt on the 26 August, was killed in action in Météren and is buried in the Météren War Cemetery. The Royal Warwicks suffered heavy losses and were withdrawn and re-formed behind the line. Tactical analysis during the First World War showed that troops who were under fire tended to digress from their line of advance and move in the direction of the offending fire. In this case, it led to two battalions of different brigades attempting to attack the same body of enemy.*

[100] *It was in this attack that a young Lieutenant Bernard Law Montgomery was shot in the chest and severely wounded. He was sent to England to recuperate and returned to France in 1916. So nearly ended the life of a General who was to earn fame at Tubruk and El Alamein during the Second World War. He was to gain further distinction at Normandy in 1944. See Appendix II for further details.*

12th Brigade requested artillery support to help fill the remainder of gap, but that resulted in the division artillery inadvertently shelling the Essex and King's Own. Under the weight of the artillery fire the line began to waver. In response the 1st Hampshire Regiment (11th Brigade), waiting in reserve, was sent forward to help fill the gap between the two brigades.

By 4:30pm the 12th Brigade had stabilised its line and although it had no reserves left, two sections of the 9th Field Company R.E. were sent immediately to assist the tired troops consolidate their positions. By early evening, the 6th Division was still some distance behind the advanced line of the 4th, with the 12th Brigade bridging the gap.

While the 12th Brigade was thus engaged, the 10th Brigade had reached the Fontaine Houck Ridge and, with the assistance of a cavalry squadron, attempted to envelop the enemy's right flank. A final assault by the 2nd Seaforth Highlanders and a company of the 2nd Royal Dublin Fusiliers managed to occupy the village of Fontaine Houck in the early evening where the trenches were found, with the exception of a few wounded, to be completely empty. Continuous rain hampered further progress and the 10th Brigade, like the 12th, was without reserves, although the 2nd Cavalry Regiment was nearby. Further attempts at advance were halted and all ground gained was entrenched.

As the offence had come to a halt, the 12th Brigade took the opportunity to close the gap between it and the 10th Brigade. The artillery had maintained constant fire on Météren and by 6:25pm, the enemy fire, emanating from that village, eased. The reduction in rifle and machine-gun fire allowed the remaining two sections of the 9th Field Company, which had been despatched to the 10th Brigade, to assist with consolidation. The rain and mist had obscured observation throughout the day so severely that neither the 29th, 32nd Artillery Brigades nor the 31st Heavy Battery, which were only brought into action late in the afternoon, was able to fire a shot. By 9:30pm, it was learned that the division had suffered nearly four hundred casualties and ambulances were sent. Only six arrived, and these made one trip each, which resulted in about one hundred wounded being left at Flêtre until late the next day.

Despite constant heavy fighting, Météren had remained uncaptured at nightfall and the fighting continued well into the night. The 2nd Lancashire Fusiliers attempted to fight their way around to the south of the village but were delayed by gardens and wire fences. An attempt was also made to approach the village along a road from the south-west, without success. The 6th Division still had great difficulty in coming into line with the 12th Brigade and towards midnight there remained confusion as to the exact location of the Cavalry Corps. That confusion resulted in orders being issued at midnight stating that the main action for the next day would focus on the capture and consolidation of Météren.

Rain and mist persisted throughout the morning of the 14th and, by midday, the 2nd Lancashire Fusiliers had successfully taken possession of Météren. Two sections of engineers were sent to put the village into a state of defence and all brigades consolidated their positions with the view of repelling counter-attacks. By swinging its right flank backwards the 12th Brigade had also established contact with the 6th Division, still some distance behind, thus completing the line.

It was originally planned to send two battalions of the 11th Brigade to Berthen to assist the cavalry with its attack on Mont Noir, north of Météren. However, by the early hours of the morning, the 1st Cavalry Division had captured the objective and by 6:35am all firing on the division front had ceased. News arrived from the cavalry, indicating that the hills north of Météren were clear as far as Westouter and Locre, to the north-east. It was also believed that, based on reports from the division Mounted Troops, the ground was clear as far as Bailleul and beyond. The ground in front of the 6th Division was also reported clear and the rain had stopped.

On receipt of that information, orders were issued for an immediate advance through Bailleul to Steenverck, to the south-east of Bailleul. The advance commenced at 12:30pm. The 12th Brigade had concentrated in Météren and joined the rest of the division in the advance but, having been to the fore in the fighting of the previous day, was allocated as rearguard. To assume positions at the rear of the division, it halted for two hours, just after leaving Météren, to allow the rest of the division to pass. The 11th Brigade, now acting as advanced guard, soon came under heavy shellfire from La Crèche, temporarily bringing progress to a halt. That delay was attributed more to the fact that the 6th Division had still not caught up, rather than the intensity of the shellfire.

The head of the 19th Brigade, attached to the 6th Division, was well ahead and its appearance in front of Bailleul and subsequent advance along the Armentières Road caused the Germans, opposing the advance of the 4th Division, to a general withdrawal. The 11th Brigade took points 77 and 40, east of Bailleul, during the afternoon and the 1st and

2nd Cavalry Brigades, operating on the line of Messines[101] - Wulverghem - Neuve Eglise, captured 100 wounded prisoners and reported the enemy infantry as being exhausted. The Division Mounted Troops also engaged German Cavalry, killed four, and captured several horses. Due to the large numbers of refugees making their way towards Armentières arrangements were made with the Gendarmes and a company of French Territorials to deal with the road traffic and possible spies[102]. Further progress was impeded as the 11th Brigade found the roads in the area of Neuve-Eglise were impassable, so III Corps ordered the division to stand fast until morning.

It was expected that the advance was to continue at 6:00am on the 15th but instructions were issued to stand fast until further notice. Drizzling rain and mist persisted for most of the day and, at 8:50pm, the 19th Hussars, patrolling ahead of the division, reported that the line of Steenweerk – Nieppe – Armentières – Houplines – Deulemont was occupied by the enemy, many of whom were busy digging their bicycles out of the mud. Warning orders arrived late in the morning to the effect that the division was to advance and occupy the line Neuve Eglise - Steenwerck - Liverrier but it was *not desired that it should get involved in a general engagement with the enemy*. The 19th Hussars were instructed to gain touch with the German rearguard immediately.

Before the advance commenced, the division was advised that the French Cavalry had already taken Steenwerck and the decision was taken to extend the advance a further five kilometres, to the line of Erquinghem - Lys – Nieppe. The intention was to take and hold the bridge at the first of those villages. Short delays were experienced while the fighting units deployed but the advance continued at 6:00am on the 16th, with the 12th Brigade marching for Nieppe and the 11th Brigade for Erquinghem.

As the advance got underway, General De Lisle, G.O.C., 1st Cavalry Division, arrived at the headquarters of the 4th Division, being under the impression that the division was not advancing until 6:00am on the following morning. On hearing that the advance had commenced, he returned immediately to his own headquarters and ordered a cavalry

---

[101] *The name 'Messines' is the Anglicised version of the more correctly named town of Mesin.*

[102] *The fear of spies crossing into British territory resulted in orders being issued, which prevented civilians from passing through the lines.*

regiment to Ploegsteert[103] to cover the left of the division. He also gave information about German trenches on the River Lys, which had been reported by his airmen.

The advance was accompanied by intermittent but determined fighting as the German rearguard attempted to slow British progress, which was equally determined to establish contact with the German main body. The resistance resulted in frequent delays as each pocket was overcome but, by 8:00pm, the oncoming darkness prevented any further advance and the division bivouacked where it was. The 19th Hussars were located at Neuve Eglise and had forwarded information to division headquarters, via the 11th Brigade, that the line of Warneton – Frelinghien – Le Touquet, to the north of Armentières, was held by the Germans. Early in the morning of the 16th, the division was warned to prepare for a further advance and that the line to be obtained was from Erquinghem to Point 63, one mile north of Ploegsteert.

We should pause at this point in the narrative to appreciate the location of the line on which the division stood on the morning of the attack. The 11th Brigade held a line from positions between the village of Sailly-sur-la-Lys, which lay south-east of Armentières on the eastern bank of the River Lys, and Nieppe, facing east on a frontage of about 3,000 yards. Directly in front of that brigade lay the river, Erquinghem village and the city of Armentières. The 12th Brigade was located at Nieppe, a short distance north west of Armentières, the possession of which was passed over to the 11th Brigade during the night of the 15th, and the 10th Brigade lay in reserve, behind the front line.

The forthcoming advance was intended to carry the right of 4th Division, the 11th Brigade, forward while the 12th Brigade extended to the left, that is, to the north. In order to achieve the extension of the line the 11th Brigade was to maintain its left flank on Nieppe and advance it right to take Erquinghem. The 12th Brigade was to extend to the left and capture the line from Nieppe, across the Belgian border, through the village of Ploegsteert and over Point 63 to Douve Farm, on the southern bank of the River Douve[104], giving a total front of some 8,000 yards. The whole manoeuvre was to be supported by the 6th Division,

---

[103] *In common with the tradition of the Tommy 'translating' Belgian and French place names to something more suitable to the British tongue Ploegsteert became Plugstreet. Plugstreet Wood (Bois de Ploegsteert), immediately east of the village was to gain notoriety for periods intense fighting in the area until April 1918.*

[104] *The River Douve flows through the valley of the same name and separates Ploegsteert, on the southern ridge and Messines, on the northern ridge.*

on the right and the Cavalry Corps on the left, which was to take Messines.

The 11th Brigade was made aware that the Germans held Pont de Nieppe and that the Erquinghem Bridge was still intact. As a result, the brigade was to secure the bridge and form a bridgehead. Sailly was also to be taken and held, but no unit of the division was to cross the bridge at Erquinghem until the 6th Division had caught up. The success of the advance depended upon the unhindered extension to the north by the 12th Brigade.

The line of attack by the 12th Brigade would require it to face the villages of Le Touquet, Le Gheer and Saint Yvon[105], the first of which was located approximately 1000 yards to the east and held by a strong body of the enemy. Lying in between these two lines was the Bois du Ploegsteert, a heavily wooded area, typical of the French and Belgian countryside. The Lancashire Fusiliers were to take and hold the line between Nieppe and Ploegsteert, while the Royal Inniskilling Fusiliers extended the line to the Chateau on top of Point 63, with the Essex Regiment continuing the line to Douve Farm.

The advance progressed well and, at first, the 11th Brigade met little resistance. The 1st Somerset Light Infantry crossed the Erquinghem Bridge unopposed, although it had been previously reported as being strongly held. The 12th Brigade also made good progress and, by 8:00pm, all objectives had been achieved. The 10th Brigade had remained in reserve near Petit Pont.

During the night of the 16th the 10th Brigade relieved the 11th Brigade and, on the following morning, the 4th and 6th Divisions continued the advance to the east, behind a screen of the 1st Cavalry Division, which moved well in front of the infantry. During the advance, the 10th Brigade occupied Armentières, still in the hands of the German rearguards and, because of the heavy house-to-house fighting, a gap gradually opened, once again, between the 4th and 6th Divisions. The Cyclist Company was charged with the responsibility of patrolling that gap and, in doing so, established contact with the 6th Division at Fleurbaix. Patrols of the Cyclist Company also reconnoitred as far forward as Quesnoy.

---

[105] *Saint Yvon, or St. Yves to the Tommy, is located, 1200 yards north of Le Gheer, on the north-east corner of the Bois du Ploegsteert, overlooking the valley of the Douve.*

While the 10th Brigade was fighting in Armentières it was informed by the local inhabitants that the main body of Germans had left at 9:00pm the previous night and moved towards Lille. By mid-morning, Armentières had been largely cleared, although determined pockets of resistance remained. It was intended that pontoon bridges would be built across the River Lys at Croix de Bas to enable the crossing of the 10th Brigade but soon after the advance began it was discovered the bridges at Erquinghem and Nieppe, still further forward, remained intact.

The need to continue the advance was foremost but the existence of some elements of the German rearguard, still in Armentières, meant that the 10th Brigade was subjected to sniping from buildings within the town, seriously affecting progress, in particular, the communications messengers. While the right flank was thus engaged, the 12th Brigade, on its journey north to assist the 2nd Cavalry Division, which was attacking east of Messines, had captured Le Douve. Further assistance was given to the cavalry by the division artillery, located on Point 63, which concentrated field gun and howitzer fire upon the area about Messines.

The 12th Brigade had also had trouble with communications and investigations revealed that the motorcycle couriers had also been subjected to the same sniping as those of the 10th Brigade as they passed through Armentières. Although the fighting was constant, the need to improve the communications resulted in the division headquarters moving forward, to Nieppe, during the afternoon and by 4:00pm the 10th Brigade had finally cleared Armentières.

As the advance continued, the 1st Royal Irish Fusiliers experienced considerable difficulty removing four Saxon infantrymen, who had refused to surrender, from a farm on the northern outskirts of Houplines, a village north-west of Armentières. In order to dislodge them, the farm was set on fire and Royal Engineers later blew it up, killing the occupants. Although the farm was eventually taken, it cost the battalion seven men killed and one wounded. Captain Kentish (Royal Irish Fusilier) and Lieutenant Corblet[106] (French Navy) distinguished themselves *"endeavouring to dislodge these desperados".*[107]Fighting continued

---

[106] *Lieutenant Corblet was a French naval officer, who was attached to the 10 Brigade headquarters as a Liaison Officer. On this occasion Lieutenant Corblet narrowly missed being killed when a bullet, fired by one of the Saxon soldiers, grazed his cheek.*

[107] *A full description of the incident at the farm is described in Appendix 'Incident at Sydney Street Farm – 17 October 1914'.*

throughout the night of the 17th as minor skirmishing took place on the outpost lines in front of the 1st Royal Irish Fusiliers at Houplines.

The River Lys, upon which the 10th Brigade stood, followed a general north-easterly path past Armentières, for many kilometres to Courtrai and beyond. East of the river, in front of the 4th Division, lay several large towns and cities, the largest of these being Tourcoing, Roubaix and Lille. These cities were major transport centres vital to the German war effort and were defended accordingly. The German High Command intended to stand along the Messines Ridge and the River Lys as the line of defence for that strategically important area. Frelinghein, one of the smaller towns, lies on the immediate eastern bank of the Lys and Le Touquet on the western bank, separated only by the width of the river.

At the time of the attack, the division faced to the north-east. The line extended from Chapel D'Armentières, just south of Armentières, and followed a northerly course along the eastern edge of Armentières to Houplines, Le Touquet and along the Le Touquet – Messines Road through Le Gheer where the line bent back, to the west, to Ploegsteert. It then turned again, to the north, past Point 63, to the River Douve. The 12th Brigade held the left, or northern flank, from the River Douve to Le Touquet while the 10th Brigade continued the line through Houplines to Chapel D'Armentières. The 11th Brigade lay in close support near Armentières.

At about 2:30am on the 19th, III Corps issued instructions requiring the two divisions of the Corps to attack down the valley of the Lys, which involved a wheel to the left by the whole Corps. In order to affect the manoeuvre, it was necessary to carry out certain preliminary operations to drive back the Germans in front of the 6th Division, which was already on the east bank of the Lys and have the 4th Division secure Frelinghien. Those allocated to the task, the Royal Warwickshire's and Seaforth Highlanders, of the 10th Brigade, were to cross to the east bank of the Lys and attack Frelinghein from the south, while the 12th Brigade was to attack from the west.

The morning of the 18th, consisted of much manoeuvring by the units involved, leading to some confusion when issuing and receiving orders, particularly in the 10th Brigade. In preparation for the attack, the headquarters of the 10th Brigade moved to Houplines station in the early hours. At 6:20am, the headquarters of the 11th Brigade moved to Nieppe and the headquarters of the 12th Brigade, with the 2nd Essex Regiment, moved to Ploegsteert. The orders required the 10th Brigade to advance north, on the eastern bank of the river while the 12th Brigade advanced east, from Ploegsteert, on the western bank, with the intention of having the two brigades meet at Frelinghein.

Minor difficulties were soon overcome and the Warwickshire's and Seaforth's crossed to the east bank early in the morning, preparatory to the attempt on Frelinghien. By 10:00am, zero hour, all was ready except that the Lancashire Fusiliers and the King's Own (12th Brigade), holding the line from Pont Rouge[108] to a point close to Le Touquet, were being subjected to heavy shelling. In the face of that shelling, the two battalions commenced their advance and, although the 12th Brigade requested artillery support to help subdue the enemy fire, the advance was bought to an eventual halt half an hour later, as it was not possible to penetrate the barrage without heavy loss. As the guns of the division registered the range of the German artillery, so the barrage weakened, allowing the Lancashire Fusiliers to continue.

Soon after, the 10th Brigade ran into difficulties in front of Frelinghien and the neighbouring 12th Brigade slowed its progress, to protect the junction between the two brigades although the 12th Brigade slowly left the 10th behind. The resistance met by the 10th Brigade ultimately required the 12th Brigade to still further delay its advance until the 10th had managed to catch up. By way of assistance, the 12th Brigade sent two companies through Houplines to join the 10th Brigade now bogged down under heavy fire, by attacking from the west.

At that point, the 12th Brigade was almost totally committed. One of its battalions, the Royal Inniskilling Fusiliers, was assisting the 1st Cavalry Division with the attack at Messines, the King's Own and Lancashire Fusiliers were attacking along the left bank of the river with the 10th Brigade. The Essex Regiment (less one company), in Ploegsteert, was the only reserve.

By midday, the 10th Brigade had fought its way to the road fork three quarters of a mile north of Ruage and had extended to the east for 1300 yards, enabling the Lancashire Fusiliers, assisted by the artillery, to continue its advance. While the 10th Brigade was in the midst of the intense fighting, the headquarters received instructions that the Germans were to be contained on the line Funquereau – Frelinghien, while the 6th Division made a concerted attack on the right.

---

[108] *Pont Rouge lies approximately mid-way between Le Gheer and Le Touquet, a distance of one mile.*

The right flank of the 4th Division was well behind that of the 6th and, in order to provide support for the exposed flank, two battalions of the 11th Brigade were ordered to attack Prevotee, on the right of the line. Once again, difficulties with communications played a part and the 11th Brigade attack was delayed until the following day. The Warwicks and Seaforth's (10th Brigade) were not able to maintain such progress that would allow it to keep level with the Lancashire Fusiliers, on the opposite bank, so the Fusiliers were instructed not to press their attack unless the 10th Brigade managed to come alongside.

To assist the 10th Brigade, the 2nd Essex Regiment, the only reserve left for the 12th Brigade, was ordered to move to Houplines. Very heavy fighting now took place along the whole front. At 6:35pm the Inniskilling Fusiliers, which had been assisting the cavalry in front of Messines, returned to the command of the 12th Brigade and was ordered to Houplines to assist the 10th Brigade. It was a precarious position as the line was very much extended and the division had few reserves.

Such was the position when, at 7:00pm, III Corps ordered that all ground taken was to be held, strong reserves were to be formed and posts established. To assist with that consolidation, additional engineers were sent forward to the front line and the 12th Brigade allocated two battalions to division reserve. Although little progress had been made, the fighting continued well into the night, mainly on the 10th Brigade front at Houplines and Frelinghien.

Orders to straighten the line and secure Deulemont and L'Epinette determined the events of the next day. The 10th Brigade was instructed to continue the attack on Frelinghien from the west with determination, while the 12th Brigade was to press against Le Touquet with the King's Own and the Lancashire Fusiliers. The remaining two battalions of the 12th Brigade, the 2nd Essex Regiment and the 2nd Royal Inniskilling Fusiliers, on their return from Houplines, were to prepare strong-points about Le Gheer to cover Point 63 from the north. The previous orders for the 11th Brigade to advance on La Prevotee were confirmed. To augment the strength of the 10th Brigade, which had lost several hundred casualties, the 2nd Rifle Brigade (11th Brigade) was temporarily attached as a reserve.

The advance began at 6:30am on the 19th and, to assist the 11th Brigade in its efforts on La Prevotee, the 10th Brigade approached Frelinghein along the river Lys. Brigadier-General Haldane, G.O.C. of the 10th Brigade, had reconnoitred the ground over which the attack would pass and pushed forward two companies of the Seaforth Highlanders along the right bank of the river while the rest of the brigade kept the Germans attention by firing on their trenches. Supported by the 37th and 88th Batteries of field artillery the two companies of Seaforth's could only proceed along the riverbank man by man but progress was made and by nightfall, both companies had occupied several houses south of Frelinghien Church. A single howitzer of the 55th Battery, close behind the battalion, gave valuable assistance by firing into selected houses from which the enemy offered resistance.

A heavy autumn mist had settled during the morning, resulting in poor visibility. The lack of clear vision prevented the King's Own and East Lancashires from providing the necessary support to the two companies of the Seaforth Highlanders, located on the eastern bank. The shrapnel shells used by the artillery also proved ineffective against the houses and the opposing artillery. To overcome the difficulties, additional howitzer support was requested and the subsequent fire of the 35th Howitzer Battery silenced two enemy guns, which had been shelling the Lancashire Fusiliers[109].

High numbers of casualties were always a concern and the 10th Brigade was advised to press on systematically through Le Touquet but was not to undertake any offensive action against Le Falot[110], only to form a strong line opposite that village against counter-attack. Although, under heavy shelling, the brigade continued to make progress and reached a point 500 yards south of Frelinghien Church. The fighting in and around Le Touquet and Frelinghien continued uninterrupted throughout the afternoon and right through the night.

The 10th Brigade was to continue the thrust for Frelinghien on the 20th with Seaforth Highlanders on the east bank and the Royal Irish Fusiliers on the western bank, to supply enfilade fire. By 6:30am, the forward movement of the two companies of Seaforth's had been generally checked by heavy fire from the town of Frelinghien and trenches to the east. However, the 1st Royal Irish Fusiliers had managed to establish themselves close to the line of enemy trenches on the western bank and subjected it to crossfire. That fire assisted the Seaforth Highlanders to work forward by way of covered approach. Whilst the Seaforth's slowly advanced, a Maxim machine-gun of the Royal Irish was directed upon

---

[109] *During the day, Major V.R. Piggot arrived to assume command of the 1st Royal Warwickshire Regiment.*

[110] *Le Falot translates, in English, to The Lantern. It was a small community of houses several hundred yards west of Le Touquet.*

the bridge at Frelinghien so as to prevent any movement of enemy troops across the river. Forward movement was slow and the smoke from two haystacks, to which the enemy had set fire, further complicated the already limited observation.

The whole area was shrouded in mist and, during the afternoon, the heavy batteries, supporting the 10th Brigade, suffered constant shellfire as the German guns searched for the British artillery. By midday, despite the difficulties, the 2nd Lancashire Fusiliers and the King's Own, which had suffered under heavy shelling, had established touch with the two companies of the Seaforth Highlanders on the opposite bank of the river and their supporting fire allowed the Seaforth's to make further progress. As they advanced they worked up close to a trench that had given them many problems and rushed it at the point of the bayonet, taking forty prisoners, about a third of which were wounded.

The advance pushed on slowly and an unoccupied German trench was also captured. Indeed, the 10th Brigade had made such progress that, at 1:15pm, the brigade artillery was able to shell the enemy's transport behind the front line. Such was the success of the 10th Brigade that, at 2:40pm, they found 100 enemy dead and captured a farm south of Houplines.

While the 10th Brigade was thus engaged, the 12th Brigade was fully occupied further north. In the early hours of the morning, an officer's patrol from the Lancashire Fusiliers had found that a barricade had been placed on the road to the east of Le Touquet, between the village and the river. By 8:00am, enemy reinforcements had arrived on the west bank in front of the 12th Brigade and, an hour later, an attack was made against the village of Le Gheer and positions between that village and St. Yvon, then held by troops of the 1st Cavalry Brigade.

The assault was firstly directed against Le Gheer at about 9:00am and resulted in the left of the King's Own being pushed back a little. Supporting troops of the Inniskilling Fusiliers were immediately sent forward and the Germans were seen to be digging trenches east of the village. By 11.00am, the attack was being pushed home and the Inniskilling Fusiliers were ordered to hold on at all costs. To assist, a company of the Essex was sent as reinforcements and a further two companies were ordered to Point 63 as reserves.

While the 10th and 12th Brigades were occupied in their attempts on Frelinghein, the 11th Brigade was formed into the divisional reserve. The brigade headquarters, then located in the Station Hotel in Armentières, ordered the 1ˢᵗ Hampshire's to relocate to the Erquinghem Road, just north of the railway, to protect them from the regular howitzer fire, regularly inflicted on the town. Similarly, the East Lancashire Regiment was sent to reinforce the 17ᵗʰ Brigade of the 6ᵗʰ Division, which had been ejected from Arabesques by the enemy.

Shortly after 1:00pm, the attacks on Le Gheer slowly subsided but the left flank of the Lancashire Fusiliers, north-west of Le Touquet, had been turned. To remedy the situation, the last two reserve companies, a company of the Essex, the Cyclists Company, assisted by a squadron of the 19ᵗʰ Hussars, were moved to Ploegsteert to reinforce the Lancashire Fusiliers.

The situation stabilised when the 11ᵗʰ Hussars arrived at 2:35pm to provide support. However, the respite soon ended when, at about 5:00pm, the enemy commenced a second, concerted attack from the north-east, this time at St. Yvon, north of Le Gheer. The Essex Regiment, with the assistance of a company of the Somerset's, took the main weight of the offensive, but both were forced to retire under the sheer weight of numbers. The attack took the Germans to within 500 yards of Le Gheer, where the momentum stalled under heavy rifle fire and, by 6:00pm, the impetus of the attack had ceased.

The 10ᵗʰ Brigade was very much hampered by poor visibility but, as the afternoon progressed, the mist cleared. While the artillery of both sides searched for the opposing batteries, buildings and farms were shelled to give assistance to the Seaforth Highlanders who were still attempting to enter Frelinghein. At about 9.30am the Seaforth's were subjected to intense bombardment and were forced to withdraw temporarily from their newly won positions. The war diary for the 10ᵗʰ Brigade on this day states *"A single gun of the 88 battery on the E of Houplines – Frelinghein Road was put out of action by some very accurate and first rate shooting on the part of a hostile battery"*.

As the advancing battalions drew closer to Frelinghein, resistance grew. The troops were constantly in action and, at about 5:00pm, the Germans launched a series of counter-attacks, firstly on the right, then at about 7:30pm in the centre of the line and then again on their right. The attacks were a part of a much larger offensive but each was brought to standstill. By 10:30pm, attacks upon the 1ˢᵗ Royal Irish Fusiliers and the 1ˢᵗ Royal Warwickshire Regiments had also been repulsed. Whilst these attacks did not appear to be carried out with the intentions of pushing back the British line, they had the effect of relieving the flanking pressure that was being applied to the Germans holding the river at

Frelinghein. The main direction of the German attack centred on the 12th Brigade about Le Gheer.

It was known that German reinforcements had detrained at Lille during the night of the 19th and had concentrated around Escobecques, just west of the Lille, in front of the 12th Brigade. In the face of such strong opposition, the division was instructed, in the small hours of the 21st that, should the division be forced back, it was to cover Armentières on the line of Bas Maisil-Le Quesne-Weg Macquart. It was to extend the line to the south of Armentières and Houplines, Le Bizet, Ploegsteert and Pt. 63, to the north. During the morning, the enemy had also attacked the 6th Division and the French Cavalry, driving them back through La Bleau, to Le Mesnis.

The morning of the 21st was inundated with rain and artillery observation became increasingly difficult as the weather deteriorated. Suspecting an attack on the division, the 1st Somerset Light Infantry marched, in the early morning, to Ploegsteert to reinforce the 12th Brigade. Such was the urgency that they were diverted from travelling via Pont de Nieppe and told to go through Le Bizet, the shortest possible route, albeit under artillery fire. To assist with the defensive lines civil labour was also recruited to assist with the digging of a support trench from Le Bizet, through Ploegsteert, to Point 63[111].

At 5.00am, the full weight of the German XIX Corps fell upon the 6th Division south of Armentières and rapidly spread north to strike the 4th Infantry and 1st Cavalry Divisions. On the 4th Division front the main weight of the assault was concentrated mainly between Le Touquet and St. Yvon and resulted in the 2nd Royal Inniskilling Fusiliers being driven out of Le Gheer at about 7:00am.

The loss of Le Gheer not only endangered the 12th Brigade positions around Ploegsteert Wood, but also imperilled the flank of the Cavalry Corps at St. Yvon. The 12th Brigade took the protective step of occupying a former line of trenches near Le Gheer, as a possible flank guard. When the East Lancashires learnt of the withdrawal, three companies were sent to occupy the reserve trenches just east and south-east of Ploegsteert. A squadron of 19th Hussars and one platoon of the Cyclist Company, which was rushed to the scene, protected the left flank. As the reinforcements arrived, the withdrawing troops of the Inniskilling

---

[111] It was not unusual for both sides to use civil labour that was available in any given area. It became common practice as the war proceeded.

Fusiliers were pressed back to Ploegsteert where they were reformed in to a reserve.

The seizure of Le Gheer by the Germans had an immediate effect on the trenches held by the King's Own, just south of Le Gheer, as rifle and machine-gun fire then enfiladed them. The King's Own took heavy losses immediately and temporarily withdrew. With the absence of the Inniskilling Fusiliers, the 19th Hussars, further still to the right, formed a defensive flank to protect their left. The Fusiliers were gathered up and led back to their positions and more losses were suffered as they returned. At 7:00am two companies of the East Lancashires, led by Captain North and armed with their machine guns, advanced through Ploegsteert Wood in preparation to recapture the trenches in Le Gheer.

Still further pressure was added when, at 9:00am, the whole British line was subjected to a concentrated attack, extending as far north as Messines and beyond. At midday, the 1st Cavalry Division, on the left of the 4th Division, requested that the guns of the 4th Division assist by shelling the enemy concentrations on its front. While the 4th Division was thus involved in defending the line, the 6th Division, fighting south of Armentières, was being pressed with determination.

The loss of Le Gheer was deemed to represent a serious danger to the support lines and all available reserves were called north from Armentières to Ploegsteert. By 10:30am, the 12th Brigade was fully committed, holding a containing line to the south, south-west and north-west of Le Gheer. All available battalions were in the fighting line with the exception of the only remaining reserve of two companies, located at Ploegsteert.

The counter-attack by Captain North's companies of East Lancashires was launched at about 11:00am. The success of the counter-attack depended upon the Inniskilling Fusiliers and Hussars holding their line and they were asked to cooperate at all costs. Steady progress was made and, to support the effort, the Somerset Light Infantry and number of dismounted cavalry, advanced south from St. Yvon to attack the German right flank. While the infantry attack was in progress, the howitzers of the 10th Brigade searched for the opposing German guns, largely responsible for the constant casualties.

A second attack, led by Colonel Anley of the 2nd Essex Regiment, was carried out at midday by a composite force of the Essex, East Lancashires, Somerset's, and elements of the 19th Hussars and succeeded in reaching the crossroads in the village. By 1:00pm, the Essex had retaken the trenches on the eastern end of Le Gheer and an effort was made to continue the attack with the possibility of enfilading the remaining enemy in the trenches still further east and cutting them off from possible retreat. The manoeuvre was successful and resulted in the capture of one hundred and fifty prisoners. The failure of the enemy to hold Le Gheer forced a general local retirement across the railway line towards Deulemont.

The only trenches remaining in enemy hands were in the immediate vicinity of the crossroads in the little village of Warnave. With the objective of capturing that remaining pocket of resistance a company of the East Lancashires, supported by a company of the Essex Regiment, advanced eastward along the River Warnave, and engaged the enemy on the western end of the village. Despite the attempts by the East Lancashires to rout them the resistance was determined but, by 3:40pm, the entire village had been occupied and consolidation commenced.

During the clearing of Warnave, fifty men of the Royal Inniskilling Fusiliers, who had been captured in the initial German attack, were recovered. While consolidating the village, the Somerset's took a further fifty prisoners which had been hiding in the houses and cellars. While the action at Warnave was being waged, the 1ˢᵗ Cavalry Division, holding Messines, was subjected to constant heavy attacks. To assist, two companies of the 2ⁿᵈ Essex Regiment and a section of Royal Engineers were sent to help with the digging of trenches and assisting with defence.

The 10ᵗʰ and 12ᵗʰ Brigades had been involved in constant fighting for four days and it was necessary to relieve the 12ᵗʰ Brigade. At 9:00pm, the two companies of the 1ˢᵗ Hampshire Regiment and one company of the 2ⁿᵈ Essex Regiment were instructed to relieve the 1st King's Own Royal Lancashire Regiment, which had faired badly and, upon relief, the exhausted troops marched to Le Bizet to form a reserve. The 2ⁿᵈ Royal Inniskilling Fusiliers were also withdrawn from Le Gheer and sent to Ploegsteert as reserves. Casualties for the 12ᵗʰ Brigade alone on this day amounted to four hundred and sixty eight all ranks and the division held a front of five and three quarter with two brigades.

The action on the left flank of the 12ᵗʰ Brigade was not yet over. At 5:00pm, the division mounted troops were again attacked at St. Yvon and was only repulsed after bitter, close-quarter fighting. In order to provide protection against further attack, a field company was sent to help strengthen the defences about the village. Further to the south, the 10ᵗʰ Brigade had enjoyed a measure of success in the face of a determined enemy although the intensity of the fighting produced heavy casualties.

While the fighting continued on all quarters of the front line, the 11th Brigade was sent to positions south of Armentières to act as Corps Reserve. Here much of the time was spent in the construction of a support line extending from L'Epinette to Houplines. Instructions were issued that all positions gained were to be held at all costs and any that was lost were to be retaken. The determination to defend the line was such that, by the early hours of the morning of the 22nd, the original line had been retaken everywhere, all losses recovered and much consolidation carried out throughout the night and next day.

Arrangements had previously been made to have the 11th Brigade relieve the 12th Brigade between the River Warnave and Le Touquet during the night of the 22nd. As the relief was carried out, it was noticed that large bodies of German troops moving north and, at about daybreak heavy firing could be heard in the direction of Messines[112]. The German offensive extended as far south as Le Gheer, which was again subjected to heavy artillery fire and infantry attack. Throughout the night, the division artillery concentrated upon the German guns in an effort to subdue the shelling being endured by the front line troops. By 5:45am on the 24th, the attack had been repulsed but casualties had been heavy on both sides. In the morning, reports estimated the number of German dead at Le Gheer at about one thousand. Amid the attacks and defence, the relief of the 12th Brigade was completed, in heavy rain, in the early hours of the 23rd and the troops spent a few hours cleaning up and receiving hot meals.

While the 4th Division faced consistent and heavy attacks south of Messines, the 6th Division was withstanding the full impact of massed assaults, particularly near Fleurbaix, south of Armentières. The 17th Brigade of that division had been sorely affected. The only possibility to provide rapid relief was the 12th Brigade, which itself, had just been relieved by the 11th Brigade. The brigade was thus called upon to march the four miles to Rue de Bois during the night of the 24th where it fell under the order of the 6th Division. The brigade was to hold a part of

---

[112] *The Cavalry Division, holding Messines, had been heavily attacked. By coincidence much of the firing that had been noted by the 11ᵗ Brigade originated from the two companies of 2ᵈ Essex Regiment and Engineers, which were temporarily attached to the Cavalry Division and manning trenches around Messines.*

the 6th Division line from Rue de Bois to the railway line near Porte Egal F^E. [113]

In preparation for the move the two companies of the 2nd Essex Regiment, which were still fighting at Messines with the 1st Cavalry Division, were ordered to rejoin the 12th Brigade at Le Bizet in readiness to march to the assistance of the 6th Division. Once the brigade had gathered, it marched for Chapel D'Armentières where it completed the relief during the night. The three brigades of the 4th Division now held a front of 14,000 yards, or eight miles.

Signs of the oncoming winter were evident as the morning of the 25th brought very heavy rain that lasted all day and well into the night. In the early hours of the morning the Royal Warwickshire Regiment, 10th Brigade, was heavily attacked and only repulsed the advancing enemy after inflicting heavy casualties with concentrated rifle and machine-gun fire. The attack did not last long but was delivered with determination and, by 4:00am, all had fallen quite. Three hours later the junction of the 12th and 16th Brigades was subjected to heavy artillery and machine-gun fire. While the shelling continued throughout the day, but no attempt at attack was made until the early evening. When the attacks commenced they were of such intensity that the men of the 1st Leicestershire Regiment, 16th Brigade, were driven from the line.

Retaliation by the 6th Division guns was extremely difficult, as they were unable to locate the opposing artillery through the heavy mist that had prevailed for most of the day. Under the intense pressure of the German assault, the positions held by 2nd Durham Light Infantry (18th Brigade)[114], became increasingly vulnerable and the commander of the battalion indicated that they could not hold on for much longer. The opinion of the 12th Brigade, expressed in later reports, indicated that it did not believe that the entire 18th Brigade would not be able to hold its positions.

While efforts were being made to restore the Leicesters to their positions, the last reserve of the 12th Brigade, the Lancashire Fusiliers were brought forward to fill the gap and occupy the vacant trenches. At about 6:00pm the 18th and 16th Brigades were again attacked all along

---

[113] *The railway line was, at that time, the most southern point to which the 4 Division extended. The location of the 12 Brigade, south of the railway, merely extended the front held by the units of the 4 Division by a further 2000 yards.*

[114] *The 2 Battalion, Durham Light Infantry Regiment, was under the temporary orders of the 12th Brigade for the purposes of defence.*

the line. It was not until well after dark that the shellfire diminished although it did not, at any time, entirely stop.

The evident risk of the 6th Division front completely failing led to the decision, by III Corps, to withdraw the whole division to a new line and preparations for the move were commenced. The retirement of the 16th and 18th Brigades to the new trench line was conducted during the night of the 25th, which enabled the relief of the long-suffering Leicester and Shropshire battalions.

Whilst the 6th Division had been subjected to the violent attempts by the enemy, the 10th Brigade, in its position about Houplines on the River Lys, had also been hard pressed. The Seaforth Highlanders were heavily shelled at Houplines and the supporting division artillery could only offer a limited response due to poor visibility and the lack of observation aircraft. The intensity of the artillery fire forced the Seaforth's to withdraw, temporarily, from their positions and only reoccupied their trenches as the fire diminished. Throughout the shelling, the hospital on the northern end of the village continued to operate, with the three female nurses, who remained at their posts, to assist with the wounded.

Throughout the 26th, the 4th, 5th and 6th Infantry Divisions and the Cavalry Corps at Messines were subjected to a long and continuous bombardment. During the evening, those divisions were ordered to hold their positions as the I[st], IVth and Cavalry Corps were scheduled to attack a considerable length of the German line to the north of the 4th Division, the next day. The 1st Cavalry Division, as part of the combined assault, was to attack in an easterly direction from Messines at 3:00pm and requested artillery support by the guns of the 4th Division.

During the night of the 27th, little activity was experienced on the 4th Division front, but German reinforcements had arrived in front of the 18th Brigade (6th Division) and, with enemy machine guns only 500 yards from the brigade flank, conditions progressively deteriorated. Division headquarters informed the 12th Brigade, that the enemy was expected to attack during the forthcoming day and, if the defences were not successful, the division would be in a bad situation.

The enemy displayed a great determination to secure the positions held by the Durham's by launching a night attack, at 10:30pm. As the attack developed, a company of the Lancashire Fusiliers was sent to a point near Des Ranques F[m] to support the Durham's and a second company followed, to support the first. The Durham's were instructed to hang on at all cost and that a force would protect their right flank should the East Yorks give way. The Germans were in large numbers and continued to mass. Desperate fighting continued for two hours but the line held and by 12:30pm, the impetus of the enemy attack had eased, except for the constant shellfire. Subsequently, as the artillery support was allocated to the 1st Cavalry Division, the 12th Brigade, suffering at the hands of the German artillery to the south, was notified that no support from the howitzers could be offered.

Congratulations were sent from the headquarters of the 4th and 6th Divisions, asking for the name of the officer responsible for the defence. It appeared that Lieutenant Beaumont had gone to the assistance of the Durham's and was instrumental in repelling the attack[115]. Amidst the heavy fighting the 12th Brigade had requested the destruction of a walled farm in front of their support line and the Royal Engineers were asked to assist. Due to the constant demand for their services, no additional engineers, beyond the two sections already allotted to them, were available. Division headquarters asked for a more detailed description of the farm and the engineers, currently attached to the brigade, were instructed to reconnoitre the position the next morning. The reconnaissance was duly conducted and established that the farm could possibly be destroyed by artillery fire. Thereafter the division artillery devoted attention to it.

Throughout the night, the troops had remained nervous and at 4:00am on the 28th, shell and rifle fire again heralded an enemy attack, followed an hour and half later by a further attack on the right flank, against the Lancashire Fusiliers and Inniskilling Fusiliers (12th Brigade). In an effort to deter the enemy from further attacks the Lancashire Fusiliers supported an attack by the East Yorkshire's, at 10am, and recovered the trenches that had been evacuated by the Leicesters the previous day. The shelling and rifle fire remained constant throughout the morning, only dying down during the afternoon. By 2:00pm, the Lancashire Fusiliers had driven some one hundred enemy from a farm on their front and had taken several prisoners.

---

[115] *During the action, Lieutenant Beaumont of the 1· King's Own Royal Lancaster Regiment, assisted by a platoon of infantry, had supported the Durhams and successfully drove back the enemy. Later, fifty-six enemy dead, two of whom had been killed on the parapet of the trench, were counted in front of the Durhams, with a further fifty-seven counted in front of the trenches of the 2· Royal Inniskilling Fusiliers.*

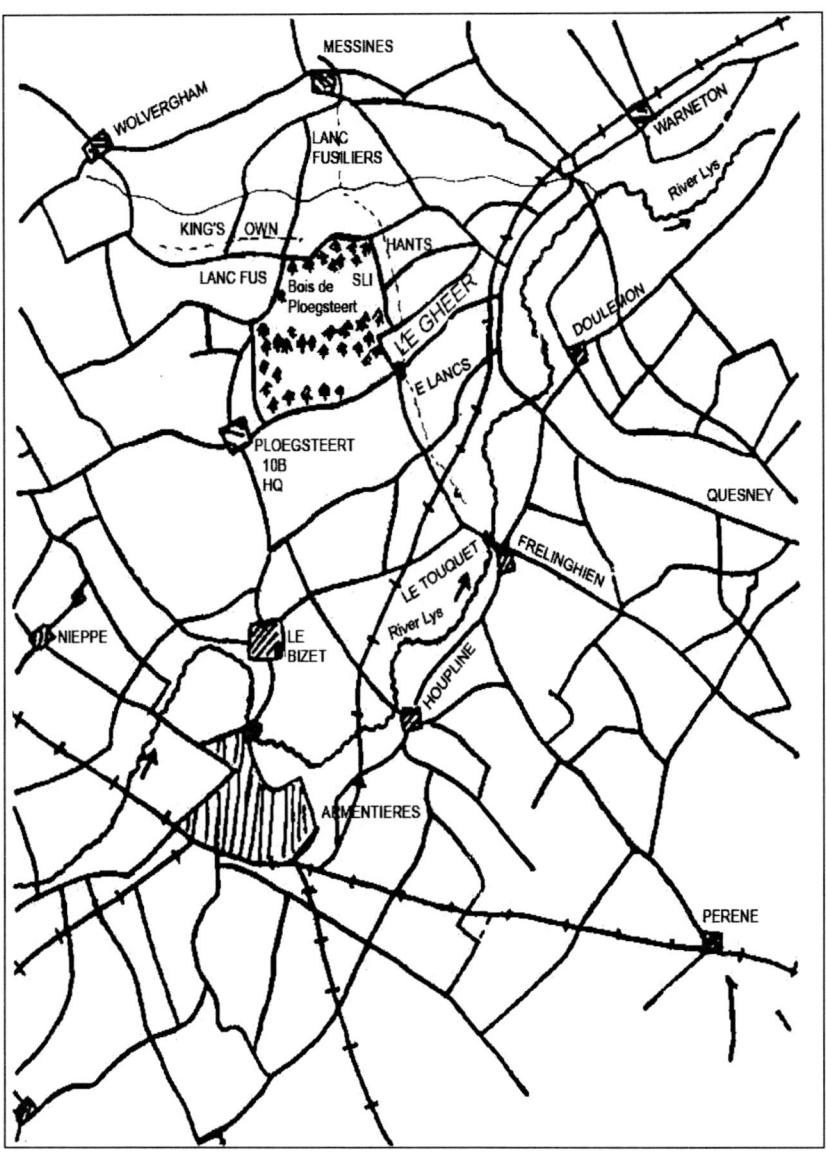

Plate 4
Diagram showing the final position of the 4th Division on the evening of the 22nd
October 1914

The 10th Brigade, fighting in front of Frelinghein, was constantly subjected to rifle and machine-gun fire from a brewery, recently occupied by the Germans, and from trenches under the south wall of that building. In an effort to subdue the fire, a howitzer, under the command of a

Lieutenant Hess, which was close behind the Seaforth Highlanders, destroyed the brewery and a loop holed wall through which enemy enfiladed the Royal Irish Rifles. Whilst the fighting around the brewery was underway, the headquarters of the 10th Brigade had reported its suspicions that information was being passed to the Germans out of Houplines. The response from division headquarters read, *"Such action as is possible has throughout been taken by GSO III in conjunction with the French local authorities, but with a town of 30,000 inhabitants and 4-5000 refugees, the difficulties presented are practically insurmountable[116]"*.

Little more action was seen during the afternoon although considerable movement of transport behind the German lines was heard. Listening posts of the 10th Brigade stated that they were under the impression that the enemy was withdrawing. Similar reports were also received from the Irish Fusiliers. Shortly after those report had been made, the 11th Brigade also reported considerable traffic moving to the south. As day dawned, the troops noted that the Germans in the trenches opposite the 4th Division were wearing grey caps with a red band, later determined to be Prussian troops, which had relieved the Saxons during the night.

The morning of the 29th produced heavy sniper fire directed upon the 2nd Essex and the artillery was called on to help by shelling No Man's Land. In compliance, the division guns fired but many of the shells dropped short and caused considerable damage to the 12th Brigade. In retaliation for the British shelling, the German artillery fired on the 12th Brigade trenches, adding to the damage. While the 12th Brigade was getting the worst of it on the 6th Division front, the 2nd Royal Dublin Fusiliers, of the 11th Brigade, holding the line at Le Gheer, were also heavily attacked, although the attempts were beaten off[117].

By the end of October the general situation confronting the British army in Belgium could, at best, be described as daunting. By the night of the 29th October 1914, the British I Corps had been heavily engaged east of Ypres and was stretched to its limits in a valiant effort to defend

---

[116] *The fear of spies among the civilian population grew to astonishing proportions during the early part of the war but little supporting evidence has been found to support the number of suspicions, which had been reported.*

[117] *New weapons and methods were constantly trialed and, during the night of the 29 the 1 East Lancashire Regiment, 11 Brigade, experimented with a new flare pistol, later reporting, "The rocket pocket pistols were very useful, whilst engaged with Germans, during the night in lighting up the ground."*

a line extending north-south across the old roman Ypres-Menin Road[118]. That road acted as the axis of advance for the German 5th Army, in its attempt to continue the push westward to the French coast. On the morning of the 30th October the left flank of the German advance was the 4th Army, which was confronting the British III Corps on a curving front from Messines to a point one and a half miles east of Armentières and then in a south-westerly direction to Fleurbaix.

On the morning of the 30th, the situation of the 1st Cavalry Division, in front of Messines, grew worse by the hour. The 119th and 125th Regiments of the German 51st Division, XIII Corps, had concentrated to the east of Messines, with the XIX Saxon Corps around Quesnoy-sur-Duêle. Considerable forces of Cavalry were also in the area of Commines and Warneton and were supported by Landwehr units. In the early afternoon, an aircraft reported five long trains having arrived at Commines and large bodies of troops between Kortekeerbeek and the railway north-west of Messines. A German observation balloon was also sighted in the direction of Frelinghein[119]. As the 1st Cavalry Division was already heavily engaged around Messines, the headquarters of that division notified the 4th Division that it would not be able to offer assistance unless absolutely necessary.

At dawn on the 30th, the 11th Brigade was subjected to heavy shelling near Le Gheer, followed immediately by an enemy infantry attack on the line between Le Gheer and Le Touquet, a distance of 2700 yards. The attack lacked coordination and, by 11:00am had come to a standstill. Enemy snipers remained increasingly active and, as the intensity of the sniping grew, the 1st Rifle Brigade had to request artillery support. That request resulted in the howitzers of the 10th Brigade being directed on several houses, from which the snipers were firing, destroying or damaging most and, although the enemy attack had failed, the 11th Brigade remained engaged with pockets of resistance around Le Gheer.

---

[118] *The numbers involved and the severity of the fighting in the Battle of Gheluvelt on the 30 October 1914 is clearly described in the History of the Seventh Division. It was in the fighting on the 29 October that a great-uncle of the authors' wife was captured. Private Joseph Green, 5384, was a member of the 1 Battalion, Royal Welsh Fusiliers, 22 Brigade, 7 Division, which was largely overrun in the area north of Zandvoorde on that day. Many of the survivors were wounded and captured. Pte Green was sent to Germany where he spent the remainder of the war in various camps. It was while he was in 24a Barrack Room, Friedrichfeld Camp near Wesel, that he formed the Greens Ragtime Band.*

[119] *The balloon was reported to have had five large balls attached, although neither Division headquarters nor III Corps knew what the signal meant.*

By 4:00pm, the 1st Cavalry and 7th Infantry Divisions, acting on the right of I Corps, had been pushed back by overwhelming numbers. A growing number of intelligence reports indicated the seriousness of the situation. Fears as to the ability of the 4th Division to hold the existing line, prompted the sending of the 9th Field Company to work on a supporting line on the eastern bank of the River Lys near Frelinghein. The trenches of the 1st Hampshire Regiment (11th Brigade), situated at Ploegsteert, had also been subjected to intense shelling and German troops were seen massing in the valley of the River Douve[120]. That suggested the possibility of concentrated attacks on the left flank of the 4th Division, where the 1st Hampshire Regiment was already engaged.

Warning messages were sent to all divisions and brigades and III Corps gave instructions to move all 4th Division reserves to the left. It was also suggested that a battalion of the 12th Brigade, still engaged south of Armentières, be moved to support the junction of the line between the 11th Brigade and the Cavalry Corps.

As result of that suggestion, the 12th Brigade was ordered to be ready to either maintain its present position, or leave the 6th Division to assist the Cavalry Corps. To prepare for the departure of the 12th Brigade, the 6th Division moved its reserves to Chapel D'Armentières. On arrival, the 1st East Yorkshire Regiment, of that division, relieved the Inniskilling Fusiliers, which then marched to Ploegsteert. Every available man was ordered to be on the left (west) bank of the Lys by daybreak.

The fighting in the Douve Valley grew in intensity throughout the 30th. Mistranslation of events took place, one example being that as the German attack developed, a message from an artillery observer stated that the line of the Somerset Light Infantry had been broken north of St. Yvon. When the headquarters of the 11th Brigade was asked to confirm if it was true, the reply stated that they were uncertain, but considered it unimportant if it had. It was later understood that the Somerset's had been pushed back by sheer weight of numbers, but had indicated that it intended to recover the lost ground. As a result, an organised attack, delivered at 8:00am, successfully recaptured the lost

---

[120] *The River Douve lay in a shallow valley, La Vallee de Douve, about mid way between the left flank of the 4 Division at Point 63 and Messines. It lay, at the time, within the boundary of the 1 Cavalry Division, but German infantry in the area could bring enfilade fire on the left of the 4 Division.*

trenches and, by 9:00am, work had commenced on restoring and reinforcing the position[121].

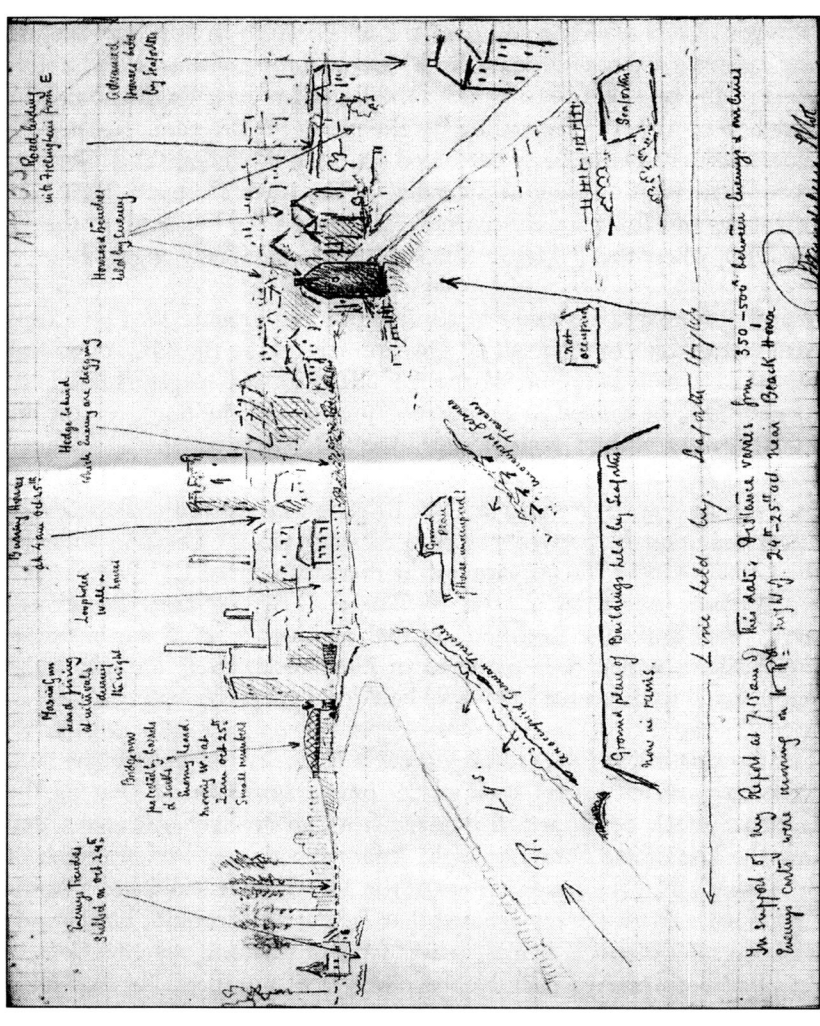

Plate 5
Sketch of the view of Frelinghein as seen by the Seaforth Highlanders during their attack o the 24th October 1914. The loop-holed wall, shown in the middle of the drawing is that referred to above.

---

[121] *During the difficulties of the day, Major Prowse of the 1st Somerset Light Infantry Regiment was recommended for immediate promotion for his work on this night and that of the 21st. The Division headquarters endorsed the recommendation and congratulated the 11th Brigade for its actions.*

In the early evening of the 30th, the 10th Brigade, still holding the line south of Le Touquet, issued warning orders to expect an attack. That attack was launched shortly after and, by 9:00pm, the entire brigade was in action, which lasted for about an hour. The sheer weight of the attack made it necessary to construct a strengthened second line and that was made possible by the arrival of the first two companies of the 2nd Lancashire Fusiliers and the remaining two companies of the Royal Inniskilling Fusiliers at Ploegsteert at about 11:00pm. To assist with the digging of the trench line, the Lancashire Fusiliers also employed local civilian labour. The number of troops available to assist was complimented by the arrival of the remaining two companies of the 2nd Lancashire Fusiliers at Ploegsteert at 5:00am on the 31st.

Upon arrival of two companies of the Inniskilling Fusiliers at Messines, a meeting of the battalion officers and General De Lisle, G.O.C., 1st Cavalry Division, took place where he spent time with the officers and explained that it was doubtful that the cavalry could withstand further attacks. He indicated his concerns to the effect that the right flank of the 1st Cavalry Division should be secured before moving his reserves to the left. It was suggested and agreed that the two companies of Inniskilling Fusiliers, having arrived at Ploegsteert at 7:00pm on the previous evening should be sent to Messines to act as support for the 1st Cavalry Division.

One company was placed in support of the right of the 1st Hampshire Regiment, located on the southern bank of the River Douve and the other placed in trenches in support of the left of the Hampshire's, immediately north of the river. It was also agreed that most of the remaining reserves of the 4th Division were to be massed on the left flank of the division line, near the junction of the two divisions. It was intended that, if the Cavalry Corps was ejected from Messines, offensive action for its re-capture should be undertaken immediately.

During the night of the 30th, the Hampshire's relieved the company of, which had been engaged for several days on the northern bank of the River Douve, with another company of the battalion. It was a relatively quiet night prior to midnight, largely free from enemy attack, although the Essex Regiment, (12th Brigade) repulsed a small attack at St. Yvon at 2:00am in the morning. To the left of the 4th Division the 119th Regiment, (51st German Division), continued its attack on Messines in the early hours of the 31st and engaged the Inniskilling Fusiliers on the River Douve. As the assault grew in intensity it gradually extended south, up the ridge towards Point 63, where it threatened the artillery. To meet the possibility of the guns being attacked, steps were taken to establish a force of reserves for action, either in the direction of St. Yvon, to the east, or Messines, to the north.

By 7:50am, the 1st Cavalry Division was being heavily pressed at Messines and requested the support of the 4th Division. The 12th Brigade could only spare the remaining two companies of the 2nd Royal Inniskilling Fusiliers because, as enemy infantry had developed an attack at St. Yvon, there was no more to give. That attack, which had been expected, was launched at 8:00am and the village was subjected to severe artillery, machine-gun and rifle fire for the remainder of the morning, although never seriously threatened with capture. When the mist cleared, about mid-morning, the artillery of both sides enjoyed clear observation and German infantry were seen entrenching in front of the 2nd Essex Regiment at St. Yvon. The whole action had been observed from enemy observation balloons aloft north-east of Frelinghien and east of Deulemont.

By 10:00am, the 1st Cavalry Division could no longer hold Messines and it informed the 4th Division that they would have to fall back to a north-south line near Wulverghem. It was intended that the withdrawal of the cavalry be carried out under the protection of a counter-attack against the advancing enemy and, to assist, the artillery support of the 4th Division was sought. To aid the attack, III Corps requested the 4th Division to gather as many reserves as possible and cooperate with the attack, to be carried out shortly before midday. At the prescribed time, the attack was launched and, initially progressed well. The Inniskilling Fusiliers pressed back the enemy infantry and the artillery observers on Point 63 recorded their entry into Messines at 12:30pm.

However, the fete of Messines was clear and the enemy effort continued to build. Aircraft reported columns of German troops moving northwest from Houtham to Commines while the 12th Brigade reported further large bodies of Germans having crossed the railway bridge at Perenchies, south-east of Armentières, and moving north. Further reports from aircraft, at about midday, indicated that the roads in the triangle of Messines – Armentières – Warneton were clear but there existed a column of Germans three miles long between Deulemont and Quesnoy, marching in the direction of Messines. By mid afternoon, the Inniskilling Fusiliers had managed to hold the trenches on the River Douve while the Germans held the ridge east of Messines, overlooking the Fusiliers.

Three companies of the Somerset Light Infantry and one company of the Hampshire Regiment held the area between St. Yvon and Le Gheer while the village itself was occupied by the 1st East Lancashire Regiment, (11th Brigade). The entire front between the two villages, approximately 1,000 yards, was heavily shelled and then attacked by a numerically superior force, but was successfully repulsed. By that time, all available troops were engaged. Consequently, a platoon of the Hampshire Regiment, fighting in front of St. Yvon, was completely overwhelmed by the greater numbers, despite the heroic defence. The weight of the attack had carried the enemy to within 100 yards of the main trench line, north of St. Yvon. No member of the platoon returned. The fighting with a determination that exercised the very character of both nations and progressively extended south of St. Yvon.

By nightfall of the 31st, a considerable quantity of German road traffic had been detected moving towards Lille and when the artillery opened fire, the sound of galloping horses was clearly heard by the troops of the neighbouring 12th Brigade. The month of October closed with bitter fighting on both sides, often in conditions of heavy rain, mud and mist. Although the division had experienced intense fighting and suffered heavy casualties, there had been few changes in the line, except on the left flank. During the night of the 31st, the Cavalry Corps, holding the Messines – Wytschaete Ridge, suffered a breakthrough near Wytschaete by a small body of the enemy. Two battalions of the Cavalry were sent to prevent any further attempt and drove the enemy from the village. The offensive against the allied line continued. Strong forces massed along the weakly held Messines – Wytschaete road and in the northeast corner of Messines.

November - 1914

It is appropriate to pause once again, to understand the events of the fighting in the early hours of the morning of the 1st November. The Cavalry Corps, fighting to the east of Messines, had been forced to withdraw through the village that stood on the crest of the ridge. To the left of the Cavalry stood the French 32nd Division and to the right, the 4th Division. The Inniskilling Fusiliers were fighting on the slopes of the northern bank of the River Douve, from the southern edge of Messines to the river, which represented the extreme left of the division line.

Adjoining the Fusiliers, on the immediate southern bank, was the Hampshire Regiment, which continued the line through to St. Yvon. These were all battalions of the 11th Brigade. The East Lancashire Fusiliers (12th Brigade) then extended the line to the south, from Le Gheer to Le Touquet where they, in turn, joined the King's Own and Rifle Brigade holding the line to Frelinghein. The 10th Brigade then held the southern part of the line with the Seaforth Highlanders, Royal Irish Fusiliers and Royal Dublin Fusiliers respectively while the Warwickshire Regiment secured the southern most point on the Armentières – Perenchies railway. At that point, the 6th Division extended the line further south.

Throughout the morning, the German efforts to take Messines and Wytschaete continued and the attacks on the left flank of the 4th Division had serious consequences. Division headquarters had received a message from the artillery at Point 63, indicating that the Cavalry Corps was in the process of retiring from Messines. As the Cavalry slowly withdrew, a gap formed between the Inniskilling Fusiliers and the right flank of the Cavalry Division. The gap grew as the cavalry continued its retirement towards Wulverghem, which resulted in the left of the Inniskilling being fully exposed to German penetration from flank and rear.

Colonel Edwards, GSO1 to division headquarters, went to see the officer commanding the 11th Brigade and, realising that the situation on the left flank was serious, requested reserves. In response to a call for assistance from the 4th Division, the 3rd Division sent a battalion, the 3rd Worcestershire Regiment, as did the 5th Division with the 1st Dorsetshire Regiment[122]. Those two battalions were ordered to Wulverghem

---

[122] *The 3 and 5 Divisions were a part of II Corps, which was fighting further to the north. Although under heavy attack, they possessed sufficient reserves to temporarily assist the 4 Division.*

with a request that they only be used if necessary. They arrived at Neuve Eglise at midday and fell under the orders of the 4th Division. Both battalions were ordered to rest, as they would be required to move at short notice. Subsequently the Worcester's were moved to Ploegsteert as brigade reserve and occupied the trenches along the southern edge of the Ploegsteert – Le Gheer road[123].

Whilst the 11th and 12th Brigades were fully occupied with attacks on their respective fronts, so the 10th Brigade, defending the line north of Armentières was being subject to similar assaults. By 2:30pm, a gap had formed between the right flank of the Rifle Brigade, fighting on the left bank of the River Lys and the river itself. To avoid the possibility of enfilading fire on the left flank of the Seaforth Highlanders, the Rifle Brigade was instructed to close the gap with haste. This was achieved, but only under great difficulties.

During the afternoon German guns, which had been brought up close to Messines, brought to bear enfilading fire upon the exposed left flank of the Inniskilling Fusiliers and Hampshire Regiments. Added to the shelling was flanking rifle and machine-gun fire from the German infantry as they advanced along the Messines ridge. The intensity of the artillery fire had made it necessary to re-adjust the line and, in the late evening, Colonel Edwards again visited the 11th Brigade and arranged to withdraw the left flank of the line to the west, to link up with the line of the Cavalry Corps. It was his recommendation that, as the retirement would now create a salient with St. Yvon at its apex, the trenches protecting that area needed to be strongly held.

Due to the extended nature of the left flank, it was decided to place the northern portion under a single command. Lieutenant-Colonel Butler, 2nd Lancashire Fusiliers, was given control of the line with Lancashire Fusiliers, Royal Inniskilling Fusiliers, and division cavalry under his control. Those units were to act as a sub-section under orders of the 11th Brigade. Colonel Edwards then proceeded to III Corps Headquarters and secured artillery assistance from the 6th Division and from II Corps. That request was followed by the arrival, at 8:00am, of a section of heavy artillery from the 6th Division. Throughout the night a reorganisation of the line, primarily on the left flank, took place as the Inniskilling Fusiliers withdrew their left flank to the west, along the River

---

[123] *The German Emperor was reported to be in the area and GHQ called for an extra effort to be made.*

Douve, to positions just east of Wulverghem while the Somerset Light Infantry relieved the hard-pressed Hampshire's.

The 12th Brigade still held a part of the 6th Division front, which had been free from attack, except for the regular shelling. The peace was short lived as, early in the morning of the 2nd, the brigade came under attack at Rue de Bois, south of Armentières, on the extreme left of the 6th Division of the line. The attempt was successfully repulsed and by 6:00am all firing had ceased. On the far left of the 4th Division line, the 11th Brigade also saw action. At 5:00am, the 1st East Lancashire Regiment suffered heavy shelling by a large gun, assumed to be a mortar, which blew away yards of trench and caused considerable damage. The bombardment continued for several hours, until the Corps heavy artillery shelled the suspected gun position and ended its activities.[124]

The fighting for Messines continued with the Germans advancing large forces against the 1st Cavalry Division and the 11th Brigade was immediately absorbed into the fighting. The attack developed quickly and by 8:00am had extended along the whole line and continued without abate all morning. The supply of German reinforcements appeared to be inexhaustible and by early afternoon Lieutenant-Colonel Butler had committed all but one company of his local reserves. In order to reinforce the line, he was authorised to call the Worcester's and the Dorset's, still resting in Neuve Eglise, to the road junction behind Point 63. The 10th Brigade also sent two companies to join the Dorset's[125].

The intensity of the fighting was such that division headquarters became increasingly concerned that the 11th Brigade would need to be replaced if the pressure on it was not relieved. The French forces had been pushed out of Wulverghem and had notified the 4th Division of a proposed counter-attack on the Messines Ridge at 7:00am on the next day, the 3rd, and instructions were issued for the artillery to support any such attempt.

The morning of the 3rd of November dawned a fine sunny day and brought a little warmth. The division experienced little activity with the

---

[124] *The weapon responsible for the shelling was the newly introduced minenwerfer, which delivered a heavy explosive through a high trajectory. The minenwerfer was readily recognised by a large and destructive explosion.*

[125] *During the evening, the 10 Brigade reported observing Germans dressed in British uniforms. The War Diary stated for this date "Can report that Germans dressed as Highlanders came to their trenches calling out 'We are Scottish Rifles, don't shoot.' They did."*

exception of the constant shelling although several sightings of German artillery movements were recorded. Little eventuated by way of the French attack and by the end of the day Messines had been lost to superior numbers, both sides having suffered heavy casualties[126].

While the fighting on the northern end of the line had consisted largely of shelling, the 10th Brigade had been heavily engaged in an enemy infantry attack about Le Gheer. The level of resistance displayed by the 10th Brigade was revealed when, after the firing had died down, about one hundred and fifty enemy dead were counted between Le Gheer and St. Yvon. The 4th Division had suffered nearly two hundred killed, due largely to the artillery fire. Daylight on the 4th revealed enemy troops entrenching in front of Messines, which attracted the attention of the 5th Division artillery.

The strain of four months of continuous fighting and constant shelling compounded by the cold and wet conditions took its toll on the troops. Sickness and disease spread rapidly with the effect that many of the fighting troops were either hospitalised or sent on other duties. The 2nd Essex Regiment, which had been in the trenches for seven days without a hot meal or cup of tea, struggled to maintain numbers and was eventually forced to request reinforcements due to the number of men being sick. Arrangements were made with the 6th Division for the Leicesters to relieve the Essex Regiment in the trenches during the night[127].

One of the difficulties experienced by the various headquarters of the division involved spurious reports of enemy activity from the brigades. Suspicion of foul play by the Germans was rife in the early months of the war and on the 5th November, the 12th Brigade reported that an aircraft flying in the area with French markings was in fact, German. A separate report was received to the effect that the artillery situated at Point 63 was being heavily shelled but this too, proved to be incorrect. A further report by a patrol of the 5th Division cavalry stated that large bodies of Germans were moving south-west towards the River Douve. However, a patrol of the 11th Brigade, sent to determine German intentions, failed to get confirmation of any such movements, but a counter-attack was prepared, should it be required. Yet again, another

---

[126] *The battle for Messines was later to be recognised in German history as the slaughter of the Innocents' due to the number of Germany's youth who died in the effort to take the ridge.*

[127] *During the day Major-General Snow, the former G.O.C. of the 4 Division, who was in Woolwich recovering from injuries after falling from his horse five weeks before, wrote to the incumbent G.O.C., Major- General Wilson, to say a formal farewell and offering congratulations to the division on its recent efforts.*

report, received from the neighbouring 6th Division, indicated that they had shot a man in British uniform walking along a German trench.

The previous weeks had brought several changes to the position of the opposing lines and attempts were made to establish the exact location of the German front line. Throughout the night of the 5th and morning of the 6th the movement of enemy horses and artillery could be detected from the lines held by the 10th and 11th Brigades, particularly in the direction of Frelinghien. Early in the morning of the 5th, the Dorset's, attached to the 11th Brigade, had sent several patrols out to observe enemy activity and one of those managed to establish touch with French forces on the River Douve. The 12th Brigade too, was busy trying to establish the enemy's situation. Two men had crawled out to within thirty yards of the German trenches and brought back a mail bag half full of letters, although none of these proved important. Just as the attempts of the 4th Division to continue the advance on the heights above Bucy-le-Long in early October were brought to a halt and trench warfare became the norm, so it was in Flanders.

The division artillery was to lend its weight to a scheduled French attack by shelling the enemy lines in front of Messines. The attack was progressively delayed throughout the morning of the 5th, firstly to 11:00am then midday and finally 3:00pm. While waiting for the attack to commence, the 3rd Cavalry Brigade was subjected to a bout of heavy enemy shelling. Despite all efforts, the guns of the 4th Division could not locate the offending artillery. As the moment of the French attack drew near, III Corps advised the 4th Division that, should the attack prove successful, the 11th Brigade was to attack and re-occupy their old trenches, north of the River Douve.

The French attack commenced at 3:00pm but faced with considerable fighting about Wytschaete, the advance failed to capture the town and the attackers dug in west of the Steenbeeck[128]. Because the German objective of capturing Messines and the ridge on which it sat had been achieved, the concerted enemy attacks of recent days slowly waned. The 4th Division had, by the 6th, settled down to a defensive role and offered artillery support for the attacks of the French Cavalry Corps and the 5th Division although much of that support was hampered by poor observation, caused by the persistent autumn mists.

---

[128] *The Steenbeeck is a small river, which flows west of Wytschaete. 'Beeck' or 'Beek' can be translated as meaning creek, or stream.*

The infantry work focused on consolidating the trench systems in preparation for winter. The diminishing enemy activity did not, however, leave the division entirely free of attack and for most of the afternoon the Dorset's, north of the wood and the Worcester's, occupying trenches east of Ploegsteert Wood, were heavily shelled. Following the shelling, the Dorset's, Worcester's, and the Rifle Brigade were attacked in the early evening, at Le Gheer, with such effect that the Worcester's were ejected from their trenches on the edge of the wood. The fog prevented any response from the artillery support and the O.C., Worcester's stated that, without artillery support, he considered the situation untenable.

Whilst the battalions located around Ploegsteert Wood were undergoing the attentions of the German artillery, orders were received for Brigadier-General Haldane, commanding the 10th Brigade, to report to I Corps Headquarters at Chateau De Trois Tours and assume command of the 3rd Division[129]. Lieutenant-Colonel Butler, C.O., 1st Somerset Light Infantry, 11th Brigade, was recommended to assume command of the 10th Brigade, but it was not to be.

Shortly after midnight on the night of the 7th, the shelling of the 11th Brigade increased and, by the early hours of the 8th, the situation had become critical. At 7:00am, the enemy attacked in large numbers between Le Gheer and St. Yvon[130]. The attackers overran approximately 500 yards of the front line trenches held by 1st Hampshire Regiment and penetrated 100 yards into Ploegsteert Wood, until stopped by desperate resistance. An immediate counter-attack recovered some of the ground but it was found impossible, without a properly prepared assault, to dislodge the enemy from the former front line.

The capture of the front line in this sector was a clear indication of the inherent difficulties in protecting the left flank of the division against a

---

[129] *Lieutenant-General Haldane later wrote in his book 'A Brigade of the Old Army 1914' about the moment of his posting; "I had, with some other brigadiers, been promoted Major-General on the 26th October, and on the 6th November was informed that I had been appointed to command the 3rd Division, which was then engaged east of Ypres. I was ordered to report myself on the 7th at the Chateau des Trois Tours near that place, where the headquarters of the First Corps were, and to which the 3rd Division was then temporarily attached. But as events turned out I was not to leave for about a fortnight, as the moment was undesirable for a change of command, and my successor in command of the 10th Infantry Brigade, Colonel MacMahon, 4th Bn. Royal Fusiliers, who was killed a few days later, had to be replaced."*

[130] *A captured officer had stated that the attack had consisted of six infantry and two Jaeger battalions.*

determined enemy. The attack had created a salient that extended from the original German trenches, across the newly captured British trenches and well forward, into the eastern edge of the wood. Further penetration would have endangered the reserve line and the rear of the artillery positions on Point 63, on the north-western corner of the wood. The Rifle Brigade was also subjected to enfilade fire from German position north of Frelinghien Church.

The division artillery fired in support of the 11th Brigade by concentrating four howitzers, twelve field guns, and one heavy howitzer in searching the German trenches along the whole front between the River Douve and the River Warnave. That gunfire was complimented by two batteries of the 14th Field Artillery Brigade, which gave supporting crossfire from near Le Bizet, while six additional howitzers engaged trenches north of Frelinghien.

To help bolster the efforts of the 11th Brigade two companies of the 2nd Ayrshire and Sutherland Highlanders were temporarily detached from the 19th Brigade, 2nd Division, and sent to Le Bizet. The arrival of the reinforcements freed up those troops holding the support line and, with the additional weight of numbers, the 11th Brigade had cleared the wood of the enemy by early afternoon, but the trench that had been captured remained in enemy hands. The heavy mist and confused nature of the fighting led to misunderstandings. At 3:04pm, the headquarters of the 6th Division reported to the 4th Division that some of the Germans fighting around Ploegsteert wood were dressed in British uniforms. It was later established they were, in fact, troops of the Hampshire Regiment, who were being driven through the wood ahead of the German attack.

The fighting around Le Gheer continued into the afternoon. The remainder of the Hampshire's, near St. Yvon, were sorely pressed and the need to re-capture the former front line was imperative, as its occupation permitted enfilade fire into the continuation of the trench line on either side. In order to make a concerted counter-attack the Inniskilling Fusiliers (12th Brigade), were allocated the task of attacking and recapturing the trench, to be accompanied by a second supporting attack by the 2nd Lancashire Fusiliers, should the attack by the Inniskilling's fail. The fighting was intense and by 9:30pm, the 1st East Lancashire Regiment was moved to the south east corner of Ploegsteert Wood to cooperate with the Inniskilling Fusiliers in their attack.

While the events at Ploegsteert Wood were taking place, the 1st Rifle Brigade, at Le Touquet, had also been subjected to attack. Throughout the morning and part of the afternoon the Rifle Brigade had been subject to constant and heavy shelling and, covered by this fire, the enemy sapped under the wire entanglements, much which had been destroyed by the shellfire.

Houses occupied by the brigade were also shelled and the weight of the attack forced many of the Rifle Brigade to retire and forfeit the trench line to the enemy. Recovery of that trench line was of utmost importance and the Cyclist Company was called upon to assist with a counter-attack at dusk. To help relieve the pressure, the 6th Division sent the 1st King's Own Yorkshire Light Infantry to Le Bizet and the 1st West Yorkshire Regiment to Chapel D'Armentières. Both were made available to the 4th Division as reserves to the 12th Brigade. The 6th Division also temporarily contributed a battery of 6" howitzers to assist with the recapture of the lost trenches.

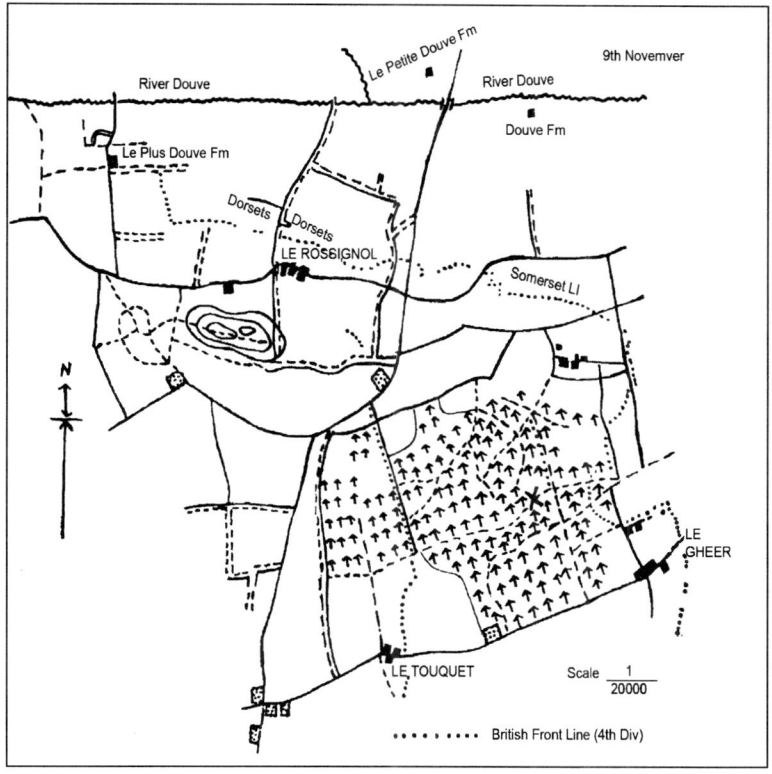

Plate 6
Diagram showing the salient formed by the German attack at Le Gheer at 7.00am on the 8 November 1914. This map was drawn on the 9 November after the tide of fighting had receded.

The determination to retake the trenches between St. Yvon and Le Gheer was marked by the arrival in Ploegsteert, at about midday on the 8th, of the 21st Brigade, 7th Division, which had been loaned to the 4th Division to help strengthen the line if necessary. Additional howitzers were also loaned for the operation, one of which was dragged up close behind the line to deal with the enemy occupied houses. The attack, originally planned to take place on the 8th, was delayed to provide for thorough preparation.

The attack by the Inniskilling Fusiliers commenced shortly before midnight on the 9th and made slow but steady progress, even in the face an attempted a counter-attack, without losing momentum. Shortly after commencing the attack, a house and one of the trenches at the southern end of those abandoned by the Worcester's, were re-taken. By 4:00am on the morning of the 10th, the right hand portion of the attack had progressed well, although the left had hung up.

The 1st East Lancashire Regiment recaptured most of the trenches, but was again driven out by enfilading artillery and machine-gun fire. The 2nd Ayrshire & Sutherland Highlanders Regiment, fighting on the left of the East Lancashires, had also advanced successfully but had diverged from the line of advance. Because of that divergence, the two battalions had advanced either side of a trench still occupied by the enemy, who then fired into the rear of the Argyll & Sutherland Highlanders. That, and the fact that they had also come up against an occupied trench, protected by wire entanglements, brought them to a halt. The 2nd Lancashire Fusiliers, advancing in the second line, took the offending trench and a farm, bayoneting the occupants of both[131].

The recapture of the trenches was followed by two strong counterattacks but the machine guns of the East Lancashires, assisted by heavy rifle fire, inflicted heavy casualties on the attackers and also caught the German supports, which were approaching in close formation. The 9.2 howitzer, "Mother", which had done sterling work on other occasions, scored two direct hits on the enemy field guns which resulted in extensive damage and a decrease in the shelling to which the Lancashire Fusiliers were subjected.

---

[131] *On the 6 January 1999 the remains of 8850, Private Harry Wilkinson, 2 Lancashire Fusiliers, were discovered in a field between the eastern edge of Ploegsteert Wood and the Le Touquet – St. Yvon Road. It was in this attack that he was killed and his burial site was on the farm mentioned above. The owner of the land was preparing the field for ploughing, which had not been touched since the end of the war. For further details about the action in which Pte. Wilkinson died see Appendix IV "Summary of 11 Brigade Action – 9 November 1914*

By 5:30pm, the 11th Brigade had brought in three hundred of their wounded. The total casualties of the 11th Brigade since the abandonment of the trenches by the Worcester's and the conclusion of the counter-attacks were one hundred and forty six all ranks killed and five hundred and four all ranks wounded and missing. Events quietened down during the evening although the 10th Brigade continued to be subjected to intermittent shelling and sniping.

It was the intentions of the 11th Brigade to continue the attack in an effort to recover the last of the lost ground but, although the Germans on their front were almost surrounded, it was postponed until the next day. The latest attack had taken several prisoners and, during interrogation, one had revealed the existence of two German regiments in Messines, artillery to the north-east of the village and a reserve division in Warneton. As a result of that information, 'Mother' was turned on Warneton.

The rest of the evening was largely occupied with the consolidation of the captured trenches and, as no engineers were available to assist, the 7th Division was asked to provide their engineers. The 4th Division now consisted of the 10th, 11th and 12th Brigades, which had suffered a long and exhausting period in the line, and a mixture of units from the 3rd, 6th and 7th Divisions. Early in the afternoon, the 6th Division, had agreed to relieve the 12th Brigade with the 1st West Yorkshire battalion, located nearby.

The strength of the German reserves in and around Lille precluded any further hope of capturing Frelinghien and in order to prevent the free passage of the enemy across the Lys it became necessary to destroy the bridges between Frelinghien and Warneton. Again, 'Mother' was called upon. The French Cavalry Corps, which had undertaken the attacks on Messines and Wytschaete, had met with little success, and withdrew when relieved by the British Cavalry Corps. The 4th Division was now holding a frontage of 8,000 yards with four thousand men in the front line and nearly two thousand, four hundred in reserve. Following an inspection of the front line by the G.O.C., it was decided that the part of the front held by the 11th Brigade was too large for one command and a complete re-organisation of the line was to be undertaken.

Arrangements were made to relieve the 12th Brigade from that part of the 6th Division front to which they had been sent on the 22nd October, although the 2nd Essex Regiment remained, temporarily, under 6th Division command. The 12th Brigade was, upon its return, to take over the section of the line from Le Touquet to Le Gheer inclusive. The 11th

Brigade was to continue the line north from Le Gheer, around St. Yvon and north as far as the Messines – Ploegsteert Road where they were to get in touch with the troops of the Cavalry Brigade. The completion of the move allowed the 11th Brigade line to be shortened, and dispensed with the need to occupy trenches that covered Point 63 from the north. Due to the complexity of restoring the various battalions to their parent brigades and the return of the two companies to the 10th Brigade, the completion of the arrangements took many telegrams and several days. Amidst the reorganisation, the 10th Brigade was heavily attacked and, although carried out with some determination, successfully repulsed. The overcrowding of Point 63 with artillery batteries had produced serious supply problems and additional sites for the guns needed to be found[132].

As a part of the reorganisation, the 21st Brigade reverted to the command of the 7th Division and the 2nd Ayrshire & Sutherland Highland Regiment was returned to the 19th Brigade. Amidst these moves, changes in officers also occurred. Lieutenant-Colonel Anley, C.O., 2nd Essex Regiment, having received a promotion to the rank of Brigadier-General, assumed command of the 11th Brigade[133]. During the evening of the 11th, the 2nd Seaforth Highlanders and 1st Royal Irish Fusiliers were subjected to heavy artillery and machine-gun fire for half an hour, although no attempt at assault was made[134]. At about the same time Lieutenant-Colonel Butler, who had been commanding the sub-section of the 11th Brigade, was presented with the Legion d'Honour from Lieutenant-General Pulteney, G.O.C., III Corps at the division head-quarters.

---

[132] *It was common practice for both sides to notify the troops of any victories by their forces in other theatres, to help maintain morale. During the night of the 10 the news of the destruction of the German cruiser Emden, by the Australian cruiser H.M.A.S. Sydney, and of the blocking of two German warships in Königsberg, Africa was promulgated to the troops.*

[133] *Colonel Anley's promotion and appointment allowed the existing C.O., Brigadier-General Hunter-Weston, who had received a promotion to the rank of Major-General on the 27. October, to arrange his departure, after minor delays, to return to go England and assume command the 29th Division.*

[134] *Contradictory reports of the event exist within the Division and brigade diaries. At 7:30am on the 12th, the 10th Brigade sent a report to Division headquarters relating the events of the attack on the 2nd Seaforth Highlanders and 1st Royal Irish Fusiliers. The report stated that the attack, supported by machine guns, came to within 100 yards of their firing line but was not pressed. It was suspected that they had inflicted heavy casualties on the enemy. This infers that an assault was indeed attempted, but failed.*

The trenches held by the 1ˢᵗ Somerset Light Infantry on the northeast corner of Ploegsteert Wood, were considered weak as, while the Somerset's commanded the high ground, it overlooked the trenches and all positions behind the line. In front was an estimated five hundred of the enemy, holding a front of about 500 yards between Le Gheer and St. Yvon in strongly entrenched positions and protected by wire and bomb proofs[135][136]. It was feared that, should the enemy take that high ground, it would offer a clear view of the 11ᵗʰ and 12ᵗʰ Brigade line.

The ground in question was under continuous shellfire, which hindered the supply of water and rations, all of which had to be carried by hand. Conditions were made worse by the late autumn mists, which obscured the vision of the artillery observers and profoundly affected the accuracy of the supporting artillery. Circumstances were most trying for the troops, who had undergone constant and heavy attacks in the previous three weeks and were continually sniped at from surrounding houses. Although the need to suppress the fire was urgent, the ground proved unfavourable to sap up to them.

The reorganisation continued throughout the remainder of the month and the difficult conditions were exacerbated by the near winter weather conditions, that of heavy rains, frost and, towards the end of the month, light snow. It was a particularly miserable period as the troops had been fighting continuously for three months, without relief, had undertaken long periods with few hot meals and could rarely secure something as simple as a cup of tea. Casualties had been heavy, with only rare opportunities to bury the dead. Amidst these trials, it was possible to experience a lighter, if not humorous, side to life in the trenches. Orders to stop shooting hares and pheasants with rifles were not taken too seriously by the troops and the instructions had to be issued several times until, eventually, those officers commanding were held responsible for failure to comply. No records exist as to how many

---

[135] "Bomb proofs" was the term attributed to overhead cover installed over trenches to prevent the effect of grenades and shrapnel.

[136] The Birdcage lay on the eastern side of the Le Touquet – Messines Road with its right flank just south of St. Yvon and the left flank near Le Gheer. It had earned the name because of the complex trench system and the very dense wire entanglements that had been constructed on the ascending face of the ridge overlooking the eastern end of Ploegsteert Wood.

of the game birds were consumed, as recovery would have been at considerable risk[137].

As the line shortened, it became possible to relieve various units and hot meals were served to those in reserve. Medical services were also provided for those suffering from the cold and wet feet. Although the artillery exchanges were constant, no major infantry actions were engaged. Trenches were prepared for the winter, a particularly arduous task as the rain constantly broke down the walls and parapets as it was quite beyond the capacity of the water pumps to drain the lines. A graphic example of the living conditions was shown when, on the 16th, the Essex Regiment reported that they had experienced great difficulties in their efforts to sap towards the enemy lines due to the number of buried Germans they came across. The casualties had been considerable and the conditions under which the troops lived were very demanding on their workload and spirit[138].

The reorganisation continued and many of the units, which had come to the assistance of the 4th Division, were returned to their parent brigades and new units joined the division to supplement its strength. The 1/5th London Regiment arrived on the 18th and was allocated to the 11th Brigade while the 2nd Monmouthshire Regiment, having arrived on the 20th, was attached to the 12th Brigade. During this period of movement and reorganisation, the first of the snowfalls occurred and continued into the evening.

Notwithstanding the conditions, it was a period of experimentation. Anti-aircraft "pom-poms" were trialed as a weapon for breaking down the parapet of German trenches but were not considered successful. Star shells, fired by the artillery, were introduced and found to be of great use. Long-range firing by the heavy artillery was undertaken and, whilst shelling Commines railway station, scored a direct hit on a train at a range of 14,000 yards. The infantry were also subjected to shelling which often destroyed the good work done on the trenches and resulted

---

[137] *News arrived of the death of Field-Marshall Lord Roberts, on the 14 November, after having visited General Headquarters and met with the Commander-in-Chief, Field-Marshall Sir John French, at St. Omer.*

[138] *It was on this day that Brigadier-General G. Hull assumed command of the 10 Brigade, thus replacing Brigadier-General Haldane, who left on the 18 to assume command of the 3 Division. Shortly after Lieutenant-Colonel Butler, CO of the 2 Lancashire Fusiliers, was promoted to the rank Brigadier-General and given command of the 32 Brigade, 11 Division, then being formed in England. He assumed that command on the 28 November.*

in much effort to consolidate. Skirmishing took place periodically as the enemy attempted to rush sections of the line, but all were repulsed.

Towards the end of the month, the amount of shelling inflicted upon the division gradually reduced as air reports showed enemy guns and troops being withdrawn from in front of the 4th and 6th Divisions. The division now held the entire line from the River Lys, just south of Le Touquet, to the River Douve, south- west of Messines, a distance of approximately 7,000 yards. Discipline was generally good but the number of court-martials in November was indicative of the difficulties under which the troops lived. There was thirty-nine court-martials many of them for drunkenness however, one was for a self-inflicted wound and six others for desertions[139].

---

[139] *The charge of desertion was one that could earn the death penalty, and it became common practise for the Courts-Martial to reduce these charges to absent without leave, which did not warrant a penalty more than detention.*

December - 1914

The first two weeks of December passed with little infantry action but both sides were subjected to constant shelling. The weather had progressively deteriorated and, amid heavy rains and mists, the ground was turned to a sea of mud and water filled shell craters. The flooding of trenches produced serious problems and there was a lack of mechanical means of removing the water. In an effort to alleviate the conditions under which the troops had to live instructions were issued to the effect that all available hands were to bale out the water by whatever means were available.

To assist with the task, the engineers, were called, but were handicapped by a chronic shortage of water pumps. On 1st December, an experiment to lower the level of the River Lys by fifteen inches was carried out by opening the lock at Houplines. Although water levels in the river decreased as a result, it did little to alleviate the seriousness of the situation. It was during this period that boarded pathways and corduroy matting was used extensively to assist passage through Ploegsteert Wood.

Despite the difficulties, the humorous character of the Tommy had not diminished. Such was the proximity of some of the trenches that troops of the Lancashire Fusiliers, 12th Brigade, offered tins of bully beef to the opposing Germans in exchange for helmets and badges. Difficulties arose once the bargaining was complete, as there always remained a disagreement as to who should come out first to fetch his share, considering the consequences of being exposed above the parapet.

Within days, the Lancashire Fusiliers reported that the Germans opposite their trenches had been replaced with a "*rather surly lot, who will not answer when spoken to*"[140]. On the 2nd December His Majesty the King, George V, accompanied by His Royal Highness, the Prince of Wales, inspected the troops in reserve and also a platoon from each of the battalions in the trenches, following which he presented D.S.O.'s and D.C.M.'s to those who had been recommended[141].

---

[140] *The troops of the 4 Division were often able to discern when a relief had taken place in the opposing line due to the communications, quite disallowed, between the two sides. The Saxon Regiments were generally affable while the Bavarians were considered dull and incommunicative.*

[141] *Distinguished Service Order and Distinguished Conduct Medal. At about the same time, information also reached the troops of the capture of General De Wet, the Boer General who had produced so many difficulties in South Africa during the Anglo-South*

The weather deteriorated even further. Heavy rain occurred daily, increasing the difficulties of drainage and trench maintenance increased accordingly. The appalling weather conditions made it difficult to locate the many snipers who fired persistently from houses and concealed loopholes. To help suppress the fire, the artillery destroyed specific houses east of Ploegsteert Wood, suspected of concealing some of the offenders. On occasions, work performed by the troops was rewarded in the most unexpected way. The 11th Brigade war diary for the 4th December states: *"the following is vouched for by the OC of the King's Own: 2 nights ago, the RE commenced putting wire in front of the new trenches of the King's Own, but as they were making the obstacle particularly strong, they were unable to finish it in one night. On going out about 10pm the next night they found the Germans had completed the work in a most satisfactory manner "*.

The severest of conditions was experienced on the 5th December when considerable effort was expended in attempting to deal with flooded trenches and collapsed parapets. The situation grew worse as the day passed and, on the 6th, two pumps and a supply of sandbags were obtained to strengthen the walls of the rapidly deteriorating trenches. Among those desperate conditions, the shelling of selected targets continued, day and night. The German artillery reciprocated with steady, sometimes heavy, shelling of the Ploegsteert – Messines Road.

However, moments of light relief existed. The enemy opposite the 2nd Monmouthshire Regiment, 12th Brigade, kindly informed them, by shouting across from their trench, that they were going to attack at 6:00pm and drive them out. They also wanted to know who was occupying the trenches instead of the 2nd Essex. Not unexpectedly, the attack failed to eventuate. Warning were also issued to all troops that the French army had recently changed the colour of their infantry uniform to a grey-blue and that the new uniform could easily be mistaken for the German field grey uniform [142].

By the 10th December, troops of the 19th (German) Saxon Corps had taken over the trenches opposite the 4th Division and their arrival was signified by intense artillery fire on the left flank of the 10th Brigade. In

---

African Campaign (1899-1901) and who had carried guerrilla attacks against the British and South Africans, in sympathy with the Germans, during the early stages of the Great War.

[142] *In keeping with the practice of informing the troops of activities in the other theatres of war news of the British naval victory off the Falklands Islands was distributed. This was followed the next day with news of the sinking of the Nuremberg.*

spite of the heavy shelling, patrols of the 10th Brigade reconnoitred a German trench 200 yards in front of their position, early in the morning of the 11th, and found it empty except for five enemy dead.

The relief of German units had taken place along considerable length of the front and the 12th Brigade had identified soldiers of the 181st Reserve Division, with the number '12' on their buttons, opposite them[143]. The period up to the evening of the 18th December was one of inactivity by the infantry, broken only by periodic shelling, which was largely directed at the 10th Brigade. Observation aircraft in the area of Wytschaete – Messines reported that there appeared to be no major movements by German forces, although a large number of buses had been seen about Wervicq, lorries and about 150 railway carriages at Commines.

Plans had been prepared by the headquarters of the 4th Division for a further attack on the small, but dangerous, salient that had remained on the eastern end of Ploegsteert Wood since the enemy attack of the 10th November. Although much ground had been regained in the earlier attack, the salient was still approximately 1000 yards wide and 300 yards deep, with the forward edge resting just inside the border of the wood. Behind the enemy front line of the salient lay the strongpoint, referred to by Tommy as the 'Birdcage'. The weather had been atrocious, with heavy rain and cold winds for many days. The ground, which had been dug over and shelled regularly by both sides, consisted of 'Flanders' clay, which adhered to every thing it touched and only drained slowly.

The area had been the scene of severe fighting ever since the arrival of the 4th Division and because of the proximity of the Birdcage to the British trenches, it was deemed necessary to capture the position as protection from such observation as it afforded the enemy. The responsibility for the capture of the salient fell to the 11th Brigade, which was holding the line in front of the salient. The plan required the 1st Hampshire Regiment, which occupied trenches immediately to the north of Le Gheer, to attack in a northerly direction, while the 1st Rifle Brigade was to attack due east, that is, directly in front of the salient. The 1st Somerset Light Infantry, on the left of the Rifle Brigade was to attack in a south–easterly direction, with the London Rifles acting in support.

---

[143] *The History of the 'Essex Regiment (2 Battalion), J.W. Burrows, 1927, p.119, states that officers and men of 'A' and 'D' Companies met a party of Germans of the 181 Regiment, 19 Saxon Corps, in No-Mans Land at 10:00am on the 10 December 1914. Whilst this is not recorded in the diaries of the Essex Regiment, it could possibly account for the ability to identify the opposing troops.*

The attack was scheduled to commence at 2.30pm on the 19th December and, in preparation, the artillery bombardment began at 10:00am, which led to immediate confusion. The 10th Brigade reported that the guns were shelling the trenches occupied by the 1st Royal Warwicks but the artillery stated that it could only be German artillery. An hour later, the 11th Brigade reported that the heavy artillery was firing on the trenches of the 1st Hampshire Regiment. This proved to be correct but the guns were also found to be under the command of that brigade.

Finally, at 2:30pm, the attack got underway and slow progress was made, eventually being held up 150yard from the objective in the face of dense wire and machine-gun fire. By 3:00pm, nearly all rifle fire on the front of the 1st Rifle Brigade (11th Brigade) had ceased. The attack had been partially successful but had left the Rifle Brigade holding a rather tenuous position due to the fact that the Somerset's, to the left of the Rifle brigade, had to breach breastworks[144], eight feet high, which stood directly in the line of their advance. From these works came heavy rifle and machine-gun fire which, added to the flanking fire from St. Yvon, brought the attack to a halt. To assist, the artillery shelled the trenches and breastworks around St. Yvon, but the shrapnel shells had little effect on the breastworks, which remained largely intact.

The task of breaching the breastworks was beyond the capacity of the Somerset's and they retired to their original start line at the edge of Ploegsteert Wood. Here they attempted to establish contact with the 1st Hampshire's, who had remained and entrenched on some of the captured ground. Being left unsupported, the Rifle Brigade retired at the same time and, in doing so, a gap formed between the adjoining flanks. In order to fill the gap and restore communications between the battalions, two platoons of the Somerset's were sent but nothing further was heard of them.

Such were the casualties that the 11th Brigade Headquarters determined that it could not consolidate the captured ground until the arrival of fresh troops. Shortly after 8:00pm, Lieutenant Pulteney, G.O.C., III Corps, arrived at the division headquarters and stopped the attack. By the morning of the 20th, the British casualties had grown to fifteen officers and three hundred and twenty other ranks killed, wounded, and

---

[144] *Breastworks were formed, during the Great War, of a 'wall' of sandbags, designed to present an obstacle to attacking troops. Traditionally, breastworks were built where the nature of the ground would not permit entrenching i.e. in very boggy or very rocky ground.*

missing[145]. There was no doubt that a good many of the casualties were caused by the artillery of the division when it shelled the Hampshire's and Somerset's and this was attributed to the "*extraordinarily bad luck of every single communications wire being cut. It is a question whether all of this cutting could have been done by the enemy's shrapnel*[146]".

As a result of the failure of the attack, the enemy spent great effort during the evening and the following day in reinforcing the position with additional troops and strengthening the wire defences, but made no attempt to advance. The concise aim of the attack, apart from re-capturing the much-needed ground, had been to draw German rein-forcements away from the French front and all assessments by III Corps suggested that it had been successful.

The next ten days were spent holding the existing positions in bitterly cold frost and torrential rain effectively bringing any chance of further offensive action to an end. The heavy rain caused the River Douve to flood until it was up to forty feet wide in places. Within the constraints of the ammunition shortage, the division artillery continued to shell tactically important points regularly.

The inclement weather kept the troops of both sides fully occupied maintaining trenches and preventing flooding. In an effort to reduce the flood levels 4th Division headquarters requested that the 6th Division open the sluice gates at Houplines, but it was learnt that they had been open for the previous three days. The only way to reduce the level was for the Germans to open the sluices at Commines. The trenches con-stantly collapsed due to the ground retaining so much water. The in-stances of trench foot and frostbite increased alarmingly and the rate of hospitalisation increased accordingly[147].

The diminishing manpower produced by these and other illnesses cre-ated great problems and, in an effort to resolve the many instances of

---

[145] *The above casualty figures included the two missing platoons, almost 100 men.*

[146] *Extract from the war diary of the 4 Division – WO95/1440*

[147] *Boxing Day was 'business as usual' and the shelling on the left of the 10 Brigade continued, but very little sniping and only the occasional shell was experienced else-where along the line. The night was very cold and no flares were sent up after dark, which gave the opportunity for many to catch up with much needed rest. During those few days the River Douve had risen another three feet and, such was the seriousness of the flooding, that trenches immediately near the river were abandoned, only to be re-covered towards the end of the month as the flood waters receded. All hopes of being home by Christmas had vanished into the mud.*

trench foot, the troops were only permitted to stand sentry duty for short periods of time and the numbers holding the trenches were reduced to bare minimums. Not withstanding the difficulties, the shelling was continuous. It caused trenches to be blown in constantly and the repairs to such damage were delayed due to the reduction in the number of available troops in the front line.

During Christmas Eve, firing by both sides decreased almost to nothing and much singing of carols was heard from the German trenches. Christmas day was fine but cold along most of the line with heavy mists in low-lying areas and a heavy frost. The atmosphere was strangely quiet and an unofficial truce was established by the approaches, at several points along the line, by unarmed German soldiers, many singing carols and carrying lanterns. Gradually the number of British troops who left trenches and met the enemy in No-Man's Land, increased, which led to an exchange of sundry courtesies[148].

On the 12th Brigade front almost no sniping and no artillery fire was experienced throughout day and, on the left, both side buried the dead between the lines. It was at first believed that a Bavarian unit had relieved the Saxon division in front of the 4th but, as the troops mingled in No Man's Land, it was found that the Saxons were still in occupation of the opposing forces. At Le Touquet, an unarmed German soldier entered the lines and asked permission to bury the dead but having been allowed inside the trench lines, he was not allowed to return.

The Seaforth's did not experience a single shot being fired in the morning mist and walked about in the open, even after the mist rose. They reported having had some trouble keeping the Germans away from their lines and put additional wire out to prevent such attempts and strengthen there position. Much of the work was carried out in the open, in broad daylight. Although the commanding officers were aware of the incidents and the complete lack of artillery fire, the truce was unauthorised and reports were called for in the ensuing days. However, the opportunity was taken by many of the field officers to gain as much information about the enemy as possible[149].

The 11th Brigade experienced similar conditions with a night entirely free from sniping followed by a day-long informal truce. The Germans,

---

[148] *The division war diary states that Christmas day was celebrated in the usual fashion.*

[149] *A full report of Christmas Day on the front line held by the 1 Hampshire Regiment is quoted in Appendix IV*

who were not allowed near the British lines, met with their British counterparts in No Man's' Land on most friendly terms, with cigars, cigarettes, and news being exchanged freely.

The opposing troops belonged to the 132nd, 133rd and 134th Regiments of XIX Saxon Corps and stated that they came from Chemnitz. It was reported that among the enemy there were some very old and many very young men. When several of the officers visited the German trenches, most partly full of water, they noted that a lot of the enemy wore gumboots. It was also noted that the trenches were very heavily manned; one man per yard in places and much valuable information was gained regarding the enemy's wire entanglements. Both sides collected and buried a great many dead.

1915 - A Period of Learning

January - 1915

January was largely considered a 'quiet period', in the sense that the division did not undertake, nor was subjected to, major offensive actions. The 12th Brigade held the right sector from the River Lys at Armentières to the railway barricade[150] near Le Touquet while the 11th Brigade continued the line through Le Gheer to St. Yvon, on the Le Touquet – Messines Road. The 10th Brigade then extended the line to the River Douve, south of Messines. Life in the trenches had settled to a routine of trench draining and maintenance, artillery actions, patrol skirmishes and the ever-present sniping. Consequent to the fraternisation on Christmas Day instructions were issued to the effect that any informal understandings with the enemy was to cease and those officers or N.C.O.'s who continued to allow such activity would be brought before a court-martial.

The weather continued to be the greater of the two enemies. Trenches, in the front and support lines, were constantly flooded and required regular baling and pumping, and the efforts of thousands of men barely influenced water levels. The river Warnave, running between Le Bizet and Le Touquet, so filled trenches in the local sector that some had to be abandoned. With occasional exceptions, the rain fell in torrents, with snow aggravating an already precarious existence and temperatures regularly below zero. To help overcome the cold, lambs-wool jerkins and woollen gloves were issued and much effort was applied to the draining and repair of the firing line along the whole front and the labour applied a heavy burden upon the infantry, which had to supply the working parties.

The trenches were subjected to constant shellfire, particularly in the region of the River Douve. The artillery fire churned most of the area into a morass in which the troops maintained a somewhat precarious defence and in which some simply disappeared. The very nature of the bog afforded an element of defence against infantry attack but presented no barrier to the predications of the artillery. The work that had to be carried out on the trenches was additional to the already dangerous task of patrolling, made particularly difficult by the ground condi-

---

[150] *The railway barricade had been constructed across the railway line north-west of Le Touquet.*

tions and poor visibility. Incidents occurred regularly, as patrols met and fired upon each other.

On occasions, 'friendly' fire, caused largely by poor visibility in the heavy mists, resulted in confusion and casualties among the troops in the front line. While it was attempting to shell the Avenue,[151] the division artillery inadvertently bombarded the Seaforth Highlanders (12th Brigade), with about fifty shells and resulted in two being killed and one wounded.

They were again subjected to further shrapnel shelling on the 2nd, with three wounded and again, on the 3rd, when shells landed behind the trenches and wounded two men. As well as suffering casualties in this manner, the Seaforth's were continuously shelled by the German artillery, particularly on the 4th, which killed one and wounded a further two. Brigade Headquarters was also subjected to the enemy shelling when, during the first week, two shells landed nearby, one of them hitting the brigade commander's car, causing considerable damage.

The continuous, heavy rain had produced further general flooding, forced most of the troops out of the trenches near Warnave and transformed the entire front into a scene of desolation. Aggravating those conditions was the equally persistent artillery fire, inflicted upon the whole front line made any degree of movement of troops, transports, and artillery an exceptional trial of endurance. It was in these conditions that the 7th Argyll and Sutherland Highland Regiment joined the 12th Brigade on the 6th January.

Point 63 was heavily shelled, fortunately without many casualties, although one man was wounded when a shell fragment removed the tip of his nose. The trenches in and around Ploegsteert Wood and the village of Ploegsteert were subjected to considerable shelling and an attempt by the Germans to shell the headquarters of the 11th Brigade resulted in one hundred and sixty nine shells landing in the area immediately behind the headquarters dug-out. The constant sniping simply added to the woes.

Notwithstanding the restrictions applied to the usage of artillery ammunition, the guns of the division responded to every enemy bom-

---

[151] The Avenue was a road, which ran northward from the Neuve Eglise – Warneton Road, to La Douve Farm, on the southern bank of the River Douve. The farm had been a strong point for the 4 Division during October but was taken by the attacking Germans on the 1 November. It remained the subject of considerable shelling until the capture of Messines by the New Zealand Division in 1917.

bardment and assisted the infantry by shelling nominated targets. Such was the case when, on the 10th, the Warwickshire's identified three German machine-gun positions, all promptly dealt with by the field guns. A similar request from the 12th Brigade to shell Frelinghien, to subdue sniping, was met with the same immediate response.

On the 12th suspicions of German mining activity opposite the railway barricade at Le Touquet, were aroused when enemy troops were seen carrying timber suitable for that purpose. In an effort to minimise possible casualties, the number of troops in the target area were thinned out and listening posts installed, manned by officers and men of the engineers. The weather continued to cause havoc with the best of arrangements. A blizzard occurred during the evening of the 17th followed by heavy falls of snow that continued into the next day, resulting in further flooding of the River Douve causing the trenches on the riverbank to be abandoned.

By the middle of the month, large movements of German troops had begun and continued for the next six weeks. Much of that was the result of the regiments in front of the division being relieved as well as a build up of forces, for a blow, which was to fall on the French line at Zonnebeke on the 25th. Sniping gained in intensity and periods of intense fire carried out by both sides.

The Kaiser's birthday was due on the 27th and the artillery requested extra ammunition to help celebrate. New and improved weapons were introduced regularly and towards the end of the month, training commenced on the new Vickers machine guns. Counter-mining at Le Touquet was also commenced and trained miners from the 2nd Monmouths were withdrawn from trench service ford employment in the mining activities.

Amidst the mining and counter-mining at Le Gheer a great deal of sniping was experienced, most of which emanated from a group of buildings east of Ploegsteert Wood. In the true tradition of the Tommy, all buildings and farms were given names, in this case, the White Estimenet[152], and the three neighbouring houses, Elger, Bennett and the Third German House, all of which proved troublesome.

---

[152] *The White Estimenet was located on the northern edge of the Birdcage and on the eastern side of the Le Touquet – Messines Road. Elger, Bennett and the Third German House were located on front of the Birdcage and on the western side of the same road.*

In response to requests from the officers in the front line, the artillery destroyed the White Estimenet with a 6" howitzer and the other three houses were seriously damaged. While the artillery was paying attention to the destruction of the houses, the Germans, using previously captured French artillery guns shelled the headquarters of the 12th Brigade.

During the last few days of January, distinguished guest were shown around the area of Ploegsteert Wood, as it was considered one of the safest locations for observing the front line. On the 28th Sir John Heilbanke, the Earl of Pembroke, paid a visit and watched the shelling, followed the next day by the First Lord of the Admiralty, Winston Churchill[153], Commander Bartholomew, R.N., and the Earl of Pembroke paid the second of several visits.

---

[153] *Ironically, after Winston Churchill lost his position of First Lord of the admiralty, following the events at Gallipoli, he served in the same area with the rank of Lieutenant-Colonel, with his headquarters in the wood in 1916.*

February - 1915

February, like January in terms of activity, did show signs of improvement with the weather. For the first week, the 'usual' shelling took place, accompanied by constant and heavy sniping. German troop movements took place and air reconnaissance reports regularly made mention of constant traffic through Menin, Lille, Tourcoing, and Roubaix. Conditions on the division front remained generally quiet although the 10th Brigade, on the River Douve, and the 12th Brigade at Le Touquet were subjected to severe shelling during the evening of the 1st.

The 12th Brigade was still struggling to complete the occupation of Le Touquet, having only made slow progress. Possession of each house was fiercely contested and, as each was taken, it was prepared to act as a sniping post. Snipers Row, as it was referred to, was finally occupied after intense house-to-house fighting on the 15th and reinforced. Whilst the 12th Brigade was fighting tenaciously for Le Touquet, it was also heavily engaged with German snipers around Rue Du Bois and Houplines, near Armentières.

Experiments were carried out on the 5th with a new 4.7" trench mortar, but it was reported *"to possess little accuracy and only produced a big flash and a lot of noise"*. The experiments continued but the general opinion was that it was unsatisfactory for the purpose. In view of the derogatory comments, trench mortar classes were commenced under a Captain Smithson in an effort to increase the proficiency of the gunners.

With the approach of spring, the division had put in hand preparations in the event of offensive action and trenches were cleaned and reinforced with wire emplacements. For the first time incendiary shells were used against the Royal Warwickshire Regiment in Ploegsteert Wood and the 10th Brigade was bombarded with shells filled with sulphur, although they failed to inflict casualties. During the 13th, the 35th Battery directed fire upon a farm in front of the line held by the Somerset Light Infantry, but the shells fell short and landed on and behind the positions of the Somerset's causing several casualties. The error was later attributed to faulty artillery observation being directed from a position at Legheim.

The succession of important guests continued and on the 14th of January Lord Selbourne visited Ploegsteert Wood to view the artillery fire. On that same day Brigadier-General Hunter-Weston, G.O.C. 11th Brigade, departed for eight days leave, while Lieutenant-Colonel Prowse assumed temporary command[154] until Brigadier-General Earl Cairns arrived to take command, five days later. The arrival of Brigadier-General Cairns allowed Lieutenant-Colonel Prowse then to depart so to assume command of the 1st Leinster's, 27th Division[155].

They also were days of developing aerial tactics and the anti-aircraft gun 'Archibald' managed to shoot down a German aircraft, seen to crash behind the German lines. Later, a second German plane dropped two bombs, one near the trenches of the Hampshire's and one near the opposing German trenches.

The 2nd Canadian Brigade, having arrived for trench training in warfare with the 11th Brigades, was subjected to sustained shelling as it marched through the village of Ploegsteert [156]. During this period, problems had been experienced in firing rifle grenades with any degree of accuracy, but Captain North (12th Brigade), had developed a technique that proved effective. He was given the responsibility of teaching the skill to the troops in the front line, a practice that proved particularly useful at Le Touquet. The troops of the Rifle Brigade applied their new-found skills during a bombardment of the German trenches, opposite the barricade, which proved effective *"judging by the squeals that were heard from the occupants"*.

Trench life was had its moments of humour. When Amelia shelled the enemy trenches in front of the Monmouths[157], the occupants responded by throwing dummies into the air. German troops in front of the

---

[154] *Brigadier-General Hunter-Weston had previously received a promotion to Major-General but had not had the opportunity to depart for his new command, the 29· Division.*

[155] *The 27· Division was under the command of Major-General T.D'O. Snow, the former commander of the 4· Division. It was on the 17· February that the 37· Field Artillery Brigade (howitzers), Royal Artillery, left the Division to become a part of the IV Corps artillery.*

[156] *The 2· Canadian Brigade was one of three brigades that constituted the 1· Canadian Division. The 1·, 2·, 3· and 4· Battalions were those that arrived on the 14· January to serve with the 11· brigade. The Canadians remained until the 25· and developed a firm working relationship with the division, a relationship that continued throughout the war.*

[157] *It was a tradition in the artillery to give each gun a name. Amelia was one of the medium (8") howitzers in the heavy artillery brigade.*

Hampshire's Battalion also made overtures of peace by shouting and holding up shovels although no attempt was made to respond[158].

Shelling of the Ploegsteert Wood increased considerably towards the end of the month with fire being concentrated in and around the wood and support trenches along the Messines – Ploegsteert road. The division artillery replied by shelling the German trenches in Warneton, Frelinghien and the Birdcage. The intensity of the shelling of the 10th Brigade, holding the left sector about the River Douve, increased considerably and on the 25th, the brigade area received over three hundred shells[159]. The end of the month was a time of reorganisation in the command of the division. Brigadier-General Hasler (the Buffs[160]) assumed permanent command of the 11th Brigade from Brigadier-General. The close of the month was marked by heavy artillery duels, especially near the Birdcage, although no infantry attacks ensued.

---

[158] *It was during this period that the health of the men was significantly affected by the poor conditions and diet, as the first case of meningitis among the troops of the 10 Brigade was diagnosed.*

[159] *On this same day, fragments of German shells, which had exploded in Ploegsteert Wood, were identified as being made of cast iron, where previously they had been manufactured from machined steel. This was translated by the front line troops as having been made by amateurs but, in fact, due to the trade restrictions imposed by naval barricade, steel supplies were kept for more important items, such as weapons.*

[160] *The Royal East Kent Regiment was commonly referred to as the Buffs, since the early eighteenth century due to the colour of the facings on their uniforms.*

March - 1915

Large German troop movements marked the first few days of March. Fifty or more trains were reported at Menin, but their direction of travel was uncertain[161] although the movement of enemy troops out of the area between Messines and Armentières did little to relieve the activity on the 4th Division front. The whole left of the 12th Brigade was subjected to increased rifle grenade attack, particularly against those holding the railway barricade. The attacks were met with fire from the heavy artillery, which aimed Amelia on the German trenches and during the night of the 3rd a corporal of the Monmouths approached a German trench and found it empty except for several dead and an officers bivouac marked '104th Regt.'[162].

From the 3rd March there was an influx of battalions, newly arrived from England, which were divided between the experienced divisions for training in trench warfare. The Nottinghamshire and Derbyshire Regiment was attached to the 10th Brigade on the 3rd of March and remained until the 9th[163], while the 48th (North Midland) Division, under Major-General Stuart Wortley, also arrived in the area of the 4th Division the following day. The brigades and battalions were spread among the corresponding units of the division, where they remained for five days.

The trenches had not drained to any substantial degree and the training was carried under the worst of conditions. The continual sniping and shelling severely hindered movement. During this period, the German artillery targeted Le Bizet, a village of some importance as a line of communications for the 4th Division and subjected it to heavy artillery fire on the 6th. In retaliation, the new 5" howitzers, recently deployed with the 32nd F.A.B, were fired against German trenches opposite the 10th Brigade.

---

[161] *Many of the German units, which left the Messines area, were bound for Poelcappelle and Langemarck in preparation of the attack that marked the beginning of the Second Battle of Ypres.*

[162] *The 104 Regiment was a part of the 88 Brigade, 40 Division.*

[163] *The 4 Division, as one of the original divisions in France was used regularly, particularly throughout 1915, to introduce new units, freshly arrived from the United Kingdom, to the vagaries of trench warfare. The general period of stay was from 5-7 days.*

The shelling and sniping continued constantly although the infantry positions remained static and, on occasions, activities occurred, which gave no immediate logical answer. On the 9th the 10th Brigade reported that "*a curious trail of light was observed at 4:15am from various parts of German trenches moving in a southerly direction.*[164]"

The higher command was aware of German troop concentrations to the north of Ypres and it was deemed necessary to ensure that the German forces were held on the division front and not thinned out to be used elsewhere. Orders were issued by III Corps that great activity was to be shown in pushing saps forward wherever possible, whilst considering their possible future use. These were not necessarily to be concealed and were intended to draw fire, thus keeping the German reserves in the area.

Every effort was made to give the impression that an attack on the division front might be impending. The artillery was also permitted to use the complete daily allowance and was to finish in the evening with a deliberate concentration on selected trenches. Consequently, during the afternoon heavy rifle and artillery fire was directed at the enemy front and support lines[165].

As a part of the programme of maintaining the enemy attention on the 4th Division line, the 11th Brigade was instructed to seize and consolidate a farm situated 200 yards east of the convent at Le Gheer. The farm stood in No Man's Land and, once captured, a communications trench was to be dug from the front line to the farm. The reason for the seizure was to break out saps north and south from the farm parallel to the 11th Brigade trenches, thus advancing the front line[166]. By 11:50pm the 11th Brigade had captured the farm and completed the communications trench, without the Germans appearing to take any notice of the event.

---

[164] *Quoted from the War Diary WO95/1441. This, of course, could have been caused by several different circumstances, but is indicative of the incidents experienced in trench warfare.*

[165] *The British attack at Neuve Chapelle, south of Armentières, commenced on the 10 March 1915. The objective of the 4 Division, acting to the north was to hold down as many of the German reserves as possible and to prevent them from moving south to reinforce the German forces confronting the British attack.*

[166] *The farm was located 150 yards south of Le Gheer.*

III Corps had notified the 4th Division that the 10th and 11th Brigades could possibly be withdrawn and sent south to positions near the Armentières - Lille Railway in order to relieve the 6th Division. The movement would actually constituted a sideslip to the south and, to fill the gap left by the movement, the 10th and 11th Brigades were to be relieved by the 84th and 83rd Infantry Brigades of the 5th Division respectively. Upon relief, the two brigades were to march south and relieve the 17th and 18th Brigades, an adjustment that would allow the 4th Division to occupy a much-reduced frontage, from the railway crossing on the Armentières – Perenchies Road to the barricade at Le Touquet.

In order to effect the relief of the 10th Brigade, the main body of the 84th Brigade marched from Bailleul to Romarin and positions north of Ploegsteert, where it stood fast for the night. The 10th Brigade handed over command at 5:30pm on the 14th and commenced its departure from the line during the night but, as the relief began, orders from 2nd Army, of which III Corps was a part, arrived and cancelled all reliefs[167]. The orders included instruction to the effect that the 1st Royal Irish Fusiliers, 1st Royal Warwickshire Regiment, 2nd Seaforth Highlanders, artillery and engineers of the division were to remain in their positions until they were relieved at time to be determined.

While the division waited for the continuation of the relief, enquiries were made by III Corps stating that several British 18-pounder[168] guns had been used against 1st Army and enquired as to when, if ever, any had been captured from the 4th Division. The reply explained that two guns of the 27th Battery had been abandoned at Ligny-en-Cambrésis during the withdrawal on the 26th of August the previous year[169].

Confirmation was soon received from III Corps that the relief of the 10th Brigade should recommence and, by 5:45am on the 16th, the 84th Brigade had taken over the line. The battalions of the 10th Brigade then assembled and marched for Armentières, however, at 12:30pm on the same day, 2nd Army again suspended all reliefs, which led to the cancel-

---

[167] The reason for the cancellation was due to the fact that 27. Division, located at St. Eloi was currently under attack. The extent of the offensive was not known and all units involved in movements were instructed to stand fast.

[168] The 18-pounder field gun had become the standard issue field gun for the British artillery during 1914.

[169] At this stage the Battle of Loos, as it became known in British history, had been fought only a week earlier by the 1. Army under General Sir Douglas Haig and it was during that attack that the captured British guns had been used.

lation of the proposed readjustment of the line. All units were instructed to return to their original positions by the night of the 17th March. Despite those orders, the 84th Brigade was to remain where it was, in the positions originally held by the 10th Brigade, under the orders of the 4th Division, until the final elements of the 10th Brigade had been relieved[170].

Final adjustments to the line were made during the night of the 16th as the 12th Brigade extended to the right as far as the crossroads at Le Gheer. Not long after having completed the move, during the early hours of the 17th, the lifting of the early morning mist revealed two hundred Germans only five hundred yards away, advancing against the right flank of the Monmouths. The battalion opened rapid fire immediately on the attackers and forced them into a reserve trench from which they were cleared in a later action. As the Seaforth Highlanders and Royal Warwickshire Regiment marched through Pont de Nieppe on their way back to Romarin, Lieutenant-General Sir H. Smith-Dorrien, G.O.C. III Corps, offered his complements on their efforts.

Both sides carried out the work of improving defences. The enemy developed and improved wire entanglements and the men of the 12th Brigade established a second barricade across the road, east of Le Touquet railway station. Late in the evening of the 17th, troops the 11th Brigade heard an unusual amount of German transport on the move but could not determine the direction of travel, movements that were also confirmed by the 6th Division. Finally, that same night, the 10th Brigade relieved the 84th Brigade and assumed command of the same trenches that it had left two days previously. Light shelling was inflicted upon the division line for most of the next day and the early hours of the 19th produced snow over the whole area.

Given the circumstances under which the troops of both sides lived, a sense of humour prevailed, as was shown at 2:10pm when the enemy, opposite the 10th Brigade, displayed a sign above their trench stating; "Bread can be obtained here without tickets." Although the enemy occasionally entreated their opposite number with light banter, those opposite the railway barricade at Le Touquet were busy with installing timber planking in their trenches. During the course of that work, a sniper of the Monmouths shot one soldier when he climbed out of his trench, and a second man, in civilian clothes, who had made the same mistake. During the night, a patrol of the East Lancashires approached

---

[170] *News of the sinking of the German warship 'Dresden' was circulated among the troops.*

a wire barricade in front of the opposing German trenches, and removed a flag without incident.

At 8:50pm on the 20th, the 4th Division was ordered to take over the right of the 5th Division as far as the Messines - Wulverghem Road and, in doing so, was to assume temporary command of the 27th Field Artillery Brigade of that division. The extension of the line meant that the 4th Division held a front from the Wulverghem – Neuve Eglise - Bailleul Road, to Chapel de Armentières. During the night of the 21st, the 10th Brigade carried out the relief the 14th Brigade, 5th Division, without interference from the enemy, but the move required a considerable reorganisation of the battalion positions, which occupied most of the next day to complete[171].

While there was movement within the British lines, large numbers of Germans also continued to move south, in the direction of Armentières, and a column of one and a half miles in length was reported by reconnaissance aircraft. As the day dawned on the 22nd, the division was subjected to a day of continuous harassment from artillery fire, which was assisted by observation balloons near Commines and St. Eloi. The shelling was responsible for setting fire to a haystack near Despier Farm and sniping throughout the night, on the 11th Brigade front, appeared to be controlled by new green flares.

The following day, patrols discovered that the enemy front line was heavily manned and that female voices had been heard in the trenches in front of the Hampshire Regiment. In the last days of the month, the 4th and 5th Lincolnshire Regiments, of the newly arrived 46th Division, were attached to the 12th Brigade for introductory training in trench warfare. What could be described as the mundane daily life in the trenches was epitomised by the activities of the last few days. Typical of the events in that period was the occasion when a bomb dropped on St. Yvon by a German plane wounded an officer and two men. The Hampshire's were also bombarded with rifle grenades from the German positions at the Birdcage. During the month of March the 11th Brigade suffered four officers and thirty-five men killed with three officers and seventy-one men wounded[172].

---

[171] That same day a second man in civilian clothes was shot in the German trenches. He appeared to be local labour used by the Germans to assist with the reinforcements of the trenches. Such labour was used by both sides throughout the war, but rarely were they used in the British front line.

[172] During the month of March the 2 Royal Irish Regiment joined the division to become a part of the 11 Brigade.

April - 1915

The first three months of 1915 had passed fitfully. During the winter, a stalemate, largely influenced by the adverse weather, had brought the opposing armies almost to a standstill. The Western Front had become a trench system extending from the Swiss Border to the Belgian coast and produced a stalemate that would endure, largely unchanged, until 1918. The High Command of both sides knew that the war could not be decided whilst ever static trench warfare continued and 'line breaking' action was deemed the only solution. Both sides were planning just such an action and spring had brought with it the opportunity. Unbeknown to the Allies, the Germans had planned a major offensive with the intention of capturing the city of Calais but, in the path of an advance to the coast, lay the Belgian City of Ypres.

New British divisions had arrived in France and undertaken introductory training in trench warfare with the more experienced divisions. The drier weather in the first two weeks of April had brought change to the 4th Division, sniping on both sides actively increased, as did the shelling of key positions by both sides, particularly with heavy artillery. On the 1st of the month, the enemy in front of the 12th Brigade celebrated the centenary of Bismarck by putting lights on the parapet, blowing bugles, and cheering loudly. Some bonfires were also seen to be burning in the direction of Pont Rouge but no offensive action eventuated and the task of trench consolidation continued apace.

Le Gheer remained a favourite target for the German artillery, which constantly shelled the village and approaches. Le Bizet, as a communications centre located several hundred yards behind the British line, had always been subjected to constant artillery fire and on the 6th, a German Taube[173] dropped six bombs on the village in which the headquarters of the 12th Brigade was located. In order to minimise the casualties amongst animals of the artillery and transport, the horses were deliberately stampeded. Although it took a considerable time to round them up and return them to the appropriate lines, the lives of many were saved.

New divisions continued to arrive in France and, on the 7th April, the 5th Gloucestershire and 4th Oxfordshire and Buckinghamshire Regiments of the 145th Brigade joined the 11th Brigade for training, and were billeted in the brewery at Ploegsteert. The 10th Brigade also un-

---

[173] *An early make of German aircraft.*

dertook the training of the 4th Berkshire Regiment of the 145th Brigade, with all three battalions remaining with the division until the 12th, when they rejoined the parent 48th division. The vagaries of the weather continued to play havoc with training and communications. High winds, which had blown all night and into the morning of the 9th April, was replaced by torrential rain that continued throughout the day and into the early evening.

The digging of the mine at Le Touquet, dug with the intention of destroying the German barricade near the railway station, was brought to an abrupt end when listening posts detected the digging of a German gallery across the front of the British mine-head. It was feared that any further digging would lead to discovery and subsequent demolition by the enemy and the fear of discovery forced the decision to explode the mine prematurely. At the end of the one hundred and ninety feet tunnel, were two explosive galleries, each between 36 and 50 feet in front of the German barricade. These were packed with 1200lb of explosives, and preparations to explode the mine were rapidly completed.

Exploding the mine was not intended to be a single event in itself. It was a part of greater plan to inflict as many casualties on the enemy as possible. The plan required that those houses and trenches in Le Touquet, occupied by the enemy, be subjected to artillery and trench mortar fire and intermittent rifle and machine-gun fire for a period of twenty minutes. This was to be followed by a pause of ten minutes, when the mine was then to be fired. Gaps had been deliberately made in the wire entanglements in front of the British line and every effort made to indicate a possible attack. It was hoped, in light of a possible attack, that the enemy would occupy the defences during the pause.

The bombardment commenced at 8:00am and ceased exactly on time, then, following the ten-minute pause, the mine was fired at 8:30am. Immediately following the explosion, all approaches to Le Touquet from behind the German lines were subjected to heavy shelling in an effort to prevent reinforcements being rushed to the village. Simultaneously the British troops broke out in cheering and opened rapid fire on the trenches and houses.

The effect of the explosion was considerable. Although there did not appear to be a large crater, a large mass of debris was formed and the wire entanglements were destroyed. The force of the explosion appeared to throw large quantities of bricks and debris in the air for a radius of about 250 yards, which inflicted some casualties on the men of the 12th Brigade. The barricade and the White House, approximately 25-30 yards behind, did not appear to be seriously damaged but a wall, from behind which German snipers would fire, was completely demolished[174]. Several other defended houses in the locality were also badly damaged. It was estimated that the entire garrison within 20 yards of the centre of the explosion had perished as well as those who had been working in the enemy mine. Several wounded were seen crawling away from the point of explosion and during the next few hours, twenty-seven stretchers were seen carried away.

The German response in the period immediately following the explosion was feeble. Very little rifle or machine-gun fire was forthcoming in retaliation, probably due to the shock and the volume of fire coming from the British line. However, considerable machine-gun and rifle fire came from the direction of Frelinghein and the German artillery fired a few rounds without causing any serious damage. Later in the evening, the railway station was shelled by the 5.9" howitzers, with little effect.

The time had come for the entire division to be relieved from the line for a rest. By the 10th April, instructions had reached the 11th Brigade to the affect that the 145th Brigade (48th Division) would relieve it on the night of the 15th. In preparation for the withdrawal the 4th Royal Berkshire, 5th Gloucestershire, and the 4th Oxfordshire and Buckinghamshire Regiments were returned to the 145th Brigade. Upon relief, the 11th Brigade was to move to the area between Nootboom and Steenwerck, approximately six miles to the west, in the direction of Hazebrouck

---

[174] *Later observation of the damage by Major Symons, 4 Company, Royal Engineers, revealed that the barricade had been "considerably shaken and considerable damage had been done to the White House, causing some walls of the building to collapse.*

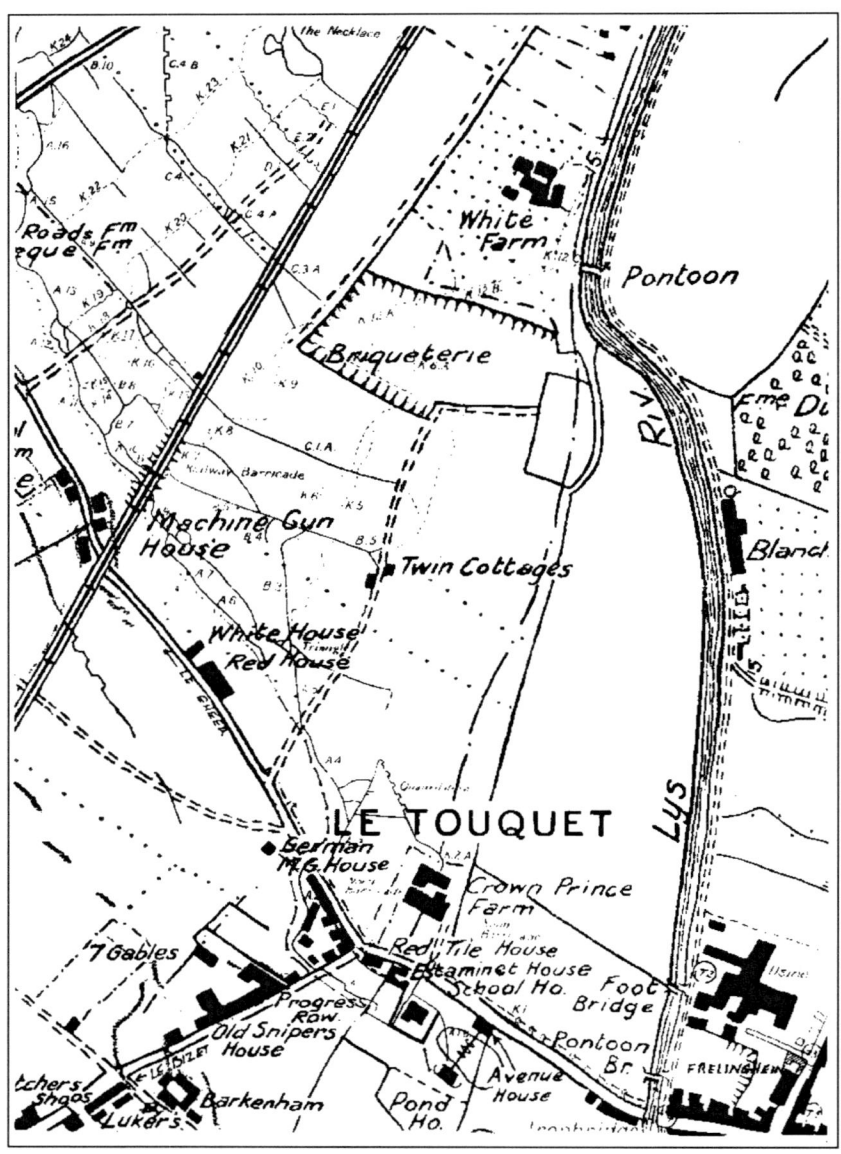

Plate 7
Diagram showing the railway line through Le Touquet and the British trench line, just to the north. The White House was the first building on the left of the road, to the south of the railway.

While preparing to depart, the shelling continued without reprieve. It was hoped that a victory might be had when, on the 13th, the division received a message that a German airship could possibly pass over and, if sighted, it was to receive 'a *warm reception*'. Although the Zeppelin eventually arrived over Ypres the following day, heading south, it was too far away for the anti aircraft guns and no action was taken. The 11th Brigade was relieved twenty-four hours early, on the night of the 14th and on completion, marched to Steenwerck for a period of rest.

Late in the afternoon of the 16th the positions of the 10th Brigade, located astride the River Douve, was shelled heavily, while preparing for relief. The 1st Royal Warwickshire Regiment was relieved amidst the shelling and marched to Bailleul where they remained until the 22nd. Having arrived at Bailleul, the village and the nearby airfield were bombed by a German airship with fifteen bombs. Although little harm was done to the airfield proper, several bombs struck the town and killed a number of civilians. The Royal Irish Fusiliers, also having been relieved, marched to Merris and the 7th Argyll and Sutherland Highlanders, who had been occupying the trenches around Point 63, followed the Irish Fusiliers the next day.

Whilst the 10th and 11th Brigades had been relieved, the 12th Brigade continued to hold the middle sector of the front between Le Gheer and Le Touquet. Mining had been undertaken by both sides in the area of the railway barricade just north-west of Le Touquet and, on the 20th, German miners were seen in a mine gallery and fired upon. Due to the proximity of the two galleries, the decision was made to explode the already prepared mine. However, the enemy took the initiative and exploded their mine first, killing the sentry standing on the opposite side of the dividing wall and partially asphyxiating Lieutenants Woodgarth and Leech. The following day the Germans were also discovered counter-mining against the left gallery at Snipers House in Le Touquet and a charge was set and fired almost immediately.

To understand the movements and actions of the 4th Division from the 22nd April to the end of May requires an appreciation of activities that were taking place on other parts of the front. At 5:00pm in the evening of the 22nd, the XXII and XXVI Reserve Corps, of the German 4th Army, under General Albrecht von Württemberg, launched a major assault on the northern sector of the Salient[175] that had formed around Ypres. The attack broke upon the 87th (French) Moroccan Territorial Division and the 45th (French) Algerian Division, which were holding the front in the region of Steenstraate – Poelcappelle, a distance of

---

[175] *The attack of the 22 April is generally referred to as 'Second Ypres' and represented the first effective use of gas as an offensive weapon since the declaration of war in August.*

141

nearly five miles. Continuing the line to the right was the Canadian Division, which extended to a point half a mile to the east of the village of Gravenstafel.

The gas barrage had caused the far left of the 87th Division, having suffered a great many casualties, to retire rapidly to positions on the west bank of the Yser Canal. The sudden retirement of the Moroccans resulted in a rolling effect, driving back the remainder of the 87th and the greater part of the French 45th Division. The blow then fell upon the left flank and rear of the Canadian Division. The Canadians, ably assisted by some units of Tirailleurs and Zouaves, fought doggedly for the next two days. With the left flank in the air and having suffered many casualties, the 2nd and 3rd Brigades, were forced to retire following a second gas attack and infantry assault against the exposed left flank. On the 25th, parts of the Canadian line gave way under the weight of these attacks, though isolated groups continued to hold the line with sorely diminished numbers. Reinforcements were urgently required and the 4th Division was one of those units called upon to assist.

The attack on Ypres had created the need to move strong reinforcements to the area as a matter of urgency. The division had been notified on the 23rd that it had to move to St. Julien, north-east of Ypres, to support the Canadians. Consequently, at 6:40am, the 10th and 11th Brigades were ordered to move three battalions to Locre and two battalions to Dranoutre where they would fall under the orders of V Corps. Having rested and refitted, the 11th Brigade marched from their billets during the morning of the 24th, entrained at the village station, and travelled to Busseboom, approximately three miles west of Ypres. Here they remained resting in a field until finally obtaining accommodation in some local farms for the night, just prior to heavy storms.

On arrival at Locre the O.C., 10th Brigade, Brigadier-General Hull, was notified that his brigade was to make a counter attack on the German line between St. Julien and Kitcheners Wood (inclusive), approximately one thousand yards to the west of the village, the next morning. Also under his command was the untried 150th (York and Durham Brigade)[176], two weakened battalions from the 13th Canadian Brigade, the 4th Canadian Battalion and units from the 28th Division. The force was to be supported by whatever artillery could be made available from any of the local divisions. In order to reach St. Julien the 10th Brigade con-

---

[176] *The Northumberland Brigade was more properly known as the 149 Brigade, 50 Division, which had only just arrived in the area.*

centrated south of Vlamertinghe[177] and late in the afternoon marched to the western outskirts of Ypres in preparation to cross the Yser Canal during the night[178].

At 7:00pm on the 24th, in heavy rain, the brigade crossed the canal and marched via St. Jean and Wieltje where Brigadier-General Hull attempted to contact the commanders of the other brigades and battalions. While in Wieltje, he issued orders to the 150th Brigade (50th Division) and 28th Division but most of the orders failed to reach their destinations until nearly midnight. The late arrival of the instructions precluded any coordinated offence. While the orders were in-transit the 10th Brigade Headquarters moved forward and finally arrived at Shell Trap Farm, just behind the G.H.Q.[179] line, at 3:00am on the 25th.

The attack was to be made with the Royal Irish Fusiliers and the Royal Dublin Fusiliers on the right and left bank of the Zanebeek Brook[180] respectively, both advancing due north on St. Julien. The Warwickshire's, supported by the 7th Argyll and Sutherland Highlanders, was to advanced in a north-westerly direction, for Kitchener's Wood, in front of which stood the remains of the 2nd Canadian Battalion. While those battalions attacked their objectives, the Seaforth Highlanders were to attack the trenches between those two points, being the grounds over which the German attack had been made.

Due to the late arrival of the 10th Brigade, the attack was scheduled to commence from behind the G.H.Q. line and would require an advance of nearly one mile, over open country. The only access through the G.H.Q. line was along several roads, which offered openings through

---

[177] *Vlamertinghe lies approximately three miles west of Ypres and was thought to be out of the range of the German artillery. This misconception soon became evident over the next few days as the Germans moved closer to Ypres, bringing Vlamertinghe within range of the heavy guns.*

[178] *For the report of the G.O.C., see Appendix V, Report on Action of 10 Brigade April 24 – May 4, 1915*

[179] *The GHQ line was a second defensive line approximately three miles behind the original front line of March 1915. It consisted of a series of trenches, which ran from a point 1400 yards west of Kitchener's Wood and extended to the south as far as Zillebeke Lake. The line arced to the east around Wieltje and Potijze and crossed the Menin Road approximately mid-way between Ypres and Hooge.*

[180] *'Beek' is the Flemish term for stream or river. The name Zanebeek Brook refers to one of the several tributaries of the Steenbeek, the main river that flows through St. Julien.*

the wire entanglements that lay in front of the trench lines. Zero hour was subjected to inevitable delays as the battalions marched to their respective starting points. The advance commenced at 5:30am, as dawn approached, and the 10th Brigade ran into difficulties immediately. Arrangements had been made for the Canadian artillery to lay a barrage on the entire front line, but at the last moment, the artillery was prevented from shelling St. Julien in the mistaken belief that Canadians troops were still in the village.

As there had been insufficient time to conduct detailed reconnaissance, heavy traffic was encountered at Wieltje, as troops and equipment passed, in defile, through the only openings in the defences. The bottleneck slowed progress but, having passed through the wire, the brigade then deployed with four battalions in the front line and one in support, all under constant shellfire.

There was no concealing the fact from the enemy that an attack was underway and, as the advance progressed, the resistance grew and, at about 6:00am, the German artillery fire concentrated on the lines of approaching troops. The battalions, advancing in lines of companies, were met by the heavy artillery fire and, as they drew within range of small arms, were also subjected to heavy machine-gun and rifle fire. The supporting artillery fire was accurate, but lacked the density to inflict serious damage on the German lines.

Despite having suffered many casualties, the Royal Irish Fusiliers and Royal Dublin's successfully secured several houses on the southern outskirts of St. Julien. The Warwicks also fought their way to within fifty yards of the German trenches, located in front of Kitcheners Wood, but the sheer number of casualties prevented a final rush. The attack on the German trench lines by the Seaforth's also suffered a similar fate, close, but too weak to capture of the positions. To assist the Warwicks, the 7th Argyll and Sutherland Highlanders moved forward, through the bombardment, and assumed positions in front of the wood in anticipation of a continuation of the attack but the offensive had lost impetus in the face of the determined resistance. To exacerbate the existing difficulties, two battalions of the Northumberland Brigade, which had been sent as reinforcements, had moved too far to the right, and extended the line, instead of reinforcing it.

At about the same time that the 10th Brigade attack ground to halt, the 11th Brigade had left its bivouacs at Busseboom. It marched to Vlamertinghe, was incorporated as a part of the V Corps Reserve, and fell under orders of the G.O.C., 1st (Canadian) Division (Lieutenant-

General E.A.H. Alderson). During a midday conference with the Division Commander, Brigadier-General Hasler, G.O.C., 11th Brigade , was instructed to move his brigade to be at St. Jean[181] by nightfall, where guides from the 2nd Canadian Brigade would meet it[182]. They would then be led into the lines held by that brigade. In accordance with those orders, the battalions of the 11th Brigade marched from Vlamertinghe, only to see the village come under heavy shelling by long-range guns.

The Canadians had been involved in constant fighting and had suffered a disproportionate number of casualties during the last three days. The remaining troops were spread out over a wide front holding the line through a series of strong points and even single shell holes. No distinct, entrenched line existed and, because of sparseness of the dispositions, the battalions of the 11th Brigade experienced great difficulties in locating the isolated groups. It was, however, believed that a mixed detachment was holding a line south of the Fortuin[183] – Mosselmakt road and it was also discovered that two battalions, the 1st Suffolk Regiment and the 12th London Regiment, were holding trenches about Fortuin, south-east of St. Julien. In order to provide continuity of the line the 10th Brigade positioned its right flank on Fortuin; in touch with the Suffolks, although a few of the 2nd Canadian Brigade (7th Canadian Battalion) was found to be manning the trenches north of the Haanebeek[184].

By 7:30am the attack of the 10th Brigade had reached its limits, having suffered casualties of more than half of the attacking strength, and the troops slowly retired during the night to a defensive line 1300 yards south of St. Julien, where they dug in. The 10th Brigade front was held by the Warwickshire's on the left and in contact with the elements of

---

[181] In 1915, St. Jean lay about three quarters of a mile north-east of Ypres on the Ypres – Poelcappelle Road and was used as a staging area for units in reserve. Today, St. Jean is almost a suburb of Ypres.

[182] At this time, the 2 Canadian Brigade was involved in desperate fighting to the east of St. Julien. The 5 Canadian Battalion was located on the far right of the brigade front, in front of Gravenstafel, two miles due east of St. Julien while the 7 Canadian Battalion was fighting several hundred yards to the north of the Haanebeek, half a mile to east of St. Julien. The 8 Canadian Battalion held parts of the line in between but further to the north.

[183] Fortuin was area name, generally signified by the intersection of the Wieltje – Gravenstafel road and the road leading to St. Julien.

[184] The Haanebeek referred to here is one of two streams of the same name and joins the Steenbeek in St. Julien. The other is just north of Frezenberg.

the 2nd and 16th Canadian Battalions, 200 yards north of Shell Trap Farm. To the right of the Warwicks stood the Seaforth Highlanders, Royal Dublin Fusiliers and the Royal Irish Fusiliers, which held the right of the brigade line, astride the Haanebeek. Throughout the night, the line was consolidated and many of the wounded taken nearly three miles to the rear.

While the 10th Brigade was withdrawing to those positions the 11th Brigade was approaching the front line from the rear. As Ypres was under constant shellfire, the 11th Brigade marched to the west of the town and, in the words of Lieutenant-Colonel F.R. Hicks, O.C. 1st Hampshire Regiment, *"We passed the blazing ruins of the city on our right where the great 17" shells were still crashing and destroying everything."*[185] On arrival at St. Jean, no sign of the Canadian guides could be found, so Brigadier Hasler, not being familiar with the area, made urgent enquiries as they marched and, amidst conflicting reports, finally located the headquarters of the 2nd Canadian Brigade. He was instructed to establish a line to the right of the 10th, as far as Berlin Wood.

Two companies of the 1st London Rifle Brigade (11th Brigade) had taken up positions on a subsidiary line about Hill 37[186], a small hill 600 yards south-east of St. Julien, thought to be near the Royal Irish Fusiliers (10th Brigade). They were accompanied by two companies of the Somerset Light Infantry to the right, the two remaining companies of the London Brigade and then 1st Hampshire Regiment, which extended the line to Berlin Wood.

On arrival at 2.30am, the battalions of the 11th Brigade were given instructions to entrench. With only an hour of darkness remaining, it was essential that the troops got underground and the tired troops dug feverishly, managing to construct trenches deep enough to offer some protection from the enemy artillery and machine-gun fire. They had barely managed to dig in before daylight but the morning mist, which provided an extra two hours of protection, assisted them. While doing so, they discovered some of the old French and Canadian trenches and utilised them for their own purposes although the trenches faced several different directions.

---

[185] *Extract from the O.C.'s report for the period of 26 April – 3 May 1915. For the full text of the report, see Appendix V, Brigade Commander 11th Brigade, 24th April & 2nd May.*

[186] *Commonly referred to as Fortuin on most British maps.*

While they were entrenching, they managed to establish touch with the 85th Brigade, (27th Division), which was holding a support line immediately behind. The enemy attacks continued throughout the night and early morning. While the Hampshire's were digging they were attacked, in the centre of the line, by a group of Germans who advanced through the early morning mist shouting "Ve Vos de Royal Fusiliers". The 'Fusiliers' were fired on and withdrew. To the left of the attack, 'A' Company, of the Hampshire, having occupied a few houses, were caught by surprise when Germans attacked and drove them from the buildings and back into the partly completed trenches, resulting in considerable confusion. Having lost several officers and men killed, Sergeant Ley, leading a handful of men, continued to offer a stout defence and prevented further enemy advance.

During consolidation, it was discovered that a gap of some 800 yards existed between the 10th and 11th Brigades. It was intended that 1/4th East Yorkshire Regiment and the 4· Yorkshire Regiment (150th Brigade), were to occupy the line immediately to the right of the 10th Brigade and, in turn, establish contact with the 11th Brigade. When attempts to establish contact with the two Yorkshire battalions failed, it was established that the battalions were still in Verlorenhoek and instructions were issued for them to hurry forward and fill the gap. While awaiting their arrival, the 1st Royal Irish Regiment (82nd Brigade, 27th Division), was sent and temporarily closed the gap between the two brigades. The two battalions of Yorkshires, having arrived after a hurried journey, relieved the Royal Irish and assumed position to the right of the Rifle Brigade, half a mile east of St. Julien and entrenched on the Fortuin – Mosselmakt road.

At about 7:00am, as the mist cleared, the precarious position of the Hampshire's became clear. They were situated at the apex of a salient, the product of a curved front, with a gap of four hundred yards to the right, to a small wood held by the Royal Irish Fusiliers. The line then extended to the left by companies, each with its left flank thrown back. With the lifting of the mist, the German artillery opened fire with guns directed from three sides. The severity of the shelling, to which the entire line was subjected, made it almost impossible to establish communications with the headquarters of the different companies. The fire prevented telephone wires being run out and, those that were connected were almost immediately cut. It was evident that the Germans held the ridges north and east, which offered them clear visibility of the entire salient, into which their guns were directed with unfailing accuracy.

In the early afternoon of the 26th, the 10th Brigade received orders to advance a battalion between Kitchener's Wood and the Wieltje – St. Julien Road, in cooperation with the Lahore Division[187], which was intending to attack to the north. Because the communications wires had been cut by artillery fire during the morning, the order to attack only arrived at 1:25pm, five minutes after the attack was scheduled to commence. As all battalions were in the front line, the Brigadier decided that it was impossible to carry out the attack and notified the Canadian Division accordingly. After much discussion, it was decided to make to attack with the 7th Argyll and Sutherland Highlanders, who were then brought forward, in line with the Lahore Division.

Time passed, but no attack eventuated, so the Argylls remained where they were. Whilst waiting for the attack of the Indian Division to develop the Northumberland Brigade (149th Brigade) had been ordered to attack St. Julien by advancing through the 10th Brigade. At the due moment, the attackers advanced in fine style but their progress was subjected to intense shelling. The fire was such that the Northumberland's were forced to halt in the 10th Brigade firing line and was withdrawn during the night. The London Rifle Brigade and Somerset's, on Hill 37, were caught by the same shelling that had brought the Northumberland's to a halt, and suffered one hundred casualties. The hill, being so exposed to infantry and artillery attack, was deemed untenable and to avoid undue casualties, the defenders were withdrawn to the support trenches.

By nightfall, the troops had been tried to their limits. After having fought and been subjected to continuous shelling and engaged in digging trenches, they were then required to carry water, dress and carry the wounded for three miles to the rear and return with ammunition and supplies. Little rest was had by anyone as the extending of the trenches could only be carried out at night.

While the 10th Brigade had been preparing to act in support of the French and Lahore Division, the 11th Brigade had been ordered to relieve the 1st Suffolk and 12th London Regiments, at Fortuin and then consolidate the line from the wood to the crossroads in front of St. Julien. The difficulties in getting instructions through to units in the front line were immense and those orders only arrived at dusk on the 27th. Patrols from the Hampshire's reconnoitred nearby farms and found

---

[187] *The Lahore Division, more properly known as the 3 Indian Infantry Division, had arrived in Marseilles, France, in September 1914 and had recently returned from Neuve Chapelle where it had fought with such heavy casualties.*

them all strongly held by the enemy. The shelling hardly ceased and it was during evening that the G.O.C., 11th Brigade, Brigadier-General Hasler, was killed by shellfire at St. Jean. Colonel Hicks assumed temporary command of the brigade while the headquarters was moved to Verlorenhoek[188].

During the evening of the following day, the 12th Brigade, still fighting to the south at Le Bizet, received warning orders to be prepared to move on the 28th. After being relieved that same morning, the brigade marched through Armentières and Nieppe to Bailleul, where it bivouacked for the evening in the fields. While the 12th Brigade was en-route, the 10th and 11th Brigades continued to consolidate the trench lines. The constant shelling was a trial for the troops as they found little time for rest. Reinforcements arrived in the form of the 8th Durham Light Infantry (151st Brigade, 50th Division), fresh from England.

The shelling of the 10th Brigade increased considerably on the 29th and the 3rd Cavalry Brigade was moved up behind the brigade to act as support in the event of enemy attack. In order to provide additional labour, the battalions of the York and Durham Brigade were divided between the battalions of the 11th Brigade. Brigadier-General Prowse, having returned from the 1st Leinsters, assumed command of the 11th Brigade. The shelling had remained heavy and after dark, the enemy raked all roads and approaches leading to St. Julien with artillery and machine-gun fire.

By the evening of the 30th, the 12th Brigade had arrived and commenced the relief of the 13th Canadian Brigade, which had been previously sent to support the 10th and 11th Brigades, some days before. Owing to the lack of guides, the relief was only carried out with the greatest of difficulty and resulted in half of the King's Own and the Royal Irish regiments getting lost. The approach to the trenches was made even more difficult by the shelling with shrapnel of the canal bridges and approaches, an action that inflicted casualties in all four battalions.

For eight days and nights, the artillery fire continued uninterrupted, while the city of Ypres was reduced to rubble by heavy artillery. At times, the 11th Brigade experienced shells landing in their trenches at the rate of 50 per minute, destroying the trenches, communication and preventing any sort of movement in daylight. Casualties were heavy and one shell, which hit the parapet of a trench, buried the headquarters staff of the Hampshire Regiment. The explosion buried the C.O., Ad-

---

[188] *Brigadier-General Julian Hasler is buried in the White House Cemetery, West-Vlaanderen, Belgium*

jutant and three orderlies, all of which were fortunate to be dug out alive. By entrenching at night, the gaps in the line were slowly connected and finally presented a somewhat unified front.

May - 1915

April had ended with a substantial advance having been made by German XXVII (27th Reserve Corps) of the 4th Army. The enemy had penetrated some three and a half miles at its deepest on a front of seven miles. The advance had taken the attackers to the British G.H.Q. line and to within less than two miles of the city of Ypres. The 4th Division was desperately fighting on a front of four miles between the La Brique – Langemarck road and Berlin Wood, half a mile east of Gravenstafel. The 2nd Essex Regiment was holding Turco Farm, on the far left of the front and located on both sides of the Langemarck road while the King's Own continued the line to the right where they were in touch with the 2nd Lancashire Fusiliers, all of the 12th Brigade.

The narrative will largely concentrate on the 12th Brigade and more specifically on a farm, then known as Shell Trap Farm[189]. On the 1st May 1915, Shell Trap Farm was occupied by the Lancashire Fusiliers and was the location at which the 12th Brigade joined with the 1st Royal Warwickshire Regiment (10th Brigade). The 2nd Seaforth Highlanders, 2nd Royal Dublin Fusiliers and the 1st Royal Irish Fusiliers then continued the line to the right respectively. The 11th Brigade continued the line from Fortuin to Berlin Wood with two companies of the London Rifle Brigade, 1st Somerset Light Infantry, the remaining two companies of the 1st Rifle Brigade, 1st Hampshire Regiment and a mixture 1/4th East Yorkshire Regiment and 2nd East Kents.

Opposing the 12th Brigade was the 38th Landwehr Brigade (52nd Reserve Regiment) while the 30th Brigade (52nd Reserve Regiment) stood opposite the 10th Brigade and the 2nd Ersatz Brigade (51st Reserve Regiment) opposed the 11th Brigade. Both sides were exhausted and had suffered large numbers of casualties, but the German High Command was aware that Ypres lay within reach and was determined to occupy the remains of the city. The forthcoming battles were to become known in British history as the Battle of Frezenberg Ridge.

Barely had the 12th Brigade completed the relief of the 13th Canadian Brigade in the early hours on the morning of the 1st May when the Brigade Headquarters was heavily shelled. The brigade occupied the left of the division front, in touch with the French 152nd Division, while the

---

[189] *Shell Trap Farm was later renamed Mouse Trap Farm, as it was thought that the name was discouraging to troops who were required to hold the position. The original name was, in fact, most appropriate.*

10th Brigade continued the line to the right, to Fortuin. As a part of that relief, the 12th Brigade also relieved the Warwickshire's and the 7th Argyle & Sutherland Highlanders, (10th Brigade). Both brigades remained under the command of the 1st Canadian Division, while the 11th Brigade, 9th Field Company and the West Lancashires, were under 4th Division command until, at 10:00am on the morning, when all Brigades reverted to the command of the 4th Division.

The delays traditionally associated with the calling up of artillery support, often resulted in missing the 'opportunity' target, so the 12th Brigade requested that the infantry be able to communicate directly with the Canadian guns. In order to facilitate those communications a Staff Captain of the Canadian Division made the necessary arrangements and the advantage of such an arrangement were about to be witnessed, as the division was soon to be subjected to a concerted German attack.

On the 2nd, the recently arrived 1st East Kent Regiment (Buffs) (16th Brigade, 6th Division)[190] relieved the Royal Irish Fusiliers in Berlin Wood and, as the German trenches in front of the 11th Brigade were seen being reinforced, all signs indicated a forthcoming attack. The expected bombardment was extremely heavy and resulted in a number of casualties in the 10th Brigade, particularly in the support and reserve lines. The fire was such that the 10th Brigade Headquarters was burnt out and the signal dugout of 11th Brigade took a direct hit, inflicting considerable damage.

It had been expected that the French division, to the left of the 12th Brigade, was to commence an attack at 3.10pm and, in preparation to give support to such an attack, the Essex and King's Own had cut the wire in front of their own positions. The supporting artillery barrage came down on time but, as the time for the French attack passed without movement, the 12th Brigade was ordered to stand fast and the Essex and King's Own were instructed to make no attempt to leave their trenches.

Instead of attacking, French troops (152nd Division) and Indian troops, (3rd Indian Division), were observed leaving the trenches and retiring to the rear and it was assumed that the Indians were being withdrawn from the line altogether[191]. An extract from the British Official History

---

[190] *The Royal East Kent Regiment had been referred to as the Buffs since 1648 following the campaign in the Netherlands against the Spanish.*

[191] *Although no official orders had been issued, planning for a withdrawal of the line to a new defensive position had been underway for several days. Shortly after the failure of*

states: *"But at 3.10pm, though fire was opened, the French infantry did not leave its trenches. A second attempt, timed for 4:40pm, equally failed to materialize, the British liaison officer with the Détachement de Belgigue reporting that the men were too tired for any further serious effort."*

In response to the withdrawal, the 2nd Monmouth Regiment of the 12th Brigade, was ordered to move forward, cross the canal and establish defensive positions at La Brique while the recently joined 1/5th South Lancashire Regiment marched from Vlamertinghe and occupied trenches at 12th Brigade headquarters, replacing the Monmouths. While carrying out those movements the brigades were subjected to intense, continuous shelling and, at 4:30pm on the 2nd, the entire division front was subjected to a heavy gas attack. The gas cloud struck the Essex and Lancashire Fusiliers severely affecting both battalions. The gas discharge was followed by an intense artillery bombardment of the trench line and only the far right of the 10th Brigade line remained unaffected. As the artillery fire lifted, German infantry attacked the centre of the 12th Brigade front. The King's Own, on whom the attack fell, returned rapid rifle and machine-gun fire and, although badly affected by the gas, managed to hold off the attackers.

The ability of the 12th Brigade to withstand such a sustained attack was substantially due to the support given by the adjoining 4th Moroccan Brigade[192] of the neighbouring French 152nd Division and the French artillery. The 152nd Division was also subjected to the attack but managed to hold the line. At 5:40pm, troops of the 12th Brigade fell back under the sheer weight of the attack and the Royal Irish Regiment reported that the line had been turned. The gas had driven the Lancashire Fusiliers and many of the Essex, out of their trenches, so nearby units were instructed to fill the gap. *"the gases were absolutely overpowering; officers and men seemed to lose their senses, most of them getting out of the trenches and reeling to the rear[193]."* A party of one officer and twelve men displayed great bravery when they refused to leave the trenches, and using whatever rifles could be found and managed to hold the attack until assistance arrived.

---

the attack in April, the British C. in C., Sir John French issued orders, for a general retirement to new defensive positions on the Frezenberg Ridge and the retirement of the Indian was in response to those orders.

[192] *Colonel Savy commanding.*

[193] *Quoted from the Essex Regiment (2 Battalion), J.W. Burrows, 1927, p. 126.*

The 7th Argylls were immediately dispatched to the left flank to support the retiring 12th Brigade, and the 3rd Cavalry Brigade made available a regiment to act as reinforcements. On arrival, the Argylls and cavalry battalions advanced through the gas cloud and occupied the vacant trenches. In doing so the advancing Germans, being caught in the open, suffered severe casualties. The total strength of the Lancashire Fusiliers was, at the time of the arrival of the Argylls, only one hundred and fifty eight, many of whom were badly affected by gas. As the Argylls and cavalry were so engaged, two companies of the Monmouths, of the 12th Brigade, which were waiting in reserve at La Brique, also moved forward, in the early evening, to assist the Essex battalion. During the action of the afternoon, a German observation aircraft was shot down over the 12th Brigade front, much to the exultation of the troops on the ground. Both battalions, the King's Own and Essex Regiment, claimed the kill.

The shelling and gas attack had also struck the 11th Brigade, affecting the troops badly. The Somerset Light Infantry and the London Rifle Brigade suffered the worst of the bombardment but no attempt was made by the enemy to attack. By 7:00pm, the bombardment had subsided to intermittent shelling. Although the German advance had been brought to a halt, large numbers of the 2nd Essex had been asphyxiated by gas, as had the London Rifle Brigade and the 2nd Royal Irish Regiment. The Irish Fusiliers were in no better condition and, in an effort to reinforce them, a company of the South Lancashires was sent from La Brique.

As the shelling eased during the evening, bodies of German soldiers were seen to concentrate in Cuisinierres Wood, against which the artillery was directed. During the night, the London Rifles inflicted casualties in several enemy working parties with heavy rifle fire. During the struggle, difficulties had been experienced with communication over the long distances between the division and brigade headquarters. In order to make communications faster, 12th Brigade Headquarters moved from the east bank of the Yser Canal to La Brique during the night.

The battering that the division had received resulted in several battalions of the Canadian Division being sent to support each of the three brigades. The 28th Division also sent a battalion of the 85th Brigade, the Durham Light Infantry and three battalions of the 84th Brigade were also made available, if required. Three battalions of the 83rd Brigade were also sent to Verlorenhoek as a reserve.

Throughout the 3rd, due to much of the artillery of the 4th Division having being withdrawn to the new line, the only artillery support available was that offered by the 146th Battery and one section of howitzers. Although two guns were destroyed by counter battery fire, the artillery worked closely with the infantry under the most trying of circumstances. One artillery observation officer was killed and all communication wires destroyed, as the enemy heavy artillery registered the battery positions. By midday, enemy troops were observed concentrating on the flanks of the 11th Brigade, with field guns in close support.

The Germans were determined to make progress and, at about 3:00pm, attacked Berlin Wood. The focus of the attack fell upon the 1st Buffs. Although they had suffered extremely heavy artillery fire, they were successful in driving back the attack by rifle and machine-gun fire alone. That outstanding action held the wood but the Buffs were so badly mauled in the initial attack that no fit men remained, all had been either killed or wounded. That left the London rifle Brigade to defend the wood and they were paid special attention by the enemy artillery. Casualties were such that the two companies on the right of the line were holding the line with only one rifle to each twelve yards of trench. However, they were not to be denied and, after determined and bitter fighting, managed to hold the ground.

After the attack had been repulsed, the enemy artillery concentrated on Berlin Wood for a second time. The fire decimated any trees left standing and reduced the area to a mass of tangled timber and shell craters. In the face of that assault, the surviving Buffs were slowly driven back to the support trench, whereupon the Germans occupied the wood and the surrounding area. The enemy then turned their attention on the Hampshire Regiment of the 11th Brigade, situated to the left of the Buffs. Troops of the 77th Landwehr Regiment (53rd Reserve Division) massed on both flanks of the battalion and gas equipment was seen being installed.

The attack, however, turned out to be a rather feeble affair. The dreaded gas failed to materialise, due to the unfavourable wind direction, and the attacking infantry were not in sufficient strength to take make an impression on the defenders. 'C' and 'D' Companies met the advance with rapid rifle and machine-gun fire and forced the attackers to retire. No further attempt was made but the continual fighting had left troops of both sides in very close proximity to one another, in some cases only a matter of yards.

The artillery fire had caused many casualties within the ranks of the 11th Brigade so, to assist the London Rifle Brigade, two companies of the 5th King's Own Regiment and two companies of the York and Lancaster Regiment (6th Division) arrived at about 2:00pm. Following the issue of a warning order at 4:00pm, the 2nd East Yorks were deployed to support the junction between the Hampshire's and the 85th Brigade, following indications that an attack, supported by gas, was expected.

While the 11th Brigade had endured repeated attacks, the 12th Brigade had also been caught in the bombardment. Early in the afternoon enemy infantry were seen massing across the whole brigade front and cutting their own wire in front of the Lancashire Fusiliers, indicative of a forthcoming attack. The French and division artillery opened rapid fire on the opposing front lines, but no attack developed.

Operation orders, issued on the 1st May, had indicated that the first phase of the readjustment of the line was to take place on the night of the 3rd. The eastern part of the salient was to be given up while the central part, held by the 12th Brigade, was to be retained and a new line in the southern portion, through Frezenberg and Hooge, was to be dug and manned. The intention of the adjustment was to shorten the line and have the 1st Canadian and 28th Divisions withdraw altogether while the 4th Division assumed responsibility for the line on the 4th May, under the command of its G.O.C., Major-General Wilson.

In accordance with those orders, the 10th and 11th Brigades were instructed to hold their present line until the movements of neighbouring division were completed. The two divisions withdrew without serious incident, given the fact that many of the front line troops were within speaking distance of their enemy but subjected to constant artillery fire. During the night of the 2nd, warning orders were issued to the 10th and 11th Brigades instructing them to be prepared to withdraw to new positions as a part of the scheduled retirement.

While no serious attempt was made by the enemy to attack any part of the 4th Division front during the night of the 2nd or the 3rd, every sign indicated the possibility of some form of offensive action. As the orders for withdrawal were being received, the Hampshire regiment (11th Brigade) and the 10th Brigade was subjected to several small attacks, each supported by the use of gas shells, although each attack was repulsed without undue difficulty.

While the withdrawal proceeded, the 12th Brigade readjusted its front and took over a part of the line held by the 10th Brigade, which then withdrew into division reserve. After having previously sent all surplus ammunition and supplies to positions behind the G.H.Q. line, the 11th Brigade finally withdrew in the early hours of the morning from under the very noses of the enemy, although having to leave some of the more seriously wounded behind.

The general nature of the retirement resulted in large volumes of wheeled transport passing along a single road and the infantry through the adjacent fields. Despite the difficulties with communications and the strain under which the men had been fighting, the troops succeeded, assisted by morning mist, in reaching the G.H.Q. line by dawn.

A withdrawal of such magnitude was readily detected by the German artillery, which turned its attention on La Brique and St. Jean as the retiring troops passed through the devastation while the shells completed the destruction of the villages around them. The conduct of the troops remained calm and ordered, a considerable achievement considering the intensity of the fighting that they had undergone only a few hours before[194].

The efforts of the enemy to continue with the attacks were constant and, late in the morning of the 4th, a party of Germans attempting to build a barricade in the recently vacated 12th Brigade trenches was driven back by a bombing party of the South Lancashire Regiment. The struggle between the two bombing parties lasted for nearly twenty-four hours and eventually each built barricades a short distance from each other and continued to exchange bombs.

The German offensive continued in the form of spasmodic local actions, which were carried out mainly by small groups but, at 9:00am on the 4th, large bodies of the enemy were seen to be massing in front of Shell Trap Farm. The division artillery broke up some of the formations but did little to delay the events of the next few hours.

The enemy artillery commenced shelling the trenches held by the 7th Argylls to the right of Shell Trap Farm. Such was the proximity of the opponents that a bombing party was ordered to barricade a communications trench leading to Shell Trap Farm from the German trenches.

---

[194] *The casualty figures for the 11 Brigade for the period of 26 April – 3 May are not clearly defined because the figures for the 1 East Lancashire Regiment have not been recorded, but the other three battalions reported a total of 34 officers and 1522 other ranks. It is not unreasonable to assume that the total figure would approximate 50 officers and about 2000 other ranks. Extracted from the Official History, France & Belgium 1915, Volume 1, p296.*

However, when the party attempted to move forward, the officer in charge was shot when attacked by a party of the enemy and the remainder of the party was driven back to Shell Trap Farm. The Argylls struggled to maintain their position in the face of the constant bombing attacks and, to assist, the South Lancashires occupied the support trenches in an effort to stabilise the line.

In an attempt to break up the attacks, the Canadian artillery concentrated its fire north and north-east of Shell Trap Farm, which proved most effective. As the assembled enemy retired under the weight of the Canadian fire, the South Lancashires inflicted heavy casualties when they directed heavy rifle and machine-gun fire on those seen retreating. By mid-afternoon, the enemy was again seen crawling forward toward the farm and attempting to dig in at a distance of 400 yards. Again, the artillery intervened.

The enemy had maintained a constant barrage on the positions held by the 12th Brigade, especially those of the South Lancashires about Shell Trap Farm and the support positions at La Brique. Of major concern was a gap of about 100 yards between the right of the 12th Brigade at Shell Trap Farm and the left of the 1st Welsh Regiment, 84th Brigade. The constant attention paid to the gap by the enemy, prompted instructions to the 84th Brigade to deny access by extending to the left and getting in touch with the 12th Brigade.

The heavy bombardment of the previous day had caused considerable damage to the trenches around the farm and great effort was put into repairing the line that night. The shelling remained constant throughout the 5th and, early in evening, the fire increased considerably on the junction of the King's Own and South Lancashires. The bombardment was immediately followed by an attack, which broke through the line and drove the defenders from their trenches. Although a request was made for two battalions to assist, such was the demand for reliefs and reinforcements that only two companies of the Monmouths were available and were sent immediately. With the addition of that assistance, the South Lancashires managed to recover the lost trenches after some severe close-quarter fighting. The South Lancashires, although back in the trenches, had been badly shaken by the shelling and the condition of the men prompted the decision to relieve the battalion.

By the morning of the 6th, the 12th Brigade, the only brigade in the line was holding a front of 1200 yards, between Shell Trap Farm and Turco Farm while the 10th Brigade held the support trenches on both banks of the canal. The 11th Brigade was in reserve in Brielen. All three brigades were subjected to continuous heavy shelling throughout the day and the German Rifle Grenadiers had clearly indicated their intentions to take Shell Trap Farm at any cost.

That night, the Monmouths took over the trenches at the farm, accompanied by a team of division bomb throwers and a trench mortar team. Shortly after the relief had been completed, men of the Monmouths captured a German of the 15th Jaegers who was attempting to cut the wire in front of their positions. Following that incident, enemy troops launched a weak attack but were beaten off with machine-gun and rifle fire, the bombers wreaking havoc amongst the attackers. With the failure of the attack, the German artillery concentrated its efforts on Shell Trap Farm[195] and, under cover of the fire enemy infantry entrenched within 200 yards of the Monmouths and King's Own.

The German command now sensed that one last major effort would give them that much sought after prize, the city of Ypres. Within the British command, there had also been expectations of an impending enemy assault and was very aware that a breakthrough would give the German 4th Army the ability to press the attack towards the coastal cities. Preparations were commenced to meet such an event.

The final effort was launched by the XXVI and XXVII Reserve Corps and the XV Corps, which fell largely upon the 27th and 28th British Divisions, to the right of the 4th Division, at 5:30am on the 8th May. The next six days were to witness some of the most savage, determined fighting and was to have lasting effects on the British army for the remainder of the war.

As the 28th Division was slowly pushed back, so the pressure on the 12th Brigade, particularly those in Shell Trap Farm, increased. The decision had been taken to relieve the 12th Brigade during the evening of the 8th. To assist, two battalions of the 10th Brigade, the 7th Argylls and the Royal Irish Fusiliers, were sent to the east bank of the canal and placed at the disposal of the 12th Brigade.

Throughout the night of the 8th, trenches and outposts were strengthened and, in the early hours of the morning, German infantry were observed carrying large packs on their backs, thought to indicate a possible gas attack. A violent bombardment commenced at 4:30am and fell on the right and centre sections of the 12th Brigade and, assisted by several

---

[195] *During this shelling Shell Trap Farm was all but obliterated. All that remained was the debris of the buildings surrounded by a moonscape of shell holes although the ground on which the farm stood remained of tactical importance to both sides.*

German observation aircraft, the shelling extended to the trenches of the 28th Division. Heavy firing could also be heard to the south. At dawn and throughout the morning the German guns concentrated on the Monmouths in Shell Trap Farm and, in an effort to reduce the number of casualties, the decision was made to hold the front line lightly and dig in behind.

The bombardment continued throughout the day and well into the night, slowly diminishing until, by midnight, all had fallen quiet but the constant shelling had left the trenches near the farm in need of much work. With exception of the Monmouths, all other units had spent a reasonably quiet day, not bothered by shelling or enemy attacks.

In recent days, the new Stokes mortar had been distributed for trial and, in an effort to break up troop concentrations that might produce an attack, the mortars, particularly those of the 12th Brigade, performed excellent work against the enemy front line. It was reported that the recently arrived trench mortars did sterling work in harassing the enemy *"with Germans running about in their trenches"*. When brought to bear the enemy was seen to run and, in doing so, was exposed to rifle and machine-gun fire.

With expectations of a major assault, two companies of the South Lancashires moved from La Brique to the support lines on the canal to reinforce the Royal Irish Fusiliers. About the same time, the Monmouths, holding Shell Trap Farm, were subjected to a gas attack. As the bombardment and gas attacks continued German troops were seen massing in front of the 28th Division and at 8:30am the German artillery lifted from the front line to shell the support lines, to the rear of both divisions, the main weight falling on the 84th Brigade.

By 10:00am, troops of the 84th were seen to be falling back along the Verlorenhoek – Ypres Road, mainly because of the effects of gas, although not in sufficient numbers to be a serious threat to the line. As these men retired, they were rallied at the G.H.Q. line and led back to the trenches. Shortly after, the 12th Brigade noted Germans massing in front of Shell Trap Farm and, in an effort to break up the enemy formations, the Canadian artillery again concentrated fire to the north and north-east of the farm.

Such were the consequences upon the attacking troops that a group about twenty of the enemy, having left their trench in front of the Essex Regiment, were met by withering rifle fire. All were either killed or wounded and none were seen to return to their starting point. As the attack developed, so the bombardment grew in intensity but the Monmouths, who had been affected by gas earlier in the morning, managed to hold the farm against all comers and had sufficient numbers, including a company of the South Lancashires, to maintain the position.

Two companies of the 5th South Lancashire Regiment (12th Brigade) and two of the 1st Royal Irish Fusiliers (10th Brigade) had been attached to the 84th Brigade (28th Division) to provide a sorely needed reinforcement. The four companies were instructed to retake Wieltje and part of the G.H.Q. line. In an effort to take the village of Wieltje the Royal Irish Fusiliers side-slipped to the right in order to put their right flank on that town but the heavy fire prevented any attempt to enter the village.

As the morning progressed, it became increasingly important to take possession of Wieltje and, at 1:00pm, the Royal Irish Fusiliers sent a further two companies to enter and secure the town and to establish communications with the troops to the south of the village. The enemy attacks grew in intensity and the 7th Argylls were sent to La Brique to support the Irish Fusiliers, who were now absorbed in some very confused, hand-to-hand fighting. The South Lancashires were also rushed forward to reinforce.

By early afternoon, the Essex had learnt from the French that bodies of the enemy were massing behind Hill 29. At about the same time the right flank of the 28th Division was driven back on Potijze and the 84th Brigade was in grave danger of giving way. In an effort to assist, the Royal Dublin Fusiliers and the 1st Royal Warwickshire's marched for Potijze where they were placed at the disposal of the 84th Brigade under Brigadier General Bols.

At about 3:30pm one company of the South Lancashires, fighting with the Royal Irish Fusiliers, attempted to sideslip to the left to cover the Essex at the farm but in doing so, were caught in the heavy shellfire, preventing further progress. As the day progressed, the volume of artillery fire increased in intensity and, at 5:00pm, German infantry again advanced against the Royal Irish, although repulsed by rifle and artillery fire.

At this point it had been established that the Germans had penetrated the line held by the 84th Brigade and that the right flank of the 2nd Monmouths was 'in the air'. A gap of 1500 yards existed between the 28th Division and 4th Divisions. As the Germans were as determined in attack as the British were in defence, the situation was now critical and demanded that the line be occupied at all costs.

At 5:30pm the 11th Brigade, resting at Oostheok Wood, was instructed to relieve the much-battered 12th Brigade on the left of the line. The 11th Brigade marched from Vlamertinghe Chateau at 7:30pm but, by the time it had reached La Brique at 9:00pm, the relief had been cancelled as the enemy was again seen massing in a farm two hundred yards to the north of Shell Trap Farm.

The difficulties involved in recalling the scattered units, while Shell Trap Farm was being subjected the heavy attacks, were too great, although two battalions were made available to the 12th Brigade should they be needed. Because of its location on a slight rise, Shell Trap Farm was the focus of enemy attempts against the 12th Brigade and the attacks grew in intensity. Such was the determination shown in the attacks along the length of the line that, by 6:45pm, the Essex Regiment was seen to retire from the trenches to the right of the remnants of the buildings at Turco Farm.

In an attempt to secure the line, a series of attacks were undertaken by the combined battalions of the 10th and 11th Brigades, while the main thrust was made by the 84th Brigade (28th Division). Unknown to the British, the German forces in front of the 28th Division were withdrawing under the weight of those attacks. As the Royal Irish Fusiliers were coming to a halt in front of Wieltje, the occupying force within that village was in the process of withdrawing to the north. The Royal Irish were not to be denied, and with further attempts, arrived at Wieltje, where they discovered village was empty and immediately established strong points around the perimeter of the village.

The second composite force, consisting of the two remaining companies of the South Lancashires and Royal Irish Fusiliers passed through Wieltje and counter-attacked astride the St. Julien – Wieltje road, where they killed or captured those enemy found in the area. On hearing of the securing of Wieltje, the commander of the 12th Brigade organised a further counter-attack consisting of a composite force of Argyll and 1/7th Sutherland Highlanders (10th Brigade) and 5th South Lancashires (12th Brigade). They advanced through the Royal Irish Fusiliers and continued along the line of the St. Julien Road, to a point about half a mile north of Wieltje.

The third and final attack was made by the East Lancashire Regiment (11th Brigade) and the 2nd Royal Dublin Fusilier (10th Brigade). The attack by those battalions was to commence on a line, which extended from Shell Trap Farm, on the left, to Wieltje, on the right. The objective was to advance and occupy that part of the G.H.Q. line that lay in front of Wieltje. The attack commenced at dark and those nearest the farm, the East Lancashires, bombed their way down the G.H.Q. line while Dublin Fusiliers swung their right flank in arc as they advanced some 400 yards.

The attack was successful, given that it had been conducted largely at night by troops untrained in the art of night fighting, and by 11:00pm the Royal Dublin Fusiliers reached the G.H.Q. line and established contact with the 84th Brigade. The whole movement was supported by the 1st Hampshire Regiment (11th Brigade) located directly behind the advancing troops and the 1st Somerset Light Infantry (11th Brigade), at La Brique.

The advance continued and by 11:45pm, had ground to a temporary halt as the infantry became involved in heavy hand-to-hand fighting, and were forced to clear the defending Germans with the bayonet. Although the attack progressed into the early hours of the 9th and all objectives had been reached, the situation remained serious.

By 3:00am, the Hampshire's had established a second line with its right on Wieltje, which extended to the west for nearly 1200 yards where it connected to the 2nd Royal Irish Regiment. With much hard, work the lines were slowly connected and consolidated as a defensive front, after which the attacks and counter-attacks diminished and the short period of quiet that followed offered an opportunity to reorganise.

All were exhausted and the battalions of all three brigades were completely mixed up. The condition of the Irish Fusiliers was such that they were withdrawn from the line during the night of the 9th and sent to La Brique to supplement the units waiting in reserve. The withdrawal of the Irish Fusiliers left the Argyll and Sutherland Highlanders and East Lancashire Regiment holding the extreme right of the line. The Royal Dublin Fusiliers and the Royal Warwickshire Regiment (10th Brigade) remained in the support line while the 11th Brigade continued the defence of the support line to the left, towards Shell Trap Farm.

As if to demonstrate the nature of the confusion experienced during the events of the afternoon of the 9th, reports had arrived at the division headquarters that two battalions of the 85th Brigade were retiring along the Verlorenhoek – Ypres road. These proved incorrect. At about this same time a report from the Royal Irish Fusiliers stated that the German troops, which had advanced on Wieltje the previous afternoon, were wearing Royal Lancashire greatcoats and wearing British packs. It is believed that these troops were, in fact, the Royal Inniskilling Fusiliers, which had taken Wieltje the previous day.

The 12th Brigade was under instructions to push on for all they were worth and support the attack by 28th Division, which was currently underway and the East Lancashires were instructed to retake the trenches, which had previously been lost by the 84th Brigade. However, despite the best of endeavours, by 2:00am on the 10th the 28th Division attack had been repulsed and pushed back to the switch line 1000 yards southeast of Wieltje.

There followed a period of quiet, which lasted for several hours, as both sides regained strength. It was to be the lull before the storm for, by 7:45am, the German artillery, with the assistance of observation aircraft, recommenced shelling the 12th Brigade front. The bombardment continued for most of the day and, at about noon the Royal Irish Regiment, at Shell Trap Farm, was heavily shelled. Three hours later German infantry again attacked the King's Own and, although the attempt was beaten off with rifle and machine-gun fire, it was a foreboding of things to come.

With the balance of probability firmly in German hands, the fate of Shell Trap Farm was soon to be decided. At 3:40pm, German artillery subjected the trenches either side of the farm to concentrated fire, which continued well into the evening. Wieltje was also subjected to the same bombardment. The 11th Brigade asked permission to relieve the 12th Brigade in the front line but it was considered too dangerous under the rain of shellfire to which the whole brigade front was subjected, until finally, at 9:00pm, conditions allowed the 11th Brigade to begin the relief.

All four battalions then held the front line. The 1st Somerset Light Infantry was holding trenches in and around Turco Farm while, to the right, lay the 1st Hampshire Regiment and the 1st Rifle Brigade was holding Shell Trap Farm. The line was then continued to the right (east) by the 1st East Lancashires and the 1/5th London Regiment (11th Brigade), which were in touch with the 18th Hussars of the 1st Cavalry Division[196], which had relieved the badly mauled 28th Division during the night of the 12th.

---

[196] *The 18th Hussars were located to the right of the Ypres – Gravenstafel road while the 1/5 London Regiment were on the left of the road.*

The 11th Brigade spent the next three days in comparative quiet, only subjected to intermittent shelling, and much effort was spent recovering trenches, which had been damaged by the German artillery. On the 11th, the Royal Warwickshire Regiment and Dublin Fusiliers, both of which had been attached to the 84th Brigade, returned to the 10th Brigade and the 29th Field Artillery Brigade rejoined the division after being attached to V Corps. Although conditions were quiet, the front line was subjected to considerable sniping. By 3:15am on the 11th, the 12th Brigade had retired to Vlamertinghe, west of Ypres.

Heavy rain fell continually throughout the night of the 12th and, at 4:30am on the morning of the 13th, the whole brigade front was subjected to a heavy bombardment, particularly on Shell Trap Farm. The shelling was followed by an infantry attack along the entire front. Although the attack was largely held off, it was by sheer weight of numbers that parties of the enemy succeeded in gaining a foothold in the trenches held by the East Lancashire Regiment and capturing a small farm nearby. Further to the right, the London Regiment and the 19th Hussars were also subjected to a massed attack and both were forced to fall back.

In an effort to stabilise the front, Brigadier-General Prowse, commanding the 11th Brigade, instructed the Essex Regiment to counterattack and recover the lost trenches. However, prior to the order arriving, the Essex Regiment had, on its own initiative, already attacked and re-occupied a portion of the trenches[197], while assisting the Hussars with rifle and machine-gun fire. Grim hand-to-hand fighting, with grenade and bayonet, continued for much of the afternoon in an effort to recover the lost trenches and it was only in the early evening that the entire line was re-captured.

In order to provide addition support for the London Rifles when required, the Royal Irish Fusiliers and Seaforth Highlanders were moved immediately to the canal bank. From there, the Irish Fusiliers were then sent directly to La Brique, where they came under the orders of the 11th Brigade. Further support was added by the 12th Brigade, which marched from Vlamertinghe to the western bank of the canal. By 12 noon, the attack had extended to the left as far as the trenches held by Somerset Light Infantry and Hampshire Regiments, that is, between

---

[197] *The trenches referred to had been totally destroyed by the German artillery fire and were little more than a series of shell holes spread at random on the original site of the trenches. It is reputed that the 2 Essex lost 180 men in the 800 yard advance from the support line to the front line.*

165

Shell Trap and Turco Farms, where sections of the line where overrun. The rifle and machine-gun fire of the defenders did, however, bring the advance to a standstill

Such had been the intensity of the fighting that the Germans had occupied Shell Trap Farm, a situation not realised, until the Inniskilling Fusiliers reported the existence of German troops in the farm the following morning, of the 14th. The War Diary of the 12th Brigade records the events, which took place at Shell Trap Farm in the morning. "*A very curious situation seems to have arisen in the farm. Germans and British were seen moving about and talking together, and eventually the British troops were moved off forward by Germans with fixed bayonets to the German lines. A Sergt. Major of the East Lancashires got out of Shell Trap Farm and ran back to the South Lancs. who were holding the Retrenchment in rear of Shell Trap. 2 platoons of the South Lancashires immediately went forward with fixed bayonets. Germans disappeared, and the South Lancs. established themselves in the farm.*" These appear to have been British troops, which had been captured during the attack[198].

The ranks of the division had thinned considerably and by mid-afternoon reinforcements had arrived in the form of the 6th and 7th Northumberland Fusiliers, of the 149th Brigade (50th Division). To add strength to the existing battalions the Northumberlands were distributed amongst the battalions of the 12th Brigade. The 6th Northumberlands were split up between the Rifle Brigade and the London Rifle Brigade while the 7th Northumberlands were divided between the King's Own and Monmouths. The battered Lancashire Fusiliers then marched to La Brique and into reserve while, with the assistance of the engineers, the Monmouths put great effort into reinforcing Shell Trap Farm.

The morning of the 15th passed quietly, apart from the occasional German reconnaissance aircraft that flew low over the division front. The aerial observation allowed the whole line to be consistently shelled and seriously limited the amount of work that could be carried out. However, after dark, the work on Shell Trap Farm continued apace. During the night, a general re-organisation took place and Division front was now lengthened to occupy that part of the line to the right of Shell Trap Farm which had previously occupied by the 1st East Lancashires

---

[198] *It appears that, while the Germans had occupied Shell Trap Farm, possibly in the evening following the attack. They did not keep possession. As the British prisoners were marched out, it appears that the German troops left with them and the farm was reoccupied by troops from the South Lancashires.*

and 1/5th London Rifle Brigade. The line now extended in a wide arc from the Ypres – Gravenstafel road, north to Shell Trap Farm and then west to Turco Farm. The 10th Brigade assumed responsibility for the line to the right of Shell Trap Farm and the 11th Brigade for that part of line to the left.

Brigadier-General Anley assumed command those troops of the 11th and 12th Brigade holding the front line during the afternoon and the 12th Brigade finally withdrew to the west bank of the canal, as the 10th Brigade took over. Each brigade established a system of reliefs, thus allowing one of the battalions to relieve another of the same brigade. Although free from enemy attack, the process of relief consumed much of the day, as Shell Trap Farm continued to be targeted by intermittent shelling. Once again the temptation to reveal a sense of humour was shown when, at 4:00pm on the 16th, the Germans put a white flag up on the parapet of their trench, opposite the Hampshire's. The artillery immediately shot it down.

In an effort to push back the German forces, which had crossed the Yser canal on the 23rd April, the French 153rd Division, on the left flank of the 4th Division, had launched an attack during the afternoon of the 15th. Partial success was achieved on the first day and the attack was continued on the 16th. To provide support for the French attack the division artillery maintained heavy fire against the German support lines, in order to prevent reinforcements being diverted to the French front. During the attack, the East Lancashires (11th Brigade), observed about fifty Germans wearing British caps and, when the French artillery was informed, the trenches were shelled intensely for about ten minutes.

Day passed to night quietly, with only occasional shelling while the last units of Canadian artillery left the 4th Division area to return to the 1st Canadian Division. One of the problems experienced by the infantry had been the occasional shelling of their positions by the Canadian artillery. In order to minimise the risk of being shelled in such a manner the next two days of the quiet period were spent establishing practices aimed at improving communications with the artillery batteries. To assist the artillery to identify the position of the front line, green canvas patches were placed on the parapets, which could be seen by the artillery observers. The following day, the 17th, the 1/2nd Monmouthshire Regiment (12th Brigade), was notified that it would be withdrawn[199].

---

[199] *The 2nd Battalion, Monmouthshire Regiment, which had joined the division on the 20 November 1914, had fought with the 4th Division through the bitter winter of 1914 and participated in the heavy fighting in front of Ploegsteert Wood. It also par-*

Sunday the 24th May began clear and fine. At 2:45am, the entire division front line was subjected to concentrated artillery fire, a heavy release of gas and heavy rifle and machine-gun fire, followed immediately by an infantry assault. *"Shortly after the attack commenced some men, mostly of the Royal Irish Regiment and 7th Argyll and Sutherland Highlanders, began to fall back from Shell Trap Farm and trenches in the vicinity. A company of the Lancashire Fusiliers was ordered forward to occupy the trenches vacated by the Royal Irish Regiment. This company, one hundred and twenty strong, pushed forward under heavy fire of Maxims[200] which had already been established in Shell Trap Farm by the Germans, but, with the exception of the Captain and thirty men who moved away to their left from their true objective, who succeeded in reaching the right of the King's Own line, the company was unable to move very far."*

The gas was very strong and had caused great discomfort as far back as the canal banks. The intensity of the attack ejected the Royal Irish Regiment from the farm and almost one hundred of the retiring troops were collected and led back to the second line trenches[201].

The 4th, 6th and 7th Northumberland Fusiliers (149th Brigade), then at Trois Tours, proceeded to the canal bank and fell under the orders of the 10th Brigade. Of these battalions, the 4th was subsequently pushed forward towards Wieltje to support the Seaforth Highlanders while the 6th and 7th remained at the canal awaiting orders. The German guns were well served by observation aircraft, which continually flew along the length of the front, indicating suitable targets.

The first attack was subjected to the fire of the entire division artillery, including that of the neighbouring French division, in an effort to stem the approach of the enemy. Such was the gravity of the situation that the Monmouth Regiment, then at Vlamertinghe, in preparation for its departure from the division, was recalled and ordered to return to the reserve lines on the eastern side of the canal. The 11th Brigade, having

---

ticipated in the Christmas truce. After leaving the 4 Division the 2 Monmouthshire Regiment was amalgamated with its sister battalions, the 1 and 3 and went on to fight with the 84 Brigade (28 Division).

[200] The Maxim machine-gun was the standard issue of machine-gun for the German Army throughout the war. It was also a part of the issue to the British Army until it was replaced with the Vickers machine-gun during late 1914 and 1915.

[201] For a further description of the attack on the 12 Brigade, see Appendix V, 12 Brigade Action 24 May 1915.

just arrived at Vlamertinghe after being relieved, also sent the Somerset's Light Infantry and the much-tried Rifle Brigade back the to the support line while the Hampshire's occupied positions along the canal bank.

The first assault was repulsed everywhere except at Shell Trap Farm. Here, due to the proximity of the two trench lines the gas was released directly into the trenches of the Dublin Fusiliers and the attackers only had to cross approximately thirty yards of No Man's Land to enter the British trenches. Elsewhere the battalions fought on for the rest of the day, handicapped as they were by the ground conditions, which had been the result of days of rain.

The enemy artillery continued to bombard trenches, roads, communications and the British guns continually, for several hours[202]. Because of the intensity of the shellfire, telephone communications were cut almost immediately and messages and reports were either late or nonexistent. To supplement the release of the gas cloud the German artillery used gas shells against the more distant targets.

Despite the heavy fighting and the best efforts of the reinforcements, the 10th Brigade had, by 4:50am, lost trenches on the right flank. Because of the confused nature of the fighting, inaccurate messages were received at the division headquarters stating that the Royal Irish Regiment and the Lancashire Fusiliers were holding trenches, when in fact they had been evacuated. On other occasions, no information could be obtained at all, especially about Shell Trap Farm.

Telephone communications had all but ceased to exist, having been cut by artillery fire and information about the action on the 12th Brigade front proved most difficult to obtain. By 6:30am, the 10th Brigade reported that Shell Trap Farm had fallen into German hands and it was intended that the 9th Argylls would be used to retake it, but they could not be found. In their absence, the Royal Warwicks attempted to retake the farm but the attack was brought to a halt by heavy machine-gun fire.

The extent of the attack required all available troops in the front line. To this end, the Seaforth Highlanders were sent from the canal bank to positions about Wieltje Farm, with two companies reinforcing the 7th Argylls, which were barely holding their own east of Wieltje. The remains of the 11th Brigade, having just arrived at Vlamertinghe, was or-

---

[202] *Gas was used extensively during the attack, as far south as the Menin Road.*

dered back to the canal but, because of the length of time that it had been in the line, the division commander chose not to use it unless absolutely necessary. By 7:00am, the Germans had taken the trenches, formerly occupied by the Royal Irish Regiment, and the communications trench leading to that position[203]. The 14th and 29th Field Artillery Brigades were instructed to commence rapid fire on these positions to form a barrier to any further advance along the captured trenches.

In an effort to recover from a slowly degenerating situation, the 12th Brigade was instructed, at 8:00am, to re-take all lost trenches, an action that would be supported by the French artillery[204] and a concerted counter-attack by the 10th Brigade was to be organised if necessary. On receipt of these orders Brigadier-Generals Anley and Hull, commanding the 10th and 12th Brigades agreed to a combined counter-attack. The attack was to be delivered by the remains of the companies of the Lancashire Fusiliers and the 1st Warwickshire's, that had been ordered forward to the division support line.

The urgency of the situation required the Lancashire Fusiliers to attack with their right on Shell Trap Farm and to cooperate with the Royal Warwickshire Regiment. The South Lancashires occupied the support line while two companies of the Monmouths were to occupy the division second line with their flank on Irish Farm. Following the artillery bombardment, the counter-attack commenced at 10:20am, but came under such heavy fire that it was unable to get forward more than 400 yards. Brigadier-General Anley considered that to achieve success, more artillery preparation would be necessary before the attack could hope to succeed.

Due to the loss of those trenches around Shell trap Farm the right flank of the King's Own had also been exposed. The Germans had dug in south-west of Shell Trap Farm. Taking advantage of the fact that the trenches they now occupied were connected directly to those held by the King's Own, enemy infantry worked along the old Royal Irish trench to within fifty yards of the communications trench connecting the two and in the direction of Canadian Farm. During the day, German attempts to push bombing parties along the trenches, against the

---

[203] *The offensive had been conducted on a wide front and had also occupied the Belle-waarde Ridge and Hooge, further to the south. The battle was to be recorded in British history by that name, the Battle of Bellewaarde Ridge.*

[204] *The French 75mm field gun, commonly referred to as simply as the 75, was renowned for its accuracy and ability to use many different kinds of ammunition. This gun also became popular among other Allied Armies.*

flank of the King's Own, were driven back by the counter-bombing. However, by midday, the supply of bombs had been consumed.

With the failure of the attack, Brigadier-Generals Anley and Hull jointly decided upon a second counter-attack, scheduled to take place at 2:00pm, under the cover of a preparatory bombardment. The counter-attack was to advance from the south with its right resting on the trenches still held by the Royal Dublin Fusiliers, thus following the same lines as the successful counter-attack delivered by the Essex Regiment against the same objective on the 13th. However, before the scheduled start time, division headquarters had received a report that the whole line, as far south as Wieltje – St. Julien Road had given way. The collapse of the line decided Brigadier-General Anley to cancel the attack, which, with the limited force available, could no longer hope to succeed[205].

At 4:50pm, a General Staff Officer from V Corps brought instructions that three French battalions were to be placed at the disposal of Brigadier-General Anley and he was directed to arrange for a counter-attack after dark. Anley immediately sent one of his Staff Officers to the headquarters of the 152nd (French) Division to get in touch with the battalions. However, shortly after, difficulties arose when V Corps advised General Anley that the French troops were not to be employed in any offensive action except in support of the 12th Brigade.

Present at the 12th Brigades headquarters, when that call was received, was Colonel Montgomery, G.S.O. I, from division headquarters. General Anley explained to him that without the ability to use the French troops in an attack, and the absence of any other body of fresh troops, there was no possibility of a counter attack being successful, as both flanks of the brigade were in the air. Due to the short night, a decision had to be made at once. Colonel Montgomery therefore arranged for a withdrawal to the support line and the French Switch[206]. Colonel Montgomery immediately returned to the division headquarters, reported the new situation and the arrangements for withdrawal, all being approved by the G.O.C.

---

[205] *The casualty rate of most of battalions involved in the fighting on the 24 was staggering. The 2 Dublin Fusiliers, 9 A&SH and the company of the Lancashire Fusiliers were all but wiped out. By that evening, those units barely mustered three hundred officers and men.*

[206] *The French Switch was a title given to a former French trench, which joined the support line the front to line near Turco Farm.*

By 2:30am on the 25th, the withdrawal of the 12th Brigade had been completed[207]. By dawn, the new division front was held by the 2nd Essex and King's Own (12th Brigade) and the Royal Warwickshire Regiment, one company of the Northumberland Fusiliers and the Royal Irish Fusiliers (10th Brigade) on the right flank. A trench had been dug connecting Wieltje Farm, in the support line, with the left of the Royal Irish Regiment. This trench had been dug and manned by the 2nd Monmouth Regiment with outposts being established at Wieltje and Cross Roads Farm.

The 4th Division was in a state of thorough disarray, with many battalions being intermixed and drastically reduced in number. The artillery was almost out of ammunition and communication between headquarters and the frontline units was non-existent. Fortunately, exhaustion on both sides had brought the battle to a standstill. German ambitions of capturing Ypres had failed and the British and French armies had stopped the offensive one and a half miles from the city boundaries. Few would argue that this day represented the demise of the British regular army.

The morning passed quietly with only a little shelling although, at 8:00am, large numbers of Germans were seen concentrating at Canadian Farm and marching in a westerly direction. After the conflict of the past few days the South Lancashire Regiment had elements of many of the regiments attached to it and the decision was made to withdraw them from the line. As the relief was carried out the troops were subjected to machine-gun fire from Shell Trap Farm, causing considerable inconvenience as they moved. As early as 3:00am on the 26th German aircraft were conducting very careful reconnaissance of the 4th Division lines and during the course of the morning enemy infantry were observed consolidating Shell Trap Farm and the trenches to left and right of Canadian Farm.

Throughout the 28th, the enemy carried out extensive sapping while their observation aircraft continued the reconnaissance flights over the lines and their artillery maintained constant fire along the entire length of the line, although no further attempt was made to attack. Such were the casualties amongst the 7th and 9th Argylls that survivors were temporarily reorganised into a single composite battalion.

On the 30th, during one of the occasional patrol actions near Forward Cottage, one patrol discovered a wounded man of the 7th Argyll and

---

[207] *The 10 and 12 Brigades withdrew approximately 900 yards to a new line located a mile north of St. Jean.*

Sutherland Highlanders on the road south of Retrenchments and brought him in. He was one of the troops injured in the German attack on the 24th May, six days before. During the night of the 31st, the 6th Division relieved a part of the 4th Division Line.

June - 1915

By late May the German offensive had ended and it was a matter of urgency to undertake a reorganisation of the line and rest the units, which had been involved. "*Apart from lack of ammunition, both sides were in need of rest, thoroughly exhausted by a long effort lasting over a month, and carried out mainly by the divisions already in the area. These, without relief, were engaged again and again until practically annihilated.*"[208]

On the morning of the 1st June, the 10th Brigade marched to Ypres and relieved the 12th Brigade in the support line, which, in turn, marched to billets, west of Vlamertinghe to act as division reserve. During the reorganization that followed, the 5th and 6th Northumberland Fusiliers returned to the 50th Division. The 6th Division had arrived at Vlamertinghe with the intention of relieving the 4th but there was to be little respite, as the division was now to take over the lines held by the French 152nd Division[209]. While awaiting relief the 11th Brigade was constantly subjected to the attentions of the enemy artillery and by 10:00am, the shelling had increased to a concentrated bombardment, particularly of those trenches held by the East Lancashires. As the morning progressed, the fire gradually diminished, although without complete respite. Many casualties were incurred in that single action.

It was under that fire that officers of the 16th Brigade, 6th Division, reconnoitred the trenches held by the Hampshire's and Rifle Brigade and successfully completed the relief the following night[210]. The two battalions then retired to La Brique and the Canal Bank respectively. The remainder of the 11th Brigade was relieved during the night of the 3rd and marched to Vlamertinghe Chateau where it joined the 12th Brigade. By 2:00am on the 5th, all reliefs had been completed and the front line

---

[208] *British Official History, Military Operations - France and Belgium 1915.*

[209] *The 152* Division was located immediately to the left of the position from which the 12* Brigade had just been relieved.*

[210] *At 6:00am on the morning of the 2nd June, the 4* Division left V Corps and transferred to the VI Corps, Major-General J. L. Keir, K.C.B., whose area of responsibility was that part of the line, which extended north-east from Ypres to Roulers. Major General Keir was later promoted to the temporary rank of Lieutenant-General on the 1* July and continued to command the VI Corps in that capacity until the 1* January 1916 when his promotion was confirmed. The Division was to remain with the VI Corps for a considerable period and enjoyed a close relationship with the 6* Division through many a stiff fight.*

battalions of the 10ᵗʰ Brigade then marched to join the Argylls and Royal Dublin's at Vlamertinghe Chateau. The brigade had been involved in some of the hardest fighting and its overall strength had been somewhat depleted in the past month. Once gathered the battalion, totalled 80 officers and 3,151 other ranks.

The relief of the French division had been scheduled to take place during the night of the 6ᵗʰ June and, in preparation, officers of the 10ᵗʰ Brigade reconnoitred the French lines during the previous day. In that interval Major-General Keir, G.O.C., VI Corps and Sir Hubert Plumer, G.O.C., 2nd Army inspected the brigade. At the prescribed time, the 12ᵗʰ Brigade moved into position on the canal bank and the general relief began at 7:00pm when the King's Own and two companies of the South Lancashires relieved a battalion of the French to the left of Turco Farm. The line was then continued to the canal by the Royal Irish Regiment and the remaining two companies of the South Lancashires while the support trench, with its right on Belle Alliance,[211] was held by 2ⁿᵈ Essex.

The relief was carried out under considerable shell and rifle fire and, upon completion; the French 90ᵗʰ Brigade temporarily remained, to occupy the trenches between the 10ᵗʰ and 12ᵗʰ Brigades. The trenches were reasonably clean, but there was no parapet or parados and very little defensive wire entanglements existed in front of the line. Improvements to the defences was very effectively prevented by the activities the enemy snipers until after nightfall and a few rifle grenades and trench mortar bombs were dropped into the trenches at random. To give greater support to the two front-line brigades, the 11ᵗʰ Brigade moved a battalion closer to the line, to Des Trois Tours Chateau.

The large-scale assaults of previous weeks were now replaced by smaller local actions, most of which took the form of sniping. Reinforcements continued to arrive in the ranks of the 10ᵗʰ Brigade and four officers and two hundred and eighty one other ranks were distributed between the various battalions. During the night of the 9ᵗʰ, the brigade managed to relieve the remainder of the French 90th Brigade while the Lancashire Fusiliers were subjected to the activities of German trench mortar, which inflicted considerable damage to the newly constructed parapets. The following day a small mine was exploded under a trench held by the Irish Fusiliers. It blew in the parapet, killed five, and wounded several others.

---

[211] *Belle Alliance was the name given by French, in 1914, to a small piece of high ground behind Turco Farm.*

Reliefs between battalions took place regularly and few units spent more than forty-eight hours in the line, although the exchange of desultory artillery and trench mortar fire, which continued for several days, resulted in a steady flow of casualties[212]. All movement in the trenches of the Hampshire Regiment was effectively curtailed by constant enemy machine-gun fire, which had been brought to bear by a battery of machine guns in fortified positions. The 2nd Heavy Artillery Regiment soon demolished the enemy position after firing twenty rounds of Lydite.

On the far left of the division line, German artillery officers maintained observation of the bridges and approaches across the canal from a tower and houses on the opposite side of the canal. To dispose of the observation posts, arrangements were made with the 9.2" guns of the Heavy Artillery Regiment to destroy the buildings, but a last minute break in communications prevented them from firing and the delay allowed the enemy to shell the canal bank at half-hourly intervals throughout the night. The destruction of the offending tower and house took place on the 13th and the enemy shelling diminished almost immediately.

The Somerset's finally suppressed the German snipers although heavy and accurate fire continued from No Man's Cottage. A decision was taken to blow up the building during the night of the 15th but the task eventually proved impossible, as the defenders gained protection against approach by nearby covering posts. In retaliation for the attention given to the building, the enemy artillery bombarded the Essex. Notwithstanding those exchanges, attempts were made to destroy No Man's Cottage with the assistance of the 26th Trench Howitzer Battery but the best of efforts produced little success.

Still determined to rid themselves of the problem, the Essex recruited the 31st Heavy Battery to the cause and two days later, on the 19th, it opened fire and, while several hits were registered, the building was not yet ready to give in and remained largely intact. The German artillery continued to retaliate by heavily shelling the area around Turco Farm for about five minutes, although no attempt at attack was made. An officer, in command of an armoured car, visited the headquarters of the 11th Brigade and offered his services but, due to the weight of the vehicle, it could not get across the canal.

During the last week of June, daily activity consisted largely of bouts of shelling along the canal bank, particularly on the left flank of the 12th

---

[212] *During this period a party of eight workers from a Glasgow ammunition factory visited the trenches to examine the effects of German artillery fire.*

Brigade and the 2nd Heavy Artillery Regiment responded by shelling the enemy about Pilkim. It was necessary to gain detailed information about the enemy and, in order to estimate the strength of the opposing forces, each brigade sent reconnaissance patrols out at night. It was soon determined that all enemy lines were held in strength, especially at night. On the 24th, the G.O.C. of the division, Major-General Wilson, was notified of his award of the K.C.B. He responded to the congratulations from the 11th Brigade, his former command, by stating; *"Many thanks for the congratulations. I look upon it as recognition of the good work done by all in the Fourth Division and I thank you for it."*

On the 27th there were indications that the Germans could possibly be mining from their part of International Trench, in front of the 11th Brigade and precautions were taken to determine the extent of the activity. A patrol of the Essex had also discovered, on that same night that No Man's Cottage, which had been the source of much recent effort, was vacant. Two days later a patrol of the Lancashire Fusiliers approached and entered the building without opposition from occupants or outposts and the Royal Engineers finally placed explosives within the building but still only achieved partial destruction.

July - 1915

On the 1st July, the 8th West Yorkshire Regiment joined the 11th Brigade. The day was largely spent allocating the West Yorks to the various battalions and improving trenches, albeit under constant shellfire. At 7:00am, the suspicions of the Seaforth Highlanders were aroused by the sounds of underground boring in front of their trenches, near an enemy saphead[213]. To prevent further mining activity, the position was assaulted with trench mortar bombs, grenades, rifles, and shellfire from the 88th Battery, inflicting several casualties on the occupants. All mining activity then appeared to stop. The Royal Engineers, satisfied that the Germans had mined into the sap, bored a hole 18' deep and exploded a charge at 2.30pm in the afternoon, destroying the enemy tunnel.

During the early hours of the following morning, German trench mortars fired in retaliation on the Seaforth Highlanders, opposite the sap, causing considerable damage to the parapets and inflicting several casualties. The contest continued as the Seaforth's retaliated with grenades and mortars against the same German sap, killing the sentry. In an effort to impede the movement of enemy infantry towards the target sap, arrangements were made with the 2nd Heavy Artillery Regiment to use the 9.2" heavy howitzer against the German trench system, referred to as Fortuin 17. The shoot was organised to take place at 6:00pm, but a break in wireless communications with the observer, forced a delay[214].

The division was subjected to occasional shelling throughout the day but little disruption was caused to the normal routine. In an effort to improve the fields of fire and observation from the front line the troops were instructed to cut the long grass and crops for a distance of fifteen yards behind the trenches and fifteen yards forward of the wire entanglements; work that was performed after dark. The night passed uneventfully, but the morning of the 3rd was followed with intermittent gas shelling. At 3:00pm, the 10th Brigade line was shelled heavily, but no offensive action followed.

That evening the shellfire grew in intensity along the centre and left sections of the line with the use of high explosive and gas. The shelling

---

[213] *A sap was a trench extending out into No Man's Land from the main firing line, often reaching out to a shell hole. They were regularly used as strong points and listening posts to act as warning for any attack by the enemy.*

[214] *Wireless, as a method of communications at this early stage of the war, was in its infancy and was subject to regular failure.*

further increased at about 5:30pm when some sixty gas shells were fired into Potijze Wood from guns in the area of Keir. The 25th Field Artillery Brigade ranged upon them and fired constantly in an effort to subdue the fire, but the shelling continued until the Somerset's were subjected to a constant, heavy bombardment. Still no attempt at attack was made. The battalion on the left of the 12th Brigade also suffered under the bombardment despite the constant efforts of the 14th and 29th Field Artillery Brigades.

During the course of the bombardment the brigades were informed that they would be relieved on the night of the 6th by the 49th (West Riding) Division. The shelling continued along the whole front during the night, especially upon the positions of the 11th Brigade, which received nearly three hundred shells from the same guns at Pilkim.

The next day, the 4th July, an attack was planned against an enemy saphead, from which so much sniper fire and bombing attacks had originated in previous days. A raiding party of the Seaforth Highlanders, under 2nd Lieutenant Rawstorne, was to attack the sap after a prearranged artillery bombardment. Accompanying the raiders, the engineers were to destroy any equipment and mine galleries that may be discovered and, when the work was completed, the party was to withdraw and return to the front line.

The saphead to be attacked consisted of a well-constructed trench, roughly rectangular, with two communications trenches that entered at each at the rear corners and led back to the main firing line. The distance between the sap and the British line was approximately fifty yards, close enough to be able to cover the distance quickly, after the confusion caused by the artillery fire.

During the evening, the 4th Siege Battery shelled the target and, after delivering twelve direct hits, the storming party left the trench, overcame wire entanglements and entered the sap. It was immediately evident that the artillery fire had caused considerable damage. The majority of the front of the sap and a part of the right hand communications trench had been destroyed, as had the machine-gun position to the right of the sap, along with the gun. Several Germans, killed by the shelling, were seen to be lying about in the sap while the remainder had fled along the communications trenches. Equipment, packs and rifles were lying everywhere, indicating that the position had been strongly held and the suddenness of the assault had allowed no time for an organised withdrawal.

While the engineers were searching for anything that required further demolition, two enemy bombing groups advanced along the left hand communications trench resulting in a bombing duel that continued for ten minutes, during which 2nd Lieutenant Rawstorne, the commander of the raiding party, was wounded. No mine galleries were found and the withdrawal was carried out quickly, all having returned to the British lines with only a few wounded. Later analysis of the event determined that the raiders had failed to drive down the communications trenches as far as was required, which allowed the enemy bombing party to get within throwing range of the main body of raiders. The sap and its defences had been destroyed and, during the night, the Germans were heard to be working on reconstruction[215].

After the enemy had reoccupied the sap, the front line of the Seaforth's was subjected to a heavy bombing exchange and constant rifle fire. In the remaining hours of darkness, German infantry retaliated by attempting to enter the trenches in the left sector of the line, but without success. The contest between the opposing troops was determined and continued throughout the 5th and the 29th Field Artillery Brigade continually shelled the German trenches and mortar positions. At 9:00pm, a Zeppelin approached from Neuve Eglise and dropped two bombs, although no damage was done.

For nearly two weeks, separate plans had been developed by the 11th Brigade for a larger attack, to be carried out by 'B' and 'C' Companies of the Rifle Brigade. It had been planned to attack a portion of trench and an adjoining sap, referred to as International Trench and International Sap, respectively. The trenches in question were situated on the far left of the 4th Division line, 200 yards east of the Yser Canal and approximately 600 yards south of the Ypres – Langemarck Railway. Ferme 14, not unlike Shell Trap Farm, lay just behind the enemy line and on the left flank of the attackers. On the right flank and about 350 yards behind the German line lay Fortin 17, a heavily fortified trench system in the support line. Between the two locations was a series of communications and support trenches that contained deep dugouts

---

[215] *For a full report of the incident, see Appendix V, Report of Raid by Seaforths 4 July 1915.*

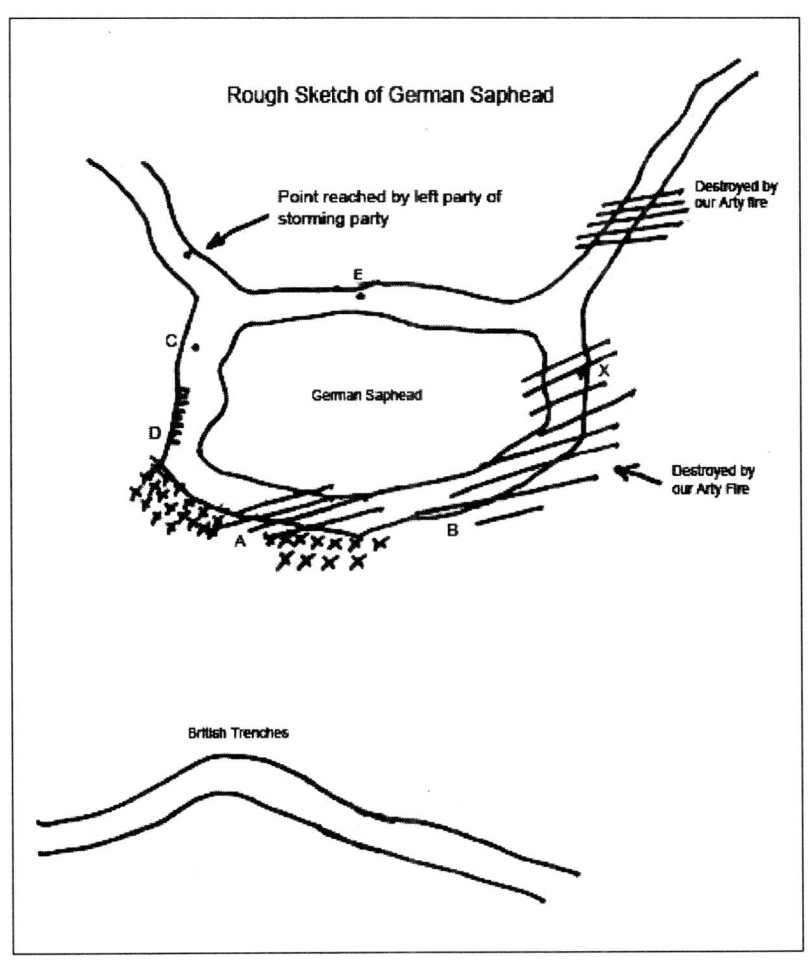

Point reached by left party of
storming party

Destroyed by
our Arty fire

E

C

German Saphead

X

D

Destroyed by
our Arty Fire

A

B

British Trenches

Plate 8
Diagram on the saphead attacked by Seaforth Highlanders on July 4, 1915.

The objective was to seize the two German trenches after a one-hour bombardment and, with the assistance of the West Lancashire Field Company, to consolidate the position and incorporate it into the British front line. The expected date of the attack was the 6th July and the two raiding companies were to be supported by two additional companies of the Somerset Light Infantry, all commanded by Lieutenant-Colonel W.W. Seymour. The task had been the subject of considerable planning. The attack was to be supported by the 18-pounders of the artillery, supplemented by French 75s[216] providing a one-hour bom-

---

[216] For the operation order and gun report of the action see Appendix V, *Operation Order No. 1 – Lt.-Col Seymour.*

bardment prior to the to zero hour. To assist the artillery observers, the troops were to carry red and yellow flags, about eighteen inches square, to mark the progress of the advance.

The night was spent quietly with a light ground mist that covered the movement of the attacking troops. At 5:00am on the 6th the division artillery, 2nd Heavy Artillery Regiment and the French 75's commenced the preliminary bombardment. The mist prevented direct observation and the artillery had to fire on previously determined bearings, which, in the event, proved accurate. Such was the artillery preparation that the heavy guns delivered the first shell directly onto the parapet of the German trench, blowing sandbags and debris high into the air. An 18-pounder field gun of the 135th Battery, which had been placed in the front line the night before, wreaked havoc on the German line when it fired one hundred shells from a distance of seventy yards, resulting in the destruction of the wire and parapet[217].

At 6:00am, the attacking companies commenced the assault and, having met little opposition, charged into the trenches without the need to negotiate wire entanglements. The bombing parties, eight teams of ten men each, preceded the infantry and immediately blocked the communications and fire trenches that led off to the east through which the enemy would need to pass, should they counter-attack. On entering the main trench, the attackers found many German troops hiding in dug-outs to avoid the artillery fire. Most of these were put to the bayonet, as were those who found themselves cut off by the blocking parties in the communications trenches, although twenty-one prisoners, of the 215th Regiment, were taken.

Barricades were constructed at the points where the newly captured trenches joined the main firing line and it was here that the attention of the bombers was focused. Because the bombing took place in the German front line, the blocking parties quickly diminished their supply of grenades and requests were made for a continuous supply, as the enemy was persistent in their attempts to overrun the barricades. Such was the intensity of the bombing exchanges that, by 9:00am, the supply of Hales Grenades was totally exhausted and VI Corps put out a call for more.

---

[217] *No casualties were suffered among the members of the gun crew and all were withdrawn after the attack had commenced. 2. Lieutenant Robinson, the gun commander, later collapsed and suffered nervous exhaustion as a result of the effort of the last few days. He recovered quickly and resumed his post. For the gun report of the action, see Appendix V, Reference procedures of 18 pr. Q.F. Gun in trenches.*

While the fighting was taking place, the supporting Somerset's managed to dig communications trenches from the newly captured position, back to the original firing line and dedicated digging parties entrenched along the edge of the road to establish a support line. While the work was hard, the Somerset's enjoyed the German cigars taken during the assault. By 7:00am the position had been consolidated and arrangements made to meet the expected counter-attacks. The observers of the 32nd Brigade, Royal Field Artillery, closely watched the enemy trenches and the batteries immediately responded to any reported movement. Shortly after completing the consolidation, a counter-attacked on the left flank was attempted but driven off. At about 10:30am the German artillery retaliated by shelling the 12th Brigade and the East Lancashires of the 11th Brigade with high explosive and gas, inflicting considerable damage on the trenches but incurring few casualties.

As the enemy recovered from the loss, organised counter-attacks were made with great determination. The French artillery observers reported Germans massing in the communications trenches around Ferme 14 but could not fire against them because the proximity to the British troops. They did, however, shell the communications trenches that ran north of the farm to prevent reinforcements arriving from that direction. Every available weapon was required to prevent penetration by the opposing bombing parties and to assist, the neighbouring 49th Division was asked to send Tovey Trench Mortars for use during the night.

The 10th Brigade, holding the line to the right of the 11th, had assisted the attack by showing bayonets above the trenches, removing wire in sections of their front, and engaging in rifle and machine-gun fire, resulting in some of the enemy artillery fire being distracted from the main objective. The shortage of grenades became increasingly serious as the fighting continued. The 10th Brigade had given its total grenade supply and requested a further two hundred.

Although the neighbouring French Division contributed a large quantity of grenades, the troops were not trained in their use and they were found to be of little value. Even though the bombing continued without interruption, the Lancashire Fusiliers and two companies of the Royal Warwickshire Regiment managed to relieve the Rifle Brigade and the Somerset's during the night. While the relief was underway, the opposing troops could be heard laying boards and driving stakes in an effort to fortify the trenches opposite the barricades.

The consumption of grenades was alarming, although the problem was partly resolved in the early hours of the 7th, when the division cyclist company prepared one thousand Mills Grenades, which had been procured from Corps reserve. Although the Cyclists were not involved directly in the fighting, they laboured under great difficulty for, as they armed the grenades, they had to carry them to the 11th Brigade Headquarters in anything that would hold them. The amount of effort required to arm and carry resulted in the supply of grenades to the trenches barely keeping pace with demand although an additional two thousand were sent by the 49th Division.

All artillery units, including the French, maintained careful watch on the German trenches for any sign of movement that might represent a build up for an assault. At 11:30am on the 7th, enemy troops again began massing to the left and rear of the captured line. In response, the 2nd Heavy Artillery Regiment shelled Ferme 14 and the surrounding area but, by 2:45pm, the East Lancashires and Warwickshire's were subjected to a determined infantry assault. The defenders met the attack with heavy rifle, machine-gun and artillery fire during which an observer for the 32nd Field Artillery Brigade, who was watching the action, saw the attack falter and then stop, without any further attempt.

The failure of the attack was confirmed at 3:00pm in a report from the Lancashire Fusiliers, which had been acting in support. The struggle for the captured trenches continued in small, personal actions, particularly at the barricades where the opposing bombing parties perpetually harried each other. In retaliation for the capture of the trenches the front line of the 11th Brigade was heavily shelled and, correspondingly, the 4th Siege Battery and the 134th Field Artillery Brigade replied, silencing the German batteries. The effort to recover the lost trenches was continued well into the evening, mainly by heavy artillery fire.

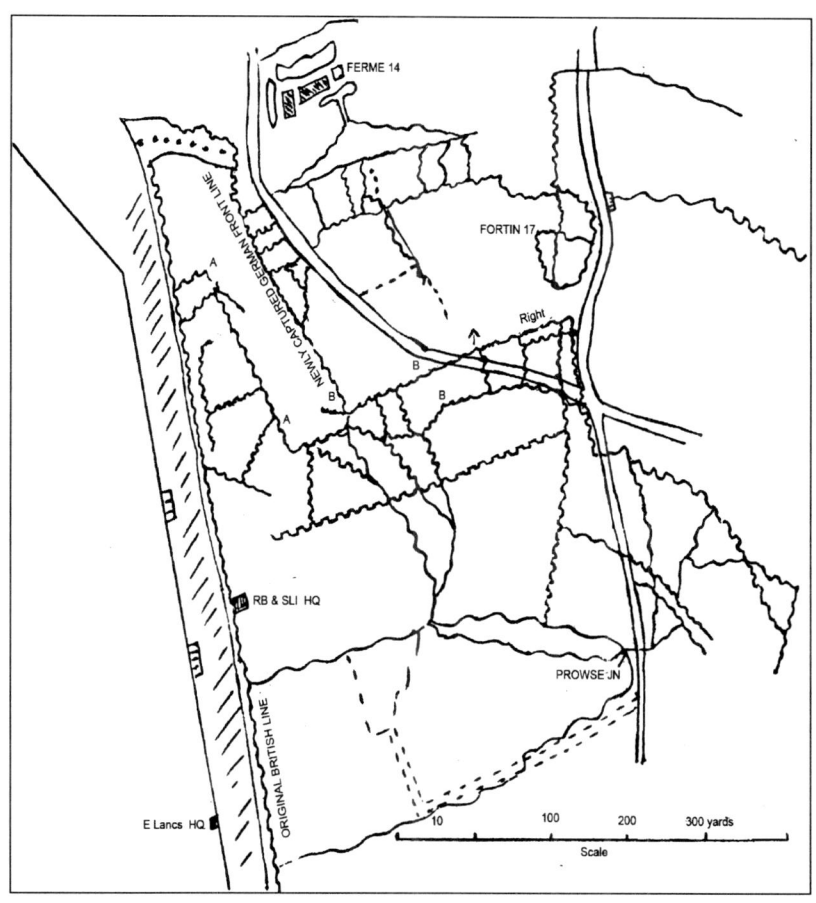

Plate 9
Sketch showing the trenches attacked and captured by the Rifle Brigade on July 6th, 1915. Those marked with A and B indicate the trenches from which the Rifle Brigade launched its' attack

It was destined, even in the midst of a concerted action, that the division was to be relieved and during the night of the 7th, the 146th Brigade (49th Division) relieved the 12th Brigade on the right of the line, which then proceeded to Proven. The struggle for the 10th and 11th Brigades continued throughout the hours of darkness and the 11th Brigade suffered under intense shelling, especially along the canal where the original front line and several battalion headquarters lay. The bombardment slowly diminished until, in the early hours of the morning, only sporadic shelling was experienced. Without warning, at 6:00am, the enemy artillery delivered a heavy bombardment on the trenches held by the 11th Brigade for a period of twenty minutes, but no infantry attack followed. Throughout the day German troops were seen massing around Ferme 14 but were dispersed by concentrated artillery fire.

Over the previous four days it had been noticed that the water level of the canal had been dropping and by the 8th it had fallen about four feet. There was no obvious reason for the fall but it produced a problem with the swing bridges, which serviced the rear areas of the 4th Division. Several attempts had been made by VI Corps to establish the cause but to no avail, and supplies of all nature were slowed as a result, including the supply of grenades for the continuing conflicts at the barriers.

The difficulty of supply of grenades could not be readily resolved and by midday, the troops holding the barriers were running desperately short. The problem was not the lack of grenades but a shortage of carriers and those who were available carried them in all manner of containers. Notwithstanding the difficulties, the division Cyclist Company managed to deliver five hundred Mills bombs while preparing the remaining reserve of five hundred for immediate use, which were soon supplemented by a further five hundred Hales Grenades.

At 2:00pm, the 11th Brigade was subjected to yet another heavy attack by German infantry and the advancing troops were subjected to the attentions of the field and heavy artillery, with devastating results. Signs that the constant attacking and repulse of the German troops was having a moral effect on the enemy were becoming evident. At 3:00pm, German officers were observed trying to rally their troops for attack but the infantry showed, in their behaviour, a marked dislike for further assaults. However, attack again, they did.

As each attempt to attack was detected, the artillery, of all calibres, was directed on the enemy trenches, an activity to which the French artillery contributed considerably. By 4:30pm, nine separate enemy attacks had been attempted, each of which were been beaten off. The shelling of the 11th brigade had caused a continuous stream of casualties, the trenches had suffered considerable damage and the troops were exhausted.

During the day instructions arrived stating that the 147th Brigade (49th Division) was to relieve the 10th Brigade during the night of the 8th. To assist the troops of the incoming division, instructions were issued that all machine guns and several 18-pounder field guns were to be left for their use. The relief was carried out successfully and by 10:00am on the 9th, the 49th Division had assumed command of the line. At 5:00pm, the Commander-in-Chief, Sir John French sent his congratulations to the division on its performance[218].

The division spent the next week, from the 11th to the 19th July, in reserve at Elverdinghe, where the troops cleaned, re-equipped and rested. On the 13th, the division was informed that it would transfer from VI Corps to VII Corps[219], effective from the 21st July. There followed, over the next few days, a series of visits to the division by Corps and Army Commanders, each accompanied by inspections of the troops. On the 14th, the Commander of the 2nd Army inspected the 10th Brigade while, on the 15th, the C. -in -C. carried out an inspection and passed on his gratitude for their recent efforts.

It was to be that the 4th Division was to leave Belgium and move south, to the Somme, to relieve the French 21st Division in the area of Vauchelles – Bertrancourt. In a move that was to occupy the next three days, the process of entraining began at Godewaerdsvelde and Cassel on the 21st and after a journey of about seven hours, the division marched to the area about Beauval, one and a half miles south of Doullens. Once ready, the troops and supporting arms then marched the two miles to the line Vauchelles – Louvencourt – Forceville – Bertrancourt, while the artillery remained about Thievres – Sarton[220].

The far right flank of the 4th Division sector lay at the Mill, in a swampy part of the River Ancre, due east of Hamel. It then passed north-west to trench 55, directly in front of the head of 'Y' Ravine, several hundred yards south of Beaumont Hamel and then continued north to a point 200 yards north of the Mailly Maillet - Serre Road, a front of nearly 5000 yards. The 10th Brigade was to assume responsibility for the right half of the line, from the Redan[221] to the Mill while the

---

[218] *During the day, news was received, with considerable elation, of the surrender of the German forces in South West Africa.*

[219] *VII Corps was, at this time, commanded by Major-General T. D'O. Snow, who had been the G.O.C. of the 4 Division at the time of its arrival in France in August 1914.*

[220] *It was about this time that the Guards Division was being formed in England. To assist in that process Lieutenant-Colonel Butler, of the Irish Guards, G.S.O.II to the division, was ordered back to the U.K. to join the new formation. Lieutenant-Colonel Butler had served in that post since the formation of the 4 Division in August 1914. He was replaced by Major Elles, the G.S.O. III, who was promoted to Lieutenant Colonel.*

[221] *The Redan was a strong point in the division line approximately 400 yards north of Beaumont Hamel. It was located directly opposite the German strong-point known as Ridge Redoubt and was separated from the main firing line by the crest of Hawthorn*

11th Brigade was to take over the left sector, as far as the Serre Road. Just after midnight on the night of the 24th, the 12th Brigade commenced the relief of the 63rd Regiment in the reserve trenches, about Auchonvillers[222]. When the brigade artillery relieved those of the French regiment, the gunners were ordered not to interfere with any of the original French gun emplacements.

An amusing incident occurred during the first day of the relief. To the right of the 12th Brigade stood the French 62nd Regiment, and the French Commandant paid a welcoming visit to the brigade headquarters. A part of the uniform of the Essex Regiment was an eagle, which commemorated the defeat of the French 6th Line Regiment and the capture of the Golden Eagle emblem at Salamanca, in July 1812[223] by the British 2/44th Regiment of Foot, later re-designated the 2nd Battalion, Essex Regiment. It was that same battalion that now relieved the successors of the French 6th Line Regiment, the 62nd Regiment. On hearing of the origins of the emblem, the Commandant immediately produced a pocket knife and removed a button from an officer's coat, stating that he wanted to keep it as a souvenir.

After having relieved the French 64th Regiment, the 10th Brigade discovered several mitrailleuse[224] detachments, of the 17th French Territorials, still occupying positions south of the Redan. French headquarters at Mailly Maillet was informed and arrangements made for their relief. On the 28th, the 8th Squadron, Royal Flying Corps, arrived at an aerodrome half a mile north-east of Marieux and fell under the command of the VII Corps for the purposes of artillery observation and reconnaissance. The Seaforth Highlanders received congratulations from the Commander-in-Chief, Sir John French, for their efforts in the attack of the 6th July.

During the 29th, the listening posts of the Seaforth's, holding positions about the Redan, discovered that German miners were at work only a little distance from their underground post and appeared to be making

---

Ridge. Because the strong points overlooked one another the area was subjected to intense mining by both British and German miners.

[222] *Auchonvillers lay immediately behind the main British line and acted as the main supply and communications centre for the following three years.*

[223] *The 62 Regiment was then known as the 6 Line Regiment*

[224] *French noun for machine gun.*

a transverse gallery under the British trenches[225]. It was determined that the enemy was mining at several different places and that the main gallery was at the same level of those of the Seaforth's trenches and only six feet away. Immediate arrangements were made to place two large charges, each of 1,000 pounds of guncotton, and several smaller charges in the event of quick action being required.

The night of the 29th was occupied with the relief of the French 62nd Regiment by the 11th Brigade while the whole line was being subjected to heavy enemy shelling, which resulted in the wounding of several men of the King's Own, 12th Brigade. Early in the evening of the 30th, the 10th Brigade front line was subjected to shelling at various times and, as it was necessary to gain information about the enemy, a patrol of the King's Own (12th Brigade) found a dummy fastened to the ground by wires. Having carefully cut the wires and, on examination, discovered that it contained two hand grenades with wires arranged to cause them to explode when pulled.

---

[225] *A transverse gallery was shaped like the head of a 'T'. A shaft would be driven from a selected position within the German trench line and then, when estimated to be under the opposing trenches, a gallery, branching left and right would be dug. The intention was to fill the transverse gallery with explosives and then tamp the main gallery with sandbags to prevent the explosion from penetrating back into the original trench.*

August - 1915

By the autumn of 1915, all hopes of the war concluding in the near future had faded away. From High Command to private soldier, there was recognition of the fact that 1915 was not to be the year in which victory would be won. The months between August and December of 1915 were considered a 'quiet' period for the division. The narrative of the following five months largely describes the daily routine and the dangers faced by the troops, interspersed with moments of short and sharp actions and sometimes, of disappointment. As winter drew closer, the weather slowly deteriorated, with regular heavy falls of rain and snow. Much time was spent digging and repairing trenches, carrying out reliefs and night patrols.

The German High Command was quite conscious of the fact that a British offensive would be in the offing in the spring of 1916 but, for the remainder of the year, any such action was precluded by the need to prepare for winter. In preparation for greater events, the front line divisions of both sides spent the last six months consolidating trench lines and supplementing artillery and air forces. Life in the trenches rapidly evolved into a defensive role, dominated by fire and counter-fire between the opposing artillery, largely directed at interfering with the work of the other.

The 1st of August was subjected to heavy rain and, in the early evening, the Seaforth Highlanders observed large bodies of German troops moving south, along Wagon Road towards Beaumont Hamel[226]. Reports from the French and the 152nd Brigade (51st Division) also stated that the enemy in front of Authuille, had cut their wire, an indication of a possible attack[227]. The accuracy of these reports raised suspicions with the headquarters of the 10th Brigade, which ordered patrols to investigate and report[228]. Little of value was discovered and the French were disregarded.

---

[226] *The road from Serre to Beaumont Hamel was referred to, on all British maps, as Wagon Road. It was the main supply route to the German front line and the centre of attention for the British artillery. It was to be a focal point for the 4th Division on the morning of the 1st July 1916.*

[227] *Authuille is situated 2000 yards south of Hamel and on the extreme right of the 10th Brigade line. The British front lay 700 yards east of the village, with the German line a further 100 yards to the east.*

[228] *By midday of the 3ʳ, there had been some discussion between the Staff Officers and brigade headquarters as to the reports, which had been received the previous day, regarding the movement of troops at Authuille. The 10ᵗ Brigade stated that it was impos-*

In the early hour of the morning of the 2nd, men of the 12th Brigade detected considerable troop movements in Beaumont Hamel between and suspected that a relief was taking place. Sounds of troop movements could also be heard in Serre, on the left flank of the division but, by morning, all was quiet, albeit with sporadic shelling. During the morning corps headquarters issued warnings to the 4th Division that it may expect a raid by German infantry on their trenches in order to establish the identity of the force in front of them. Being aware that raids of this nature had been carried out in this area, when occupied by the French, all troops on the move were instructed to be properly armed and equipped for immediate action.

Previously held suspicions that the Germans were continuing to mine in the region of the Redan were confirmed by listening posts and, in readiness, explosive charges were prepared with the intention of destroying the tunnel when required. Neither raid nor mine explosion was experienced and the remainder of the month was spent quietly, with only the occasional shelling and the perpetual reliefs. In an effort to establish the technologies used by the Germans, VII Corps put out calls for unexploded gas shells so that experts could examine them. The artillery was also busy as it participated in shelling various targets and carrying out registration shoots on a variety of locations for future reference.

From time to time suspicions had been raised about the presence of possible enemy observation posts. The Seaforth Highlanders had noted a mysterious hay cart, which they assumed was a camouflaged vehicle, being seen at various places and, soon after its appearance, a field gun would commence firing from that direction. Little was proven as to the role the hay cart played in any of the artillery actions but the cart soon disappeared.

The period of quiet was used as an opportunity to train troops in the use of new weapons and to practice new tactics, which had been learnt from the bitter lessons of previous battles. The Mills bomb was a relatively new introduction to the soldier's armoury and lessons in its proper use were initiated, but not without difficulties. During the training courses, there occurred several instances of premature explosion, one of which wounded Captain Massey Westrop of the division

---

sible for any troops, German or British, to have been there. However, the three officers who had made the initial report restated having seen German troops in the area. Further investigations by patrols of the 11· Brigade, which had been out during the night, stated that the wire in front of the German lines was uncut and had, in fact, been strengthened.

Cyclist Company and twelve men of the Royal Dublin Fusiliers and the constant casualty rate caused the cessation of all practice. The Lewis gun had had also reached the division and training was provided for dedicated gun teams.

The front line troops were subjected to heavy sniping on occasions, although the response from those affected was swift and accurate. There were times that the sniping was such that the artillery was asked to intervene. During the 2nd August, the 128th Battery laid fire on one of the positions from which sniping was heaviest and managed to bring the practice to a halt.

Temporary relief from the tedium of trench life was delivered on the 8th, when it was announced that an increase of the allotment for leave to sixty officers and men was then effective. Leave was generally granted for five days and many were able to return to the U.K. to see the friends and family that they had last seen in August 1914, twelve months before. Some were granted leave of only a few days, allowing them to visit Paris, or spend time in Amiens, a communications and rest centre.

The 4th Division, like many other experienced divisions, spent considerable time providing instruction to units of the new divisions as they arrived from the United Kingdom. On the 9th, two companies of the Royal Irish Rifles were attached to the 11th Brigade and entered the trenches for the first time. One company was attached to the East Lancashires and the other to the Somerset Light Infantry and, for many, the introduction to trench life was a rude awakening as the heavens opened and caused considerable damage to the trenches through flooding. The intensity of the rain made the conduct of reliefs and the carrying of supplies extremely difficult, but did not prevent the necessary patrolling, during which a private of the 119th Regiment was captured[229].

Early in the morning of the 13th, a patrol of one officer and two N.C.O.'s from 'C' Company, 1st Royal Irish Fusiliers was surprised by an eight man German patrol. The action resulted in all three being wounded, while the officer and one of the N.C.O.'s were missing[230].

---

[229] The 119 Regiment was a part of the German 51st Division, which had fought against the 4th Division in front of Ploegsteert Wood in October and November 1914 during the Battle of Messines.

[230] For details of this action, see Appendix V 'Report of Patrol Action, 13 August 1915'. Lieutenant Hector Adolphus Hugh Warnock, aged 22, the patrol leader was killed in this action and is buried in the Achiet-Le-Grand cemetery extension. He was a member of the 4 Battalion, Royal Irish Fusiliers but had been attached to the 1 Battalion at the time of the action. There is no evidence of Corporal Stevenson or Corporal Murray, the

The officer commanding the patrol, Lieutenant Warnock, was seen to shoot one of the enemy and Corporal Murray shot two others. The third N.C.O., Corporal Stevenson, was last seen charging the enemy patrol. He failed to return. The remainder of the enemy patrol then approached the lines of the Irish Fusiliers and fired into the trench, which resulted in the wounding of one man. The fire was returned and two of that patrol were seen to be hit. Earlier that evening men of the Royal Dublin Fusiliers had heard shouting from the German trenches saying, "Hello the Dublin's, send over three N.C.O.'s, we want to give ourselves up". That sort of provocation was generally met with rifle fire.

On the 16th, VII Corps advised all Divisions that two men dressed in British and French uniforms had entered the X Corps area making enquiries about the defences. Upon enquiry as to their identity, it was noted that the two had disappeared and orders were issued that anyone not able to produce significant identity should be arrested. On the same day, the Germans posted a notice above their trenches in front of the 4th Division stating, "It is untrue that we kill blessed men and prisoners."

Light shelling of the back areas was experienced throughout the month, with Auchonvillers and Mailly Maillet being prime targets. The bombardment of the trenches was constant and an incident of the Dublin Fusiliers being shelled from several heavy trench mortars was a matter of course in daily events. The mortar fire 'blew in' about fifteen yards of the parapet and buried two men, both eventually being recovered and a third man, reported missing, was also assumed to have been buried. Although the constant artillery fire and sniping aggravated life for those in the trenches, the greatest enemy was the heavy rain, which fell periodically, flooding trenches and causing great difficulties with communications, food and ammunition supply and was a cause of constant repairs.

A severe shortage of artillery ammunition had existed since the declaration of war and on the afternoon of the 17th, the president and two delegates of the Federation of Trade Unions were escorted around the lines of the 10th Brigade to examine the effects of the shelling. During the visit, the support trenches near Hamel, on the right sector of the division front, were heavily shelled with high explosive and the counter-fire by both sides continued without abate. In an effort to conserve the remaining supplies, orders were issued on the 20th that no 13pdr. high explosive ammunition was to be used except in the case of emergency and not at all by the anti-aircraft guns.

---

remaining two members of the patrol, having been killed during the war. Extracted from the Commonwealth War Graves Commission web site.

During the night of 22ⁿᵈ, the 4ᵗʰ Division extended to the left and took over trenches held by two battalions of the 48ᵗʰ Division. When completed, the Division held a line of 6,500 yards, with two brigades in the firing line and one in reserve. During that same night, a patrol of the Seaforth Highlanders encountered a German covering party that was protecting a working party in front of their lines. After an exchange of rifle fire the patrol withdrew without having suffered any casualties. It was also discovered that the Germans were using a new 4" trench mortar, which they fired against the 10ᵗʰ Brigade with great effect. The projectile was about one foot long and weighed approximately five pounds, but produced an explosion out of all proportion to its size.

As well as relieving elements of the 48ᵗʰ Division, arrangements had been made for the 12ᵗʰ Brigade to relieve two battalions of the 143ʳᵈ Brigade (51ˢᵗ Division) on the immediate right of the 4ᵗʰ Division. The 2nd Essex Battalion completed that relief during the night of the 24ᵗʰ, resulting in the line being extended to approximately 8,500 yards. On the 26ᵗʰ, the division celebrated the anniversary of its first action at Haucourt and Ligny, during the battle of Le Cateau, twelve months before, but few of the original men of the division were left to enjoy the celebration.

Much effort was needed to consolidate the trenches taken over from the 143ʳᵈ Brigade, many of were old French and German trenches. On the 27ᵗʰ, units of the 37ᵗʰ Division were attached to the 4ᵗʰ for instruction in trench warfare and remained with the division until the 5ᵗʰ September. Little action was recorded for the remainder of the month apart from occasional shelling of the trenches. Casualties for the month of August totalled two hundred and sixty officers and men killed, wounded and missing.

Patrolling at night was always a test of an individual's nerve and the nocturnal activities of both sides led to regular contacts. An example of the trials faced by the officer and his men was clearly demonstrated on the night of the 31ˢᵗ August when a patrol of the Hampshire Regiment attempted a reconnaissance of the Mound[231]. After setting out from the starting point, the patrol encountered and engaged a German patrol and was forced to retire in the direction of the British line. While doing so, a second German patrol was sighted on their flank and, realising that they were outnumbered, withdrew quietly and reached the front line without casualty.

---

[231] The Mound was, as the name implies, was a small piece of high ground, which permitted observation over both trench lines. It was located in No Man's Land, on the far left of division line, in front of Luke Copse.

September - 1915

September continued in the same manner as August and consisted mainly of artillery exchanges in counter-battery and harassing fire, while the troops undertook a cycle of front line service and relief and working parties spent much of their time consolidating trench lines, wiring and constructing dugouts. Confronting the division were a number of German strong points, each of which necessitated the constant attention of the artillery while those positions along the British front line, considered by the Germans as being a threat or abnormally exposed, received the attentions of the enemy guns.

Separate incidents serve to demonstrate what constituted 'normal' nocturnal activities. The machine guns and Lewis guns of the 11th Brigade engaged a German patrol near the railway line, south of Hamel and forced it to withdraw, having inflicted several casualties. At the same time working parties of the 11th Brigade were harassed continually by German artillery, machine-gun and rifle fire and at point 371, near the area known as Mary Redan, about 300 yards south of Y Ravine, German and British working parties exchanged rifle fire.

Night patrolling was not the only activity to try the nerves. During August, there had been some alarm, and considerable discussion, when it was discovered that the enemy had undertaken mining operation at Point 335, midway between Hawthorn Redoubt and the Quadrilateral, north of Beaumont Hamel. Listening posts of the 12th Brigade had detected the sound of underground digging and drawn conclusions as to the extent and distance to which the mine galleries had reached.

Guided by the Royal Engineers and mining experts, experienced miners, drafted from within the ranks, dug a mine, which led to a 'T' head gallery from which a series of four further shafts were then driven forward. The forward galleries were then prepared with explosive charges, consisting of two 1000lb charges of ammonal and several smaller charges. Although one of the smaller charges failed to detonate, the explosion, fired at 3:50am on the 1st September, totally destroyed the main gallery of the German works and travelled along the access tunnel with such force that flames were observed in the German trenches.

So incensed were the enemy that the opposing artillery immediately retaliated by firing thirty rounds of 4.2" and 6" shells at the brigade trenches. The shelling continued throughout the day with the more than 100 artillery and mortar shells being fired at the 12th Brigade. As the resultant crater was within bombing distance of both lines, it remained unmanned by either side. The war diary of the 12th Brigades records for this date that the Germans were '*very irritated*'.

Occasionally events took place that could not immediately be explained. At 6:35pm in the evening, a string of 30-40 flares rose from the German line in perfect formation, although no explosion was heard when they were launched. On reaching a height of about 100 feet, they all went out and a column of white smoke was observed 30-40 feet from the same point. It was assumed that the flares had been secured to a line and launched by a rocket.

The village of Hamel was located on the extreme southern end of the division line and, at the beginning of September, was held by the 11th Brigade. On the 2nd, the trenches in and about Hamel were shelled by enemy 5.9" howitzers and a heavy trench mortar, the bulk of which was directed upon the railway signal box south of the village, then being used as a British artillery observation post. By way of retaliation, the division artillery concentrated on Point 379, a German trench system just north of Hamel with field guns and howitzers, a duel that lasted well into the afternoon. As evening approached, the howitzers changed targets and maintained a steady and accurate fire on Point 382, a mill east of Hamel.

The trench mortars of the 11th Brigade continued the bombardment into the morning of the next day, firing on a German supply dump near the railway. Fourteen light and heavy bombs were fired and, although two failed to explode, those that did caused considerable damage. Added to the constant shelling was the perpetual sniping fire, which came from trees in front of the brigade. Due to the difficulty in establishing the exact whereabouts of the snipers, the artillery was called to fire shrapnel into the area, immediately suppressing the sniping.

That night, the 2nd September, the 10th Brigade relieved the 12th Brigade[232] under heavy artillery fire as the enemy observers had noticed the movement of the Seaforth Highlanders. Upon completion, the entire brigade line was subjected to heavy sniper fire in which the German artillery also participated, three shells exploding in the trenches held by the Seaforth's, without causing casualties. The trenches about Lasigny Farm were also subjected to intermittent shelling and the occasional shell was fired on Auchonvillers.

---

[232] *The 12 Brigade held a broader front than the 11 Brigade and required relief on a brigade scale. The 11 Brigade did not require all battalions in the line simultaneously and conducted inter-battalion reliefs.*

The 12th Brigade went into rest billets where it formed a bombing school with about sixty men. The school was deemed so effective that it continued for the remainder of the time that the division remained in that part of the sector and was continued by the other brigades, as their time for relief arrived. The success of the bombing school led to the formation of other training facilities and during the ensuing months, each was improved to provide training for signals, machine guns, gas warfare, and for practicing methods of attack.

The two front line brigades were kept fully occupied. During the night of the 3rd, the 11th Brigade experimented with signal rockets, which made the German observers nervous, causing them to fire large numbers of their own flares. The snipers in the front line took advantage of the light offered by the flares and the results were often signalled by the enemy. The constant rain, which turned the shell torn ground into a morass of water filled craters and ankle deep mud, seriously hampered patrols. Those patrols that managed to enter No-Man's Land found the German lines relatively quiet, although enemy snipers, to the right of the Warwicks, remained active.

Conversations across No Man's Land between the troops of the opposing forces continued. An officer of the Warwickshire's heard a German call from his trench "We are Saxons and you are Anglo-Saxons. What are we fighting one another for?" The voice from the German line also referred to the British troops as the King's, indicating that the enemy was not aware that the Warwicks had relieved the King's Own. The reply was a single rifle shot.

In the locality of 'Y' Ravine, enemy working parties, busy strengthening and wiring the defences, had placed a dummy on their parapet. To prevent work in that area and, possibly to prove their marksmanship, the artillery knocked off the dummy and damaged the trench with a single shot[233]. The Seaforth Highlanders, located on the extreme left of the division, in front of Serre, had noted several enemy parties working on saps. One was dispersed with rifle fire and a second fired on by the division howitzers and caused considerable damage with several direct hits.

---

[233] *"Y" Ravine is a gully, which leads down a hill west of Beaumont Hamel and was large enough to provide a measure of protection for the occupying German troops from direct observation. The ravine was quite large and housed several hundred troops as well as providing a line of communication with the various headquarters in the village. Such was the importance of the ravine that the German defenders applied considerable effort in its defence. The nature of the defence was to prove a barrier to the 29 Division in its attack on the 1 July 1916 and to the 51 Highland Division in the following September. It is now a part of the Canadian Memorial Park.*

The retaliation by the German artillery also inflicted much damage on the parapets of the trenches held by the Seaforth's.

The nocturnal activities of both sides continued unabated, with exchanges of fire between patrols, working parties and the occasional shelling. The war diaries of the battalions constantly refer to the number of patrols carried out and the fact that not all patrols engaged the enemy. Many were very quiet occasions, only with statements about the condition of the enemy wire and the hearing of enemy working parties.

On the 4th, the headquarters of the 112th Brigade (37th Division) and the 8th East Lancashires (112th Brigade) departed from the 12th Brigade, to whom they had been attached for instruction. There existed, among the officers of the 12th Brigade, the sentiment that the 8th Lancashires had not reached the standard that would be required of it when engaged with the enemy.

Although the following week featured little, apart from the usual shelling, sniping, patrolling and trench work, major changes took place in the command of the 4th Division. The G.O.C. of the division, Sir H.F.M. Wilson K.C.B. was given command of the XI Corps and Brigadier-General Anley, O.C. 12th Brigade, assumed temporary command of the division[234] while awaiting the assignation of a permanent commander. While the changes in command were taking place, the 11th Brigade responded to an earlier request from VII Corps headquarters for suggestions for an attack. It proposed that they should attack the German communication trenches, which supplied the fortified position of Beaumont Hamel.

It was suggested that the attack should extend from Point 369, south of 'Y' Ravine, to Point 362, which intersected the southern face of 'Y' Ravine, about half way along its length. The proposed line covered the edge of the Ravine to the crest of the spur to the south, a distance of about 400 yards. The reasons for the attack was given as offering the advantage of holding the ridge which would offer command of the entire length of the ravine and enable enfilading fire on Beaumont Hamel. It was proposed that the attack could proceed down the slope and the ravine towards the village with the intention of taking the second and

---

[234]At the time of appointment, Major-General Wilson's command was temporary but his promotion to Lieutenant-General and the appointment to the XII Corps was confirmed on the 28 October. The command of the 4 Division then passed to Major-General Hon. W. Lambton C.V.O., C.B., C.M.G., and D.S.O.

third line of trenches, but should stop short of the village, and the heavy defences within[235].

The plan called for the artillery to destroy the lines of wire in front of each trench line to permit the advance to capture all three lines. During the bombardment, it was expected that, because of the proximity of the three lines, the artillery would be able to shell all three as a singles operation. It was suggested that the attack be made on a three-battalion front with two battalions in reserve while the attack should be accompanied by 15–18 bombing parties, to be divided between the communications trenches.

It was also foreseen that the attacking brigade would need to be relieved by a fresh brigade in order to consolidate the new lines and dig five communications trenches from the existing British line, to join up with the captured trenches. The difficulty, which was readily recognised, lay in the distance that the new trenches would have to be dug. It was also understood that the attack and the later consolidation would be observed from the direction of the Thiepval ridge, then in German hands, which overlooked the whole area.

While the plan was being considered, life pursued the normal routine. A patrol of one officer and two men of the Dublin Fusiliers encountered a twenty man German patrol during the night of the 7th and, waiting until the enemy was only twenty yards away, opened fire, with two of the enemy seen to fall. The patrol then withdrew with one of their number wounded. A later patrol, attempting to identify the opposing division, found blood at the scene but no sign of the enemy.

During the early hours of the 10th, the 10th Brigade was relieved from the trenches and the incoming 12th Brigade was issued with secret instructions to make such preparations as to give the German the impression that an attack was to be launched from their front. Over the course of the next four nights dummy assembly trenches were dug east of Lasigny Farm and to the north of Tenderloin Street. Saps were also commenced at regular intervals along the front line. In the midst of this work, the arrival of the 12th Cheshire Regiment (66th Brigade, 22nd Division) for training also meant those units of the 12th Brigade were in-

---

[235] *The slope referred to is a steep hill, at the base of which lies Beaumont Hamel. It was down that same slope that the 2 South Wales Borders, 2 Royal Fusiliers, 1 Border Regiment and the 1 Newfoundland Regiment (86 Brigade, 29 Division) advanced to their fete on the 1 July 1916, during the British offensive, referred to as the Battle of Albert.*

volved in giving instruction. The increased activity did not interfere with normal operations, the patrols continued each night and the Germans working parties offered regular targets for the machine gun and artillery fire.

The snipers of the 11th Brigade devoted great attention to the opposing enemy snipers and did much to diminish the harassing fire. The snipers then turned their attention to the German second line, bringing all movement to a halt. In an effort to beat down the fire, the enemy traversed machine-gun fire along the front line and, on the night of the 11th, subjected the lines of communications, behind the division front, to artillery fire for an hour and a half.

That shelling seriously disrupted the movement of supplies and troops to and from the front. That same night two Alsatian deserters surrendered to a patrol of the Hampshire's and, when interrogated, stated that an attack on the 4th Division line, in the neighbourhood of Serre, was planned for the 15th. All brigades were warned against a possible assault and in anticipation, two Lewis guns of the 12th Cheshire's were placed at Lasigny Farm.

The 15th came and went without any sign of an attack but, the King's Own, in the trenches near Serre, reported the sounds of mining. An officer of the engineers was sent to the area and he spent considerable time at the listening posts but could not verify any such activity. The following day, the 12th Brigade was relieved by the 10th, in the course of normal rotation, and although the 12th Brigade was considered 'at rest', it was required to supply one thousand, six hundred men for working parties.

Patrolling by both sides was aggressive, particularly on the left of the division front. During the night of the 19th, a German patrol approached the trenches of the Seaforth Highlanders and attacked with rifle fire and bombs. Although the snipers of the battalion drove the attacking party back it was not before two of the Seaforth's had been wounded. During the course of the action, the enemy patrol was seen to accidentally shoot one of its own. A second enemy patrol also bombed a sap occupied by men of the Dublin Fusiliers, but they too were driven back by rifle fire and, judging by the shouting, suffered casualties. A patrol of the Dublin's, having encountered an enemy patrol of about ten men, and forced the enemy to withdraw after throwing two grenades.

Tensions along the whole front line steadily increased and, in order to deliver as much damage upon the opposition as possible, the division artillery adopted a more offensive attitude, bombarding those villages behind the enemy lines, which were acting as rest areas and centres of communication[236]. It was with some amusement that a haystack, located northeast of Auchonvillers, and became a focal point for the German artillery.

Although it was not being used as a British artillery observation point, the enemy paid particular attention to it and it was only with the eighteenth round that it was hit and it was the twenty-sixth round that set it on fire. It had been noticed during the day that a board had been placed near their front line and later that night a patrol of the Dublin's went out to recover it. I doing so, a bell rang and the defenders threw four grenades, albeit without causing casualties.

It was time to learn something of the enemy defensive preparations and during the night of the 24th, every effort was made to keep the gaps in the German wire open with the artillery, machine-gun fire and bombing parties. Upon examination by patrols, it was realised that the gaps that had been cut in the wire were not good and that some of the wire on the inner side of the wire entanglements remained uncut and would present an obstacle to advancing troops.

The Essex Regiment also attempted to create an impression of an impending attack. Two large gaps were cut in the wire in front of the battalion, a normal precursor to an attack, and the artillery carried out the a wire cutting exercise in front of 'Y' Ravine but, with little success. The response from the German artillery was negligible.

Attempts were also made by patrols and artillery to draw enemy fire but those efforts also proved inconclusive. While the Germans made no real effort to respond, their attempts to repair the damage to the wire were met by heavy machine-gun and rifle fire. Over a period of several days and nights attempts were made to provoke the Germans but they would not be drawn into exposing their positions, although patrols could hear them talking in their trenches.

Some times the fighting took on a very personal character. An incident took place at the Mill, just east of Hamel when a patrol consisting of a Sergeant Redmayne and two Lance Corporals, Arrowsmith and Brown,

---

[236] *Lord Kitchener arrived behind the lines of the 4 Division on the 21 and inspected the 1 Hampshire Regiment of the 11 Brigade, and the 2 Essex of the 12 Brigade.*

of the 1st East Lancashire Regiment, who were near the Mill, encountered a lone German soldier. The War Diary for the 23rd September quotes: *"the German was only 6' from Sergeant Redmayne and was first to fire. The Sergeant immediately fired causing the Bosche a severe wound in the arm. The German then fired again missing the Sergeant by inches. They closed and the prisoner was brought in."*

That action was carried out in broad daylight and in full view of the enemy. When the prisoner was finally taken into the British line it was determined that he was in the 99th Zabern Regiment. That capture, seen by all, resulted in heavy exchanges of artillery fire in retaliation[237]. The last few days of the month passed quietly with only the normal shelling and sniping. Throughout September, the division had suffered casualties of one officer, thirty eight other ranks killed, and seven officers and one hundred and ninety seven other ranks wounded.

---

[237] *Sergeant Miles Benjamin Redmayne, 18575, was killed in the attack of the 1· July 1916. He has no known grave and is remembered on the Thiepval Memorial.*

October - 1915

The transition from September to October was noticeably unspectacular, notable only for units of the various new battalions, accompanied by their headquarters, being regularly attached to the three brigades of the division for a period of training. Because the purpose of the training was to teach officers and ranks alike, the effects of trench life, the visitors became active members of the division and undertook the responsibilities that would be expected of them once they had returned to their own division. The enemy was ever active and the duties of patrolling, digging, and reliefs were an endless part of daily life.

As winter approached, the weather deteriorated and produced conditions that were to become synonymous with the Somme. Rain and mist were reminiscent of the winter period of 1914 with flooded trenches, disease, and periods of bitterly cold weather. Artillery bombardments, sniping, patrolling and sickness all inflicted upon the ranks and foot inspections become a part of the normal routine in an attempt at preventing trench-foot. So it was to be for the next four months. In order to avoid the description of repetitive detail the following narrative will focus on highlighting those incidents, which best describe the winter months of 1915.

In keeping with the practice of new units being attached to the division, the 1/1st London Field Artillery Brigade (36th Division) arrived on the 9th October, attached to the very experienced 29th Field Artillery Brigade for instruction. The brigade went into action immediately and played an important part in the artillery actions in the following week. The following day the 8th and 9th Royal Irish Rifles, 107th Brigade (36th Division) were attached to the 11th and 12th Brigades respectively.

The fire and counter fire of the artillery and trench mortars continued constantly throughout the month, gradually growing in intensity. On the 11th, whilst the 10th Brigade was in reserve, the first large party departed for leave to the United Kingdom[238]. On the 16th, Rifleman Exgar of the 8th Royal Irish Rifles was reported as "mysteriously disappeared" and rumour had it that he might have been a spy. Three nights later, a lone German got into one of the 10th Brigade trenches, killed one man

---

[238] *Usually the leave period was for five days. In this period, the soldier would need to find transport to Calais and travel to Dover. He would then have to make his way home, anywhere in the U.K., and repeat the journey back to his unit. Returning late could often result in being charged.*

and wounded a further two, before making his escape. The only trace of his presence was his cap, which he had left behind.

At 5:40am on the 22nd, a small mine was fired by the enemy in front of the Redan and, although little damage was done and no casualties were reported, the artillery retaliated with a heavy shelling of the German trenches. Two days later, a patrol of the South Lancashires encountered a German patrol in the early hours of the morning and, after a quick and violent action, both patrols retired. Because of the nature of these actions, it was difficult to identify those who were killed, missing, or injured and it was later discovered that the officer commanding the patrol was missing.

His Majesty, King George V, French President Poincare and Lieutenant, HRH, The Prince of Wales inspected the 10th Brigade in the grounds of the Chateau at Acheux on the 25th in bitterly cold weather. The decision was made that, to further assist with the training of the 36th Division, the 12th Brigade should be temporarily attached to that division and that the 107th Brigade, of that division, should join the 4th Division. The exchange of units took affect on the 4th of November.

November - 1915

November was little different to the previous two months, with the overall situation being generally quiet, interrupted only by the intermittent shelling. The first two weeks produced heavy rain, which compounded the already abominable conditions in the trenches and dugouts and making roads almost impassable.

On the 4th, the 12th Brigade marched to the 36th Division area. It left Varennes at 9:00am and marched via Toutencourt, Merisart, and arrived at Rubempré and Septonville at about 12:15pm, where they went into billets for the night. The following day, the 5th, Brigade Headquarters signal section and the 82nd Trench Mortar Battery marched via Talmas to Canaples, while the Essex and King's Own proceeded to Beavaz and St. Leger, where they fell under the command of the 109th and 108th Brigades respectively. The 1/5th South Lancashire Regiment, 2nd Lancashire Fusiliers, and the 10th Field Ambulance followed them, on the same day.

To replace them, the 11th and 14th Royal Irish Rifles (36th Division) joined the 4th Division for instruction and, by the 6th November, the remaining battalions, the 10th and 15th Royal Irish Rifles, of the 107th Brigade, had assumed positions in the trenches with the 11th Brigade. The process of re-arranging the units was undertaken in periods of heavy shelling. The division artillery consistently turned its attention on Beaumont Hamel, Beaucort, Serre, and Grandcourt while the Germans concentrated equally on Mailly Maillet, Auchonvillers and Englebelmer, all being important communications centres for reliefs and supplies

Both sides were heavily involved in mining, and on the 10th, the 2nd Royal Inniskilling Fusiliers reported the sounds of digging under trench 54, 400 yards west of the head of 'Y' Ravine and precautions were taken in the event of the mine being exploded. On the 15th of November, the whole area was subjected to heavy snowfalls, followed by bright sunlight, only top have the weather turn bad, the following day, to heavy rain and two downfalls of snow. Amidst the rain and snow, the artillery exchanges continued, causing considerable damage to trenches and communications.

The last ten days of November were punctuated with close quarter patrol engagements, especially in the area of the Redan. A patrol of the Royal Irish Rifles met a strong German patrol on the night of the 19th. The officer commanding the patrol, a Lieutenant Shillington, was wounded and the remainder, due to their inferiority in numbers, withdrew. A later patrol went out but could find no sign of the officer. Ten days later a note was found tied to a bush in No-Man's Land, having been left by a German patrol, which read *"Lieut. Shillington prisoner and in good health"*.

Towards the end of the month the 36th Division assumed responsibility for the northern sector of the 4th Division line while the southern sector was temporarily taken over by the 48th Division, thus allowing the 4th Division to retire completely from the line for a short but well deserved rest. The month ended on a familiar note, considerable shelling, and consistent rain. The rain had been so consistent that the movement of the ground caused land slips in the area of the Redan causing extensive damage to the trenches, dugouts and telephone wires, half filling the trenches with water and mud.

December - 1915

The ground conditions were appalling and, as the opportunity for major offensives had passed, neither side exercised any real offensive initiative. Both sides faced each other in passive aggression and attention turned to the preparation of trenches and communications for the cold, wet months, which lay ahead. The prospect of the troops having to live in entrenched position on a largely stagnant front, caused much time and energy to be applied to the installation of overhead cover in sections of the trenches and ensuring that protection was available to those troops in billets. The building up of the armies for the coming of a spring offensive progressed steadily with the arrival of the Territorial divisions and the training of the new troops took considerable effort, as did the accumulation of artillery ammunition and the guns.

Offensive activity on the 4th Division front now took the form of artillery exchanges and sniping and, during the first few days, various parts of the frontline were subjected to considerable German trench mortar fire. During the artillery exchanges, weaknesses in the fuses used in the 18-pounder ammunition were discovered. The introduction of the Graze 100 fuse brought with it an unpredictability of performance and the gunners experienced several occasions when the shell would prematurely explode in the barrel of the gun. In the first two weeks of December two guns were destroyed in this manner, when, as much as three feet of the barrels were blown off, wounding several gunners. Quite often the shell would fail to explode on impact and much of the effectiveness of the artillery bombardment was lost.

Notwithstanding the problems with the ammunition, the combined guns of the 4th and 51st Divisions undertook a bombardment of Thiepval on the 7th, delivered with great accuracy. The German artillery retaliated by firing on the trenches and artillery positions of both divisions, for the rest of the day. The exchanges continued into the 8th, as the guns of the division turned their attention upon the opposing trenches, inflicting considerable damage. Aircraft of both sides were also active, with artillery observation and the occasional bombing of trenches and rear areas. On the 6th, a British and German plane were seen to fall behind the German lines, each after executing damage upon the other.

An example of the strain experienced by all fighting troops in this kind of warfare was clearly displayed on the 11th when, at 1:00am, a German soldier was seen inside the wire entanglements in front of the trenches of the 10th Brigade. He was called on three times to surrender but failed to do so and was shot by one of the defenders. When his body was re-covered, it was found that he was a member of the 66th Regiment and was not wearing any equipment. Sniping on both sides continued al-most relentlessly and German soldiers, seen walking along the parapet of their trenches near the Redan, caused by the constant flooding, were regular targets. Snipers of the 10th Brigade shot most of them and the artillery and machine-gun ensured that no one could leave their trenches. This was a period of extreme difficulty for the troops in the front line.

The 12th Brigade was busy training the battalions of the 36th Division in the rear areas. Instruction focused largely on the use of the tube hel-met[239], formations of bombing parties and practising rapid fire. Corps, division and brigade commanders attended a demonstration of wire cutting with bullets by members of the Hampshire Regiment[240] and on the 10th December, the 11th and 14th Battalions of the Royal Irish Rifles were withdrawn and returned to the 109th Brigade. The Essex Regiment and 2nd Lancashire Fusiliers returned from the 108th Brigade and re-joined the 12th Brigade, while the 82nd Trench Mortar Battery departed from the 36th Division and was temporarily attached to the 48th Divi-sion. In freezing conditions a battalion of the 30th Division, was at-tached for its introduction to trench warfare.

The enemy had continued their subterranean activities and, at 7:00am on the 21st, they fired a mine in front of the Redan. Although the ex-plosion blew in No. 2 Gallery of the opposing British mine, it caused very little other damage and no casualties were incurred, but created an atmosphere of 'not knowing where the next one was'. One of the changes that came into effect a few days before Christmas was the for-mation of the Brigade machine-gun companies as a result of the lessons learned in previous actions.

Unlike the Christmas of the 1914, there was no unofficial truce or frat-ernisation between the opposing troops, as orders had been issued promising severe punishment for any act of collaboration. Thus, the

---

[239] *The Tube Helmet was a gas helmet consisting of a canvas hood that fitted over the head and tucked under the collar. A tube in front of the mouth facilitated breathing and talc lenses provided partial visibility. Most troops found these very uncomfortable and hot.*

[240] *The process involved a wire cutter being fitted to the rifle, which, theoretically, placed the wire across the muzzle, the objective being to have the bullet cut the wire. The results were not very promising and several of the wire cutters broke under the concussion and many others simply fell off.*

fighting carried on, although Christmas day passed without incident. As an indication of the worst kind of enemy that the troops had to face lies in the casualty figures for the 10th Brigade for the month of December. Of the five hundred and twenty six all ranks declared as casualties, fifty-eight were reported killed, wounded, and missing due to enemy action. The balance were victims of the climate, most being cases of trench foot[241].

[241] *Trench-foot was a very painful circulatory complaint of the feet and legs caused by extended period of exposure to water and mud. In weather conditions typical of the end of 1914 and 1915, the troops regularly had to stand in mud and water, often near freezing, for extended periods of time. The feet would remain constantly wet, leading to some serious cases of gangrene, occasionally resulting in amputation.*

1916 - Lessons Applied

January – 1916

By January 1916, the 4th Division had been serving in France for sixteen months. It had engaged in all major engagements and was, at the beginning of the month, in the relatively quiet Somme area, holding the line from Authuille, on the eastern bank of the Ancre River, to a point midway between Serre and Hebuterne. The division was disposed such that the 11th Brigade was holding the area between Authuille and the Redan whilst the 107th Brigade continued the line to the Serre - Mailly Maillet road and the 10th Brigade then extended the line as far as the Puisieux Road. Incorporated into the British line, in that section just north of Serre, stood four wooded Copses, appropriately named Mathew, Mark, Luke, and John. The area in which those woods stood was to become the centre of attention for both sides and the tenacity with which that part of the line was defended, by both side, was to increase over the forthcoming six months.

New Years day was subjected to constant rain that saturated every aspect of life and the artillery exchanges ploughed the terrain into a bog and produced a steady flow of casualties. In parts of the line, the German and British trenches were located within mining distance of each other, especially true in the area of the Redan Ridge[242]. The digging of mines under the trench lines of the opposing armies was continuous and in an effort to destroy British mining activity, German engineers fired a camoflet[243] under the Redan on the first day of the month, but failed to inflict the desired damage. The line was also subjected to sudden periods of shelling, countered by bombardments of the German front line by the division guns.

The artillery exchanges were perpetual, sometimes without serious effect, and at other times with devastating results. While the rain slowly

---

[242] *The Redan Ridge was a spur of the main Hawthorne ridge, which protruded into the German area of occupation in the region almost midway between Beaumont Hamel and Serre. Because the ridge offered advantages of observation, it was heavily defended. British and German alike subjected the area to constant mining. Because of the hilly nature of the local geography, mining activities extended as far as the lines in front of Serre and, to a lesser degree, near Hamel.*

[243] *A camoflet was the name given to a small charge of explosives used to damage an opponents' mine gallery.*

turned the ground into slush, the snipers of both sides were very active and wrought heavy casualties. On the morning of the 4th, the German artillery bombarded Hamel with an estimated two thousand 5.9" and 4.2" howitzer shells over a period of five hours, which resulted in the death of six and the wounding of sixteen. The village was destroyed, it's passing marked only by small heaps of rubble.

Having visited devastation upon the village, the guns then lifted, to concentrate on trenches to the north of the village. As the barrage rolled on, intense enemy rifle fire was opened upon the trenches north of Hamel and was only quelled when the division artillery retaliated by shelling the German front line. The British guns also fired on St. Pierre Divion, behind the German lines, where much of the enemy artillery was located, ultimately suppressing the fire.

The bombardment had caused considerable damage to the northern trenches, particularly trenches 38 and 39 and resulted in the deaths of nine men and the wounding of thirteen. In retaliation the division artillery and the Heavy Artillery Group concentrated on Beaucourt, St. Pierre Divion, and the German trenches, during the course of the following day. The German guns again retaliated by turning their attention on Hamel and Mesnil. The exchanges continued for the next few days, and on many occasions, were supplemented by trench mortar attacks against opposing trenches and villages.

The fighting along the whole front constituted an amalgam of small and desperately fought contacts with the enemy[244]. Offensive mining continued throughout, each side watching the other for signs that might reveal the entrances to the mines. At the end of the first week, a considerable number of German troops were observed carrying heavy timbers, suitable for mining, near the Mound, in front of Luke Copse. The following day sounds of mining were heard in the area about Mathew Copse, 100 yards to the south[245] of Luke.

The troops of both sides were aggressive and during the evening of the 7th, a working party of the 10th Brigade, wiring in front of the firing line, were subjected to rifle and machine-gun fire. In order to get to

---

[244] For a copy of an Intelligence report on one of the patrol actions, see Appendix VI, "Report of Patrol Action - 11 Brigade - 8 January 1916".

[245] It was on this front that the 36 Division was to suffer such heavy casualties in July 1916. In January of that year, the area was held on the left flank of the line held by the 4 Division.

grips with the working party, an enemy party also came out and bombed the group. The covering party returned fire and grenades until both sides withdrew, taking their casualties with them. That nature of nocturnal confrontation was typical of the fighting throughout the winter period, although the weather and ground conditions generally made it impossible to surprise the opposition and, such was the intensity of the underground activity that both sides regularly fired mines.

The troops had learnt very early in the war to identify what was considered a 'quiet day'. With the exception of the normal bombing and shelling, the next few days were spent in comparative quiet, notwithstanding heavy shelling to which the 10th Brigade was subjected on the 10th[246], when it suffered an estimated two hundred and eighty 5.9" howitzer shells. On that same day, while the fighting on the left of the line was perpetual, considerable activity was also observed in the area of the Quadrilateral[247]. Several days' later two German infantrymen of the 180th Jaeger Regiment attempted to enter trench 84, 300 yards north of the Serre Road, but were detected by the sentries and both were killed.

Until the middle of January, parts of the German front line had not been clearly visible from the British line, as both lines lay on opposite sides of the Hawthorn Ridge. In order to prevent the enemy from taking the high ground and allowing them observation over the support trenches to the north, a new fire trench 500 yards long and 150 yards forward of the original line was dug on the crest of the ridge. The operation was very carefully planned and carried out by the 8th and 10th Battalions of the 107th Brigade. A double row of wire entanglements was erected and the trenches dug and occupied by dawn, and it was doubted if the enemy were aware that it had been dug.

Located in the German trench system, on Hawthorn Ridge, was a German strongpoint referred to, in British intelligence reports, as the Hawthorn Redoubt[248]. It presented a serious obstacle in the event of a British advance and, in order to gain an understanding of the strength of the redoubt the division artillery concentrated its fire on the position

---

[246] *The 1/5 South Lancashire Regiment, which had served with the 4 Division since February 1915, left on the 15 to join the 166 Brigade of the re-formed 55 Division. They were replaced by the 2 West Riding Regiment and attached to the 12 Brigade.*

[247] *The Quadrilateral was a natural, fortified salient in the German front line, which sat astride the Beaumont Hamel - Serre Road. That strong-point was to produce major difficulties for the 4 Division in July 1916.*

[248] *The Hawthorn redoubt, like the Quadrilateral, was fortified network of trenches designed to provide concentrated fire, in the event of an attack.*

at about midday on the 19th. The German artillery replied by shelling the new front line and Auchonvillers. Having assessed the difficulties in dealing with such an obstacle, major mining operations were commenced with the objective of placing a mine directly below the strongpoint. The resultant explosion, on the 1st July, is recorded later in this volume.

Occasionally small incidents occurred that were of a personal nature. At 8:00am on the 20th, a German soldier shouted to the troops of the 10th Brigade in Luke Copse and then fired a rifle grenade, which failed to explode. When it was picked up, it was discovered that it had no detonator and was filled with cuttings from a German picture magazine. The diary of the 10th Brigade states *"the pictures are uncomplimentary to our Army and Highlanders in particular"*. The remainder of the month was spent under the usual shelling and the division had suffered casualties of twelve officers and one hundred and ninety men killed or missing.

February - 1916

Although the 10th Brigade had been holding the line north of the Mailly Maillet – Serre Road that part of the line still remained the responsibility of the 48th Division, on whose behalf the 10th Brigade had been acting. It was intended that the line should now be reorganised. By late January, the 12th Brigade had fulfilled its training obligations and, amidst the shelling, the division received Operation Order No. 27, giving instructions for the relief of the 4th Division, by the 36th Division, in that part of line south of the Mailly Maillet – Serre Road.

In preparation for the relief, the 12th Brigade, then acting as support troops for VII Corps, was recalled to rejoin the division and relieve the 10th Brigade in the front line. To do that, the 12th Brigade was to be temporarily placed under the command of the 48th Division. On the 4th, the 12th Brigade and the 10th Field Ambulance returned to the 4th Division area and relieved the 10th Brigade during the night of the 5th. It assumed responsibility for the northern sector of the line, between Serre and Hebuterne, with headquarters in Mailly Maillet. The 107th Brigade and its associated 110th Field Ambulance was also returned to the 36th Division. The 10th Brigade then retired to the support line.

While the 12th Brigade was taking over from the 10th Brigade, the 11th Brigade was also relieved by the 108th Brigade (36th Division) during the night of the 6th, following which the 36th Division assumed command of the front at midday on the 7th. In order to give the 36th Division an artillery capacity, the 4th Division artillery remained in the area for a further month, until the artillery of the 36th Division was ready to take over. The supporting units of the 4th Division continued the withdrawal, leaving the 12th Brigade in the firing line between the 48th and 36th Divisions. The last withdrawal was that of the headquarters of the 4th Division, which retired to Couin during the 7th.

The 10th and 11th Brigades marched to the Lucheux area where they received reinforcements, many taking leave. From the 10th February to the 16th March, the two brigades enjoyed a period of rest, after six months of continuous front line service. Although the greater part of the month was spent behind the lines, the two brigades had suffered casualties of nine killed and twenty wounded[249] in the first week.

---

[249] *While the 10 and 11 Brigades were at rest the 12 Brigade was still serving with the 36 Division*

For the 12th Brigade, still in the front line, action continued without break. The brigade front, facing due east, was divided into two sectors, north and south, each held by a battalion and relieved by a second battalion on a regular basis. Suspicions of German mining under Luke Copse were strengthened when a listening post heard the sounds of digging underground and immediate precautions were taken. The front line was also subjected to an enemy raid. Between the 5th and 18th February the brigade was the target of regular artillery fire and sniping.

The opposing German 52nd Division was in an offensive mood and inflicted a steady flow of casualties upon those in the front line. Rarely did hours go by without sections of the lines or communications trenches being subject to heavy and accurate artillery and howitzer fire. The enemy machine-gunners had the locations of listening posts, trenches and saps clearly marked and subjected them to constant fire. The business of sniping had been refined to a science by both sides and the practice of exposing oneself, even for the briefest moment, would attract the attention of a sniper. The intensity of the fighting grew and nights were interspersed with patrol exchanges and working parties being constantly subjected to artillery, machine-gun and rifle fire. In the early hours of the morning of the 15th, the enemy was observed bringing a mortar into the remains of Serre village and, within minutes, several mortar shells were fired into the trenches with great accuracy.

After having relieved the King's Own in the front line on the 16th, the Lancashire Fusiliers were immediately subjected to heavy machine-gun fire and later, fired on by a five-man patrol after which the shelling increased, particularly on Monk, Robroy and Exma trenches. That same night, a party of Germans was seen to penetrate the British wire and was fired upon heavily by troops of the Essex regiment. One of those soldiers was seen to throw down his rifle and indicate that he wished to surrender.

When brought into the line it was revealed that he was of the 66th Regiment of the 52nd Division and, upon interrogation, revealed that he had been looking for an opportunity to surrender, as he was Pole who had been called up for military service. As his occupation was that of a carpenter, he had been attached to the pioneers who were in the area working on German dugouts. When he was given the opportunity to go out with another man and fix the wire in front of the German line he took his chance and approached the British line, even though he had been told that the British shot their prisoners.

Serious things were afoot for the Lancashire Fusiliers as, at 5:30pm in the evening of the 19th, German artillery heavily shelled the front line of the 12th Brigade and then lifted onto the communications trenches. As the guns lifted, an enemy raiding party attempted to enter trenches 82, 83 and 84, a series of posts that constituted the front line and each being defended by fourteen to eighteen men. Posts 2, 3, 4, 5 were fully occupied but number 6 had been obliterated by earlier fire from a minenwerfer and was now only guarded by a few men in a nearby crater.

The acting Sergeant Major of 'D' Company reported seeing about 100 of the enemy penetrating the wire in front of post number 4, where he deployed a Lewis gun. To prevent a possible penetration into the trenches by the enemy, a barricade was hurriedly established in the communications trench and a support platoon held ready to move forward as soon as the enemy artillery fire ceased. The battalion commander, upon receipt of the report by the Company commander, ordered that fire should be withheld until the artillery opened fire but, if it took longer that fifteen minutes, the machine guns and all other weapons that could be brought to bear, should commence firing. As soon as the division guns began firing the German artillery retaliated and continued to fire until about 7:15pm.

Numbers of wounded men returned along the communications trench with reports that the Germans had entered the posts and were bayoneting the men. The garrison of number 5 post, commanded by a sergeant, also returned, an action that was later investigated. Two parties of officers and men were sent forward to reinforce those in the front line but were under orders to build a barricade in the communications trench if the posts were found to be occupied. On arrival, the parties met no opposition as the enemy raiding party had already retired. It was discovered that twelve men were missing although it was not clear whether they had been captured or blown to pieces during the bombardment.

Later investigations by the division commander concluded that the rifle was not used properly. It appeared, from all reports, that the men preferred the bomb to the rifle and that the infantryman had failed to use the rifle in its intended role, thus allowing the enemy to get very close and, when in large numbers, to overrun the position. The commanding officer ordered that the rifle was to be considered the primary weapon and that rifle fire should have been opened immediately, retirement being the last option. He also determined that the defences had not been wired properly and had left areas that could be easily penetrated by a determined enemy. As a part of the investigation surrounding the circumstances of the raid it was found that a German officer, killed in the raid, was carrying a bomb containing a flammable liquid. He also wore khaki puttees, old boots, and khaki trousers with a red stripe down the side. He was later buried in front of trench 83.

The steel helmet had only been recently issued and was not popular with the troops due to its weight but, towards the end of the month, the advantages were demonstrated when a soldier's life was saved when a bullet bounced off his helmet, leaving a large hole. Slowly the winter temperatures began to warm, and the frozen ground slowly thawed, causing trench walls to collapse and reducing the whole area to a deplorable state.

March - 1916

After fourteen months service, the 1/7th Argyle and Sutherland High-landers left the division on the 1st of March, to join the 51st (Highland) Division, which was now fighting in the line at Hamel. By the 5th, the 12th Brigade was finally relieved by the 144th Brigade of the 48th Division. On this same day, the artillery of the 4th Division was relieved by that of the 36th Division and all units rejoined the main body of the 4th Division in rest.

On the 14th March, the division received Operation Order No. 28 instructing it to relieve the 37th Division in positions a few miles to the north, between the 18th and 20th March[250]. Setting out immediately, the brigades marched the eight miles to Foncquevillers, north of Gommecourt Wood, where the Royal Dublin Fusiliers and the Royal Irish Fusiliers (10th Brigade) relieved the 6th, 7th and 8th Leicesters (110th Brigade), during the night the 17th. The brigade immediately encountered a considerable number of German patrols and almost constant machine-gun fire.

During night of the 18th, the East Lancashires and the Somerset Light Infantry (11th Brigade) relieved the 112th Brigade on the right of the division line. The following night, the 19th, under a dull and wet sky, the Royal Warwickshire's and Lancashire Fusiliers (10th Brigade) relieved the 111th Brigade. Throughout that period, the Germans were seen to be hard at work every night, reinforcing the front line with wire and strong outposts. The artillery exchanges were continuous, the two sides engaged in bombarding the opposing trenches with rifle grenades and trench mortars while the snipers of both sides attempted to gain the initiative. Patrol encounters involved bombing and counter bombing and the whole area was a danger to anyone who carelessly exposed himself. It was noted that there was considerable activity in and behind the German lines as they prepared for an inevitable attack in the spring.

The German defenders were on the *qui vive* and, at 2:00pm on the 21st, enemy troops opposite the 11th Brigade, opened heavy rifle fire on a British aeroplane, but the troops of the brigade brought heavy rifle and machine-gun fire on the offending trenches and successfully suppressed the firing. By mid-afternoon of that same day, it was reported that a

---

[250] *The orders were to relieve the 37· Division "south of Arras". In fact, the location was only several miles to the north and was to be the scene of desperate fighting in July 1916.*

trolley could be heard moving on tracks in the German trenches and, when it stopped, shellfire was opened on the trenches of the 11th Brigade. It was determined that the shells were 13cm and it was believed that a howitzer might have been mounted on the trolley.

In the dark hours of the next morning, a small party of the enemy attempted to enter the trenches occupied by the Somerset Light Infantry but were ejected by an equally small group of sentries and an officer[251]. During the course of the raid two sentries were wounded, one of whom later died, while several German raiders were killed and wounded. Patrols constantly attempted to ambush each other and affect attacks on opposing working parties. Trenches 93 and 96 were subjected to heavy shelling by 5.9" howitzers and caused considerable damage, while the British snipers spent much of their time harassing the German working parties.

---

[251] *For reports on this incident, see appendix VI "Report of an attempted raid on trench 65".*

April - 1916

At the beginning of April the 4th Division was in the line with 55th Division on its left. From the 1st of the month to the 11th, the division artillery, acting in conjunction with the 55th Division, assumed a more offensive role and conducted regular bombardments of the German trenches and villages to the rear. The artillery was prepared for the inevitable retaliation and consistently fired on the German batteries whenever they could be located, while the troops worked endlessly in strengthening the defences and patrolling No-Man's Land.

The 11th Brigade was holding the line just north of Gommecourt Wood with the Somerset Light Infantry and East Lancashires. Life had settled to a lively pattern of trench warfare, with the opposing enemy using a 77mm field gun to snipe at any movements along the Foncquevillers – La Brayelle road. Heavy transport was heard in the wood during most nights and the front line had experienced considerable trench mortar fire.

The constant patrolling soon established that the Germans, although they had their moments of activity, were not particularly alert on most occasions. On occasions, patrols were able to work up quite close to the enemy outposts. The working parties of both sides were constantly shelled and dispersed with artillery and machine-gun fire. During one of those moments a minor disaster was averted when a nose cone from a German shell struck a box of small arms ammunition, but failed to cause an explosion.

In order to identify the opposing division, a party of the King's Own Royal Lancashire Regiment (12th Brigade), raided a German sap in the early hours of the 12th. The party, supported by the 126th and 127th batteries of artillery, and the 12/1st Trench Mortar Battery, entered the sap after the wire cutting party had demolished the heavy wire entanglements using two Bangalore Torpedoes. The German trenches were very deep and in parts inundated with water. When the raid commenced many of the defending Germans, believed to number about twenty, ran into the deep dugouts. They were bombed with grenades but none were captured, although six were killed in the trenches. The raid was carried out over a period of fifty minutes and, on retiring, the party brought with them a gas helmet, a rifle and several grenades, having suffered only one officer and three men with slight wounds[252].

---

[252] See Appendix VI "Report of Raid by 1 King's Own - 12 April 1916".

Further provocation was carried out later in the day when the division artillery shelled the trenches opposite the 10th Brigade. Neither the raid nor the shelling appeared to attract the expected retaliation. It was determined however, that those enemy guns that did fire were firing from the southern corner of Adinper Wood. The next few days remained relatively quiet, interspersed with the customary shelling and patrol activity and, during the night of the 13th, a German patrol of about ten men approached the wire in front of the 11th Brigade. Following detection of their presence, the sentries opened fire and the patrol retired without further engagement. It was later found that they had left two white flags planted in the ground in front of the wire entanglements.

After several days planning, a further raid was carried out on the 17th by troops of the 10th Brigade, this time in broad daylight. The raiders successfully destroyed what was thought to be a mine entrance and a machine-gun emplacement, killed some fifteen German officers and men, and then returned safely. Again, surprisingly little retaliation was experienced, although the German artillery had previously been quite active during the day, which resulted in two men suffering from shock[253]. For the remainder of the month, nightly patrolling replaced the excitement of trench raids and the month drew to close on a note of good news; that the 4th Division was to be relieved by the 37th Division between the 1st and 3rd of May.

---

[253] *By 1916, the trauma suffered by soldiers who had been exposed to extended periods of shell-fire and battle, described as shell-shock was, by this time, understood and viewed somewhat sympathetically. The condition had previously been considered as an act of cowardice.*

May - 1916

It is now appropriate to pause in order to understand some of the momentous changes and decisions that had taken place in recent months, which would affect the future for the 4th Division and, indeed, many other divisions. On the 19th of December 1915, the Commander-in-Chief of the British Expeditionary Force, Field-Marshal Sir John French returned to the United Kingdom and General Sir Douglas Haig, formerly the G.O.C. of the British 1st Army, assumed the supreme command of the British Army in France. He at once set about reorganising his forces for the forthcoming year. On the 21st January 1916, General Falkenhayn, commanding the German 5th Army launched an attack at Verdun, east of Paris, which was to consume the French army in what was arguably the most intense and lethal battle that was to be undertaken by French forces in the war.

As the Battle of Verdun progressed, growing pressure was placed on Haig to assist the French by engaging the Germans to the north, in an attempt to draw German forces away from Verdun. The concept of an attack on the Germans from the British sector had been growing for some months but it was felt by the High Command that the British would not be ready until later in the year and possibly 1917. However, as the lifeblood of the French army drained at Verdun, the need for the British army to act was inevitable. Haig commenced a systematic process of preparation and the 4th Division was a component part in what was to become a major British campaign.

On the 1st, the retirement from the line began when the 111th Brigade relieved the 10th Brigade during the evening, although the battalions occupying the support lines were relieved at 10:00am, under considerable shellfire, and retired to Halloy. At 7:00pm, the relief of the front line battalions commenced. The following evening, the 112th Brigade relieved 11th Brigade, which then marched into billets, allowing the division to continue with training and re-equipment.

On the 4th of May, the division was informed that it was to leave VII Corps and join VIII Corps, then forming behind the southern sector of the British Line. The transfer was to take effect on the 7th of May, three days hence and, to achieve that transition, Operation Order No.31 was issued which instructed the 12th Brigade to move to the area Bertrancourt-Beaussart on the 7th. Accompanying that move, the 29th and 14th Field Artillery Brigades also marched out of Grouches to a line, which stretched from Lemaillars to Mezerolles, while division headquarters moved to Ribencourt, east of Doullens, well behind the line. On that same day the 1/1 Durham Field Company and the 1/1st Renfrew Field Company, Royal Engineers, was attached to the 12th Brigade. The 11th Brigade moved to the St. Requier training ground on the 15th.

What followed was a fortnight of intensive training for the whole division and each brigade undertook rehearsals in tactical manoeuvres, practice attacks, communications with contact aircraft and signalling under battle conditions using signal lamps and flags. By the 19th, when Operational Order No. 33 arrived ordering the division to prepare to move, all was ready, but there remained much work to be done in preparing the support and communications lines. After the 11th Brigade had completed its training, the 2nd Royal Irish Regiment, which had served with the 4th Division since early in 1915, left the division to join the 7th Division.

From the 19th to the 31st of May the 11th and 12th Brigades moved to several different locations, often retracing there steps, but finally arriving at billets in the area of Lemeillard - Boisberques - Autheux - Occoches - Outrebois – Mezerolles, in company with the artillery. For the month of May, the division suffered casualties of one officer and five men killed and three officers and thirty-seven men wounded, nearly all on the first day of the month, before the relief.

June - 1916

At the beginning of June, the line originally held by the 4th Division was being held by the 31st and 29th Divisions. In preparation for a major assault upon the German lines, it was intended that the 4th Division would assume responsibility for a part of the line located between those two divisions. To do that, the 4th Division was to relieve the 86th Brigade, holding the right of the 31st Division line and the 92nd Brigade, which was holding left of the 29th Division line. That effectively allowed the 4th Division to come into line between the two aforementioned divisions on a single brigade front.

Although division and corps commanders were well aware of that a major British assault was afoot, most troops were aware of an increasing number of divisions in the area and of movement behind the lines. Although the division remained at rest until 3rd of June, the move of the 10th Brigade, on the 4th, to Warnimont Wood and Bus les Artois, as corps reserve, signalled a more general move by the division[254]. While the 10th Brigade was on the move division headquarters received instructions to relieve parts of the line held by the 29th and 31st Divisions on the night of the 14th June[255].

It was the intention to maintain the 11th and 12th Brigades close behind the line, while the 10th Brigade, then in corps reserve, would take over the desired frontage. The forward movement of the 11th and 12th Brigades commenced from Yvrench and Yvrencheux on the 9th, when they marched to Beaumetz and Bernaville, respectively, for the night. The following day, the 12th Brigade marched to Beauvil, where the battalions went into billets behind the front line and provided large working parties to assist the front line troops by digging new assembly trenches and access roads.

Much effort was put into the wiring of the new positions and preparing communications trenches. As the date of the relief drew nearer, the 12th Brigade moved closer to Bertrancourt on the 14th, where a mud model of the German lines had been made, to clarify the objectives of the

---

[254] *On the 3 June 1916 Brigadier-General Anley, G.O.C. 12 Brigade, was awarded the C.B. and was ordered back to England to receive his award.*

[255] *This placed the 4 Division in between the 29 and 31 Divisions. Those movements were the final manoeuvrings of the Divisions for the assault. It was with these two Divisions on either flank that the 4 Division was to make it fateful advance at dawn on the 1 July.*

forthcoming assault. The officers and men spent considerable time understanding the tactics and, on the 17th, the division practised its part in the attack on a scale model (33:1) of the German front.

While the 12th Brigade was thus employed, the 10th Brigade approached the line from the rear and relieved the 1st Lancashire Fusiliers (86th Brigade, 29th Division) with the 2nd Royal Dublin Fusiliers, while the 2nd Seaforth Highlanders relieved the East Yorkshire Regiment, 92nd Brigade (31st Division). The other two brigades remained in support about Auchonvillers.

The line now held represented the frontage on which the division was to attack, from just north of the Mailly Mallet - Serre Road to a point 1400 yards south, immediately next to the northern edge of Beaumont Hamel. The advance was to take the division due east, across the Redan Ridge and a shallow valley, which separated the two opposing lines, with the objective of seizing and holding the three lines of German trenches. Accompanying the 4th division would be the 29th Division on the right and 31st Division on the left. Following is a brief description of the terrain over which the division was to advance and the difficulties to be faced.

The right-hand boundary, between the 29th and 4th Divisions, was represented by an imaginary line which extended almost due east, through the very northern edge of Beaumont Hamel, where it crossed the German frontline, 400 yards ahead. The enemy front line consisted of three, almost parallel, trenches, intersected at regular intervals by communication trenches, many of which ran in a south-easterly direction to connect with the second line of defence, Munich Trench. The boundary then extended due east for 1300 yard, where it crossed the Puisieux-Beaucort road and finished on the enemy third line, Puisieux Trench, a further 850 yards, in all, 2550 yards.

The left flank boundary, joining the 31st Division, was defined by a line, which started 500 yards north of intersection of the Hebuterne Road and the Serre - Mailly-Maillet road and met the enemy front line 200 yards away, 650 yards south of Serre. The enemy trench system was designed similarly to those near Beaumont Hamel, but the defensive line was some 600 yards deep. The second line, Munich Trench, ran south from Serre and crossed the division boundary a further 400 yards ahead. From Munich Trench the boundary swept, in large curve to the north-east for 1800 yards before striking Puisieux Trench, the third line of defence, on the Puisieux-Beaucort road, 1000 yards south of Puisieux.

The attacking battalions of the 11th Brigade, advancing to the east, were to leave their trenches near the crest of the main Hawthorn Ridge, descend to a second lower ridge, Redan Ridge, traverse the valley and attack and the trenches of the German front line. They were then required to continue the advance, up the opposite slope, cross Wagon Road[256], on the Serre-Beaucourt Ridge and capture Munich Trench. When Munich Trench had been occupied, the following 10th and 12th Brigades were to pass through and capture the third line Puisieux Trench. The total distance to be covered was nearly two and a half miles.

Incorporated into the German front line were two strong points, the Quadrilateral and Ridge Redoubt[257]. The Quadrilateral[258] was situated towards the left of the division front, while Ridge Redoubt was closer to the centre. That line was flanked by Serre, a heavily fortified village with a dominating field of fire, which covered the approaches of the 31st Division and the left of the 4th Division particularly in the area around the Quadrilateral. A similar situation existed on the right. Beaumont Hamel, also heavily fortified, was directly in front of the 29th Division, but could enfilade the right of the 4th Division.

On the 18th June, the 4th Division issued Operation Order No. 38, which detailed the attack, the tactics and the timetables to be employed[259]. It was an attack with limited objectives and was to be carried out under the cover of the artillery, which would be located in a man-

---

[256] *Wagon Road lay approximately 1000 yards behind the German front line and joined Serre with Beaumont Hamel. It ran along the crest of the Serre-Beaucourt Ridge for most of the distance and offered a perfect view of the valley between the German and British lines. It was one of the main supply lines for the German on this part of the front and was a regular target for the division artillery, especially when a relief was taking place.*

[257] *Ridge Redoubt was a German strong-point situated opposite the centre of the divisional line. The machine guns firing from this position were never neutralised and continued to wreak havoc among the attacking troops of all three brigades for the entire day.*

[258] *The Official History gives an interesting description of the Quadrilateral. "The Quadrilateral, referred to as the "Heidenkopf", the name of a local German commander, lay on the Serre – Mailly-Maillet road. It was the remnant of a former German front line, which once ran through Matthew Copse and Touvent farm. In the previous fighting of 1915 the French had pushed Germans back closer to Serre, but the Heidenkopf had held firm, and consequently now formed a pronounced salient in No Mans Land."*

[259] *For a full copy of the order, see Appendix VI, "Operation Order No.38".*

ner that placed them within range of all pre-determined targets and could offer fire support for the period of consolidation to follow. It was not intended that it should result in a general breakthrough.

The initial assault was to be carried out by the 11th Brigade across the entire division front at 7:30am on a day to be determined, immediately upon the artillery barrage lifting from the German front line. The plans called for the attacking brigade to assault and occupy the first and second line of German trenches and, when secured, the 10th and 12th Brigades were to follow, one beside the other, at 8:30am. The 12th Brigade was to attack on the left, closest to Serre, while the 10th was to advance on the right, next to Beaumont Hamel, the dividing line being approximately 250 yards north of the Redan Redoubt. Both brigades were to advance through the 11th Brigade and capture the third line of German trenches on a final frontage of about 1700 yards.

The German High Command was well aware of the forthcoming attack and had been taking considerable preparations since late 1915. Opposing the 4th Division was the German 26th Reserve Division, a Bavarian Division of the XIV Reserve Corps, which held a frontage from Serre, on the northern flank, to a point just south of Ovillers, on the Albert – Bapaume Road. Immediately in front of the 4th Division was the 121st Regiment (26th Reserve Division), which covered most of the front to be attacked.

The trenches and roads, used by the 4th Division, were subjected to intermittent shelling while the enemy guns registered on a range of targets. The next three days were occupied with conferences of the division staff officers to finalise the scheme of attack with the brigade and battalion commanders. At that point, the original date for the attack had been determined as the 29th June by G.H.Q. The hour of the attack was referred to as 'Zero' hour and was originally planned for midnight (0:00)[260].

Five days had been allocated to the artillery preparation, each given letters dating from the 24th to the 28th, 'U', 'V', 'W', 'X', 'Y' respectively, and the day of the assault was nominated as 'Z' day, the 29th. The artillery was to achieve certain objectives on each of those days by as the targets changed in accordance with a pre-determined timetable and target schedule.

---

[260] *The date and time of the attack was changed on the 28 to 7:30am on the 1 July.*

All batteries of the attacking divisions, supplemented by those supplied by the supporting divisions were to participate in the barrage. Each battery was assigned a set of prioritized targets to be engaged by a pre-determined number of rounds of a particular type. When the target had been bombarded according to the plan, the gun, or battery, would then change targets. Because the guns required maintenance, crews required rest and ammunition had to be brought forward, there were periods, sometimes long periods, between the separate engagements. It was not until just prior to the attack that every gun fired continuously, with the aim of causing maximum damage. That bombardment described later by the soldiers in the trenches as sometimes reaching terrifying levels as it increased in intensity.

Those battalions, which were not in the front line, continued to practice the attack, although subjected to enemy artillery fire. Just after 10:00pm on the 25th the Special Brigade, a unit attached for the purpose of the operating gas equipment, released gas from cylinders in the front line trenches with the intention of harassing the Germans. The wind was not entirely in their favour although for nearly and hour the gas crept over the German trenches while the enemy artillery responded by shelling No Man's Land and the ground between the front line and support line.

By 11:00pm, the wind had changed direction and slowly blew the gas back over the brigade front line. This was aggravated by the fact that a shell fragment had damaged one of the gas cylinders and caused it to leak into the trenches, causing the trench to be evacuated. The gas caused several casualties, particularly among the men of the Special Brigade, and prevented the reoccupation of trenches until 2:00am on the following morning, because of the risk of residual gas.

Late in the morning of the 26th, patrols of the Somerset Light Infantry reconnoitred the enemy wire and reported that that the wire was well cut although hostile shelling prevented any approach to the Quadrilateral. That same shelling had also prevented patrols of the East Lancashire and Royal Warwickshire Regiments from reaching the enemy front line and, as the end of the month approached, the intensity of the shellfire steadily increased. Due to the intensity of the German artillery and the movement behind the enemy lines, it was apparent that German High Command was well informed as to the British intentions.

During a conference, held by Major-General Lambton with his brigade commanders, it was revealed that the attack, scheduled for 12:30am the next morning, was to be delayed until 7:30am on the 1st July. So that the impact of the previous five days of bombardment would not be lost because of the date change, the artillery was instructed to continue until the morning of the 1st July. For the assault troops, the intervening days were spent testing weapons, ammunition, and completing a myriad of tasks.

In the expectation of the forthcoming attack, the enemy was completely alert to the danger and met every attempt at penetration by patrol or raiding party, with intense artillery and machine-gun fire. When the Somerset Light Infantry attempted to raid the German trenches to the south of the Quadrilateral, they were met with the heavy fire, to which No Man's Land was subjected at the slightest provocation. An attempt by the Rifle Brigade to raid the German trenches on the night of the 29th also failed when they encountered very heavy gauge wire that had not been cut by the artillery and defied all efforts to be cut with double wire cutters. When discovered, they were fired upon by rifle and artillery fire, which precluded any chance of success and resulted in the wounding of three of the raiders.

A second patrol of the Somerset Light Infantry experienced similar difficulties in their attempts to negotiate the protective wire. When five yards from the front trench, the defenders opened fire, killing one of the men and wounding one of the officers and two other ranks. The enemy artillery retaliated immediately and placed a barrage between the patrol and its own front line, thus forcing them to wait in shell holes for half an hour before successfully retiring. While the Somerset's were engaged in the raid, an officer approached the German wire at Lone Tree and discovered that, although parts of the wire entanglements had been cut quite well, there remained sections that still represented an obstacle to attacking troops. Several patrols of the East Lancashires and 8th Warwicks also reported that the wire entanglements were poorly cut.

At about 10:30pm on the night of the 30th, amid constant rain, wind, artillery and machine-gun fire, the troops of the 10th and 12th Brigades began their march forward, towards the starting line. The approach was quite difficult in certain areas, as the ground become very muddy, which was made steadily worse by the constant shelling. The bombardment of the Sucrerie and Auchonvillers Roads caused few casualties, but created great confusion, in the middle of which the 1/6th and 1/8th Royal Warwickshire Regiment arrived, having been attached to the 11th Brigade for the initial attack. Because of the damage caused to the jumping off trenches, behind the main front line, the assaulting companies were disposed in the front line in the early hours of the morning of the 30th [261]. By 3:00am, the battalions had arrived and were given breakfast and, in some cases, a rum ration.

It is now appropriate to understand the full extent of the task set out before the 4th Division, to be executed within the next few hours, and the order of battle. As previously mentioned, two Warwickshire battalions, the 1/6th and 1/8th, had been attached to the 11th Brigade from the 143rd Brigade (48th Division), which stood in the rear to support the attack where necessary. The 11th Brigade, responsible for capturing the first two trench lines, was to lead the attack with three battalions, the 8th Warwickshire Regiment, 1st Rifle Brigade and the 1st East Lancashire Regiment and capture the enemy front line. Once captured, a second line of assault troops, the 1st Hampshire Regiment, 1st Somerset Light Infantry and the 6th Royal Warwickshire Regiment, were to pass over the first line and capture and consolidate the support line, described on British maps as Munich Trench.

When the 11th Brigade had signalled the capture of the second objective, the combined attack of the 10th and 12th Brigades was to pass over both previous objectives and take the third and final objective, the German reserve line. The 12th Brigade was to advance on the left of the line with the 10th Brigade on the right. The advance required the 12th Brigade to extend its left flank partially across the front of the 31st Division, which was to attack on the left of the 4th Division, in order to present a defensive flank towards Serre. Once the third line had been captured, all positions were to be consolidated in the expectation of a counter-attack. The order of advance is demonstrated in the model below.

---

[261] *Because of overcrowding and severe damaged caused to those trenches, many of which were abandoned, many of the troops started their attack from the front line.*

1st Objective – German Front line

11th Brigade – 7:30am

| 8th | 1st | 1st |
| R. Warwickshire Reg. | Rifle Brigade | East Lancashire Reg. |

2nd Objective – German Second Line

11th Brigade – 7:40am

| 6th | 1st | 1st |
| R. Warwickshire Reg. | Somerset Light Infantry | Hampshire Reg. |

3rd Objective – German Third Line

12th Brigade - 10th Brigade - 9:00am

| 1st | 2nd | | 2nd | 2nd |
| King's Own | Essex Reg. | | Seaforth Highlanders | Dublin Fus. |

| 2nd | 2nd | 1st | 1st |
| Lanc. Fus. | Duke of Wellingtons | R. Warwickshire Reg. | Irish Fus. |

Plate 10
Diagram of the formation in which the 4th Division was to attack from the Hawthorn Ridge, on the 1st July 1916.

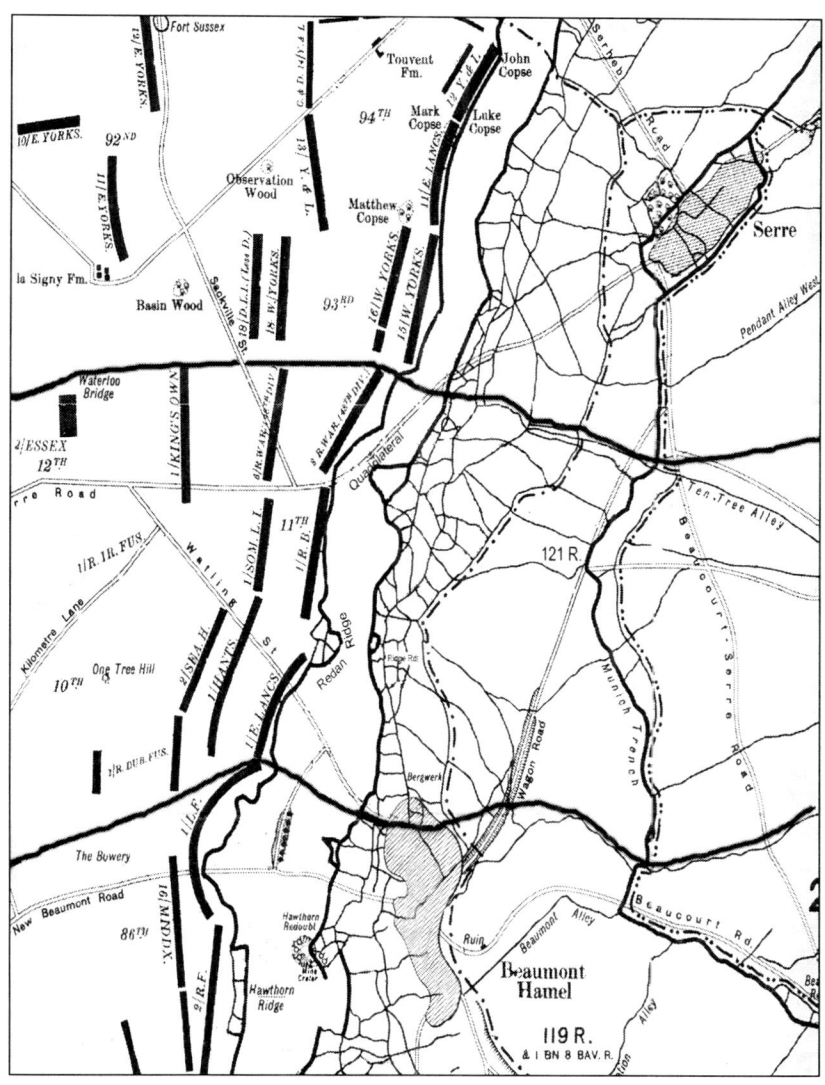

Plate 11
The ground over which the 4 Division attacked on the 1 July 1916.

July - 1916

Due to the confused nature of the fighting on the 1ˢᵗ July, and the mixing of the various units, the assault is best related by concentrating on each brigade in the order of attack, from right to left. The artillery concentrated every available gun on the German front line for several hours before Zero hour. An extract of a statement by Germany's General von Below, commander of the German 2ⁿᵈ Army, against which the British army on the Somme now stood, gives a clear picture of the effects of the last hours of the British bombardment. *"what we experienced surpassed all previous conception. The enemy's fire never ceased for an hour. It fell night and day on the front line and tore frightful gaps in the ranks of the defenders. It fell on the approaches to the front line and made all movement towards the front hell. In fell on the rearward trenches and battery positions and smashed men and material in a manner never seen before or since. It repeatedly reached the even the resting battalions behind the front and occasioned there terrible losses. Our artillery was powerless against it … In the Somme fighting of 1916 there was sprit of heroism which was never again found in the division, however conspicuous its fighting powers remained until the end of the war."* [262]

At 7:20am, ten minutes before zero hour, two events took place that would have a lasting effect on the day's events and develop diverse opinions on the High Command for many years. Firstly, a mine under the Hawthorn Redoubt, in front of the 29ᵗʰ Division and close to the right flank of the 4ᵗʰ Division, was fired by order of Lieutenant-General Hunter-Weston, commander of VIII Corps[263]. It was believed that the destruction and capture of the redoubt prior to the main attack would remove a major obstacle to the advancing infantry. The explosion destroyed the strong point and all in it, but the ten-minute delay permitted the neighbouring German troops, better situated to man and hold the crater than the men of the 2ⁿᵈ Royal Fusiliers (29ᵗʰ Division), to retake the crater and confront the Fusiliers when the attack commenced. The occupation of the crater by the enemy resulted in the ad-

---

[262] *Extracted from the British Official History, Military Operations, France and Belgium 1916, p494.*

[263] *With the approval of G.H.Q. The controversy over that premature explosion is still much discussed today*

vancing troops having great difficulty in overcoming what was thought would be an easily achieved objective[264].

The second action involved the lifting of the artillery barrage from the German front line, which occurred at the same time as the mine explosion. As the guns elevated their range to fire upon the enemy support line, the assaulting troops were forming up into their attack formations in No Man's Land. In those critical few minutes, between the lifting of the barrage and zero hour, the German infantry left their deep bunkers and dugouts, re-manned the ruins of their trenches, and opened a withering rifle and machine-gun fire on the exposed troops. The fire from the enemy front and support lines was supplemented by heavy enfilade fire from Ridge Redoubt, Ten Tree Alley, Beaumont Hamel and Serre. As the machine-gun fire struck the struggling attackers, the German artillery laid a barrage on No Man's Land, the British front line and the support lines. *"This barrage was put down in "crumps" on a small length of trench, and after about ten minutes shifted to another. So severe were its results that for fifty yards behind the front no solid ground was left, nothing but a wilderness of shell holes[265]."*

Problems for the attacking infantry continued. Four minutes before the scheduled attack, that is, at 7:26am, the 1st East Lancashires, on the far right of the first wave, commenced the advance and were immediately caught in the concentrated machine-gun fire from Ridge Redoubt, on their left and Beaumont Hamel, on their right. A report by the 11th Brigade, dated the 6th July 1916, stated; *"Only three platoons of the left Company succeeded in entering the German trenches, the remainder of the Battalion never got beyond the German wire. It is reported that this was uncut in places."* The fate of those who entered the trenches was not known at the time of the writing of that report but it was reported that half an hour after reaching the German line three Very lights were seen indicated that they had reached their objective.

Three minutes later, at 7:29am, the Rifle Brigade commenced its attack in the centre of the first wave. The company on the right was immediately caught in machine-gun fire from the direction of Ridge Redoubt and was prevented from reaching the German front trench at the expected point. The company had veered to the left, in the direction of

---

[264] *The British Official History gives a very concise description of the events leading up to capture of what is now known a Hawthorne Crater. See Military Operations Belgium and France, 1916, Volume I, pp 430 – 432.*

[265] *Quoted from the Official History 'Operations in Belgium and France 1916, p 438.*

that fire, and effected entry into the enemy front line near the Quadrilateral and slowly fought through to trenches beyond.

As they progressed, they were engaged by German bombing parties, which had approached along trenches that led from Ridge Redoubt, after having emerged from deep dugouts after elements of the leading battalions had passed. The resistance of those groups resulted in hostile fire coming from the rear. The inability of the reinforcements to cross No Man's Land, prevented by the intense artillery and machine-gun fire, left most of the leading wave momentarily isolated. However, although constantly engaged against those diverse groups, the Rifle Brigade managed to hold out in various parts of the captured trenches until about 3:00pm.

On the left flank, the 8th Royal Warwickshire's commenced its advance at 7:30am, zero hour but, in the face of extremely heavy machine-gun fire from Serre, only reached a line of shell holes in front of the German wire. One of the first difficulties that the Warwicks faced was the capture of the Quadrilateral, on the right of the battalion. *"The Germans had realized that, in the event of a General offensive, the work (Quadrilateral), owing to its prominent position, could no longer be permanently held, and they had therefore mined it with the idea of blowing it up as soon as the British entered. On the 1st July Heidenkopf was only defended by one machine-gun and a few engineers who were to fire the mine. At the moment of assault, however the machine-gun jammed, and, by some error, the engineers blew the mine too soon, with the result that they and the machine-gun crew were blown up with the redoubt before the British reached it. The effect of the explosion was greater than calculated, for it blocked up many of the German dug-outs near by, so that the assaulting infantry were able to overrun the whole position of No. 3 Company, the right company of the 121st Reserve Regiment, which held this sector of the defences."*

The official history goes on to say, *"One effect of the mine was to obscure all views of Serre and Puisieux from the front line for quite a long time."* The intense machine-gun fire coming from the left brought the Warwicks to a halt and they remained in those positions until after dark when they withdrew to the start line. At 7:40am, the second wave commenced the attack in support of those battalions that had gone before them. The 1st Hampshire Regiment, advancing in support of the East Lancashires, was immediately met by the same concentrated machine-gun and artillery fire. Such was the intensity of that fire that the entire battalion failed to get across No Man's Land and remained in scant protection of the shell craters that were so common between the two front lines. The combined fire of the German artillery and the machine-gun and rifle fire from Beaumont Hamel and Munich Trench had killed or wounded every officer and a large number of men.

To the left of the Hampshire's was the 1ˢᵗ Somerset Light Infantry, which had advanced in support of the Rifle Brigade. They were met with the same concentration of fire from Beaumont Hamel and Ridge Redoubt and also suffered considerable losses while crossing No Man's Land, but small groups managed to reach the remnants of the Rifle Brigade still fighting in the communications and rearmost trenches of the front line. Even together, they were insufficient in numbers to make further progress and were driven back to the German front line, to the left of the Quadrilateral[266], by enemy bombing parties. With many officers and N.C.O.'s killed or wounded, confusion existed as to which trenches had been taken and, in order to establish the true situation, Brigadier-General Prowse, G.O.C., 11ᵗʰ Brigade had advanced with his brigade into the trenches.

The 6ᵗʰ Warwickshire's, on the far left of the second wave, advanced into No Man's Land along with the Somerset's and Hampshire's. They were to support the 8ᵗʰ Warwickshire's, but were immediately met by the same very heavy machine-gun fire from Serre that had inflicted so many casualties on the 8ᵗʰ Warwickshire's. The companies attacking on the far left flank suffered very heavily indeed and few managed to enter the German front line at all. However, those a little further to the right, which were protected by the nature of the ground, had not been subjected to the worst of the fire. They managed to enter and pass the German front trench and proceeded to the support trenches a little further on where they joined elements of the 8ᵗʰ Warwicks. They then continued forward, managed to take several small trenches and sections of the third trench of the German front line. Here, intense fighting took place, mainly conducted by almost continuous bombing, and casualties mounted quickly. The Germans, attacking along communications trenches from Munich Trench, the second line of defence, bombed their way towards the front line and encountering the Warwicks as they went.

In the one and half hours between the initial attack of the 11ᵗʰ Brigade and the supporting attacks of the 10ᵗʰ and 12ᵗʰ Brigades, the German artillery had laid a heavy barrage on the British front line and No Man's Land. In that period, it was planned that the 11ᵗʰ Brigade would have captured the German front line and second line system and the com-

---

[266] *The site of the Quadrilateral is now the location for the Serre No. 2 British Cemetery, established towards the end of the war.*

munications trenches with which they were joined. By the scheduled time for the attack of the 10h and 12th Brigades the 11th Brigade had in fact only captured the parts of the front line and were being heavily attacked from front and flank.

In preparation for the attack, the 10th Brigade, led by the Royal Dublin Fusiliers and the Seaforth Highlanders and the 12th Brigade, with 2nd Essex and the 1st King's Own, advanced from the assembly trenches, preceded by fighting patrols at 9:00am. Having reached the British front line, both brigades suffered considerable casualties as they lined the trenches waiting for the signal to advance. At that time, the German artillery had concentrated on the trenches. When the whistles blew, they mounted the parapet and moved into No Man's Land, where the attacking battalions were forced to advance through the enemy barrage, resulting in many casualties, before reaching the enemy front line.

Once through the barrage, the Dublin Fusiliers and the Seaforth Highlanders were subjected to fire from Beaumont Hamel, the same fire that had devastated the East Lancashires and Hampshire's. The leading companies of the Dublin's suffered extremely heavy casualties and those companies, which had not left the trench with the first wave, were immediately ordered to halt and remain in the front line until the position became clearer. Orders were hurriedly sent to the other battalions, namely the 1st Royal Warwickshire Regiment and the Royal Irish Fusiliers, which were approaching from behind the British front line, instructing them to stop on the Tenderloin – Mount Joy line and await further orders. Those orders did not reach the Seaforth Highlanders and they pressed on, albeit moving more to the left than was intended, in order to avoid the machine-gun fire from Beaumont Hamel and entered the German trenches and joined the troops of the 11th Brigade.

Although it was acknowledged that the attack had been seriously delayed, the headquarters of the 10th Brigade had attempted to obtain an assessment of the conditions in the German front line. Hand-to-hand fighting was taking place in most of the trenches and a machine-gun and artillery barrage had been placed on and in front of the British Front line. Instructions had been sent to the Seaforth Highlanders to bomb down the trenches in a southerly direction, towards Beaumont Hamel, to relieve the pressure on the East Lancashires and Hampshire's. As occurred so many times that day, those instructions were never received and the rapidly thinning ranks of the Seaforth's were subjected to strong German counter-attacks by bombing parties on both flanks.

The 12th Brigade, having advanced behind the left-hand company of the Rifle Brigade and the 6th Warwicks, experienced difficulties almost immediately. The troops left the trenches very quickly, making it difficult for the battalion and company commanders to be fully aware of the locations of each of the various units. To compound the situation, the commanding officers and the adjutants of the King's Own and 2nd Essex were all wounded very early in the assault, which caused an immediate breakdown in communications between the companies.

It had been intended that the 12th Brigade should use two wireless sets to facilitate communications between the permanent Brigade Headquarters and the forward headquarters observation post. As the brigade moved forward to its starting point, the second set was damaged beyond repair by machine-gun fire, thus isolating the Brigade Headquarters from the forthcoming events. The order to halt in the front line trenches was not received by many men of the forward companies of the King's Own and Essex battalions and the remainder continued as planned.

Those companies continued to advance over the British front line and enter the German trenches near the Quadrilateral. Although having suffered under the barrage, they managed to get support to the scattered groups of the 11th Brigade, which were barely holding their own. Those of the Essex and King's Own were now mixed up with the troops of the 11th Brigade, and communications had completely broken down. By the time the runners found them, they had been fighting in the German trenches for over an hour. The G.O.C of the 12th Brigade had tried to contact Brigadier-General Prowse by telephone, but staff officers of the 11th Brigade Headquarters informed him that they were under the impression that the Brigadier had occupied the German second line, with his troops.

Telephone cables were broken almost as they were laid and they were impossible to repair under such heavy fire. The information that did reach the rear area, through wounded and stragglers, was generally vague and, in many case, completely incoherent. The war diary of the 12th Brigade states: "*Confused incoherent messages were coming from wounded who were streaming up Roman Road passed (sic) Brigade HQ from which it was impossible to establish more than that some portions of the King's Own and Essex had probably reached, if not passed Munich Trench.*" The lack of communications prevented the troops, fighting in the German front line, from requesting or receiving continuous supplies of bombs and ammunition and many officers in the trenches found themselves responsible for troops from several battalions, often from different brigades.

It was not until 9:25am that the O.C. Duke of Wellington's received the order to halt. He immediately despatched runners to the advanced company and successfully stopped three of the four companies, but the fourth company, having already passed the British front line, continued the advance as far as the German front line. The O.C., Lancashire Fusiliers, did not receive the order to halt at all, due to the runners being either wounded or killed[267].

Communications with those troops in the German front line were almost impossible as the artillery and machine-gun fire over the intervening ground between the two front lines prevented all movement except in a small area to the right of the Quadrilateral. Not only was the 4th Division in serious difficulties but, by 10:00am, it was clear to Major-General Lambton that the attacks of the 29th Division, on the right and those of the 31st Division, on the left, were not making any significant progress.

A report from the Somerset's, received at the 12th Brigade Headquarters at 10:36am stated that they had gained their objective in the centre[268]. Runners were sent immediately to the King's Own and Essex in an effort to establish their progress, but none returned. Shortly after, the wounded commander of one of the companies of the Duke of Wellington's reported to the headquarters of the 12th Brigade. He reported that his company was in the Quadrilateral and had reached the second trench of the German frontline. He stated that they were with remnants of the Lancashire Fusiliers, on his right and some of the King's Own and Essex, further forward.

Within minutes of receiving that report, a message, sent by signalling lamp by Lieutenant-Colonel Freeth of the Lancashire Fusiliers, was received by 12th Brigade headquarters, which stated: *"the advance was slow but practical and that casualties had been severe and that reinforcements were required"*.

---

[267] *The casualty rate amongst the runners was extremely high, given the artillery and machine-gun fire they were forced to negotiate and many that had been sent to various brigade and battalion headquarters were never seen again. The losses suffered by the runners was one of contributing factors in the failure of companies and battalions failing to carry out the orders of the commanding officers. Although they suffered severely, the runners played a major part in the events of the day.*

[268] *The Somersets, Warwickshires and Hampshire's were to capture the German second line of defence, Munich Trench.*

Communications with the King's Own and Essex, in the third trench line, was non-existent and several attempts to establish contact failed. Their situation was completely unknown, although some reports suggest that, by 11:00am, small groups had carried on to Munich Trench and others, as far as Pendant Copse. Gradually those troops of the 11th and 12th Brigades, which had reached Munich Trench, were pushed back and, by midday, almost all were again fighting in the German front line. Those who were in the more distant trenches were not seen nor heard of again.

The resistance of the German 121st Regiment soon developed into concerted counter-attack, made by large numbers of troops that had come from Munich Trench, Serre and Beaumont Hamel, as reinforcements. As they bombed their way down the many communications trenches, the attack developed into a more general movement against the left flank of the 12th Brigade. The enemy fought with great determination and drove the Essex back by bombing from front and flank. By midday, most of the fighting was concentrated in the front line system, with the greater effort focused in the area of the Quadrilateral

An attempt was made to resist the efforts of the German reinforcements coming from Beaumont Hamel. The Seaforth's and Dublin's on the right flank, were now deeply involved in hand to hand fighting in the German front line. They were ordered, at 12:00pm, to attack the trenches referred to as 86, 91 and 88, which joined the first and second trenches of the German front line near the village. The attack was to commence at 12:30pm and accompany a fresh attack by the 29th Division. The Dublin's had suffered crushing casualties and were ordered to assemble as many men as could be recovered, return to the British line, and gather in their original assembly trenches.

Due to the loss of many of the officers and N.C.O.'s, Colonels Hopkins and Freeth remained with the troops and did much to organise the defence of the captured line. Overcrowding in the second line of German trenches and the inability to consolidate the line was largely instrumental in the decision to withdraw to the first line at the base of the Quadrilateral. Lieutenant-Colonel Freeth was ordered to consolidate the line using the fragments of the various battalions.

Many acts of courage were shown throughout the fighting, one case in particular was Lieutenant Brown, 12th machine-gun Company, who gathered his four guns and consolidated them in the Quadrilateral, working the guns with effect until, one by one, they and their crews were disabled. He managed to hold on until 2:00am on the following morning, before having to withdraw.

By 1:00pm, the attack on Beaumont Hamel by the 29th Division, had irretrievably failed. The division had suffered immense losses and lacked the strength to achieve the capture of the village. The attack of the 31st Division, in front of Serre had failed with similar losses, although it was believed that several small groups had entered the village. The 4th Division had only taken the Quadrilateral and much of the German front line. Although the troops of the 4th Division continued to occupy the enemy front line, Germans reinforcements were brought forward from the support lines in numbers that the mixed troops of the division were unable to withstand.

The Seaforth's, on the right of the division line, were forced to give up the third trench, a part of the German first line, due to the casualty rate and a shortage of bombs. The shortage of ammunition, bombs and water was taking its toll and at about 1:30pm the observer for the 32nd Artillery Brigade sighted a visual signal from the Quadrilateral requesting more bombs. Five hundred were immediately despatched but these failed to get through, as most of the carriers were either killed or wounded while crossing No Man's Land. Shortly after, a company of Royal Irish Fusiliers was ordered to reinforce the Seaforth's and, upon leaving their trenches just north of Redan, was immediately confronted by intense machine-gun fire. A further attempt was made at 4:00pm when a second company succeeded in crossing, by moving further to the north, opposite the Quadrilateral and took with them an additional five hundred bombs for the Seaforth's.

In an effort to impose some organisation into the fighting, the G.O.C., 12th Brigade, ordered Lieutenant-Colonel Bray, O.C., Duke of Wellington's, to reorganise his battalion in the British front line trenches, along with other troops that were available. By 2:30pm, the reorganisation was complete, made a little easier by the slackening of the artillery fire and the fact that two hundred men of the Pioneer Battalion had just joined the brigade in the trenches. At 3:00pm, more bombs were sent to the Quadrilateral, which was now held by an amalgamation of troops from the Somerset's, Lancashire Fusiliers, King's Own and Seaforth's, all under the command of O.C. Seaforth's.

By mid afternoon, Major General Lambton realised that the objectives set for VIII Corps could not be achieved. He directed the 12th Brigade to hold and consolidate the captured German line while the remainder of the mixed troops were brought back into the British front line and reorganised under Lieutenant-Colonel Bray. It was inevitable that withdrawal was necessary and, at 6:30pm, the G.O.C., 12th Brigade ordered the division reserve to form defensive flanks on either side of the Quadrilateral in order to facilitate the withdrawal of the men of the 12th Brigade. While the organisation of those troops that remained in the German trenches was under way, the fragmented elements of the 11th Brigade were retired from the front line. The brigade marched immediately to Bertrancourt and later to Mailly Maillet, for rest and reorganisation.

Throughout the remainder of the afternoon and evening, the Lancashire Fusiliers, Seaforth Highlanders and elements of the 11th Brigade continued to hold those parts of the line that had been captured on the right flank. Although additional support was sent in the form of two companies of the Irish Fusiliers, it was found impossible to move forward on the extreme left flank, because of the machine-gun fire from Serre. The enemy machine-guns now commanded a field of fire that covered those troops in the captured trenches, the British front line and support trenches.

The flanking forces managed to hold out until about midnight when all but one company of the Irish Fusiliers were evacuated successfully and returned to the British lines. 'D' Company, of the Irish Fusiliers, did not receive the order to withdraw until 8:45am on the following day. They continued to fight until 11:00am on the 2nd, when they withdrew, bringing all of their wounded except one, who was recovered that evening, as well as three German prisoners and some captured material.

After midnight, the German artillery remained quiet, but their focus lay on the area of trenches held by the 10th Brigade, which was subjected to intermittent, but heavy artillery and trench mortar bombardment. The opposing infantry remained nervous and when a patrol of the 10th Brigade attempted to approach the German front line between Points 27 and 45, in the early hours of the morning of the 2nd, they were driven back by heavy rifle and machine-gun fire.[269] It was thought that no men remained in the Quadrilateral, although it was known that a large number of wounded were in an old dugout, twenty yards outside the British front line. They were brought in during the night, as were a number of wounded lying out in No Man's Land. The task of collecting the dead and wounded continued throughout the night and much

---

[269] *For casualty figures of the 4 Division for the 1 July 1916, see Appendix IV 'Casualty list for 1 July, 1916.'*

effort was exerted treating those in need and getting them to field ambulances and casualty clearing stations.

At about 10:00am on the 2nd, large numbers of the enemy were observed travelling from Grévillers to Irles, east of Beaumont Hamel and the possibility of counter-attack appeared probable. Two hours later fresh troops were seen entering the front line opposite the division, dressed in light blue uniforms and carrying packs. To meet such a possibility the whole morning was spent repairing and strengthening the trenches. To forestall an attack the division artillery shelled the German lines at 3:30pm and again at 6:30pm while German artillery retaliated by shelling the British lines at 9:30pm with lachrymatory shells[270]. That evening, the enemy were seen wearing steel helmets and clean uniforms. Many were also carrying containers, thought to be Flamenwerfers[271].

Despite what appeared to be preparations for an attack, none eventuated and the work of consolidating the trenches continued for several days, as did the task of sorting out the troops into their respective battalions and brigades. The high number of casualties among officers complicated the task of reorganisation and, wherever officers could be found, they were given command of a unit. Others, capable of responsibility, were also placed in command of bodies of troops. At 5:00am in the morning of the 3rd, five men of the 11th Brigade entered the British trenches held by the 10th Brigade. They had been lying in shell holes and within the German front line after being buried by the bombardment during the initial attack two days before.

That evening additional German troops were seen marching from the direction of Bapaume and Achiet-Le-Grand. The movement was interpreted as being preparations for an attack and instructions issued to ensure that all wiring was completed on the front and support lines and the parapets were to be repaired with utmost haste. During the preparation for possible counter-attacks, the 6th and 8th Royal Warwickshire Regiment returned to the 48th Division.

The 29th Division had suffered heavily during the attack and, on the 4th, the 1st Royal Warwickshire Regiment and Royal Irish Fusiliers of the 10th Brigade, sideslipped to the right and relieved two battalions of that division, a process only completed in the evening, owing largely to the heavy rain. The 10th Brigade Headquarters and the remainder of the

---

[270] The term 'Lachrymatory' is described as 'causing tears'. This term was initially applied to shells, which carried Chlorine, but was later applied to most forms of gas.

[271] Flame-throwers

brigade then retired into billets in Mailly Maillet to act as support of the front line battalions. The part of the line held by the Warwickshire's and Irish Fusiliers was subjected to constant, heavy artillery and machine-gun fire from Beaumont Hamel, especially in the area of the Sunken Road.

Although most nights were deluged with heavy rain, the nocturnal activities of patrols established that the enemy had carried out very little work on their trenches with exception of those holding the Hawthorn Crater. Much work had been put into the strengthening of that position from where it was suspected that mining had commenced. The position was heavily fortified and, when three shells from a trench mortar were fired into the crater, a considerable amount of timber was seen to fly into the air. As the day's passed, German activity increased and machine guns fired all along the division front while artillery and trench mortars concentrated fire on particular trenches.

An inspection of the trenches by the G.O.C., 12th Brigade, found them in very poor condition, a result of the damage from enemy shellfire and the fact that the troops were living in water up to their knees. The inspection also revealed that gas cylinders in the Redan Redoubt were leaking, which had resulted in two officers of the Lancashire Fusiliers being gassed. As a result, orders were issued for all empty gas cylinders to be buried.

During the afternoon of the 5th, a Red Cross party ventured into No Man's Land in search of any remaining wounded and recovered of a further eight men. It was to the credit of the opposing Germans that their respect for the Red Cross flag was demonstrated by withholding all fire as the party carried out its duties.

During the night of the 6th, preparations were made for the release of a smoke cloud from the trenches of the 12th Brigade, although the release was cancelled at the last moment. Despite the cancellation, a German shell landed in a dump of smoke candles, started a fire and released a cloud on the left of the brigade front. Suspecting the possibility of an attack, the German artillery reacted with a heavy barrage on the front line trenches and inflicted several casualties. The bombardment continued throughout the following day and into the early hours of the morning of the 8th, being particularly heavy near the Sunken Road. That provoked a response from the division artillery which shelled the German front line and known artillery positions.

The Germans continued to neglect trench defences and patrols of the Essex and Lancashire Fusiliers, in the late morning of the 8th, confirmed that the wire defences were negligible and that a portion of the line was not manned at all. The events of the last week had not dampened the offensive spirit of the troops and a bombing raid on enemy positions in front of the 12th Brigade had been planned for several days. At 1:30am on the morning of the 9th, the raiding party, under Lieutenant Waghorne, left the line at a point north of the Redan, with the aim of entering the German trenches opposite. When only ten yards from the enemy front line, the patrol encountered deep wire. Although it had been cut in many places by the artillery, it remained thick enough to prevent them from rushing the position and the patrol withdrew after being fired on by sentries.

The 11th Brigade, which had been withdrawn from the front line on the evening of the 1st, re-entered on the 10th and relieved the 12th Brigade. Upon retirement, the 12th Brigade then marched to Bertrancourt, where it commenced a training programme and the re-opened bombing and signal schools.

It had been decided to test the enemy's preparedness for a further attack. During the evening of the 12th, a working party of eight hundred and thirty-two men of the 10th Brigade, carried 200 cylinders of gas forward to the lines of the 11th Brigade, the last one being delivered at 3:30am on the 13th. The gas was discharged between 10:00 and 10:15pm the following evening, which was then followed by a heavy bombardment by the division artillery for an hour, between 2:30 and 3:30am on the 14th. While the bombardment was underway, a smoke cloud was released at 3:10am, followed immediately by a barrage of the German front lines by all division machine guns, thus simulating an attack. The response was an immediate German artillery barrage on the British support lines.

The 4th Division had been warned that it was to be relieved by the 12th Division on the 21st of the month and the last few days were spent completing the consolidation work and the digging of new lines. Not unusually, the German artillery and machine guns paid considerable attention to the new work made that much more difficult by the saturated ground. In an effort to suppress much of the enemy fire, the division machine guns concentrated fire on Wagon Road, behind and parallel to the German lines, which was used as a line of communications with the trenches in and around Beaumont Hamel.

The process of relief commenced at 1:30pm on the 21st and the 12th Brigade retired to Vauchelles while the 10th and 11th Brigades marched for Beauval. While there, they received large drafts of reinforcements, the standards of which were viewed by the hardened troops of the 11th Brigade as being very low. The division had recovered considerably from its losses and undertook intensive training that produced a considerable positive effect on morale.

For the moment, the division had seen the last of the Somme and VII Corps was destined to return to the Flanders area of Belgium. Entraining at Doullens between the 22nd and 26th of the month, the five hour trip took them to Cassel, thirteen miles east of Poperinghe, an area with which they were already familiar. The war diary of the 1st Hampshire Regiment states *"Those of us who were in Flanders before shewed no zeal at renewing our acquaintance with this part of the world."*

On arrival, the 11th Brigade marched directly to the canal bank, to the north of Ypres, where, together with the 10th Brigade, they relieved the 3rd and 1st Brigades (Guards Division) respectively[272], while the 12th Brigade remained in Poperinghe as division Reserve[273]. Both of the forward brigades maintained support positions on the Canal while two battalions of each held the forward trenches facing east, towards St. Julien. The 29th Division, which had fought on the right of the 4th and suffered so severely in front of Beaumont Hamel, had also moved to Belgium and was once again, to the right of the 4th Division.

The first few days were spent in comparative quiet as the troops consolidated the trenches and introduced the new reinforcements to the vagaries of trench warfare. The activities in which the men of the 4th Division had been involved fourteen months before in this area had changed very little. The shelling of the division lines was spasmodic until the 30th, when they were subjected to constant shellfire for most of the day.

Patrol activity by the Royal Warwickshire's and Royal Irish Fusiliers prompted instant reaction from the German defenders wherever they were met. Several patrols were able to establish the nature of work being

---

[272] *The lines that the 4 Division now took over from the Guards Division, were those in which they had relieved the French 152 Division on the 7 June 1915, twelve months before.*

[273] *Whether by coincidence or design the Division had returned to the same area in which it fought with such difficulty during the battle since known as Second Ypres in April - May 1915. They returned to what were the same positions.*

carried out by the enemy and gained a fair picture of the defensive nature of the German lines. As a part of that reconnaissance work an officer left the line during the night of the 30th, to reconnoitre the enemy lines on the northern end of the Estimenet. On approaching the trench, he discovered that it was unmanned and entered without interference. He proceeded along the trench, discovered a steel helmet in a dugout, and then encountered a barricade covered by wire, which blocked further progress. He returned to the British lines unharmed and without having been discovered.

The month of July had not been good for the 4th Division. It had started with high hopes of success in its first offensive efforts and had suffered badly. The total casualties for July amounted to three hundred and three officers and five thousand, five hundred and eighty seven other ranks killed wounded and missing.

August - 1916

The first week of August continued in much the same manner as the closing days of the previous month. The troops of both front line brigades were fully occupied in the daily routine of trench maintenance, night patrols, and sniping. The artillery of both sides remained in deadlock, resulting in the trenches being continuously damaged and in need of repair. Enemy working parties were targets for the Lewis gunners and night patrols regularly engaged in ambush and attack, largely bombing one another and repelling attempts at attack by rifle fire. An example of the nature of patrol work was demonstrated during the night of the 1st, when a German patrol was seen to approach the front line of the 10th Brigade and throw grenades. However, the patrol withdrew quickly when fired on.

Whilst there was no attempt by either side to undertake large-scale offensives, the trenches of both sides were constantly inundated by fire of various kinds. The enemy machine guns were always active and played upon the parapets wherever movement was detected.

While the two line brigades were actively engaged, the troops of the 12th Brigade were undertaking training courses in any one of the many schools that had been developed in the rear area and were now mandatory for all divisions. Training in every aspect of trench warfare was now available and all units not engaged in defence were under instruction to ensure that the appropriate numbers of troops were allocated to training. Schools were available for instruction in bombing, signals, machine gun, Lewis gun, artillery, map reading and many other subjects and were conducted with one objective; to ensure that the British soldier was enabled to assume the initiative in any situation in which he may find himself.

Action at the front was highlighted constantly by incidents such the Allied aircraft, thought to be French, which was brought down by German anti-aircraft fire on the 3rd August in that part of No Man's Land, which lay in front of the 11th Brigade. German troops were soon seen near the wreckage and were dispersed by rifle fire. At 9:30pm, a patrol of the Rifle Brigade was sent to inspect the wreckage. On their arrival they discovered that that the Germans had dug a sap out to the plane and removed everything of value, including the engine.

Night patrols were about the only form of direct contact between the opposing sides and efforts were made to inflict damage and surprise wherever possible. Not all were successful. A patrol of the 10th Brigade encountered a German patrol in No Man's Land during the night of the 3rd. The enemy, having seen the British patrol, threw several grenades and attempted to rush forward but four bombs, thrown by the British patrol, appeared to have been effective, as it was stated in the report on the incident that *"it was suspected by the groans that casualties had been inflicted"*.

Not withstanding the dangers that were a part of daily routine, the troops had settled into a pattern of activity, which, all too easily, became the "way of life". On the 6th, considerable damage to the front line trenches was inflicted when Cross Roads Farm was subjected to shelling by fifty high explosive 5.9" shells. That same night a patrol of the 2nd Battalion, (238th Reserve Regiment, 52nd Reserve Division) attempted to raid Mortejeest Trench but was driven off, leaving one dead and one who later died of his wounds[274].

The threat of a gas attack was ever-present and, during the night of the 8th, while the 10th Brigade was in the process of relieving the 11th Brigade, the opposing enemy unexpectedly released a cloud of gas on a frontage of approximately 500 yards. The gas was carried on a light breeze in the direction of Boezinghe and the effect was exacerbated by the close proximity of the German and British trenches, allowing the gas to strike with little warning.

As the men were in full marching order, many experienced difficulty putting on their gas masks. The fact that there was a double garrison in the trenches caused widespread casualties with about two hundred men being affected immediately. Due to atmospheric conditions, the gas cloud separated into two, one flowing down the Colne Valley, supplemented by a number of gas shells, whilst the other part travelled in a north-westerly direction over the front line. A small party of about forty Germans followed the gas cloud but was beaten off by rifle and machine-gun fire.

That attack was followed up by a concentrated artillery bombardment of the 11th Brigade front, supported by trench mortars and rifle grenades and the shelling followed the gas into the Colne Valley, in the area of Barnsle Road. The gas used in the attack was very strong and resulted in several men being killed immediately. Approximately forty men had put their gas helmets on and walked about 200 yards to the

---

[274] *The 238th Reserve Regiment, 52nd Reserve Division, was the same regiment and division that confronted the 4. Division on the 25. April 1915, between Kitchener's Wood and St. Julien.*

rear before being overcome and all were found dead. All officers and N.C.O.'s in the immediate area were affected and casualties continued to occur during the following few days as the dugouts and clothes were saturated with residual gas.

Again, it was time for the 4th Division to leave the line and, on the night of the 19th August, the 38th Division commenced the relief, which continued until the 21st. As the last units withdrew, the entire division proceeded to relieve the 3rd Canadian Division, which signified a transfer to the Canadian Corps. The German artillery was considerably more active on the canal front[275] and both sides were engaged in constant and heavy artillery exchanges. Mining activity was also a feature of fighting in the area, the Germans firing a small mine, without causing any damage. Two days later the 10th Brigade reciprocated, also without causing damage to the enemy. While the effects of the mines were negligible, the trench mortar fire was much more effective and caused considerable damaged to parapet and trench.

Within days of the arrival of the 4th Division in the Canadian line, orders were received notifying the division that it was to be relieved by the 1st Australian Division. That relief commenced during the night of the 31st August, when the 2nd Australian Brigade relieved the 12th Brigade in the reserve area, which allowed it to then proceed to Poperinghe. The 10th and 11th Brigades, having been relieved by the 1st and 3rd Australian Brigades respectively, followed immediately.

---

[275] *Yser Canal*

September – 1916

The 1st Australian Division had assumed command of the trench line from the Ypres-Commines Canal to Trench 55, a distance of some 3000 yards where it joined with 38th Division, which in turn, extended the line to the Ypres-Menin Road. The 38th Division was due to be relieved by the 2nd Australian Division, but that division had not yet arrived in the area. As a temporary measure, the 4th Division was instructed to carry out that relief and the 10th Brigade, less one battalion, moved to Proven to act in support, while the remaining battalion marched to Poperinghe to join the 11th and 12th Brigades. The 12th Brigade commenced the relief on the night of the 3rd, replacing the 114th Brigade and the 11th Brigade completed the process on the following night, the 4th, when the last of the 38th Division units left the line.

No sooner had the division occupied the trenches than it was advised that the 2nd Australian Division, which was then arriving in Poperinghe, would relieve it on the night of the 10th. The division held the line without serious incident until the 2nd Australian Division arrived and assumed positions in the line. When all was complete, the 4th Division returned to Poperinghe and continued to march towards the coast where it arrived at Esqelbecq[276] on the 11th. Here they remained in rest and in training until the 17th September.

During its stay at Esqelbecq, the 11th Brigade participated in an exercise of official deception. The purpose of the exercise was to give the impression to curious eyes that British troops were departing from Dunkerque for other fronts. On the 12th the 11th Brigade, accompanied by the 29th Artillery Brigade, 12th Field Ambulance and 3rd Company Division Train was required to march to Dunkerque and participate in an exercise under the command of Admiral Bacon, Commodore of the Dover Patrol. 600-800 men boarded six or seven drifters at Dunkerque and field guns and limbers (less the horse teams) were loaded onto the deck of a Monitor. Having completed the process, the troops and guns were disembarked during the afternoon. The process was repeated again on the 13th and 14th after which the entire column returned to the division area on the 15th.

On the 16th, orders were received for the division to leave its artillery behind and entrain immediately for a move back to the Somme. The movement to the south began on the 17th and proceeded to the area of

---

[276] *Esqelbecq is in northern France about mid-way between Poperinge, Belgium and Dunkerque, France.*

Villers Bocage and Bertangles, several miles north of Amiens. There they remained in rest, until the 24th, when the division transferred to the XIV Corps. The whole division commenced to advance in stages, until it was aligned along a front extending from Daours to Vaux-sur-Somme, directly east of Amiens and stretching along the Somme River with the junction of the Ancre River in its centre, where it remained in Corps reserve.

October - 1916

It is appropriate, at this point, to summarise the events that had occurred on the Somme since the divisions' departure in August. The attack, launched by the British and French Armies on the 1st July, had failed in the northern sector of the British line. It was in that part in which the 4th Division had participated, without success, and suffered so severely.

The attack of the British XV Corps, against the German 28th Reserve Division, on the southern sector of the line, had been more successful. The corps had been actively engaged and had continued the advance in a north-easterly direction, towards Bapaume, although heavily contested by the German II Army. By the end of the September, the British XIV Corps ran almost due east, through the northern limits of Gueudecourt, curved south-east, along the northern outskirts of Lesboeufs, to meet the French line just east of that village. For the purpose of this history, the following narrative shall remain with the 4th Division in the immediate area of Lesboeufs[277].

On the 1st October, the 4th Army issued warning orders instructing XIV Corps, consisting of the 4th and 6th Divisions, to attack the line of Le Transloy – Thilloy – Warlencourt – Eucort, on the 10th October, although later delays caused the date to be delayed for two days. The plan required both divisions to attack side by side, with the 4th Division advancing on a 1,600-yard frontage, on the right of the Corps line against, the 18th Regiment (German 9th Reserve Division). In that role, it was to maintain contact with the French 18th Division[278] to the right and the 6th Division on the left. The objectives were the capture of Le Transloy by the 6th Division and the German defence system, to the east of that village, by the 4th Division.

The ground between Lesboeufs and le Transloy constitutes a wide, shallow valley, with a series of low spurs, which penetrate from the south and radiate from the crest of a ridge on which Lesboeufs and neighbouring Morval sit. The villages are joined by a road that transverses the valley in a wide, sweeping curve to the west and is intersected from the left by the Gueudecourt - Le Transloy road, at about 1500 yards towards Le Transloy. Both roads were sunken in sections and

---

[277] *The action at Lesboeufs was fought only ten miles from the southward route that the Division had followed during the retreat of August 1914, a little over two years before.*

[278] *French VI Army.*

provided enfilade fire on any troops approaching directly from Lesboeufs. The terrain over which the two attacking brigades were to advance was open, but heavily entrenched and torn by the constant shelling of the opposing artillery.

The 4th Division was to attack, in a north-easterly direction, on a two-brigade front, from trenches immediately in front, that is to the north, of Lesboeufs. The start line consisted of a single trench, known as Thistle Trench, to the west of Lesboeufs, and as Shamrock Trench, to the east. Slightly ahead of Thistle Trench lay Windy Trench, which had been a German outpost, but had passed into British hands well before the attack. The 10th Brigade was to advance on the right of the line, with its right flank joining the French and its left flank joining the 12th Brigade, 100 yards to the right of the Lesboeufs - le Transloy Road. The 12th Brigade was to continue the line for approximately 400 yards, where it joined with the 6th Division. The 11th Brigade would remain in support[279]. The French 18th Division and the British 6th Division each had its' own objectives.

The 12th Brigade was to advance from Thistle and Windy Trenches with two battalions, while the 10th Brigade was to start its attack from a single line, Shamrock Trench, also with two battalions. The advance would carry the two brigades diagonally across the front of the particularly heavily defended town of le Transloy to the final objective, a line of trenches to the east of that village. To achieve the objective, the attack, firstly, had to capture a series of German trenches, approximately 500–600 yards from the start line.

To reach the first objective, the 10th Brigade had to overcome a series of trenches, Foggy, Dewdrop and Hazy, which lay across the line of advance. These were not long trenches but were heavily defended and situated in such a manner as to offer enfilade fire on an attacking force. Foggy Trench was located approximately 270 yards forward of the British front line while Dewdrop Trench lay a further 200 yards and Hazy Trench 300 yards yet again. To the left of Hazy trench was two fortified positions simply referred to as the Strongpoint and the Gunpits. Rainy Trench, lying on the boundary of the two brigades, was located to the left of Dewdrop and both allowed access to the Gunpits and the Strong Point[280].

---

[279] It was the 11. Brigade, which led the attack on 1. July, on the Redan Ridge, about six miles from their current location.

[280] After the capture of the trenches, Rainy and Dewdrop were joined up by the British troops and the whole system became known as Dewdrop Trench.

The advance of the 12th Brigade would have to confront an even stronger defensive line, referred to as Spectrum Trench, some 600 yards ahead of the start line. Spectrum trench crossed the boundary between the 4th and 6th Divisions, where it was referred to as Rainbow Trench and was to produce serious problems during the advance. There existed several other smaller defensive trenches and they will be addressed as the advance progresses. The second objective was a strongly held series of trenches in front of le Transloy. The line was located on rising ground towards the village and commanded excellent observation over the entire area to be traversed by the three divisions.

The first week was spent in training and moving to the support positions in preparation for the relief of the 56th Division. The relief occurred on the 9th October, the 10th and 12th Brigades having relieved the 168th and 167th Brigades respectively in the front line, while the 11th Brigade relieved the 169th Brigade in the support line. During and after the relief, the German artillery was very active, concentrating particularly on the sunken road just to the rear of the font line[281].

During that first day, the 9th, the 6th Division conducted a 'Chinese'[282] attack, which immediately attracted the full attention of the German artillery, and the entire 6th Division line was heavily bombarded. The shelling also concentrated on parts of the road leading into the trenches in front of Lesboeufs. The barrage increased in intensity in the short period of three minutes and gradually crept back to Needle Trench, some 300 hundred yards behind the village. During the two days preceding the attack, the British artillery had shelled the German lines and the bombardment increased in intensity whenever it struck the objectives of the forthcoming attack. The German artillery always responded in kind and caused casualties in the two front line brigades.

The attack was scheduled to start at 2:05am on the 12th October and, for several hours before, heavy rain had fallen, resulting in the ground turning into a bog. At the prescribed time, a concentrated artillery bombardment was directed on the enemy front line and the two attacking brigades advanced. Because of the cloud cover, the night was very dark and maintaining direction and formation proved extremely

---

[281] *This period was marked by considerable air activity by German aircraft spotting for the artillery.*

[282] *A 'Chinese' attack was term given to an exercise, which was intended to give the enemy the impression that an attack was underway. This was generally meant to give him little rest and to assist in discovering his exact positions.*

difficult, making the observation of the progress of the attack by Forward Observation Officers almost impossible. The 10th Brigade attacked on a two-battalion front led by the 1st Royal Warwickshire Regiment on the right and the Royal Irish Fusiliers to their left, in touch with the 2nd Duke of Wellington's Regiment (12th Brigade), who were in turn, accompanied on the left, by the 2nd Lancashire Fusiliers.

The centre and right of the Warwickshire Regiment proceeded smoothly to the objective, capturing Frosty and Hazy Trenches and entrenched about 100 yards forward of the captured line. However, the left of the Warwickshire's was met with heavy machine-gun fire, which prevented the capture of the Gunpits. At the same time, the Royal Irish Fusiliers, to the left of the Warwicks, had advanced too quickly and ran into their own barrage, causing casualties. The leading elements retired slightly to avoid the barrage but were met by the same machine-gun fire that confronted the Warwicks. That fire prevented the capture of the Strong Point.

The right of the Royal Irish Fusiliers, having met such intense resistance, retired to their assembly trench, accompanied by some of the Warwickshire's, who had also been caught in the fire. The retirement resulted in a gap forming between the two battalions and, in an effort to overcome the resistance, two companies of the Dublin Fusiliers, acting in support of the Irish Fusiliers, were sent forward to renew the attack, but were driven back by the intensity of the fire. It was clear that further progress was dependent upon the capture of the Strong Point and the Gunpits.

The Duke of Wellington's (12th Brigade), having advanced from Windy and Thistle Trenches, successfully crossed Spectrum Trench, where it left a clearance party and proceeded, with two companies, to move forward to their objective, the high ground, on the extreme left, overlooking le Transloy. Having reached the appropriate line, the two leading companies faced determined counter-attacks but were too weak to hold the ground and were forced to withdraw. The diary for this date states; "*A considerable proportion of these two companies were cut off by the enemy and did not return to our line*". The Lancashires, on the far left of the 12th Brigade, were due to start twenty minutes after the remainder but were held up by the heavy machine-gun fire.

Plate 11
Ordinance Survey map showing the line of attack of the 4th Division on the 12thth October 1916.

Throughout the day the struggle continued, often hand-to-hand, with constant bombing and, getting reinforcements to the forward troops, still holding their gains, was difficult until after dark. The wounded often lay in positions that were too dangerous to attempt recovery. At about 5:40pm the Germans counter-attacked the Warwicks, on the right, but the attempt was repulsed with rifle and machine-gun fire. During the night the positions captured by the Warwicks were consolidated with a defensive right flank thrown back to join up with the French, who had been held up due to the intensity of fire on their front.

Following a request by the O.C., 10th Brigade, to comply with the established line of the Warwickshire's, the French immediately sent troops forward and established outposts. The individual posts were joined together over the course of the next few days to form part of the new front line.

Portions of the objective had been reached and held but, because the exact positions of the rather fragmented groups of infantry could not be verified, the artillery barrage line could not be brought back to support them. The night of the 12th was spent quietly while both sides reconciled their own positions, although the German artillery shelled Lesboeufs and the right of the line held by the Warwicks. The 6th Division had made progress similar to that of the 4th Division but had suffered heavy shelling on Rainbow Trench throughout the night. Every attempt was made by both divisions to consolidate the gains over the next two days. The effort on that first day of the attack was great but the cost high, thirty-two officers and one thousand, four hundred and fourteen men killed and wounded.

At 6:30pm on the 14th, a surprise assault on the Gunpits, Rainy, and Dewdrop Trenches was made by the Royal Dublin Fusiliers and Seaforth Highlanders without the support of the artillery, but the attempt was driven back by machine-gun fire. One company of the Seaforth's had reached the northern Gunpits and Rainy Trench but were unable to maintain their position when counter-attacked by bombing parties. It appears that the rear lines of the Seaforth's had lost direction in the dark and arrived too late to repulse the counter-attacks. Rainy Trench was abandoned, as it was impossible for the artillery to bombard Dewdrop Trench without endangering those in Rainy Trench.

The Dublin Fusiliers' attack on the southern Gunpits also failed and caused heavy shelling by the German artillery on Lesboeufs, the front line, and support lines. Later reports, on the 15th, revealed that the Seaforth's had reached to within 120 yards of the Gunpits before being discovered and the leading wave had entered the pits but were bombed out by enemy infantry as they emerged from the dug-outs and Dewdrop trench. Two days later the 12th Brigade undertook a bombing attack on Dewdrop Trench but failed to make progress.

After four days of constant fighting, the exhausted troops of the Royal Irish Fusiliers and Warwickshire's (10th Brigade) were relieved by the Rifle Brigade and 1st East Lancashires (11th Brigade). The remaining units of the 10th Brigade holding the front line were also relieved, amid regular artillery fire, on the night of the 16th. When the relief was complete, the 10th Brigade retired into division reserve. The artillery fire continued throughout the next day as the German 5.9" howitzers concentrated on Shamrock and Thistle trenches, resulting in nineteen casualties in the 12th Brigade alone. The fire also seriously damaged Shamrock trench for about 300 yards on the northern end, making it practically impassable in daylight.

The second phase of the attack was ordered to continue on the 18th. The 4th Division was to continue with the objective of reaching and capturing those parts of the enemy line that had not been secured in the original attack of the 12th. On this occasion, the attack was to be made by the 11th Brigade on the right and the 12th Brigade on the left. The division was to capture the trenches Hazy, Frosty, Dewdrop, the Gunpits and those parts of Spectrum Trench, which were still in German hands.

The 12th Brigade was to advance with one battalion, the King's Own Royal Lancaster Regiment, with the responsibility of capturing Spectrum trench up to the point where it joined Dewdrop at the Lesboeufs - le Transloy Road. During that advance, the machine-gun Company and the Trench Mortar Battery were allocated special tasks to assist and six machine guns were to be located in Shin Alley to support the attack. Four of those guns were to traverse the ground about 4-500 yards behind Spectrum and Dewdrop Trenches, through which the Germans reinforcements passed. The remaining two guns were to sweep the trenches around the le Transloy Cemetery, referred to as Cemetery Circle[283], and the trenches to the left of the cemetery.

Two additional guns, firing from Spectrum Trench, were to sweep Zenith Trench, 150 yards behind Spectrum, to prevent reinforcements coming from the west. Those guns were to fire constantly for thirty minutes after zero hour. Four trench mortars were to be located off Currie Trench, just outside the division boundary and in the 6th Division area. Two of these guns were to fire into those parts of Spectrum Trench that were held by the Germans, from a distance of about 150 yards while the remaining two were to fire on the sunken road, immediately behind Dewdrop Trench. To add weight to the attack the King's Own was to be supported by two companies of the 2nd Essex in Cow Trench, behind Lesboeufs.

---

[283] *The author visited the two villages in 2004 and was clearly impressed with the view from the trench lines at the cemetery. The civil cemetery is located halfway up the hill alongside the Lesboeufs – Le Transloy road and on the southern outskirts of the village. The location offered the defending infantry a view of all movement in the intervening area for distance up to 2000 yards.*

The 18th began with rain and at 3:40am, zero hour, the division artillery commenced an intense barrage on the German lines. Under cover of this barrage, the King's Own advanced, but experienced great difficulty moving over the wet ground, which had been churned to mud by the constant shelling. By 4:00am, the King's Own had taken possession of about 90 yards of Spectrum trench and, as the morning progressed, the shelling turned into an artillery duel between the opposing sides. The 11th Brigade was being hard-pressed in the vicinity of the Gunpits and, by 9.00pm, the 12th Brigade had assumed responsibility for a part of the 11th Brigade area, to the right of the Lesboeufs - le Transloy Road. The King's Own achieved some of the objectives allocated to them, without casualties, but stubborn opposition and heavy shelling prevented the complete capture of Spectrum Trench.

The supporting 1st Rifle Brigade had assembled on the right hand end of Burnaby Trench and extended to the right as far as the German trenches with 'C', 'I' and 'B' Companies, on a three-company front of nearly 600 yards facing Frosty, Hazy, the Strong Point and the Gunpits. "A" Company was to advance behind "I" and "B" Companies in order to add depth to the attack. To the left of the Rifle Brigade, the East Lancashire Regiment assembled in Burnaby Trench and extended a further 500 yards to the left facing Rainy and Dewdrop Trenches.

The rush to reach the enemy lines resulted in a considerable mixing of troops as the front waves got held up by intense machine-gun fire. In the poor light "I" Company of the Rifle Brigade became dislocated from the main attack and veered to the left and then, in an effort to correct the mistake, back to the right. Realising that they had passed their objective, they then turned around and approached the Gunpits from the rear. In their endeavours to return to their correct position, they encountered a series of shell holes, which had been partially joined and fortified. "I" Company rushed the position, taking about twenty prisoners and a leading patrol destroyed two machine guns further ahead.

Not having the numbers to send the prisoners to the rear, the company continued, taking the prisoners with them, and approached the Gunpits and Strongpoint. A German officer in the Gunpits came out under the impression that the approaching Germans were reinforcements. He was shot and considerable hand-to-hand fighting ensued in which "I" Company suffered heavy casualties. Of the total strength of "I" Company, only about fifty men managed to return to the front line in Burnaby Trench.

Having advanced through the heavy machine-gun fire, the East Lanca-shires managed to reach Dewdrop Trench, only to find it empty. Once in the trench, the guns of the 4th Division artillery shelled the East Lancashire's resulting in heavy casualties amongst the officers and N.C.O.'s, resulting in heavy casualties amongst the officers and N.C.O.'s. A report by the G.O.C. (11ᵗʰ Brigade) after the event stated; *"I consider that the cause of failure was primarily due to the slippery state of the ground and darkness of the night. The men did not reach their objectives in a fit state to fight. If the night had been fine like the preceding nights portions of the objectives would probably have been held. The state of the ground caused great disorganisation, and disor-ganisation at night with indifferently trained Officers, N.C.O.'s and men, makes the consolidation of such a position very difficult. Sec-ondly, there is no real objective to go for. All the enemy trenches were practically destroyed - in most places unrecognisable as such. The Ger-mans probably have some fifteen to twenty machine guns chiefly in shell holes placed irregularly so that at no time does our creeping or stationary barrage silence the whole lot."* No mention of the 'friendly' artillery fire.

The next two days were spent under constant enemy artillery fire. Those of the East Lancashires who were able, withdrew to the assembly trenches. The positions captured on the 18ᵗʰ were consolidated while XIV Corps planned a renewal of the attack. The operation orders for the attack, issued on the 20ᵗʰ, indicated that the French 18ᵗʰ Division, fighting on the right of the 4ᵗʰ, was to attack at the same date and time.

The date of the attack was determined as the 23ʳᵈ October and it was to achieve two objectives. The first was to complete the removal of the remains of the enemy from Rainy, Dewdrop and the remaining part of Spectrum Trenches, and establish secure positions a little past that line, referred to as the Brown Line. The second objective was to advance the line to a position immediately in front of le Transloy. It was intended that the new line would lie 250-300 yards in front of the village, ex-tending from the junction of the le Transloy - Lesboeufs Road and the le Transloy-Gueudecourt Road, to the right as far as the le Transloy–Sailly-Saillisel Road, a front of nearly 1000 yards. The objective was re-ferred to as the Yellow Line. The offensive was to be preceded by a continuous bombardment of the German positions for several days.

To add further weight to the attack, the 28ᵗʰ Brigade (8ᵗʰ Division), which had been temporarily attached to the 4ᵗʰ Division for the attack and the 2ⁿᵈ Seaforth Highlanders (10ᵗʰ Brigade) were both attached to the 12ᵗʰ Brigade. The 12ᵗʰ Brigade was to attack on a three-battalion front, using a line drawn from the north-east corner of Lesboeufs to the eastern side of le Transloy, as the right boundary and the normal boundary with the 6th Division, as the left boundary.

The 11th Brigade was also provided with reinforcements, with the addition of Royal Dublin Fusiliers and Royal Warwickshire Regiment, (10th Brigade). In preparation for the assault the 28th Brigade relieved the far left of the 12th Brigade on the night of the 20th. In turn, the 12th Brigade side slipped to the right and took over a large part of the 11th Brigade area, leaving the 11th Brigade holding the right half of the line.

Next to the 28th Brigade, three battalions, the 2nd Essex (less two companies) on the right, the Lancashire Fusiliers in the centre and the King's Own (less two companies in the left) were to attack on the 12th Brigade front. It was intended that, having reached the Brown Line, the Lancashire Fusiliers would remain there and consolidate the position while the Essex and King's Own continued the advance to the Yellow Line. Whilst the Essex and King's Own were establishing the new line, the Lancashire Fusiliers were to mop-up Rainy, Dewdrop and other small trenches and shell holes.

While the 12th Brigade was thus engaged, the 11th Brigade was to attack on the right of the division and maintain contact with the French 18th Division. The Brigade was to advance with the 1st Hampshire Regiment on the far right and the Dublin Fusiliers to their left, supported respectively by the Rifle Brigade and the Warwickshire's. The Hampshire's were to form up in a series of trenches Frosty -Antelope - Andrews Post - Foggy and part of Thunder Trench while the Dublin's assembled in Burnaby - Foggy - and half of a new trench to Andrews Post.

The attack was to commence at 11.30am, zero hour, with an intense creeping artillery barrage, planned to advance at the rate of 50 yards per minute. The intentions were that the three assaulting battalions would advance at the double until the leading wave was close to the creeping barrage and follow it across the first objective after which it would stop. The first three waves of the Essex and King's Own were to cross the enemy trenches and entrench on the Brown Line, behind the protection of the barrage. The advance was then to continue behind the barrage until the Yellow Line had been reached, whereupon the new line would be consolidated while the barrage remained in place.

As the advance was to begin, a company of the Duke of Wellington's and two Lewis guns were to leave the assembly trench, Spectrum Trench, and clear the sunken Lesboeufs - le Transloy Road, 100 yards to the right. This involved special parties from the Dukes clearing each of the dugouts, which had been dug into the sides of the cutting, and then garrisoning the area.

Much effort was made in preparing the brigades for the attack and, on the day before, the division was advised that it would be relieved by the 33rd Division, during the nights of the 23rd and 24th. Preparations for the attack continued throughout the night as the troops moved into the assembly trenches where instructions were given that they were to lie down and remain still, should an enemy aircraft approach the area.

As the hour approached, the attack was delayed until 2:30pm as dawn revealed a heavy mist, which prevented the artillery from observing the progress. At the prescribed time, the guns opened a heavy bombardment of the German lines and the enemy artillery immediately responded by heavily shelling Lesboeufs and the trenches to the east of the village but both brigades had got away quickly and avoided most of the shellfire.

The enemy barrage was accompanied by intense machine-gun and rifle fire but, due to the mist, little could be seen of the progress of the attackers. The 11th Brigade immediately ran into the heavy small arms fire, most of which was coming from Boritska Trench, near to Frosty Trench and from gun positions beyond, but a few men managed to occupy the end of Boritska Trench, followed later by its complete occupation.

The capture of the Gunpits by the Dublin Fusiliers was a harrowing experience as they were stopped 30 yards from the objective by fire coming from within. The 11th Brigade diary for the 23rd records *"....but fired by the example of Sergt. Downie who charged a German machine-gun the Battalion again advanced and cleared a part of the Gunpits and the strong point to the Eastwards destroying several machine guns."* The Warwicks were to advance through the Dublin Fusiliers but became involved in hand-to-hand fighting, resulting in the complete mixing of the two battalions. A part of this force attempted to continue the advance but, as both flanks were in the air and the men were under heavy machine-gun fire from both Dewdrop and Boritska trenches, no progress could be made.

All attempts by the troops to the right of the Hampshire's failed because of the very heavy fire, but some of the Hampshire's and Rifle Brigade worked forward and established a line east of Frosty Trench. The line was further extended during the night, the Hampshire's managing to link up with the Dublin Fusiliers in the Gunpits.

The 12th Brigade could not capture Dewdrop Trench although it was believed that a few men of the Essex Regiment had reached and passed over it in pursuit of the first objective. By 3:20pm, reports were received stating that those men of the Essex battalion, which had continued onwards were seen digging in on the Brown Line but they were unable to hold their gains against the heavy machine-gun fire. Reports about this incident were conflicting as few, if any, of those men returned.

Most of that fire appeared to be coming from Dewdrop Trench and the Seaforth's, King's Own and Essex concentrated all efforts on the capture of that line. However, the best efforts of those battalions were put to the test by the wet, muddy conditions and in finding sufficient men in the mist. The King's Own finally took a further 60 yards of Spectrum Trench but was not able to reach the sunken road on the left, from which much of the fire originated.

The failure of the 12th Brigade to achieve its objective appeared to be directly attributable to the heavy machine-gun fire coming from the north and north-west. The delays caused by the heavy fighting prevented the infantry from following the barrage, which quickly disappeared into the mist. It was impossible to obtain accurate information as to the whereabouts of the leading troops and, therefore, the artillery was unable to shorten the range for fear of shelling their own troops.

The poor visibility caused considerable confusion among the troops and various headquarters. Further attempts were made throughout the afternoon to attack Dewdrop but the withering machine-gun fire defeated all such efforts. As night approached, it was evident that the attack had failed and all units were withdrawn to the original front line. It was only as the troops returned that the gravity of the failure became clear.

The 12th Brigade had suffered three officers and one hundred and twenty eight men killed, eight officers and five hundred and thirty seven men wounded and one officer and two hundred and twenty nine men missing. The only gain made by that brigade was an additional 60 yards of Spectrum trench being taken and held. The 11th Brigade had managed to take and hold most of the Gunpits and the Strong Point. To ensure the security of those gains, during the night the captured positions were joined by communication trenches to allow access to the relieving troops.

The following day, the 24th, the division line was subject to the special attentions of the enemy artillery, which continued for the whole day and well into the night, as the 33rd Division commenced the relief. The 10th Brigade, acting in support, had been relieved the previous night, the 23rd, by the 19th Brigade. During the night of the 24th, the 100th and 98th Brigades relieved the 11th and 12th Brigades respectively. As each relief was completed the brigades retired from the line, the 10th Brigade marching to the Sandpits Camp, while the 11th marched to Trônes Wood and the 12th to Briqueterie.

November – 1916

November was inauspicious as some of the troops and many officers were granted home leave. The weather remained mostly fine but cool, even cold enough to experience periodical snowfalls. In the need to recover from the losses and occupy those who remained, a full schedule of training was undertaken in every form of trench fighting required of the British soldier. Reinforcements were absorbed into all battalions and, on the 15th, the Royal Dublin Fusiliers, who had been a part of the 10th Brigade since mobilisation in August of 1914, were transferred to the 16th Division, and replaced by the Household Battalion.

On the 28th November the XV Corps, of which the 4th Division was now a part, issued Operation Orders stating that the Corps would relieve French XX Corps (5th French Army), located between Rancourt and Sailley-Saillisel, 4000 yards south of le Transloy, where the division had fought the previous month. This part of the line was considered 'quiet' and the opposing forces, whilst attempting to destroy the enemy whenever the opportunity presented itself, were quite content to allow life to carry on without any large scale offensive actions or artillery duels.

December - 1916

By the 1st December, the division was once again on the move to assume positions in the front line. The 10th Brigade marched for Argoeuves, reaching that village the following afternoon. It entrained at Oisemont on the 3rd and travelled through Amiens and Corbie to Méricourt l'Abbé, where they detrained and marched east to Morlancourt, where they spent the night in billets. The following four days were spent marching to camps in the areas north of Bray as the whole division moved forward in stages. The movement slowly took them eastward and passed through the same areas as in the previous move to Lesboeufs, two months earlier.

They were now bound for Maricourt, seven miles south of Lesboeufs and 10 miles from the Redan, where they fought six months earlier. Maricourt was at the northern most limit of the French line, where it met the southern end of the British Line, eight miles north-west of Pérrone. In early 1917, the area north and south of Pérrone was considered a 'quiet' area, that is, an area where divisions could be sent after serving on the very active fronts such as the Somme and Flanders. The French army had occupied that part of the line since 1914, and the British were asked to take over some of the line so that the French had some time to rest and refit.

The 4th Division carried the relief on the night of 7th December and assumed responsibility for that part of the line, which overlapped the boundary of the 39th and 11th Divisions (French XX Corps). The 12th Brigade relieved the right hand brigade of the 39th French Division while the 10th Brigade relieved the left hand Brigade of the French 11th Division. While those reliefs were being completed, the 33rd (British) Division relieved the remainder of 11th French Division.

Certain readjustments were necessary to complete operations, so the 10th Brigade side slipped to the right and took over those trenches held by the left brigade of the 33rd Division on the night of the 10th December. Once settled in the area, life in the trenches continued in much the same manner as before, that of a constant cycle of battalion reliefs and spasmodic shelling by both sides. The pattern prevailed until the 20th, when the German artillery became very active and paid special attention to Frégicourt, albeit a temporary intervention.

Little activity was experienced and only occasional shelling by the Germans in the general direction of Rancourt, just to the right of the 4th Division. By the 11th, the Germans had increased the rate of shellfire on the Bapaume - Péronne Road and all trenches west of that road, including those in the area of the 4th Division. This steadily increased over next nine days until it was consistently heavy. Aggravating the shelling was the rain, which fell steadily and, at times, in torrents, until the trench walls collapsed at random.

During the 23rd, the 10th Brigade relieved the 12th Brigade and the following night three Russians, soldiers in the German Army, walked in to the line held by that brigade and surrendered. Towards the end of the month, there was very little enemy activity except in the air where, on the 26th, several encounters between Allied and German aircraft took place resulting in two enemy aeroplanes being shot down. The last day of 1916 saw the 4th Division relieved by the 8th Division and pass into XV Corps Reserve at Bray, on the River Somme.

1917 - Hopes Rise

January -1917

The first two weeks of January were dedicated to training and improvement of physical fitness. During that period, the division undertook several changes. New reinforcements arrived and, as Christmas day had been spent in the trenches under shellfire, a belated celebration was held on the 7th, all personnel having the day off. Shortly after, on the 11th, Brigadier-General Carton De Wiart V.C., D.S.O., joined the division and assumed command of the 12th Brigade after having commanded the 8th Battalion, Gloucestershire Regiment (19th Division).

Operation orders were issued on the 13th, stating that the British XV Corps was to relieve the French IX Corps and, as a part of that relief, the 4th Division was to relieve the French 18th Division[234] on a line between Rancourt and Bouchavesnes, north of Pérrone. The new lines were adjacent to the positions the division had held in December, an area used to reinforce and train many British divisions after having served more active area. The German Army used the area for the same purpose and it was not unusual to find opposing divisions in the same area, after having faced one another in combat elsewhere.

The division commenced its departure from the training grounds on the 14th and arrived behind the French lines at Bouchavesnes, two days later. Upon arrival, the 11th Brigade relieved a Regiment of the 35th French Brigade and the 10th Brigade relieved a Regiment of the 36th Brigade (12th Brigade), the following day. The 18th and 19th were occupied with trench maintenance and completing the relief of the French artillery. During the evening of the 20th the Seaforth Highlanders of the 10th Brigade were subjected to heavy shelling by the German artillery, and division guns retaliated by bombarding the German front line trenches. So trench life went on.

In the very cold weather, often accompanied by regular snowfalls, constant patrol activity, periodic artillery fire and the considerable aerial activity, kept the troops on the alert. The presence of such an abundance of German and Allied aircraft in the area led to many a display of aerial combat, resulting in consistent losses on both sides. On the 23rd a

---

[234] It was the French 18th Division that had fought next to the 4th Division at le Transloy in October of the previous year.

German aircraft was brought down by anti-aircraft fire and landed behind the British lines at Hopital Farm and shortly after, a second aircraft was forced down behind the enemy lines by two French planes.

As a result of the influx of divisions coming into the area, it was intended to shorten the line being held by the 4th Division to a one-brigade front. On the night of the 23rd a portion of the front being held by the 10th Brigade, on the southern sector of the division line, was taken over by the 98th Brigade (33rd Division). To allow the 10th Brigade to withdraw completely the 11th Brigade extended its right and established contact with the 98th. The 10th Brigade then returned to Bray Camp 112. Shortly after its arrival, the camp was attacked by a single German aircraft, which dropped a number of bombs and inflicted several casualties.

During the period in Bray, large working parties were made available to the 178th Tunnelling Company, which had been attached to the division, to establish large, deep dug-outs for the accommodation and protection of the troops. The supply of local water was insufficient to supply the needs of a division and the Tunnelling Company utilised the many springs in the area to help meet the daily consumption.

German observation aircraft continually circled over the division artillery batteries, which were concentrating on the German trenches and line of communications. The information passed to the enemy batteries resulted in constant duelling between the opposing artillery. The regular air activity pitted aircraft against aircraft and it was during this period that the Royal Flying Corps suffered some of its highest losses of the war.

February - 1917

The 12th Brigade relieved the 11th Brigade on the first day of the month and, as the relief took place, both brigades were subjected to regular shelling and, in an effort to distract the enemy artillery, the division guns retaliated by shelling the opposing batteries and trench lines. In an environment of increasing tensions, the constant patrolling of the 4th Division had made the enemy infantry sensitive to the possibility of attack and remained alert, firing with rifle and machine-gun at every opportunity.

Early in the morning of the 3rd, the German artillery subjected Sap 16[285] to a severe bombardment and at 5:00am a raiding party of about twenty, all dressed in white, approached. They successfully entered the sap and bombed down to the main line, turned right (north) for a short distance where they were met by determined resistance and driven out. As they left they attempted to take four men prisoners, but they were having none of it and managed to escape whilst the raiders were retiring. The enemy party left behind three dead and one wounded while a further four were shot in No Man's Land. British casualties were one officer wounded, later dieing as a result of his injuries, six other ranks killed, and seven other ranks wounded, mostly by the earlier artillery fire.

The British artillery retaliated against the German front line trenches during the following day and caused considerable damage. Normally this would have resulted in an angry response by the German artillery but, on this occasion, the enemy remained relatively quiet. The soldier's day was filled with attacks by rifle-grenade, artillery exchanges, working parties and night patrols. Harassment was conducted by sides, often without confirmed results. During the night of the 4th, a patrol of one officer and two O.R.'s of the Duke of Wellington's carried out a raid on an occupied enemy advanced post by throwing eight bombs and then withdrew.

On the 7th, instructions were received stating that, on the 10th of the month, the 4th Division was to take over a part of the line north of Bouchavesnes from the 8th Division. Accordingly, the 10th Brigade was to sideslip to the left, or north, towards Rancourt, and relieve the 24th Brigade. The movement of the 10th Brigade was carried out in a period

---

[285] *Saps, or frontline outposts, were often numbered instead of named. Often they were numbered from right to left and the locations were only available on the most detailed of local maps.*

marked by considerable aerial activity by both sides and the ground troops stood witness to intense combat between opposing aircraft in which many were seen to fall.

The division was due for relief and on the night of the 20th January the right hand sector of the 10th Brigade was relieved by the 100th and 19th Brigades (33rd Division) while the 11th Brigade was relieved by the 23rd and 25th Brigades (8th Division). Following withdrawal, all three Brigades returned to the Corbie area and remained in headquarters reserve.

March -1917

March was to bring a brutal new event into the life of the 4th Division. In November of 1916, a conference of military representatives from all of the Allied powers had met at the French General Headquarters at Chantilly to decide a general plan of strategy for the forthcoming year. From that meeting came the plans of the British Commander-in-Chief, General Douglas Haig, for the events that were to take place in 1917.

His plan was to commence operations against the German line, between the Rivers Scarpe and Ancre, in an attempt to straighten a salient in the Allied line, which had formed between the two rivers, a result of the British effort on the Somme during 1916. He then intended to transfer the offensive to the Flanders area in Belgium and attack the German line along the Messines - Wytschaete Ridge and the high ground north-eastwards, through Passchendaele. The southern attack, at Arras, was to involve the British 5th Army attacking the salient from the south, that is, from the Ancre, and for the British 3rd Army to attack from the north, about Arras.

Due to a readjustment to the French plans, a consequence of General Nivelle having assumed the role of French Commander-in-Chief, Haig was instructed by the British Government to alter his initial plan. The modified plan involved the British army attacking at Arras on a much wider front than was envisaged in Haigs' initial plan and to support the French offensive, due to commence a week later. The plan was dependent upon there being no major changes of the German front positions before the attack. However, during the month of March, the German forces had undertaken a controlled and deliberate withdrawal, on the front between Arras and Soissons, to the Hindenburgh line (also known to the Germans as the Siegfried line), a move which effectively eliminated the salient, the subject of the British attack. The 5th Army was then given the responsibility of pursuing the enemy and confronting the German forces in their new positions.

In order to offer continued support for Neville's' offensive, it was the wish of the British government to continue the offensive about Arras and it was to this part of the front that the 4th Division moved. On the 3rd of March, Operation Order No. 13 was issued, which required the division to commence its march, the following day, to the training area near Abbeville. The movement lasted until the 7th when the 10th Brigade marched into billets in the area around Mézerolles - Remaisnil - Villers l'Hôpital, the 11th Brigade at Buire au Bois - Rougefay and the 12th Brigade in the area of Vaulx - Gennes-Ivergany, where the brigades commenced training. The programme was constant and addressed the skills that would be needed in what was perceived to become mobile warfare.

On the 20th, division headquarters received instructions to move the area controlled by the XVII Corps (Lt.-Gen. Sir F. I. Maxse). XVII Corps was to consist of the 9th, 34th, 51st and 4th Divisions, all a part of the British Fifth Army, commanded by General Sir Hubert Gough. As the troops continued training, orders were issued which defined the role and responsibilities of the various divisions involved. In order to understand the order of battle General Haigs' own words are quoted: *"The main attack was entrusted to the Third and First Armies under the command of General Sir E. H. Allenby, and General Sir H. S. Horne, respectively.*

Four Army Corps (the VII., VI., XVII and XVIII Corps, under the command of, respectively, Lieut.-Generals Sir T. D'O. Snow[286], J.A.L. Haldane[287], Sir C. Fergusson and Sir F. I. Maxse) were placed at the disposal of General Allenby, with an additional Army Corps Headquarters (the XIX. Corps, Lieut. -General H. E. Watts) to be used as occasion might demand. Cavalry also (the Cavalry Corps, Lieut. -General Sir C. T. Mc.Kavanagh) was brought up into the Third Army area, in case the development of the battle should give rise to an opportunity for the employment of mounted troops on a considerable scale."[288]

On the 20th Preliminary Instructions No. 2 was issued which, in part, stated: *"The 4th Division will, with the 9th, 34th and 51st Divisions, form part of the XVII Corps and take part in the operations of the Third Army.*

The primary object of the operation of the XVII Corps is to capture the German 3rd System of trenches which runs from the River SCARPE, East of ATHIES, through LE POINT DU JOUR - MAISON DE LA COTE - COMMANDANTS HOUSE.

---

[286] *Lieutenant-General Snow commanded the 4 Division at the time of mobilisation (then a Major General) until September 1914.*

[287] *Lieutenant-General Haldane commanded the 10 Brigade, under Maj.-General Snow, at the time of mobilisation.*

[288] *Quoted from Sir Douglas Haigs, Despatches, J. H. Boraston, C.B., O.B.E. and printed by J. M. Dent & Sons Ltd., London, p87.*

When this line has been captured a further advance will be made South of LE POINT DU JOUR to capture the southern portion of VIMY RIDGE, the 4th System of the trenches West of Fampoux, and the village of Fampoux.

The VI Corps will be operating on the right of the XVII Corps.
The Boundary between XVII and VI Corps throughout is the River SCARPE.

The Canadian Corps will be operating on the left of the XVII Corps.

The German 3rd System of Trenches (Brown line) on the front of the XVII Corps will be captured by the 9th, 34th and 51st Divisions (from right to left in the order given), the 4th Division being in Reserve in rear of the 9th Division.

The 4th Division will pass through the 9th Division, capture the 4th German Trench system, and the village of FAMPOUX, and establish itself on the Green line (vide Map A)." [289]

Geographically, Arras is located south of Lille and lies between the River Scarpe, on its northern boundary, and the Valenciennes - Amiens Railway on the southern boundary. The German Army occupied a north-south line extending from the Belgian town of Ypres, stretching south through Armentières, Lens and east of Arras, where it curved south-east to Péronne and then eastwards to the Swiss border. Germans forces had occupied Arras during the invasion of 1914 but had been pushed back by the French until, by 1917, the line was located approximately 1500 yards to the east of Arras. The XVII Corps held the line, opposing the German lines from the River Scarpe, north to Lievin. The 9th Division held the southern flank of the corps line, from the Scarpe to Biache St. Chantecler, 3000 yards to the north and it was there that the 4th Division was to arrive, to support and attack with the 9th.

---

[289] *For a full description of the orders, see Appendix VII "Preliminary Instructions No.2". Extract of War Diary WO95/1491*

April -1917

During the early months of 1917, the German forces south of Arras had fallen back on the Hindenburgh line while those to the north maintained the line of late 1916. The British 3rd Army was to attack the enemy defences on the line Croisilles - Commandants House, capture the Hindenburgh line and press through towards Biaches St. Vaast. To the left, or north, the 1st Army was to attack simultaneously with a view to capturing Vimy Ridge, north of Commandants House. XVII Corps was confronted with formidable defences, which consisted of four well-defended trench systems, which constituted the Hindenburgh line. By early April, the part of the British front line held by the 9th Division, soon to be assumed by the 4th Division, lay on the immediate eastern edge of Arras. The River Scarpe, on the northern edge of the city, flowed from the north, near Lille, in a wide southerly arc and approached Arras from the east.

In front of that part of the British line for which the 9th Division was responsible, lay the first of the German defensive lines, referred to in British military jargon, the Black line. It was three well-planned and defended trench lines located approximately 800 yards in front of the British line and some five hundred yards deep. One thousand yards beyond lay the Blue line, a strongly fortified railway embankment and cutting, which offered protection from artillery fire and gave complete observation over the intervening ground.

The third line of defences, the Brown line, sometimes referred to as the 3rd German Trench System, lay approximately 1000 yards behind the Blue line and extended from le Point Du Jour, on the extreme left of the line of advance, to Athiens on the River Scarpe. The Brown line was situated on the forward slope of the Point Du Jour Ridge and consisted of three well-prepared trenches, heavily wired throughout and commanded a clear field of fire between it and the Blue line. A further two thousand yards behind the Brown line lay a fourth formidable line referred to as the 4th German Trench System.

That line of defences extended from Gavrelle, to the left and 1500 yards outside of the division line of attack, to the River Scarpe, which it crossed 200 yards in front of the village of Fampuox, and then to Wancourt, 6000 yards south of the river. As it was situated to the rear of the Point Du Jour Ridge, it was not visible from the British front line, although the British High Command was well aware of its presence from aerial photographs. It was a deep system of defences consisting of fire and support trenches and constructed with deep dugouts for the defenders. To the rear of the 4th German Trench System lay two sunken roads, both capable of offering a fifth line of resistance if necessary.

Once past these obstacles the division was to take and hold the fortified village of Fampoux, the first objective of the 4th Division, and the heavily defended Hyderabad Redoubt[290]. It was then to continue to the Green line, a line about 1000 yards east of Fampoux, between Gavrelle and Roeux, which offered observation over the plain of Douai. In order to allow the troops to identify which part of the battlefield they were passing, the attacking divisions were instructed to carry notices marked, appropriately, as "Black line", "Blue line" and "Brown line" and were to be installed as each objective was taken.

The XVII Corps plan required the 9th Division to attack on the northern bank of the River Scarpe, with its right flank on the river and its left on Biache St. Chantecler. The 34th and 51st Divisions were to attack on the left of the 9th Division respectively with the objective of capturing the continuation of the Black, Brown and Blue lines. The 4th Division was to follow the 9th Division and, once it had reached the Brown line, advance through and capture the 4th German Trench System and the Green line. To achieve these last objectives, the 11th and 12th Brigades were to lead the assault while the 10th Brigade, with two battalions behind each of the attacking brigades, was to support the advance.

The 12th Brigade was to commence the advance with its right flank on the River Scarpe and extend to the left, to meet the 11th Brigade approximately 1500 yards to the north. That line, in turn, was to extend further to the left, to a line, which intersected and crossed the Arras – Gavrelle Road near le Pont Du Jour[291]. Zero hour was set for 5:30am on the 8th April but, due to the necessity of getting all of the units into position, some of which could not arrive until after zero hour, the date was postponed for 24 hours, until the 9th.

To assist with the initial advance, an artillery preparation was to take place on V, W, X and Y days, four days before the attack and was to commence at 6:30am each day. Fifteen minutes before the bombard-

---

[290] *The Hyderabad Redoubt was the name given to a German strongpoint located just behind the 4 German Trench System that offered covering fire on Fampoux and on No Mans Land south of the river.*

[291] *Point-Du-Jour was the site of a house on the St. Laurent-Blagny – Gavrelle road. While in German hands, the location was converted to a redoubt. I t was finally captured by the 34 Division on the first day of the attack, the 9 April 1917.*

ment on the first day, the 5th, gas was to be released in a north-easterly direction, followed by the bombardment.

While plans were being finalised, training continued for the troops until the 5th of April, when orders were issued for the division to move to the area of Haute-Avenges, some seven miles north west of Arras. The artillery commenced its' preliminary bombardments and gas was again released on the morning of the 6th using Livens Projectors. At 1:30pm, a practice barrage was laid on the German front line and specific targets in the rear areas, to confirm that all guns were registered on their specific targets. The long-range guns fired on Gavrelle, Farbus and Les Montauban, which caused considerable damage and started several fires.

On the 7th, the 10th Brigade marched to Bethosart, the 11th to Hermanville and the 12th to Y Huts, a camp that had been constructed for the accommodation of troops. The War Diary for the 11th Brigade states, for that date, *"This move marks the commencement of the brigade up to battle."* During the night of the 7th, raids were carried out against selected enemy trenches. Those raids faced severe fighting but three wounded prisoners were captured. During the early hours of the 8th the whole division moved to the assembly areas of St. Nicholas, just to the north of Arras and St. Catherine, where large quantities of supplies and materials had been delivered in previous days. The movement of troops to their allocated areas was effected without difficulty.

The day was spent moving to new locations, which caused some concern, as the 10th and 11th Brigades were required to cross the paths of the Cavalry and troops of other divisions, which were moving forward. However, the difficulties were resolved quickly and the 11th Brigade began concentrating around Maroeuil. In preparation for the forthcoming events, the headquarters of the 4th Division moved closer to the line, to Etrun.

To understand the following events, a description of the plans and expectations of the 4th Division is appropriate. At the commencement of the bombardment at zero hour, the 9th Division, accompanied by the 34th and 51st Division to its left, was to immediately advance. The bombardment was also to act as a signal for the brigades of the 4th Division to depart the camps and march for the assembly point in the Rolincourt Valley.

Upon notification of the capture of the Blue line by the 9th Division, the assaulting brigades of the 4th Division were to march in column of route to the Blue line, deploy into fighting formations and locate on their individual battle fronts. Forty-five minutes after the 9th Division had left the Blue line, the leading brigades of the 4th Division were to advance in support.

It was intended that the 9th Division assault was to take the Brown line 8 hours after zero hour, 1:30pm. It was expected that the advance of the 4th Division from the Blue line to the Brown line would take about 30 minutes to cover the one mile between the two positions. On arrival at the Brown line, the brigades were then to take a short time to assume their final fighting deployment for the 3300 yards advance to the Green line. Once ready, the two leading brigades would then advance and take the 4th German System 12 hours after zero hour, 5:30pm.

For the ease of understanding, the remaining narrative will concentrate on the activities of the 9th and 4th Divisions which were facing the newly arrived Bavarian 14th Division (1st Bavarian Reserve Corps - General Ritter von Fasbender).

On the day before the attack the O.C. 12th Brigade, Brigadier-General De Wiart V.C., D.S.O., was slightly wounded by shrapnel but his injuries were such that he continued with his duties. At 5:30am on the 9th the artillery of seven artillery brigades, of all sizes and calibres commenced the opening bombardment and maintained an almost perfect barrage, right up to the Brown line. At the same time the leading 26th and 27th Brigades (9th Division) left their trenches and advanced under the cover of a machine-gun barrage.

That barrage represented the signal for the brigades of the 4th Division to commence the march from Maroeuil, X Camp and Y Camp through Anzin St. Aubin - St. Catherine - St. Nicholas - Rolincourt Valley, a march of about two hours, where they assembled in preparation of moving to the Blue line. The 12th Brigade remained in the area about St. Nicholas until the order arrived to commence the advance.

The German artillery response to the bombardment was not heavy and, by 6:15am troops of the 9th Division had entered and captured the first objective, the Black line, confirmation of which was received by the contact aeroplanes of the R.F.C. By 7:55am, the troops of the 9th Division were approaching the Blue line and completed the capture shortly after. The capture of that line was the signal for the 11th and 12th Brigades to commence their march to reach that line at 12:10pm. Accordingly, the 12th Brigade moved to Forrester Redoubt, next to the 26th Brigade.

Once on the Blue line the two brigades deployed into their fighting formations and commenced the advance immediately. The 12th Brigade advance was held up by the slow progress of the 26th Brigade, and the exposure caused by such a slow advance inflicted nearly 150 casualties. The progress of the 9th Division slowed down as resistance grew and at 12:55pm, the 4th Division received orders to give the 9th Division close support at the Brown line.

By 3:25pm, the 9th Division had completed the capture of the Brown line and Athies, where the attacking brigades remained to consolidate and convert the German line into defensive positions. Shortly after, at 3:50pm, the 11th and 12th Brigades crossed the trenches of the Brown line and continued the assault under the cover of a creeping barrage[292]. As the two brigades reached the 4th German System, it had become apparent that the 34th Division, to the left of the 11th Brigade, had been slowed in its advance by the enemy resistance. To protect the left flank of the division, the East Lancashire Regiment (11th Brigade), following behind the Hampshire's, formed a defensive flank facing north and extending back from 4th German System to Point Du Jour, a distance of some 500 yards. The advance continued and, upon cresting the Point Du Jour ridge, the troops could see scattered parties of Germans and at least one gun, streaming towards Gavrelle. Long-range machine-gun fire was opened upon the retiring gun, but failed to stop the flight.

The 12th Brigade had advanced with the King's Own Royal Lancashire Regiment, Lancashire Fusiliers and Essex Regiments, which successfully captured that part of the 4th German Trench System that lay immediately west of Fampoux without undue difficulty. It appeared that the lack of resistance was largely due to the demoralisation of the defenders. A certain amount of rifle and machine-gun fire was experienced but, with few exceptions, the German troops holding the front line surrendered, while those in the support lines retired to the east and were shot down as they fled. The War Diary of the 4th Division records that *"The prisoners went to the rear at top speed without waiting for any escort."*

Circumstances on the 11th Brigade front were considerably more difficult. It was soon discovered that the artillery fire had barely damaged the wire defences, in front of the enemy trenches but, while the trenches were well constructed, they were not heavily defended. After forcing the wire defences by passing through the access gaps or climbing over it, troops of the Somerset Light Infantry and Hampshire's took possession of the trenches and shot those enemies who tried to resist.

---

[292] *Six artillery brigades delivered the barrage and, as the 7· was moving forward, the barrage thinned a little.*

Artillery fire coming from the north-west, in front of the adjoining divisions and was relatively light but other field guns, firing from between Point Du Jour and Gavrelle, subjected the Somerset's and Hampshire's to heavy and accurate fire. Enemy gunners worked their guns until the British troops were within several hundred yards and, in an attempt to give time for the guns to get away, German infantry counter-attacked with grenades and rifles.

The attempts were in vain and many of the guns were captured, along with the bodies of several gunners. After the opposition from the field guns had been overcome, the troops concentrated efforts on establishing a double line of strong points. As they dug in, the German artillery recovered its composure and subjected the stationary troops to constant shellfire. It was during this period of consolidation that Lieutenant-Colonel Burke of the East Lancashires was killed[293].

While the Somerset's had been attacking towards Point Du Jour, the Rifle Brigade, following behind, had crossed the Brown line twenty-five minutes behind the assaulting brigades. While passing through the wire of the 4th German System and in the confines of the sunken road, the advancing lines were subjected to heavy artillery fire and suffered considerable casualties. The Rifle Brigade was responsible for the capture of the Hyderabad Redoubt. As they approached, it was discovered that the guns had hardly touched the redoubt and the wire was uncut. Undeterred, the position was rushed at about 5:15pm by the leading platoon whereupon the occupants, like earlier incidents, promptly surrendered.

Patrols were immediately pushed forward but encountered heavy machine-gun and rifle fire from the direction of the Inn, near Roeux and from German infantry lying in the open between the redoubt and the Gavrelle - Roeux Road. In the face of that fire and the failure to establish outposts east of the Redoubt, the decision was made to consolidate the newly captured position.

Previous reports of German reinforcements advancing from Fresnes towards Gavrelle appeared correct and it was the arrival of those troops, of the 18th German Division, which rallied the defenders. Those reserves, accompanied by the remainder of the survivors of the 4th German System, were subjected to heavy rifle and machine-gun fire from

---

[293] *Lt.-Col. Charles James Burke, D.S.O., 2 Battalion, Royal Irish Regiment, was attached as Commanding Officer of the 1 Battalion, East Lancashire Regimen t at the time of his death. He arrived in France in August 1914 as the Commanding Officer of the No.2 Squadron, Royal Flying Corps, before rejoining his the infantry. He is buried in the Point-Du-Jour military Cemetery, Athies.*

which they suffered heavy casualties. Just before dark a counter-attack, of an estimated strength of two battalions, was seen approaching, in three lines, from the direction of Gavrelle but was brought to a standstill under the combined machine-gun and rifle fire of the Rifle Brigade, Hampshire's and the supporting artillery.

Whilst the 11th Brigade was struggling to secure its objectives on the left flank, the 12th Brigade was also fully occupied on the right flank. The brigade continued its initial success, capturing prisoners in Cam Trench and a considerable number in the ravine east of Athies. Like the 11th Brigade, the troops of the 12th Brigade had found that the wire in front of the 4th German System had been barely touched but little opposition was met. Some of the enemy advanced and surrendered whilst the majority fled eastward, towards Gavrelle. As the troops cut their way through the wire, they were subjected to the fire from several machine guns but the crews were shot down by Lewis Gun fire, and a further two hundred and thirty were captured.

The next objective for the 12th Brigade was the capture of Fampoux with the 2nd West Riding Regiment. Fampoux is located on the northern bank of the River Scarpe and was covered by fire from the high ground of the of the Scarpe valley, from both side of the river and from Greenland Hill, located 1000 yards behind the Black line. By 5:30pm, the German artillery had shelled the eastern edge of the village albeit, without seriously hampering progress. As the troops of the King's Own proceeded through the village, those few enemies who remained hidden in houses were bombed into submission and by 7:00pm, Fampoux had fallen.

As the King's Own emerged from the eastern end of the town, they were met by heavy enfilade fire from machine guns on the southern bank of the river. To subdue the fire, Vickers machine guns were brought forward, mounted in the upper storeys of the buildings, and brought to bear on the shallow trenches in front of the village and on the guns on the opposite side of the river. Five stokes mortars were also brought forward but did not have the range to reach suitable targets.

The 10th Brigade, acting in support, was used largely for carrying engineering supplies, ammunition and water to the two fighting brigades, acting as stretcher-bearers on their return. Enemy resistance grew steadily and the fighting continued well into the night, with neither brigade succeeding to capture the Green line. When darkness fell, the Germans dug in on the lower north-east and southern faces of the hill on which the Hyderabad Redoubt stood, four hundred yards from the main redoubt.

During the evening a patrol of four Prussians of the 31st Regiment (18th Division), endeavoured to enter the redoubt to recover documents which had been left behind during the withdrawal, but were captured. By days end, the 11th Brigade had captured an estimated three hundred and fifty officers and men including a General, the headquarters of whom was located in the sunken road. They had also shot another General while he endeavoured to retrieve his motor car on the Pont Du Jour - Gavrelle Road.

XVII Corps issued instructions to the effect that every effort was to be made to secure the high ground east of Fampoux and provide support for VI Corps in the advance at 8:00am the following day. As a part of that attack, the 4th, 34th and 51st Divisions were required to complete the capture of the Green line, and consolidate those positions that offered the best observation over the Douai Plain. To help support the forthcoming attack, five of the seven brigades of artillery were moved forward during the night to new positions, allowing the more distant targets to be engaged.

The wet weather made telephone communications with the brigades extremely difficult, as it caused leakage on the lines. The failure of much of the voice communications prompted the division commander to visit each of the brigadiers to give personal instructions for the next day. The 12th Brigade was to seize the railway station, chemical works and the village of Roeux[294]. The attack was to commence at 3:00pm, as that was the earliest that all arrangements could be completed. Despite the effort taken to ensure that the brigades were clear as to their instructions, the orders were suddenly cancelled at about 1:30pm, as the Cavalry was to launch an assault on Greenland Hill, with the intention of ultimately pressing through to Biaches St. Vaast, Fresnes and Oppy.

The order, stopping the attack, arrived too late to prevent the 1st King's Own and 2nd Duke of Wellington's, having already advanced from the

---

[294] *Roeux is located on the banks of the River Scarpe, 800 yards east of Fampoux and is separated from the river by a sharp incline from the river to the edge of the village. That steep rise produces something of a narrow valley and those who entered the valley were exposed to fire from the opposite side the river. The ground within that valley still shows the effect of the dense artillery bombardment to which it was subjected. The railway station and chemical works, both substantial buildings, and the cemetery were located to the north of Roeux, separated by relatively open land and offered considerable enfilade fire to troops passing between those positions.*

start line. The two battalions were immediately met with heavy rifle and machine-gun fire and suffered considerable casualties. In an effort to capture and hold the high ground, as instructed, strong fighting patrols of the 11th Brigade entered No Man's' Land while others attempted to bomb up the front line, to broaden the front for the cavalry. The patrols from the 1st Somerset Light Infantry and 1st Hampshire Regiment were also met with heavy machine-gun fire *"and were practically annihilated before they had gone 200 yards*[295]*"*. While the 4th Division was attempting to secure the ground for attack by the cavalry, the 1st Cavalry Brigade had reached Fampoux, immediately behind the 12th Brigade, where the advancing lines were subjected to intense shelling and forced to retire to the western outskirts of the village.

During the afternoon repeated attempts were made by units of the 11th Brigade to push forward towards the Inn[296], on the far left flank and reach the railway embankment, but they too were subjected to concentrated fire, with the subsequent heavy losses resulting in neither objective being taken. During the evening of the 10th, amid heavy snow, the enemy launched a counter-attack by bombing up the trenches of the 4th German System. The fighting was particularly grim and only the hardiest determination beat off the assault with bomb and rifle fire. A second, later counter-attack was attempted by enemy troops advancing along the Plouvain - Fampoux Road, but again, the effort was stopped with the assistance of the machine guns and artillery. During the night, the Lancashire Regiment managed to advance the line, by digging, under some very difficult conditions, a series of strong points.

The German 14th Division was now being reinforced and presented firm resistance to any further attempt at attack. Enemy resistance had grown rapidly and several counter-attacks, supported by effective artillery fire, had taken place and defeated all attempts with concentrated machine-gun fire, of the two line brigades to advance their positions.

At 9:30pm on the 10th, the division received orders that the advance was to continue the following morning, with the objective of capturing Greenland Hill and Plouvain[297], thus opening the way for yet another

---

[295] *Quoted from the 11· Brigade war diary for April 1917*

[296] *The Inn stood 1500 yards south of Gavrelle on the Roeux – Gavrelle road.*

[297] *Greenland hill was a piece of high ground the stood approximately 15 feet (4.5 meters) above an otherwise relatively flat plain. I presented perfect visibility over the surrounding terrain and was located 2,500 yards in front of the existing British line. Plouvain was a village, approximately the same size as Roeux and situated 1500 yards southeast of Greenland Hill and 3000 yards east of Roeux.*

attempt by the cavalry. While the 10th and 12th Brigades were to carry out the attack, the 11th Brigade was to form a defensive flank facing north, as the 4th Division was still situated well ahead of those other divisions attacking on either flank.

The country between Fampoux and the station was then, as it is now, perfectly open and commanded to the south by the railway embankment and Mount Pleasant Wood, both strong German positions. To the north, the ground slopes gently up to the Inn, round which the enemy had organised strong points. When attacking from Fampoux and the sunken road to the north, the troops would have to deploy from what is practically a defile, the exits of which were swept by converging machine-gun fire. It was recognised that, should the enemy decide to maintain their positions during the next day, as seemed likely, any attack would be rendered especially difficult by the impossibility of assembling troops under cover. Division staff officers realised that artillery support for such a venture would be essential in dealing with the many strong points, which enfiladed the almost level ground.

The operation orders only reached the three Brigade Headquarters after midnight and gave instructions to continue the efforts to gain additional ground, wherever possible. The 11th and 12th Brigades had been fighting and digging continuously for forty eight hours in heavy snow and it was deemed necessary to bring up fresh troops to deal with the Green line, the only troops available being the 10th Brigade. The battalions of the 10th Brigade had been carrying supplies and consolidating trenches since the attack began on the 9th and, as it was necessary to get to the assembly positions over unknown ground, it was only possible to move in morning daylight hours.

As zero hour had been fixed for 12:00 noon of the 11th, at least six hours of bombardment was deemed necessary if it was to be effective and, to get the guns into range for the barrage, all available field artillery moved forward during the night. The very success of the operation depended on the preparation by the heavy artillery and the plan of attack required the Corps heavy artillery to concentrate on the station, Inn, Chateau and other known strong points, from daybreak onwards. The movement of heavy ammunition was aggravated by the constant snowstorms, which had made the tracks almost impassable and the heavy artillery was compelled to fire largely by map bearings, a method of bombardment that had proved inefficient on previous occasions.

As the day progressed, while the artillery attempted to soften the strong points, the infantry faced increasing difficulties in assembling for the attack. The only possible places that offered safety from the ravages of the German artillery were in Fampoux and the sunken road that ran north to the Hyderabad Redoubt. The only route through the village was already under heavy enemy shellfire and the entrance to the sunken road, which was in full view of the German artillery observers, had been registered by the enemy's guns.

An indication of the difficulties with communications and the need to execute decisions at short notice is clearly described in the War Diary of the Seaforth Highlanders for the 11th April[298] with reference to the 10th Brigade Operation Order No.18. *"The substance of the 10th Brigade orders was afterwards embodied in an Bn. Order. This order being written as opportunity offered during the halts on the way up to the position of assembly, for the attack. It was issued in an incomplete state to enable OC Coys to explain the order to their platoon and section commanders and to give the General instructions for the attack to their men. This had to be done during the move from the Brown line to the point of assembly, there being no other opportunity of doing so. Further orders were issued when the Bn reached the ground north of the Athies - Fampoux Road in H.16.c........"*

"During the movement of the Seaforth Highlanders to the assembly point west of the Hyderabad Redoubt the Battalion came under constant M.G. fire which was described as 'considerable but harmless' as the Coys were under cover of the trench, but the enemy's shellfire on the road and entrance to the trench was accurate and a nuisance......owing to the narrowness of the trench and the shell fire it took the remainder of the time before zero hour to get the Coys distributed on their correct frontages."

To get into the jump-off positions, the Seaforth Highlanders and Royal Irish advanced in fours down the Athies - Fampoux Road as far as the cross roads and by 10:00am the 10th Brigade had assembled on the western edge of the village of Fampoux. As the two battalions passed through the village, they were subjected to heavy shellfire in which they lost several casualties and, on arrival at the sunken road, east of the village, it was discovered that it too was being shelled. Chancing the bombardment, the brigade proceeded along the sunken road to the Hyderabad Redoubt, the rear of the column stopping at the junction of the road and the trench, which led to the redoubt.

---

[298] *Diary WO95/1483, National Archives, Kew.*

While the 10th Brigade was struggling to get to the start line, the 12th Brigade assembled on the ground to the south of the Athies - Fampoux Road, between the road and the river. By 11:00am, the battalions were in position but had been observed by two German aircraft, which had flown over the sunken road. Being impossible to miss the massed troops, the machines immediately returned over the German lines and, shortly after 11:00am, artillery fire began to fall all around the area of the sunken road[299].

Notwithstanding the artillery fire, the attack commenced at 12 noon. The Seaforth's advanced on a three-company front accompanied by the Royal Irish, on a two-company front. The intention was to leave the remaining companies in the Green line, the start line, to continue the consolidation and to act as a reserve. *"At zero - 3 minutes all was now in order and when zero came the coy's advanced into the barrage. They were immediately subjected to intense machine-gun fire and a barrage on the road and on the redoubt. The line was a little bunched on the right and left but it eased off and became a good line before reaching the artillery barrage. This barrage was very weak but, whatever its strength had been it would have been of little assistance until it had reached the area from which the machine-gun fire was coming i.e. the General line I.13.c central - I7.a.1.9. and the ground on the enemy's rear of that line. This situation, the sighting of the enemy's machine guns beyond the barrage area in invisible and unknown positions was responsible mainly to the failure of the attack as it had been responsible for the failure of many attacks during the later stages of the Battle of the Somme. Until some system of dealing with this tactical problem is devised the enemy will continue to cause heavy casualties among attacking infantry.[300] "*

As the Seaforth's and Royal Irish emerged from the village, they immediately came against heavy machine-gun fire, which appeared to emanate from the Inn, the Chemical Works, railway station, the Chateau and the railway embankment, all of which were the objectives of the attack. That fire swept the ground over which the battalions were to attack, from front and flank. As the machine-gun fire struck the advancing battalions, the enemy artillery placed a barrage on the sunken road, where the Royal Warwickshire Regiment and the Household Battalion were assembling.

---

[299] *It was in this area during 1917 and 1918 that the German fighter pilot, Manfred von Richtofen, claimed many of his victories. April 1917 saw the appearance of the Richtofen Circus, in which were many names that were to become well known in later years.*

[300] *Extract from an officer's report of the events of the 11·.*

The advancing ranks of the Seaforth's and Royal Irish were soon thinned by the raking machine-gun fire but the advance continued and, for a while, it appeared that the right flank of the 10th Brigade might reach the Gavrelle - Roeux Road. One platoon of the Royal Irish Fusiliers, under the command of a wounded officer, reached a spot within 200 yards of the railway station and gained cover from the railway embankment. However, in the face of intense fire and in danger of being surrounded by numbers of the enemy, the platoon was forced to fall back. *"That position was the farthest point reached by the battalion. Looking back, a long line of dead Seaforth's could be seen stretching forward from Hyderabad Redoubt to the platoon at the railway embankment"*.

On the left, a party continued to hold a trench for some time, until all ammunition was exhausted and, in the face of a counter-attack, was forced back. Very few returned, the remainder, including the officer, being either killed or captured. The Royal Warwickshire Regiment and the Household Battalion, constituting the second wave of the 10th Brigade attack, were meant to advance from the start line, west of Fampoux, at zero plus ten minutes (11:10am) and pass through the first objective at zero plus 40 minutes. As they commenced the attack both battalions were caught in the same artillery fire as the forward battalions and were unable to reach the leading troops.

While the 10th Brigade was thus engaged, the attack of the 12th Brigade, advancing between the river and left of the 10th Brigade, was led by the 2nd Lancashire Fusiliers, nearest the river and the 2nd West Riding Regiment on the left. Initially the attack proceeded well and the German trenches immediately in front were quickly taken, along with about 40 prisoners. The railway embankment was then captured and several machine guns destroyed.

Here the attack ground to a halt, as it was impossible to cross the embankment under heavy machine-gun fire coming from the station, the grounds of the Chateau, the cemetery and the distant Mount Pleasant Wood. Try as it did, the artillery was unable to subdue the many machine-gun positions, and the advance could go no further. To defend against counter-attack, the line reached was consolidated and a post was pushed forward into a small wood while a second party made its way to second wood. The two posts were subjected to such continuous machine-gun fire that the second position was withdrawn during the night.

To support the forward brigades, now well advanced, the 11th Brigade had followed behind and formed a northward facing defensive flank from the Hyderabad Redoubt to the left flank of the 10th Brigade. As the 11th Brigade was already holding a 2000-yard line from Pont Du Jour, it was decided that only one battalion of that brigade, the 1st Somerset Light Infantry, should be used in the main attack. Starting from the Hyderabad Redoubt, the Somerset's were also subjected to artillery and machine-gun fire. Attacking on a one-company front, they succeeded in pushing forward nearly three hundred yards but when unable to advance further, dug in where they stood. To protect the advance, a party bombed its way down a communications trench, which ran east from the Redoubt.

As the Somerset's advanced, the Hampshire's bombed their way up to Honey Trench in an effort to extend the flank and to keep up with the Somerset's. The 1st East Lancashires also managed to advance 400 yards along the Gavrelle road where, under galling fire, they were forced to halt. The day continued with all units digging a new line where they had been stopped. During the night, officers' patrols penetrated No Man's' Land and established contact with the enemy. Those patrols formed a forward screen of outposts to enable the stretcher-bearers to recover a large number of wounded and established four posts, manned with Lewis Guns. The East Lancashires used the darkness to establish a third series of strong points. The division had suffered heavily as result of the attack, with a total of one thousand four hundred and eight officers and other ranks[301].

On the 12th April, the 9th Division, which had remained behind the 4th, was asked to repeat the attack of the previous day. To assist, the Hampshire's were ordered to continue to bomb up the 4th German Trench System as far as possible. At 1:30pm the bombing parties commenced their attack and were immediately met with heavy rifle and machine-gun fire from the flanks. Although subjected to the same fire, the posts that had been placed out the previous night were maintained until the attack of the 9th Division had commenced, when they were shelled out by the British guns as they delivered the bombardment ahead of the attacking troops. The shelling killed two and wounded four, as well as putting a Lewis gun out of action.

The coming of spring brought with it conditions that thawed the frozen ground and, as the battalions assembled for the attack, the trenches were collapsing under the enemy artillery fire and provided little cover

---

[301] *For further analysis of the days events see Appendix VII "General Remark on the attack of the 4 Division 11 April 1917."*

for the troops. As the advance began, the 1st Rifle Brigade was to form a defensive flank from the 4th German System to the Inn but was immediately caught in flank and front by machine-gun fire with the loss of two officers and fifty-one other ranks in the first 100-200 yards. Such was the resistance that the attack of the 9th Division failed.

The 9th Division held the line from the Scarpe to the Hyderabad Redoubt, which allowed the 12th Brigade to withdraw, whilst the 11th Brigade continued to the Gavrelle Road. The 13th and 14th were days of few operations except for the East Lancashires advancing their posts some 100 yards ahead of the old position. During that period, the German artillery subjected the lines and battery positions, particularly those of the 32nd Artillery Brigade, to considerable gas shelling which inflicted several casualties.

The inclement weather now intervened to make ground conditions impossible. In preparation for a proposed attack on the 21st, the Hampshire's were, on the 15th, ordered to bomb up the 4th Trench System to Hilly Trench. To assist, the heavy artillery subjected the objective to three and a half hours of constant bombardment while the Hampshire's worked along the trenches under cover of a creeping barrage of 4.5" howitzers, which advanced at the rate of 100 yards every 6 minutes. The bombardment turned the trenches into a sea of deep mud through which the infantry could not penetrate and an attempt to advance over the open was caught in both flanks by rifle and machine-gun fire.

Following that failure, the 11th Brigade was relieved from the line by the 10th Brigade and withdrew to the Blue and Black Lines to act as support where it was again subjected to constant and, sometimes, heavy artillery fire. The attack, scheduled for the 21st of the month, was subsequently postponed to the 23rd and ultimately carried out by the 37th Division. The 10th Brigade, however, spent the next five days advancing their trenches and constructing assembly trenches in preparation for the forthcoming attack. Subjected to heavy artillery fire amid constant rain and snow, the men laboured hard to prepare the lines for the incoming 37th Division.

During the night of the 20th April, the 10th Brigade was relived and the 4th Division finally left the line and retired into the VIII Corps rest area, south of the River Scarpe. When the division was assembled, a roll call established that the fighting brigades had suffered a loss of one hundred and nine officers and two thousand four hundred and ninety other ranks since the commencement of the attack on the 9th April. Those figures did not include casualties suffered by the division artillery, Engineers and Pioneers.

Notwithstanding the cost in casualties, the division had gained a considerable achievement. In the nineteen days that that the division served in the line they had effected an advance of some six thousand yards along the River Scarpe, the farthest most point reached by any of the attacking division. XVII Corps had broken clearly through the much-vaunted Hindenburgh line and partly through the Mericourt - Vendin line, the Green line, which had acted as the support line to the Hindenburgh line. In doing so the division captured 45 guns of all sizes, 3 Trench Mortars, 15 machine-guns and several thousand prisoners.

During the last week of April, whilst the 4th Division was resting and refitting, the battle of attrition was continued in other areas, by other divisions. On the 23/24th April the 30th, 50th, 15th and 29th Divisions had all advanced through bitter fighting towards Cambrai. North of the River Scarpe, the 51st Division was heavily engaged in the area of Roeux Wood and the Chemical Works. The 37th Division, which had relieved the 4th, had made progress and reached the buildings west of Roeux Station, and had established positions on the western slopes of Greenland Hill, north of the Railway. The 63rd (Royal Naval Division) had also captured Gavrelle, a brilliant achievement.

Those advances had been made in the face of heavy and determined German counter-attacks, in which they too suffered very heavy losses. Despite severe fighting on both sides, the 37th Division, faced with constant counter-attacks, could make little or no further headway against Roeux. The 63rd Division, at Gavrelle, was subjected to five heavy counter-attacks on the 23rd and a further three times on the following day but the division held on, with the support of the artillery. Further attempts were made by British forces on April 28th in order to absorb the attention of the German forces on the Arras front while the French Army continued the offensive on the Aisne and in Champagne. The Germans attempted many powerful and determined counter-attacks on Gavrelle during the last remaining days of April but, in desperate hand-to-hand fighting, the Canadians managed to take Arleux-en-Gohelle and the 37th Division continued with slow progress on Greenland Hill.

May - 1917

The 4th Division was destined to return to the Arras front to continue the offensive. On the 2nd May, Division headquarters issued Operation Orders No. 31, stating that that the division was to participate in a general attack by XIII, XVII and VI Corps on the line Fresnes - Les-Montauban - Plouvain during the morning of the 3rd May. The plan required the 4th Division to attack on the right of the corps front with two brigades in line and its right flank on the River Scarpe. The 9th Division was to attack on the left while the 17th Division followed in support. The dividing line between the two divisions was to be Hyderabad Redoubt - Clyde-Cut. The planned called for the 10th Brigade, supplemented by the Somerset Light Infantry (11th Brigade), to advance on the right of the line while the 12th Brigade, supplemented by the 1st Rifle Brigade (11th Brigade), was to advance on the left.

The objectives were three heavily defended lines referred to as the Black, Blue and Red lines, which extended across the line of attack, the farthest being nearly 2,500 yards in front. Before the 4th Division lay Roeux (on the Black line) with Plouvain some 2000 yards further beyond (on the Red line), to the east with a series of strong trenches in between (the Blue Line).

For a better understanding, a description of Roeux is appropriate. The village lies on the northern bank of the River Scarpe, in one of the many loops created by the meandering path of the river. In 1917, the village consisted of two parts, divided by a small area of less densely populated land in which stood the communal cemetery. Corona Trench was a long and heavily defended communication trench, lay on the high ground just north of the cemetery and afforded a field of fire over all ground lying to the south towards the village and enfiladed any troops passing through the village.

The northern part of Reoux stood astride a railway line, which ran north-east towards Douai, and was heavily defended by trench systems and fortified cellars and dug-outs. On the railway line and in the centre of the northern part of the village lay the station, again heavily defended. To the north of the village lay Crook and Crow trenches, names allocated by the British, which were communication trenches that joined the German front line to the second line of defence, Cupid Trench, to the east or behind the main line.

The northern half contained the chemical works and a number of well-built houses lying on either side of the Gavrelle - Roeux Road. The principal building was the chateau, constructed in the manner typical of such homes, with very thick stone walls and extensive cellars. East of the buildings lay two large factories and a quarry in which dug-outs had been provided. Between the Chateau and the cemetery to the south, were a number of houses, which joined the cemetery to the main part of Roeux. The northern part of the village lay well down the forward slope of the Greenland Hill - Delbar Wood Ridge.

The southern part of the village lay on the River Scarpe, which had been canalised many years before, leaving a small area between the canal and the main body of the river, which consisted of large slow-flowing bodies of water, interspersed with areas of shallow marsh. Immediately to the west of Roeux, lay the heavily defended lay Roeux Wood.

The area around Roeux presented special difficulties for attacking troops. In order to deploy for the attack, they had to move down the forward slope of the Point Du Jour - Fampoux Spur or along the Scarpe Valley, both of which were clearly visible from Windmill Hill. Similarly, with the exception of a covered approach in the Scarpe Valley, the movement of German troops was also visible to the British observers. From the cemetery, the ground sloped down steeply to the river and the southern part of Roeux, on the opposite side of the ridge, was not visible at all from the British lines.

The local geography indicated, as was apt to happen, that troops attacking Roeux from the west would also be subjected to intense machine-gun fire from enemy positions on the south bank of the Scarpe. On previous occasions, attempts to attack from the area of the cemetery had failed with heavy loss and it was therefore decided not to attack directly from the west, the line of approach, until the village had been turned from the north.

The Blue line lay approximately mid way between Roeux and Plouvain, a distance of nearly one thousand yards. It consisted of a trench line that ran along the forward contour of high ground and commanded a large proportion of the open country before it, as far as Roeux. Delbar and Hausa Woods, to the east of the village, were in a commanding position, with the ground sloping from Hausa Wood to the Scarpe and a large quarry near Hausa Wood was used by the enemy as an assembly area for troops. The ground behind the ridge sloped to the east, towards Plouvain and was not visible from the British lines and it was believed, correctly, that many artillery batteries occupied those slopes.

One other feature, which added considerably to the difficulty of attacking the Blue and Red lines, was the railway line running diagonally across the line of advance of the 4th Division. The railway embankment extended several hundred yards east of the station where it entered a deep cutting and a number of machine-gun emplacements were known to have been constructed along its length. The troops of the 4th Division, which were to conform with the movements of the 9th Division, north of the railway, were to form a defensive flank facing south along the cutting until the troops attacking south of the railway, at a slower rate, had drawn level with them.

The enemy had made good use of time to strengthen the positions on both the Blue and Red lines. Behind the Chateau there had been constructed a strong machine-gun dug-out protected by seven feet of concrete, providing emplacements for four machine guns, all capable of sweeping the country behind the Chateau, up to the railway, to the north and the cemetery, to the south. This portion of the village had been assaulted on previous occasions and, although some troops had entered, they were unable hold it. The buildings had suffered from the British artillery fire and the Germans had spent considerable time and energy on the construction of trenches and dugouts.

The attack was to include the capture of the northern portion of the village of Roeux, including the chemical works and station buildings to a line just to the east of that part of the village, the Black line. It was also to capture the Trench system on the high ground near Hausa and Delbar Woods, the Blue line, as well as piercing the defences around Plouvain, the Red line. At the time of planning, none of these operations were perceived as overly difficult, if executed with deliberation. It was not planned that the Somerset's should take the southern part of Roeux in the initial attack, but left to a later assault. Thus was the task that lay before the 4th Division.

The planning of the attack by the 4th Division was complicated by that of the 9th Division. Unlike the 4th, the 9th Division was to advance across a considerable distance of flat, open country, exposing the attacking troops to retaliatory action by the enemy and, to avoid unnecessary casualties, it was essential that the attacking brigades cross the open ground as quickly as possible. The rapid movement required considerable coordination of the creeping barrage to ensure that it suited both divisions as well as the neighbouring XIII Corps, to the north and VI Corps, to the south.

The attack was to commence, along the whole front, at 3:45am on the 3rd May and, on reaching the Black line the leading waves of the assaulting brigades were to halt for twenty minutes. Strong 'mopping up' parties were to be left to deal with any remaining defenders in the buildings, before moving on behind the barrage. Having reached the Blue line, a further halt of thirty minutes was to be made to enable the battalions detailed for the capture of the final objective, to pass through. The battalion detailed to attack the southern portion of Roeux was to advance from the front line when the right flank of the assaulting troops had reached the crossroads near the eastern end of the village.

Throughout the preliminary planning, concerns were expressed about the ability of the 4th Division to fulfil its role. The division had suffered considerable losses in previous weeks and those numbers had not been made up. It was intended that the 10th Brigade should advance with eighty one officers and one thousand, five hundred and eighty three other ranks while the 12th Brigade mustered eighty officers and one thousand, nine hundred and forty one other ranks, approximately half-strength for both Brigades. From these numbers men also had to be designated as stretcher-bearers and carriers, thus reducing, even further, the number of available fighting troops.

It was not the intention to take the southern part of Reoux as a part of the main attack. That part of the town and the intervening ground to the north of the village, was to be captured in a separate undertaking by the Somerset Light Infantry, when the northern part of the town and associated railway had been captured. Due to the level of resistance offered on the sloping ground between the railway station and the Chateau on previous occasions, that part of the line was to be shelled systematically until Z day, to subdue the defenders.

The 12th Brigade moved into the line during the night of the 30th April. The 2nd Lancashire Fusiliers were astride the railway line, facing directly at the northern part of Roeux whilst the 2nd Essex was deployed to the left of the Lancashires. The Duke of Wellington's lay in front of Fampoux in support of the two leading battalions while the King's Own were further back, in the 4th German Trench System, as reserve. The heavy artillery bombarded the buildings on the northern edge of Roeux throughout the 2nd but failed to engage the western edge of the town and the houses on the north western corner. By midnight on the 2nd the assaulting brigades were in position, having brought the Duke of Wellington's up behind the Lancashire Fusiliers and the King's Own to positions north of the railway.

The 10th Brigade deployed on a three-battalion front. The 1st Royal Warwickshire Regiment on the left, followed by the 1st Royal Irish Fusiliers, the Household Battalion in the centre, followed by the Seaforth Highlanders and the Somerset Light Infantry to the right, advancing twenty minutes after zero hour with the sole objective of capturing Roeux. Before Roeux lay Roeux Wood, which stood directly in the line of advance of the Somerset's. It had been reported several times that the artillery had not paid the wood the attention that would be needed to ensure the successful assault of the right flank, but without effect.

At 3:45am, zero hour, the artillery bombardment commenced ahead of the infantry start line and remained in that position for thirty minutes, thus allowing the infantry to leave the trenches and deploy. At 4:15am, the barrage slowly moved forward while the infantry followed. The advancing lines of the 10th Brigade experienced difficulties almost immediately. As the morning was unusually dark, troops of Household Battalion, with the responsibility of capturing the cemetery, soon lost their way. The advancing companies of the battalion became completely disorganised whilst subjected to the heavy short-range machine-gun fire.

Following behind the Household Battalion, the Seaforth Highlanders were decimated by the machine-gun fire, but groups of men reached the Black line and continued the advance, as scheduled, behind the barrage towards the Blue line. On reaching that line, the remnants of the battalion moved to the right, until the left of the line was just opposite the north-west corner of Delbar Wood. There they halted, as ordered, until zero + 85 minutes, 5:10am, when the attack on the Red line, east of Hausa and Delbar Woods and immediately west of Plouvain, was due to commence. The attack failed owing to the fact that both flanks of the Seaforth Highlanders were 'in the air', unsupported by the other battalions, which had been held up before the Black line. Under heavy fire and with little ability to reply, the Seaforth's were forced to withdraw, although few managed to get back.

Those of the Household and Seaforth battalions who remained, being unable to advance further, endeavoured to establish themselves close up to the cemetery but owing to enfilade fire from the Chateau found it impossible to remain and were withdrawn to their original front line. One party of the Seaforth's had dug in midway between the Cemetery and Roeux Wood where they maintained their positions under very heavy fire.

To their left, the Warwicks had also met with strong opposition, but small groups of the first wave managed to get through to the Black line and attempted to consolidate. The second wave came to a halt in the face of machine-gun fire from the Chateau grounds and the houses further to the south. Like so many of the leading units, those who were designated to 'mop-up' the Chateau had also lost direction in the dark. The smoke and the dust from the barrage made visibility almost impossible. They failed to find their objectives, which allowed the enemy to direct intense machine-gun and rifle fire and to inflict such very heavy casualties upon the Warwicks and Seaforth's. The remnants of Warwicks dug in where they lay, on a line from the west of the Chateau to the railway embankment, and remained there until after dark, when they were recalled.

The 12th Brigade was a little more fortunate in its endeavours. South of the railway line the attack at first succeeded, and two companies of the Lancashire Fusiliers, Duke of Wellington's and part of the King's Own Royal Lancaster Regiment, followed the creeping barrage through the northern part of the village, many reaching as far as the Blue line. One of the wounded survivors later stated that he had reached a position overlooking Plouvain, where they came under heavy enfilading machine-gun fire from the railway cutting and Hausa Wood, losing all of their officers.

Finding themselves unsupported and with both flanks in the air, the survivors withdrew to the Black line and endeavoured to dig in. The enemy emerged from hidden dug-outs and cellars and gradually overpowered the men, who were taking cover in any hole or trench that offered protection. A few of the posts managed to hold out until nightfall but were withdrawn to allow a new bombardment to be carried out. Those responsible for mopping up had established themselves in houses between the railway and the Chateau but, as the latter had not been taken, the fire that was inflicted on the troops of the 10th Brigade was also directed on those in the houses. As soon as there was sufficient light, snipers and machine guns in the Chateau and in the house north of the railway made communications impossible.

On the northern side of the railway, the Lancashire Fusiliers were held up almost immediately by heavy machine-gun fire coming from houses that had not been dealt with by the heavy artillery. The machine guns were concentrated at the crossroads and inflicted heavy losses. An attempt was made to outflank the buildings by passing around to the left but, against such fire, no effective progress could be made. The King's Own, following the Lancashire Fusiliers, ran into the same fire and suffered immediate, heavy losses and the remnants of both battalions and part of the Carrier Company took up position in Calabar and Clover trenches.

On the extreme left, the Essex were reported to have entered Crow and Crook trenches and were thought to have pushed further on. Information was difficult to obtain and, as no one had returned, little was learnt of the attack by the Essex until nightfall. The attack of the 9th Division had met with no better fortune than that of the 4th Division. It appears that, in the darkness, the right flank of the 9th Division had lost direction and advanced across the front of the Essex Regiment.

According to plan, the Somerset Light Infantry commenced the advance against the southern portion of Roeux twenty minutes after zero hour. Like the other units before them, they immediately lost their way and as they passed through Roeux Wood the enemy machine guns, concealed in the undergrowth, took a severe toll but, notwithstanding the heavy casualties, the left company of the Somerset's managed to reach the outskirts of the village. At 5:00am there were reports that troops were at the eastern end of Roeux but, being completely disorganised, were unable to hold their positions. In response, a battalion of the 11th Brigade was placed at the disposal of the O.C., 10th Brigade but, as the remainder of the Somerset's was retiring to their start trenches, the reinforcements were not deployed.

By dawn, it was clear that the attack was not progressing as planned and the apparent failure was reported to XVII Corps. Subsequent reports from various sources tended to show that in some places it had been partially successful and particular trenches, Crook and Crow and the northern end of Roeux had been taken. At 8:35am orders were received from XVII Corps that the attack was not to be pressed, but an attempt was to be made to capture the cemetery, Corona Trench and to re-take the northern half of Roeux. The C.O. 12th Brigade, was consulted and was of the opinion that it would not be possible to organise an attack before dark, and that the brigade on his left, could do nothing to assist. At 10:05am and again at 12:40pm, after receipt of the news that about one hundred men were believed to be dug in on the Black line, further instructions were received from the XVII Corps, suggesting the employment of all available troops to make good the ground gained.

At 10:30am, the enemy counter-attacked from the direction of Delbar and Hausa Woods, but the attempt was brought to a standstill by artillery fire. Half an hour later, after some concerted effort, troops of the 12th Brigade has cleared the buildings south of the railway, with the exception of the Chateau and one or two houses east of the Roeux –

Gavrelle road. They had also established themselves in the unoccupied portion of Calabar Trench.

The 10th Brigade had also been ordered to clear up the situation on its right. It was not considered advisable to take any further action on this flank until an evening attack could be organised and to that end, instructions were issued for strong patrols to be sent out to obtain information necessary for the organising an attack.

At 2:20pm, a German force, estimated at two battalions, made a second and more determined counter-attack in two waves from Delbar and Hausa Woods. The attack started from the east, swept over the Black Line north of Roeux and then swung to the north, up the slight depression east of the Chateau, crossed the railway between Cupid trench and the station and then into Crook and Crow trenches. A portion actually effected a lodgement in Clover trench but was later bombed out. The British artillery retaliated and the remainder of the first wave took cover in the trenches in and to the north of the railway cutting, whilst the second wave was all but annihilated by the artillery fire.

In order to eject the enemy from their newfound positions, the 1st Hampshire Regiment, the only reserve left, together with the 1st Rifle Brigade, placed at the disposal of the 12th Brigade. The Hampshire's were sent along the trenches east of Fampoux as reinforcements, while the Rifle Brigade was instructed to endeavour to reach the men cut off in front. The Hampshire's had been drawn upon for carrying parties and other support duties and the troops available for fighting did not amount to more than two companies.

The only way that they could hope to reach the Black line was to attack through the northern part of Roeux, a venture that could not be carried out during daylight hours. At 5:00pm, the Corps Commander visited division headquarters and, after discussion with the Division Commander, ordered an attack to be carried out after dark with a view to extricating any men surviving near the Chateau, or beyond.

Orders were issued for counter-attack and all other spare troops were made available to 12th Brigade Commander, who was given a free hand. The time of the attack was fixed for 11:00pm and, due to the uncertainty of the location of any men lying in front of the Black line, was to be conducted without an artillery bombardment.

The preparations commenced at dusk, when the remnants of the Seaforth Highlanders were sent to relieve the Household Battalion in

Ceylon Trench, close to the railway line. As the battalion commander, adjutant, medical officer and three other officers had all became casualties to a single shell, Company Sergeant Major Fraser assumed responsibility. The preparations included the Rifle Brigade taking over those trenches that had been gained on the western edge of the village and had been allocated the task of attacking the Chateau, but the 12th Brigade experienced difficulties collecting and assembling the troops in the darkness, resulting in delay.

While the 10th Brigade was assembling, the enemy occupants of the Chateau attacked with bombs and machine-gun fire and drove Warwickshire's out of nearby trenches. Although 10th Brigade attack allowed the Warwicks to again advance and reoccupy the trenches, they were unable to maintain the position in the face of heavy enfilade fire from the Chateau.

The general attack of the 10th Brigade only succeeded in establishing a line of posts in advance of the original line, from west of the cemetery to the River Scarpe, which were kept under constant enemy fire. With the exception of the new posts and a captured portion of Crook and Crow Trenches, the troops were back in their original lines by 10:30pm. The attack by the Rifle Brigade, which eventuated at 3:00am on the following morning, was no more successful than the earlier efforts and suffered under the intense machine-gun fire. The remnants of the battalion finally withdrew to Ceylon Trench.

The fighting troops of the 4th Division had spent a hard day and had displayed great gallantry in their efforts to capture the Red line. By days end a total of eighty prisoners and several machine guns had been captured but had lost a total of one hundred and seven officers and two thousand and nine men killed, wounded or missing. Considerable analysis of the failure of the attack took place over the next week and determined five principal causes.

It was deemed that the preliminary artillery barrage was inadequate and had not provided sufficient cover for the advancing troops, nor sufficiently destroyed those obstacles that confronted them. The distance to be covered was too great for the available number of assaulting troops[302]. The fact that a night attack was attempted without having given sufficient time to prepare, resulted in the rate of advance of the artillery bar-

---

[302] *The deficiency in numbers was largely due to the losses from the April operations, which had not been replaced and a cadre of experienced troops from each battalion had also been left in the assembly areas, in keeping with military policy.*

rage, which was based on daylight operations, outdistancing the attacking troops. Finally, the failure of those troops, charged with the responsibility for the 'mopping up' in the dark, offered those enemy troops, which had been overlooked, the opportunity to bring concentrated fire to bear from flank and rear.

The division held the few gains for the next five days using mixed elements of the various participating units, which remained under constant artillery bombardment and machine-gun fire. On the 5th the heavy artillery undertook the bombardment of those buildings south of the railway line, in an effort to suppress the constant sniping and machine-gun fire. Although generally effective, the shelling missed the houses at the crossroads, north of the station, from which a dangerous enfilade fire was constantly played upon any movement - *"Again this was reported without result[303]"*. At 9:45pm in the evening, patrols of the King's own were sent to establish posts in Crook and Crow trenches but were met by heavy machine-gun fire[304].

In an effort to reorganise the mixed units, the King's Own took over Cam and Clyde Trenches from the Essex, allowing them (the Essex) to retire to trenches east of Fampoux. Here they reorganised and assumed the role of support battalion to the division. The Royal Warwicks (10th Brigade) and the Lancashire Fusiliers (12th Brigade) were also withdrawn to the 4th German System, to finally get a little rest.

During the 6th, intermittent shelling of the German lines by the British artillery took place, but the infantry of both sides spent the day in relative quiet. That night, a patrol of the 12th Trench Mortar Battery found four minenwerfers near the crossroads with a large store of ammunition.

---

[303] *Quoted from the War Diary of the 12 Brigade, WO95/1503. The diaries regularly express frustration at the performance of the artillery during the actions of April and May.*

[304] *The strategy behind the plans drawn up by General Haig involved opening an offensive in Flanders. That process had commenced on the 5 May when it was deemed that the British and French Armies around Arras had secured all achievable objectives and the campaign was officially drawn to a close. Further operations in the Arras area, which involved the 4 Division, had been initiated in order to maintain German focus and resources on the Somme while other divisions were transferred to Flanders. The German forces in Flanders had not participated in the withdrawal witnessed on the Somme and the last half of 1917 found the opposing armies confronting each other on much the same lines as those established in late 1915. Much serious fighting had taken place all along the front especially around Hill 60 and Wytschaete and it was determined that a great effort should be made to deny the Germans the advantages of the high ground, overlooking the Ypres Plain and the use of the port facilities at Antwerp.*

Much of the ammunition was brought in and used in two previously captured minenwerfers, located in the quarry. During the course of the next few days two of the four minenwerfers were brought in, along with the remaining ammunition and the remaining two were rendered useless. Because of the resultant mortar fire, the German shelling increased during the night and, at times, became intense, especially on the support and reserve trenches. The spasmodic nature of the fighting continued into the 7th and 8th with extensive use of gas shells. Fresh assembly trenches were dug and communications trenches deepened.

A proposal by the G.O.C, 4th Division, for a further attack was approved by XVII Corps, but was postponed to the 11th, when the 17th Division could be brought in to attack on the left of the 4th Division. Operation Order No. 34, detailing the attack by the 4th Division was issued on the 10th and, the 12th Brigade was relieved by the 50th Brigade (17th Division) during the evening to allow the 12th Brigade to reorganise[305].

The plan required the division to attack on a 1300-yard frontage with all three brigades. The plan required the 10th and 11th Brigades, reinforced by those units of the 12th Brigade, which had been reorganised with such men as could be obtained, to carry out the advance. The fighting strength of the each of the brigades at the commencement of battle were little more that the average battalion. The 10th Brigade had six hundred and ninety seven officers and men, the 11th one thousand and fifty nine all ranks and the 12th Brigade had six hundred and eighty eight all ranks[306].

The King's Own came under the orders of the 10th Brigade at 10:00am on the morning of the 11th, to act as support for that brigade. To support the attack of the 11th Brigade, the Lancashire Fusiliers and two platoons of the Royal Warwickshire Regiment were moved up to the 4th German System at 5:00pm. That combined force was to capture Roeux, the cemetery, Corona and Cupid trenches.

The commitment of all fighting troops to the forthcoming attack left the division without a reserve. In order to provide support for such a

---

[305] As the brigade prepared to leave the trenches, a British aeroplane was brought down in the front line whilst engaging a German aircraft.

[306] The average strength of a brigade would normally be about 4000 men. The fighting strength of the 4 Division now amounted to a total of something less than 2500 infantry.

weakened force, the 152nd Brigade (51st Division) was placed at the disposal of the division commander, on condition that it was only to be used in an emergency. In the event of the division being reduced by casualties and not able to hold the line, two battalions of the 152nd Brigade were moved up behind the attacking brigades to be available to go into the line on the night of the 11th, before the attack. Additional to the 152nd Brigade, two companies of the 6th Dorsetshire Regiment (50th Brigade, 17th Division) were also placed at the disposal of 11th Brigade Commander, to prolong the front of attack to the north.

It was anticipated that the capture of the northern part of Roeux would draw down the concentrated fire of all of the enemy artillery that could be brought to bear, and would most likely be followed by heavy counter-attacks. Traditionally, all previous attacks had been made at or about dawn, at the time at which the enemy would be most alert. To limit the potential enemy retaliation, the attack was planned to commence in the evening of the 11th May. By attacking in the evening and establishing a line beyond the village it was hoped that the enemy would be left in uncertainty as to the situation during the night, and the troops would thus be given time to dig themselves in.

The difficulty of executing an evening attack lay in the assembly of the attacking troops in daylight. To overcome the possibility of the movement being seen by the enemy observers and enemy aeroplanes, the brigades were to enter the trenches during the previous evening and remain still during daylight hours. The advantages to be gained by an evening attack were, however, considered to justify the risks and zero hour was fixed for 7:30pm, 11th May. All possible arrangements were made to reduce the danger of discovery by deepening trenches, under cutting parapets, mounting anti-aircraft machine guns and Lewis guns and arranging for aeroplane patrols[307].

To prepare the ground, over which the attack was to be made, the artillery was to form a creeping barrage, using all of the artillery of the 4th Division and units of the 12th and 17th Divisions. The 12th Division was to advance along the south bank of the Scarpe, that is, on the right flank of the 4th Division, whilst the 17th Division was to advance on the left flank. The barrage was to be supplied by the field artillery distributed at the rate of one gun per 7 yards of front and supplemented by all available howitzers and Stokes trench mortars. Targets ahead of the barrage were to be dealt with by the heavy artillery, under headquarters

---

[307] *In the event, although enemy aeroplanes flew along the trenches at a low altitude, the unusual number of troops in trenches does not appear to have been noticed.*

command, which were responsible for dealing with strong points and those areas to the rear that might contain machine guns.

Arrangements were also made for thirty percent of the attacking troops be allocated the task of mopping up the strong points, with parties being ordered not to move from those position for several hours after the attack. To provide against counter-attack, machine guns were to moved forward immediately upon capture of the objectives. To each machine-gun was attached a party of Royal Engineers, which was to advance, from the assembly area, with the gun and were not to leave it until it was secure. Pioneers were allocated to consolidation and to connect communication trenches during the night.

In accordance with the plan, the brigades moved to the assembly trenches, Calabar, Ceylon and, directly in front of the cemetery, Cusp Trench, throughout the night of the 10th. The heavy artillery continued the usual slow bombardment and the enemy guns undertook the customary retaliation. The afternoon was hot, and at zero hour, the sun was shining into the eyes of the enemy.

Precisely on time, an intense barrage of artillery and machine-gun fire commenced. The barrage was almost perfect and allowed the attacking troops to leave the trenches and form up without loss. All three waves of the assaulting infantry left the trenches before the enemy barrage arrived and during the advance only one enemy machine-gun opened fire, from the southern end of Roeux. The 12th Division had laid a smoke barrage on the southern side of the river, which attracted the greater part of the German artillery effort.

The attack proceeded according to plan and the enemy appeared to have thought that the barrage was merely the usual practice and, with few exceptions, did not attempt to leave his shelters until too late. Once again, the Seaforth Highlanders advanced behind the Household Battalion and, advancing as quickly as possible, got up close behind. At one point the right of the Seaforth's, under the command of 2nd Lieutenant McCormack, actually moved to the front of the advance.

At first, all went well and the Seaforth's were soon in amongst the houses and dugouts. They attacked with bomb and bayonet and, having inflicted severe losses on the defenders, prisoners soon began to march to the rear in large numbers. The German barrage was slow in arriving and fell largely on the valley between Colne Trench and the canal, although Ceylon Trench and Pleasant Wood also received considerable attention. In one instance a machine-gun Officer, a Sapper N.C.O. and several of a machine-gun detachment were killed, but the remainder of the detachment and the remaining Sappers not only brought the gun back into action but also a captured German gun.

After dark, it soon became obvious that the enemy still occupied some of the buildings and sniping and machine-gun fire caused several casualties. In the darkness, it was difficult to determine from which houses the fire originated. Messages soon began to arrive at the Brigade Headquarters stating that the objectives had been taken with little opposition and with few casualties.

The fighting continued into the night and a company of the King's Own was sent forward to assist the Seaforth's in clearing the houses, dugouts and galleries, but progress was difficult in the dark. The work of clearing the houses continued into the morning of the 12th, in which about seventy prisoners, including seven officers, one of which was a doctor, and all of his staff was taken. In the quarry behind the Chateau alone over, two hundred prisoners were taken and many more bombed in their dugouts. It also appeared that the artillery barrage had killed a considerable number when trying to escape eastwards.

Many of the casualties within the attacking brigades had been caused by the infantry advancing into their own supporting barrage, which was inevitable in the thick smoke caused by the bursting shrapnel. Only on the right flank near the cemetery was any serious opposition experienced. *"On this side there are many more houses than are shown on the map, and possibly owing to this, a portion of the right Battalion appears to have mistaken the cross roads in I.19.d for their real Objective, the cross roads in I.19.b. At the former they captured a number of prisoners including a battalion Commander and his Staff, but a considerable gap was left between them and the rest of the battalion which was digging in east of the cemetery."*

The mistake was discovered in time by a report from a contact aeroplane at about 9:00pm and a company of the Royal Warwickshire Regiment and second from the King's Own were sent forward to rectify the situation. However, the enemy maintained an obstinate defence in the cemetery buildings and continued to cause a number of casualties, including the Brigade Major of the Seaforth Highlanders who had gone forward to assess the situation. To resolve the problem, the officer commanding the Seaforth's collected a party from his own and other battalions in the neighbourhood and organised a bombing attack upon the buildings, eventually driving the Germans into cellars where the survivors, five officers and seventy other ranks, surrendered.

By 11:00pm, a continuous fire trench had been dug along the entire 11th Brigade front to a depth of six feet, and by 5:00am the whole objective had been secured and consolidated, with a large number of machine guns in position. Posts, placed in front of the line and manned by Lewis guns, prevented any attempts by the German to interfere with the consolidation. The new front line required further improvements and instructions were issued to advance the line as far as the railway crossing, in association with the advance of the 17th Division, the following day. This action involved a short advance of about 200 yards on the northern end of the line and was to take place on the morning of the 12th May.

The attack, carried out by the East Lancashire Regiment, Somerset Light Infantry and the Rifle Brigade, commenced at 6:30am and the objective captured and consolidated without difficulty. The 17th Division had, however, met with stronger opposition and advanced only where the right flank of the division joined with the Rifle Brigade. As the work of consolidation continued more prisoners, found hiding in cellars and dugouts, were captured. The westerly movement of German reinforcements through Vitry was reported and, to meet the threat of possible counter-attack, a line from Roeux to the River Scarpe was established. Units of almost every battalion in the division, the total not exceeding 2000 rifles, now held the front line.

Exhaustion was making itself felt as the men had either been fighting or digging for more than 36 hours and it was deemed necessary, in the light of the possibility of fresh counter-attacks, to relieve the 4th Division. Thus, on the night of the 12th the two forward battalions of the 152nd Brigade (51st division) were ordered to relieve the entire front line. The remaining two battalions of the 152nd Brigade were also to move forward and man the support line.

The relief depended on the 17th Division completing the operation to straighten the line by advancing into line with the left flank of the 4th Division. The advance commenced at 10:00pm and caused considerable artillery fire to fall along the whole line, including that of the 4th Division. While the advance got under way, a post of the Royal Warwickshire Regiment observed a force of about 150 Germans moving east along the northern outskirts of Roeux. When the Lewis guns opened fire, fifty of the enemy surrendered and came into the British lines, while the remainder fled. Those who had surrendered were identified as the 11th Company of the 360th Regiment (4th Ersatz Division), which had been holding Roeux Wood.

The relief was completed shortly after, although a considerable number of casualties had been sustained as a result of the shelling. The Royal Engineers and Pioneers of the 4th Division assisted the incoming battalions of the 152nd Brigade in the task of consolidation, as they joined up the trenches and wired the line. The 1/5th Seaforth's (152nd Brigade) assumed the defence of the line from Roeux to the Scarpe. On relief, the 10th and 12th Brigades moved back to Arras, where they embussed for the rest area around Penin. The 11th Brigade assembled near the railway cutting and marched into Arras where it remained overnight, moving into billets with the remainder of the division the following day.

During the operations of the 11th/12th the division was responsible for the capture of a total seven hundred and seventy six prisoners, although not all reached the prisoner-of-war cage to the rear. A proportion of them became casualties as they passed through the shell swept area on their way back. It was estimated that two battalions of the 360th and 362nd Regiments (4th Ersatz Division), were killed during the attacks as many of their dead were found in trenches and lying in the open and at least one machine-gun company was known to have been annihilated.

A third battalion, which came up on the night of the 12th to act as support, was badly handled by the division artillery until it withdrew during the 13th and was caught, a second time, near Delbar Wood, although exact casualty figures are not known. The 4th Division suffered, over the two days of assault, total casualties twenty eight officers and five hundred and eleven other ranks, killed, wounded and missing.

The division remained in the Penin area for four weeks for a much-needed rest, although not as many reinforcements were received as was required to bring it up to strength. The battalions then undertook considerable re-organisation and training. During this period the G.O.C. of 3rd Army, General Sir E. Allenby congratulated the division on its performance in the last two months.

June - 1917

The division remained in the area of Penin until the 12th of June. During this period several awards for gallantry were presented, among those was Private G. Garwood who received the Military Medal. However, on the 9th, the 4th Division received orders requiring the 11th and 12th Brigades to relieve the 9th Division on the nights of the 12th and 13th of June, this time on the southern bank of the river. On the night of the 10th, the 12th Brigade moved into Arras from where officers reconnoitred the area around Bayonet, Crossbow, Wrist and the northern parts of Scabbard Trenches.

The 11th Brigade then joined the 12th Brigade in Arras the following night, but was instructed to take over the line on the northern bank of the Scarpe. The relief of the 9th Division took place on the nights of 12th and 13th when the 12th Brigade relieved the 27th Brigade and the 11th Brigade relieved the 26th Brigade respectively. Whilst the 12th Brigade was carrying out the relief, the 10th Brigade moved to Arras as support.

As the reliefs took place, reconnaissance by forward patrols revealed that the Germans held the line with a series of posts in shell holes, well in advance of the main line and that the area around Scabbard and Rifle Trenches had been badly damaged and were no longer used. The trenches to the west were also found to contain many of the dead from previous battles and little or no attempt had been made to bury them. That task fell to the pioneer battalion as the process of consolidation began.

For the next ten days, the 11th Brigade, on the northern bank, was subjected to considerable shelling, mainly about the Chemical Works, Roeux and the old 4th German Trench System. Once again the division undertook the training of the new, incoming divisions and, on the 19th, the 3/4th Queens Own (Royal West Kent Regiment) was attached to the 4th Division for training in trench warfare. 'C' and 'D' Companies of the Queens Own were attached to the 11th Brigade while 'A' and 'B' companies were attached to the 10th Brigade, which had relieved the 12th Brigade during the night. Throughout that period, the area experienced considerable thunderstorms, making the task of trench work and the installation of wire increasingly difficult.

Amid the drudgery of work parties and night patrols there were periods of offensive action designed to gather vital information. Plans had been made to conduct a raid by the Royal Irish Fusiliers (10th Brigade) on the night of the 24th. The plans required that a raiding party, consisting of four officers, sixty other ranks and two Lewis gun teams, was to raid the system of shell holes opposite Croft Trench. Those shell holes were in two loose lines approximately seventy three yards apart and acted as advanced posts to the German front line, which consisted of Carrot, Cyprus and Candy Trenches, located in front, that is, to the west of Hausa and Delbar Woods. That line of trenches was, in fact, the Blue line objective of the attacks of the previous month.

A description of the shell holes, given after the raid by Captain G.P.M. Hornidge, O.C. of the raiding party, is applicable here. *"The system appears to be one of enlarged shell holes about 12 feet in diameter and 8ft.deep; No revetment work has been done. In every hole a few steps have been cut into the side nearest our line, wide enough to allow two men to recline against the side. In a few cases the tops of the steps have been sandbagged round. Some of the shell holes on the right and centre have been connected by trenches about 2 feet deep, but no attempt has been made to form a trench line. These trenches appear to have been dug solely to provide communication and not with any idea of forming an organised defensive system. Neither near these enlarged shell holes or these shallow trenches was any excavated earth observed; it had apparently been carried some distance, as no one reports having walked over soft earth, or having seen what looked like a filled in shell hole. Near the centre of the 2nd objective a machine-gun emplacement was found but no gun. Some of the holes contained small shelters in the sides, in which were a few hand grenades and some bread and jam."*

The plan required that the assaulting troops should assemble in Crete Trench before the night of the raid and then move to Croft Trench 30 minutes before zero hour. At the prescribed time an artillery barrage was to be laid on the German front line and shell holes. On the commencement of the barrage, the assaulting troops were to leave their trench in two lines, approach the first line of shell holes and enter them as the barrage lifted one and a half minutes later. The first wave had one minute to establish the Lewis Guns as flank protection while the second wave of troops passed through to capture the second line of shell holes.

The barrage was then to lift and maintain a protection against any attempt by the enemy to reinforce from the main line. The troops then only had a matter of minutes to search for any documents, take prisoners and begin the withdrawal of the second wave through the first, returning to the starting trench. The second line was then to be followed immediately by the first wave and all were to be back in the in the front line within eleven minutes. In an effort to practice the assault, the selected party from the Royal Irish Fusiliers conducted a practice raid in the rear area during the day of the 22nd.

While the 10th Brigade was busy with the consolidation and preparation for the raid north of the Scarpe, the 11th Brigade was equally busy preparing for an assault by the Rifle Brigade, south of the Scarpe. The enterprise was in accordance with 11th Brigade Operation Order No. 103, which required a company of the Rifle Brigade, to advance behind a barrage and capture a German trench near the junction of Pelves Lane and the track leading across the canal to Roeux. Two platoons were to act as the first wave and they were to be followed by a third platoon acting in support. The fourth platoon was directed to protect the right flank of the attacking force by taking covering positions facing east. In order to ensure that communications were established with the new position as quickly as possible, a platoon of the 3/4th Queens Own were to dig a communication trench from Finger Trench to the newly captured position. The heavy artillery was to commence firing upon specified targets at the same time as the field guns commenced the barrage. During this period of planning and practice, the front and support lines were subjected to constant shelling and the equally constant rain.

The hour of the assault had been set for 10:20pm on the night of the 23rd and in preparation for the attack, the artillery concentrated on cutting the wire in front of the German positions for two days before zero hour. The Rifle Brigade sent out patrols each night to check the progress being made with the wire cutting and reported to the affirmative. On schedule the bombardment commenced and two minutes later the assaulting wave left Finger Trench and advanced in two lines, followed closely by the covering party from Elbow Trench. As the first wave reached the objective, the covering party passed through to form a covering line ahead of the attacking wave. A machine-gun barrage, provided by the 11th Machine-Gun Company, supported the movement. It swept the road leading out of Roeux, selected buildings and other roads and approaches. That fire later proved to be most effective.

Immediately upon the commencement of the barrage and while the attacking troops were leaving Finger Trench the platoon of the 3/4th Queens Own began digging the new communications trench quickly, in spite of the retaliatory machine-gun fire. The attention that the British artillery had been paying to the wire had made the Germans aware of an impending attack and, in response to the barrage, the German machine gunners commenced intense fire but were quickly beaten down by the artillery and trench mortars.

The objective was reached and taken without serious complication, although temporary delays were experienced in those places where the wire had not been cut as completely as required, especially on the right. The covering party also experienced slight difficulties with wire but soon took up the required positions, 60 yards east of the objective and, in fact, in front of the line laid down in the plan. The leading wave took the objective in the face of hostile machine-gun fire and an intense German bombardment, which arrived almost at the same time as the British barrage.

All went according to plan until about half an hour after the capture of the position. Consolidation work was under way when the officer in charge of the consolidation work gave the instruction to retire. No reason was established for the order but it resulted in the covering party withdrawing, forcing the assaulting troops to return to their original trench. By 11:00pm all were back where they started. The Rifle Brigade suffered five men killed, thirty-two wounded and seven missing, without any casualties among the officers. The only prisoners taken were one officer and six other ranks, all of which stated that they had suffered very heavy casualties from the machine-gun fire and it was claimed that the attacking troops had bayoneted 25 of the enemy. All reports on the attack reflected the success achieved, particularly by the machine-gun barrage. The Lancashire Fusiliers undertook constant patrolling after the withdrawal but found that the trench was strongly held, with the occupants consolidating the position.

Following the withdrawal of the Rifle Brigade, the 11th Brigade was subjected to constant artillery and machine-gun fire throughout the 24th. It was now the turn of the Royal Irish Fusiliers to put into effect the raid previously planned. Thirty minutes before zero hour all troops were in their prescribed positions, in absolute silence. All of those engaged in the raid were arranged in sections, each with their own particular objectives. About one minute before zero the heavy artillery, which had been allocated particular targets, commenced firing and the shell fire was taken by many of the waiting troops as being the opening barrage, particularly those on the left of the raiding party.

Some of these parties advance immediately and were well out into No Man's Land when the scheduled barrage fell amongst them, causing casualties. When the leading troops got to within 20 yards of the first objective they were met with machine-gun fire that originated from Cyprus trench. The Lewis gunners were alert to attempts by the enemy to get reinforcements to assist those in the shell holes and about five were seen to run up from the second objective; all were seen to fall before the fire of the guns. Trip wires about eighteen inches high and four feet deep were encountered approximately ten yards in front of the objective, but were found to be thin enough for the troops to pick their way through. As they approached the shell holes several of the enemy were seen to run to the rear.

On the right and centre of the raiding party all of the shell holes on the first objective were found to be empty but, of those on the left, five were occupied. After a brief but determined skirmish, three prisoners were taken and a further three killed. On advancing to the second objective, considerable rifle and machine-gun fire was opened from neighbouring shell holes and again trip wire was encountered. This did not prevent a number of shell holes being attacked, leaving thirteen enemy dead. A German officer, climbing out of a shell hole with his revolver was killed as he attempted to rally the retreating troops, amongst which the Lewis guns wreaked destruction.

Hurried inspections of the shell holes took place and the retirement began almost immediately but, as the troops returned over No Man's Land, five German were seen to advance and the Lewis guns once again took their toll. It was later realised that these men were unarmed and were attempting to surrender, but the fact that they were wearing great coats made them appear armed. The Royal Irish Fusiliers suffered the loss of two officers and ten other ranks missing and five other ranks wounded.

A gas discharge by the 10th Brigade, north of the Scarpe was originally planned to take place on the night of the 23rd but the positions containing the projectors, Croft Trench, was shelled heavily by the German artillery shelled, damaging several of the projectors. It was thought possible that the Germans had observed the projectors and suspected some form attack.

Because of the damage caused by the shelling, the discharge was delayed until the night of the 25th when, at 2:00am 450 drums were discharged using Livens Projectors, against the German trenches in the region of the Windmill, Chalk Pit, Hausa Wood and Delbar Woods. The attack was accompanied by the fire of a stokes mortar bombardment and the only response solicited by this attack was the firing of a few rifle grenades and several pink flares.

The perpetual artillery exchanges continued and the nocturnal prowling of the patrols produced regular minor skirmishes throughout the remainder of the month. On the 25th, the division was informed that it was to extend its right flank further to the south, closer to the river and assume responsibility for a portion of the line then held the 12th Division (VI Corps). The movement began during the night of the 26th when the 10th Brigade, on the northern bank of the river, was relieved by the 52nd Brigade (17th Division). The brigade then side-slipped to the south and took responsibility for a part of the 11th Brigade area. The 12th Brigade then took over the 11th Brigade area south of the Scarpe on the night of the 27th and later also relieved the 25th Brigade of the 12th Division as requested. The 11th Brigade then withdrew to Arras.

July - 1917

With the division astride the Scarpe, trench life continued without relief. The daily routine may have been mundane for the troops, but never boring. The German artillery maintained continuous and concentrated shellfire on the front and support lines and the lines of communication, punctuated by periods of intense artillery fire by both sides. The first two weeks were spent consolidating the lines that had been taken over from the 12th and 17th Divisions. The practice of gathering information, probing for a weakness or finding an opportunity to execute damage upon the enemy was conducted by perpetual patrolling. On the 5th, a company of the 3/10th Middlesex Regiment was attached to the King's Own and West Riding Regiments (12th Brigade) for four days instruction in trench warfare.

The daily events were largely directed at deluding the enemy as to the British intentions and, on the 6th, in an attempt to convince the enemy that the front line was under attack, the division artillery placed a heavy barrage on the German front line. Such was the soldiers' familiarity with this nature of fighting that the opposing German artillery and infantry took very little interest and offered little reply. The 11th was marked by heavy trench mortar exchanges between batteries in and about the opposing front lines.

Planning was commenced on a series of raids, which were to be carried out on both sides of the river [308]. Several days earlier instructions had been issued to the 10th Brigade to conduct a bombardment of the German shell holes in an area approximating a rectangle of 200 yards by about 100 yards, using Thermite shells, fired by 4" Stokes Mortars[309]. The bombardment was to be carried out at 12:30am on the night of the 12th and was to last a total of three minutes. On completion of the bombardment, two patrols of the Household Battalion were to scrutinise the ground directly in front of the left sector of the area affected by the bombardment, with the objective of killing any enemy found and identifying the opposing troops. They were also to assess the effects of Thermite in the preliminary bombardment.

---

[308] *During the course of the planning, Lieutenant-Colonel O.C. Borrett, D.S.O., temporarily commanding the 12 Brigade, left the division to assume command of the 197 Brigade (66 Division). He was replaced by Lieutenant-Colonel A. G. Horsfall, D.S.O.*

[309] *Thermite is a chemical compound formulated to produce an explosion of high-temperature, not unlike Phosphorous.*

In order to suppress any suspicion by the enemy of impending action, the engineers provided temporary covered accommodation for the patrols and supporting infantry in the front line. The whole operation was to be supported by artillery and machine-gun barrage with the intention of preventing any enemy escaping from the area affected. The artillery barrage was to include a mixture of various kinds of gas shells, wind direction permitting, on the eastern edge of the 'box' formed by the barrage.

Whilst these plans were being finalised, the 12th Brigade had determined to raid Arrow Trench on the south side of the Scarpe. Arrow Trench was a trench 250 yards long, which ran north-east to south-west across the Pelves - Monchy Road. The northern end of the trench had been terminated with a 'T' sap, which ran north - south for about 30 yards each way. The trench was thought to be in bad condition and only manned on the north 'T' sap. The timing of the raid was arranged to take advantage of the distraction to the German artillery caused by the bombardment on the north side of the river.

An earlier patrol had defined the defences of the sap as being one machine and the crew of four, along with six other men living in dug-outs a little further along the trench. It was also thought that the machine-gun was withdrawn to a safer position during the day.

The raid was to be carried out, on the night of the 12th, under the command of 2nd Lieutenant C. H. Stanley, accompanied by two N.C.O.'s and fourteen other ranks of the 2nd Essex Regiment (12th Brigade). The objective was to capture the machine-gun and kill the crew, capture prisoners for identification and bomb the shelters and then re-assemble at Brigade Headquarters upon their return. One section of seven men, under Sergeant Goodall, was to capture the machine-gun while the second section under Corporal Russell was responsible for the capture of the remaining infantry.

The troops, armed only with a rifle and fixed bayonet, twenty rounds of ammunition and two No.5 Mills bombs were, at zero hour, 12:31am, to crawl out of their trenches and extend into a line at fifty yards distance from the objective. They were then to crawl until they were within rushing distance of the sap then, on a given signal, rush the positions. Having only five minutes to complete their responsibilities they were then to return to the line on the firing of blue rockets. The whole operation was to be supported by the 12th Brigade machine-gun Company and the trench mortars.

At 12:30am, the mortars of the 10th Brigade commenced the Thermite bombardment, accompanied by the artillery and machine guns. The Thermite appeared to be quite effective although there appeared to be considerable irregularities in the ammunition. The mortars soon come under intense fire from the German trench mortars and suffered several casualties, but gallant action by 2nd Lieutenant Dea and Lance Corporal Harley, in serving their mortars, contributed to the effectiveness of the bombardment.

The two patrols departed four minutes after the commencement and remained out in the area for forty and fifty minutes. Patrol "A", consisting of one officer and eight other ranks, including a Lewis gun, left the front line, at the junction of Croft and Colombo trenches and moved in a north-easterly direction to inspect a line of shell holes. Changing direction, the patrol then moved south and followed the shell holes, turning again to the north-west, after meeting patrol 'B'. On its return, the patrol discovered a defended shell hole in which was a long dead German.

Patrol 'B', one officer and six men, started from Colombo Trench and proceeded south-east, almost reaching the Roeux - Plouvain Road, to a point 30-40 yards in front of the poplars, which lined the road, it encountered wire about 3 feet high and quite thick. While in the area, an enemy soldier was seen running to the rear. Turning to the north-west, they met the patrol 'A' and encountered a small trench about 12 feet long, which had two layers of sandbags around the edge, covered with soil.

They also found a fortified shell hole, which had apparently been used as a bombing post, as a collection of new bombs were found lying on top of the rim, ready for use. It was agreed that the Thermite had had little effect. During their stay, they met no opposition, although they were subjected to light, long distance rifle fire and a single machine-gun directed on the parapet of the British front line. The patrol then returned to Colombo Trench.

Meanwhile, south of the Scarpe, the Essex had carried out their raid. At the prescribed time, one minute after the commencement of the bombardment on the northern side of the river, the raiders of the Essex Regiment left the trenches and made their way to the 'T' sap. On arrival, they discovered that the enemy had completely evacuated the position although two Germans were seen to retire from a position further up Arrow trench, carrying what was thought to be an ammunition belt. Due to the extremely poor condition of the trench, the patrol carried out no further action. Although no attempt at retaliation was made during the raid, there remained the blue rockets, which acted as a signal for several enemy machine guns to fire intermittently along the front line and a single shell was fired into the sap that had just been vacated. When the signal for withdrawal was seen the patrol returned without having suffered any casualties.

On the 13th, the division received a warning order that the Germans may retire to the east, to the Drocourt - Queant line and that attention must be paid to any movement that indicated that such a withdrawal could be underway. There was however, no such movement and Arras was subjected to an early morning bombing by several German planes.

In an attempt to keep the enemy in a state of anxiety, several attempts were made to give the impression that a raid was in progress. By utilising the artillery to bombard a trench and form a box barrage around it, just as would be done in the event of a raid, it was seen as a method of inflicting casualties and wearing out the opposition. The exercise was carried out against Devils Trench, south of the Scarpe, on the 20th and again on the 25th. To supplement that strategy, the 1st Hampshire Regiment (11th Brigade) conducted a real raid against Devils Trench at 10:45pm on the 26th, with a party consisting of three officers, one warrant officer and seventy other ranks, accompanied by seven engineers. Their intention was to enter and exploit Devils Trench with the aim of capturing a suspected machine-gun emplacement and identify the opposition.

The raiding party was divided into three groups, each allocated to special parts of the trench and a fourth to deal with the machine-gun post. In preparation for the final assault each group crept out into No Man's Land twenty minutes before zero and formed up in two lines, 30 yards in front of the British main line. Howitzer fire had previously cut the wire in front of the German trench and, at zero hour, an artillery barrage was put down in front of and to the flanks of the area to be raided. At the same time, the parties advanced behind a rolling barrage.

All suspected machine-gun posts were kept under artillery and mortar fire while a machine-gun barrage was maintained to protect the flanks of the raiders. Five and a half minutes after zero, the raiding party entered the enemy trench and saw several of the enemy, believed that they had been caught in the artillery barrage, running to the rear while others were seen to move off to the flanks.

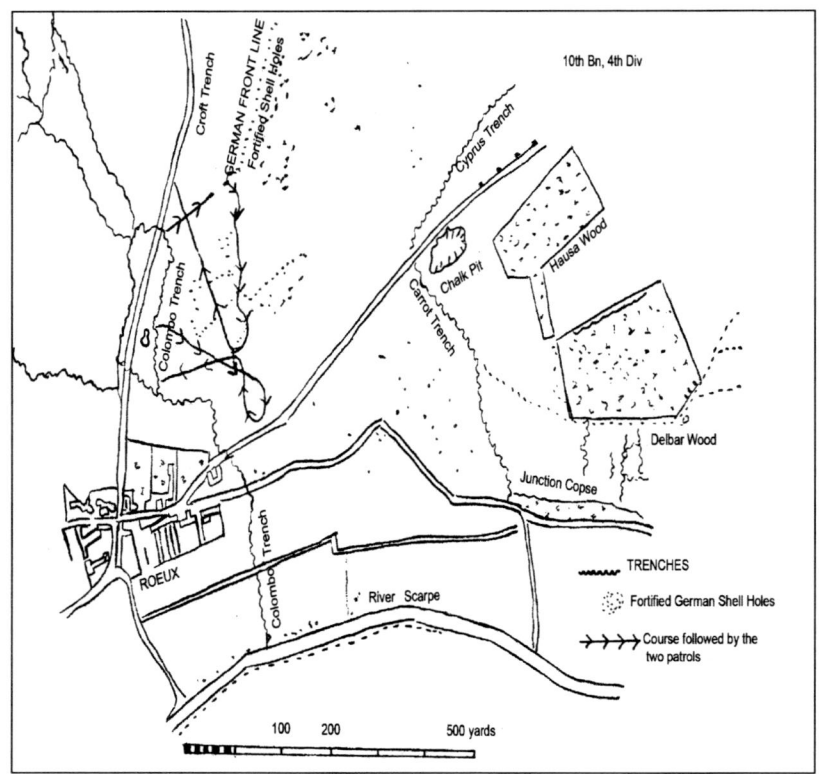

Plate 12
Direction followed by the two patrols of the Household Battalion, 10th Brigade, after the bombardment using Thermite shells on the morning of the 13th July 1917.

The party allocated to capturing the machine-gun post continued the advance but got lost because of difficulties locating the communication trench leading to the post. After having advanced for 100 yards and finding nothing, they returned and rejoined the main body, which had cleared the badly damaged Devils Trench.

In retaliation, the enemy began to bomb along trenches on the left flank of the raiders, an attempt that was immediately repulsed by the left flank bombing party. Fourteen minutes after the commencement of the raid the officers in charge of the flank parties reported that all was clear and two minutes later the first signal for withdrawal was fired. All, except the three officers and three bombing sections, acting as a rearguard, withdrew successfully to the British front line.

Shortly after, a second signal indicated withdrawal for the rearguard parties, as the prisoners had already been escorted to the British lines.

The enemy appeared to have been taken completely by surprise and the prisoners stated that the British artillery and machine-gun barrage had prevented them from using their own machine-gun or rifle fire to prevent the raid. The German artillery responded only lightly, with the majority of shells landing behind the support line.

The whole trenches system was found to be in very bad condition, with no permanent dug-outs and only one unmanned concrete machine-gun post, which was promptly destroyed by the engineers. Although the raiding party suffered lightly, one killed, two missing and three wounded, many enemy dead and several wounded were found in the trenches. The wounded, one N.C.O. and three other ranks of the 9th Company, 3rd Battalion, 163rd Infantry Regiment (17th Infantry Reserve Division) were all returned to the British lines under escort and provide much valuable information about troop movements opposite the 11th Brigade. The last few days of the month were spent under very active artillery fire, day and night, amidst which the 12th Brigade finally relieved the 11th Brigade during the night of the 31st.

August - 1917

The nature of the fighting had evolved, during the previous two months, into static trench warfare as Germans reinforcements arrived. It is worth noting that, at this time, circumstances were occurring on other fronts that directly effected activities on the Western Front. Russia's imperial political system was collapsing and the mood of revolution prevailed. The turmoil in Russia was having an effect on the preparedness of the Russian Army to continue the fight and resulted in a diminishing threat to the German and Austrian Armies on that front. As a result, the strategic focus turned to the Western front, as it was perceived, correctly, that Germany would begin diverting many divisions, intended for Russia, to the Western Front. Others followed, directly from Russia, later in the year.

As the greater strategic movements were taking place, the activities on raids and active patrolling punctuated the 4th Division front. The division had been a part of the holding operations that General Haig had used whilst large forces were transferred north, to Flanders[310]. The German line on the Arras front had stabilised, leaving the enemy in a position of strength. Many of the divisions that were acting in support on that line had been drawn from 'quieter' fronts and the actions of June and July were designed largely to keep them there.

The front line brigades, the 10th, north of the river and the 11th to the south, were constantly subjected to the shelling of trench lines but minor incidents occurred which encouraged the troops to adopt an aggressive policy of 'peaceful penetration'[311]. The division War Diary offers an example of a particular event, which occurred on the 11th Brigade front on the first day of the month, the likes of which occurred regularly. *"During the afternoon a corporal crawled out from sap A (I.25.d.15.30) to the enemy's wire and found a German bomb. He threw it into the enemy's trench where it exploded. No action by the enemy followed."* The usual inter-battalion reliefs were a part of trench life, but on the evening of the 1st, the Royal Irish Fusiliers were relieved from their po-

---

[310] *The attack in Flanders, referred to as 'Third Ypres', commenced on the 31·July. It was to continue for some months in indescribable conditions that are now synonymous with the name 'Passchendaele'. The offensive officially ended on the 6· November 1917 with the capture of the village by that name.*

[311] *'Peaceful penetration' was the name given to the art of approaching an enemy post and killing or capturing the occupants and removing their weapons in broad daylight.*

sition on the 10th Brigade line for reasons that affected all in the division.

It was with great regret among the troops that, on the 2nd of August, the 1st Royal Irish Fusiliers (10th Brigade), left the division to become a part of the 36th Division, an all-Irish division. The battalion had served with the 4th Division for six years and had fought with the 10th Brigade since the beginning of the war where it provided sterling service. The departure was sorely felt amongst all ranks and the battalion was played to the railway station by the massed bands of the division. There, the Corps Commander and the G.O.C. of the division addressed them, expressing their regret. In their place arrived the 3/10th Middlesex Regiment[312].

Events continued as usual and the front line experienced heavy shelling throughout the night and into the next day, causing considerable damage to Elbow and Ceylon Trenches, but did not prevent further expeditions by individual patrols. A daylight patrol crawled out of the front line to a position close to the German wire and shot a man walking down the trench. To this there was no response from the enemy.

The steady flow of British divisions to Flanders required the 12th Division, fighting on the right of the 4th, to withdraw from the line. To enable the withdrawal, the 10th Brigade was ordered to take over a part of the positions then held by the 12th Brigade, on the south side of the river, on the 8th. The 12th Brigade was then to side slip and assume responsibility for a part of the area held by the 12th Division. For the 10th Brigade to assume the required position, it was necessary for the entire brigade to move to the right and straddle the river. The 45th Brigade (15th Division), situated to the left of the 4th Division, was to occupy that part of the front line being vacated by the 10th Brigade. While officers of the 45th Brigade reconnoitred the area, they were subjected to considerable German trench mortar fire, which had been directed at Archie Trench.

In the interim, the full moon had made patrolling at night extremely dangerous but was, on one occasion, used to advantage. On the night of the 5th, an attempt was made by the 11th Brigade to carry out an inspection of the German trenches under the protection of an artillery

---

[312] *The 3/10 Battalion was formed in May 1915. It was attached to the 67 Division (Home Counties) in which it served until arriving in France in June 1917. After serving with the 9 Division for a short period it was attached to the 10 Brigade, 4 Division on the 2 August 1917.*

barrage but the attempt failed, largely due to the machine-gun fire directed upon them from trench and shell hole.

The two days were fully occupied with small ventures carried out by individuals and small groups in an attempt to wear down the opposition. Two snipers of the Lancashire Fusiliers crawled out and discovered two German snipers who had been giving trouble from their positions in No Man's Land. One was dispensed with and nothing further was heard from the other while, at about the same time, a deserter of the 76th Reserve Infantry Regiment entered the British line and surrendered. The brigades undertook regular patrol work whenever the opportunity presented itself and, in accordance with the policy of constantly gathering new information, the patrols paid considerable attention to the wire entanglements in front of the German lines.

The 12th Brigade, in discussions with the 12th Division, agreed to carry out a daylight raid on the German position opposite Bit Lane, to protect the left flank of the 36th Brigade while it attacked enemy positions on its own front. The operation was planned for the morning of the 8th, and to assist the operation, the artillery immediately commenced wire cutting. While the planning was underway on the front line, those to the rear enjoyed the 4th Division Sports Day, held on the 7th August and was attended by those troops that were in reserve and at rest. The event was reported a great success.

All preparations had been finalised for the raid, which consisted of elements of the 2nd Essex and 2nd West Riding Regiments. The plans were always at the mercy of the weather and the morning of the 8th was shrouded in a heavy mist, forcing the decision to postpone the raid for 24 hours. The mist did not lift until about 10:00am but, once gone, the visibility was perfect and the artillery of both side engaged in active shelling of the opposition for the remainder of the day.

Notwithstanding the constant fire, the division artillery and trench mortars continued cutting the wire in front of the trenches to be raided after which night patrols had reported the wire having been cut successfully. At about 6:00pm on the night of the 8th, after heavy rains that had flooded many of the trenches, a large German party raided trenches on the left of the Royal Warwickshire Regiment, causing nearly sixty casualties, but were then beaten back with bombs, rifles and bayonets.

Zero hour was set for 7:45am and was preceded by a bombardment by the field and heavy artillery that had commenced at 6:30am. The guns fired on selected targets and, at 7:45am they formed a rather thin barrage behind which the infantry was to advance. The German artillery responded immediately to the artillery fire by placing a barrage on the front and support lines, which caught the waiting troops by surprise and inflicted early casualties.

The raiding party consisted of seven officers and one hundred and eighty other ranks of the 2nd Essex, two officers and thirty other ranks of the 2nd West Riding Regiment and four detachments, each of three sappers of the 9th Field Company. In accordance with the plan, the raiders advanced from the trenches and the party from the West Riding Regiment, having only suffered light casualties, reached and entered Arrow Trench, south of Bit Lane, to find it unoccupied.

Those of the Essex Regiment were not so fortunate, they were immediately subjected to heavy machine-gun fire and suffered heavily. German troops were seen to climb upon the parapet of their trenches to fire machine guns and rifle grenades as well as throwing bombs. Lewis guns engaged those troops with effect and drove back some of the more adventurous enemy, who had come forward from their trenches and manned shell holes.

Watching the raid take place were troops of the 10th Brigade, located on the opposite side of the river. They immediately offered support by firing across the river from Roeux Wood but some of this fire caught the flank troops and inflicted seven casualties. It was soon conceded that the raid was not going to succeed and the order to withdraw was given. Given the number of casualties, mainly the result of the machine-gun fire, it was some time before the situation was cleared up.

Wounded and unwounded trickled into the front line for most of the night. The total number of casualties amounted to eight officers and eighty-eight men killed, wounded and missing. The attack of the 12th Division, to the right of the 12th Brigade, was only partly successful but did achieve certain objectives as intended. Shortly after midnight the raid was followed up by the division artillery, which bombarded Angel and Devils trench, known to be fully occupied by enemy infantry.

August was a period of constant aerial battles and on the 11th, at about 8:00am, three German aircraft were engaged by five British aeroplanes above the troops of the 4th Division. One of the enemy aircraft was seen to crash and a second was driven down. That night the 3/10th Middlesex Regiment relieved the 1st Royal Warwickshire Regiment (10th Brigade).

The 14th proved to be a busy day for both front line brigades when, at 1:30am a strong enemy patrol of twenty men approached the wire in front of the 12th Brigade. When seen, they were engaged with rifle fire and grenades, which drove them off after leaving casualties. Early in the morning of the 14th, a patrol of the Middlesex Regiment, Major O'Neill, a sergeant and two men, captured and brought in two German prisoners from one of the forward posts located in front of No. 1 Post, on the northern side of the river.

At 3:00pm on the same day Archie Trench and others nearby, held by the enemy, was bombarded by trench mortars, 4.5" and 9.5" howitzers with heavy and accurate fire. On the second burst of fire, eight of the enemy were seen to leave the trench and advance towards the front line of the 12th Brigade. The field guns of the division, waiting for targets, ranged onto the advancing men and shepherded them towards the British wire where they were subjected to concentrated shrapnel fire and suffered many casualties. One of those men was shepherded right up against the wire and was captured that evening by a patrol sent to retrieve him. He belonged to the 76th Reserve Infantry Regiment (17th Reserve Division).

As two battalions each of the 10th and 12th Brigades then held the front line, the remaining battalions were either in support or in reserve. Taking advantage of the break, the Household Battalion took the opportunity to hold an aquatic sports day in weather, described by the war division diary as *of an unpredictable nature*. Such events provided relief from the strains experienced in the front line and the monotony of training and marching when behind the lines and acted as a source of great amusement and competitiveness for all concerned.

Whilst the 10th Brigade was busy on the northern side of the River Scarpe, the 11th Brigade, having been in rest since the beginning of the month, relieved the 12th Brigade on the southern side. It was a period of re-organisation of the line, in preparation for the withdrawal of the division and, once again, the 10th Brigade was instructed to take responsibility for a portion of the line from the 11th Brigade on the 18th. During the course of the 17th, the G.O.C., XVII Corps[313] and the Division Commander visited the 11th Brigade in the line. The G.O.C., III Army and the Corps Commander again visited the brigade, the following day, during which medals and awards were presented. Immediately after the visit and in accordance with orders, the Seaforth Highlanders took over a part of the line held by the Rifle Brigade, south of the Scarpe, while

---

[313] *The G.O.C. of XVII Corps was the former commander of the 4 Division, Major-General T. D'O. Snow.*

the 11th Brigade extended its line to the edge of the Northern Twin Copse, relieved the last of the 12th Division.

That movement effectively widened the frontage of the 4th Division, with the 10th Brigade straddled across the river as far as Scabbard Alley. During the move a German Corporal of the 8th Company, 76th Reserve Infantry Regiment (17th Reserve Division) was killed when found alone in a shell hole behind the line of outposts early in the morning. That night a patrol of the Household Battalion encountered a German patrol and, in the exchange, suffered one man wounded and a second missing. Two nights later, a patrol of the Householder managed to approach an enemy working party and inflicted heavy casualties through rifle and Lewis gunfire.

The response arrived in the form of artillery and mortar fire on the front line, which caused considerable damage and inflicted several casualties. It was followed the next day, by trench mortar fire, during a heavy storm, which inflicted further damage to trenches on the north side of the river.

Patrol actions were a feature of nocturnal activity in No Man's Land and one incident typifies the constant threat that fighting patrols presented to the troops of both sides. During the evening of the 25th, several patrols of the Household Battalion managed to get behind the German front line and, approaching them from the rear, causing considerable damage and casualties amongst the unsuspecting enemy. That same night, a German raid was affected against No's. 2 and 3 Posts, on the northern side of the river and it was only after some determined fighting that the attempt was driven off by rifle and machine-gun fire.

The remainder of the month was 'quiet by frontline standards, with a high wind, which preventing all artillery fire. The wind did not affect the aggressive patrol work and an enemy soldier was killed just outside the wire in front of the Middlesex Regiment. On the 30th, the division was advised that it would be withdrawn into Army Reserve for rest and training. The order detailed that the 4th Division would be relieved by the 15th Division and would then retire to the Adinper Area where it was to fall under the orders of VI Corps. The relief was to commence in the first few days of September. Rather than take their ammunition with them when relieved, the trench mortars laid a heavy bombardment on the German front line during the afternoon of the 31st. This attracted retaliatory fire on Cabbage and Corona Trenches, on the northern side of the river, but failed to inflict any casualties.

September - 1917

Amidst the preparations for retirement from the line, time was still found to grant leave to officers and men. Brigadier-General Pritchard, C.M.G., O.C. 10th Brigade, departed for leave to England on the first day of the month, replaced temporarily by the commanding officer of the Seaforth Highlanders, Lieutenant-Colonel R. Lang, M.C. The first few days were relatively quiet with occasional shelling and counter-fire and the night patrol work was made difficult by a full moon that provided ample light all over the battlefield. On the 1st of the month the 12th Brigade relieved the 11th Brigade on the south bank of the river, in cold and windy conditions.

On the 4th, staff officers of the 45th Brigade (15th Division) arrived to reconnoitre the lines held by the 10th Brigade, with a view to continuing the relief of the brigade in the forthcoming days. During this inspection, the German trench mortars concentrated considerable fire on Archie Trench. The evening of the 4th remained too light for patrolling, so the next few nights remained free of interference from enemy attacks.

While the 10th Brigade was preparing to leave the line, the 11th Brigade, which had been in division reserve, marched for the Homier training area on the Somme. The relief commenced on the night of the 6th when the Royal Warwickshire and Middlesex Regiment (10th Brigade), acting in support to the front line battalions, marched to Bailleulval[314]. The remainder of the brigade marched after the 45th Brigade had completed the relief of the front line battalions. The 12th Brigade followed the 10th after being relieved on the 7th.

It was in this period that considerable effort was put into the training and the battalions practised new methods of attack. From the 9th - 12th, the troops were practised in platoon and company exercises, which consisted of musketry, fire and control, attacking from a trench line and methods employed in attacking a strongpoint. Emphasis was placed on the use of the rifle as the primary offensive weapon in an attack, instead of the grenade[315].

---

[314] *That area was referred to as the Adinfer Training Grounds.*

[315] *It is interesting to note that, while in the training camp, those of the Hampshire Regiment that had served with the division in the attack of the 1st July 1916 were taken by bus to Mailly Maillet, on the 9. Here, they were allowed to view Beaumont Hamel and the area of the Redan Ridge, over which they had attacked with such heavy casualties.*

On the 12th, the G.O.C., Major-General Lambton suffered severe injuries after falling from his horse while crossing a concealed shell hole on the training ground. The injuries were incurred as the horse rolled bodily over him[316] and were to prevent him from returning to command the 4th Division. Two days later Major-General T. G. Matheson assumed command. The time spent in the training grounds was not all hard work. During its stay, the 10th Brigade held its sports days and football matches leading up to the finals being held on the 19th [317].

On the 13th, the division artillery commenced its move to the XIV Corps area in Belgium and, in the course of the following week, the infantry brigades marched to the Mondicourt area where they entrained for St. Omer, the final stage of the trip, taking the division to Proven. On arrival, the 4th Division fell under the command of XIV Corps, Fifth Army (Lt.-General Gough). The troops remained in billets and underwent further training and re-equipping. On the 24th of September the division was advised that it would be required to relieve the 20th Division on the 28th and assume its position on the right of the headquarters front in the area about Langemarck[318].

A brief appreciation of the events, which had occurred in Flanders while the division was fighting at Arras, is appropriate at this point. The attacks on the Arras front had commenced on the 9th April and by the 15th of that month most of the objectives set out by the Commander-in-Chief of the British Forces in France, General Haig, had been achieved. German reinforcements had been moved from various parts of the Western Front to resist the British advance to the east of Arras and the French attacks had failed.

Many of the reinforcement had been moved from the Flanders area in Belgium, and offered an opportunity for Haig to carry out his long-desired assault in the north, with the objective of denying the Germans

---

[316] *Co-incidentally, the first G.O.C. of the Division, Maj.-General Snow, suffered similar injuries when he fell from his horse during the battle of the Marne on the 8 September 1914 near La Ferté.*

[317] *Unfortunately no record remains of the results of the any of the sports finals.*

[318] *Not much had changed in Flanders since the Division had last served in the area. When the relief took place between the 28 and 30 September they took over trenches lines only several hundred yards ahead of the same trenches that they had held 12 months previously, in September 1916. At the time of the division arriving at Langemark, the battle for Passchendaele was reaching its zenith, under conditions that are now well known and the advance that the 4 Division was about to embark upon, was a part of Haigs' offensive on Passchendaele.*

access to the coast. After the 15th, April several of the divisions in the Arras area were moved to Flanders in preparation for the attack which was to, hopefully, place the Germans at a strategic disadvantage before the expected arrival of the many divisions from the Eastern front. The 2nd and 5th Armies were given the task of carrying out the attack, commencing on the 31st June with major operations on the Messines Ridge on the 7th of July and Lombarttze, on the 10th July, on the coast.

By the 26th of September, the division headquarters had arrived at Langemarck and received orders from XIV Corps, stating that the 4th Division was to participate in an attack, in conjunction with its sister division, the 29th. The orders were immediately promulgated to the infantry brigades so that they would be prepared for offensive action upon entering the front line[319].

Even while the troops waited in the training camps they could not entirely escape the attention of the enemy. On the 28th a German aeroplane bombed the camp in which the 11th Brigade was staying, wounding one man. That evening, the 12th Brigade relieved the 61st Brigade (20th Division) in the front line while the 11th Brigade moved into immediate support along the Yser Canal after having relieved the 59th Brigade (20th Division). The 10th Brigade moved into the division support area and relieved the 61st Brigade the following night.

---

[319] *See Appendix VII, 4 Division Order No. 61.*

October - 1917

The planned attack of the XIV and XVIII Corps, of the 5th Army, was to commence at 5:20am on the 9th October. The 4th Division, attacking on the right of the 29th Division, was to advance on a two-brigade front of 800 yards, in a north-easterly direction. The left flank (10th Brigade) was to start from a point 100 yards south of the Langemarck – Poelcappelle road, west of the cemetery and extend 300 yards to the east, to Louis F[m]. The right flank (11th brigade), was continue the line to the south-east for a further 500 yards, almost to the Langemarck-Poelcappelle road

It had not been determined which German division was facing the 4th Division. It was known that the 208th Division had been in the line until the 23rd September. It was also thought that it may have been relieved by the 40th Division, due to heavy casualties.

Operation Order No. 61[320] described the first objective to be taken in the advance towards the final object, the Blue line. Described as the Green Dotted line, the position extended to the Retar Cross Roads, on the Poelcappelle - Langemarck Road, 500 yards south-west of Poelcappelle and extended north through Kangaroo Farm, Lemnos House and then north west to the intended line of the last objective on the Langemarck-Turon Crossing Junction road.

The final objective was the capture of the Blue line[321], a line extending between a point, on the right, just east of the Poelcappelle-le 5 Chimes Road, about 400 yards north east of Poelcappelle, to a point approximately 250 yards north-north-east of 19 Metre Hill, on the left. The objective occupied a curved frontage, approximately 1300 yards distant from the start line.

The beginning of October found the 4th Division holding the line with the 12th Brigade while the other two remained in the support and reserve lines. During the night of the 1st October, the division began a process of deployment into the positions that would form the order of battle for the forthcoming attack. The front, held by the 12th Brigade, represented the entire division front. As evening fell the 1st Rifle Brigade (11th Brigade) and the 2nd Seaforth Highlanders (10th Brigade) which

---

[320] See Appendix VII, '4 Division Operation Order No. 61 for details.

[321] The 4 Division diaries describes the final object as the Blue Line but the map used by the division in the planning of the attack referred to the final objective as the Green line. The reader should take both as being the same objective.

was under temporary command of the 11th Brigade, relieved the 12th Brigade, which then retired to the reserve positions that had just been vacated by the 11th Brigade. This now split the front line into those areas of responsibility from which each of the attacking brigades would be advancing.

While the remaining three battalions of the 11th Brigade moved forward into three separate lines, one behind the other. Behind the Rifle Brigade was the 1st Hampshire's, on the Yser Canal[322]. In reserve, further to the rear, were the 1st Somerset's and further again, in Elverdinghe, was the 1st East Lancashires. The Seaforth Highlanders had moved forward with and under the command of the 11th Brigade for the purpose of movement and occupation of 10th Brigade sector of the line. Once completed the G.O.C., 10th Brigade then assumed command of the Seaforth's and during the night of the 3rd, the remainder of the 10th Brigade, moved forward and assumed final positions next to the 11th Brigade. The next two days were spent quietly as late orders were issued and the men wrote letters and prepared their equipment for the attack.

The balance of the 10th Brigade remained in the support area. The manoeuvrings of the attacking brigades were not yet complete. The intention was to have the 12th Brigade take over the front line again, now that the attacking troops were familiar with the ground over which they would have to advance and give the assaulting brigades a period of rest before the event. To this end the 11th Brigade extended its left and relieved the Seaforth Highlanders in the front line, which then withdrew to the support area along the canal. During the following day, the 7th, the 12th Brigade relieved Rifle Brigade in the front line, which, in turn, retired to the reserve area.

---

[322] *The trenches that the Hampshire's occupied were those that the Division had occupied in September 1916, 12 months before.*

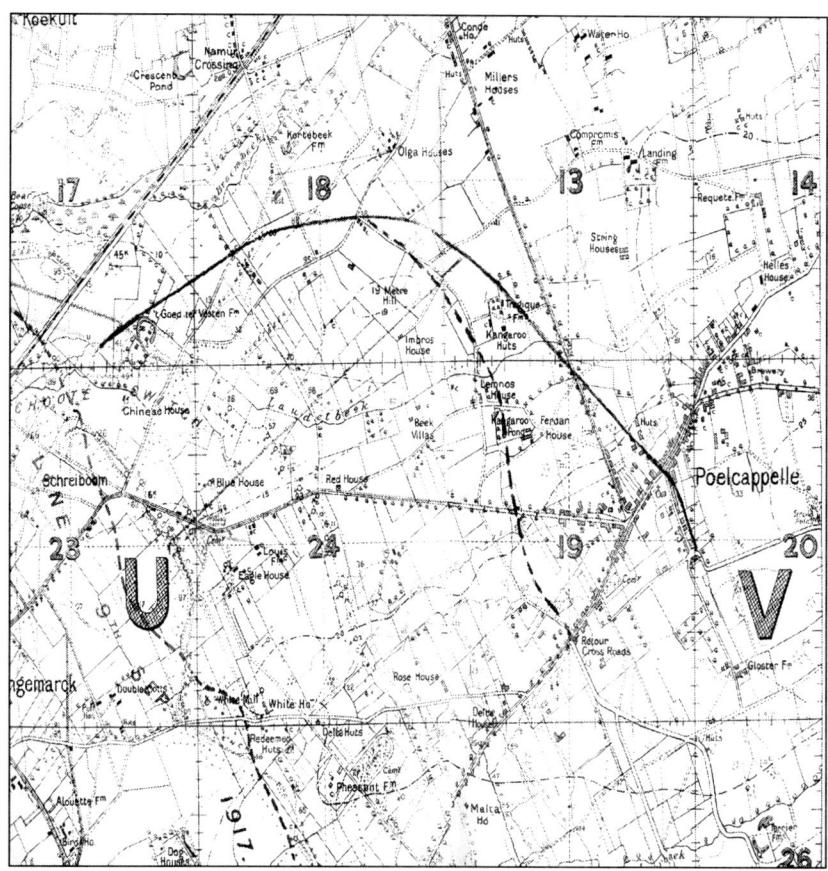

Plate 13
An extract of the original 4th Division map showing the start line and the two objectives to be captured.

Following a short period of rest, the movements back to the line began on the 8th, with the 10th Brigade moving forward and taking up positions immediately behind the 12th Brigade in the front line. The 11th Brigade also moved forward thus placing the two attacking brigades immediately behind the reserve brigade, through which they would pass at zero hour. The 11th Brigade, on the right of the line, had placed the 1st Somerset Light Infantry on the far right of the front, accompanied by the 1st Hampshire Regiment to its left. Further to the left of the Hampshire's was the 2nd Seaforth Highland Regiment (10th Brigade). The remaining battalions of each brigade were located in successive lines to the rear and were to move forward at zero hour.

All remained quiet throughout the night of the 8th and all battalions were in position by 4:00am on the 9th, almost without loss. Zero hour had been set at 6:00am. From 5:00am, the German artillery commenced general shelling of the lines and specific areas. Langemarck and Steenbeek, both communications centres to the rear and considerable lengths of the front line were subjected to periods of concentrated fire. The shellfire grew in intensity until 6:00am when the attacking brigades advanced, on that dark and showery morning, under the cover of a creeping barrage. Each of the battalions advanced with two companies leading, each company led by a platoon. The German artillery responded with only moderate fire although several early casualties were incurred due to shelling and machine-gun fire.

General progress was good and Kangaroo Trench[323] was captured with very few casualties[324] and resulted in the capture of about thirty-five prisoners and a machine-gun, about fifteen minutes after the commencement of the attack. Once past Kangaroo Trench the attack continued to proceed smoothly, although the advancing platoons of the 2nd Seaforth's encountered the Laudetbeek Marsh, which lay on both sides of parts of the Laudetbeek[325], some 200 yards past Kangaroo Trench. The boggy nature and the need to circumvent some of the worst parts caused an immediate loss of direction and some time was spent before the advancing men could be re-aligned in the direction of the attack.

The leading companies of the Seaforth Highlanders continued without serious casualties until they reached Beek Street, a German trench 150 yards further on from the Laudetbeek. Here they came under heavy machine-gun fire from the left and suffered heavy casualties. The commander of the left Company, that is, closest to the fire, and six of the eight platoon commanders were killed or wounded within minutes. That fire was slowly over come and the Seaforth's then pushed on to reach the first objective, 19 Metre Hill. It was there that their troubles started.

---

[323] *Kangaroo Trench was the name given to an almost continuous German trench, which extended across the front of the Divisions line of attack at a distance of between 350 and 475 yards distant from the starting line.*

[324] *Most of the casualties were caused by the troops advancing too close to their own creeping barrage. Experience had shown that it was the one method of attack, which offered the best chance of entering the enemy lines before they could recover from the shellfire. As the British soldier got used to that method of attack, it became the standard method of assault and the casualties were accepted as the consequence of following the barrage at such close quarters.*

[325] *'Beek', a noun of the Flemish language, is best translated in English as stream'.*

While the 10th Brigade was attacking its objectives, the 11th Brigade was having something of an easier time. During the advance, resistance gradually increased and the Hampshire's faced only light opposition while the Somerset's ran into some solid resistance from a track running south from Lemnos House[326]. The resistance came from German troops firing from large piles of stones along the track. They were soon dealt with and the remnants retired to Lemnos House proper, from where they were only cleared after the house was bombarded with rifle grenades.

As the Somerset's were clearing the building, they were subjected to considerable machine-gun fire from Ferdan House, two hundred yards to the right and ahead of the line set as the first objective. They met further determined resistance from a concrete 'pill box[327]' situated along the Poelcappelle - Langemarck Road. The pill box was kept under covering fire from a Lewis gun while troops of the Somerset's manoeuvred around either flank and captured it, taking sixteen prisoners and two machine guns. Most battalions had achieved the first objective by about 7:00am.

Having reached the Green Dotted line, the attacking troops paused for about an hour behind the standing barrage while the headquarters of Seaforth Highlanders took the opportunity to move forward to Kangaroo Trench, in order to shorten communications with the fighting troops. The artillery barrage, behind which the advancing battalions had halted, was very ragged and many shells were falling short. The Hampshire's, which had only experienced slight resistance, apart from long-range rifle fire and some shelling, had gained the first objective and was waiting for the Seaforth's and Somerset's to come into line. Due to the number of shorts falls by the artillery, they were forced to withdraw from their line and retire to a position level with the struggling Seaforth's.

The artillery fire had caused an unacceptable number of casualties amongst the Hampshire's and again later, with the other battalions. Prisoners of the 371st Infantry Regiment, 13th and 10th Bavarian Infan-

---

[326] *Lemnos House was the name given to a house located between a track leading almost due east to Poelcappelle and the Laudetbeek. The house was located approximately in the centre of the 11 Brigade advance and almost on the 1 objective for that brigade.*

[327] *The 'pill box' was a term given to German concrete fortifications, which generally held one or more machine guns. At first these presented serious problems to advancing infantry and artillery until tactics for overcoming them were developed and adopted by most of the Allied armies.*

try Regiments began passing through Adelphi,[328] on their way to the prisoners' cage, at about 7:30am. A wounded officer of the Seaforth Highlanders, returning to the rear, reported that the attack had made satisfactory progress. The nature of the attack had caused supporting units to become mixed up with the attacking battalions, but all remained in good order and maintained touch with the flanking units of the 11th and 29th Divisions.

At this point of the narrative, we will return to the 10th Brigade, which had reached a line, thought to be the position of the first objective, 19 Metre Hill, and were consolidating under heavy fire from the left. At this stage, the left of the 10th Brigade was forward of the neighbouring 87th Brigade (29th Division) and the front line of that brigade had successfully advanced to the first objective, with the exception of the right flank, where it joined with the 10th Brigade. That situation resulted in heavy fire, which not only held up the 87th Brigade, but also inflicted many casualties on the exposed flank of the 10th Brigade. Because of the interference from the flank, orders were sent to the 3/10th Middlesex Regiment to move forward to Eagle Trench[329] and employ one company to fill in the gap, facing to the left, as a flank guard.

Late in the morning, the O.C. 2nd Seaforth's, realised that both his flanks were unprotected. The left flank had, by this time drawn the entire 3/10th Middlesex Regiment into the fighting and the right flank had been counter-attacked, separating it from the left of the 11th Brigade. He also realised that his forward line was two hundred yards short of the objective. At about 10:00am the artillery observers had intercepted a message from the O.C., 'D' Company of the Seaforth Highlanders that stated; *"Am on reverse slope of 19 Metre Hill - Capt. Ward, O.C. assaulting Coy. going strong, refused help from me - troubled by machine-gun fire from left flank - from O.C. 'D' Coy."* The situation was further complicated by the fact that no one could define exactly where the individual groups of fighting troops were located. However, a report from a contact aircraft did indicate that isolated outposts had reached the first objective. This information was immediately sent to the O.C. Seaforth's and Middlesex Regiment. The Middlesex had requested urgent reinforcements for the left flank and, in response, a company of

---

[328] *Adelphi was the name given to the collection point behind the starting line, which was dedicated to the gathering of the prisoners of war, where they were handed over to the Military Police for on-forwarding.*

[329] *Eagle Trench was a newly captured trench on the extreme left of the 10 Brigade and situated slightly to the rear of the Seaforths.*

the Royal Warwickshire Regiment was ordered to proceed to Eagle Trench to act as support.

At 1:55pm, a large body of German infantry counter-attacked the left of the 10th Brigade. Heavy fighting ensued and eventually the attackers were driven off with rifle and machine-gun fire. The Seaforth's suffered heavy artillery fire and faced large numbers of the enemy and, although the attack had been repulsed, the continuous fighting forced the leading elements of the Seaforth Highlanders, on 19 Metre Hill and now without officers, to withdraw. They were, however, assisted by the Somerset's (11th Brigade), which was holding Tragique Farm and stone heaps on the opposite side of the Poelcappelle - Langemarck Road. Those troops, assisted by several captured machine guns, fired into the flank and rear of the attacking enemy, seriously hampering their movements.

During the early afternoon the East Lancashire Regiment, 11th Brigade, had been sent forward to assist the 10th Brigade on 19 Metre Hill. On arrival, Captain Tinling, of the East Lancashire Regiment, realised that the withdrawal was taking place and led his company forward, engaged the advancing enemy and brought them to a halt. Despite continued intense fighting and shelling the positions on the hill remained in the hands of the East Lancashires.

During that action, Captain Tinling had given instructions to a Sergeant Cottam that 19 Metre Hill was to be held at all costs. Soon after giving these instructions, Captain Tinling was killed[330]. In accordance with those orders, Sergeant Cottam and the remaining sixty men of the company established themselves on the forward slope of the hill, fighting off a counter-attack with rifle and Lewis gun fire. He and his small force remained in shell holes under heavy artillery fire, directed by a German observation aircraft, for a further forty eight hours. When relieved he had not been in touch with his battalion for the entire period.

While the left of the Seaforth's was forced to withdraw slightly, the withdrawal of the right flank had forced the left of the neighbouring Hampshire's to withdraw to Imbros House, immediately to the right of 19 Metre Hill. At about 2:40pm, shortly after these events, the O.C., Royal Warwickshire Regiment, was ordered to move the remainder of

---

[330] *Captain George Evelyn Tinling, M.C., 1 Battalion, East Lancashire Regiment, was killed on the 4 October 1917. His body was never recovered and he is remembered on the Tyne Cot Memorial, Belgium. Extract from the Commonwealth War Graves Commission web site.*

the battalion forward to Eagle Trench and, from that position, to retake 19 Metre Hill.

The three companies of the Royal Warwicks arrived at the assault positions at about 5:00pm and, after reorganising, advance at 5:50pm. They advance with two companies in line and the third in support. *"The two leading Companies soon came under Rifle and machine-gun fire from the left and an officers patrol was sent out on that flank which captured two Pill Boxes with 1 Officer and 7 O.R. at U.18.c.4.5. (This was on the Broombeek Street trench line[331]) A further advance of 200 yards was made and touch was made with a post of the 11th Brigade, location uncertain. As it was not dark, there were no signs of either the 2nd Seaforth Highlanders or 3/10th Middlesex Regt., and the Support Company was moved up on the left to fill the gap, which still appeared to exist. This Company eventually gained touch with the 1st Royal Dublin Fusiliers at U.18.c.4.6 at 3.15am on the 5th. The advance of this battalion at dusk was most opportune. It was well directed and well executed, and the battalion succeeded in filling a gap which might have led to serious consequences had a determined counter-attack been launched against this flank during the night.[332]"*

While the 10th Brigade was thus occupied, the 11th Brigade, having paused to re-organise on the first objective for the scheduled hour, continued with their advance. As the barrage increased in preparation, the formation gathered behind the barrage was again seriously shelled by those, which fell short and suffered a considerable number of casualties.

The right of the Somerset's was directed on Ferdan House, from which constant machine-gun fire had been inflicted upon the waiting troops. With the cooperation of a Stokes mortar of the neighbouring 33rd Brigade (11th Division), a party of the Somerset's worked around to the left while a party of the East Lancashire Regiment worked to the right and rushed the house. That small assault netted two officers and thirty men, two machine guns and two trench mortars. The capture of the house allowed the advance to continue until it reached a line that extended from the right of the 10th Brigade, through Tragique Farm to the south eastern edge of Poelcappelle.

---

[331] Comments in brackets are those of the author. Broombeek Street was a German trench line on the left of the 10· Brigade and in the area of the 11· Division. Because that Division had not reached that point, the enemy infantry in the trench system were able to bring heavy flanking fire on the 10· Brigade from the left.

[332] Extract from the War Diary (WO95/1480) of the 10· Brigade.

By late in the evening the division had reached and consolidated the second objective and continued to hold it throughout the following day, the 5th. The line of the 10th Brigade front was held *"with mixed bodies of 2nd Seaforth Highlanders and 3/10th Middlesex Regt. in support in Beek Street and Kangaroo Trench. Some of the Royal Dublin Fusiliers were subsequently found to be supporting this line on the left flank and, and there is no doubt that their Right Post mistook the ground and, although they believed themselves on their final objective, were always some 350 yards short of it, thereby uncovering the flank of this brigade. "*

"It is certain that the Seaforth Highlanders advanced over 19 Metre Hill to the 1st objective during the course of the initial advance. The advance was carried out with great gallantry in the face of heavy machine-gun fire and in spite of several casualties. The number of missing testifies to the fact that all those men who reached the first objective were killed or wounded, except the few who were in touch with the 11th Brigade and who eventually withdrew to the line shewn on Map "C".[333] "

Throughout the night of the 4th, much effort was applied to locating the various units, consolidating lines and getting reinforcements forward. The greatest difficulty was sorting out the troops of the companies and battalions, now mixed and getting them into satisfactory defensive positions. The momentum of the attack had taken individual groups in all directions, most occupying dislocated shell holes. The clearing of the dead and wounded, re-establishment of communications and the planning of the activities of the next day, occupied most of the night.

The greatest of difficulties were experienced in establishing the exact location of the brigade fronts. The War Diary of the 10th Brigade, for the 5th October, clearly demonstrated the difficulties of using contact aeroplanes for such work; *"This aeroplane information was inaccurate as was most of the aeroplane information received during the day. This information probably represents a few groups of men but is not a sound guide to locating the actual line of resistance with a view to working out barrage lines for further operations."* Again on the 6th the difficulties continued: *"Most of the day in determining the exact brigade front and those of the brigades on either side. "*

---

[333] *Quoted from the War Diary (WO95/1480) of the 10 Brigade.*

During the 5th the whole area was subjected to regular showers of rain and, with the exception of the 'normal' shelling, the fighting remained quiet on both sides. Amid the confusion of unit locations, staff officers were totally occupied with issues of the relief of the two assaulting brigades. In the early hours of the 4th, Operation Order No. 64 was issued in an effort to remedy the situation. It gave instructions to the affect that the 12th Brigade was to relieve the 10th and 11th Brigades, thus giving them the opportunity to withdraw and re-equip. It was soon realised that, due to the isolation of many of the small groups and the difficulty of communicating with them, the order would not be able to be carried out fully.

To clarify the situation and to ensure that all units were assembled, division headquarters issued Operational Order No. 65 on the morning of the 5th, which cancelled the previous order and issued new instructions. It required the 11th Brigade, on the night of the 6th, to extend to the left and assume responsibility for the area then held by the 10th Brigade. On relief, the 10th Brigade was to withdraw to the assembly area, referred to as the Malakoff area, located on the eastern Bank of the Yser Canal[334] and reorganise.

During the move, those parts of the Royal Warwickshire Regiment and Royal Dublin Fusiliers, which had extended in the area of the 29th Division, were to be relieved by units of that division, resulting in some changes to the boundary between the 4th and 29th Divisions. Once the relief of the 10th Brigade was complete, the 11th Brigade was then to be relieved by the 12th Brigade on the night of the 7th, and return to the assembly area.

Amidst the difficulties experienced in locating the front line, Operation Order No. 66 was issued on the 6th, stating that a continuation of the attack would take place on the 9th. The order informed the brigade commanders that the Germans had suffered heavy casualties in the attack of the 4th and that the XIV Corps, was to continue the attack with three divisions in the line. The order of battle required the 4th Division to attack on the right of the corps front, accompanied by the 9th Division in the centre and the Guard Division on the left, each to attack on a one-brigade front. The 4th Division was to be led by the 12th Brigade, the 10th Brigade advancing in support and the 11th Brigade in reserve. To the right, the neighbouring 11th Division was to lead with the 32nd Brigade.

---

[334] *It was here that the Division first assembled on arrival in Belgium on the 26 of the previous month.*

The attack was to commence from the Green line, the final objective of the previous attack, at 5:20am, and proceed in two bounds. The first bound was an advance of some 400 yards, to the Purple Dotted line. The second bound was to advance a further 800 yards to the Purple line[335]. The whole attack was to be assisted by a creeping artillery barrage, moving at the rate of 100 yards in four minutes, supported by a machine-gun barrage. The brigade was to pause for forty-five minutes on the first objective in order to re-organise and consolidate the position. It was intended that the 12th Brigade and the adjoining 32nd Brigade (11th Division) were to be assisted by tanks in the last stage of the attack. However, difficulties befell the tanks, preventing their participation.

Contact aeroplanes were to fly over the front line approximately every hour and twenty minutes after the initial assault with the aim of establishing the positions of the troops and the progress of the attack. The troops on the ground were to light red flares when the plane sounded its Klaxon horn or on the dropping of white flares. A second aircraft was to watch, throughout the day, for approaching bodies of German troops. To inform the commanders on the ground, the "counter-attack" aircraft was to drop smoke bombs in the area of the front line towards which the enemy was moving. The bomb was designed to burst about 100 feet below the aircraft and descend slowly, leaving a trail of brown smoke.

Concerns about the repetition of errors experienced in the attack of the 4th October were expressed when notes were issued by 12th Brigade headquarters, which stated that it was imperative to keep direction, thus preventing the confusion of units being mixed up. It also stated that, if companies should suffer casualties, they were to fight it out with rifle fire and not send back for reinforcements. Bodies of supporting troops were allocated with the specific purpose of fighting off any enemy counter-attacks, but the front line units were told that they should deal with such attacks and that *"it should be a matter of pride to do so without calling for reinforcements."*

Operation Orders required the 1st Royal Warwickshire Regiment and Household Battalion (10th Brigade) to act in conjunction with the 12th Brigade. Both were to move forwards at zero hour and occupy the line of Ferdan House - 19 Metre Hill and, on arrival, would then fall under

---

[335] *For the reader who is unfamiliar with military terminology, the colours given refer to lines drawn on the maps and issued to those officers who were to lead their men to the appropriate objective. The lines translated to map references, hence physical positions on the ground.*

command of the 12th Brigade. During the evening of the 8th, the 12th Brigade moved forward from Stray farm to the start line without the German artillery or machine guns showing any signs of alarm, apart from their normal activities. Unknown to the 4th Division, the German 6th Bavarian Division, which had taken the brunt of the attack, had been relieved during the night of the 8th, by the 227th Division.

Under very cold and clear conditions, in a field of battle covered with mud and shell holes full of water, zero hour arrived. At 5:30am, 9th October, the 12th Brigade advanced on a two-battalion front with the 2nd Essex on the right and 2nd Lancashire Fusiliers on the left. Following closely behind were the 2nd Duke of Wellington's, as support and the King's Own further behind, acting as brigade reserve. The morning was very dark but the Essex and Lancashires Fusiliers got away well, with the German barrage arriving four minutes later, behind the assaulting brigade.

By 6:30am, one hour after the commencement of the attack, the Lancashire fusiliers had reached the first objective. Five minutes later, the Essex had reached a point east of Meunier House, an advance that was verified by a contact aeroplane and reported to brigade headquarters. It was during that advance that the commanding officer of the Duke of Wellington's, Lieutenant-Colonel Horsfall[336], was killed. The 11th Division, attacking on the right of the 4th, had been held up in front of Helles House, just north of Poelcappelle, as the infantry debauched from the village.

Although the 11th Division had captured Poelcappelle, the momentum of the attack had left pockets of resistance in the village. The Brewery still contained enemy troops, which had not been cleared, and such was the fire from the building that it brought the 11th Division to a temporary halt. The interruption endangered the right flank of the Essex with enfilade fire and to prevent that fire from forcing a withdrawal of the right flank, the Household battalion was sent forward to assist.

As the leading battalions continued towards the final objective, it met heavy machine-gun fire as they neared the railway. That fire originated from a fortified house referred to as Millers House, on the left flank of the advance. Millers House was soon overcome but, in doing so, the Lancashire Fusiliers had suffered approximately one hundred and fifty casualties. While the Fusiliers were dealing with Millers House, the Es-

---

[336] *Lieutenant-Colonel Alfred Garnett Horsfall, aged 41 years, is buried in Bard Cottage Cemetery, Belgium.*

sex was facing stern opposition from Meunier House and, a little later, from the Brewery. To add to the existing difficulties, the Essex received reports of German reinforcements approaching 1000 yards on the left. Those troops eventually came into view in the early part of the afternoon and approached the Lancashire Fusiliers from the direction of Senegal F^m and Water House.

As considerable difficulties were experienced getting reports back to brigade headquarters, the situation remained obscure to the various battalion commanders. Notwithstanding the intermittent receipt of reports, it was correctly determined that the attacking battalions had passed the first objective and were progressing towards the second.

Contributing to that understanding were the reports, delivered by contact aeroplanes, which stated that flares were seen just short of the line of String Houses - Requette F^m - Helles House. A message was also received from the 2nd Essex, delivered by pigeon, at about the same time, indicating that the Essex were north east of the Poelcappelle - le 5 Chemins Road. That report also stated that although touch had been lost with two of the companies, it was felt that they were in shell holes in front of the main line of advance. Attempts by the C.O., 2nd Essex, to get forward with the companies were thwarted by the intense shelling and sniping[337].

However, by 12:30pm, it was evident that the advance had been held up and the artillery was uncertain as to where the barrage was to be placed. At 1:15pm, orders were issued by division headquarters to the Lancashire Fusiliers and Essex, limiting the advance to the line between Requette F^m and Water House, where the line was to be secured and touch established with the troops on both flanks.

Later in the afternoon, the C.O., King's Own, confirmed that that the Lancashire Fusiliers definitely did not hold Compromis or Landing Farms and confirmed that a gap of about two hundred yards existed between the right flank of the Essex and the 11th Division. He left instructions with the C.O., Essex, to close the gap and advance the line as far as possible at dusk. To assist with that move, a company of the King's Own was sent forward.

As the afternoon progressed, the fighting diminished, but the line had not been fully secured and, by 6:30pm, it was quiet enough to send the

---

[337] Casualties with the Essex were estimated at about two hundred by early afternoon.

Household battalion to Stray Farm. Both sides were exhausted and the German artillery had reduced its activity to bouts of occasional shelling. To the 4th Division, the situation was now clear and, during the evening, Operation Order No. 68 was issued, stating that the attack would be renewed on the 12th.

During the night of the 10th, the Household Battalion and the Royal Warwickshire Regiment (10th Brigade) relieved the two attacking battalions and at 4:30am on the morning of the 11th, the German artillery commenced shelling the Poelcappelle - le 5 Chemins Road heavily and continued until daylight. German snipers were also active throughout the day, as were enemy aircraft, which flew well into the night, but no attempt was made to re-take any of the lost ground. The enemy artillery maintained constant fire along the supply lines and the front line throughout the night of the 11th.

Before summarising the events of the forthcoming attack, the objectives and order of battle require some understanding. The 10th and the 11th Brigades had led the attack of the 4th October and the 12th Brigade had led the attack of the 9th, all a part of the same offensive, as was the projected attack of the 12th October. The objective, as described in Operation Order No. 68 issued on the 9th, was the Purple line, a line approximately 200 yards beyond the Green line of the first attack. The advance was to be supported by a creeping barrage, moving at a rate of 100 yards in eight minutes.

During the 11th, an amendment to Operation Order No. 68 was issued, which redefined the attack as having to take two objectives and changed the description of those objectives as the Green line and the Red line. The attacking force, whilst of brigade strength under the command of G.O.C., 12th Brigade, was to be a composite force consisting of the Household Battalion and Royal Warwickshire Regiment, (10th Brigade) and the 1st King's Own and 1st Rifle Brigade (12th Brigade). The advance was to be led by the Household Battalion on the right and the Warwickshire Regiment on the left with the King's Own following in support and the Rifle Brigade in reserve.

The final objective, the Green line, remained as first defined in the original order. The Red line, or first objective was, in fact, a line of Requette F^m - Bower House while the final objective was the line Requette F^m - Water House. That represented an advance by the left flank, swinging on the right flank at Requette F^m, of about five hundred yards. On the right of the 4th Division was now, the 18th Division and it was intended it should establish contact with the 4th Division at Requette

F^m. To the left was the 17th Division, which in turn, was to remain in touch with the 4th at Water F^m. The total advance was to take place on a 750-yard front with a right-hand swing. The arrangement for the artillery barrage remained substantially unchanged but was to begin to creep from the Green line towards the final objective one hour and forty minutes after zero hour.

Zero hour had been set at 5:25am. During the night, intervals of heavy showers feel, leaving the battlefield a sea of mud. The night was relatively quiet as the leading battalions moved up to the jump-off tape, although Langemarck had been subject some gas shelling. On time, the barrage commenced and, at 5:33am, the leading battalions left their trenches. The advance on the left proceeded smoothly and by 6:20am, the leading companies of the supporting Rifle Brigade had crossed the Poelcappelle - le 5 Chemins Road. At about the same time the leading Household Battalion was attacking Requette F^m. The fighting was intense, the leading companies of the Household Battalion were subjected to heavy machine-gun fire, and contact with the left hand battalion of the 18th Division, to the right of the Household Battalion, was lost.

Notwithstanding the aggressive nature of the fighting, the Householders, after having captured Requette F^m, were subjected to constant heavy machine-gun fire from the Brewery and Helles House. To suppress the flanking fire emanating from the village, the King's Own formed a defensive flank facing Poelcappelle. To support the King's Own, the Rifle Brigade moved forward and added to the concentration of fire. At 6:50am a message was received at 12th Brigade H.Q. *"verbal message from support coy. stated first objective taken, in touch with the Warwicks"*. While the Rifle Brigade was thus engaged on the right of the brigade, the Warwicks, which was pushing on towards the second objective in the face of moderate opposition took Senegal F^m on the left.

By 7:25am, two hours after the commencement of the attack, a company of the Household Battalion, having met little opposition, had reached a farm about 150 yards north of Requette F^m in close proximity to the second objective. During the action in front of Poelcappelle, the G.O.C., 12th Brigade sent his thanks to the Rifle Brigade for their efforts and reports and stated that Requette F^m must be held at all costs.

Slow progress was still being made on the left flank where a German strong point was captured, along with twenty prisoners. When the artillery lifted to allow the battalions to approach the final objective, the companies on the left of the Essex were able to advance in line with the Warwicks, in the face of stiff, but not insurmountable, opposition. The

Warwicks continued to progress and established positions 400 yards in front of Landing F^m. From that point, they pushed past Bower F^m, passed 100 yards ahead of Besace F^m, and continued on to Memling F^m where they established contact with the 17th Division. By 8:30am, the Warwicks had taken Besace F^m, the final objective for that battalion. Although subjected to a heavy counter-attack, all attempts to eject them from the farm were repulsed.

However, the two companies on the right of the Essex were at a complete standstill, subjected to the intense fire from the Brewery. By late morning, the casualties among the Household Battalion, caused by the same fire, were such that the remnants of the battalion were reorganised into a single company as only four officers were left. To assist with the attack, the 34th Division, in reserve, made two battalions available to the 4th Division and they were instructed to relieve the Royal Warwickshire's and the remnants of the Household Battalion, which were then to retire to Stray F^m in the reserve area.

Soon after midday, German troops were seen to be massing in the north east corner of Poelcappelle and in the area about Helles House, which eventuated in a counter attack. Outnumbered, the Warwicks were driven from Requette F^m. The Rifle Brigade was immediately ordered to provide two platoons to assist the Household Battalion retake the farm. The fighting was intense and at 7:00pm the Household Battalion sent back a message stating that the two platoons of the Rifle Brigade were not strong enough and requested the support of a fresh company. However, due to the late hour and diminishing light, orders were issued to stop all further offensive action against the farm.

The weather deteriorated as the evening progressed and during the night the two battalions of the 103rd Brigade, (34th Division) relieved the Warwickshire's and Essex, which then proceeded the L2^{338} rest area during the early hours of the morning. Due to the confusion caused by the fighting near Poelcappelle, the positions of the Household Battalion and Rifle Brigade were little known to Brigade Headquarters and relief of those two battalions before daylight was prevented by the weather.

The following day, the King's Own and Rifle Brigade were ordered to make their own way back independently in daylight and, those that remained, were relieved during the night. All units then retired from

---

[338] The L2 area was located about Poperinge, about 8 kilometres east of Ypres and had been an assembly area for the British divisions fighting in the Flanders area since the beginning of the war.

the field of battle and marched to the L2 area where they were assembled into their respective brigade formations. The 4th Division was not destined to participate in any further fighting in front of Passchendaele and on the 14th October, the 12th Brigade marched to Elverdinghe Station, entrained for Proven and marched into the P3 rest camp. There it remained until the 16th.

During the period of fighting, from the 4th to the 12th of October, the division had captured an estimated 300 prisoners but had itself, suffered casualties of one hundred and fifty seven officers and three thousand, four hundred and twelve other ranks. The G.O.C forwarded a memorandum to the brigade commanders, to be read out to all troops of the division, thanking and congratulating them for the effort that had been put in during the month of October. That was followed by congratulatory messages from the commanding officers of Third and Fifth Armies during the course the month[339].

Between the 17th and 20th of the month, the division entrained at Hopoutre and Peselhoek and travelled to Duisans, in the area of Arras, France, and fell under the command of the XVII Corps. During the move the G.O.C., Major-General Matheson, fell ill and departed for England, being temporarily replaced by Brigadier-General A.G. Pritchard, G.O.C., 10th Brigade. Corps Operation Order No.71 required the 4th Division to relieve the 12th Division in the area of Monchy le Preux, that is, south of the River Scarpe and the next few days were spent drilling and training until the 24th when the relief commenced.

In consistent rain, the 10th Brigade relieved the right of the line, that is, the 37th Brigade and the 11th Brigade relieved the left, while the 12th stood in reserve. When the two front line battalions arrived in the trenches they found them in terrible condition, several of them collapsing as a result of the heavy rain and much work was done before they were considered reasonable. The division was in the line with old friends, the 51st Division to its right and the 15th Division to the left; divisions with which it had fought in April and May of 1917.

The front was quiet and experienced only intermittent shelling. Large working parties were provided by the 2nd Essex to assist the Commander, Royal Engineers, to rebuild the communications, roads, railways and bridges, most of which had been destroyed in the fighting of the last six months. On the 28th, the 12th Brigade was loaned temporar-

---

[339] For full details of the memorandum, see Appendix VII, 'To all Ranks of the 4 Division'.

ily to the 51ˢᵗ Division to assist with its own relief, as not all of the incoming 34ᵗʰ Division had yet arrived. While the 34ᵗʰ Division relieved the 153ʳᵈ and 152ⁿᵈ Brigades, the 12ᵗʰ Brigade was then relieved by the 154ᵗʰ, immediately south of the Arras - Cambrai Road.

The division artillery took every opportunity shell the opposing enemy however, the shelling attracted determined retaliation and resulted in the loss of ten men of the 12ᵗʰ Brigade alone[340].

---

[340] *Major-General Scott and ten officers of the American 1 Division were attached, 26 October, for twelve days for familiarisation with the front line.*

November - 1917

The division remained in the front line for the entire month, one of the wettest November's for several years. The opposing German division also remained relatively quiet, broken only by periods of artillery exchange and regular inter-battalion reliefs. The 12th Brigade had been temporarily attached to the 51st Division in the latter part of November and, after being relieved by the 102nd Brigade (34th Division) it returned to the 4th Division reserve area on the 1st of the month where it remained until the 8th.

The activities during November consisted of constant patrolling, interspersed with several raids, the first of which occurred at 1:40am in the morning of the 4th, when an enemy raiding party attempted to enter the trenches on the left of the 1st Hampshire Regiment[341]. *"Advancing towards Sap 4 in two parties of 25 each. At 1.35am much shouting had been heard in the German trenches. It was believed that they had difficulty in getting the raiding party to advance. At about the same time a heavy barrage was put down on the whole brigade front and support lines. Our guns immediately opened fire on their barrage lines[342]. The raiding party did not reach the wire and were dispersed by rifle and Lewis gun fire.[343]"*

During the German barrage two officers who had been attached to the 11th Trench Mortar Battery were killed as they walked along Dale Trench towards the front line by a single 10.5cm shrapnel shell[344]. By 2:10am, all was quiet and at 4:00am, patrols were sent out in an effort to establish the identity of the enemy from the dead and wounded, but no trace at all could be found of the attackers.

---

[341] *On the 4 November, the 11 Brigade was holding the right sector (half) of the Division line, with the 10 Brigade to its left. The brigade was holding the sector with the 1 Rifle Brigade on the right and the 1 Hampshire Regiment on the left, connecting with the 10 Brigade. As a result, the raid struck the company holding the junction with the 10 Brigade.*

[342] *The artillery was allocated lines on which to fire, known as barrage lines, in the event of an attack by the enemy.*

[343] *Extract of the 11 Brigade War Diary WO95/1492*

[344] *Lieutenant N. F. Button, Somerset Light Infantry and 2nd Lieutenant F.H. Haden, Rifle Brigade.*

The daylight hours proved fatal to any one careless enough to expose any part of themselves to the enemy, as many very efficient snipers watched the lines perpetually and the German artillery would fire on the slightest movement. The difficulties of daylight movement resulted in a heavy reliance on night patrolling, a significant part of the daily trench life and, as the full moon approached movement, even at night, made those nocturnal activities quite dangerous.

The 12th Brigade relieved the 11th Brigade during the night of the 8th, a movement that attracted the attention of the German artillery and trench mortars, although few casualties were suffered and the relief was completed by daylight. Apart from the occasional patrol contact, neither side conducted any serious offensive action and the front remained quiet, only interrupted by bursts of artillery and trench mortar fire on selected parts of the front.

Between the 8th and the 13th November, the front line battalions sent several patrols every night. Their purpose was to seek information, such as the strength of the German wire, identification of the enemy, discovering and firing upon working parties, and many other activities. The artillery of both sides conducted sporadic shelling of front and support line trenches, much of it using gas shells. The opposing trench mortar batteries often engaged in counter battery fire and bombardment of the trenches. Casualties for that period amounted to nearly thirty officers and men, largely from the effects of the gas.

Within a few days of the arrival of the division, plans had been formulated for a raid to be carried out and on the night of the 16th. The Lancashires were allocated the task of raiding Long Trench, a part of the German front line located nearly 1,200 yards due east of Monchy le Preux and 400 yards north of the Monchy le Preux - Boiry - Notre Dame Road. Long Trench was approximately 220 yards in length and was joined from the rear by Poodle Trench, a communication trench that approached from the north-east.

The raiders were not to spend more than 15 minutes in the enemy trench, the objective being to obtain identification and cause as many casualties as could be achieved. Four machine guns of the 12th machine-gun Company and three of the 234th Machine Company were to give fire support to the raid. The artillery barrage was to fall on Poodle Trench to prevent reinforcements from approaching during the twenty-minute raid.

The raiding party failed to reach the enemy lines. Led by 2nd Lieutenant Walden and consisting of twenty other ranks, the party was caught in withering machine-gun and artillery fire before reaching the enemy wire. Under such intense fire and the fact that 2nd Lieutenant Walden had been killed early in the advance, the survivors of the party made their way back to the front line[345].

That same night, a patrol of the 2nd Essex Regiment, consisting of one sergeant and thirty other ranks left the front line at No. 4 sap, to the south of 2nd Lieutenant Waldens' raiding party, at 10:30pm and disappeared into the night. At 11:15pm, bombs were heard to explode in No Man's Land, followed by rifle fire. As the patrol did not return at the required time a further patrol was sent out to find them but no sign of the original patrol was ever found.

After the failure of the raid by the Lancashire Fusiliers, orders were immediately issued for a further raid, this time, by the King's Own the following night, the 17th. That raid was, again, to be made against Long Trench, at the junction with Hen Trench and only a few yards to the south of that of the Lancashire Fusiliers. The raid was to be led by Lieutenant White and consist of two officers and twenty-five other ranks. The party was broken into three groups, 'A', 'B' and 'C'. 'A' group was to act on the right of the raid and consisted of one officer and eight O.R.'s., 'B' consisted of one Sergeant and eight O.R.'s and 'C' an officer and eight O.R.'s. The whole action was to be supported with the, well-practiced formula of a creeping barrage and massed machine guns.

At 7:15pm on the evening of the 17th the party advanced under the barrage and passed through the enemy wire. *"'A' Party, under Lieutenant White on reaching the German trench, worked up it in a northerly direction for about 30 yards when they found 2 Germans in a shelter. They took them prisoner, and as the left party did not appear to be advancing towards them they withdrew. Lieut. White had one prisoner and two of his party had the other. The latter were missing until 2 am on the 18th instant, when one of the two came in wounded. He reported that a bomb had fallen among them, had killed the German prisoner and wounded the other man and himself.*

'B' Party, under a Sergt. reached a point within 10 yards of Long Trench when a hostile machine-gun opened fire. A bomb was thrown by one of the party and two Germans jumped up. These were both

---

[345] 2 Lt. Rand Edwin John Walden, 2 Battalion, Lancashire Fusiliers, is buried in the Monchy British Cemetery.

shot. The Sergt., having been delayed by machine-gun fire, considered the time allowed was up, so he brought his party back.

'C' Party " The covering party" split in half during the advance. The left portion returned to our lines when 'A' party under Lieut. White withdrew. The right portion, however, would appear to have lost its way and is still missing. Careful search has been made over the ground, both after the raid and on the night of the 18th/19th, but no trace has been found of the missing men.[346]"

The raid, while it achieved some of its objectives, resulted in Lieutenant Hart and six O.R.'s missing, and the prisoner was identified as belonging to the 179th Infantry Regiment (24th Division)[347]. The enemy, of course, did not take a raid of this nature without a measure of response. The German artillery had responded immediately to the opening British barrage of high explosive and smoke by heavily shelling the support line and the western end of Monchy le Preux.

The 10th Brigade, although at rest in the reserve area, had been involved in the planning of a substantial raid scheduled for the 20th of the month. To that end, on the 11th, a conference was held between the division and brigade commanders to arrive at objectives and methods of carrying out the raid. As a result, orders were issued to the Royal Warwickshire Regiment to prepare for the raid[348].

The trenches to be raided were located on the left of the division front, then held by the 11th Brigade, south-east of Monchy le Preux, where the opposing lines were approximately 200 yards apart. The German frontline was referred to, on British maps, as Strap Trench and the support trench as Buckle Trench. The two were joined by several communication trenches, one of which ran back well into the rear area for about 1200 yards, where it joined with another communication trench,

---

[346] Extracted from the War Diary of the 12 Brigade WO95/1503.

[347] As a result of the bravery shown in this raid several awards were later made. No. 241474 Pte A. Halton was awarded a Victoria Cross. Military Medals were awarded to No. 17005 L/Cpl F. Wady, No. 25223 Pte. R. J. Law, No. 20081 Pte. B. T. Tift and No. 27983 L/Cpl B. Taylor, all of the King' Own. The author wonders if the number of high-level awards earned in the space of fifteen minutes could possibly represent the maximum ever awarded in such a short time.

[348] In November 1917 the front line extended in a north-south direction, approximately 1200 yards to the east of Monchy le Preux.

named Beetle. Strap trench had many small saps extending forward, as was the practice of both sides.

To appreciate the conditions under which the troops were living, it should be remembered that, at the end of 1917, the whole of the Western Front had been subjected to some of the heaviest rains experienced for many years. The ground conditions were such that moving from on point to another, sometimes only a matter of a few yards, would consume considerable time and effort[349]. The condition of trenches and dugouts regularly defeated attempts at repair and drainage.

The raiding party was to consist of four officers and one hundred and fifty three other ranks, approximately equivalent to the strength of one company with supporting arms. Although the raid was to last no more than twelve minutes, the plan required that certain objectives were to be achieved. It was desired to obtain identification of the units that were opposite the division, to inflict as many casualties on the their opponents as possible and to capture and destroy material. The area to be the subject of attention was a section of Strap and Buckle Trenches and the associated saps. Located north east of the junction of Monchy le Preux - St. Robart Factory Road and the road, known as Spire Lane, running south east from Boiry Notre-Dame, it was located approximately 800 yards north of the Arras- Cambrai Road.

Preparations commenced immediately and those who were to participate in the raid commenced to dig practice trenches in a training area, to the rear. From the 13th, the Warwickshire's practiced the actions that would be involved and, on the 16th, carried out a demonstration raid for the Corps Commander. The plan for the raid introduced an element that had not been used in any previous raid carried out by the 4th Division, the use of dummies[350].

Zero hour had been set for 6:20am on the 20th. While the raiders practised their skills, the artillery and trench mortars commenced, on the 18th, to cut the wire and shell the enemy frontline. During the night of the 18th, the 10th Brigade moved forward and relieved the 11th Brigade. At 1:30am on the 20th, the raiding party left Fosse Farm, where they

---

[349] *Conditions in front of Monchy le Preux were comparable with those in front of Passchendaele, which had been captured by the Canadians only a few days before.*

[350] *The technique of using dummies for deception was used extensively in the final advance of 1918 and even more so during the Second World War. For further information on the use of the dummies, see Appendix VII, 'Instructions No.4 to 10 Brigade Operation Order No. 80.'*

had been billeted during the training and proceeded to the front line where exits from the trench had been pre-prepared. The party consisted of five smaller groups named 'V' to 'Z', each with their own designated exit and all were in position by 3:20am.

At the designated time the artillery barrage fell on the barrage line. On that part of the line in front of 'Z' party, the barrage landed on both sides of the trench and several guns continued to fire short throughout the raid, causing several casualties in the leading wave. The barrage was the signal for the Household Battalion to raise the dummies, which drew considerable artillery fire, damaging to the decoys. The remainder of the German barrage, although being delivered very quickly, fell behind the front and support lines without causing any appreciable damage. The first wave of raiders left the trenches immediately and quickly caught up to the barrage.

The wire in front of the German front line had been well cut in many places and the raiders passed through without undue difficulty. The trenches had been badly damaged by the artillery and the party faced very little opposition. Those few enemy troops that were met were quickly dispensed with and several were killed when explosive charges were thrown into dugouts and the few snipers that fired from Bat Trench were driven out, along with several bombers.

The following waves entered the trenches and destroyed dugouts and any equipment that was to be found. It appeared that the front line trenches were held lightly during the day and fully manned at night, in the event of any British attack. As there were few occupants holding the trenches, no prisoners were captured nor were any of the dead found to be wearing shoulder straps or regimental numbers.

As the raiding party retuned to the front line, a strong party of Germans, estimated at about sixty in all, attempted to follow the retiring raiders across No Man's Land but were driven back by concentrated Lewis gun fire from the Household Battalion. Following the raid, the gaps that had been cut in the wire to allow the raiding party to pass, were replaced. The officer commanding the working party, Lieutenant Nivell and an O.R. was wounded by machine-gun fire from the German lines during in the execution of that work[351].

---

[351] As the raid took place, events of a much larger nature also commenced when, at zero hour, a general attack commenced further south, on a six-mile front in front of Cambrai.

The last ten days of November were occupied with the rather mundane activities of trench repair, patrolling and changes within the brigades. On the 21st, the G.O.C., 10th Brigade, Brigadier-General Pritchard, was sent to the rear, to a rest station, with *'blood poisoned hands and thoroughly run down'*. Colonel R. Laing of the Seaforth Highlanders temporarily replaced him until Brigadier-General Green, D.S.O., arrived on the 27th to assume command of the 10th Brigade. On the 23rd, Brigadier-General De Wiart, V.C., D.S.O., and G.O.C., of the 12th Brigade was wounded during heavy shelling by artillery and trench mortars.

On the 24th of the month, the 11th Brigade relieved the 12th Brigade and found that the trenches were in terrible condition as a result of flooding. However, work continued and patrols that returned during the evening reported hearing the Germans passing verbal messages from shell hole to shell hole and listening to the messages was found helpful to the intelligence staff. Patrols, which were sent specifically to capture a prisoner for identification, regularly reported that no Germans could be found in No Man's Land[352].

On the 19th, the division headquarters had been advised that the 4th Division was to relieve the 18th Division. To assist with the relief, located to the left of the 4th Division, the 11th Brigade side slipped to the left and relieved the 44th Brigade, placing the left flank of the brigade in Scabbard Trench. Accompanying that move, the 10th Brigade also slipped to the left and relieved the right of the 11th Brigade.

The last few days witnessed the abandonment of trenches in areas that were incapable of being maintained because of the rain and snow. On the 30th, the division began a practice that was developed two years earlier, on Gallipoli, known then as the 'silent stunt'. The intention was to mystify the enemy as to the British intentions. Orders were issued to the effect that no gunfire of any nature was to be carried out for specific periods. This had the effect of provoking the enemy artillery to shell the front and support lines heavily throughout the day using mustard gas but failed to inflict casualties.

---

[352] *It was interesting to note that the War Diary of the 11th Brigade made mention of the fact that as at the 22nd of November, a limited number of residents of Arras were allowed to return to the city. Priority was given to those who were most able help rebuild the town.*

December -1917

During the month of December, the division maintained the offensive spirit and conducted several raids, designed to keep the enemy alert during one of the coldest winters in living memory. On the 1st of December, following previous instructions, a bombardment, using Stokes mortars with gas shells, was conducted against the German trenches by the No. 1 Special Company of the Royal Engineers. Four sections of mortars, each with specific targets, fired a sequence of Thermite and gas shells over a fifteen-minute period on the Bois Du Vert[353].

For thirty seconds, immediately before zero, all mortars fired five rounds of Thermite, followed at zero by thirteen rounds of chlorine gas shells per mortar, in rapid fire. For the next twelve minutes, the firing was intermittent; using a mixture of gas shells and for the last minute and a half, by rapid fire of chlorine gas was again fired. Supporting the mortar bombardment, all available artillery and machine guns opened fire on the communications trenches and roads east of the wood while harassing fire was maintained for the remainder of the night.

The bombardment resulted in the evacuation of the resident German troops but, because of the residual gas, no patrol could enter the area until about 4:00 am. When a patrol of the 2nd East Lancashire Regiment investigated, it found that the wood was deserted, although two dead, identified as belonging to the 133rd Regiment (24th Saxon Division) were found. A little later, a German soldier of the 179th Regiment, of the same division, who was carrying rations and had evidently lost his way, stumbled into the front line of the East Lancashires.

The period following the gas attack settled into one of perpetual shelling trenches and the opposing artillery. The troops were generally engaged in the daily routine of inter-battalion reliefs, trench maintenance, patrol work and sniping. In the early hours of the morning of the 3rd, following the relief of the 11th Brigade by the 10th, the left of the brigade was subjected to a heavy bombardment. Lasting for twenty minutes and, although it was believed that the shelling heralded an assault, no attempt was made by the enemy to approach the front line.

XVII Corps had passed a warning to the divisions in the line that it was possible that the Germans would make and attempt to recover those

---

[353] *The Bois Du Vert was located approximately 300 yards behind the German front line and 1400 yards north of St. Rohart Factory.*

parts of the Hindenburgh line[354] that had were lost in April. It was suggested that the date of the attack was most likely to be the 9th December and instructed all divisions to institute a defensive plan. The plan required the attack to be repelled, with no ground to be given at all. During the night of the 8th, all battalions that were acting as reserves were moved into their battle positions. All machine-gun posts were manned continuously and the reserve brigades were ready to move at a moment's notice. As the evening progressed, the artillery of all sizes stood to and all working parties rejoined parent units. The 4th Division remained in this state of readiness until the evening of the 9th but no sign of attack became apparent so all divisions stood down at 5:00pm and life returned to normal.

The weather continued to deteriorate over the next five days, resulting in a diminishing of enemy activity and a corresponding increase in effort to maintain the trenches in a defensive condition. The weather created great difficulties in the trenches, with deep mud and water in the lines and No Man's Land, which had turned into a quagmire, although it did not prevent the best attempts of both sides to maintain contact with their opponents.

On the 12th, the headquarters of the 12th Brigade issued Operation Order No. 3, requiring the 2nd Essex Regiment to carry out a raid on the German front line, Strap Trench, in front of the Bois Du Vert. The raid was to be carried out by a party of one officer and twenty men with the objectives of capturing a prisoner and doing as much damage as possible in the 15 minutes permitted. The operation was to be supported by trench mortars, machine-guns and Lewis guns which would be firing on the parapets of the German trenches within a three hundred yard radius of the target trench. Smoke was also to be used to help mask the activities of the raiding party. Meanwhile, on the 13th, a small party of Germans was observed outside the wire of a forward sap held by and outpost party of the 10th Brigade. Rifle and machine-gun fire was immediately directed on the enemy and brought the patrol to a halt.

After the raiding party had been selected, several days of practice were conducted and, at 1:00pm on the 15th, the party, under Lieutenant Miller, left the trench near Sap 4 and advance to the German trench

---

[354] *The German line of defence that had been built during 1916 to act as a barrier to any Allied attempt to dislodge the German Army. The Germans knew it by the name of the Siegfried line. It was the first set of trenches taken by the 9 Division on the 9 April 1917.*

under the cover of the barrage. As the raiders approached the German line, it was noticed that there was very little wire protecting the front and support lines and that the artillery had seriously damaged the firing line. Upon entering the trench, the raiders proceeded for a considerable distance, as far back as Buckle Trench, without finding any enemy at all, although it had been noticed that the occupants of nearby trenches retired in the direction of the Bois Du Vert as soon as the bombardment began.

The trench was poorly constructed, only about three feet deep in places and possessed no dugouts or machine-gun defences. Six minutes after the raid commenced a light barrage landed on the support line of the 10th Brigade. No prisoners were to be found, so the party withdrew according to schedule. The response from the German artillery remained quiet until about 2:00pm when the support lines where heavily shelled.

The following few days remained relatively quiet although the bad weather continued, almost unabated. Trenches had continued to deteriorate and, as the spasmodic shelling contributed to the poor conditions, many trenches became uninhabitable. It was not until the 18th that conditions began to improve and any attempt could be made at repairing the worst of trenches.

The activity of reconstruction continued until the evening of the 21st when a German raiding party conducted a raid on a post held by the Household Battalion. The raid commenced at 5:15pm with a heavy artillery and trench mortar barrage falling on the front and support lines of the 10th Brigade and extended for about 50 yards north and south of Sap 12. The artillery fire was supplemented by machine-gun fire aimed directly at the sap. Five minutes later, the machine-gun fire stopped and a party of approximately thirty Germans rushed from two sides. As the raiders approached, Lewis guns, situated just west of the sap, in a shell crater, opened fire, supplemented by the Lewis guns of the 1st East Lancashire Regiment. The concentration of the fire prevented most of the raiders from approaching the sap but four or five Germans managed to enter and seize one of the occupants.

Corporal Davis, leading the remaining garrison of the sap, attacked the raiders with the bayonet and put them to flight. One German was killed and remained where he fell, but the others escaped through a gap in the side of the sap that had been caused by a shell. On their return, the raiders were struck by minenwerfers, fired inadvertently at them, and scattered them, although none were seen to fall. The German barrage slowly died down until at about 5:45pm all was quiet. The dead German was identified as being a part of the 6th Company, 179th Infantry Regiment (24th Infantry Division). One Officer, 2nd Lieutenant Bird[355] of the Household Battalion was killed and two N.C.O.'s and four men wounded during the raid.

Two days later it was the turn of the 1st Warwickshire Regiment to be subject of the German intentions. At 6:18pm on the 23rd, 'Y' Sap, manned by a party of Warwicks, was subjected to a slow fire from heavy trench mortars. The fire grew in intensity, supplemented by light trench mortars and howitzers. Scabbard Alley and Support Trench took the brunt of the shelling whilst Bayonet Wexford and Musket Trenches were contained by 5.9" howitzer fire. Again, the front line was subjected to heavy machine-gun fire as was both sides of 'Y' Sap. Five minutes later two parties of the enemy, each estimated at about twenty strong, approached the sap from the northeast and the east. The northern party was seen first and driven off by heavy rifle and machine-gun fire but, whilst that party was thus engaged, the second party managed to enter the head of the sap, overpowered the occupants and disappeared.

The Lewis gun team nearest the post, being totally occupied with the first group did not realise what had happened and it was not until an N.C.O. moved up the trench that it was realised that it was empty and immediately brought additional troops up to occupy it. A further casualty, a member of a listening party that had been sent out about midway between 'Y' and 'X' Saps, was suffered when they were caught in the barrage, resulting in one man being reported missing. The casualty rate was heavy with four killed, two suffering from shell shock, seventeen suffering from wounds or gassing and nine missing, a total of thirty-two. With the front line blown in, in many places, the damage was considerable.

An officer's patrol entered No Man's Land at 7:15pm in search of dead or wounded but could not proceed far as many of the patrol were affected by residual gas. A further patrol followed at 4:00am in the morning of the next day but found nothing and many of the second patrol were also affected by gas in the shell holes. The rest of month remained relatively quiet, accompanied by the usual spasmodic shelling and mortar fire. So the year closed on a note of great achievement, but great loss.

---

[355] *2. Lt. J.W. Bird, Household Battalion, is buried in the Faubourg d'Amiens Cemetery, at Arras and it is possible that his body may not have been recovered immediately and he was buried after the Armistice.*

1918 – Victory from Defeat

January - 1918

January remained cold and unpredictable, the weather controlling much of the daily activities. The battlefield remained a frozen glacis of mud and ice-covered craters, constantly churned over by the regular shellfire in forward and rear areas. Despite the conditions, the division artillery maintained a constant fire upon points of importance behind the German lines, turning the landscape into a quagmire. Under those difficult conditions, the German frontline troops made considerable effort to fraternise with their British opponents by calling out and encouraging the men to engage in conversation, but the efforts were generally met with total silence or a bombardment by trench mortar or machine-gun fire.

By the 4th of January, the weather had further deteriorated and, by nightfall, had turned into five days of torrential rain. The constant rain thawed the ground and turned it into a bog that made movement an absolute trial of strength and patience. Both sides suffered a similar fate, marked by a noticeable decrease of infantry activity and the artillery slowly sank into the mud. The troops spent most of their time attempting to drain the trenches and prevent the walls from collapsing; shades of the 1914 winter in Ploegsteert Wood.

The support of large numbers of troops in the front line called for vast effort and, as rations were only reaching the front line in limited quantities, a reduction in numbers was the only solution. Many trenches were deemed uninhabitable and, as any serious attack by either side was out of the question, the numbers of troops in the front and support lines were to be reduced to that necessary for maintenance. An immediate consequence of the reduced numbers living in the rather squalid conditions was seen in a proportionate reduction in trench foot and related diseases.

Although the ground conditions made the simplest of movement difficult, the opportunity to harass the enemy was always taken whenever possible. The machine guns and mortars of the frontline brigades were played upon their opponents who were regularly forced to expose themselves, due to the conditions in the trenches. The artillery took every opportunity to fire upon the opposing lines, as the opportunities arose.

Most trenches were partially full of half-frozen mud and water in which the troops had to stand, for their own protection against the enemy fire.

Incidents continued to occur which demonstrated the determination with which both sides fought. On the 13th, a small party of enemy troops was observed outside the wire, in front of a forward sap of the 10th Brigade but the outpost party occupying the sap, prevented entry with the support of machine-gun and mortar fire. That same night, it was only with the greatest of difficulty that the 11th Brigade managed to relieve the 12th Brigade before daybreak. Working parties were immediately appointed to the task of cleaning up the support line in the second defensive system but rain defeated all attempts and, as tracks and roads were impassable, many miles of Duexboard[356] were laid to facilitate troop movement over the muddy terrain and within the trenches.

With all of the difficulties of trench drainage and rebuilding, reliefs and shellfire, every opportunity to strike at the enemy was taken. In the middle of the month, heavy mists had prevented observation by the artillery and infantry alike. Although difficulties were experienced with direct observation, it became evident that there was considerable movement in the German line, much of it in the open. Ground conditions prevented patrol work in No Man's Land and much reliance was placed on the artillery to take advantage of such targets.

By the 18th, the weather showed signs of clearing and extensive efforts were made to restore order to the trenches. The improvement in the weather also brought renewed activity by the artillery and aircraft of both sides and allowed for limited patrolling of No Man's Land. The 12th Brigade had relieved the 10th Brigade on the night of the 18th and, although the brigade had moved into Arras for rest, large working parties had to be found to assist with the reconstruction work.

Aerial combat was a common occurrence above the front line, and on the 24th, three British aircraft were seen to fall, north of the Scarpe. Several days' later two stretcher-bearers of the 12th Brigade gave chase to a German soldier, seen in No Man's Land, while they were walking along a trench. They seized the nearest rifles and bayonets and chased the hapless German almost up to the enemy wire where he was finally caught and returned has prisoner. It eventuated that he belonged to the

---

[356] *More commonly known to the Allied soldier as Duckboards, these were constructed of timber slats nailed to supporting timbers, not unlike the modern pallet, and laid in rows over difficult or soft ground to aid the passage of troops.*

179th Infantry regiment of the 24th Division, regular opponents of the 4th Division.

In January, a re-organisation of the structure of the army took effect. Up to late 1917, the British army and that of most of the Dominion forces were structured on the traditional British model of four battalions to the brigade and three brigades to the division. Largely for political reasons caused by the casualty rate, many battalions were unable to obtain sufficient reinforcements to maintain wartime strength. Among the several changes that were instituted, was a reduction in the number of battalions per brigade to three, the remainder being re-assigned, to reinforce where necessary.

Much regret was experienced by the troops who had to leave for another brigade or division, after having fought together for so long. Many were simply disbanded and troops distributed amongst other battalions. The camaraderie formed by months and years of fighting and living under such conditions was a strong emotional influence among the troops and many a case was pleaded to hold units together.

The realities of the situation prevailed and the 4th Division was no exception. On the 27th January, instructions were received to the effect that the Household Battalion and the 3/10th Middlesex Regiment were to be disbanded and distributed between the other battalions whilst the 2nd Duke of Wellington's was to be transferred from the 12th to the 10th Brigade. The most regrettable event to complete the change was the transfer of the 1st Lancashire Regiment from the 4th Division to the 34th Division[357].

The re-organisation was not restricted to the infantry alone. The three machine-gun companies, which had been an integral part of the brigade structure since inception, were amalgamated as a single machine-gun battalion under the command of Lieutenant-Colonel Somerville. Whilst the loss of the personal identity of those units affected by this change was a point of regret, the re-organisation of the division was smooth and most remained within the ranks of the parent division. The

---

[357] *The East Lancs., as they were affectionately known, was one of the constituent units of the 11· Brigade for many years before the outbreak of war. The battalion had gone to France with the Division on the 23· August 1914 and fought through every battle in which the Division was involved. It had lost many casualties in the name of the 4· Division and the transfer of the battalion was felt through all ranks. The battalion did, however, continue its illustrious career with the 34· Division, and lived up its hard won reputation, earned with the 4·.*

changes were to come into effect when the division was relieved from the line in February.

Meanwhile, the daily activities of the division continued with increased shelling and mortar exchanges, while the struggle continued with the reconstruction of trenches in ground that remained waterlogged. At the close of the month, the 10th and 12th Brigades were holding the left and right of the line respectively and suffered some inconvenience from night-flying German aircraft, which bombed trenches and engaged British planes overhead. The 11th Brigade remained in Arras in reserve and received orders on the 30th which stated that the division would be relieved from the line by the 15th Division between the 5th and 9th of February.

February - 1918

The structural changes started to take effect from the first day of February. While the 10th and 12th Brigades were engaged in the front line activities, the 11th Brigade was saying farewell to the 1st East Lancashire Regiment. The battalion was inspected and addressed by its Commanding Officer, Brigadier-General T. H. Wade and was read a farewell message from the G.O.C. 4th Division, Major-General Matheson, who expressed his appreciation for the services of the battalion and his regret at its departure. On completion of the formalities, the battalion marched for the 34th Division, escorted for a part of the way, by the massed bands of the division.

In accordance with the policy of the Commander-in-Chief, that all troops who were out of the line should participate in various schools and training courses, the 11th Brigade partook of a constant schedule of training in musketry, route marching, use of the Lewis gun, grenade throwing, signals and many others. The brigade also supplied large working parties to assist with the reconstruction of the trenches and communication lines. During that period of activity, several awards were also made. Sergeant Coke of the 1st Rifle Brigade received a bar to his Military Medal and Corporal Saunders of the same battalion was awarded the Military Medal.

Action at the front was continuous and on the 2nd, the 2nd Duke of Wellington's conducted a raid against a complex of German trenches in broad daylight. Directly in front of the line held by the Dukes lay the German front line trenches, referred to as Strap and the support line, Buckle, previously raided by the Warwickshire's, on the 20th November 1917, six weeks before.

The raid, carried out at 8:30am, was directed on Strap and Buckle Trenches between the two communication trenches, Bat and Badger. The raiding party consisted of two officers, 2nd Lieutenant N. G. Coldwell[358], who acted as raid commander, 2nd Lieutenant R. A. McDowall, sixty other ranks and four stretcher-bearers. A barrage was laid down by artillery, trench mortars and machines guns, and was described as "*perfect*" by the raid commander.

---

[358] *26 years old Lieut. N.G. Coldwell, survived the raid but died on the 16 May 1918 while the battalion was serving with the 10 Brigade, fighting on the La Bassee canal. It would appear that he died of wounds in one of the many hospitals that were located in Etaples during the First World War. He is buried in the Etaples Military Cemetery.*

Behind the barrage, the raiding party entered Strap Trench where they killed four of the enemy and captured a further five, uninjured. The party then moved up Bat and Badger and entered Buckle where it was observed that the remainder of the garrison was retiring along the length of Badger. The remaining enemy made an attempt at retaliation, but before they arrived in Buckle and Strap Trenches, the raiding party had returned to the British line. It was estimated that the enemy suffered approximately thirty casualties killed, missing and wounded. The raiding party also suffered, with two missing, one believed killed and one believed to be wounded and lying in a shell hole. A further eleven returned wounded.

Well after the raid was completed, two Sergeants left the front line trench, in full view of the enemy and brought in the wounded man. The prisoners were identified with the 130th Infantry Regiment (24th Division) and, when examined, gave a considerable amount of information about the strengths and dispositions of the division.

There was little reaction from the enemy until, at about 10:30pm, when the front and support lines suffered heavy shelling of trench mortars, various calibre artillery and gas shells for about thirty minutes in the area from which the raid had been launched. It was not clear whether the enemy had attacked, but a lone German was seen near the wire and shot. He was brought in later, severely wounded but, before dying from the his injuries, he stated that he had been born in Württemberg and was a part of the 314th Pioneer Company. Later in the evening, five separate patrols went out between 11:30pm and 4:10am in an effort to establish what activity was being undertaken but no enemy were met, nor could any trace of the missing man be found.

The next two days passed without incident and the relief of the division commenced on the 5th, with the 11th Brigade being relieved by the 44th and 45th Brigades (15th Division). Once the relief had been completed, the brigade then marched to the Wallus training ground. That same evening, the 12th Brigade was relieved by the 44th, while the 10th Brigade was relieved the following night, the 6th, by the 45th Brigade.

In accordance with the departure of the 3/10th Middlesex Regiment on the 8th, the battalion was inspected by the G.O.C. and, following the customary farewell speech, the battalion then marched to the Corps Depot and disbanded. The Middlesex Regiment was followed two days later by the Household Battalion, which was broken up on the 10th and left the division, some going to the Foot Guards and the balance being absorbed into the ranks of the Household Cavalry. With the process of reorganisation completed, the division commenced a period of training and re-equipping.

On the 18th, the division received a warning that it was to relieve the Guards Division in the centre section of the headquarters front. While the Staff officers of the 10th Brigade carried out a reconnaissance of the new line, the remainder of the division continued with constant training, interrupted only for a presentation of a Guard of Honour for the Commander-in-Chief, General Haig, who visited Arras on the 22nd. The Guard was made up of one company of each battalion of the 10th Brigade and was assembled for inspection at the 4th Division headquarters.

While the division was out of the line, the battalions were kept fully occupied. They carried out a schedule of re-equipment and cleaning and, in order to maintain fitness, undertook route marching and bayonet practice. Tuition in Lewis gunnery, machine-gun drills and musketry practice was conducted to improve skills and learn new techniques that were constantly being developed. Training was interspersed with periods of leave, locally and to the United Kingdom and several competitions were arranged to establish the best rifle team in the division.

Division headquarters staff and those of the three brigades engaged in an exercise, under the instruction by the headquarters staff of XVII Corps. It was directed at establishing a common practice of headquarters conduct in action and in reserve. Conferences were held for the officers to discuss the effects of the re-organisation and re-equipping of the division, while each brigade, accompanied by the supporting arms, undertook exercises on the training grounds and supplied large bodies of men for working parties.

March - 1918

It had been acknowledged by the British High Command that, as a direct result of the collapse of the Russian army in the socialist revolution of October 1917, German divisions would be transferred from the East to the Western Front, in an effort to force a decision on the Allies. British intelligence became aware of that movement in January of 1918 as new divisions began to appear on the Western and Italian Fronts. The westward movement gained momentum and resulted in a steady build up which eventually tipped the scales of numerical superiority in favour of the Central powers. The difficulty for the British High Command lay not in the fact that they were aware of the forthcoming offensive, but in not knowing where the blow was to fall. However, all army commanders were warned for a major attack.

Events were to show that it was to fall initially upon the junction of the French and British armies and, in the British sector, largely upon Lieutenant-General Gough's 5th Army. What is now known of the German preparations shows that a large number of the divisions that had been withdrawn from Russia had been training for the occasion, several hundred kilometres behind the Western Font. The attacking divisions were constituted largely of hand picked troops, trained in the art of rapid infiltration, a method not used extensively on the Western Front.

The British defensive system, on the Arras front, was based on the extensive German works that had previously been the Hindenburgh line and the secondary lines beyond. Since the capture of those lines twelve months before, much effort had turned the captured area into a defensive line facing the last remaining German defence works, referred to as the Drocourt-Quéant Switch. Considerable effort had been made to convert the system to British defensive needs, although the positions south of the Scarpe had only been newly dug. By mid-March much of preparations for the anticipated attack had been completed.

The defences on the Arras front consisted of three trench systems, one behind the other, each separated with a gap determined by geographic and tactical needs, generally 500 – 1000 yards apart and each had been wired to offer defence from the east. The lines were known as the first, second and third systems, which were reinforced with a fourth and final line in front of Arras, the original British front line, referred to as the Army line. What was not foreseen was the scale of the attack and the methods to be employed.

The first two days of March were very cold, with occasional snowfalls and, with the division in headquarters reserve, every effort was made to improve the fighting capacity of the troops through constant training. Schools were conducted for instruction in new fighting methods and to reinforce some of the past practices. Many of the new tactics included actions to be taken against enemy tanks and an emphasis was placed on marksmanship. To ensure maximum readiness for the expected attack, several warning orders were issued as practice to bring the division to a state of readiness. Information gathered from prisoners and other sources indicated that the offensive would be launched on the 13th March.

As the date approached all Allied forces were ordered to a state of readiness and the brigades of the 4th Division were instructed to be ready to move any time from 5:00am on the 13th and be prepared to go to any one of several possible locations in the area. No attack eventuated and the divisions were stood down on the 14th. After a few days, the 4th Division was instructed to relieve the Guards Division in the front line, during the night of the 20th in much the same position as the line reached by the 4th Division in May of the previous year.

In preparation for the relief, the whole division departed the training area on the 19th January and marched into billets in and around Arras. During the night of the 20th, the 10th Brigade relieved the 3rd Guards Brigade in the Roeux sector, that is, astride the River Scarpe with its right in touch with the 46th Brigade of the 15th Division. The 2nd Duke of Wellington's assumed its position in the front line on the northern bank, while the Royal Warwickshire Regiment took over positions on the south bank, in touch with the Dukes. The 11th Brigade continued the line to the left and relieved the 1st Guards Brigade in the centre of the line with the King's Own and the 12th Brigade relieved the 2nd Guards Brigade with the 2nd Essex Regiment.

The night and early morning of the 21st was covered in a heavy mist, which made observation difficult for the infantry and almost impossible for the artillery. Barely had the Guards Division cleared the lines when, at 5:00am, the German artillery commenced an intense barrage on the front and support lines and rear areas[359], concentrating largely on the

---

[359] *Artillery technology had advanced at a similar pace on both sides during the war. The German artillery used, for the first time on a large scale, a technique that was to be used so effectively by the British army in August of 1918. The technique, referred to by the British artillery as silent registration, allowed guns to range on selected targets without the need to fire ranging shots. The effects were considerable whenever used on a grand scale.*

battery positions and the Scarpe Valley. Large quantities of gas and high explosive shell were fired for three hours, only to slowly diminish at about 8:00am. At the commencement of the bombardment, the Guards Division was just reaching Arras and was caught in some of the long range shelling.

The artillery bombardment was not followed by the expected infantry attack[360], although consistent shelling of selected targets continued until 10:30am after which it ceased altogether. After the initial bombardment, the day remained relatively quiet, although the troops remained alert in the expectation of an assault. As the day progressed reports arrived which clarified the situation in other sectors of the front, especially that of the 5th Army which had taken the brunt of the offensive.

The front line and supply lines were shelled constantly over the next two days and, in an effort to reduce casualties, division headquarters issued orders that the first defensive line should be evacuated during the day and held only by isolated posts and Lewis gun positions, but re-occupied at night. Any attempt by the enemy to enter the vacant line was to be dealt with immediately by the artillery. Despite best efforts, the Germans soon realised that the front line was empty and sent patrols, many of which managed to enter the vacated trench line. The first attempts were met and ejected almost immediately, although the incursions continued frequently, particularly in the areas held by the King's' Own and the Somerset Light Infantry. Signs of enemy activity increased and reports on the 23rd indicated a build-up in numbers of enemy troops in front of the 11th Brigade.

The general attack had spread to the north and the enemy took advantage of any opportunity to advance their line, resulting in considerable forward movement on the southern bank of the river. The 15th Division, fighting on the right of the 10th Brigade, had been driven back, resulting in the right flank of the 4th Division being exposed to attack. By mid-afternoon, it was clear that Monchy le Preux and the first and second defensive lines had been occupied by the Germans as far as Welford and Bayonet Trench, very close to the southern bank of the River Scarpe.

In order to assist, the 10th Brigade side-slipped to the right and took over the unfinished trenches of the 46th Brigade, allowing it to with-

---

[360] *The main assault was delivered further to the south, where the artillery barrage was accompanied by the rapid infiltration of the front line at several points. It was not until the mist lifted that the extent of the attack was truly determined.*

draw and regain contact with the main body of the 15th Division. The newly acquired trenches faced to the south-east and the 10th Brigade found it necessary to extend a defensive right flank on their right to cover the gap between the two divisions. Enemy activity soon extended across the Scarpe and by 7:00pm, enemy troops were seen working in front of the wire. They were fired on by the trench mortars of the 11th Brigade, but no attack eventuated and by 10:00pm all had fallen quiet, the night was spent quietly in a heavy mist although the sounds of constant work could be heard in the German trenches.

The period between the 24th and the 26th remained one of consolidation by both sides although opposing patrols clashed constantly at night. Several prisoners, captured on the 24th by one of the patrols, stated that the Germans were preparing to attack near the Cambrai Road. A second statement from prisoners captured on the 25th indicated that an attack was to be made north of the Scarpe. In order to interrupt any intended attack, arrangements were made with the artillery to shell the German front line at 5:00am the following morning. Although the artillery fire was prompt and accurate, no offensive effort on behalf of the enemy was noted. At 2:50am on the morning of the 26th, a heavy bombardment by 4.2" and 5" howitzers fell on the trench at the junction of the 11th and 12th Brigades for a period of ten minutes. When the shelling ceased, a raiding party of about fifteen enemy infantry was forced back by Lewis gun and rifle fire from the Hampshire's and King's Own.

Several reports had been received of German troops, dressed in British khaki, having attempted to approach the front line but were fired upon. At 7:30pm in the evening of the 26th, a soldier of the 11th Brigade, in Ceylon Trench, was fired on by a man dressed in a British uniform and, immediately after, bombs were thrown. Several enemy troops were also engaged by supporting infantry, resulting in one of the attackers being wounded. Later the same day, Germans, dressed as British Officers, were seen offering money for information.

Information given by prisoners indicated a pending attack with the objective of recapturing Vimy Ridge[361]. In order to shorten the line held by the 10th Brigade, the 11th Brigade extended two hundred yards to the right and relieved the Seaforth Highlanders. All units were warned of possible action and, at 3:00am on the 28th, the German artillery commenced a bombardment of the headquarters positions, using guns of all

---

[361] *Vimy Ridge had remained in German hands since the early stages of the war. The Canadian attack of the 9 April 1917 captured the ridge and much of the ground as far forward as Lens. The ridge was desired by both sides for the view it offered over the lines of the opposing forces.*

calibres and the liberal use of high explosive and gas. Initially the shelling was largely restricted to the third defensive line, north of the Scarpe and the valley in which the River Scarpe flows.

The shelling fell upon the rear and support positions until about 3:30am when it suddenly increased and concentrated on the front line. By 4:30am, the shelling on the first and second lines was intense and, shortly after, was extended south of the river, where the line of 15th Division was also targeted. During the bombardment, German infantry, in front of the 12th Brigade, were seen cutting their own wire. Clearly an attack was forthcoming and two companies of the King's Own were hurried forward to Mississippi and Missouri trenches to support the Essex Regiment in the front line.

The bombardment continued until 7:20am as the artillery shelled the defences and cut the wire for the infantry. At that hour the enemy left their trenches and attacked westward, on both sides of the river. The attacking troops quickly broke through the front line to the right of the 12th Brigade, which resulted in the Essex slowly being pushed back. Pressure on the left flank slowly forced the line to give way but the centre and the right, that is the 11th Brigade and 10th Brigade, managed to hold, albeit under the increasing weight of the attack. The line held by the 11th Brigade, Cadiz, Camel, Coot Trenches and Stoke Avenue, as far as the Fampoux Lock, remained intact while the 10th Brigade continued to hold up the attack with determined defence of every shell hole and trench.

By 9:30am, the impetus of the attack had faltered but, massed formations of reinforcements could be seen advancing down the western face of Greenland Hill, behind the German lines, while others concentrated in the valley below. The Lancashire Fusiliers fought for every foot of ground in the face of enemy troops bombing down Naval Trench towards the Gavrelle Road. Steadily the 11th Brigade was pushed back on the Hyderabad Redoubt[362] and, although it had lost touch with the 12th Brigade on the left, was still in contact with the 10th Brigade, on its right. German infantry were also seen to enter Humid and Harry Trenches, on the left of the 12th Brigade, further weakening an already failing left flank.

---

[362] *The Hyderabad Redoubt was a strong point in the German 2 line of defence during the British offensive twelve months before. The redoubt was originally captured by the 10 Brigade and thereafter remained within the 2 line of defence of the British lines.*

In an effort to delay the advance, the officer commanding the machine-guns of 'D' Company, Machine Gun Battalion, which was located in Missouri Trench, was given instructions to hold on at all costs, to prevent further penetration on that flank. Although subjected to artillery and machine-gun fire those guns fired almost continuously, but by 10:30am, four of the guns had been knocked out. Because of the reduced fire from the machine-guns, the King's Own were ordered to take over the defence of Mississippi and Missouri Trenches.

Shortly after the attack commenced, a Provisional Battalion was formed, which consisted of three field companies of engineers, the Pioneer Battalion and men from the transport lines, all of whom reported to the C.O., Royal Engineers. At 10:00am, the three field companies were sent to the Army line, which extended from the river, northwards to Point Du Jour[363]. The Pioneers and transport troops were sent to the south bank where they extended the Army line to the south and established contact with the 15th Division.

By mid-morning, the Duke of Wellington's (10th Brigade) were continuing to hold the line about Roeux. With the right flank secure and the 11th Brigade fighting for every foot of ground, the attack on the right was brought to a standstill. However, the enemy continued to make slow progress on the left against the 12th Brigade. The sheer number of enemy reinforcements prevailed, slowly forcing the 11th Brigade back, in sympathy with the 12th Brigade. The same pressure caused the Seaforth Highlanders (10th Brigade), opposite Roeux, to withdraw. German infantry managed to penetrate the junction of the 11th and 12th Brigades, about Cadiz Trench and forced the 11th Brigade to throw back a defensive flank to Havanna Trench, thus producing a gap between the two brigades, through which the enemy filtered. Such was the intensity of the fighting on the 12th Brigade front that, by 1:00am, all trench mortars were out of action.

In an attempt to close the gap between the two brigades, a company of the 1st Rifle Brigade was sent along Zion Trench to Havanna Trench and, as the company moved forward, infantry of the Hampshire's (11th Brigade) bombed their way up Havanna Trench. Elements of the 12th Brigade simultaneously bombed their way in the opposite direction, down the trench, in an effort to force the enemy to withdraw. By

---

[363] *The Army Line was the original German trench line that ran from Athies, on the northern bank of the River Scarpe, to Point0Du-Jour, on the St. Laurent – Gavrelle road. It was the original 'Blur Line' which was captured by the 9 Division on April 9 1917 and where the 4 Division continued the advance thereafter. It continued south across the river, the original 'Artillerie Shutzstelling' line.*

1:30pm, the company of the Rifle Brigade had reached Jutland Trench and the commanding officer, appreciating the situation, ordered the company to attack and successfully drove the enemy out.

South of the Scarpe, the main weight of the German attack had fallen on the 15th Division and had carried through, almost to the Cambrai Road and forced the division back. As the 15th Division withdrew, the right flank of the Royal Warwickshire Regiment, 10th Brigade, holding Lancer Trench, in the second line, was exposed to enemy penetration. The efforts of the Warwickshire's, isolated on the southern bank of the river to maintain a line with the Duke of Wellington's on the northern bank, are worthy of mention.

Attempts to penetrate the weakened right flank were not long in coming and, although the Warwickshire's extended a defensive flank, it could not cover the distance between their own right and the left of the 15th Division, now back on the Army line, 2600 yards to the rear. After having fought off two most determined attacks, they were slowly forced to retire. The Warwickshire's fought hard but fell back on the Third System of trenches, that is, towards Italian Trench, between Lancer and Invergordon, where they made yet another stand against a very determined enemy.

At midday, the situation of the 4th Division was one of forced retirement with German infantry penetrating around both flanks of the 12th Brigade, circumventing the right flank of the 10th Brigade and the 11th Brigade withdrawing in sympathy with both. Only elements of the Lancashire Fusiliers, twenty men of the Tunnelling Company and some troops of the King's Own were holding the support line of Trent – Hyderabad – Mississippi – Missouri – Logic and Stoke Avenue. In an effort to alleviate the situation the three field companies of the provisional battalion were sent to Missouri Trench to reinforce those who were still holding out.

Later in the afternoon, the Warwickshire's organised a successful counter-attack on Invergordon Trench, but were finally defeated by the division artillery, which shelled the trench and those Warwicks in it. As the Warwicks retired, the Duke of Wellington's, fighting on the northern bank of the river, found it necessary to withdraw in order to maintain touch. That was achieved without any interference from the enemy and the Dukes formed a defensive flank along the Arras – Douai railway, facing south-east across the Scarpe. Shortly after midday the Provisional Battalion was ordered to send four of its six companies along the Athies

- Fampoux Road as far as Cam Valley and drive back any of the enemy who had pushed forward along the line of the river.

The enemy attacks weakened throughout the early afternoon and by 2:15pm had been definitely halted and, while minor conflicts occurred, no further attempt was made to break through the British line. The division to the left had established on the 2nd defensive line, namely, the Bailleul – Willerval line, while the two brigades of the 4th Division, that is the 12th and 11th Brigades respectively, continued that line through Trent, Hyderabad, Havana, Camel and Coot Trenches to the Railway line. From that point the 10th Brigade had formed a defensive flank to the south-east.

As the capture of the Arras – Cambrai Road represented the main enemy objective in the Arras sector, the 15th Division remained the focus of the German attention. In an effort to relieve some of the pressure on the 15th Division, the 10th Brigade was ordered to counter-attack in a south-easterly direction, against the Germans right flank, south of the River Scarpe. As the attack slowly developed, individual outbreaks of determined bombing occurred on those fronts held by the 11th and 12th Brigades. In the locality of Cadiz Trench, at about 4:00pm, such activity was carried out with equal ferocity on both sides, but was finally repulsed by the men of the Hampshire Regiment and, as the enemy withdrew over the open, they attracted concentrated fire from a Lewis gun in Havanna Trench. It was later reported that that particular gun had inflicted fifty killed or wounded upon the retiring enemy.

Shortly after, the C.O., Hampshire's, sent a request for additional troops to hold the left of the 11th Brigade and, in response, a company of the Seaforth's (10th Brigade) was sent forward to cover the defensive flanks along the railway. By late afternoon the spasmodic fighting on the fronts of the 11th and 12th Brigade had also quietened down. At about 7:30pm the 11th Brigade was instructed to adjust the line by withdrawing to the line Fampoux – Lock – Stoke Avenue to comply with the lines held by the brigades on either side, the adjustment being completed by 1:50am of the following morning.

South of the Scarpe, the 10th Brigade was still heavily engaged. To stabilise the line on the right, a combined force consisting of the Duke of Yorks, two companies of the 21st West Yorkshire Regiment and the 7/8th King's Own Scottish Borderers of the 46th Brigade (15th Division), launched a counter-attack, at 6:30pm, on the enemy positions about the river. The attack was met by machine-gun fire, but a line was successfully established on the high ground[364] overlooking Battery Valley. That combined attack represented the last serious engagement and the fighting on the right settled down to exchanges of spasmodic machine-gun and artillery fire.

Throughout the night, much effort was spent reorganising the scattered units and returning them to their own brigades. The work continued into the next day, the 29th, amidst cold and rainy weather. Substantial movements behind the German lines were detected by the troops in the front line and called on the artillery to shell the areas concerned. The right of the 10th Brigade was strengthened when the Warwickshire's established a line of pits in front of the Duke of Wellington's, while the trenches were consolidated for defence.

The final two days passed without any serious fighting, although the artillery of both sides was constantly engaged in fire and counter-fire. The British batteries focused attention on counter battery work, while the German artillery concentrated much of its efforts on the 3rd line of defences. The division had suffered heavily during the action of the 28th, with the loss of 60 officers and approximately 1800 men to all causes. It also had lost fifteen machine guns, thirty-nine Lewis guns, eleven Stokes Mortars, two anti-tank guns and four 6" mortars.

---

[364] *Orange 102 Hill*

April - 1918

Notwithstanding the events of the 28th, the full impact of the German offensive of the 21st March had not been fully felt by the 4th Division. To the south, the main blow of the offensive had struck the British 5th Army, under General Gough and had forced the III, XVIII, XIX and VII Corps to retire, ultimately, to the west through Albert, only stopping in front of Amiens. The danger to the junction of the French and British armies was critical and the conflict continued, through various phases, until mid July. The 4th Division, still fighting north of Arras, now became engaged in a long and debilitating fight, which tested the sheer stamina of both sides.

The actions in which the 4th Division had been involved had diminished the capacity of the battalions to produce sufficient volume of fire to repel a substantial attack. The reduction of offensive capacity had been recognised in the events of the last few days, as the action on the 28th March had resulted in the loss of many valuable machine guns, thus reducing the ability of the battalions to produce the required firepower. To address the situation, the decision was taken to substantially increase the number of machine guns of the establishment. On the 1st April, many of theses guns began to arrive in the form of the 7th machine-gun Squadron, which had been retained by XVII Corps headquarters in headquarters reserve.

Forward and rear areas were subject to constant and heavy artillery fire, with Feuchy and Lemon Trenches and Battery Valley, south of the River Scarpe, marked for special attention. German aircraft activity was at its peak, aeroplanes were constantly overhead and moving above ground without being seen was impossible. At 5:30am on the 1st of April, one of these planes flew over the British front line and shot down four observation balloons in flames, all of which were situated in front in the XVII and VI Corps areas.

Although the artillery and aircraft were constantly engaged, the situation on the ground remained relatively quiet until 5:30am in the morning of the 2nd when an enemy force, estimated at about two companies, attacked a small salient in the front line. The attack resulted in desperate hand-to-hand fighting after the bombing stops in Troy Trench had been forced but, with determination, the enemy was finally ejected. Two wounded German prisoners were captured during the mêlée, one from the 9th Reserve Infantry Regiment and the other from the 188th Infantry Regiment (187th Division). The attack had been carried out without any preliminary bombardment, but the German artillery and trench mortars, following the withdrawal of the attackers, subjected the British trenches to heavy shelling.

Following the attack, orders were issued emphasising the fact that *"every inch of ground must be fought for"* and that no retirement was possible. The last remaining line of resistance, the Army line south of the Scarpe and the 3rd defensive system, was to be held at all costs. To assist with the defence, arrangements were made to have the 46th Brigade (15th Division) take over the line on the south bank of the river from the Warwicks and Duke of Wellington's during the night of the 3rd. The artillery fire was constant, measured only by its varying intensity on any given day. The relief was carried out satisfactorily in rain and very poor visibility, without interference from the enemy, although some shelling was experienced.

During the night of the 4th, three soldiers of the 28th Reserve Infantry Regiment were captured outside the wire, which indicated that the opposing 24th Division had not been relieved, as thought. Information given by those prisoners also indicated that the enemy was planning an attack on the morning of the 6th. That statement was supported by a heavy barrage during the morning of the 5th, which fell on the front line, north and south of the river and lasted until 10:30am, when it diminished to desultory bombardments of selected targets of choice.

That night the fighting troops, assisted by a company of Pioneers, joined the outpost line into a continuous trench system. The night remained quiet until the shelling commenced in the early hours of the morning in which Pudding and Lemon Trenches were targeted and, in preparation for a possible attack, all units were placed on stand-to at 4:30am on the 6th. When, by 8:30am, no attack had eventuated, the troops were stood down. During the day the O.C., 10th Brigade, Brigadier-General H. W. Grun, D.S.O. relinquished his command[365]. The troops in the trenches were treated to the spectacle of aerial combat between a German and British plane over the trenches, resulting in the enemy aircraft being brought down behind the German lines and was seen to crash near Greenland Hill.

Relief, at last, was in sight for the division when the 1st Canadian Brigade was placed at the disposal of the 4th Division, with accompanying instructions that the whole division would be relieved by the 1st Canadian Division on the 8th of the month. The division was also notified that the entire XVII Corps was to leave the 3rd Army and join the 1st

---

[365] *No established reason.*

Army on the La Bassee Canal, north of Lens. As the division prepared to leave the field at Arras, the entire area was subjected to saturation artillery fire

During the night of the 8th, the 12th Brigade was relieved by the Provisional Battalion, which was then incorporated into the 2nd Canadian Brigade along with other mixed details. The 10th and 11th Brigades were relieved on the night of the 9th by the 1st and 3rd Canadian Brigades respectively after which the 10th Brigade retired to Agnes-Les-Duisans, the 11th to 'Y' Huts, north of Arras and the 12th Brigade marched to Simencourt. Even though the division was out of the line, it was not exempt from the persistent shelling. During its stay at 'Y' Huts, the 11th Brigade was subjected to fire from the German heavy artillery, which resulted in the Royal Warwickshire Regiment having to move to Agnes-Les-Duisans.

Although the infantry had been withdrawn from the line, the artillery, after being relieved by the Canadian gunners, was required to relocate to other parts of the line and remain in action under the orders of the Commander, Royal Artillery (56th Division). Such was the pressing need for artillery that, on the 10th, XVII Corps issued orders instructing the 29th Brigade artillery, a part of the 4th Division, to be transferred to the command of 56th Division. The 32nd Brigade also fell under the command of the 15th Division.

Events on other parts of the British front had placed great strain on available resources and, at 6:35pm on the 11th, a warning was issued to the 4th Division to be ready to march to the Bruary area at four hours notice. At 8:00am the following morning, the infantry brigades were ordered to move by bus to Lilliers, north of Lens, while the brigade transports were to move by road. The 11th Brigade embussed at 12:00am, the 10th Brigade at 1:00pm and the 12th Brigade at 2:00pm. While the departure was carried out according to orders, the instructions regarding the debussing points failed to reach the brigades whilst they were en-route, which resulted in the brigades being dispersed over a wide area.

The 11th Brigade arrived at Gonnehem, four miles north-west of Bethune, as required and fell under the temporary orders of the 3rd Division. The 10th Brigade debussed along the Busnes – Lilliers Road with its head on Busnes and many of the smaller units, machine-gun companies, engineers and pioneers formed up on various roads about Lilliers. As the 11th Brigade had arrived in the 3rd Division area, it immediately relieved the 2nd Suffolk Regiment (76th Brigade), on the canal bank on the left sector of the division front[366]. The remainder of the division was placed in I Corps reserve until all other units had arrived. Due to the confusion, the provision of accommodation proved difficult and many of the infantry had to find accommodation, with the brigade transport, wherever possible.

The 4th Division was to spend several months of heavy and, sometimes, close fighting in this area. To understand the area, a description of the ground to be held by the division is given here. Prior to the arrival of the 4th Division the Germans had attacked, as a part of the March offensive, to the south of Armentières, took Merville on the 11th and penetrated further to the south on the 12th. On that day, the enemy thrust through Riez Du Vinage and, in an effort to cross the La Bassee Canal, were confronted by the 3rd and 51st Divisions on a three mile line of the canal from the point at which it swung north, at Bethune.

The German thrust was largely prevented from reaching the canal by the gallant action of the 255th Brigade, Royal Field Artillery, of the latter division[367]. The divisions were located with 61st and 3rd Divisions fighting on the western bank and the 51st Division, in between the other two, on the eastern bank. It was upon these three divisions that the full weight of the enemy attack had fallen.

The 51st Division had stopped the German assault, on its part of the front, within yards of the canal, but only at a very high cost in casualties. Because of the inability of that division to offer continued resistance, it was decided to withdraw it from the line and, to fill the gap, the 3rd Division extended to the left and assumed responsibility for a part of the line. The 61st Division, located to the left of the 51st, extended to the right and took over the left of the 51st Division line.

The 4th Division arrived in the area to take over a part of the much-stretched 3rd Division front, thus allowing the safe withdrawal of the 51[st][368]. The momentum of the German attack had been held on both flanks by the 3rd and 61st Division but had pushed the 51st back to the canal bank, forming a large salient. The line extended south, from Baquerolles [Fm] to the southern most edge of the Bois de Pacaut, only

---

[366] *The 3 Division held the entire divisional front with one brigade. The remaining two brigades were located in the support and reserve lines, to the rear of the front line. At the time of the arrival of the 4 Division, the front line was located on the southern bank of the La Bassee Canal, seven miles north of Lens.*
[367] *Extracted from Sir Douglas Haig's Despatches, J.H. Boraston, C.B., O.B.E., Published by J.M. Dent & Sons Ltd, 1920, pp225-226.*

[368] *The 4 Division assumed responsibility for what had been the 51st Division Front.*

100 yards from the canal, then northeast to about le Cix Marmuse, a total distance of nearly four miles.

Barely had the 10th Brigade begun to settle down when it was ordered to take over the right sector of the 3rd Division during the night of the 13th. After considerable difficulty in reaching its destination, it completed the relief of the 76th Brigade at 1:00am, with the 11th Brigade situated on the left and the 8th Brigade (3rd Division) on the right. The 12th Brigade remained in reserve about La Valee. The two front-line brigades were ordered to establish contact with the enemy who were found located in the Bois de Pacaut and Riez Du Vinage. To this end, during the night of the 14th, both brigades commenced active patrolling and captured a German artillery officer with several O.R.'s and a light machine gun. The village of Riez Du Vinage, which was forward of the right of the division front line, had been taken by the Germans prior to the arrival of the 4th Division and it was the task of the 11th Brigade to recapture the village.

The attack was carried out by two battalions, the 1st Hampshire Regiment and the 1st Somerset Light Infantry, to the left and right respectively. The Hampshire's met with little opposition and only suffered three casualties but the Somerset's were not so fortunate. Whilst both battalions were successful in achieving the objective, the Somerset's met determined resistance on the right, suffering the loss of one officer and eighty-seven other rank.

The entire village was captured, with the exception of a small group of houses, which were not included in the plan of attack. Also captured were five officers, one hundred and thirty two other ranks, a British battery of 4.5" howitzers and five 18-pounder field guns that had been lost in the original German assault on the 28th March. The division line now extended along the eastern edge of Riez and turned across the northern face of the village, to meet the 61st Division, some distance to left.

Following the attack, the night remained quiet but the peace did not to last long. Early in the afternoon of the 15th, the 10th Brigade, with the support of the 11th Brigade, was instructed to re-capture the wood. To facilitate the attack, the Royal Engineers constructed a pontoon bridge across the canal to allow the assaulting troops to cross quickly. With the 10th Brigade on the right and the 11th on the left, the artillery barrage came down at the specified time but damaged the pontoon bridge.

While the bridge was being repaired, the 2nd Duke of Wellington's managed to cross and commence the advance on the left of the line, but the few Warwickshire's got across and those that did, failed to make any substantial progress. The Duke of Wellington's reached a line about 200 yards ahead of the Somerset Light Infantry but was then ordered to withdraw, as their presence masked the fire of the 11th Brigade. By the time the bridge was finally repaired, the enemy machine guns were firing in barrage.

At the junction of the 4th and 61st Divisions, a salient protruded into the British front line, a position held in strength by the enemy. In conjunction with the action to capture the Bois Du Pacaut, it was decided to take the salient and straighten the line. The troops on the right flank of the 61st Division successfully captured the houses near Riez, which had not been previously taken by the Hampshire's, by advancing and wheeling to the left. The advance of the Hampshire's, co-operating with the 61st Division, also proceeded smoothly but, in the face of stern resistance, the 61st Division could not hold the position thus gained and was forced to withdraw.

The withdrawal had left the Hampshire's exposed to close range rifle fire and, as it was felt that being exposed did not achieve any military objective, they too, were ordered to withdraw to the original line. The total casualties suffered by the two brigades amounted to twenty-five officers and five hundred and four other ranks, most only with slight injuries. Captured prisoners stated that casualties had been great, caused by the heavy machine-gun fire. As a result of the fighting, the 10th Brigade front had become considerably confused and the opportunity was taken to reorganise during the night of the 16th.

The following morning, the line of the canal and Mt. Bernenchon, in the 12th Brigade area, was subjected to intense shelling. Riez was subjected to similar treatment in the afternoon, followed by an attempt of a small party of German infantry to enter the village, but they beaten back by concentrated Lewis gun and rifle fire. Later that the evening information was given, by a prisoner from the 16th Division, that a determined attack was to be delivered upon the 4th Division with the objective of capturing the whole line of the canal. It was believed that the small attack on Riez that afternoon was an attempt to draw fire to disclose the positions to be attacked.

In possession of that information, the 11th Brigade was instructed to send a battalion to the bank of the canal at once and, in the event of a serious attack, was to counter-attack immediately. The remaining two battalions were to assemble along the Hinges – Mt. Bernenchon Road. By 1:00am on the 18th, a bombardment of the area south of the canal had commenced and grew in intensity until 4:00am.

In anticipation of an attack, the 10th Brigade requested that a battalion of the 11th Brigade move up into support as soon as possible. To do that, the 11th Brigade moved two battalions forward, one to Mt. Bernenchon and one to Hinges to support the 12th Brigade and 10th Brigade respectively and were to counter-attack on their own initiative, in the event of the enemy crossing the canal. The remaining battalion was sent to Gonnehem.

By 2:45am, the S.O.S. signal was seen in front of Riez twice and, at 3:55am and 4:10am, the same signal was seen from Pont-De-L'Hinges. A message from the Seaforth Highlanders stated that the enemy had been seen collecting in the south-west corner of the wood at 3:45am. A report from the Lancashire Fusiliers indicated that, up to 4:00am, no infantry action had taken place nor had any rifle or machine-gun fire been heard. A little later, at 4:15am, an attack developed from the southern and south-western edges of the Bois de Pacaut. A determined attempt by the enemy to reach the canal was driven off by the bridge-head post and a party of the Renfrew Field Company, which had been wiring on the northern side of the canal. A second attempt was made shortly after by a party of about 20 German infantry, also driven off with rifle and Lewis guns.

As soon as it became evident that the enemy was attacking in strength, the engineers destroyed the bridges at Pont Diminges, the drawbridge and pontoon bridges. The King's Own was attacked heavily later in the morning, with the right flank being particularly affected. Because of the intensity of the fighting, the situation of the King's Own remained quite obscure until late in the morning, when it became evident that they had held their line and defeated the attempts to break through.

Throughout the morning, a steady flow of prisoners passed through the line from the wood. Many of those driven to cover in their attempt to cross the bridge also surrendered to the bridgehead post. Several of the enemy, who had penetrated into Riez during the attack, were also captured on the south-west side of the village. The situation on the right flank of the 10th Brigade was not clear to division headquarters either so, at 1:00pm, a contact aeroplane was sent to determine the location of the forward troops. The initial report from the aircraft proved incorrect and a second plane was sent at 6:00pm, followed by a personal inspection by the commanding officer of the battalion involved.

By late afternoon, the front had quietened down and the two battalions of the 11th Brigade were sent back to their billets with orders to be prepared to move at short notice. The German artillery remained noticeably quiet. Parts of Riez had been occupied in the early part of the day and, after consultation with the G.O.C. the 12th Brigade commander decided to re-take the village during the night and arrangements were made for a rolling barrage to be laid, as protection to the advancing troops. Promptly, at 8:00pm, the barrage came down and the advance commenced. By 9:30pm, the village had been re-captured and the 12th Brigade had re-established in the original lines to the north and northeast of the town. During that attack, fifteen prisoners and a light machine-gun were captured.

The division had captured a total of one hundred and thirty nine prisoners, including three officers, in the days fighting. Information obtained from those prisoners indicated that the attack had been carried out by five battalions of the 470th and 471st Infantry Regiments with a sixth battalion meant to exploit any success that might have been achieved in the Riez sector. Patrols, which had been active during the night of the 18th, reported that the Germans were attempting to dig in about 15 yards inside the southern end of the Bois Du Pacaut and to the left of the wood.

Generally, the 19th remained relatively quiet except for an incident that demonstrated the confused nature of the fighting of the previous day. During the morning, the 2nd Essex had assumed responsibility for a section of the 12th Brigade front and it was soon realised that a pocket of resistance still existed in the village. An assault on the house in question was organised resulting in the capture of a further three officers and sixty other ranks, which had been overlooked in the recent fighting. As the prisoners were being marched back from the front, twenty-one were shot by German infantry firing from the wood. Only forty-two were brought out alive.

At 2:30am on the 20th, Riez was again subjected to an attack from the direction of the wood but, having successfully penetrated through the outpost line, the attempt was finally beaten off, leaving only small pockets of the enemy to offer resistance. At 4:15am, a second attempt was made, which resulted in the right of the line being pressed back slightly. At 9:30am, a contact aeroplane established the extent to which the line had retired and confirmed that the enemy had gained possession of the western edge of the wood.

To help resolve the situation, the 11th Brigade was brought forward to hold the line of the canal across the breadth of the division area and relieved the 10th Brigade. To further assist, a brigade of the 3rd Division took over a part of the canal line during the afternoon and relieved elements of the 11th Brigade for more pressing tasks.

The fighting continued into the evening, when the 2nd Essex Regiment (12th Brigade) attacked Riez with the aim of regaining those parts of the village, which had been lost during the earlier fighting. The contest was intense but, by 1:30am in the morning of the 21st, the entire village had been secured and the line extended as far as the bend in the canal. The very personal nature of the fighting in the dark, is shown by the fact that the Essex Regiment reported having killed four of the enemy in the house on the outskirts of the village and captured three prisoners.

During the night of the 20th, a patrol of the 1st Hampshire's captured a machine-gun and two of the crew between the canal and the wood. The Lancashire Fusiliers also undertook aggressive patrolling and a single patrol of one officer and five men rushed and captured an enemy outpost, killing five and capturing a further four, with their machine gun. Other patrols constantly engaged enemy working parties. Such engagements warranted fighting patrols getting in close contact with the enemy but considerable sniping and machine-gun fire, originating from a lone house, prevented parties of the Hampshire Regiment from crossing the canal.

During the morning of the 21st, prisoners of the 486th Infantry Regiment, who had been captured in the wood, were paid special attention by British interrogators and it was learned that a Guard Division was to relieve the incumbent 239th Infantry Division that evening. The division was then to deliver an attack on the morning of the 22nd. During the afternoon of the 21^{st,} the 11th Brigade was instructed to clear the southern portion of the Bois Du Pacaut at 5:15am in the morning of the 22nd and to establish itself on the line of the La Pennerie – Riez Road. The attack was to be accompanied by an intense artillery barrage on the northern portion of the wood and other selected targets and a projection of gas was to be delivered by 'G' Special Company if a favourable wind was blowing.

The 10th Brigade, Pioneer battalion and the Field Companies also made preparations to meet the possible enemy attack by taking up a line on the Clarence River, south and north of Gonnehem respectively. To facilitate that move, the engineers built a gangway over the demolished Pont D'Hinge, although it was destroyed by enemy artillery and had to be rebuilt. During the night of the 21st, the canal bank was shelled intermittently and patrols of the Rifle Brigade reported the establishment of enemy outposts and the fact that working parties were digging inside the perimeter of the outposts.

By 10:00am, the 1st Rifle Brigade and 1st Hampshire Regiment (11th Brigade) had carried out the attack on the wood and taken all objectives, except for a portion in the centre of the Hampshire's line, where the assault had been held up by hidden machine guns. To overcome the difficulties, the flanking companies worked their way up the side of the gullies and trench mortars were used to clear the area. Whilst the 11th Brigade continued its struggle, the 12th Brigade was instructed to assist the 61st Division with an attack at 4:30am on the 23rd. The objective of the 12th Brigade was to capture the road east of the canal, behind a creeping barrage. On completion of the attack, the 10th Brigade was then to relieve the 12th on the new line.

It would appear, according to information gained from newly captured prisoners, that the relief of the 239th Division by the Guard Division had not taken place. The enemy made no attempt at attack in the morning of the 22nd although, during the day, small groups of German infantry were observed moving up to Le Vert Bois Farm from which an attack was later attempted against La Pennerie. That attack was subjected to concentrated artillery fire and broken up before it reached the village. In the early afternoon, the German artillery delivered a very heavy bombardment of the canal line and the southern end of the Bois Du Pacaut, held now by the 11th Brigade, as well as on Gonnehem and Annoy.

By 4:00pm, the 1st Hampshire's had completed clearing the resistance in the centre of its line and finally secured the La Pennerie – Riez Road. Harassing fire was directed on the canal crossings throughout the night and the canal bank subjected to heavy shelling for a period of three hours, while the division batteries at Bellevue were shelled with gas.

As planned, the 61st Division attacked on the morning of the 23rd. The 12th Brigade reported having taken the road five minutes after the commencement of the attack, with the exception of the Lancashire Fusiliers, which had met determined resistance from intense rifle and machine-gun fire, directed from Le Cornet Malo. During the attack, twenty-one prisoners of the 456th Infantry Regiment (235th Infantry Division) were captured and stated that they had only been in the line for two hours when the attack fell upon them. By 7:00am, the 61st Division had also captured its objectives, along with some sixty men and five officers of the 456th Infantry Regiment.

The situation on the right of the 12th Brigade was unclear. A considerable number of casualties had been incurred due to the high volume of sniping from isolated pockets of the enemy. Those groups had been overlooked when clearing the ground and it was believed that they were creeping forward to snipe from the rear. A contact aeroplane confirmed that the enemy had penetrated between Riez and La Pierre au Beure and had broken through the front line. In the light of those events, the relief of the 12th Brigade was delayed for twenty-four hours and arrangements made to remove those of the enemy who had penetrated the line.

All attempts by the 12th Brigade to secure the area north of Riez proved extremely difficult because of the problems with identifying the location of the German snipers. To minimise casualties, all troops north of the railway line, that is, between the railway line and the Riez – La Pierre au Beurre Road, were withdrawn to the line of the railway. The German artillery was also busy during the night of the 23rd, shelling the new lines, the canal bank and Riez. The division artillery responded at 10:30pm and 4:30am by shelling the known German batteries.

The line held by the 4th Division now stretched over a considerable distance but, during the morning of the 24th, orders were received to the effect that, on the night of the 25th, 4th Division was also to assume responsibility for a part of the 61st Division front. The 3rd Division was then to take over apart of the 4th Division line on the night of the 26th. At dawn on the 25th, the 61st Division was attacked, but the combined artillery of the 61st and 4th Divisions broke up the formations, resulting in the capture of five enemy officers and sixty other ranks of the 455th Infantry Regiment, without loss of the line.

After the front had settled down, the opportunity was taken to relieve a portion of the 61st Division line. The 10th Brigade also relieved the 12th Brigade, all carried out under heavy shelling, particularly along the canal bank. The remainder of the day passed quietly and allowed the final movement of the 3rd Division to be completed without interference. Once again the fighting capacity of the division had been reduced by the high casualty rates suffered in recent events[369]. In an effort to main-

---

[369] *Many of the troops, earmarked for transport to France as reinforcements, had been prevented from leaving due to political decisions in Westminster. Tens of thousands of troops were available but not being permitted to sail, meant that the fighting divisions*

tain its fighting capabilities, all light machine guns were required to be supplied to the front line units and be ready for action at all times. Total casualties for the 4th Division during the month of April amounted to one hundred and twenty-seven officers and one thousand, nine hundred and thirty four other ranks.

were denied the required reinforcements. That decision was later rescinded to allow sufficient forces for the forthcoming offensive.

May - 1918

May remained relatively quiet, albeit with the regular shelling and counter-battery fire from both sides. The canal bank remained one of the most dangerous locations on the 4th Division front, due to the extensive use of gas against the front line and the artillery positions. The German artillery used shells containing several different gasses, some of which had been introduced in recent months. Those gasses, Blue Cross and Yellow Cross, were particularly debilitating and invariably fatal to the unwary.

The nocturnal activities of both sides, consolidating trenches and wire defences, patrol contacts and minor incursions on opposing outposts, inevitably resulted in engagement. At about 2:00am on the 2nd an enemy patrol attacked a wiring party of the 10th Brigade and, although driven off by rifle fire, failed to provide identification. The battery positions around Gonnehem, Belleverive and Langy experienced regular heavy shelling and on the 3rd, suffered severely. It was not unusual to get lost in the dark and on the night of the 4th, one of a party manning an outpost of the 11th Brigade, located in the Bois Du Pacaut, shot a lone enemy soldier of the Bodyguard Regiment.

On the 5th, orders were issued for the 'G' Special Company of the Royal Engineers to conduct a gas attack against the village of Le Coronet Malo[370]. The attack, to be carried out using gas projectors, was to be carried out when the wind was favourable and be supported by the artillery, which was to fire on the target periodically. As events happened, the wind was suitable that same night and the attack was arranged to commence just after midnight of the 5th. It was, however, delayed due to the need to re-adjust brigade boundaries, as it was thought that the gas would present a danger to the moving troops.

The area of the Bois du Pacaut was to be heavily contested for some time to come, as the southern perimeter of the wood extended to within 80 yards of the canal and offered cover for a large body of assaulting troops. To provide an element of resistance and to give warning of such an attack, the outpost line of the 11th Brigade was pushed forward, within the wood, during the night of the 5th. The following night, a patrol of the Lancashire Fusiliers reported having approached right up to the enemy wire and found the trenches unoccupied.

---

[370] *Le Coronet Malo was a village on the northern boundary of the Bois Du Pacaut.*

At about midnight on the 7th, division headquarters received a letter from I Corps stating the it was in possession of information, from a reliable source, that the Germans were preparing for an attack on the 10th or 11th, following a three-hour bombardment, to start at 10:30pm. The objective of the attack was to gain the line of the canal before dawn. However, patrols sent out during the night of the 8th found that houses and strong points, usually manned, were unoccupied, although the enemy artillery fire falling on Mt. Bernenchon, the canal bank and Riez Du Vinage, was heavier than usual.

In the expectation of the foreseen attack, a conference between the G.O.C. and the brigade commanders agreed that the brigades occupying the front line were to do so with three battalions instead of the usual two. The 12th Brigade, acting in support, placed two companies at the disposal of the 10th Brigade, on the left of the line while it also manned the 2nd and 3rd lines of defence during the night of the 9th.

While the infantry were taking up the positions, a projection of gas was to be carried out by 'M' and 'G' Special Companies of the Royal Engineers. Gas cylinders were to be used against Baquerolles Fm, 1500 yards due north of Riez Du Vinage, and the projectors against the extreme right of the line. The gas attack was fired at 2:00am on the morning of the 9th and covered both areas in dense clouds of gas, causing the volume of rifle and machine-gun fire to decrease considerably. A little later, at 3:50am, a telephone message from headquarters indicated that the German attack was expected that same morning and that the objective was Bethune, to the south.

Shortly after the receipt of that message, the German artillery commenced heavy shelling of the division battery areas, but left the front line untouched, although Gonnehem suffered heavy gas shelling for a three-hour period from 3:00am. Apart from the shelling, no sign of offensive action was seen and the 9th passed quietly, although the front line received the full benefit of the German artillery during the course of the evening. During the course of that bombardment, a single German shell destroyed a dump of gas shells, causing considerable concern, but few casualties.

Apart from the usual shelling, the next two days passed relatively quietly. On the 11th, a patrol of the 10th Brigade discovered a pile of enemy infantry packs, with the identification marks of the 6th Company, 469th Infantry Regiment, in a recently occupied bivouac. At about the same time, 'M' Special Company discharged 100 cylinders of gas near a group of farms 1000 yards north of Riez. As the gas drifted across the rear area behind the German lines, warning rockets were seen being fired. The German artillery retaliated to that attack by shelling the front line but patrols continued to report the absence of German troops in the houses normally used by snipers and machine guns.

At that stage of the war 'peaceful penetration' had become a pastime for most of the British Army on the Western Front. The troops of the 4th Division were no exception and, at 8:30am on the 15th, the 2nd Duke of Wellington's captured two prisoners out of a small group of the enemy who were manning an outpost. The raiding party consisted of one N.C.O. and six men who rushed the post, made the capture and re-tired, without suffering any casualties. When interrogated the prisoners were identified as belonging to the 4th Company (1st Battalion) which had relieved its sister battalion, the 3rd, on the morning of the 12th. They also stated that the 54th and 61st Reserve Infantry Regiments (35th Division), of their division, had come into the line on the night of the 14th but knew nothing of the German intentions.

In the early hours of the 16th, a patrol of the 2nd Essex Regiment shot a lone enemy soldier when he approached a house while the patrol was in occupation. This attracted the attention of his comrades, eight of whom then approached the house. The patrol barely had time to cut off a shoulder strap, which identified the 456th Infantry Regiment (235th Division) and withdraw before being attacked. Later in the morning, a second house was seen to be on fire as result of being struck by a red rocket, fired by the Germans. Because of the fire, fourteen enemy troops were seen to leave the building, four of which were shot as a re-sult of the rifle and machine-gun fire from the British lines. It proved impossible to secure identification, as the building was burnt to the ground.

A little later, a two-seater German aeroplane was brought down behind the 4th Division lines and it was found that the occupants were wounded. They expressed that fear existed amongst the German com-mand that a British attack was expected along this part of the front.

Little action, other than desultory artillery fire, was seen for several days, as both sides drew breath. During that period, a British plane, having fallen victim to enemy fire, crashed in flames behind the 3rd de-fence line on the 17th, the plane and pilot being destroyed by fire. At 3:15am the following day, a post of the 11th Brigade, located just north of the La Bassee Canal, was attacked by an enemy raiding party, sup-ported by heavy machine-gun and light mortar fire. The raiders were driven off, but not before causing casualties among outpost party, with one killed and eight wounded. A second attempt was made a party of about twenty raiders to enter trenches of the 11th Brigade but was beaten off by the concentrated fire of Lewis guns.

Mustard gas was used extensively against the support trenches, south of the canal, during heavy shelling in the early hours of the morning of the 20th, which resulted in a large number of casualties within the 12th Brigade. The closing days of the month were punctuated with blow and counter-blow by both side and at about midnight of the 30th, a determined attempt by a German raiding party was made on an outpost of the 10th Brigade in the Bois Du Pacaut. The attack, made under very heavy machine-gun fire, was repulsed only after severe hand-to-hand fighting, which left four dead and one wounded.

June - 1918

Throughout May and June there had been clear indications that the Germans were going to great lengths to strengthen their line in front of the 4th Division. The volume of shelling by both sides steadily increased, particularly with the use of gas. On the 1st of June, Le Vert Lannot, located on the right flank of the 4th Division, was shelled with an estimated 3000 - 4000 gas shells between 3:00am and 4:15am and made the area completely uninhabitable for a considerable time. Late in the evening of the same day, the 12th Brigade attempted a small-scale raid on enemy outposts in the orchard, on the western side of Riez Du Vinage, but the raiding party was beaten back by heavy fire and superior numbers.

All indications pointed to the fact that the enemy facing the division was prepared for British attempts at penetration and was in an aggressive mood. The possibility of an enemy attack was ever-present and, in order to prevent the possibility of a breakthrough, the 12th Portuguese Infantry Battalion, which was billeted at C'Antrainne, was placed at the disposal of the G.O.C., should the rear lines need to be manned. Patrols of both sides were constantly active.

In order to establish the identity of the enemy formation opposite the division, the Somerset Light Infantry carried out a daring attempt to capture a prisoner during the night of the 7th. At about 7:30pm, a patrol of one officer and six men occupied a house in a small farm located on the road, running north from Riez Du Vinage to Bacuerolles Fm. In front of the farm and on the opposite side of the road were the remains of the small village of La Pierre au Beure, through which a narrow road ran to join the Riez Road. An enemy patrol approached the house but stopped at the road junction and set up a machine gun, opening heavy fire down the road leading into the north of Riez Du Vinage.

The patrol remained quiet as a body of troops, estimated at about 200, arrived in small parties and commenced work in the enclosure to the left of the house occupied by the patrol. At 10:45pm, seven German soldiers entered the yard of the house, which blocked the only remaining exit. The patrol opened fire, shooting one and killed the other six with grenades. The farmhouse was immediately subjected to fire from machine guns and light mortars and the patrol rapidly withdrew, albeit without having secured identification, and returned to the front at about 11:20am without casualty. Upon the return of the patrol, Lewis gunfire was opened on the house and surrounding area.

Several hours later, quantities of gas were projected into the German front line resulting in many casualties. The response from German artillery was immediate, laying a heavy bombardment on the support and reserve lines, Mt. Bernenchon and the canal bank. It had been suspected that the enemy had been creating dumps of ammunition behind their front line and concerted efforts by the division artillery were made to destroy the dumps during the evening of the 9th June, with a barrage on a 1,000-yard front. The bombardment resulted in constant heavy artillery exchanges for some days. Most of that retaliation was directed on the canal bank and the ruins of Riez Du Vinage.

The constant attempts by raiding parties and patrols to establish the identity of the other side kept those in the front line and outpost line nervous. An attempt by the 2nd Seaforth's to raid an enemy post, on the western edge of the Bois de Pacaut failed, as the occupants were on the qui vivre, droving off the raiders and inflicting several casualties. Similarly, a patrol of the Warwickshire's was also driven off by heavy fire when it approached a German outpost next to the Hinges – Boheme Road.

For a number of weeks, the neighbouring 3rd Division had been planning to advance the front line and had arranged for the 4th Division to support the attack by adjusting its right flank in sympathy with left of the 3rd Division. The date for the assault had been set for 11:45pm on the 14th and, at that hour, 'M' Special Company was to barrage the Bois de Pacaut with 300 chlorine gas cylinders fired from projectors. In the event, the attack of the 3rd Division was entirely successful and resulted in the capture of four officers and one hundred and eighty nine other ranks. The enemy response was the intense shelling of Hinges for the rest of the day.

Not all attempts to conduct raids against the enemy lines met with failure. While the 3rd Division was engaged in the business of advancing its line, a patrol of the 1st Rifle Brigade (11th Brigade) carried out a daring enterprise. The patrol, consisting of a Sergeant, one Corporal and two men, left the line at 7:50am to clear the front line of enemy shell holes. That patrol, after much hard fighting, captured twenty prisoners, several machine guns and killed a further twenty.

In order to have the infantry and the air force better understand the requirements of the other services, I Corps arranged for officers of 21st Squadron, R.A.F. and of the divisions to spend time with each organisation for periods of three days. During that period, German aircraft were almost continuously over the British Lines. By mid-month, the

German shelling of the British line had increased considerably, with hardly a moment when some part of the front line or rear area was not subjected to shellfire.

The following day a similar venture was carried out, in daylight, by a small patrol of the 1st King's Own (12th Brigade). Crawling through a corn crop, they encountered an enemy post, unprotected by wire and situated approximately 500 yards north east of Riez Du Vinage. The post consisted of a trench with three shelters, the garrison was found to be asleep and the entrance to each shelter, housing two men each, was covered with a waterproof sheet. The report of the raid quotes *"The post was entered, rifles removed, two telephone wires cut, before men were aroused, two Huns were pulled out and passed back, one of the remainder showed fight by throwing a stick bomb so he, along with the rest of the others were disposed of. The noise aroused neighbouring posts who commenced to throw stick bombs. These posts were engaged and our withdrawal effected."*

As the patrol made its way back it gave the signal for a protective barrage to be brought down and trench mortars and machine guns commenced firing immediately, followed closely by artillery support. A shell silenced one machine gun and a second machine-gun was engaged by the Lewis gun, located less than 100 yards away. Unfortunately, one of the prisoners was killed on the return journey, while the other proved to be of the 17th Reserve Infantry Regiment, a new identification. Incidents like these encouraged a growing sense of ascendancy over the enemy amongst the officers and men of all battalions.

On the 19th June, a further reorganisation of the British Army took place in which battalions were to be reduced from the normal establishment strength of nine hundred and ninety-six all ranks to nine hundred. The orders, which instigated that process, also indicated that it would be a temporary measure and it was likely that the numbers would return to normal[371]. During the last half of 1918, influenza had begun to appear among the fighting troops of all armies on the Western front[372] and, on the 21st June, the G.O.C. (4th Division), Major-General Matheson, was restricted to his bed as result of the virus.

---

[371] *It should be noted that many battalion's strengths were below these levels due to casualties, sickness and transfers.*

[372] *This epidemic was to spread, during 1919, worldwide and was to assume catastrophic proportions.*

The possibility of a further enemy attack on the British line was still very real and plans for the defence of the division line, as a part of the headquarters front, were constantly revised. As a consequence of such revisions, the decision to dig new lines, based on the lines of assembly for any counter-attack that may be required, was taken. That decision led to a new defensive scheme being implemented on the 23rd. The re-organisation of battalions and defence schemes was only a part of a far larger review and, on the 25th, instructions were issued indicating that the 5th Army would be assuming command of the XI and XIII Corps in the 1st July.

July - 1918

Before discussing the activities of July, a summary of the strategic events, which had occurred on the Western Front since March, require elaboration. The large-scale German offensive, which had been launched on the 21ˢᵗ March 1918, had largely come to a halt, with the exception of localised attempts to breakthrough on the Somme and in the French sector, to the east. The last serious attempt was made on the 15ᵗʰ July in the area about Reims[373].

For some time the Commander-in-Chief of the Allied Armies, Marshall Joffre[374], in conjunction with the commanders of the Allied armies, had been planning a major offensive, with the objective of breaking the stalemate of trench warfare and bringing the war to an end. To that end, the reserves, mainly French and several divisions of the Americans, were being formed well to the rear of the front line. As the impetus of the German offensive slowly diminished, much re-organisation of the battered British Army was undertaken. The British Army had suffered such severe losses that eight front-line divisions were reduced to cadres, incapable of further combat until the arrival of reinforcements from the United Kingdom.

Interchanges of divisions between the French and British added some-what to the security of the reserve lines but did little to restore strength to the British forces. As reinforcements flowed from the United Kingdom and other fronts, particularly Italy and the Middle East, a revitalisation of the British army took place during the months of May, June and July. The German attack, although it had stopped by the end of May, had produced considerable, and in some instances, very serious interruptions to the lines of communications that had existed prior the 21ˢᵗ March and the French and British Armies had lost substantial portions of strategically important ground. The remainder of the British Army, consisting of about forty-five under-strength infantry divisions, was gradually reinforced, albeit with insufficiently trained and inexperienced young recruits.

---

[373] *The German attack was launched on a grand scale and consisted of the last large body of reinforcements available for offensive action and it became clear to the French and British High Commands that this was to be the last German attempt at a decision of the Western Front.*

[374] *Appointed as Allied Commander-in-Chief on the 29 March 1918.*

By July, as a result of several large scale, but local attacks, conducted at various points along the British front, during the previous months, the British Army undertook substantial change. Supplies, reinforcements and most important of all, guns and tanks were arriving in growing numbers. During the month of July a change in the behaviour of the German opponents was noted; it was possible for small patrols to extend into areas without serious opposition that had not been previously deemed safe and return with large numbers of prisoners. The minor operations of 'peaceful penetration' were producing large numbers of prisoners and information. Most importantly of all, large local operations against sections of the German line, sometimes involving an assault of headquarters strength, were succeeding beyond expectation and producing large quantities of prisoners. Signs of a change in the morale of the German soldier was becoming evident.

The troops of the 4th Division spent the first few days of July quietly. The 10th Brigade departed the front line on the 2nd, after being relieved by the 11th Brigade. The following day a body of Germans, estimated at about fifty strong, attacked a patrol of the 2nd Essex, on the far left of the division front. The patrol found that it was in danger of being surrounded. However, following determined fighting, it withdrew and then fired upon the enemy, causing considerable casualties. Patrol engagements occurred daily and sometimes several times in a day. The 2nd Essex met with strong opposition near the western edge of the Bois de Pacaut and withdrew under heavy fire, the officer being killed and two men wounded.

Small incidents occurred which indicated a subtle change in the conduct of the individual enemy soldier. On the 4th July, a prisoner of 23rd Reserve Field Artillery Regiment was taken and stated that he was looking for his battery in No Man's Land[375]. The division had achieved such superiority that much of the patrol and raiding operations could be conducted during the daylight hours. At 9:30am on the 6th, a raiding party of the 2nd Lancashire Fusiliers, one officer and twenty six other ranks, carried out a raid on a German shell hole outpost and captured three men of the 1st Battalion, 38th Reserve Infantry Regiment (12th Division). The German artillery did not retaliate until 9:45am, when the Bois de Pacaut was shelled heavily for forty minutes. Several days later, the Bois de Pacaut was subjected to a gas shelling by the 'M' Special Company when it fired three hundred and forty five gas mortar shell shells into the northern half of the wood and parts of the German salient.

---

[375] It was a common occurrence for a soldier to get lost in an area where great devastation had occurred, especially at night.

Aggressive patrolling, raiding and gas shelling was conducted perpetually and, on the 15th, the 2nd Essex sent a patrol into the area between le Rues-Les Vache and La Bierre-au-Beure, on the western flank of the salient. Here they saw a party of Germans, about 50 strong, advancing along the road joining the two villages. The patrol opened fire on the approaching enemy, who immediately attempted to surround the patrol. After withdrawing to safe distance it was estimated that the German party had suffered one killed and six wounded.

The attempts at raiding were becoming bolder and were directed at greater objectives. Signs of demoralisation within the enemy ranks were now abundant and, in an effort to exacerbate the process, the 2nd Duke of Wellington's prepared for a raid on a large scale. The raiding party consisted of five officers and two hundred and one other ranks, formed into four platoons, including eight stretcher-bearers and three Royal Engineers. The party was to leave the trenches, situated on the western edge of the Bois de Pacaut and extend along the road on the northwestern edge of the wood, a distance of about 750 yards, clearing any German posts, trenches and shell holes as they proceeded. Upon arriving at the road, the entire line was to face left, advance through the wood in a southeasterly direction, and clear all positions that might be encountered. The whole operation was to be carried out in twenty minutes.

The raiding party had trained for the assault at Busnettes and during the early evening, the entire party left their billets and proceeded to march the eight kilometres, in small groups of about ten men, to the La Bassee Canal, using different routes. From there, in two's and three's, they crossed the canal immediately to the rear of the wood and moved directly to the 'jumping off' position, the last group arriving at 1:45pm. The parapet of the assembly trench had previously been heightened to prevent enemy observation and twenty lanes had been cut through the wire in preparation. So that the crossing of the German wire was executed with minimal delay, three of the four platoons were to act as the first wave while the fourth platoon advanced across in the open, in rear of the first wave.

At 2:30am, the barrage came down exactly on target and cut the wire so effectively that the troops did not need to use wire cutters. The first wave mounted the parapet as the barrage descended and the four platoons advanced in file as groups, the first platoon stopping sixty yards behind the barrage as it shelled the objectives. As the barrage lifted to the next line the platoons rushed a series of shell holes and a machine-gun post, to the left of the road. As there was a distinct lack of resistance, the remaining platoons proceeded to their objectives on schedule. The signal to execute the second phase of the attack, which was signalled by the blowing of horns, was given thirteen minutes after zero hour and the line the turned and passed into the wood, sometimes with difficulty owing to patches of thick undergrowth. A small number of the raiding party advanced behind the main line in the event of any the enemy revealing themselves after the first line had passed. The advance finally reached the British front line at 2:50am.

At first, the enemy appeared surprised and confused by the intensity of the barrage. Those caught in it either ran to the rear, or were quickly overrun by the advancing raiders. Those who were able to escape the barrage offered only light resistance. At the completion of the operation, twenty-nine prisoners had been captured and one machine gun. It was estimated that a further seventy had been killed or injured by the raiding party or artillery and three machine guns destroyed. The raiding party had not escaped lightly. At a final count, the casualties amounted to five killed and twenty-five wounded with a further two missing, believed killed. The raid had, as well as causing considerable damage to houses, dugouts and outposts, a lasting moral effect on the enemy.

The next few days remained quiet until the 21st, when two hundred drums of gas were projected against the German trenches and posts in the southern sector of the Bois de Pacaut. That same night a patrol captured a prisoner who was identified as belonging to the 38th Reserve Infantry Regiment (12th Division). The capture of prisoners occurred regularly and on the 23rd, a patrol of the Somerset Light Infantry, rushed a post in the heart of the wood, capturing four prisoners of the 51st Reserve Infantry Regiment. Later in the afternoon, a patrol of the Hampshire Regiment captured two more prisoners, of the same Regiment, from the same post. To further demoralise the enemy, two hundred drums of chlorine gas were projected into trenches on the northern corner of Riez Du Vinage, late in the evening.

Amid that activity, a British aeroplane was brought down in No Man's Land in front of the 12th Brigade. With covering fire from the infantry, the pilot set fire to his plane and retired safely to the British lines. For the next four days, the aggressive incursion continued and patrols of the 2nd Essex, 2nd Lancashire Fusiliers, Somerset Light Infantry and the Rifle Brigade all captured prisoners. Although the last two days of the month were spent quietly, the offensive spirit of the British soldier was at its height and was soon to be called upon.

August - 1918

By the beginning of August there were clear signs of a German withdrawal along parts of the whole front. The French and Americans had been attacking on the southern part of the line for nearly two months and suspicions of a withdrawal taking place on the 4th Division front was confirmed by the High Command in the early days of the month. Apart from general patrol activity, the line remained quiet. On the 1st, L'Eclere, in the rear area, was shelled occasionally by a long-range gun. The shelling grew in intensity overnight as Mt. Bernenchon received periodic fire and L'Eclere again became the target of the long-range guns the following day. The latter shelling caused considerable casualties among the Lancashire Fusiliers whom were resting in billets, killing five. Because of the danger, the battalion was ordered to move to Busnettes and Cantrainne.

During the night of the 4th, patrols of the Rifle Brigade discovered that the enemy outposts on their front were deserted and the Royal Air Force reported that the machine-gun and anti-aircraft fire had also diminished considerably. In conformity with normal practice, the canal bank was shelled on the same day but it was noted that a long-range gun was responsible, not the normal artillery fire. The 12th Brigade also reported that the enemy outposts on the brigade front were also deserted. However, the enemy in front of the 10th Brigade, in and around the Bois De Pacaut, remained in their outpost line and continued to resist. Patrols extended further afield and one, of the 12th Brigade, managed to secure two prisoners of the 100th Reserve Infantry Regiment (23rd Division) almost 500 yards behind the original German front line.

On the 4th August, 4th Division headquarters issued Operation Order No. 141 that confirmed that the Germans were withdrawing and that the brigades were to follow up. The procedure for such an advance was defined such: *"The brigades were to continue with constant patrolling but were not to be content with negative reports. Should a patrol proceed to a given distance and not find any enemy, then once support for the patrol had arrived, the patrol is to continue until contact has been established. Once touch was gained it was not to be lost. Patrols were to stay out and, if necessary, be reinforced. Patrols were to carry telephone and pigeons to enable rapid communications"*

This indicated that the division was preparing for a cautious advance and accordingly, some of artillery was moved forward to provide support for the advanced patrols and preparations were put in place for an advance of a larger scale. The advance was confirmed on the 6th by Operation Order No. 143, requiring the advance to be carried out in stages, each step being a distance of 500 – 700 yards, whilst maintaining contact with the divisions on the two flanks. The nature of the advance was to be determined very much by the advancing brigades, while keeping the division headquarters informed.

During the 6th, much effort was devoted to patrolling on the whole division front. This soon established that the Germans had withdrawn much sooner on the left than they had on the right. During that period, patrols had proceeded some 1000 yards behind the enemy front line in broad daylight without meeting any serious resistance. Le Cornet Malo, 1400 yards from the point of the salient, was reached during the night of the 6th. The following day, patrols penetrated past that village and encountered isolated machine guns, which offered some resistance. At 11:30pm on the 7th, two deserters of the 2nd Guard Reserve Infantry Regiment (1st Guard Reserve Division) were captured on the extreme right of the 12th Brigade line. Information given by the prisoners indicated that the Germans were holding a line approximately 1000 yards east of the Bois De Pacaut by groups of piquets, which consisted of one N.C.O. and eight men, armed with a light machine-gun and rifles.

The main first line of defence was reported to be 1000 yards further to the east located in a series of disconnected trenches. The forward piquets were to retire onto the defence line, which was held by several companies, in the event of attack. It was believed that the Germans were intending to retire to the Canal de la Lawe, upon which they would stand[376]. The prisoners also stated that the 1st Guard Reserve Division was too weak to attempt an attack and that the companies of the regiments were only about 50 – 60 strong, each with four machine guns.

Patrols, continuing to probe, found that the enemy piquets offered stiff resistance and, on the 8th, several of the outposts were captured by the Seaforth Highlanders who, with one company, captured 23 prisoners and five machine guns, killing a others[377]. When attempting to cross the

---

[376] *The Canal de la Lawe is situated approximately 50-60 yards to the east of the Lawe River. The river, in turn, intersects the La Bassee Canal to the south of the 4 Division line and runs, firstly, in a north-westerly direction until it reaches about the mid point of the Division front and then turns almost 90 degrees to follow a north easterly course. The distance from the Division front, on the 7 August 1918, to the bend of the Canal de la Lawe was approximately 6000 yards.*

[377] *Early in the morning of the previous day, the 8 August, the V Army, consisting of one British, two Australian and one Canadian Corps, Supported by French and British Corps on either flank launched an attack in the Valley of the Somme. It was this attack*

Quentin Road the Seaforth's suffered a considerable number of casualties due to heavy machine-gun fire originating from Quentin and beyond. The company commander was severely injured in that fire and the command of the company passed to the officer commanding the Support Company.

Notwithstanding the level of resistance, the advance continued and resulted in the surrounding and eventual capture of two groups of the enemy lying in ditches and shell holes. Bombs initially killed several of those and, in the face of serious attack, the remainder surrendered. Those who retired were subjected to heavy Lewis gun and rifle fire. German snipers in Boheme and Pacaut inflicted consistent casualties as the patrols advanced. Once across the road, the company advance a further seventy yards and dug in so that the dead and wounded could be attended to. In the advance, the Seaforth's lost a total of fifteen killed and wounded.

The prisoners were identified as belonging to the 3rd Company, 1st Battalion, 102nd Reserve Infantry Regiment (23rd Division) and reported that the 1st Battalion had entered the line during the early hours of the morning of the 8th, only to be engaged by the Seaforth's a few hours later. They had lost touch with those on their flanks and had been completely surprised. One stated that they had not had time to set up their machine guns before being surrounded. It eventuated that the rearward movement of the enemy was being carried out in order to withdraw from the salient, which had been formed in the initial attack and was intended to straighten the line. They also stated that their division artillery had withdrawn eastward and there was an expectation that the whole division was to be withdrawn because it was too weak.

By the 9th August, the division had advanced well past the intended final line, following the German withdrawal. During the morning, the enemy launched two local counter-attacks on the extreme right of the division line, each being driven off with the assistance of the artillery. As the advance had progressed beyond expectations, the whole line required reorganising. The 11th Brigade moved into the line and relieved the 10th Brigade. The order in which the brigades held their portion of the line was changed so that a single battalion of each of the two front line brigades held the line of outposts, while the remaining battalions remained in support. During the night of the 10th patrols worked well ahead of the outpost line without encountering any enemy, although

---

that clearly indicated that the German Army could no longer maintain its position on the Western Front.

the Bois de Pacaut and the canal bank continued to receive heavy shelling.

The division continued the advance on the 11th and reached the line of the Hinges Road capturing two prisoners, one from the 102nd Reserve Infantry Regiment (23rd Reserve Division). One had crawled through a field of corn to the shell hole that he had previously occupied, only to find that an English outpost had established there and subsequently surrendered. He stated that the 23rd Division was too weak to attack and that they were all sick of the war. The second prisoner, of the 101st Reserve Infantry Regiment, had got lost in the British shelling, encountered a British patrol and surrendered.

By the end of the day the 4th Division had made a substantial advance, particularly on the left and in the centre of the salient. The right had progressed in line but the whole line of advance pivoted on the right flank so the distances covered were not as great of those on the left. By the 14th, the German withdrawal from the salient was complete and the 4th Division settled on the line reached on the 12th, with only minor adjustments.

The defence instructions stated that the new line was to be was to be broken into three defensive systems, each supporting the line in front. The area was to consist of an outer cover of piquets, a line of outposts, reserves and a line of supports, which constituted the main front line. The purpose of the defences was to progressively weaken a concerted enemy attack at the outpost line, which would then effect a fighting withdrawal to the second line of outposts and, if necessary, to the main line. It was intended that any attack would be fought to the last on the support line but, apart from severe gas attacks on the canal bank, Riez and the wood, neither side undertook any further offensive action

It was clear that the enemy was preparing for further withdrawals as, in the few days up to the 19th, explosions could be seen and heard as structures were destroyed, including the big chimney stacks in Merville, to the left of the division. The destruction continued throughout the night, destroying anything of value. The observation aircraft and artillery observers reported the destruction of roads, bridges and buildings but, patrols investigating the German line on the night of the 18th saw no sign of further withdrawal and reported the front as being strongly held.

By 8:00am on the 19th, however, patrols of the Rifle Brigade were able to penetrate the German defences without interference. By 1:00pm the right flank of the Rifle Brigade had reached Paradise Road, a road passing through the village of Paradise, 300 yards due east of the front line. By 3:00pm, the line of the 11th Brigade had been considerably advanced, but the 10th Brigade had barely moved as it was being subjected to heavy artillery fire.

On the 20th, orders were issued indicating that the 'Green line', that is the line beyond which the patrols should extend, had been moved further to the east and represented an advance of 1500 yards. The orders instructed patrols to keep contact with the enemy and, any area of ground evacuated by the enemy was, initially, to be secured by the patrol until supporting troops had moved forward to occupy the area. The patrol was then to continue its pursuit of the retiring enemy. Should an isolated German post be discovered, a combined artillery and trench mortar barrage was be brought down upon the post, after which scouts were to approach the post and call the patrol, if the garrison was prepared to surrender[378]. That method permitted patrols to stay out in No Man's Land for extended periods, while the main body of the division maintained a slow, but steady advance.

XIII Corps informed the 4th Division that it would be relieved by the 19th and 74th Divisions on the 21st. At that time, the 19th Division was advancing on the right of the 4th Division, with the 74th on the left and, at the prescribed time, both of those divisions were to sideslip to the left and right respectively to relieve the two front line brigades. During the night of the 19th, the Seaforth Highlanders, after relieving the Royal Warwickshire Regiment, advanced in line with the 19th Division and captured ten prisoners while the left of the 19th Division also captured a further forty. By midday, the leading brigades, the 10th and 11th, had advanced approximately 1000 yards.

Interrogation of the prisoners revealed that they belonged to the 4th Company, 1st Battalion, 64th Reserve Infantry Regiment (1st Guard Reserve Division) and had been sent to relieve a piquet of the 2nd Guards Reserve Infantry Regiment but could not find it and had got lost. They had been subjected to infantry fire from flank and rear, not realising that they had been surrounded and decided to surrender. They stated that they were to stay in contact with the enemy and retire, if necessary, but they expressed doubts as to how far they were to remain in advance of the their division or how far they had to retire. One of the prisoners indicated that the division would hold a line in front of the River Lawe, but also felt that it would retire further to the east. He also indicated

---

[378] *This method was adopted in order to minimise the already growing casualty rate.*

that, as the huts and roads had been repaired near Aubers, the division would discontinue its retirement in that area.

A new line, the Second Green Line, had been reached by midday on the 20th and patrols took the liberty of moving in all directions but most were held up by machine-gun and trench mortar fire along the Abbey Road, 500 yards beyond the Second Green Line. The advance had been swift. In the early afternoon further orders were issued, defining the positions of the Third and Fourth Green Lines. The night of the 20th passed quietly, with the exception of occasional gas shelling and, by the following morning, it was discovered that the Germans intended to make a strong stand along the Abbey Road with machine guns, trench mortars and rifle fire.

Little forward movement was made during the 21st and only minor adjustments were made. In the early hours of the 23rd, a large body of enemy attacked the forward posts of the 11th Brigade, forcing them back about 700 yards but, by 9:30am, a counter-attack had regained the positions and allowed some consolidation. Whilst the thrust and counter-thrust was taking place, the 12th Brigade, in division reserve, was relieved by the 231st Brigade of the 74th Division. In the latter half of the day, the 11th Brigade was relieved and marched to the Ames area in the rear, followed by the 10th Brigade on the 24th.

The division had been fighting in the front line, on the La Bassee Canal for five months, the only break being the move from Arras to Lilliers, which took several days. In that five-month period, the division had suffered heavy casualties and, although it had received some reinforcements, it had left the field of battle very much weakened. It was, however, to be called upon again, to give of it's best. No sooner had the 10th Brigade reached the concentration point in the rear area, than the division received orders to entrain, commencing at 7:00am on the 25th, for transporting to the area about St. Pol, where it would become the reserve for the 1st Army. It was back to Arras for the 4th Division.

The movement of the division was affected without delay or mishap and it arrived at it destination during the afternoon of the same day, immediately falling under orders of the Canadian Corps. Its arrival at St. Pol signalled another move to Villers-au-Bois on the 26th, to make way for the Cavalry Corps, which needed the accommodation for its men and horses.

At this point, we should pause for a moment, to recall events on the Arras front since the departure of the 4th Division. On the 8th April

1918, the division was relieved by the 1ˢᵗ Canadian Division, south of the River Scarpe[379]. By early August, the German army had begun what was to be the final withdrawal from occupied France and Belgium. The Canadian Corps, like all other formations, had pursued the retreating enemy with great success. The Germans, on that particular part of the front, had retired in the face of the aggressive Canadians, to the Drocourt - Quéant line, a secondary, but powerful, defensive system, behind the main Hindenburgh line.

At the time of the arrival of the 4ᵗʰ Division, the Canadian Corps had made a substantial advance on the southern side of the Scarpe with the 2ⁿᵈ and 3ʳᵈ Canadian Divisions, which had taken them in a southeasterly direction, towards Cambrai. They had taken possession of the advanced line of the Drocourt – Quéant line and were now approaching the main defensive lines of that system. The 51ˢᵗ British Division, another long standing fighting partner of the 4ᵗʰ Division, having followed the German retirement from the La Bassee Canal, had also returned to Arras and advanced on the northern bank of the Scarpe and was now approaching Greenland Hill. It was all familiar ground to the 4ᵗʰ Division.

In the early hours on the 27ᵗʰ August, the division received orders to concentrate east of Arras, preparatory to relieving the 3ʳᵈ Canadian Division during the night of the 28ᵗʰ. The two Canadian divisions were to continue the advance during the 28ᵗʰ and the 4ᵗʰ Division was to carry out the relief as the advance slowed for the night. At the same time, the 1ˢᵗ Canadian Division was to relieve the 2ⁿᵈ Canadian Division. The boundary between the two divisions was to be the centre of the Arras – Cambrai Road.

The Composite Brigade[380] was placed at the disposal of the G.O.C., 4ᵗʰ Division[381] and was to form a left flank guard on the southern bank of the River Scarpe. A minor difficulty arose from the fact that the Canadians had carried out such a substantial advance that buses had to be

---

[379] *It was the 1 Canadian Division, then referred to simply as the Canadian Division, that the 4 Division fought with and finally relieved, at St. Julien on the 23 April 1915, during the first German gas attack at Langemark, Belgium.*

[380] *Consisting of the 1st Canadian Motor machine-gun Brigade, 101st machine-gun Battalion and the Canadian Cyclist Battalion, under the command of Brigadier-General Brutinel.*

[381] *French born Brigadier-General Raymond Brutinel, CB, CMG, DSO., was responsible for the formation of the Canadian machine-gun Corps in 1916.*

brought in to transport the troops of the 4th Division to areas close to the front line[382].

The relief of the 3rd Canadian Division was completed without difficulty and by 8:30am on the 29th, the 4th Division was holding a line of nearly 10,000 yards, facing the villages of Eating and Sailly-en-Ostrevent, both some distance ahead. The right flank rested on the Arras – Cambrai Road, slightly west of Marquion and extended to the Boiry-Notre-Dame – Sailly-en-Ostrevent Road. The 11th Brigade held the right, or southern sector of the line, in touch with the 2nd Canadian Brigade, while the 10th Brigade held the left flank and maintained contact with the Provisional Brigade, which continued the line to the River Scarpe.

The 10th and 11th Brigades joined in one of the old German outpost trenches of the Drocourt – Quéant line, while the 12th Brigade remained in reserve, in some of the old British trenches, east of Monchy-le-Preux. During the course of the day, the 39th machine-gun Battalion was attached to the division and, in turn, was attached to the Provisional Brigade as a part of the flank guard.

Upon completion of the relief, the 4th Division continued the advance. During that advance, the Provisional Brigade carried out a brilliant action against a body of entrenched enemy, resulting in the capture of several prisoners and nine artillery batteries, each of four guns. Two of those guns were only 500 yards behind the front line, to fire on any advancing tanks. The prisoners belonged to the 71st Field Artillery Regiment (35th Division) and information supplied by them fully described the condition of the division. The 61st Regiment consisted of three seriously under strength companies and was no longer considered a regiment, while the 176th Regiment was completely exhausted.

Patrols continued to maintain contact with the retiring enemy throughout the night and the following day, the 30th. As the advance continued, the leading battalions approached one of the many natural waterways, Trinquis Brook, behind which lay Sailly-en-Ostrevent[383].

---

[382] *The movement of such a large body of troops by vehicle close to the front line was assisted largely by the fact that the Allied air forces had mastered the skies above the battlefield with the introduction of new models of fighter aircraft. That factor permitted considerable daylight movements, which would have been impossible several months before.*

[383] *Sailly-en-Ostrevent lay in a large bend of the Trinquis Brook (River on some maps) which flowed along the southern edge of the village in a westerly direction and turned abruptly north, 500 yards to the west of the town. The village was very heavily de-*

The village represented a fortified obstruction on the left flank of the division while, 1500 yards further to the south, lay the similarly fortified town of Etaing, in front of which lay the Sensée River[384]. With the support of the machine guns of the Composite Brigade, the 10th Brigade crossed the Trinquis Brook and managed to occupy the village after particularly difficult hand-to-hand fighting. Once the village had been secured, the Composite Brigade was relieved by the 33rd Brigade (11th Division) and rejoined its parent division.

As the 4th Division emerged from Sailly-en-Ostrevent, the front line was subjected to intense shelling, which inflicted a considerable number of casualties upon the two front line brigades. The 2nd Duke of Wellington's and the 1st Royal Warwickshire Regiment (10th Brigade) were assembling to pursue the advance when the bombardment landed in amongst the massed companies. It was, however, necessary to continue and the brigades, still recovering from the confusion, resumed the advance at 4:00pm, under the cover of an artillery barrage. The advance secured a line from St. Servins F^m, 700 yards east of Haucourt, to the northern edge of Eterpigny Wood, while securing nearly one hundred and fifty prisoners from two different divisions. However, the latest advance had produced a sharp salient in the line and, because of the risk of an attack being made against it, the salient was evacuated during the evening.

Information given by the prisoners indicated that one of the two divisions facing the 4th Division, the 58th Division, was exhausted and of poor quality with an average battalion strength, in the 103rd Reserve Infantry Regiment, as little as 50 men per company. Also facing the 4th Division was the 4th Ersatz Division, which had just arrived at the front and consisted of the 360th, 621st and 214th Reserve Infantry Regiments, all very weak and with company strengths of about sixty men[385]. The 1st Guard Reserve Division, also very weak, had just arrived in the area[386].

---

fended, but could be attacked from the west and the south and was subjected to accurate shelling from both of those directions.

[384] The Sensée River should not be confused with Canal de la Sensée, which lies about five miles to the west of Etaing.

[385] The 4 Ersatz Division and two other divisions, the 20 and 12 Reserve Divisions, which were currently behind the front line, had faced the 4 Division in the area of the Bois Du Pacaut earlier in the year.

[386] The 1 Guards Division had also met the 4 Division in Pacaut Wood only weeks before.

It became clear in the interviews that the enemy intended to stand on the Drocourt – Quéant line.

Based on that information, orders were issued, on the 31ˢᵗ August, for an attack to be made upon the German lines on the immediate front. The Drocourt - Quéant line, sometimes referred to as the Drocourt – Quéant Switch, consisted of two heavily wired trench systems, joined by communication trenches that ran to the rear. The whole system included deep dugouts, capable of holding many troops, each of which had direct access to the firing line. Like the Hindenburgh line, it was intended to act as a barrier against an Allied advance and allow Germany to retain the territorial gains that lay behind.

The Allies were well aware that it represented the last entrenched and organised line of resistance upon which the German Army could stand. It was understood that, once the Drocourt – Quéant line had been penetrated, it would help precipitate a general withdrawal from the entire Western Front, leaving few strategic points upon which a stand could be made, west of the Rhine River. The German High Command was also aware of the fact that if it could resist any attack on that line for the next six to eight weeks, the winter would prevent any further Allied offensive action until the spring of 1919. The strategic importance of the Drocourt – Quéant line and the remainder of the Hindenburgh line was clear in the minds of both sides.

The 4ᵗʰ Division was to carry out the attack on the left of the Canadian Corps, in company with the 11ᵗʰ British Division and the 4ᵗʰ Canadian Division, on the left and right respectively. The objectives, as in most offensives, were lines of tactical importance drawn on the area map and for the purposes of attack, were indicated by the Red, Green, Blue and Brown lines. The Red line represented the support line of the Drocourt – Quéant line.

The 4ᵗʰ Division was to attack and hold the first three of those lines on a total frontage of 2400 yards. It was to avoid the village of Etaing until the Red line had been secured. Thereafter, the division was to concentrate its attention upon Etaing, by attacking from the south and the south-west. Once Etaing had been engaged, the reserve brigade was to pass through the leading brigades and advance to the Green and Blue lines, the high ground overlooking the Sensée River[387].

---

[387] *The Sensée River flowed on a north-westerly path in front of Etaing and then turned to the south-east in a large curve, in which Etaing was located. This meant that the troops of the 4 Division had to cross the Sensée in order to attack Etaing and then continue to the second crossing of the same river, some two and half miles to the east.*

The reserve brigade of the 4th Division, once through the Red Line, was to adopt a rather informal attack by concentrating small units onto any centres of resistance on the high ground and the smaller villages. While those areas were thus engaged, the remainder of the brigade was to get across the Sensée River and capture the village of Lécluse, several miles to the east.

Lécluse lay on the western bank of the Sensée and was protected by the heavily fortified Bois de Lécluse. Immediately behind the village lay a wide expanse of the Sensée River, mainly marsh, with large deep pools. The Blue line lay on the high ground on the eastern bank of the river overlooking Hamel[388] and the sloping ground to the east and was contained within the next loop of the river. The line was to be held in such a manner that would prevent any of the enemy from getting across the river from east or west.

While the 4th Division was thus engaged, the 4th Canadian Division was to storm the line next to the 4th Division and, once through, was to spread out, with its right on the Arras – Cambrai Road. It was intended that the 11th Division should participate in the formal attack, but was to swing its right flank in line with the advance of the 4th Division to create a flank guard.

In preparation for the attack, the 12th Brigade was to relieve the 11th Brigade on the 1st of September, which, in turn, would act as the reserve brigade. The whole attack was to be carried out under the cover of a creeping barrage, incorporating a considerable quantity of smoke shells. The two attacking brigades were to be supported by sixteen tanks, eight to each and it was made perfectly clear that, should a delay occur with the tanks, the infantry was to continue, regardless.

Just prior to the commencement of the attack, information gathered from recently captured prisoners clarified the position of the German forces opposing the 4th Division. The German 46th Division had been broken up and the troops distributed amongst various other divisions. The 4th Ersatz Division had received some of those reinforcements, bringing the battalion strengths up to about fifty men. The line was being held by the 4th Ersatz and the 26th Reserve Division, both seriously under strength.

---

[388] *Not to be confused with the village of Hamel, on the Ancre River, in which the division had been severely handled by the German artillery in late 1915.*

The attack had been planned for the 2nd September and, in the interim, the 10th and 12th Brigades were participating in constant offensive patrolling. At 2:30pm on the 31st, the 2nd Duke of Wellington's attempted to retake St. Servins Fm. However, the attack failed under heavy machine-gun fire, emanating from the farm buildings. A second attack was organised, again by the Duke of Wellington's, this time assisted by the Seaforth Highlanders. That second attempt was successful, resulting in the capture of the farm and a large area of surrounding ground, including a sunken road south of Eterpigny. Also captured in the attack was two officers, fifty-four other ranks and eight machine guns. The location reached by that attack carried with it the advantage of placing the 12th Brigade largely on the 'jumping off' line for the forthcoming attack on Etaing. That night, the plan of attack was altered, due to the number of casualties incurred in recent days.

September - 1918

In order that the advance could be conducted on a narrower front, the Canadian 1st Division took over a part of the 4th Division line in the early hours of 1st September, by extending across the Arras - Cambrai road. While the reorganisation was underway, the 12th Brigade relieved the 11th Brigade. The casualty rate and the lack of reinforcements had seriously weakened the 4th Division. So serious was the problem that difficulties were experienced when the right flank of the 10th Brigade was not able to establish contact with the left flank of the Canadians. The only solution was to have the 10th Canadian Brigade relieve the 10th Brigade on the right of the division line.

During the morning of the 1st, patrols had continued to penetrate the German outpost line, resulting in the capture of a further four officers, fifty-three other ranks and three machine guns. Information given by the prisoners revealed that the front trench of the Drocourt – Quéant line was the most heavily defended and contained very deep dugouts, each capable of holding about twenty men while the lines to the rear had been badly damaged by artillery fire and were only lightly held.

The demands upon the Canadians were as serious as those on the 4th Division and a last minute reorganisation occurred at 6:45pm on the 1st, when the 11th Brigade took over the right-flank responsibilities from the Canadian 10th Brigade. That meant that the division was to carry out the attack with the 12th Brigade on the left and the 11th Brigade on the right. The 12th Brigade had also been allocated the additional task of capturing the village of Etaing. It was the intention that, while the 12th Brigade was thus employed, the 11th Brigade would to continue the advance to the Green line, the final objective. The much-battered 10th Brigade was to remain as reserve to the two forward brigades. The final date and time for the attack had been confirmed as 4:55am on the 2nd.

At 5:00am on the 2nd September, the 11th and 12th Brigades advanced under the cover of a rolling barrage and, by a little after 6:00am, the King's Own (12th Brigade) had occupied the first two enemy trenches, having taken one prisoner in the first line and fifty in the second. By 6:30am, the Canadians had occupied Dury. The fact that the prisoners were from a combination of divisions, the 360th and 362nd Infantry Regiments (4th Ersatz Division), the 28th Infantry Regiment (6th Division) and the 15th Reserve Infantry Regiment (26th Reserve Division)[389]

---

[389] *This indicated that the opposing Divisions were so weak as to require several Divisions to hold a front equivalent to one British brigade.*

revealed the extent of the weakness of the enemy facing the attacking brigades. Statements from the prisoners indicated that the morale of the opposing enemy had totally collapsed.

At 7:45am, German tanks were seen moving along the Arras – Cambrai Road, where the second defensive trench crossed, but presented no problems to the troops, then moving around Moulins Damiens, on the southern flank. The advance was temporarily checked at the 3rd line, as the enemy had received reinforcements but, with the assistance of tanks, each searching for targets, the opposition was soon overcome. By 9:00am, contact aircraft had confirmed that the first objective had been taken and that troops were occupying the ground further to the north. The Rifle Brigade had also made very good progress but encountered heavy machine-gun fire from Prospect F^m.

By noon, the advance stood on a line, which extended from a point 700 yards south of Dury, around the eastern outskirts of that village to a point approximately 1500 yard to the north. Having broken through the Drocourt – Quéant line, the attacking brigades had captured thirty-one officers and one thousand and forty two other ranks but there re-mained parts of the line, which defied all attempts at capture. A stretch of trench of about 1300 yards due north of Dury and sections of the support line behind and 600 yards to the east were held in strength. The artillery had offered to shell any part of the line upon request and those strong points were nominated. Following an intense bombard-ment and equally intense fighting, the recalcitrant trenches were cap-tured. Because of that fighting, the units of the leading brigades were mixed up and before continuing, a reorganisation was required.

When completed, the 12th Brigade then turned its attention to the vil-lage of Etaing while the 11th Brigade completed the capture of isolated points of resistance. Located on the extreme left flank of the brigade, Etaing lay on the southern bank of the Sensée River and the Germans had applied much effort to its fortification. In its efforts to capture the village, the 12th Brigade struggled against heavy machine-gun and artil-lery fire throughout the afternoon and evening, resulting in only partial capture of the town. The 11th Brigade also experienced similar difficul-ties clearing the remaining trench line to the south-east of Etaing, but the fighting diminished as darkness fell.

The two brigades were instructed to recommence the attack at 5:00am on the next morning, the 3rd and arrangements were completed with the artillery to support that attack. Several hours before the scheduled attack, the 11th Brigade was instructed to withhold its attack on the trenches until the 12th Brigade had secured Etaing, but was to continue, should the enemy attempt to withdraw.

On schedule, the artillery barrage fell and the 12th Brigade advance began. By 6:00am, the 2nd Essex reported, through the artillery Forward Observation Officer, that Etaing had been cleared. Shortly after, the remains of the village were subjected to a heavy German gas bombardment. Prisoners captured in the attack revealed that the German Army was in the process of carrying out a major withdrawal on that part of the Canadian Corps front. As a result, the 11th Brigade continued the advance immediately.

By 7:00am, demolition explosions were again heard behind the German lines, one of them being the bridge between Tortéquenne and Lécluse nearly two miles to the north-east of the start line. As those explosions were occurring, the two leading brigades were approaching Lécluse and signs of the enemy withdrawal were abundant. The observation balloons, which had been a feature of the landscape for some time, had been withdrawn a considerable distance. Empty trenches and sundry equipment lay scattered about and the destruction of all tactical points, bridges, road junctions, railways and many buildings had been demolished.

By 8:00am, the division headquarters was again on the move. The Canadians had reached Récourt, nearly five thousand yards from the original start line, having captured seventy seven prisoners and occupied the Bois de Récourt, due north of the village. The 4th Division had matched the Canadians step-for-step, but difficulties were then encountered. The rapid advance of the forward troops of the fighting brigades, the associated headquarters were left well behind and communications between the two, being so far stretched, often failed altogether. The only voice communications was by telephone and the fire of the German artillery and the forward movement of the division artillery, continually cut the lines.

By mid-morning, the Somerset Light Infantry had entered Lécluse, but were subjected to the fire of a single German 77mm field gun, firing over open sights, from Tortéquenne, on the northern bank of the river. Having reached that point, the division was notified that it would be relieved by the 1st Canadian Division that night. Because the advancing battalions had again become mixed up, it was found easier to relieve the troops in a particular area rather than by battalion. The division was now approaching the Canal de la Sensée, some four thousand yards in front and could clearly hear the demolition of the bridges over the canal and the associated waterways.

Between 4-5:00pm on the 3rd, the 11th and 12th Brigades were relieved by the Canadians, and travelled by bus to the area about Monchy Breton, twenty miles east of Lens. Congratulations poured into the division headquarters from First army, Fifth army and the Canadian Corps. The G.O.C. visited the badly battered 10th Brigade and paid special thanks to the Rifle Brigade (11th Brigade) for their outstanding efforts.

The following two weeks was fully occupied with re-equipping, re-training for open warfare and absorbing new reinforcements. During that period, exhausted as the troops were, there existed a subdued optimism about the possibility of the war coming to and end and, for the first time in four years, there was a consensus that the German Army had been broken. While the division had been resting, the Canadian Corps had crossed the Canal de la Sensée, the last major defensive position before the Canal Du Nord, approximately ten miles to the east.

On the 15th September, the 4th Division received orders to return to the front line, this time with the XXII (British) Corps, which had been fighting to the north of the Canadians, between the Scarpe Canal and the Sensée River. The XXII Corps had not progressed as far as the Canadians because of a later starting date and had only advanced at the rate of the German withdrawal but was yet to participate in a formal attack upon the retiring enemy.

The 4th Division was to assume its position in the line on the northern bank of the Sensée River, opposite the point from which it had previously commenced the advance on the 2nd of the month, opposite Etaing. On the 18th, the 10th Brigade moved forward by bus and relieved the 167th Brigade (56th Division) the 11th Brigade relieved the 33rd Brigade (11th Division), effectively taking over the centre of the XXII Corps line.

It is necessary to understand the area in which the 4th Division was then located, before pursuing the narrative of subsequent events. The division faced east with its right, or southern flank, on the northern bank of the Sensée River and its left, or northern flank, resting on the southern bank of the Scarpe Canal. Located on the extreme right flank and 400 yards in front of the line, lay the village of Sailly-en-Ostrevent, still in German hands. On the extreme left flank and sitting astride the Scarpe Canal lay Vitry-en-Artois. The ground between the two villages, upon which the front line was located, was part way up a ridge of high ground crested by several hills. The reverse slope descended for a distance of 5,500 yards to the Canal De La Sensée, which directly intersected the line of advance.

The two canals, the Sensée and the Scarpe joined on what was to be the left flank of the division when it finally reached the Sensée Canal. Like so many of the rivers of northern France, the Sensée River, which constituted the southern boundary of the division, followed a large winding course, sometimes with several miles between the peak of one bend and the trough of the next. Lying in the intervening country between the Sensée River and the Scarpe Canal lay several small villages, typical of the quiet rural French countryside. The 4th Division stood in the western corner of a large triangle, the apex of which pointed to the north. The River Sensée and its tributaries, the River Trinquis and the Trinquis Brook, representing the base of the triangle, while the Scarpe Canal and the Canal De La Sensée representing the converging sides.

The expectation of an enemy withdrawal was central to all planning. On the 21st of September, instructions were issued to all divisions of XXII Corps, advising what course of action was to be taken in the event of such a withdrawal. Special emphasis was placed on small search parties of Royal Engineers, attached to the advancing infantry, with the responsibility for clearing out deep dugouts, cellars, houses and crossroads of booby-traps. To assist with advanced exploitation, ahead of the advancing divisions, a troop of XXII Corps Cavalry was attached to division headquarters.

The few days following the arrival of the division were spent establishing the exact location of the front and, during that period, the division experienced intermittent shelling with Blue Cross gas. The days were inactive until the 24th when, at 2:00am, a party of about thirty of the enemy raided an outpost located to oversee the Pont de Vaches, a bridge over the Trinquis River, between Valley Wood, to the north and Sailly-en-Ostrevent. During the raid, the Lewis gun of the outpost garrison jammed and, after some stiff fighting, the garrison party withdrew, leaving three wounded in enemy hands.

A second attempt was made by a party of about ten Germans but they were driven off, leaving a wounded prisoner, believed to belong to the 10th Company, 3rd Battalion, 36th Reserve Infantry Regiment (214th Division). No further raids were attempted and the day passed quietly. The nocturnal prowling of the patrols, at which the troops were so adept, took many of them into the enemy outpost line. A patrol of the 1st Hampshire Regiment met an outpost, killed four of the occupying party and returned with valuable information about the state of the opposing defences.

In an effort to keep the enemy alert and unsure of British intentions, arrangements were made to carry out a 'chinese attack' at 5:35am on the 27th. The purpose was to establish in the enemy, a sense of being attacked, without revealing the point of attack. Arrangements were made for extensive smoke screens, created largely by the use of captured smoke canisters and an artillery bombardment to be carried out on the German front line, south of Vitry-en-Artois. Use was also made of 100 dummies, to be shown above the parapet during the 'attack' so that, under the cover of the distraction, the engineers could throw a bridge across the Trinquis Brook, a tributary of the Trinquis River, south-east of Biache St. Vaast.

At the prescribed time, the artillery laid the smoke screen and the barrage. The whole demonstration lasted for about an hour and attracted a certain amount of fire, most of which soon died down. The remaining few days of September were spent quietly.

October - 1918

October commenced as September had closed, quietly. During the evening of the 1st, a soldier of the British 63rd (Naval) Division, who had been held as a prisoner of war in Sailly-en-Ostrevent, entered the lines of the 4th Division, after having escaped. Due to his imprisonment he was not able to offer any valuable information except that Sailly contained very few of the enemy, which supported the fact most the shelling that took place intermittently was delivered by long-range guns and enemy aircraft, which dropped bombs during the night.

Considerable activity had been seen along the Tortéquenne – Hamel Road throughout the next day and, as the days passed, the enemy in front of the 4th Division became increasingly active, with minor raids and patrol actions becoming more frequent. Although most of the attempts were successfully driven off, it was evident that the whole German line was sparsely held. The subject of peace was on the lips of all and the proposal for ending the war, sent to the United States by the German Government, was common knowledge within the ranks.

Such was the fluid situation on the British front that the 4th Division was made aware that it was required elsewhere. At 4:00pm on the 11th, division headquarters received a warning to be prepared to move the next day, to the area about Bourlon Notre Dame, five miles west of Cambrai. While immediate arrangements we made to transport the 10th and 11th Brigades by bus to the area about Fontaine Notre Dame, the 12th Brigade travelled to the area north-east of Cambrai, between the Cambrai – Saulzoir Road and the Canal de l'Escaut.

The reason for the move was to relieve the 49th Division and, in preparation for an expected counter-attack against that division, the 10th Brigade was placed on two hours notice to act in support. The division, still in 1st Army reserve, commenced moving forward on the 13th and arrived in the Cambrai area about midday. During the course of the next day, tragedy befell the division.

The G.O.C., 4th Division, Major-General Lipsitt and his staff had gone forward to carry out a reconnaissance. Accompanied by the G.O.C, 12th Brigade, Brigadier-General MacNaughter and an officer of the 49th Division, the party proceeded to reconnoitre the front line. Well forward of the outpost line, Major-General Lipsitt was struck in the face by a machine-gun bullet as he was crawling down a slope to view the crossing of the River Selle between, Haspres and Saulzoir. He managed to stagger back to a wood but died almost immediately. Consequently, Brigadier-General MacNaughter, the senior Brigadier, assumed temporary command of the division[390].

Since the commencement of the offensive in August, the advance had thrust at different points along the British and French fronts. The principle of the overall offensive had been to draw the ever-diminishing enemy reserves to the point of the line that was under attack and, as the resistance grew, to strike elsewhere along the front, with the same objective in mind. Accordingly, the XXII Corps had been acting in concert with the headquarters of the First Army, north of Cambrai.

The combined effects of the multiple blows of the Second, Third, Fourth and Fifth Armies, supplemented by the naval blockade of German ports, had culminated in a diminishing of the ability of the German Army to maintain a substantial resistance anywhere along the entire Western Front. The French and American armies had been striking, in much the same manner, for some time in the Champagne region with a cumulative effect.

The time had now arrived for a general advance by all Allied armies with the objective of concluding the war. The 4th Division was to advance on the right of the XVII corps front, with the 51st Division on its left and 19th Division on the its right. Those divisions had worked closely together since 1916 and were well practiced in cooperation.

During the night of the 17th, the 4th Division relieved the 49th with the 10th and 11th Brigades taking over the right and left of the line respectively. Operation Order No.167 was issued instructing the division to continue the advance, the objective of the attack being the crossing of the River Selle by XXII Corps while acting as the left flank guard to the XVII Corps, which was responsible for the main thrust of the attack.

The 4th Division, advancing on a frontage of approximately 3,500 yards, was to cross the River Selle, which ran along the western boundaries of Saulzoir and Hastres, capture both towns and then continue in a north-easterly direction to take and hold the high ground, approximately 1000 yards beyond. The 10th Brigade, being on the right of the

---

[390] *The funeral of Major-General Lipsitt, CB, CMG, took place at Quéant at 3:00pm. The arrangements for the funeral were made by the 3ʳ Canadian Division, which he had commanded for two and a half years. Among those present were G.O.C., 1ˢ Army, G.O.C., Canadian Corps, G.O.C, XXII Corps, and representatives of the 4th Division, Canadian Corps, 3ʳ Canadian Division and Major, H.R.H, The Prince of Wales. Brigadier-General C.H.T. Lucas, D.S.O., C.M.G, Royal Berkshire Regiment and Inspector of Military Units, arrived to take command of the Division.*

division line, was allocated the task of capturing Saulzoir and the 11th Brigade was to take Haspres.

Some 3000 yards to the east of the River Selle, in the area of Avesnes-le-Sec, the division faced several difficulties in the approach to the start line. The attacking brigades had to advance for that distance and cross the river whilst under fire from the villages and surrounding area. The Selle was a relatively wide watercourse that followed a twisting, serpentine course across the line of advance. It flowed directly in front of Saulzoir, where it bounded the western edge of the town and then continued north, where it flowed through the middle of Haspres. The river was thought to be heavily defended, as was the railway line embankment, which followed the course of the river, crossing it midway between the towns. The approach was relatively flat for the first 1000 yards, then descended a gradual decline for a further 1000 yards, then rose to a low ridge, from where it further descended to the riverbank. At the base of the first slope lay Montrécourt Wood, in front of and about mid way between Haspres and Saulzoir.

Zero hour was set for 12:30am on the 20th for the 11th Brigade and 2:00am for the 10th. Delays prevented the 11th Brigade advance but, at 2:00am, the 10th Brigade rose from the trenches and advanced quickly down the slope behind a rolling barrage, crossed the Selle and took Saulzoir, immediately pushing on and occupied the high ground behind, all without opposition or casualty. Due to the ease with which the assault was carried out and that Haspres was also unoccupied, the advance of the 11th Brigade was delayed until later in the afternoon. When the advance was executed the brigade walked the distance and occupied its objectives without a barrage or a single casualty. Orders were issued immediately for the division to push forward and occupy a line of outposts on the forward slopes west of the River Ecaillon, which carried the division line some 8,000 yards further forward, clearing the deserted village of Verchain in the process.

On the 21st, patrols continued to push forward and the whole division followed, discovering that bridges over the River Ecaillon had been destroyed and only meeting resistance about Monchaux-sur-Ecaillon, where they ran into machine-gun fire from the railway embankment, 1000 yards to the north of the village. The division was advancing at such a pace that the 11th Brigade had lost contact with the 51st Division, which was fighting its way through a series of villages, south-west of Valenciennes. The 10th Brigade had also lost touch with the 19th Division, which was engaged south of the Chaussée Road.

The division approached the southern outskirts of Valenciennes, and the enemy was withdrawing quickly, leaving only small pockets of resistance. The late hour of the day brought the division to a halt just west of the River Ecaillon, where night positions were taken up and orders issued, a rapid crossing of the river be necessary. The casualties for the day amounted to forty-eight all ranks.

A brief mention should be made here as to the nature of the advance. By necessity, in a narrative of a division in action, the focus is generally on the forward fighting troops and the conflicts and difficulties that they experience. The fighting brigades generally had time to pause while waiting for the artillery and other services to follow, or for the flanking divisions to draw up in line. However, the artillery, ammunition columns, ambulances and a considerable number of other branches struggled day and night with tasks involved in rebuilding river crossings, repairing mined road junctions, and clearing streets and roads for the transport to get the heavy loads forward. All of this was performed, quite often, whilst under enemy machine-gun and artillery fire. The supply of hot food presented never ending difficulties as the troops, especially those manning outposts and forward patrols, were often considerable distances ahead of the main body.

Preparations began in the early hours of the 22nd for a continuation of the advance. Initially, the objective was the capture of Monchaux and the securing of a line 2000 yards north-east of that village. The preparations for the attack on Monchaux were finalised and, as a result, the final line of advance was extended to include the capture of Quérénaing, 4000 yards due east of Monchaux, on the right of the advance. As the advance was to progress, the division front was to narrow substantially, to about 3000 yards. The time of the attack was set for 4:00am on the 24th, before which the 19th Division, on the right of the 4th, was relieved by the 61st Division.

At zero hour, the barrage came down exactly as scheduled and the two leading brigades moved forward, in line with 51st and 61st Divisions. Little opposition was met and the River Ecaillon was crossed, partly by using bridges and partly by swimming. By 6:00am, the first objective, the eastern bank of the river from Monchaux, on the left, to Sommaing, on the right was secured. The second objective, the high ground north-east of Monchaux and Verchain was taken at about midday and by day's end the line rested before Quérénaing, having captured 800 prisoners of the 10th Ersatz and 11th Divisions. The division had suffered approximately 500 casualties, mainly due to machine-gun and artillery fire and congratulations from the Corps Commander were received during the evening.

During the night of the 24th, the 12th Brigade again took over the line and, because of the narrow front, relieved both front line brigades, although the 10th Brigade maintained a flank guard on the right flank until the 61st Division had caught up. The enemy retreat had now become a route and all divisions found that the pace of advance quite unrelenting. The policy, passed from the Commander-in-Chief, to corps and division headquarters, was to remain in contact with the enemy with advanced patrols and to carry out the assault wherever resistance was met. The instructions to the 12th Brigade stated that, should the advance proceed satisfactorily, the reserve battalion to the brigade should pass through and continue the exploitation.

The following morning found the 12th Brigade on the move, under a protective barrage and successfully occupied Delfericiere F[m] and the village of Quérénaing. Having faced little opposition, all objectives were taken by late morning and, as the afternoon progressed, the 12th Brigade received instructions for new objectives. As each new line was reached, a new objective was set. Following that procedure, the advance continued quickly, so quickly indeed, that once the 4th Division had reached the Valenciennes – le Quesnoy Railway, further forward movement ceased, to allow the 61st Division, which was also advancing quickly, to catch up. As the two divisions met at the railway, a large body of Germans pressed a counter-attack against the front line but the effort was repulsed with heavy fire.

Following the attack, the 12th Brigade was required to take and hold the high ground overlooking the River Rhonelle, on the line of the Artres – Famars Road. Once that line had been reached, it was to send patrols across the river and secure a bridgehead for the crossing of the remainder of the division. However, the brigade had suffered casualties in the advance and during the night of the 25th it remained on the line of the railway where much re-organisation was undertaken.

Badly needed hot meals and ammunition was brought forward and the wounded evacuated. At 10:00am on the following morning, the advance resumed and, by early afternoon, had reached the Artres – Famars Road and patrols immediately cleared the intervening ground. Two platoons of the Lancashire Fusiliers crossed, under light fire and took the high ground on the east bank. That secured the bridge over the River Rhonelle, situated on the eastern end of Artres, with an outpost of the Lancashires.

The 12th Brigade now overlooked the town of Présau, which lay in a low valley astride the Jenlain – Aulnoy Road and on the Eau de Saméon stream. In an effort to regain the heights above Présau, a large body of German infantry counter-attacked, forcing the Lancashires off the ridge and back to the bridgehead. The attack failed to penetrate the line around the bridge, although the brigade line, from the bridge to the left flank, which was held by the 2nd Essex, was heavily shelled with gas. The attack also concentrated on the leading brigade of the 51st Division, to the left of the 4th.

The weight of the attack on that division was heavy enough to push the front line back to the railway line, although the ground was recovered during the evening. The 12th Brigade had suffered 250 casualties during the course of the days fighting, about 50 of them as result of the gas shelling. The days advance had also taken heavy toll of the enemy, with the capture of six officers and eighty three men of the 76th Reserve Infantry Regiment (111th Division) and three hundred and sixty nine men of the 369th and 371st Reserve Infantry Regiments (10th Ersatz Division).

The 12th Brigade received the congratulations of the corps and division commanders, who informed all three brigades that they would not be immediately required to carry out any further operations for securing additional ground east of the River Rhonelle. As the division stood stationary astride the Rhonelle the neighbouring 61st Division subjected Artres, on the extreme right flank of the 4th Division, and the high ground beyond, to an intense artillery bombardment to discourage any further attempt at counter-attacks[391].

To assist the much-weakened 12th Brigade to hold and consolidate the gains, two companies of the 11th Brigade were placed at the disposal of the 12th and assisted in the final clearing of the ground, which sloped down to the western side of the river. To this end several strong patrols were sent out during the course of the 26th, returning with several prisoners who had concealed themselves in the earlier attack.

For any further advance to take place, it was essential that the bridgehead be expanded to allow a crossing of the entire division. To assist with this task troops of the 61st Division had been passed over the bridge and extended to the right for 1000 yards to secure ground for the passage of that division. Whilst the 4th and 61st Divisions were undertaking the broadening of the bridgehead the 51st Division was again

---

[391] *It was exactly this point that Lieutenant-Colonel Montgomery had reached, in his reconnaissance on the 25 August 1914, while trying to find the advancing Germans.*

subjected to a second counter-attack, which drove its advanced troops out of Famars, although intense close quarter fighting saw the village back in the hands of the 51st by late morning.

The German command had decided to stand on the Rhonelle River and, during the afternoon of the 26th, subjected the entire corps line to very heavy gas shelling. Not withstanding the show of resistance, the patrols were not to be denied and approached the high ground east of Artres, while patrols of the 61st Division approached from the west. That action surrounded a large number of the enemy who were located on the crest of the ridge. Prisoners were taken from the 76th Infantry Regiment (111th Division) and again from the 369th and 371st Reserve Infantry Regiments (10th Ersatz Division), with very little fighting.

Interrogation of the prisoners revealed that the company strength of the two opposing divisions had been reduce to about 30-40 men and had been seriously weakened as a result of the recent fighting. It was also stated that the divisions had been instructed to hold the line on the Rhonelle River, to allow time for the construction of defensive positions between Mons and Maubeuge, approximately 50 miles to the east. The constant moving and fighting had resulted in a large number of the troops of the 12th Brigade having occupied positions in the area of the 61st Division and units of that division were sent to relieve them. During the night of the 28th, the 11th Brigade moved forward and relieved the 12th Brigade while the 49th Division relieved the badly battered 51st Division.

As the relief was underway, Operation Order No. 4 arrived, detailing the recommencement of the offensive on the 30th October. The attack was to be carried out in conjunction with the 49th Division and was to capture Présau and the high ground to the north, with the intention of turning the eastern flank of the German defences in Valenciennes, 4000 yards to the north. Présau lay about 3,500 yards in front and the ground behind the village rose sharply to the crest of a hill overlooking the surrounding countryside and all roads leading to the north-east, towards Mons. It was these lines of communications that the XXII Corps desired to cut, possibly forcing the surrender of the town garrison.

The attack, to be carried out by the 11th Brigade, was to be covered by a rolling barrage delivered by nine brigades of artillery. Additional to the artillery fire, forty-eight guns of the machine-gun Battalion were to provide barrage fire, once the heights had been reached. Upon the capture of the high ground, patrols were to extend out immediately, with the aim of capturing the German artillery batteries thought to be in the area. In the early hours of the 30th the start date was postponed for two days, to the 1st November. It was on the 30th October that the troops learned of the signing of an armistice with Austria and Turkey.

November - 1918

At 5:15am on the 1st November, the barrage fell upon the German out-post line, on the eastern side of the Rhonelle River. Three minutes later the troops of the 11th Brigade, the Rifle Brigade on the right and Hampshire Regiment on the left, rose and attacked across the river, advancing upon Présau and, by 9:00am the village had been taken, with only minimal casualties. As the troops 'mopped up' the village, a heavy German counter-attack, in which the Rifle Brigade suffered consider-able casualties in close hand-to-hand fighting, forced the 11th Brigade to vacate the town.

That afternoon the brigade was forced further back to the Présau – Aulnoy Road, 500 yards west of Présau. The enemy attack on the 11th Brigade, including several tanks, extended to the south and confronted the leading brigades of the 61st and 49th Divisions. Such was the weight of the attack that many of the enemy troops penetrated the line of the 4th Division, only to find it difficult to withdraw due to fire from their rear. The confused fighting resulted in the capture of seven hundred and thirty of the enemy, all belonging to a mixture of regiments, the 214th (49th Division) and 111th (28th Reserve Division).

During the night, a battalion of the 10th Brigade moved from Saulzoir to positions behind the 11th Brigade and, in conjunction with King's Own (12th Brigade), was to attack on the morning of the 2nd and retake the objectives of the first assault. Subsequently, orders were issued that, following the attack and capture of the heights, the 11th Division would relieve the leading battalions.

At 5:30am on the 2nd, the 11th Brigade advanced and carried the line through Présau and eastward until, at 10:30am; the line lay 300 yards east of the village. The attack also extended for 3,000 yards to the north-west, having taken all of the high ground in a single movement. It was estimated that thirty-four officers and seven hundred and fifty other ranks were captured, among them two battalion commanders and three battalion staff officers of the 110th Reserve Infantry Regiment. The capture also included five guns and two tanks. Once established upon the ridge, the 11th Division completed the relief of the entire 4th Division.

The capture of Présau was to be last active engagement of the 4th Division. The 3rd and 4th of November saw the division resting and re-equipping in corps reserve, although the infantry brigades had to maintain the forward movement to remain in contact with the front line divisions. The troops did little more that march forward, behind the 11th Division as it maintained a steady advance. On the 7th the division signal section intercepted wireless messages from Germans and French sources that announced the arrival of the German delegates to discuss the terms of the armistice. Those messages had been intercepted on the division radios and forwarded to headquarters, which was unaware of the events.

Further wireless messages, passing between the German peace delegation and the German headquarters were intercepted, stating that the Allies had demanded a definite reply by Monday morning, the 11th November. The messages were intercepted in a continuous flow and on the 9th one of the message stated that Rittmeister Von Helldorf, the bearer of the Allied terms, had been delayed in crossing the German lines and was eventually despatched by aircraft. The fighting on the western front continued, with extensive advances being made along the whole line. The 4th Division continued to follow in the path of the 11th. Late on the 9th a wireless message was intercepted indicating that the end was near - the Kaiser had abdicated.

The engineers were required to move forward on the 9th to assist with the repairs to bridges over the Grand Honnelle, a distance of nearly forty miles north-west of the River Rhonelle, where the 4th Division had been relieved. The corps had advanced that distance in seven days marching, dragging guns, food, ammunition and a full range of other services needed for support.

On the 10th, the 4th Division was instructed to retire and concentrate in the area of Présau – Saultain – Curgies, south-west of Valenciennes, in the area of the its last offensive. Late on the 10th, a wireless message was intercepted stating that the German government had accepted the terms of the armistice, followed by a further message indicating that it had been signed at 5:00am on the 11th and was to come into force at 11:00am. The division had finished its war twenty-four hours before the armistice came into effect and, as that hour passed the battlefield fell silent.

Many words have been written about the hours following the 11:00am cease-fire. The end had been accepted in the home countries with great joy and celebration, but the troops on the front accepted the change from war to peace in a quiet state of reflection. Little celebration was to be seen - too much had passed.

1919 - Demobilisation

On the 12th November, instructions were received to the effect that the 4th Division, as a unit of XXII Corps, was to transfer to the 2nd Army and form a part of the force that was to move forward and occupy German territory. During the remainder of November, army life carried on. Time was spent in maintaining a schedule of training, cleaning, inspections, conferences and considerable effort was put into salvaging the detritus of war. For a short period, immediately after the cease-fire, the conduct of some troops deteriorated sufficiently to warrant the officers of the division taking special efforts to re-establish military discipline amongst the troops[392]. The division was also was kept occupied in preparing for several ceremonial parades and schedule of sports events.

Early in December, the instructions to prepare for departure to the 2nd Army were withdrawn and, instead of the entire division being sent to Germany, volunteers were called for and, once accepted, those men were transferred to the 2nd Army and incorporated into associated units. Several hundred men volunteered.

The civil authorities in the United Kingdom had given considerable thought to the planning for demobilisation as early as 1916 and wished to avoid the difficulties experienced in the demobilisation of soldiers following previous campaigns. A system of priority was established, based on length of service, civil occupation, marital status and those who wished to remain in the army[393].

The process of demobilisation of the 4th Division commenced almost at the time of the armistice coming into force and continued until completed in July of 1919. The rate of release averaged approximately one hundred and fifty per week and slowly the units decreased in size. For those who remained in France, waiting their turn to return home, the days were filled with regular route marches, training and cleaning. A very large part of each week was spent in competitive sports and assisting the local inhabitants to re-settle into their villages and farms.

The various brigades and battalions held dances, directed at maintaining friendly relations with the French population and much effort was

---

[392] *See Appendix VIII – 1918 'Orders about disorderly conduct 11 November 1918'.*

[393] *For a full description of the methods employed in demobilisation, see Appendix VIII -1918 'Demobilization and Reconstruction'.*

put into helping with the reconstruction of vital communications such as bridges, roads and railways. Christmas day saw the remaining troops of the brigades celebrate, amidst cold but fine weather, with a hearty evening meal, described by the diarist of the 11th Brigade as a 'good day'.

On the 6th January, the division moved to the area of Binche – La Louviere, east of Mons, where the troops settled down to billets and pleasant relations with the inhabitants. The area offered little opportunity for training as it consisted of mines, slag heaps and rural areas of winter crops. In February, the G.O.C., Major-General C. H. Tindall Lucas C.M.G., D.S.O., said farewell to the division and returned, along with most of the brigade commanders, to England. By the end of February the 4th Division stood at strength of six hundred and twenty-eight officers and three thousand, eight hundred and ten men. The slow process of demobilisation continued throughout the following months, interspersed with the presentation of awards, sports events and social activities. The last remaining cadres were transported from Boulogne in July, marking the end of the existence of the 4th Division as a fighting force.

Appendices
Introduction

The appendices contain many reports and operational orders issued before and after particular actions of the 4th Division. The information contained therein has been drawn directly from the original documents held within the diaries of the 4th Division and those of its associated brigades and battalions. Many of the reports were written by officers on the day of the event or within a short period after, as part of their reporting obligations, one exception being a report written as late as 1930, well after the action under discussion. The purpose of including the documents is to allow the reader to 'hear' the words of those who were directly involved in the actions describe herein.

The contents of the reports and orders have been transcribed in the exactly the same manner as they were originally typed or hand-written by the authors. Many contain typographical and grammatical errors, when compared to the grammar of today, and every attempt has been made to ensure that those errors of style have been retained in the transcription. Care has been taken to ensure that no errors have been introduced by the author, which could then be understood as being that of the original writer. However, the responsibility of any deviations from the original documents is entirely that of the author. I believe that the reports and orders transmit the mood and motives of the officers, both senior and junior and, with the wisdom of hindsight, it is most informative to read the words of the participants, many of which were written whilst still in the trenches.

The struggles undertaken by the 4th Division between the years of 1914 to 1919 are described in detail in the history above. During those years, something like 60,000 or more men passed through the ranks of the division, some to fall and others to return to a changed world and some to a life of fame and public recognition.

Throughout the course of the war the 4th Division was to have several Commanding Officers, of which Major- General T. D'O. Snow was the first. The next few pages are meant to give a brief profile of each the G.O.C.'s and the Brigade Commanders who commanded the 10th, 11th and 12th Brigades in those first hectic days and were later to become influential figures in their own right. As well as those destined to fame through a military career, there were those who were to gain international recognition for literary talent.

There were cases of those whose careers were extinguished and lost in a life of obscurity, those who made mistakes but survived to assume a higher level of achievement and, most notably, those who found fame, not with the sword, but with the pen. Some of the historic figures that were associated with the division through the course of the war are described herein; many are names now well known to history.

Author

Appendix I – Primary Sources

Headquarters	Diary
WO/1439-40 (1914)	General Staff
WO5/1441-43 (1915)	General Staff
WO5/1444-45 (1916)	General Staff
WO5/1446-47 (1917)	General Staff
WO5/1448 (1918-19)	General Staff

10th Brigade

WO5/1477 (1914)	Headquarters
WO5/1478 (1915-1916)	Headquarters
WO5/1479 (1916/1917)	Headquarters
WO5/1480 (1917-1919)	Headquarters
WO95/1481(1914-1916)	7th Argyle and Sutherland Highlanders Battalion & Household Battalion
WO5/1481 (1916-1919)	2nd Duke of Wellington Regiment
(1914-1916)	2nd Dublin Fusiliers Battalion
WO5/1482 (1914-1917)	1st Royal Irish Fusiliers
(1917-1918)	3/10 Middlesex Regiment
W05/1483 (1914-1919)	2nd Seaforth Highlander Battalion
W05/1484 (1914-1919)	1st Royal Warwickshire Regiment

11th Infantry Brigade

WO95/1495	1st Hampshire Regiment
WO95/1496	1st Rifle Brigade
WO95/1498	1st East Lancashire Regiment

12th Infantry Brigade

WO95/1505	2nd Essex Regiment
WO95/1505	2nd Royal Inniskilling Fusiliers
WO95/1507	2nd Lancashire Fusiliers

Divisional Units

WO95/1751	'B' Squadron 19th Hussars
WO95/1472 (1918-1919)	4th Battery Machine Gun Corps
WO95/1473 1914-1919)	10th Field Ambulance

Appendix II – Commanding Profiles
Major-General Thomas D'Oyly Snow, KCB, KCMG.

Thomas D'Oyly Snow was born in Newton Valence, Hampshire, on the 5th May 1858 and was educated at Eton and Cambridge. Upon graduation, he enlisted in the 1st Battalion, 13th Regiment of Foot (Prince Albert's Somerset Light Infantry) as a 2nd Lieutenant. He joined the battalion in Zululand in 1879 as a part of the British Relief Force where he participated in the deciding actions against the Zulu nation. In 1884-85, he was an officer in the Egyptian Expedition, which engaged in the unsuccessful effort to relieve Khartoum, in the Sudan, and save General Gordon. During that campaign, he fought at Abu Klea and El Gubat, where he was seriously wounded. In 1885, he was promoted to the rank of Captain, followed in 1887 by the appointment to the position of Adjutant of the 1st Battalion, Somerset Light Infantry, while based at Colchester.

In 1893, after serving with the 1st Battalion on Gibraltar, where he transferred to the 2nd Battalion, which was returning from Egypt, and attended the Staff College, Sandhurst, as a student. Upon graduation, he was posted to the Headquarters Staff of the Somerset Light Infantry. On the 1st May 1897, he was promoted to the rank of Major and transferred to the staff of the Inniskilling Fusiliers in Omagh, Ireland. By July 1898, he was a Brigade-Major on the staff of the Egypt Expeditionary Force, under General Kitchener, during which he fought at Athara, on the way to Khartoum. Following the Egyptian Expedition, he was promoted, in November 1898, to the rank of Lieutenant Colonel of the Royal Inniskilling Fusiliers.

From 1910-11, he commanded the 11th Infantry Brigade, 4th Division, with the rank of Brigadier-General and then assumed full command, as Major General, of the 4th Division from late 1911 to September 1914. It was under his command that the division went France, fought its first battle at Le Cateau, undertook the retreat from Mons, and participated in the advance of September 1914 over the river Marne. It was during the crossing of the Marne, on the 9th September, that Major-General Snow suffered a serious pelvic injury after being thrown from his horse. Following his recovery, he assumed command of the 27th Division in November of 1914, a command he retained until June 1915, and during which he was awarded the KCB. He led the 27th Division in some of the most violent fighting in the Second Battle of Ypres during April and May 1915 during which gas was introduced as an offensive weapon.

Following his departure from the 27th Division, he assumed command of VII Corps and was responsible for the attack on the northern end of the British line in the 1st July 1916 offensive, in front of Gommecourt. The VII Corps also participated in the Battle of Arras in April 1917 and the German counter attack at Cambrai in December 1917. It was during the tumultuous times of late 1917 that he received the KCMG for service rendered to the nation. He was promoted to Lieutenant General and assumed command of Western Command in the United Kingdom. From 1919–29 he held the post of Colonel of the Somerset Light Infantry regiment.

During the war Lieutenant-General Snow was affectionately known by two nicknames – 'slush' and the more familiar 'snowball', much favoured by his friend, Sir Henry Wilson. Like many wartime leaders, he was the subject of considerable criticism, some of which may not be justified. However, as the commander of troops during some of the largest and most intense battles of the Great War, criticism was unavoidable. He died on the 30th August 1940, during a later world crisis, and is buried in the Brookwood Cemetery, Surrey, United Kingdom.

Lieutenant-General Sir Aylmer Gould Hunter-Weston, K.C.B., D.S.O., O.St.J.

Aylmer Gould Hunter-Weston was born on the 23rd September 1864 in Edinburgh, Scotland, the son of and Jane (nee Hunter) and Lieutenant-Colonel Gould Weston. Although little is known of his years of education, he received a commission, as a Lieutenant, in the Royal Engineers on the 15th February 1884, at the age of nineteen. He was posted to the North West Frontier where participated in the 1st Miranzai Expedition in 1891 and, following promotion to the rank of Captain on the 1st April 1892, participated in the Waziristan Expedition of 1894/95 as the officer commanding two companies of Sappers and Miners. During that expedition he received a minor wound and was twice mentioned in despatches, published in the London Gazette on the 14th June and the 2nd July 1895. Further promotion soon followed and, on the 28th August 1895, he was promoted to Brevet Major.

Following his service in India, he was posted, for a period of seven months, between the 8th April 1896 and the 28th November 1896, in Egypt as a Staff Officer on special service on the staff of General Kitchener. During his stay he participated in the expedition to Dongola and saw action on the 7th July. As result of that action, he was again mentioned in despatches on the 3rd November 1896. His next posting was to South Africa, between the 11th July 1900 and 23rd September 1901, where he served as Deputy Assistant Adjutant General and Commander Royal Engineers. He later served as a Staff Officer to Lieutenant-General Sir John French, then commander of the Cavalry Division.

During his service in South Africa, between February and May 1900 he partook in the actions in relief of Kimberley, the Orange Free State at Paardeberg (17th – 26th February), Poplar Grove, Dreifontein, Karee Siding, Vet River (5th – 6th May) and the Zand River. His also participated in actions in the Transvaal and the Cape Colony, which earned him further mentions in despatches, Gazetted on the 4th May 1900 and the 8th February 1901.

He also returned to England, on the 5th September 1900, for an unknown period. The day after the completion of his service in South Africa, he received a promotion to Brevet Lieutenant-Colonel, on the 29th November 1900 and was awarded the Queen's Medal with seven clasps. He returned to England and assumed the role of General Staff Officer, Grade II (Deputy Assistant Adjutant General) at the headquarters of Eastern Command, IV Army Corps, between the 1st September 1904 and the 17th June 1908. It was in that period of time that he married Grace Strang-Steel, in 1905. On the 29th November 1906, he received a promotion to the rank of Brevet Colonel, confirmed on the 18th June 1908.

On that same day, he received an appointment as General Staff Officer, Grade I, in Headquarters, Scottish Command, a position he held until the 5th March 1911. He also inherited the title of 27th Laird of Hunterstone, following the death of his mother, Jane Hunter-Weston, that same year and made a member of the Order of the Bath.

On the 6th March he transferred to the War Office in London, as G.S.O. I., and became the Assistant Director of military training, a post he served until the 13th January 1914. On the 1st February of that year, he assumed the temporary rank of Brigadier-General and was appointed Commander of the 11th Brigade, 4th Division, a position he held until the 4th August when his promotion was confirmed. He remained with the 11th Brigade until the 12th March 1915. As the commander of the 11th Brigade, he travelled to France with the division on the 22nd August 1914. His brigade fought through the Battle of Le Cateau, the Retreat, the Battles of the Marne and Aisne, partook of the advance against Armentières and the Battle of Messines.

On the 29th October 1914 He received a promotion to the rank Major-General and assumed the command of the 29th Division, which fought a Cape Helles in the Dardenelles in 1915. In July of that year, he returned to the United Kingdom for a medical condition. He was promoted to the rank of Lieutenant-General on the 24th May 1916 and given the command of the VIII Corps, then on the Somme.

In October 1916, he contested and won the by-elections for the Scottish seat of North Ayrshire. He then entered the House Commons. Following the Armistice, Lieutenant-General Hunter-Weston resigned his commission in 1919 to continue his political career, which continued until 1935. Following an accident at his ancestral home, Hunterston, Ayrshire, he died on 18 March 1940

During the war he was mentioned in despatches on eight separate occasions, Gazetted on the 19th October and 30th November 1914, 6th July 1915, 6th January 1916, 4th January and 11th December 1917, 20th May and 20th December 1918. He had been awarded the Belgian Order of the Crown (2nd Class), The Legion of Honour (3rd Class), Belgian War Cross, 1914-14 Star and clasp and the British War Medal.

Lieutenant-General James Aylmer Lowthorpe Haldane D.S.O., C.B., K.C.B., Grand Officier de l'Ordre de la Couronne, Legion of Honour, Croix de Guerre (French and Belgian). O. St. J.

Born in Edinburgh, Scotland, on the 17th November 1862 to Doctor Daniel Rutherford Haldane and Mrs. Charlotte Elizabeth Haldane (nee Lowthorpe), James Aylmer Lowthorpe Haldane, was Educated at the Edinburgh Academy and Wimbledon. After graduating from the Royal Military College, Sandhurst he was commissioned as a Lieutenant in the Gordon Highlanders on the 9th September 1882.

Six years later, on the 1st September 1888, he was appointed to the position of Adjutant of the Gordon Highlanders, holding the posting until the 31st January 1892. Posted to India, He was promoted to Captain on the 8th April 1892 where he participated in the Waziristan Expedition, 1894-95 and in the relief operations in Chitral in 1895. Following those campaigns, he served as the Aide-de-Camp to Lieutenant-General Sir William Lockhart, between 1st April 1896 and 6th April 1898 during which he participated in the Tirah Expedition. During that expedition, he was present at the actions of Chagra Kotal and Dargai, and at the capture of the Sampagha and Arhanga Passes.

He also participated in the reconnaissance of the Saran Sar and the resultant action on the 9th November 1897, the actions around Dwatoi on the 24th of that same month. He saw further actions against the Khani Khel Chamkanis and the operations in the Bara and Bazar Valleys between the 7th and 30th December 1897. He was Mentioned in Despatches [London Gazette, 5th April 1898], received two clasps, and was created a Companion of the Distinguished Service Order [London Gazette, 20th May 1898] with "James Aylmer Lowthorpe Haldane, Captain, Gordon Highlanders. In recognition of services during the recent operations on the North-West Frontier of India". The Queen, at Windsor, presented the insignia to him on the 25th June 1898.

As the need for British to serve in South Africa arose in1899, he served with the 2nd Gordon Highlanders throughout the campaign. The events in which he participated were many, the first being the operations in Nepal. He took part in the operations at Elandslaagte (Natal) in 1899, where he was severely wounded and Laings Nek between the 6th and 9th June 1900. During the last half 1900, he fought in the Transvaal, east of Pretoria, between July and November 1900, and participated in the fighting at Belfast on 20th to 27th August and at Lydenberg, between the 5th and 8th September. He was mentioned in Despatches and Gazetted on the 8th February 1901. He received the Queen's Medal with four clasps.

Following the recent fighting, he was attached, as Staff Captain to the intelligence department of Army headquarters on the 27th June 1901. He was promoted to Major on the 23rd July 1902. Promotion came quickly and the following day, the 24th July 1902, he received a further promotion to the rank of Brevet Lieutenant-Colonel. He received a posting, on the 1st July 1903, to the position of Deputy Assistant Quartermaster General of intelligence, a responsibility he retained until 28th October 1906.

On the 11th February 1904, he was attached to the Japanese Army in Manchuria, during the Russo-Japanese campaign and received the Japanese War Medal and clasp, the Order of the Sacred Treasure, 3rd Class. Following his time with the Japanese, he received a further promotion, on the 11th January 1906, to Brevet Colonel with the temporary rank of Brigadier-General and was created a CB.

Between the 29th October 1906 and 23rd September 1909 he retained several positions at the Army Headquarters, that of Assistant Director of Military Operations, General Staff Officer, Grade 1 and General Staff Officer, Grade 1, at the War Office. On the 1st October 1909 he joined the General Staff, Eastern Command and on the 28th April 1912 took command of the 10th Brigade, 4th Division, a part of Eastern Command. When the 4th Division moved to France on the 23rd August 1914, Brigadier-General Haldane and his brigade suffered severely in the Battle of Le Cateau.

On the 28th November 1914, following his promotion to Major-General, he assumed command of the 3rd Division until the 8th August 1916, when took command of VI Corps. He finally received his promotion to Lieutenant-General on the 1st January 1919. From 1920 to 1922 he assumed the command of the British army in Mesopotamia and retired from the army in 1925. He died in 1950.

General Henry Seymour Rawlinson, 1st Baron Rawlinson of Trent, G.C.B., G.C.S.I., G.C.V.O, K.C.M.G.

Born in Trent Manor, Dorset on the 20th February 1864, son of soldier and diplomat Sir Henry Creswicke Rawlinson, Henry Rawlinson was educated at Eton and Sandhurst. He received a commission as Lieutenant in the Kings Royal Rifle Corps on the 6th February 1884, while in India. His first engagement was as Aide-de-Camp to the Commander-in-Chief in the East Indies, Lord Roberts, between the 28th November 1885 and to the 30th January 1890. During his stay in the India, he participated in the Myanmar expedition of 1886–87, during the Burma uprising.

During a period in the United Kingdom, was promoted to the rank of Captain on the 4th November 1891 and then transferred to the Coldstream Guards on 20th July 1892. Between the 19th November 1895 and the 1st January 1898 he acted as Brigade-Major at Aldershot. Shortly after, on the 24th January 1898, he was posted to Egypt where he acted as Deputy Assistant Adjutant General to the headquarters of General Kitchener during the advance and battle of Omdurman.

His appointment in Egypt concluded on the 21st October 1898 and was promoted to the rank of Major with the Coldstream Guards on the 25th January 1899 and received a Brevet of Lieutenant-Colonel, the next day. Promotion came quickly and, on the 26th June of the that same year he was promoted to Brevet Colonel and, on the 16th September, he was transferred, as Deputy Assistant Adjutant General, to the British Headquarters in Natal, South Africa. He held the post of D.A.A.G. until the 12th October 1902, when he was promoted to the position of Assistant Adjutant General, South Africa.

On the 1st April 1903, his rank of Colonel was confirmed and he was posted as Assistant Adjutant General for Military Education and Training a position he maintained until the 4th of December that same year. On the 5th December he assumed the position of Commander of the Staff College, Sandhurst where he remained until the 1st March 1907, when he was promoted to Brigadier–General and given command of the 2nd Infantry Brigade at Aldershot. Although he remained a brigade commander until the 9th August 1910, he had previously been promoted, on the 10th May of that year to the rank of Major-General.

Having completed his posting with 2nd Brigade, he assumed command of the 3rd Division, Southern Command, on the 1st June 1910, a posting in which he remained until the 31st May 1914. The day after Britain's declaration of war Major-General Rawlinson assumed the short-term responsibility of Director of Recruitment at the War Office, London, until the 19th September 1914. As a result of and accident suffered by the G.O.C., 4th Division, Brigadier-General H.F.M. Wilson (see above) had assumed the command of the Division. While Brigadier-General Wilson's command was being confirmed, Major-General Rawlinson assumed temporary command from the 21st September to the 4th October 1914, when he returned the command to the newly promoted Major-General Wilson.

On the day of his leaving the 4th Division appointment, Major-General Rawlinson received the temporary rank of Lieutenant-General and assumed command of IV Corps the following day, the 5th October 1914. He maintained the command of IV Corps until the 21st December 1915, was promoted to General on the 22nd December and assumed temporary command of 1st Army on the same day. Having expressed his opinions on the tactics used on the Western Front, he was transferred to Gallipoli to finalize the last of the British withdrawal from the peninsular.

Having succeeded beyond expectation, he was recalled to France and given the command of the 4th Army. He assumed that command on the 5th February 1916 until the 8th November 1917, in which time he participated in the Battle of the Somme and the subsequent actions in defence on the southern part of the British line. Between the 9th November 1917 and 18th February he commanded the British 2nd Army during the process of transferring to the Italian Front. Following the departure of the 2nd Army, General Rawlinson was assigned as the British Military Representative to the Supreme War Council at Versailles, France. That was soon followed up with the four-day command of the 5th Army on the 28th March, while waiting for General Birdwood to assume command.

Upon leaving the 5th Army, he assumed, again, the command of the 4th Army, a post in which he remained until 23rd March 1919. Following his return to England, he became the Aid-de-Camp to King George V, assumed command of British forces in Russia on the 4th August 1919, returning to the U.K. on the 14th November of that same year. Immediately upon his return, he accepted command as Commander-in-Chief of the Aldershot command and finally, transferred to India as Commander-in-Chief on the 21st November 1920. He died in India on the 20th February 1925, his 65th birthday while playing cricket.

Field-Marshal Bernard Law Montgomery, KG, GCB, DSO, PC.

Born in Kennington, London on the 17th November 1887, son of the Reverend Henry Montgomery, he was one of nine children. He was educated at St. Paul's School, London and, after graduating from the Royal Military Academy he was commission as a Lieutenant in the 1st Battalion Royal Warwickshire Regiment on the 19th September 1908.

After serving in India for five years, he returned to the United Kingdom in 1913. On the 22nd August 1914, he sailed from Southampton aboard the S.S. *Caledonia* bound for Boulogne, France and the Western Front. He participated in the Battle of Le Cateau, the British retreat from Mons and the advance of the 4th Division in September of 1914

Montgomery was granted a promotion to Lieutenant (temporary Captain) on the 14th September 1914 while fighting on the heights of Chivres, above the River Aisne. The 4th Division then moved to northern France and, as a part of III Corps, advanced upon on Armentières in October of the same year. On the 13th October, he received a serious gunshot wound to the chest and leg while involved in house-to-house fighting in Méteren, near Bailleul. The following day, when it was realized that the wound was not mortal, he was promoted to Captain. He was transported back to England for recuperation and, while in hospital, was awarded the Distinguished Service Order for his leadership.

Upon recovery, he was posted, on the 12th February, as Brigade Major to the 47th Division, whilst still in the United Kingdom. When the division moved to France in March 1915 where he served as General Staff Officer (Grade II) between 22nd January 1917 and 15th July 1918 with the temporary rank of Major (Brevet).

On the 16th July 1918, he was granted the rank of Brevet Lieutenant-Colonel and made the General Staff Officer (Grade I), a responsibility he maintained until the 4th April 1919. During the war he had been Mentioned in Despatches, each included in the London Gazette, on the 17th February 1915, 4th January and 11th December 1917, 20th May 1918, 20th December 1918 and the 5th July 1919. He had also been awarded Croix de Guerre (France), 1914 Star and clasp, British War Medal and the Victory Medal.

After hostilities ceased, elements of the British army moved into Germany and Montgomery assumed the position of General Staff Officer

(Grade II) with the rank of temporary (Brevet) Major in the Army of the Rhine until the 2nd September 1919. He continued his military career as a battalion commander when was then delegated to the rank of temporary Lieutenant-Colonel of the 17th Royal Fusiliers on the 19th September 1919, in Germany.

On returning to the United Kingdom, he trained at the army's Staff College in Surrey. Upon graduation, he was appointed Brigade Major in Ireland between 5th January 1921 and as Brigade Major to the 17th Brigade, 24th Division, Southern Command on the 24th May 1922. He assumed the role of General Staff Officer (Grade II) in Northern Command on the 11th May 1923 and the Deputy Assistant Adjutant General to the Staff College on the 23rd January 1926. During his tenancy as the college, he married Elizabeth Carver. On the 1st January 1931 the rank of Brevet Colonel was bestowed upon Montgomery, thus having his full rank of Lieutenant-Colonel confirmed two weeks later, on the 17th.

From the 29th June 1934 he assumed the role of General Staff Officer (Grade I) at the Staff College in Quetta, Colonial India[394], Following the confirmation his rank of Colonel. He remained in Quetta until the 28th June 1937, when he returned to the United Kingdom to receive his promotion to Brevet Brigadier-General and his appointment to the command of the 9th Infantry Brigade, on the 5th August 1937. Ten months later, on the 21st May 1938, a further promoted to Major-General was confirmed and he assumed command of the 8th Division in Palestine.

As the inevitability of war with Germany became evident, he returned to Britain and assumed command of the 3rd Division, Southern Command, on the 28th August 1939. The 3rd Division, as a part of the British Expeditionary Force, saw action in Belgium but later withdrew from Dunkirk in May 1940. Upon his return, he was rewarded with the C.B. and on the 22nd July of that year he was promoted to acting Lieutenant-General and given command of V Corps a post held until April 1941. He then assumed command of XII Corps until the 24th December 1941.

The following day, Christmas Day, he was given the responsibility of General Officer Commanding South East Command, a post that he held until the 9th August 1942. The next day he was sent to North Af-

---

[394] *Quetta was, in 1934, a part of the British colonial sub-continent. In 1947 colonial India was partitioned, creating the nation of present-day Pakistan, in which Quetta now lies.*

rica and assumed command of the British 8th Army from Sir Claude Auchinleck. Two months later, on the 16th October, that his rank of Lieutenant-General was confirmed. Three weeks later, on the 11th November 1942, he was promoted to a full General. During the period of his command, he captured, in conjunction with Anglo-US army, the occupied territories of North Africa and commanded the British forces in the Invasion of Sicily and Italy. His abrasive nature sometimes alienated him from the respect that the many Americans and his British colleagues enjoyed.

The Allies had been planning for the invasion of Europe Since 1942. In accordance with that plan, Montgomery returned to the United Kingdom in December 1943, to assume command of the 21st Army group on the 6th January 1944. Promoted to the ultimate rank of Field-Marshall on the 1st September 1944, he continued to hold the command of the 21st Army Group until the 25th May 1945. He was then appointed the Commander-in-Chief of the British Occupation Forces in Germany and also sat as the British Member of the Allied Control Council for a month.

Be was appointed the Chief of the Imperial General Staff at the War Office in London on the 26th June 1946 where he remained until the 1st November 1948. He then assumed the role of Chairman of the Western Europe Commanders-in-Chief Committee. He then became the Deputy Supreme Commander, Allied Commanders in Europe until the 19th September 1958.

Field-Marshall Bernard Law Montgomery was presented with many awards and honours from Britain, U.S.A., Poland, U.S.S.R., Denmark, The Netherlands, Belgium, Czechoslovakia, Ethiopa and Norway. He retired from public service on the 18th September 1968 and died on the 24th March 1976, aged 89 years. He is buried in the Churchyard of the Holy Cross Church, Binstead, on the Isle of Wight.

Captain Bruce Bairnsfather

Bruce Bairnsfather was born in Muree, India in 1888, the son of Lieutenant Thomas Bairnsfather and Amelia Every. Educated in India and Stratford-upon-Avon, United Kingdom, he enlisted in the army and was posted to the Royal Warwickshire Regiment. Not suited to military life, he left the army and pursued a career in the world of art by creating advertising posters for commercial interests.

He enlisted at the outbreak of the war and rejoined the 1st Battalion of his old regiment, the Warwickshire's. Promotion was rapid and he was soon promoted to the rank of Lieutenant. The battalion went to war as a part of the 10th Brigade, 4th Division and he participated in the most traumatic moments in the history of the division. He partook of the fighting during the battle of Le Cateau on the 26th August 1914. In that battle the 1st Warwickshire's suffered incredible losses and only managed to withdraw under those most difficult of circumstances. He participated in the retreat to the area south of the River Marne, the advance back across the Marne and Aisne.

He moved with the Division in October 1914 to the area of Plugstreet would and participated in the Christmas Truce, an action for which, as an officer, he got into much trouble. It was the period in which the battalion served in Plugstreet Wood that demonstrated his ability to express himself through his art. As a machine-gunner, he was deeply affected by the nature of the fighting and he turned to expressing the plight of those in the trenches in his cartoons. It was through the London magazine, The Bystander, where Bairnsfather received the accolades attributed to his drawings.

He had been badly gassed and received a shrapnel wound during the fighting in front of Ypres in 1915 and was sent back to the London General Hospital to recuperate. Due to his condition he never again returned to the front but spent the remainder of his service on the Isle of Wight, with a training battalion, where he was promoted to Captain. While there, he wrote several articles and sketched for some of the larger papers and magazines. It was here that he created the character of Old Bill and his Fragments from France cartoons.

He was also in great demand by the French and Italians. After the war his reputation continued with several stage productions and films included his favourite character, Old Bill and his Fragments from France cartoons. His reputation followed throughout the Second World War when he was appointed to the American Forces as a cartoonist. He fame carried into many theatres, Newspapers and public commentaries in later post-war years. Captain Bruce Bairnsfather died in 1959, aged 71years.

Lieutenant-Colonel J.F. Elkington, D.S.O, Medaille Militaire, Croix de Guerre with Palm.

Born on the 3rd February 1866 in Jamaica. "The story of John Ford Elkington is one of dishonour, courage and heroism. He was one of five sons and one daughter born to Lt. General John Henry Ford Elkington and Margaret Elkington (formerly Jamieson) whose family had a strong Army tradition and background.

John Ford Elkington was Educated at Elizabeth College, Guernsey and the Royal Military Academy. He joined his father's regiment, the Royal Warwickshire's in 1886, being promoted to Captain in six years. In 1898 he volunteered and served in Nigeria but was invalided home with malaria. He was in the South Africa War from 1900 to 1902. In February 1907 he was serving with the 3rd Battalion in South Africa. Between 1900 and 1912 he served in India. In 1910 he was promoted to Lieutenant Colonel and returned to take command of the Shorncliffe Camp in February 1914."

On the 26th August 1914 the 4th Division, as a part of II Corps, stood on the Cambrai – Le Cateau Road as the left flank division. Here they faced the might of the German the German 2nd Cavalry Division and, later in the day, the German IV Reserve Corps. The days' fighting was intense and demanded the every bit of skill and stamina from the troops. Totally exhausted and close to capture the last elements of the front line troops of the 10th Brigade, the 1st Royal Warwickshire Regiment and the 2nd Royal Dublin Fusiliers made their way through Haucourt and attempted to follow the main body of the Division. The condition of the officers and men was one of nearing a state of collapse but, in separate groups, made there way to St. Quentin, south of Cambrai. Travelling largely by night the groups underwent great difficulties and was in a state of total exhaustion on the arrival at St. Quentin.

Quote: "As darkness fell it was almost impossible to keep the men together and it was under these conditions that Elkington met a fellow Colonel [Mainwaring] also trying to keep his own men together. He arrived in the vicinity of a village called St. Quentin where he hoped to obtain food and supplies for his men. Here a crucial event took place, which was to alter the whole of Elkington and Mainwaring's careers. Some confusion arose about the presence of the British Troops and the Marie of St. Quentin felt that their being there would endanger the lives of the women and children, should the Germans, now in the vicinity, shell the village and kill the innocent residents for helping them.

Elkington had decided that they would meet the Germans not in the town but behind the Railway Station to avoid involving the many women and children in the village.

Here some confusion arose because Mainwaring, who visited the Marie accompanied by an interpreter, whilst trying to arrange for food and a train for the men, signed a paper promising not to fight in the town in return for the food. Meanwhile Elkington was with his troops at the station in an attempt to find a train. That paper was crucial to the case of both officers Colonels at their Courts Martial later.

Elkington arrived at the Railway station and put his men in one shed and their arms, which could easily be reached if needed, in another. Here for a short while they were allowed to rest whilst having a little bread to share. Finally he got his men away and proceeded to Noyon, whereby he took command of his battalion again and fought with them for two days. Shortly after, he was arrested and put on a charge of 'Cowardice and Conspiring to Surrender' the charge saying that he conspired to surrender to the enemy by the signing of the paper. He was acquitted of the Cowardice charge, but the other charge was upheld and he was dishonourably discharged from the Army losing his rank."

Those events led to the subsequent arrest and court-martial of both officers with resulting in their dismissal from the service, Lieutenant-Colonel Elkington went on to join the French Foreign Legion and was severely wounded in fighting around Vimy. In October 1916, after his return to the UK for recuperation, he was summoned to Buckingham Palace by the King where he received the Distinguished Service Order after have been granted a pardon in August of that year. "Despite often being in pain from his injury, he now took an interest in local affairs. He regularly took his seat on the Kingsclere Bench; started a men's club and became chairman of Newbury District Hospital[395]". Lieutenant-Colonel J. F. Elkington died on the 27th June 1944, aged 78 years and is buried in the churchyard Burghclere, Hampshire, United Kingdom.

---

[395] Quoted from the Elkington Family website:
www.elkingtonfamily.com/Johnfordelkington.htm, with the kind permission of the Webmaster.

Brigadier-General Adrian Carton De Wiart V.C., D.S.O., K.B.E., C.B.,C.M.G., Croix d'Officier de la Couronne, Croix de Guerre(Belgium& France), Legion de Honneur, Cross of Valour (Poland).

Born on 5th May 1880 in Brussels, Belgium, on the 5th May 1880 to Belgian barrister, Leon Carton De Wiart. He was educated in Belgium and at the Oratory School, then in Edgbaston, Birmingham and Oxford University. Not being the academic type, he left Oxford and joined the Army as a trooper in 1900. During his initial service he was sent to South Africa where he was seriously wounded with a gunshot a lung. Upon returning to England to recuperate he, again, returned to the university at Oxford, but received a commission in the Imperial Light Horse and returned to South Africa where he engaged in military action. In 1901 he transferred to the 4th Dragoon Guards with a regular commission. During the South African campaign he received the Queens Medal with three clasps.

Following the conclusion of the war he transferrd to India in 1902 and later, returned to peacetime South Africa where he was appointed as Aide-de-Camp to the Commander-in-Chief, Sir Henry Hilyard. Upon his return to England he married Countess Frederica Fugger von Babenhausen in 1908

At the outbreak of the Great War in 1914 he was sent to Somiland where he was attached to the Somaliland Camel Corps. He fought in the action at Shimber Berris where he suffered a gunshot wound to the face, losing his left eye. He was transferred to France where he commanded, among others, the 8th Gloucester Regiment of the 19th Division. He served in many areas and suffered wounds in many of the camapigns in which he fought. He suffered serious wounds to the body and lost his left hand. He assumed command of the 12th Brigade, 4th Division, on the 9th January 1917.

Following the end of hostilities in 1918 was sent to Poland, as a General, with the British Military Mission where he assumed command from General Botha. In1921 he resigned his commission although he remained resident in Poland, until the outbreak of the Second World War when he was re-appointed head of the Polish Military Mission. In September 1939, the Military Mission left Poland and, after a circuitous and dangerous journey made his way back to England.

His career, during the war, involved command of the 61st Division in the United Kingdom, command of a combined force which fought in Norway and after a difficult evacuation, arrived in Scapa Flow. After a period in Ireland with the 61st Division, He was appointed, on the 5th April 1941, to command the British Military Mission in Yugoslavia. However, while en-route to his appointment, he was taken prisoner in North Africa after the aircraft in which he was travelling crashed.

Following his release in 1943, he was sent to China to act as Churchill's personal representative to Chiang Kai-Shek. He died on the 5th June 1963 in Killinardrish in County Cork, Ireland.

Appendix III – Changes to 4th Division 1914-1918

Mounted Troops

14th April 1915:B Squadron, 19th Hussars transferred to the 9th Cavalry Brigade, 1st Cavalry Division.

10th Brigade

21st May 1915: Receive 1/9th Battalion Argyll and Sutherland Highlanders.

22nd Jul 1915: 1/9th Battalion Argyll and Sutherland Highlanders transferred to Corps Troops

2nd Aug 1917:3/10th Battalion Middlesex Regiment transferred to the 10th Brigade

2nd Aug 1917: 1st Battalion Royal Irish Fusiliers transferred to the 36th Division.

20th Feb 1918: 3/10th Battalion Middlesex Regiment was disbanded.

1st Mar 1916: 1/7th Battalion Argyll and Sutherland Highlanders. Transferred to the 51st Division. .

15th Nov 1916: 2nd Battalion Royal Dublin Fusiliers transferred to the 16th Division.

17th Nov 1916: Received Household Battalion.

10th Feb 1918: Household Battalion. - Disbanded.

11th Brigade

17th Nov 1914: Received 1/5th Battalion London Regiment.

19th May 1915: 1/5th Battalion London Regiment transferred to the GHQ Troops.

26th Jul 1915: Received 2nd Battalion Royal Irish Regiment.

22nd May 1916: 2nd Battalion Royal Irish Regiment transferred to the 7th Division.

1st Feb 1918: 1st Battalion East Lancashire Regiment transferred to the 34th Division.

12th Brigade

Exchanged with the 107th Brigade, 36th Division from 05 Nov 1915 until 03 Feb 1916. All the Battalions that were serving with the Brigade at that time went to the 36th Division.

16th Feb 1915: Received 1/5th Battalion South Lancashire Regiment.

14th Mar 1915: Received 2nd Battalion Royal Irish Fusiliers

26th Jul 1915: 2nd Battalion Royal Irish Fusiliers transferred to the 11th Brigade, 4th Division.

26th Jul 1915: 2nd Battalion Royal Inniskilling Fusiliers transferred to GHQ Troops.

5th Nov 1915: 1/5th Battalion South Lancashire Regiment Transferred to the 36th Division.

5th Nov 1915: 2nd Battalion Essex Regiment transferred to the 109th Brigade, 36th Division.

5th Nov 1915: 1/2nd Battalion Monmouthshire Regiment transferred to the 36th Division.

5th Nov 1915: Received 8th Battalion Royal Irish Rifles.

5th Nov 1915: Received 9th Battalion Royal Irish Rifles.

5th Nov 1915: Received 10th Battalion Royal Irish Rifles.

5th Nov 1915: Received 15th Battalion Royal Irish Rifles.

3rd Feb 1916: Received 2nd Battalion Duke of Wellington's Regiment.

3rd Feb 1916: 8th Battalion Royal Irish Rifles transferred to the 36th Division.

3rd Feb 1916: 9th Battalion Royal Irish Rifles transferred to the 36th Division.

3rd Feb 1916: 10th Battalion Royal Irish Rifles transferred to the 36th Division.

3rd Feb 1916: 15th Battalion Royal Irish Rifles transferred to the 36th Division.

10th Feb 1918: 2nd Battalion Duke of Wellington's Regiment transferred to the 10th Brigade, 4th Division.

Pioneers

21st Jun 1916: Received 21st Battalion West Yorkshire Regiment attached.

11th Nov 1918: 21st Battalion West Yorkshire Regiment detached.

Royal Field Artillery

XIV Brigade

8th Feb 1915: 39th Battery transferred to the XIX Brigade, 27th Division.

21st May 1916: Received 86th (Howitzer) Battery.

14th Jan 1917: 68th Battery transferred to the Army Field Artillery.

14th Jan 1917: 86th (Howitzer) Battery transferred to the XXXII Brigade.

14th Jan 1917: 88th Battery transferred to the Army Field Artillery.

XXIX Brigade

21st May 1916: Received 128th (Howitzer) Battery.

XXXII Brigade

21st May 1916: Received D (Howitzer) Battery.

14th Jan 1917: Received 86th (Howitzer) Battery.

14th Jan 1917: D (Howitzer) Battery broken up, sections rejoined their original batteries - 86th and 128th (Howitzer) batteries.

XXXVII (Howitzer) Brigade (17 Feb 1915 transferred to Corps Troops).
28th Nov 1914: 55th (Howitzer) Battery attached to the 7th Division.
17th Feb 1915: 31st (Howitzer) Battery transferred to Corps Troops.
17th Feb 1915: 35th (Howitzer) Battery transferred to Corps Troops.

CXXVII (Howitzer) Brigade Formed 06 Aug 1915.
6th Aug 1915: Received 86th (Howitzer) Battery.
6th Aug 1915: Received 128th (Howitzer) Battery.
21st May 1916: CXXVII (Howitzer) Brigade broken up
21st May 1916: 86th (Howitzer) Battery transferred to XIV Brigade.
21st May 1916: 128th (Howitzer) Battery transferred to XXIX Brigade.

Royal Garrison Artillery
29th April 1915: 31st Heavy Battery transferred to the No 2 Group Heavy Artillery Reserve.

Appendix IV – 1914 – Orders and Reports

Division HQ: Action of Ligny - Haucourt - 26th August 1914

CAMBRAI sheet and sketch map attached.

To explain the position and action of the 4th Division on 26th August, it is necessary to state briefly the orders receive and issued on the evening of 25th August, which caused a great part of the 4th Division to arrive in its position north of Haucourt and Ligny about dawn on the 26th August, whilst still executing a flank march from Briastre.

Preliminary movements on the evening of 25th and morning of 26th August.

2.   On the 25th August the 4th Div. was ordered to cover the withdrawal of the rear guard of the 3rd Div. and 19th Inf. Bde., on a position on high ground west of Briastre and wait till the whole of these formations and the Cavalry Division were clear.

3.   The rearguard of the 3rd Division was very late, and great difficulty was incurred in getting touch with the 19th Bde. and Cav. Div. It was however decided that the duty of the 4th Div. was to remain where it was till all the troops of the 3rd Div. and 19th Bde., had passed through, and a communication to this effect was sent to General Murray.

4.   This view was confirmed by a private letter from General Wilson. This letter, later confirmed by Op. Order NO.8 of 25th, added that it was the intention of G.H.Q. that the Army should retire to the line Le Catelet - Beaurevoir, the 4th Div. to begin the retirement at 7 a.m. 26th August from approximately the line Caudry - Waimbaix. The rest of the force was to conform.

5.   On the these orders Div. Orders wore issued at 5 P.M. for the 4th Div. to take up a position for the night on the line Caudry (excl) - Fontaine Au Pire – Wambaix - Knell just south of Seranviller.

6.   The 3rd Div. began to pass through at Briastre about 2 p.m. and the 11th Bde of 4th Div. took over rearguard at 3.15 p.m. The10th Bde., being on the left of 11th Bde. on high ground about Pt. 119.

7.   No trace had yet been obtained as regards the position of 19th Bde. and Cav. Div.

8.   At 6.10 p.m. definite news of the 19th Bde. was received but the 7th Bde. (rearguard of the 3rd Div.) was still far behind and large parts of the Cav. Div. transport and guns and also those of 3rd Div. were passing Briastre and Viesly. 4th Div. H.Q. were at Point 129. Viesly.

9.   At 6.15 p.m. G.H.Q. was Informed of the situation and units ordered to be ready to retire to the position detailed as soon as the rearguard was clear of Briastre.

10.   The line to be occupied was at this time changed to the following: -
11th Inf. Bde. Fontaine Au Fire to the railway station at Cattenières.
12th Inf. Bde. to continue the line to Waimbaix.
10th Inf. Bde. still to go in reserve at Haucourt.

11.   This movement was successfully carried out by units of the 4th Div., but, owing to the amount of transport of Cav. Div. and 3rd Div., which passed through Viesly, the movement of the rearguard of the 4th Div., was delayed till after midnight. The result was that the 3 brigades did not get on to the position detailed in Op. Order No.1 of 25th till about daylights that is between 3.30 and 5.30 a.m.

12.   Infantry posts were put out by brigades to cover entrenching, but the only available mounted troops were elsewhere and thus no one was available to give sufficient warning of the advance of hostile troops. This resulted in several of these advanced posts being surprised by machine-gun fire and annihilated.

First Phase. 5.30 a.m. to 10 a.m.

13.   It is first necessary to state that about 6 a.m. when Op. Orders were being issued from Div. H.Q. at Haucourt to carry out the retirement laid down in Op. Order No. 8 of 7 p.m. of 25th from G.H.Q. and O.A. 304/26th, received at 5.28 am. 26th August, a message was received from the Second Corps to say that it could not retire and that it was going to fight on its present position, and asking the 4th Div. to protect its left as far as Haucourt.

14.   A reply was at once sent to say the 4th Div. would do as was asked, and General Bowes, (he arrived shortly after 6 am.) a representative of G.S. at G.H.Q., then with 4th Div. was informed of the decision.

Orders were then issued for the position to be; taken up and strongly entrenched.

11th Bde, from Le Coquelet Fe. to railway about South of <u>0</u> of Fontaine.

12th Bde. to carry on from left of 11th Bde. to Mont D'Esnes, just N.W. of Esnes.

10th Bde. in reserve at Haucourt. Divisional Artillery and 2 brigades east of Esnes and 2 brigades at Ligny. In most cases however these orders, owing to the entire absence of communication, except mounted orderlies, did not reach their destination.

15.   About 6 a.m. it became apparent that the Germans had sent forward cavalry and guns accompanied by detachments of infantry and machine guns in motors.

These advanced parties were very cleverly handled and as already stated partially surprised the posts who were covering the troops entrenching. Some battalions suffered severely especially the Kings Own of the 12th Bde., who were fired on by maxims at close range from near Cattenières railway station.

16.   The village of Haucourt, where 4th Div. H.Q. still were, was now, (7.30 to 8a.m.) under fire of guns and long range rifle fire and a considerable number of stragglers from the front line were dribbling into the village. It was at this time that Captain D'Esterre, A.D.C. to G.O.C. was wounded, and several men also. Some of the Div. Staff immediately collected the stragglers and took them back into the firing line.

17.   The G.O.C. himself proceeded, towards Cattenières in a motor, but could go only a short way, and went to the position which the 14th F.A.B, had taken up just S.W. of Haucourt as soon as it heard the attack begin. Here G.O.C. was joined by the Div. Staff and by means of them issued orders. No other means of communication were available.

18.   The following dispositions were made:-
G.O.C., R.A. brought up part of the artillery, who were already on their way from Ligny, to get into the positions assigned to them overnight.

The 14 F.A.B. which had already reached Haucourt, on the ridge S.W. of Haucourt, facing north and north-west to support the 12th Brigade.

29th F.A.B. at, and to the east of, Haucourt to support 11th and 12th Brigades. 32nd and 37th F.A.B's to remain at Ligny for the present.

19.   Two battalions of 10th Bde. were kept in reserve south of Haucourt till it was seen that the left of the Div. was safe as it seemed probable, from reports received, that the enemy might work round our left by Seranvillers-Crevecoeur-surl'Escaut and Esnes.

The greater part of the other two battalions of the 10th Brigade had become committed to a counter-attack with the 12th Brigade against the ridge north of Haucourt and were not disengaged for some time

About 8 a.m. the 32nd F.A.B. also came into action with two batteries on the spur S.W. of Ligny, a third battery, at first in reserve, being later on employed at Ligny as shewn below. 37 F.A.B. came into action under cover west of the village Caullery.

20.   The line of the 12th Brigade and part of the 10th Brigade was formed on the ridge N. and N.E. of Longsart, its right near the railway.

21.   On the other flank the 11th Brigade which halted at north end of Fontaine Au Pire from 2.45 a.m. to 4.15 am. was also attacked while moving into position by rifle, machine gun and artillery fire. It however held off the attack with 2 battalions while moving the other 2 into a position South of Fontaine Au Pire on the general line detailed for the Brigade to hold.

22.   The position was taken up with Carrieres as its centre, its left ran S.W. to and across the railway, its extreme left on the edge of the plateau its right ran and S.'9. the extreme flank being covered by troops 6cheloned behind it along the railways but not in touch with Second Corps. Heavy shrapnel and machine-gun fire was turned against this position but the 11th Brigade successfully held its own all day, attacks being chiefly directed from the north-west and north-east. This determined defence by the 11th Brigade was of the greatest possible value not only to the 4th Div., but to the whole line.

23.   The 4th Div. thanks to their resistance was now in position to resist further attacks, especial attention still being paid to any signs of attack from the west. The front the Div. extended approximately from the road running south to Ligny through the second E. of Carrieres to

the railway along the crest of the ridge and thence westwards along the ridge north of Longsart.

This left part of the position had to be given up about 9a.m. and the main line then ran south-west from the railway through Haucourt to Point 137. Half of 2 battalions (Essex and Inniskillings) however remained on the line of the Harcourt-Esnes road till the 12th Brigade again advanced to its old Position at 3 P.m.

Second Phase.   10 a.m. to 3 P.M.

As pointed out above the 12th Brigade had been compelled to retire towards the line Haucourt - Pt. 137, where it was well placed on high ground with a good field of fire; the right in Haucourt and 2 half battalions in advance of the main line on the Haucourt - Esnes road. The 12th Brigade was reinforced about 11 o/clock by the Royal Irish Fusiliers from the reserve and the fire of a battery of the 14th F.A.B. was turned to the westward to support it. At this period communication between the 12th Brigade and Divisional H.Q's was temporarily lost.

24.   A proportion of the Royal Dublin Fusiliers and of the Warwick Reg. (10th Bde) who were still about Haucourt, were ordered to advance to a position north of Haucourt on each side of the stream running north to the east of Haucourt.

25.   Division al HQ's were at this time on the high ground south of Haucourt near the reserve, but moved to a point near the second E of Le Chemin Vert about noon. About 12,10 p.m. it was decided to push troops into Ligny in case the 11th Brigade should have to fall back, as it was realised that the loss of Ligny would mean a break in the general line of defence and would affect not only the 4th Div. but the troops on the right as well.

A Staff officer was sent down from Div. H.Q. to organize the defence of Ligny.

26.   The 135th Batty. was placed close in front of the village of Ligny covering a stretch of open ground which lay behind the position held by the 11th Bde and over which the enemy would have to advance if he followed up the retirement of the 11th Brigade. In addition to the Battery, 200 men, chiefly Som L.I., were collected and placed in charge of a Captain of that regiment to support the guns, and a Cavalry machine-gun section which had come to help the Div. was also placed in the village.

27.   Between 12 and 1 p.m. the 11th Bde. was still holding its own on the ridge about Carrieres although it was severely and consistently shelled and its trenches raked by machine guns, while the Div. Arty. could do nothing to keep this shrapnel fire down, nor could support be given by other infantry. Its right however had still not been able to get touch with the 3rd Div.

28.   At about 12.45 p.m. 12th Bde. was ordered to place Selvigny in a state of defence so as to save troops which were to be sent to Div. H.Q. as a reserve. This order was not received.

29.   It should be here mentioned that the last remaining battalion of the 10th Brigade at first held in reserve, had been sent out to extend the left of the 10th Brigade thus leaving no reserves in hand. The situation was then reported to G.H.Q.

30.   The Artillery was in the positions shewn in R.A, report and sketch map.

31.   The importance of Ligny as a tactical point to hold at the last extremity was now very evident, and the 10th Brigade were also asked to send any men they could spare to reinforce its garrison.

32.   It was however not possible to carry these orders out and the garrison of 200 men, six guns and two machine guns at Ligny remained as before until the 11th Brigade retired back to the village.

33.   At 1.20 p.m. two battalions of the 19th Brigade, Royal Welsh Fusiliers and Scottish Rifles were placed at the disposal of the 4th Div. and were ordered to take up a position at east end of Ligny, and in the wood SE of Ligny, and also at. The windmill near the wood S.E. of Ligny. These two battalions were however withdrawn to help the 5th Div. before the above order reached them.

34.   A further attempt was made to get touch with 3rd Div. and the situation explained to them. Soon after 1 p.m. a Staff officer was sent to carry this out.

35.   At 1.35 p.m. a farther report was sent to the 3rd Div. and they were urged to hold on as there was no apparent need to retire. The 11th Brigade having held its own successfully and there being no signs of a flank movement from the west.

36.   On the left flank about 3 p.m. the 12th Brigade advanced past Longsart towards its original position in order to Withdraw as many of the wounded as possible, and was successful in removing a considerable number.

Third Phase.   3 p.m. to 12 p.m.

News was however soon afterwards received from a Staff officer who had been sent to Ligny that the 3rd Div. had retired out of Caudry towards Montigny and that the east of Ligny was open to the enemy, and the garrison of Ligny, and the right of the 11th Brigade in a dangerous position if the enemy advanced. The following steps were then taken to rectify the position.

37.   About 3 p.m. the 11th Brigade had been told by a Staff officer verbally that if it's position became too difficult it was to retire on to the prepared position at Ligny.

38.   The 3rd Div. having retired and his position in danger of being turned General Hunter-Weston therefore decided to retire.

This retirement was successfully accomplished under cover of guns of 32nd F.A.B. and the garrison of Ligny, and the number of casualties, considering the shellfire to which they were exposed, was not very great. The enemy then attacked Ligny but were easily repulsed.

39.   Meanwhile at 3:40 p.m. another message was sent to the 12th Brigade and received by them at 4.30 p.m. to hold Selvigny and put it in a state of defence. The Brigade then retired from the Haucourt - Esnes line to Selvigny which it put in a state of defence.

40.   A detachment of the King's Own under Major Parker remained In Haucourt until 9p.m. and successfully encountered 150 Germans with the bayonet and finally retired practically unmolested rejoining the 12th Brigade on the afternoon of the 27th.

41.   Soon after it was reported that the 3rd Div. had had to retire to Clary. This exposed the rear of the village of Ligny and it was considered necessary that the 4th Div. should conform to the movement or its line would be turned and the garrison at Ligny which now include the 11th Brigade would be out off.

42.   The general idea for the retirement was for the most advanced units to retire through supporting points established on the high

ground east of Caullery and at Selvigny, the former being held by artillery, the latter by 12th Brigade supported by artillery. The infantry to be withdrawn under cover of fire from these points on to the line of retirement through Walincourt - Malincourt to La Catelet as given by G.H.Q, which it will be seen from the map was, to commence with, about parallel to the line of battle.

43.   The 11th Brigade and troops in Ligny to move first to the high ground-3/4 mile north of the S. of Deheries, then the l0th Brigade to the high ground near Soval Chateau-Hurlemont Ferme. The 12th Brigade meanwhile holding on to Selvigny and the artillery taking up one covering position after another commencing with the high ground just east of Caullery, batteries passing through each other in turn to the high ground 3/4 mile north of Deheries. The Division to assemble in that neighbourhood and then to continue its retirement through Malincourt.

44.   Orders were therefore Issued at 3.40 p.m. to the l0th Brigade which was wrongly believed to be N.W., of Caullery or Haucourt, to retire up the valley between Haucourt and Caullery try to the high ground south of Sorval Chateau. This order was received about 5 p.m.

45.   Similar orders were, sent to the Dublin Fusiliers, 10th Brigade in their advanced position north of Caullery.

46.   A slight modification in the order of retirement was now made on receipt of information from G.O.C. 12th Brigade who was then at Hurlements Fermes with Div. H.Q. that General Haldane was on the left of 12th Brigade near Selvigny.

47.   The G.O.C. 12th Brigade was told to tell General Haldane, to act as rearguard to the whole Div. when the retirement began. This verbal message reached General Haldane just after he had received the first one (A.M. 27. APP.25) quoted and was not carried out as had been intended by Div.   H.Q's as General Haldane understood the verbal message to be only a repetition of the order directing him on Sorval Chateau and not as it really was, a modification of the above quoted order, in so far as it gave him a new direction on Walincourt and Malincourt, instead of on high ground south of Sorval Chateau. The result was that General Haldane, with two battalions instead of moving S.W. after the rest of the Division, moved south-east to begin with. He then halted until he could find out whether the retirement had begun and thus lost touch. He later ascertained from inhabitants and stragglers the direction which the Div. had taken and followed it up some 5 or 6 hour

s in rear along the same route through Malincourt and Vendhuille, and rejoined the Div, with his two battalions on the 27th August near Roisel.

48. At 4.p.m. A message was sent to the 11th Brigade and received at 5 p.m. to retire on l'Epine Daiubigny Ferme, which order was carried out by a part of the Brigade but a considerable part retired south instead of S.W* and were away from the Div. till they rejoined in two parties on the 27th and 28th August between Harcourt and Voyenne.

49. The retirement on to Sorval Chateau - Hurlement Fe and thence to high ground 3/4 mile N. of Deheries was carried out successfully and unmolested with such troops as were available including the whole of the Div, Arty. except two guns.

50. The enemy did not follow up at all till after dark, but wasted an immense amount of ammunition in shelling the places where our troops had been till dark without hitting anyone.

51. The retirement of the Artillery from their advanced position was carried out with perfect order, and, considering the fire that was turned on them as soon as they began to move, the losses were small.

52. As regards the loss of the two guns, see R.A. report on the gallant action of Major Vallentin's batter, which certainly deserves special mention.

53. The artillery finally retired to a position of assembly in the hollow, just north of S of Deheries,

54. As explained above General Haldane, with two battalions of the l0th Brigade, should now have formed, the rearguard when the Div. moved off towards Le Catelet, but for reasons already given, he did not do so.

55. Soon after dark, that is about 8 p.m. the Div. moved off towards Le Catelet through Malincourt and Villers-Outreaux from its final place of assembly about Selvigny and Deheries, the 12th Brigade, leading followed by the whole of the artillery and portions of the 10th and 11th Brigade.

56. One of the Div. Staff was left at the road junction at the OU of Maison de Walincourt to see the last of the troops through and formed a small infantry rearguard to follow on after the guns.

57.   The infantry though still cheerful, were by this time thoroughly tired and as many as possible were carried on the limbers and wagons of the four artillery brigades. The composite regiment of Household Cavalry brought up the rear. A little later orders as to precautions to be taken at Vendhuille where the Div. halted at midnight, and orders for further retirement at 5.30 a.m. on 27th were issued at 11.50 p.m.

CONCLUDING REMARKS.
Before closing this report there are I think a few points which require explanation, if the difficulties under which the 4th Div. laboured during, these operations are to be appreciated.

The cause of the absence of so large a part of the Div. from the main body -from the evening of the 26th until the afternoon of 27th and the morning of 28th was chiefly due to the fact that the first part of the line of retirement was almost parallel to the line on which the Div. fought a severe action all day, whilst troops of the neighbouring Div. could be seen retiring directly to the rear. Moreover, the Div. went into action on the 26th August with 3 Brigades of Infantry and 4 of artillery but without any Signal Coy, Div. Cav. Div. Cyclists. Field Ambulances. Fd Cos. R.F. rain or Div. Amn. Col. It was therefore severely handicapped in almost every respect.

The absence of the Signal Co. rendered the control of subordinate units on a front of some five miles a great deal of which was under heavy shell and rifle fire, a most difficult and arduous task, and owing to the heavy state of the ground as a result of the previous night's rain the horses of the staff soon became tired. By the time the, retirement began it was impossible for them to go to direct units on the right road of retirement, and, if it had not been for the assistance most willingly given by the composite regiment of household Cavalry under Col. Cook, many more men would have bean absent from the Division on the night of 26th/27th.

The absence of the Fd. Cos. was felt very much when the villages of Haucourt, Ligny and Selvigny had to be put in a state of defence, but I must record the fact that this was very efficiently done by the infantry so far as the means available allowed

The chief cause of the partial surprise of some of the covering troops whilst the Div. was entrenching the position had been ordered to occupy and of the losses incurred early in the day by the 4th. Div. was that the Div. was without its mounted troops. The only mounted troops that the Div. had on the evening of the 25th was a small party of Irish

Horse who however were on the night of 25th and morning of 26th at Bevillers in touch with an advance party of Germans, the result being that the covering parties consisted of infantry only who, it is obvious could be posted only a short way in front of the working parties.

The absence of all Field Ambulances from the beginning of the operations on the 25th August until the 29th was perhaps a greater handicap than would appear at first sight, and was responsible for a great deal of the straggling that took place during the 27th and following days. Many of the wounded and sick would in the ordinary course have been treated and evacuated on the field, but as it was very many of the slightly wounded and the sick accompanied the Div. on its retirement and were carried on artillery wagons and impressed carts. That had bad results in two ways. Firstly, it affected for the time being the march discipline of the units and secondly, it was responsible for tiring out the artillery horses, many of the guns and wagons carrying, for several days up to 8 sick and wounded men. It was also difficult under the circumstances to, weed out those who were really sick from those who were merely stragglers.

In spite of these handicaps the 4th Div. thanks to the staunchness of the infantry and the accurate fire and discipline of the artillery, was able to hold its own against very superior numbers and was only compelled to retire by the fact that its right flank was in danger owing to the retirement of troops its right.

It may be of interest to add a table shewing the marches of the 4th Division during its retirement from Solesmes until the advance from Brie Comte Robert commenced.

Action at Haucourt – 26th August, 1914

Report of Capt. Wheeler, Temporary Commander of Royal Dublin Fusiliers
Report dated 4.9.1914

At 6:15am the R. Duf. Fus. were formed up N.E. of Haucourt when gunfire was opened on them from the high ground N. of Haucourt. The battalion moved in a S. direction in artillery formation to take up a new position. After crossing the Ligny – Haucourt Road 'A' and 'D' Co.'s and a platoon of 'B' were entrenched to form a firing line and support the remaining forming a reserve. 'C' Co. was ordered to watch the left flank. At this time the battalion was not in touch with the 10th Brigade but a message stating the position was sent to the 4th Division who approved.

At about 1pm orders were received (verbally) from 4th Div. that there would be no retirement. Owing to the configuration of the ground touch was lost with the firing line and the companies concerned had not yet rejoined the battalion – no further information is at hand.

The reserves were shelled from 2pm onwards.

At 4:25pm a message was sent to the 10th Inf. Brig. and IV Division asking for advice as to what to do. Owing to the infantry in the neighbourhood having withdrawn and our guns ceased firing we were informed to that the guns had been withdrawn and we had better get away as best we could. This was done at about 5:30pm, one platoon of 'C' Company being the last infantry to leave the position.

No orders having been received as to the direction of the next position to be taken up parties withdrew in every direction, each selecting the route that appeared advisable.

No detachments have yet reported.

Brigade Report: 10th Brigade Action at Haucourt 26th August, 1914

By Brigadier-General Haldane
Report dated 9.9.1914

I marched at the head of the column, with the divisional GOC, led by the 1st Line transport. The infantry became detached. I reported to the Division HQ but did not know where my troops were. I was ordered to accompany the GOC on his personal reconnaissance of the division positions. Before the reconnaissance was finished the Germans had launched their attack. This prevented me reaching his brigade. The infantry of the 10th Brigade dispersed, on being attacked, in the immediate vicinity of their positions (between Ligny and Haucourt). I was not aware of this. On hearing the first shots, I bade leave of the GOC and hastened to the eastern side of Haucourt, Where I ordered the 1st Seaforth Highlanders and 1st Royal Irish Fusiliers to act under my orders. This reserve was used to protect the left flank of the division, who were engaged at times throughout the day. The Germans failed to deliver a serious attack on the left flank due to, in my view, the existence of these two battalions.

The remaining two brigades (2nd Royal Dublin Fusiliers and 1st Royal Warwickshire Regiment) were committed to an attack on the advancing Germans in company with troops of the 12th Brigade against the ridge N. of Harcourt. In this action the R. War. R. Led by Col. Elkington suffered casualties including 8 officers, 3 of which were company commanders. Some of the Dub. Fus. Remained on the ridge near a round water tower E. of Harcourt and held the village and trenches N. of the tower.

I attempted to establish contact with these two advanced battalions but could only speak with Major Sheraton of the Dublin Fusiliers, and he did not know where the CO was. At about 3:30pm my Staff Captain informed that Col. Elkington was in the valley to the N.E. of Harcourt. I moved in order to establish contact with Elkington, and noticed that the troops on the hill N.E. of Harcourt were maintaining their position and those in the valley had begun to retire in the direction of Ligny. Heavy German artillery fire was fired on both of those positions. The troops (Dub. Fus.) in the valley were showing signs of unsteadiness so the staff officer accompanying me remained with them to steady them while I went to the troops at the tower, and then took positions to the rear, close to Harcourt, accompanied by the OC 29th FAB. Col. Stockwell, GOC 29th FAB, began to withdraw his batteries, whereupon the Germans directed shellfire on them and a company of R. Irish Fus. This artillery caused a few casualties as those in front of Harcourt were few in number. I was not aware of the fact that Haucourt was still held by the 4th Division and thought that the German artillery was in support of their attack on the village and ground to the south of it.

Shortly before 5pm I received orders to cover the withdrawal of the division and to move the rearguard by the valley between Conillerie (?) and Selvigny. In order to carry out this movement I had to move the two battalions I had with me to the flank over ground exposed to artillery fire, close to where the other two battalions had been in action all day. In spite of receiving several casualties this move was carried out sucessfully but were forced to leave the dead and wounded on the field as there was no transport for them. The 10th Brigade withdrew under fire, reaching the positions allocated after dark.

The 10th Brigade HQ enquired as to whether they were to hold their ground or retire. Div. HQ had only been temporarily situated in Malincourt and the Brigade Major, sent out confirm these orders, found the HQ had moved 'to an unknown place'. When he tried to return to Brigade HQ he could find it in the dark and rain, so proceeded in a direction that he thought I would take in retiring. The brigade had in fact remained in their position in order to maintain security for the division. I, in accordance with my orders, had decided that, in the absence of orders. I would remain where I was until 3:30am of the 27th so as not to compromise the withdrawal of the division.

About midnight of the 26th a French civilian from Clery informed me that a body of Germans wearing helmets, which he described, had entered that village a short time before, broken into the houses and prepared to bivouac. They had seized him but he escaped. He was allowed to proceed south.

At 3:00am the 10th Brigade stood to arms and all wounded, about 20, were taken to Hurlemont farm. A company of the Seaforth Highlanders, under the command of Capt. Bailley, had become separated from the battalion during the withdrawal from shelling and did not bivouac with the brigade on the night of the 26th.

At 5:45am the 10th Brigade withdrew about 1 mile towards Malincourt and sent the adjutant of the Sea. H. to Malincourt. He returned at 5:45am and stated that the inhabitants had informed me the last of the brigade had passed through the village at about midnight. The brigade proceeded to follow the division by ascertaining its direction at each village i.e. Malincourt – Villiers – Outreaux – Anbencheul to Gouy, where the brigade stopped to give the men water. Proceeding to Vendhuille the brigade picked up two stragglers who told them that the last of the division had passed through 2 hours before. At Vendhuille an ASC officer informed me that he had seen cavalry about 2 miles to the south. I ordered him to drive me to them, and the brigade to follow, and met up with the 4th Life Guards at Letombois Farm, near Lempire and spoke to Col. Cook who stopped their withdrawal their withdrawal and sent a section to Vendhuille to protect the withdrawal of the 10th Brigade. Continued their march at Roisel. I then went to Hancourt and found the rest of the Brigade.

Account of Action of the 11ᵗʰ Brigade on the 26ᵗʰ August, 1914

Lt. General Sir Aylmer Hunter-Weston

After a continuous night march from Briastre one and a half miles south of Solesmes, the 11ᵗʰ Infantry Brigade halted for one and a half hours at the northern end of Fontaine-Au-Pire at 2:45am on the 26thAugust, 1914. At 4:14am as the Brigade was about to resume its march, rifle, machine gun, and shell fire was opened on the outposts west of the village of Beauvois. While the Rifle Brigade held off this attack from the north and north-west, the Som. L.I. were pushed forward into the southern end of Beauvois to hold off the enemy to the north-east and to ensure that the safe passage of all wheeled vehicles to the east of them, and to the south from the halting place, being impassable owing to the wet. Under cover of these two battalions, the other two battalions of the brigade moved south and took up a position on the ridge of which Carrieres (the quarry), ½ a mile to the south west of the village of Fontaine-Au-Pire is the centre. All the transport was successfully got away but owing to the necessity of having to stick to the roads, the 1ˢᵗ line transport had to go a long way round before it could again approach the infantry. The 2ⁿᵈ line transport was ordered back to Selvigny which it reached safely in due course. Under the cover of the fire of the 1ˢᵗ Hampshire Regiment the two advanced battalions retired on La Carrieres. The Somerset L.I. (1½ companies) occupying the eastern end of The Quarry while a company of the E. Lancs occupied the western end. The Somerset's prolonged their own line from La Carriere to the south-east, sending two companies back towards Ligny to entrench a position north of that town.

The three remaining companies of the E. Lancs. also retired to the slope north of Ligny. West and south-west of Carriere the line was taken up by the Hampshire's whose left rested on the edge of the plateau south of the railway line. The brigade having thus established itself on the Carriere Ridge the companies of the E. Lancs. and Somerset's were recalled from their covering positions north of Ligny and formed local reserves on the west and east flanks of the Carriere position. Against the 11ᵗʰ Infantry Brigade the enemy concentrated a very heavy fire both from field guns and machine-guns. The rifle fire was not heavy as the cavalry, and afterwards the infantry kept at a respectful distance and did not venture to show themselves on the smooth glasis-like slope, which lay in front of the position. The hostile infantry however worked around both flanks, attacking from the north-west along the railway and on the north-east establishing themselves on the southern outskirts of the village. The enemy fire was uninterrupted and severe, and on four occasions caused the troops in the more advanced positions to retire, on each occasion though, they were either led back or replaced by fresh troops and the position was successfully maintained. At about 3:00pm the 5th Division, having returned from Caudry. It was seen to hold the Carrieres position any longer would lead to the brigade being taken in reverse. In accordance therefore with divisional instructions the brigade prepared to retire to Ligny. This retirement was carefully organised with close co-operation between the infantry and artillery, which later took up positions in and to the west of Ligny, ready to cover our retirement. The infantry, with the Rifle Brigade, left on the positions as rearguard, was formed up in lines on dead ground south of the Ravine Warnelle, whence on the command being given, it moved off in good order towards the village of Ligny.

Each battalion was given a definite objective, viz: - E. Lancs to right centre of the village, Somerset to eastern end of the village. The Rifle Brigade following towards the left centre. The shrapnel fire on our troops was very severe, notwithstanding the support given by our guns. There were a good number of casualties but considering the way the whole ground was plastered with shrapnel bullets it was surprising that the casualties were not greater. On arrival at Ligny, the battalion reformed in the localities that had been allocated to them and took up the defence of the front edge of their respective portion of the village. As soon as the rearguard quitted the Carrieres position the German infantry, which up to that time had kept themselves carefully concealed, advanced in large numbers on the Caudry side of that position. These afforded excellent targets to our artillery and their formations were speedily broken up by our shrapnel fire. Shortly after the brigade had established itself at Ligny an attack an attack was made on the northeast and east of the village by German infantry. This attack was pushed in twice, but on each occasion was repulsed with heavy loss. Shortly before 5pm the brigade was ordered to retire via Caullery towards Malincourt. This retirement having to be conducted under heavy artillery the formation adopted was that a small column of fours each as far as possible under and officer. After passing Caullery the enemy's pursuit by artillery fire died away owing, as we afterwards learnt, to the attack on the Germans from the north-west by a French Corps. In connection with the above very trying operations, I should like to bring to notice the good services of the following officers, N.C.O.'s, and men.

Major Rickman   Rifle Brigade. -
This officer was unfortunately killed in this action.
Capt. G.F. Boyd D.S.O.   Leinster Regiment-'Brig. Major'

Capt. Hon. L.C. Pock	Hants. Reg.
Lt. Col. Le Marchant	E. Lancs. Reg.
Capt. Prittie	Rifle Brigade
Major Prowse	Som. L.I.
Capt. Connellan	Hants. Reg. (now local
Major)	
Capt. Hon. Morgan-Grenville	Rifle Brigade
Capt. Jones Mortimer	Som. L.I.
Capt. W.H.N. Freeston	Som L.I.
Maj. Salmon	Rifle Brigade
No. 29 CQMS Hedges	Rifle Brigade
9699 Corp. J. Lismore	E. Lancs. R.
7504 Corp. F. Wilcox	Som.L.I.
8805 Pte. J. Holloway	Hants. Reg.

The total casualties in this action amounts to about 30 officers and 1,115 other ranks.

A.H. Hunter-Weston
Date 16/9/14

Action of the 11th Brigade on the night of 12-13th September, 1914

Lt. General Sir Aylmer Hunter-Weston - Report dated 1930

At 7pm on the 12th September, 1914, out arrival at Septmonts in heavy rain, after marching all day, the 11th Brigade received orders that it was to hat and get food and then to push on, and if possible, to seize the crossing over the River Aisne at Venizel. While the brigade was getting such food as was possible, three officers were sent forward with a local guide, the junior infantry officer to reconnoitre the route and to report on the state of the bridge, and the senior infantry officers to remain in observation at the bridge, and if possible to find out whether the enemy were holding the other side.

Owing to the crowded state of the village of Septmonts and the heavy rain, it was difficult for the troops to get shelter or to get at the cooks waggons. At 11pm however the brigade started its advance, which had to be conducted by the commander by the map, as he junior officer reconnoitring officer who returned to guide the column was completely exhausted and incapable either of movement or of coherent speech. He had unfortunately dismissed the local guide.

On arriving at Venizel Bridge the R.E. reconnoitring officer reported that one of the four big charges placed to destroy the bridge had failed to explode and that though the main girders on each side of the south span were cut the reinforced concrete of the roadway were holding the bridge sufficiently to enable the bridge to be used. The senior infantry reconnoitring officer (Lieut. W Thurn, 1st Hants Regt.) reported that a German patrol had fired on him on the north bank, but that it had retired.

The 1st Hants, 1st Rifle Brigade, 1st Som. L. I., and 1st E. Lancs were therefore passed across the centre of bridge carefully in single file at two paces interval covered by an advanced party of the Hants. This took a long time and it was not till 3am that the brigade had crossed and assembled on the other side. In order to hold the crossing of the river at Venizel effectively, it was in the opinion of the Brigadier necessary to hold the heights above Bucy-Le-Long, which dominates the bridge and the flat ground between those heights and the river. He therefore ordered the brigade to advance to the attack of those heights and to seize them at the point of the bayonet.

The leading battalion, the 1ˢᵗ Hants, were ordered to take the central spur on which is La Montaigne Fᵐ. The Somerset's were given the left and far N.W. of Busy and the Rifle Brig. the right spur N. of St. Marguerite. The E. Lancs., being kept in reserve, south of the centre of Bucy-Le-Long.

Thanks to the boldness of the movement it was completely successful, and the heights were seized the heights were seized and entrenched without opposition, the enemy making no attempt to hold the trenches they had dug on the flat ground overlooking the bridge. The Germans were completely surprised and those that were met retired immediately onto the main body who were employed in digging the retired line of trenches along the top of the plateau which then became their main line.

Our men, on gaining the crests of the southern slopes of the hills immediately themselves and have maintained themselves there ever since.

The distance covered by this rear battalion this day and night exceeded thirty miles. The operation of crossing the plain and crossing the heights was very well carried out by the three battalions.

Situation Summary of 11th Brigade for 13th September, 1914

Situation

As it presented itself to the Commander of the 11th Infantry Brigade, 4th Division, British Army, at 1 a.m. (midnight), on the 13th September 1914, when he arrived at the head of his brigade at Venizel Bridge, over the River Aisne, East of Soissons, France.

SUMMARY OF RELEVANT PAST HISTORY:

Up to 7 pm., 12th September.

The 11th Infantry Brigade had been continuously fighting and marching since the 24th August. The Brigade had suffered heavy casualties in officers and men, and all were physically exhausted by the continuous fighting and marching both in the retreat from north of Le Cateau to Brie-Compt-Robert, 16 miles south east of Paris, and in the subsequent advance, including the heavy fighting at La Ferte.

Throughout the day of the 12th September, the Brigade had been continuously on the move on bad roads and in terribly wet weather. It left Passy-en-Valois at 8 a.m., and reached Septmonts at 7 p.m. after many short halts, which, though inevitable owing to the actions of the troops in front, were none the less annoying and extremely fatiguing both on officers and men. On arrival at Septmonts, the Brigade was ordered to get such rest and food as possible, but owing to the congestion in that little village, very little rest could be obtained, and owing to the rain, the cooks' wagons with the food were difficult to get at. By this time, therefore, both officers and men wear near the limit of physical endurance.

On the other side of the balance sheet, however had to be put the fact that this Brigade, like all the rest of the "Old Contemptibles" was very highly disciplined and had a magnificent espirit-de-corps. The "Brigade spirit" had been enhanced by the splendid behaviour of the Brigade in the fighting near Solesmes, south-west of Mons; in the Battle of Le Cateau, where the Brigade formed extreme the left of the British Line; by the splendid discipline it had maintained during the retreat from Solesmes to brie-Comte-Robert and by the exhilarating effect of the sudden turn at that place from retreat to advance. The Brigade was also greatly bucked-up by its success at La-Ferte, where during the battle of the Marne it had successfully driven back the Germans and made a brilliant crossing.

At Septmonts, 7 to 11 p.m., 12th September:

From Septmonts the Brigade Commander had gone to Carri-ere-l'Evecque where the 4th Division Headquarters were established. Here, after talking with the Divisional General and the General Staff, it was decided that he should pushed forward with his Brigade, and, if possible, seize a crossing over the River Aisne at Venizel Bridge.

On his return to the Brigade at Septmonts, the Brigadier, after giving orders for the Brigade to advance at 11 p.m., sent forward three reconnoitring officers with a reliable local guide to reconnoitre the road to Venizel Bridge. The Senior Infantry Reconnoitring Officer was ordered to remain in the vicinity of the Bridge and to find out all that he could on that vicinity. The Royal Engineer Officer. If were possible for him to get actually to the Bridge, was to determine was to determine how it could best be repaired. The Junior Infantry Reconnoitring Officer was to bring back to the brigadier the Senior Officer's report on the situation, and thereafter with the local guide was to lead the brigade through the night to the Bridge by the route they would have twice traversed.

Advance from Septmonts to Venizel Bridge:

The Head of the Brigade commenced its advance from Septmonts at 11 p.m., as ordered, and shortly after passing Carriere-l'Evecque, the Junior Reconnoitring Officer was met returning from the Bridge. He was, however, so completely exhausted that he was practically incapable of either of further movement or even of coherent speech. Moreover, in his exhaustion and consequent temporary mental aberration he had unfortunately dismissed the only available local guide. He was not to be blamed for this, for he and all other officers and men of the brigade had undergone immense and continuous exertion and were at the limit of human endurance.

The Reconnoitring Officer being thus hors-de-combat, The Brigade Major having been wounded and in hospital, and the Acting Brigade Major and Staff Captain both being otherwise occupied, the brigade had to be led by the Brigadier, who fortunately was well used to night work from his experience in the South African War, where he had led six night raids and on two occasions gone right through the enemy's outpost lines and cut the railway behind their main body.

Arrival of Brigadier and Head of Column at Venizel Bridge at 1 a.m., 13th September 1914.

Notwithstanding that the night was very dark and wet and the roads muddy and difficult, the head of the Brigade reached the vicinity of Venizel Bridge on the River Aisne, some 5-miles east of Soissons, at 1 a.m. Here the Brigadier was met by his two Reconnoitring Officers.

The Infantry Officer informed him that there were fresh German trenches close to the bridge on the south bank, but they did not appear to be occupied; that a German patrol had fired on him from the north bank but had apparently retired. The Engineer Officer reported that one of the four big charges placed to destroy the bridge had failed to explode and that, although the main girders on each side of the main span were cut, the reinforced concrete of the roadway would probably be sufficiently strong to enable the bridge to be used, if great care was taken not to put too much weight on the span at one time, but tat there was considerable risk that the bridge might give way without warning.

PROBLEM FOR DECISION BY BRIGADIER:

The main factors that the Brigadier had to take into consideration in making his decision as to the future action of his Brigade were:

The possibility of getting troops across the river:

His own inspection of the Bridge confirmed the report of the Engineer Officer that to get the troops across the bridge was possible, but that it must be a very slow and tedious job involving very considerable risk.

Position of adjacent British and French Troops:

As regards our own and allied troops, it was know that the French were advancing towards Soissons some mile to the west (left), but it was believed that they were still some miles distance from that town. Immediately behind the 11th Infantry Brigade on the heights to the South of the Aisne River Plain were the other two brigades of the 4th Division. To the East (right) was the rest of the British Expeditionary Force, but at some considerable away, and still well South of the River.

The Enemy:

The Germans, though retreating, were in great force and were known to be close in front. It seemed certain hat they would dispute the passage of so important a river as the river Aisne.

Topography:

Though on such a pitch dark night it was impossible to see any of the surrounding country, the map showed that the country of about a couple of miles to the north of the bridge was quit flat, and that the country then rose steeply to the plateaux of the Aisne Heights North of Bucy, and that these Northern Heights completely dominated the Riverain Plain[396].

5. The Weather and the Time:

---

[396] *I believe that this is meant to read "River Aisne Plain"*

The night was wet and dark; the time 1 a.m., in the middle of the night, with still four hours of darkness before sunrise.

6. The Condition of his troops:

The condition of his troops has been given above.

7. Possible Course open to him:

(a) to hold a Bridge Head near the Bridge:

This would safely hold the Bridge, and would have successfully carried out his orders. His troops would be safely dug-in by daylight, and his troops in these trenches would be covered by the Divisional Artillery from good positions on the Southern Heights.

But, on the other hand, to hold the bridge by a bridge head near the Bridge would place the rest of the division and other Troops who had to follow his Brigade, in a very unfavourable position, for the German Artillery from the Northern Heights could dominate both river crossing and the Riverain Plain North and South of the River. And to cross the open plain and storm the formidable, and by then strongly entrenched Northern Heights, would be an operation very costly in life.

(b) to attempt to traverse the Riverain Plain and to storm and hold the Northern Heights under cover of darkness:

This course, if successful, would assure the passage of the rest of the Force, and would have an immensely beneficial effect on the operations of our Higher Command.

But was it possible. Only about four hours of darkness remained before sunrise. The weather was appalling; the distance to the Northern Heights considerable. To get the Brigade across the Bridge must necessarily take a long time.

The brigade was much reduced in strength by casualties during the long-continued fighting. The officers and men were greatly exhausted by their long-continued exertions.

BRIGADIER'S DECISION:

Judged By the standards of Peace, or of ordinary men, the task was impossible. But in the Lexicon of the British Army there is no such word as Impossible, as we proved by the result both here, at the Battle of the Aisne, and later at the Original Landing on the Gallipoli Peninsula.

The Brigade and its Commander had great confidence in each other. They had served together both in Peace and in War. The Commander knew his men. He knew how fit and how well trained they were. He knew that with such troops the Impossible could be achieved. He therefore unhesitatingly and immediately decided to take the Risk to gain the big Result. The Brigadier gave the orders. It was the wonderful and splendid troops who carried through this desperate task and accomplished it with complete success.

SUBSEQUENT HISTORY:

The leading troops of the leading battalion (1st Hants) immediately on their arrival were passed carefully across the precarious roadway, advanced over the evacuated German trenches near the Bridge, and moved on to take up a covering position well to the North.

After them, slowly and in single file at two paces interval, breaking step, passed the rest of the 1st Hants., the 1st Somerset's, and the 1st Rifle Brigade, the 1st East Lancs following in reserve.

The ammunition carts had to be unloaded, and their contents passed over by hand. In these precarious circumstances the crossing took along time, and it was not until 3 a.m. that the Brigade had had crossed and had assembled on the northern side of the River.

While the crossing was being completed, the Brigadier explained in detail his plans to his battalion commanders and officers. The brigade was to advance and seize the Heights North of the River at the point of the bayonet. The intervening flat ground between the river and the heights was to be traversed as rapidly as possible, o as to ensure that the heights could be reached before daybreak. The leading battalion, the 1st Hants, were ordered to take the central spur on which lies La Montaigne Farm. The Somerset Light Infantry were to take the left ad were to seize the spur North-West of Bucy. The Rifle Brigade were to take the right and were to seize the spur North of St. Marguerite, the East Lancs being kept in reserve and to move to a position South of the centre of the village of Bucy-Le-Long.

Thanks to the boldness of the movement it was completely successful, and the Heights were seized and entrenched without opposition. The enemy made no attempt to hold the trenches they had dug on the flat ground, nor the trenches on the top of the edge of the Plateaux overlooking the Riverain Plain which they had evidently intended for their main positions. The Germans were completely surprised, and those who were met retired immediately on the Main Body, who were employed in digging the retired trenches some hundreds of yards behind the front edge of the plateaux. This retired line of trenches therefore became their Main Line.

Our men, on gaining the crests of the hills which overlooked the Riverain Plain and formed the Southern edge of the plateaux of the Aisne Heights, immediately entrenched themselves and formed a very strong position, for while the front line trenches were pushed forward on the comparatively flat ground on the top of the plateaux, the Reserves were in all cases completely sheltered just over and below the crests of the Heights. Indeed in the very steep slopes of these rocky heights there were many caves which gave admirable and comfortable shelter to our troops.

The operation of crossing the plain and seizing these Heights was carried out by the three leading battalions in a way which reflected the greatest credit both on the leadership of the officers and on the endurance and soldierly qualities of the men. This Brigade was by many hours the first Allied formation to cross the Aisne. The distance covered by the brigade on this day and night exceeded thirty miles.

The whole of the day of the 13th September and the night of the 13/14th were spent in strenuous work digging trenches. By the morning of the 14th the position may rightly be described as strong.

During he following night the battalions were sifted out and the 4th Division got into its final position, with the 11th Infantry Brigade on the left in contact with the French; the 10th Brigade in the centre; and the 12th Infantry Brigade on the right. The Bucy Heights thus taken on the night of the 12/13th continued to be held by the 4th Division during the Battle of the Aisne, until relieved by the French on the 7th October, when the Division moved North by march and train to take part in the fighting in Flanders.

Incident at Sydney Street Farm – 17th October 1914

"On reaching Houplines, I found that the delay was being caused by a few determined men who were holding a farmhouse on the roadside, from which all efforts to dislodge them had failed. Already one of the best company commanders of the Royal Irish Fusiliers, Captain Carbery[397], had been killed, while several men of the regiment had lost their lives in gallant efforts to shoot down the desperados at close range or draw back into cover such of their comrades a had been wounded and were unable to move.

Unfortunately this day the advanced guard, for some reason unknown, had no guns allotted to it, and there was no immediate prospect of clearing the obstruction by bringing down the walls on the heads of the unpleasant occupants. I therefore ordered the building to be set on fire, and suggested to the advanced guard commander the possibility of blowing it up as well, a procedure which, however, did not find favour, as to approach the house by daylight and lay a charge at a vulnerable point meant almost certain death to anyone who might make the attempt.

As it was getting dark, I ordered outposts to be thrown out and rode back to Armentières, where I enjoyed the hospitality of the Maire, Monsieur Henri Chas, at his fine house in the rue Sadi Carnot.

Dinner was hardly over when Lieutenant Corblet of the French Navy, who was attached to headquarters of the 4th Division and who had been with my advanced guard during the day, arrived and asked to see me.

He had just come from what we called "Sydney Street" Farm, where he had tried to parley with the occupants, receiving a bullet in reply which scared his cheek. Then with a gallant private of the Irish Fusiliers he had tried to gain a door whence he hoped to take the enemy in rear and finish with him. This ruse had failed, and the soldier who had volunteered to help had fallen dead in his arms. After the attempts to close with the obstinate holders of the farm, who seemed determined to sell

---

[397] *Captain Miles Bertie Cunninghame Carbery, aged 37, commander of C Company, 1st Battalion, Royal Irish Fusilier was killed in action on the 17th October by sniper fire from the buildings at Sydney Farm. He was the son of Son of the late Mr. and Mrs. W. E. Carbery, Eastbourne, Camberley and is buried in the Houplines Communal Cemetery extension, France. Extracted from the Commonwealth War Graves Commission web site*

their lives as dearly as they could, were ordered to case, and a ring of men was drawn round the place, making egress unobserved impossible.

Lieutenant Corblet told me that he had seen no signs to make him think that it was intended to blow up the building, but he strongly recommended that a howitzer, with high explosive shell, should be obtained and that herewith and end should be put to a somewhat ridiculous situation.

I went to headquarters of the 4th Division, and as a howitzer was not readily available forthcoming, obtained an 18-pounder gun, which did not reach the scene of action until 11 p.m.

When I arrived there some time earlier, I found that the building, which surrounded three side of a small courtyard, was still burning and that from that side of it which overlooked the road, shots were fired whenever anyone incautiously stepped from the surrounding gloom into the area illuminated by the flames. Captain R. Kentish of the Royal Irish Fusiliers, who had headed several gallant attempts to settle with the Saxon occupants – for Saxon soldiers they later proved to be – and save from the burning debris men who had fallen wounded close to the building, told me that a charge had been laid and would soon be ready for firing, and that this was expected to blow down the wall facing the road. he had a party of men in the ditch prepared to open fire and prevent escape on that side.

All being ready, we withdrew to the shelter of and avenue of trees close to the farm, and a moment later a loud explosion took place, followed shortly after by the thud of bricks and timber. Kentish and I ran around to the roadside facing the room which, full of burning matter, was now exposed to view. His men were firing fiercely into the flames, whence, strange to relate, shots came back and other sounds were heard. Soon all was over and the three determined holders of the farm were forever silenced; but in the morning a fourth, whose cries were heard during the night, was removed, wounded and somewhat burnt, to hospital.

It seems probable that the brave defenders of the building were under the delusion that their throats would be cut if captured, and for that reason had fought so tenaciously, for, from statements made by several prisoners, it had come to our knowledge that this preposterous idea had been spread by German officers in order to discourage their men from surrendering[398]."

---

[398] *Quoted from 'A Brigade of the Old Army 1914', Lieutenant-General Sir Aylmer Haldane K.C.B., D.S.O., Edward Arnold 1920, pp 131-134.*

Summary of 11th Brigade Action - 9th November, 1914

"As the shells crashed into La Hutte, German guns and infantry also began to pay close attention to British defences on the eastern side of Plugstreet Wood and it was all that the B.E.F could do to hold their ground. One of the exhausted units in the front line during this period was the 2nd Lancashire Fusiliers who, as part of the 4th Divisions 12th Brigade, had already seen action at Le Cateau, the Marne, The Aisne and Armentières since arriving in France on the 23rd August.

By early November the Commanding Officer of the battalion, Lt.-Col. R.H.K. Butler, had set up his headquarters in one of the buildings on the Ploegsteert – Messines Road known to the troops at this time as 'Hyde Park Corner'. It was here that Butler's staff, which included Captain Hugh Elles, the man who was to command the Tank Corps at Cambrai in November 1917, reorganised the remnants of numerous smashed units and sent them back to the line.

A German attack focused on Le Pelerin on the 7th November failed to crack the British front line, but a salient was created when the defenders were pushed back to the fringes of the wood. There were numerous attempts to regain the lost ground through a series of attacks that continued until mid-December, but none were successful and many casualties were sustained. The remains of one man that fell during this period, Private Harry Wilkinson of the 2/Lancashier Fusiliers, have only recently been discovered in a Le Pelerin field. Wilkinson died in an assault launched against the salient at 2320 hours on the 9th when two companies of the 2/Argyll and Sutherland Highlanders attacked via Edgar Farm towards the northern shoulder of the salient.

In the darkness and confusion of battle the Highlanders missed the German front line and the Lancashire Fusiliers in support had to tackle the emerging enemy with the bayonet and establish themselves in some buildings just beyond. After taking up a defensive posture, however, they were enfiladed from German positions that had not been secured by other British units in attack and the position become untenable. By dawn the Fusiliers had been forced back to their own front line and the 29-year-old Wilkinson, together with four comrades was dead.

Intriguingly, the Lancashire Fusiliers' Annual 1914 reported that these men were 'Buried behind the Trenches', but Wilkinsons's remains, identified by his rusted identity tags, were found in a shallow grave, together with a rum bottle and pipe in what would have been No Mans Land."

Lloyd Clark
RMC, Sandurst

Christmas Truce – 1st Hampshire Regiment

"Report on proceedings to the front of Hampshire Regiment trench on Christmas Day"

"The night 24/25th was particularly free sniping to our own front, the enemy were singing Christmas carols and their national songs. About 10 am on Christmas morning I was making a sketch of the trench under cover of fog, when I saw several of the enemy approaching from the trench north of our T piece. I shouted out for them to halt, not firing as the enemy was without arm, this was complied with and I sent forward a patrol to state that they must approach no nearer and return to their trench. Soon after more of the enemy were seen approaching from their main trench to the east of our position, these men also were halted and a patrol sent forward. As the patrol seemed unable to induce enemy to return to their trenches and more were seen approaching. I went forward and asked to se an officer. An officer came forward, but I failed to make him understand me, and interpreter however was soon procured and the enemy asked that there should be no shooting and that they should be allowed to bury their dead of which there were a considerable number a short way in front of their trench. This request I granted as by this time considerable numbers were walking about outside their trenches. A spot was indicated just by there foremost dead which I informed them that if they passed I would be compelled to open fire and that after dusk I should open fire an anyone outside the trench. The enemy agreed to these conditions and kept to them throughout the day. Towards evening what looked like a Staff officer appeared and ordered all back to the trenches, which order was immediately complied with. To our right front a gathering of some two to three hundred men of both sides took place, the men exchanging gifts, handing over enemy's dead, from near our trenches, and even exchanging rifles. Throughout the day I kept the garrison of my trench from contact with the enemy the men not being allowed out of the trench on the enemy's side. I gained the following information as regards the enemy and his trenches and dispositions.

The men were well clothed and seemed well supplied, every man was wearing a pair of gumboots. The regiments represented were 132/133 and some with F.A. under a crown, the great majority belonging to the 133rd regiment. The men seemed in age to range between nineteen and forty-five. The seemed very simple-minded creatures and were much elated over alleged victories in Russia. They stated they wished the war would soon finish but were confident of them selves. The strength to our immediate front I estimated to be about one man to every two yards except on right front, where they appeared to be much stronger there being about one mane per yard looking over the parapet even after a considerable number had left the trench.

The wire in front of the enemy's trenches was mounted on wooden frames with cross pieces at either end three foot high, the men appeared to have no difficulty in steeping over these. I could not see if there was trip wire in addition. The trenches seemed to be in good condition, the men jumped in from the parapet with splashing about, the trenches are loopholed about eighteen inches off the ground (in the front trench) these were about ten feet apart. Three lines of trenches were observed, the rear line being about one hundred yards from the front line, these were connected up by communications trenches. There appeared to be wire netting over the trenches coming about the parapet. A fortified house about (will get this later) yards in rear of the enemy's barricade on the north side of Le Gheer road was observed. I could see no Maxim guns or emplacements.

J B M Becket Capt.
OCC Coy
Hampshire Regiment

Christmas Truce – 1st Somerset Light Infantry Regiment

"C" Form (Quadruplicate). Army Form C. 2123 A.

MESSAGES AND SIGNALS. No. of Message.

Charges to Pay. £ s d — Office Stamp. 24 25-12-14

Service Instructions.

Handed in at the SLI Office at 6.10 p.m. Received here at 6.30 p.m.

TO 11th Bde

Sender's Number	Day of Month	In reply to Number	AAA
SL 14	25th	—	

No shelling or sniping today aaa Was able to recover today the bodies of CAPT MAUD and CAPT ORR from within GERMAN lines also LT HENSONS body and those of many N C Os and men aaa Last night good progress was made with breastwork behind left trench

FROM SOMERSETS

PLACE

TIME 6 PM

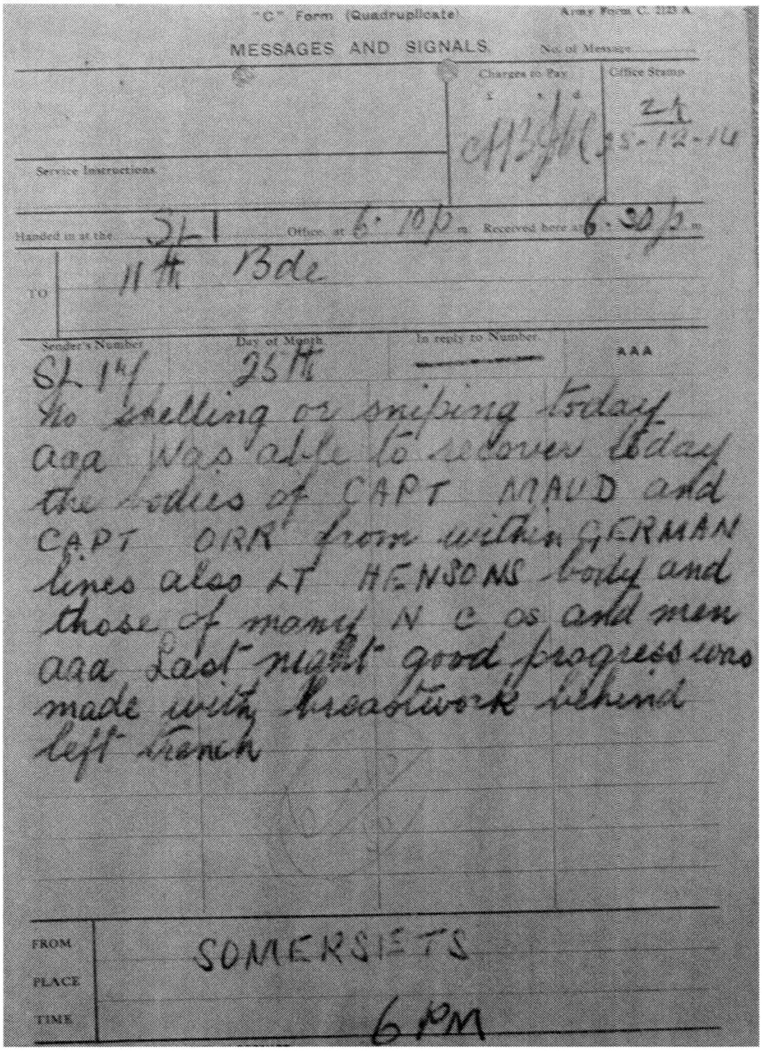

Plate 14

Message sent from the H.Q. of the Somerset Light Infantry at 6:00pm on Christmas Day 1914, towards the end of the truce.

Appendix V – 1915 – Orders and Reports

Report on Action of 10th Brigade April 24th – May 4th 1915

Reference Belgium Sheet 28
IV Division

The following is a report on the action of the 10th Infantry Brigade, and some attached units, from April 24th to May 4th: -

On the morning of April 24th I was informed by the Canadian Division that my Brigade would make a counter-attack next day on the German line from Saint Julien to the wood in C.17.a both inclusive, the attack to be supported by the Canadian Division Artillery. On this I moved the Brigade to a position just west of Ypres ready to cross the Canal at dark.

At about 3-30pm I received Canadian Division Operation Orders No. 10, and finding that my command was considerably enlarged I asked for an extra Staff Officer; Major MacBrian of the Canadian Division Staff was attached to me and his services during the whole of the next day were extremely useful, in fact without him, as my Brigade Major was wounded early in the day, I should have been much handicapped. I take this opportunity to notice the names of Lt-Col Lamb and Major C.H. Mitchell of the Canadian General Staff who were with me on the 25th as Liaison Officers both of whom rendered good service at the critical moments.

On receipt of the Operation Orders I endeavoured to get in touch with the various units placed under my command, I saw Brig. Gen. Burstall, C.R.A., and also Brig.-Gen. J. Riddell commanding Northumberland Brigade and explained my plan of action to them. As there was no opportunity for any previous reconnaissance and I did not know the ground I had to issue my orders of the map.

The Brigade moved across the Canal at midnight halting with it head at the junction of roads in C.28.b where I had a conference of Commanding Officers; I had previously told them the general plan and they had made Company Commanders fully conversant with situation. On arrival WIELTJE I found that, owing to congestion of the traffic on the SAINT JULIEN – YPRES road and the whole Brigade having to defile by two roads only through the wire in front of the G.H.Q. line, that it would be impossible to commence the attack before 5-30am.

At WEILTJE I gave the following orders verbally to Commanding Officers – Battalions to move through the wire and deploy for the attack on the line FORTUIN – farm in c.-16-c. – four Battalions in front line with a Battalion in support of the left flank and the North-

umberland Brigade in support of right flank. Objective SAINT JU-
LIEN village, the wood and enemy's trenches between these points.
Two Battalions the Royal Irish Fusiliers were and Royal Dublin Fusiliers were directed on SAINT JULIEN the R Ir. Fus on the right of the
ZANEBEEK BROOK, the R. Dub. Fus. on the left. The R. War. Regt.
were directed on the wood in C.17.a, the A. & S. Highrs. supporting
them, the left attack was under the orders of Colonel A.J. Poole, Commanding R. War. R.

The Seaforth Highlanders to move on the German trenches
between the wood and SAINT JULIEN connecting the right and left
attacks.

The Brigade deployed in good order with few casualties. I had
arranged with the C.R.A. Canadian Division for a preliminary bombardment of the wood and ST. JULIEN and trenches between these
points but at the last moment had to cancel the order to fire on St. Julien as I was informed that the Canadians were still in the village. The
artillery fire was good but there was not enough of it to seriously damage the enemy who were entrenched in a very strong position.

As soon as the Infantry advance commenced it was met by
heavy rifle fire and machine gun fire, the attack on SAINT JULIEN
pressed forward and in spite of heavy casualties, occupied the southern
most houses of St. Julien. The attack on the wood was pushed to within
40^x or 50^x of the German trenches and the centre attack was up in line.
Heavy artillery and rifle fire now, at 6. a.m., held up the whole line, the
left was reinforced by the 7th A. & S. Highlanders and at 6-15 a.m. I
directed two Battalions of the Northumberland Brigade to rein force
the attack on St. Julien keeping east of the ZANEBEEK brook; these
two Battalions went forward but losing direction came up a good way
to the right of my attack and so extended the line instead of thickening
it.

The attack at 7-30 a.m. had reached its limit and the Brigade
began slowly to retire on to the line it eventually held where it dug itself
in. I did not put in the remaining two Battalions of the Northumberland Brigade as I saw it would not be possible to carry the enemy's line
under the heavy fire to which the attack subjected, also, in the event of
the enemy making a strong attack on my depleted line, I considered it
necessary to keep to keep these two Battalions in hand for offensive action. At 9 a.m. I placed one of these Bns. Under the orders Brig.-Gen.
Commanding 3rd Canadian Brigade as a support for his left flank. The
casualties up to now had been very heavy, nearly 50% so I ordered the
ground already gained to be made good, the Brigade was able to maintain the position it had taken up and to consolidate and reorganize after
dark.

I had not yet got in touch with the two Battalions York & Durham Brigade which were supposed to be on my right connecting up with the 2nd Canadian Brigade but at 10 a.m. I heard that they were at VERLORENHOEK and that the 85th Brigade had been asked to send them forward to fill the gap (Can. Div. G.375)

This was done as later on I found them on my right.

Although the attack failed the object of checking any further of the enemy was attained, the line which the Brigade occupied on April 25th being held until the early morning of May 4th when the Brigade was moved to reserve.

I attribute the want of success to the heavy artillery and machine gun fire of the enemy which our artillery were unable to deal with, the enemy's infantry did not at any time show a bold offensive and it is probable that they had had enough for this day. The attack was also severely handicapped by having to be made over ground that was new to the troops and there being no time for previous reconnaissance. It was necessary to make the attack at daylight as the deployment had to be made in front of the G.H.Q. line, which was heavily wired. This could only be done in the dark as the exits through the wire were few and under direct observation from the enemy's trenches.

I wish to bring to notice the gallantry of the whole Brigade on this day. All Battalions were well and accurately led on their objectives and there was no confusion in the deployment. I regret that the casualties were so heavy, 73 officers and 2346 rank and file. The names of Officers and men whom I wish to bring to notice will be found in Appendix 'A'. I attach a rough sketch showing position held by the brigade on the night of 25th/26th.

Under Canadian Division Operation Order No.11, issued at 6-15p.m. on 25th, my Command was broken up and reduced to my own Brigade and a Battalion of the Royal Irish Regt. My right was ordered to connect up with General Bulfins troops on the St. Julien – FORTUIN road. I ordered the Royal Irish Regt. to prolong my right and get in touch with the 11th Brigade who were holding the section to my right, this they were unable to do as the left of the 11th Brigade did not extend to the junction named in the orders. However, two Battalions of the York and Durham Brigade were found in a position to the right of the road and these were in touch with 11th Brigade on their right so there was no gap in the general line.

April 26th. At 1.25 p.m. I received Canadian Division Operation Order No.12 issued at 12-30 p.m. para. 3 of which ordered me to advance one Battalion between the wood in C.10.d and the WIELTJE – SAINT JULIEN road to co-operate with the Lahore Division who were attacking in a northerly direction with their right on the wood, according to orders this Division would be deployed at 1-20 p.m. As all my Battalions were in the front and wires had been cut during the morning it was impossible to carry out this order and I so informed the Canadian Division. I went up with my staff to my firing line and had arranged by 2-30 p.m. to send the 7th Argyll and Sutherland Highlanders forward as soon as I saw the attack of the Lahore Division develop against the wood, this attack never went forward against the wood so I did not advance my Battalion.

The Northumberland Brigade which had been ordered to attack St. Julien at the same time, moved forward with great dash behind my right and centre but owing to heavy shell fire did not progress beyond my firing line where it remained till dusk and was then withdrawn. At night I made a slight alteration in my line drawing back the Royal Irish Regt. in to line with the Royal Irish Fusiliers and the Durham & York Battalion on my right.

April 27th & 28th. Nothing happened on my front except that it was subjected to continuous shelling.

There was rather more shelling, the 3rd Cavalry Brigade came up in support in rear of my right and I arranged with Brig.-Gen. J. VAUGHAN the steps to be taken in case of attack.

April 30th. Shelling continued all day.

At night a Battalion of the 12th Inf. Brigade relieved my two left Battalions, the R. War. R. and 7th A. & S. Highrs., who were drawn back in support.

May 1st. A good deal of shelling in rear of my line, my support Battalions having some casualties and my Headquarters being burnt out.

May 2nd. The morning was very quiet and hardly any shelling but at 5 p.m. the enemy made an attack using gas which struck the whole of my line except my right which only got a small dose, the 12th Brigade on my left were also heavily gassed. My line held fast but as I saw troops on my left coming back I sent the 7th A. & s. Highrs. up on my left and at the same time arranged with Gen. Vaughan 3rd Cavalry Brigade to send up a Regiment to the threatened point, these two units arrived at the same time and at once occupied the trenches which had been vacated, catching the enemy in the open and inflicting severe loss. The way in which these units went through the gas was worthy of great praise and they certainly saved the situation. I should like to bring to the notice the excellent work and close co-operation of the 3rd Cavalry Brigade; on the two previous nights they had dug defended posts covering WIELTJE and the approaches to it which would have been invaluable if the enemy had broken through in that direction.

May 3rd. Some attacks were made on our front but they were easily checked, the wind was strong and in the wrong direction as regards the enemy so no gas was used, a good many gas shells were fired but the result was nil. On the night of the 3rd/4th the Brigade was withdrawn into reserve, the operation which began at 1 a.m. was carried out successfully with no casualties; previous to the withdrawal all surplus ammunition and trench stores were removed behind the G.H.Q. lines. The Royal Irish Regt. returned to its own Brigade. I should like to say how much I appreciate the willing work of this Battalion, they came under my orders late on the evening of April 25th when there was still some confusion and uncertainty of what troops were actually on my right. Colonel GLOSTER Commanding on arrival south of FOR-TUIN found that he could not get touch with the troops on his right or left and so very rightly decided to take up a position covering FOR-TUIN for the night, I desire to bring this officers name forward for notice.

I attach a list of recommendations which I hope may be favourably considered, the Brigade has had a hard nine days losing during that period over 50% of officers and men and merits reward.

This report is not as complete as I should wish but owing to my G.S. clerk having been gassed and gone to hospital with some of the records on him a great deal has had to written from memory. I have sent a motor cyclist chasing over the country after him but have not yet recovered the papers and do not like to delay the report any longer.

Brigade Commander 11th Brigade, 24th April & 2nd May.

On Saturday the 24th April, the 11th Inf. Brig. left rest billets near Bailleul and moved to VLAMERTINGHE where in came into Corps Reserve under orders of G.O.C., V Corps.

At midday Sunday, 25th April, the V Corps sent for the Brigadier and after explaining the situation, sent him to G.O.C. 28th Division (Canadian Division) under whose orders the Brigade were to act.

The 11th Inf. Brig. were ordered to move so as to reach ST. JEAN at dusk. The 2nd Canadian Brigade were to find guides at ST JEAN to guide the 11th Brigade into the line held by the 2nd Canadian Brigade.

The 2nd Canadian Infantry Brigade did not find any guides, and it was not till 10 p.m. that the conflicting reports of the whereabouts of the so-called line of defence could be cleared up.

The situation was then found to be as follows:

Left of 85th Brigade were holding wood in D.10.c.

A detachment of mixed troops about 400 all told were believed to be holding a line south of the FORTUIN-MOSSELMAKT road.

The 1st Suffolk Regt. and the 12th London Regt. were entrenched about FORTUIN.

The 2nd Canadian Brigade had practically disappeared from the trenches north of the HANNABECK.

The 10th Inf. Brig. were holding a line in C.17 with their right on FORTUIN.

At 10 p.m. the Hants were sent to get touch with the 85th Brigade in D.10.c. They were to establish touch with the 85th Brigade's left and entrench on the line of the FORTUIN-MOSSELMAKT road pushing patrols down to Cross Roads in D.14.a

At 10.30 p.m. the 11th Inf. Brig. moved from ST JEAN on FORTUIN. The Rif. Brig. deployed and took up a position in the subsidiary line about Hill 37. D.20.a. with two companies of Som.L.I. on their right.

The Som.L.I. less two companies and the L.R.B. dug in square D.19. The troops were in position half-an-hour before daylight.

During the 26ᵗʰ the Rif. Brig. and two companies Som.L.I. on Hill 37 were heavily shelled from north, north-east and south-east, losing about 100 casualties.

At dusk 26ᵗʰ, the L.R.B. were moved to D.20.b and entrenched. Shelling continued all night. Two companies Som.L.I. rejoined their Battalion in support. The Hants entrenched from wood D.10.o to HANNABECK.

Communications during daylight was extremely difficult.

On 27ᵗʰ, the 11ᵗʰ Inf. Brig. was ordered to relieved the mixed detachment about D.15.c. and the Suffolk Regt and London Regt. at FORTUIN: also to consolidate their line from wood D.10.o to cross road C.18.0.

Orders could only be got through at dusk. The line was reconnoitred and farm in D.14.a were found to be strongly held by the enemy.

General Hasler was killed by a shell in ST JEAN.
Col. HICKS took command of the Brigade and H.Q. were moved to VERLORENHOEK

On 28ᵗʰ, the Hants improved their line by putting some buildings in square D.15.a in a state of defence.
The Rif. Brig. dig themselves in between the HANNABECK at square D.14.b.8.4 and Road junction at D.14.b.3.2.

The Som.L.I. dug themselves in with their right in touch with the Rif. Brig. and their left at D.13.b.3.2.

Two battalions of the York and Durham Brigade continued the line to road junction C.18.b.

On 29ᵗʰ at dusk, the battalions of York and Durhams Brigade were split up, two companies being sent to each of the 4 battalions of the 11ᵗʰ Infantry Brigade.

The front was re-allotted and occupied as follows.
Hants & 2 Coys. 4/E. Yorks from wood D.10.o to farms in D.15.a.3.8. both exclusive.

Rif. Brig. and 2 Coys 4/E. Yorks from above road farms to road junctionD.14.d.4.4.

Som.L.I. & 2 Coys.4/E.Yorks from above road junction to D.13.b.3.2.

L.R.B & 2 Coys 4/E.Yorks from D.13.b.3.2. to road junction C.18.d

Brigadier-General C.B. PROWSE took over command of the 11th Brigade on 29th April.

During the 30th April and 1st May, the shelling was very heavy, no part of the line was entirely free from it.

During the night of 1st-2nd, the shelling all over the area was very severe. H.Q. of the Brigade had a shell in the signal dug-out on the afternoon of the 1st.

The E. Lancs arrived at 10.30p.m. on the 29th and were moved into support at ZEVENKOTE.

About 4.45p.m. 2nd May very heavy shelling commenced on front line held by Som.L.I. and L.R.B. as well as on 10th Inf. Brig and 11th Brig.H.Q. VERLORENHOEK.

The Germans used gases but no infantry attack was made. The shelling eased down about 7 p.m.

Reports were received of Germans collecting in the BOIS DE CUISINIERES in front of the wood D.10.c. and in D.8.

The L.R.B. suffered very heavily during the worst of the shelling. They did very good execution on the German working parties during the night and sent in two prisoners.

The Som.L.I. suffered less than the L.R.B. but were considered knocked about.

The G.O.C. 85th Brigade reported that the D.L.I. Brig., 3 Bns 84th Brig., 1Bn. 85th Brig., were available in support and 3Bns. 83rd Brig. were ordered to VERLORENHOEK.

The position of affairs at midnight 2nd-3rd was as follows:

The Hants with the Roy. Fus. in support were in touch with the left of the 85th Brigade. The German were known to have been collecting on their front.

The Rif. Brig. supported by 2 Coys. of 84th brig had had a very heavy shelling.

The Som.L.I. with one company of the E.Lancs had been heavily shelled and a certain amount of gas had affected the left companies.

The L.R.B. had been very severely shelled, suffering heavily. They also had suffered from gas.

There was every indication of attacks on both flanks of the line held by the 11th Brigade and also on the centre of the line.

All the morning of the 3rd the shelling continued.

The artillery support was entirely inadequate, consisting as it did only of 146 F.A.Brig with one section Howitzers attached.

Lt-Col Rundle worked his guns in the very closest co-operation with the infantry and did more than could expected of him, although 2 guns were destroyed about 10 a.m., an observation officer killed, and all wires blown down. His batteries were registered by the enemy's heavy artillery.

At noon the situation was that the enemy had been seen to concentrate on both flanks of the 11th Brig. line and to bring up guns into close support of his infantry.

The battalions in the front line especially the Rif. Brig. had again been subjected to very heavy and accurate shell fire.

A report was received from R.F.A., Middlesex Regt. and Som.L.I. about noon that 2 companies of right of the Rifle Brigade had been very badly cut up – one part of the trenches being manned by 1 rifleman per 12 yards, but they still held fast.

At 2 p.m. the situation was much the same but two companies of the 5th Kings Own Regt and 2 companies of the York and Lancaster Regt were sent up to support the Rif. Brig. This made the situation a serious one as these troops were required to hold the 2nd line to cover the withdrawal of the 28th Division and 11th Inf. Brig. that night.

About 4 p.m. a message was received from the Hants stating that wood D.10.c. had been carried by the enemy and that a further attack was impending and the enemy apparently going to use gas.

At 4.12 p.m. orders were given to the 2/E.Yorks to move to support junction of 11th and 85th Brigades.

At 7 p.m. the situation had not changed. The East Lancs (less two companies) were on their way up to release the battalions of 83rd Brig. Three Battalions of the 27th Division were at or near VERLOREN-HOEK watching the left of the 11th Brigade.

In spite of the continuous strain on all ranks and the difficulty of getting orders to battalions till after dusk the withdrawal was successfully accomplished, which speaks very highly for the discipline maintained and the regimental leading.

The casualties suffered by the Brig during this period covered by this report are attached.

The 11th Infantry Brigade held all their trenches and one and all refused to give an inch.

Brig-Gen.
Commdg 11th Infy.Brig.

Report from Major Symons-Mine explosion at Le Touquet 9/4/1915

4th Division

At 8-30 am I exploded the mine in LE TOUQUET.

Charge of 1200 lbs was taken from barrels and put in sandbags.
These were then taken by trolly up to the junction and then by hand up to the chamber prepared before. The filling of the sandbags from barrels took 2 hours, loading 2 hours and tamping 12 hours. I tamped 70 feet with air spaces. I did not see the result but bricks were thrown as far back as far as our Barricades. A few of our men have been hit with these bricks. The mine appears to have brought down most of the wall facing Sniper's Houses. Owing to gas I do not think it will be safe to investigate our galleries for 36 hours, but judging from reports I am afraid they must be damaged. Captain Edwards and two men were "gassed" during the tamping but have recovered. I think considerable damage must have been done to whatever was behind the front German walls although the barricade itself did not appear to be much damaged. It is quite sure that with large charges under brickwork one must be under cover or a considerable distance back.

9/4/15

Sd. C.B.O.Symons, Major.
Commdg, 7th Fd. Co. R.E.

Operations at Le Touquet 9th April 1915 - Explosion of Mine.

Report of Operations 9-4-1915 – Explosion of Mine
12th Infantry Brigade No. G. 64.
G.O.C. 12th Brigade

Owing to the fact that the enemy were on the point of discovering the mine by means of a counter mine, it became necessary to fire it prematurely, and at a time when the explosion could not be a prelude to an infantry attack.

In these circumstances all that could be hoped for was
Kill a number of Germans.

Weaken the enemy's defences, and ascertain his dispositions with a view to facilitating an attack on LE TOUQUET in the future.

Learn by experience the effect of a heavy explosion on the defending troops and the precautions necessary for the safety of the attackers.

2. THE PLAN
The mine was fired at 8-30.a.m. the earliest possible moment after the discovery of the approach of the German Counter Mine.

Previous to the explosion the enemy's trenches and defended houses in the neighbourhood of LE TOUQUET were subjected to bombardment by Artillery and trench mortars, and to burst of fire. The bombardment lasted for twenty minutes; there was then a pause for ten minutes.

During the night some gaps were purposely cut made in our barbed wire entanglements.

In the early morning two companies of Infantry were extended and advanced towards the subsidiary line of trenches to the West of LE TOUQUET. By this means it was hoped that the enemy would anticipate an attack and man his defences in strength during the pause before the mine exploded.

Immediately after the explosion the Artillery were ordered to turn their fire onto the approaches of LE TOUQUET with a view of attacking the enemy's reinforcements should he attempt to bring any up.

3. THE EFFECTS OF THE EXPLOSION

The effect in material was considerable. The "White House" was practically demolished, and other defended houses were badly damaged. The full value of the damage cannot at present be estimated, but it is hoped that further advance has been facilitated.

The enemy's casualties are unknown. It is thought that the whole garrison within a radius of 20 yards of the centre of the explosion must have perished besides any men working in the enemy's mine. A few wounded men were observed crawling away. And between 1.p.m. and 5.p.m. twenty seven men on stretchers were carried away.

The enemy's wire entanglement in the immediate neighbourhood of the explosion was destroyed. No large crater appears to have been made, but a large mass of debris was formed which would have been a more or less difficult obstacle to a rapid advance.

The force of the explosion threw a large number of bricks and stones into the air. It appears necessary for all troops within a distance of 250 yards at least, to be provided with overhead protection.

The ENEMY'S DISPOSITIONS.

There is nothing to indicate the strength of the enemy holding LE TOUQUET and the trenches near the village. In the morning the smoke of the usual number of fires were observed.

The enemy's Infantry holding the hostile front line only fired a comparatively few rounds. Usually in our trenches in this portion of the line it is unsafe to show above the top of the parapet; directly after the explosion the troops opened a heavy rifle fir from over the top of the parapet and suffered practically no casualties. It seems possible that the surprise of the explosion to the enemy may have given our men the advantage of a start in the opening of the fire, and once that fire was started, he found it impossible to fire back.

A hostile machine gun and a considerable rifle fire opened from FRELINGHIEN. The machine Gun was located. If in the future a further advance is attempted, it would seem necessary to arrange a heavy rifle fire, as well as artillery fire against the village.

The enemy's artillery fired a few rounds but did little damage. Accurate shrapnel fire was opened, after the explosion, on the houses in our possession in LE TOUQUET, but not until after a delay of sufficient length to have enabled our troops to have crossed the ground between the opposing defences without loss. The majority of rounds appear to have been fired against the houses at some distance from the front line apparently with a view to preventing reinforcements.

In the evening the enemy opened a heavy bombardment on LE TOUQUET Ry. Station and Battalion Head Quarters with 5.9" Howitzers. They did comparatively little damage.

Explosion of the Mine at Le Touquet

===

GGG/180

This mine of which you have been given details in the mining report, had on the 8th instant reached a distance of 190 feet with the main shaft, as reported in my GGG/180 of the 8th instant.

From the noise of trollies moving and other signs it was evident that either a German mine was being run close to the head of our mine shaft, or else that the Germans had discovered and were preparing a counter mine. In either case no time was to be lost, and orders were issued that all work should cease in our line, and that 1200lbs of gunpowder should be placed in it and well tamped, so that, if possible the side gallery should be saved.

It was calculated that the head of our mine was within 40 to 45 feet away from the enemy's barricade, which was it's main objective, and it was calculated that if the explosion was successful the crator would reach just short of the barricade, but that it would bring down the nearest German House and loopholed wall, facing our Sniper's Houses.

With the object of blowing up as many Germans as possible it was decided to make a demonstration with infantry and artillery so as to cause the Germans to man their defences, and orders with this object were issued by G.O.C., 12th Brigade.

The time of the explosion was settled between Major Symons R.E. in charge of the mine, and the Brigadier Commanding 12th Brigade, and depended entirely on how long the tamping, etc., took.

Major Symon's report giving these was sent to you this morning.

It was finally decided to blow up the mine at 8.30am and at 8 o'clock demonstration began.

A member of the Divisional Staff went down to witness the results of the explosion, from the forward trench about 200 yards from the end of the mine, just in front of Barkham farm.

He reported as follows:-
"Bombardment commenced at 8 am, the 5 inch howitzers firing at Pond House, and the 18 pr at the trench north of Le Tourqet. The trench mortar situated in the corner of Sniper's Houses bombed the

breastwork in front of the Estimenet House with considerable success. The infantry opened fire all along the line, in the neighbourhood of Le Touquet.

The enemy's rifle fire was completely subdued by ours, but one or more Machine Guns opened fire the Houses in Frelinghien, south of the Lys.

At 8.30 am, precisely an enormous explosion took place, a cloud of smoke shout upwards, and with it, timber, bricks and earth, and it is hoped some Germans. Some of the bricks were thrown as far back as our own barricade and Barkham Farm, that is to say, about 250 yards from the mine.

Most of the men were under cover, but the anxiety to see the explosion caused some of them to expose themselves, and a few of them were hit by falling bricks."

It is impossible to say how many Germans were blown up, or injured, by the explosion, but the result was apparently satisfactory. The main object of exploding the mine was to blow up the enemy's mine and there is every probability that this objective was achieved.

The force of the explosion apparently just reached the barricade, but did not seriously damage it. On the other hand, it blew down a large part of the loopholed wall, facing the Sniper's Houses, which had been much strengthened by the Germans, and must have been held by them at the time of the explosion.

After the smoke had drifted away a huge mass of rubble and a large crater could be seen.

Only one German body was seen and this was that of a wounded man, which was pulled in by his comrades out of the crater. Two or three other Germans who were apparently attempting to dig something up in the crater, were fired at and disappeared.

So far as can be ascertained, the calculations as to the position of the head of our mine was correct, as the edge of the crater reached just about where it was expected to be. It will probably not be safe to enter the mine for 36 hours, and so it has been impossible to ascertain so far whether our side gallery has been damaged. This will, however, be done as soon as possible.

There was little retaliation by the Germans in the shape of gun fire, but they fired at certain points of our communication trench, leading up to Le Touquet, with Little Willies and Rifle Grenades, thus indicating what that they considered to be our vulnerable points. These places can be easily rendered bombproof, and this information will be of great information to us.

It is hoped shortly to forward to you the names of certain officers and men who have carried out to a successful finish a very difficult task. Not only was mining carried out through very difficult soil and much hampered by water, but during the last 48 hours they have been carrying out a very dangerous task, in close proximity to the enemy, and liable to be blown up at any moment, as there is no doubt that the Germans were working extremely hard in order to anticipate us.

= = = = = = = =

Since writing the above, a report has been received which shews that 17 German wounded have been seen crossing Frelinghien bridge, from Le Touquet.

9/4/15
Major-General,

Commanding 4th Division.

Brigade Commander 11th Brigade, 24th April & 2nd May.

On Saturday the 24th April, the 11th Inf. Brig. left rest billets near Bailleul and moved to VLAMERTINGHE where in came into Corps Reserve under orders of G.O.C., V Corps.

At midday Sunday, 25th April, the V Corps sent for the Brigadier and after explaining the situation, sent him to G.O.C. 28th Division (Canadian Division) under whose orders the Brigade were to act.

The 11th Inf. Brig. were ordered to move so as to reach ST JEAN at dusk. The 2nd Canadian Brigade were to find guides at ST JEAN to guide the 11th Brigade into the line held by the 2nd Canadian Brigade.

The 2nd Canadian Infantry Brigade did not find any guides, and it was not till 10 p.m. that the conflicting reports of the whereabouts of the so-called line of defence could be cleared up.

The situation was then found to be as follows:

Left of 85th Brigade were holding wood in D.10.c.

A detachment of mixed troops about 400 all told were believed to be holding a line south of the FORTUIN-MOSSELMAKT road.

The 1st Suffolk Regt. and the 12th London Regt. were entrenched about FORTUIN.

The 2nd Canadian Brigade had practically disappeared from the trenches north of the HANNABECK.

The 10th Inf. Brig. were holding a line in C.17 with their right on FORTUIN.

At 10 p.m. the Hants were sent to get touch with the 85th Brigade in D.10.c. They were to establish touch with the 85th Brigade's left and entrench on the line of the FORTUIN-MOSSELMAKT road pushing patrols down to Cross Roads in D.14.a
At 10.30 p.m. the 11th Inf. Brig. moved from ST JEAN on FORTUIN. The Rif. Brig. deployed and took up a position in the subsidiary line about Hill 37. D.20.a. with two companies of Som.L.I. on their right.

The Som.L.I. less two companies and the L.R.B. dug in square D.19. The troops were in position half-an-hour before daylight.

During the 26th the Rif. Brig. and two companies Som.L.I. on Hill 37 were heavily shelled from north, north-east and south-east, losing about 100 casualties.

At dusk 26th, the L.R.B. were moved to D.20.b and entrenched. Shelling continued all night. Two companies Som.L.I. rejoined their Battalion in support. The Hants entrenched from wood D.10.o to HANNABECK.

Communications during daylight was extremely difficult.

On 27th, the 11th Inf. Brig. was ordered to relieved the mixed detachment about D.15.c. and the Suffolk Regt and London Regt. at FORTUIN: also to consolidate their line from wood D.10.o to cross road C.18.0.
Orders could only be got through at dusk. The line was reconnoitred and farm inD.14.a were found to be strongly held by the enemy.

General Hasler was killed by a shell in ST JEAN.
Col. HICKS took command of the Brigade and H.Q. were moved to VERLORENHOEK

On 28th, the Hants improved their line by putting some buildings in square D.15.a in a state of defence.
The Rif. Brig. dig themselves in between the HANNABECK at square D.14.b.8.4 and Road junction at D.14.b.3.2.

The Som.L.I. dug themselves in with their right in touch with the Rif. Brig. and their left at D.13.b.3.2.

Two battalions of the York and Durham Brigade continued the line to road junction C.18.b.
On 29th at dusk, the battalions of York and Durhams Brigade were split up, two companies being sent to each of the 4 battalions of the 11th Infantry Brigade.
The front was re-allotted and occupied as follows.

Hants & 2 Coys. 4/E. Yorks from wood D.10.o to farms in D.15.a.3.8. both exclusive.

Rif. Brig. and 2 Coys 4/E. Yorks from above road farms to road junction D.14.d.4.4.

Som.L.I. & 2 Coys.4/E.Yorks from above road junction to D.13.b.3.2.
L.R.B & 2 Coys 4/E.Yorks from D.13.b.3.2. to road junction C.18.d

Brigadier-General C.B. PROWSE took over command of the 11th Brigade on 29th April.

During the 30th April and 1st May, the shelling was very heavy, no part of the line was entirely free from it.

During the night of 1st-2nd, the shelling all over the area was very severe. H.Q. of the Brigade had a shell in the signal dug-out on the afternoon of the 1st.
The E. Lancs arrived at 10.30p.m. on the 29th and were moved into support at ZEVENKOTE.

About 4.45p.m. 2nd May very heavy shelling commenced on front line held by Som.L.I. and L.R.B. as well as on 10th Inf. Brig and 11th Brig.H.Q. VERLORENHOEK.
The Germans used gases but no infantry attack was made. The shelling eased down about 7 p.m.

Reports were received of Germans collecting in the BOIS DE CUIS-INIERES in front of the wood D.10.c. and in D.8.

The L.R.B. suffered very heavily during the worst of the shelling. They did very good execution on the German working parties during the night and sent in two prisoners.

The Som.L.I. suffered less than the L.R.B. but were considered knocked about.

The G.O.C. 85th Brigade reported that the D.L.I. Brig., 3 Bns 84th Brig., 1Bn. 85th Brig., were available in support and 3Bns. 83rd Brig. were ordered to VERLORENHOEK.
The position of affairs at midnight 2nd-3rd was as follows:

The Hants with the Roy. Fus. in support were in touch with the left of the 85th Brigade. The German were known to have been collecting on their front.

The Rif. Brig. supported by 2 Coys. of 84th brig had had a very heavy shelling.

The Som.L.I. with one company of the E.Lancs had been heavily shelled and a certain amount of gas had affected the left companies.

The L.R.B. had been very severely shelled, suffering heavily.
They also had suffered from gas.

There was every indication of attacks on both flanks of the line held by the 11th Brigade and also on the centre of the line.

All the morning of the 3rd the shelling continued.
The artillery support was entirely inadequate, consisting as it did only of 146 F.A.Brig with one section Howitzers attached.

Lt-Col Rundle worked his guns in the very closest co-operation with the infantry and did more than could expected of him, although 2 guns were destroyed about 10 a.m., an observation officer killed, and all wires blown down. His batteries were registered by the enemy's heavy artillery.

At noon the situation was that the enemy had been seen to concentrate on both flanks of the 11th Brig. line and to bring up guns into close support of his infantry.

The battalions in the front line especially the Rif. Brig. had again been subjected to very heavy and accurate shell fire.

A report was received from R.F.A., Middlesex Regt. and Som.L.I. about noon that 2 companies of right of the Rifle Brigade had been very badly cut up – one part of the trenches being manned by 1 rifleman per 12 yards, but they still held fast.

At 2 p.m. the situation was much the same but two companies of the 5th Kings Own Regt and 2 companies of the York and Lancaster Regt were sent up to support the Rif. Brig. This made the situation a serious one as these troops were required to hold the 2nd line to cover the withdrawal of the 28th Division and 11th Inf. Brig. that night.

About 4 p.m. a message was received from the Hants stating that wood D.10.c. had been carried by the enemy and that a further attack was impending and the enemy apparently going to use gas.

At 4.12 p.m. orders were given to the 2/E.Yorks to move to support junction of 11th and 85th Brigades.

At 7 p.m. the situation had not changed. The East Lancs (less two companies) were on their way up to release the battalions of 83rd Brig. Three Battalions of the 27th Division were at or near VERLOREN-HOEK watching the left of the 11th Brigade.

In spite of the continuous strain on all ranks and the difficulty of getting orders to battalions till after dusk the withdrawal was successfully accomplished, which speaks very highly for the discipline maintained and the regimental leading.

The casualties suffered by the Brig during this period covered by this report are attached.

The 11th Infantry Brigade held all their trenches and one and all refused to give an inch.

Brig-Gen.
Commdg 11th Infy.Brig.

Report 1st Hampshire Regiment- 25th April, 1915

1st HAMPSHIRE REGIMENT
Written By Lieut –Colonel F.R. Hicks, O.C., Battalion.
Move from Ploegsteert to Ypres.

To understand the narrative a rough sketch of the situation round Ypres is necessary. When Ypres was held during the fierce fighting of October – November 1914, it made a big salient from out line, stretching out some four miles east of the City, while at the south at St. Eloi our line was under three miles away. At the north, the Salient was less pronounced.

On the 22nd April 1915 the French line on the Canadian left gave way completely, retiring behind the canal. The Canadian left was in the air. Fighting hard, the Canadians fell back slowly and on the 25th were holding the dotted line on the sketch. But that evening they broke and there was a gap some three miles wide between our regular troops, just north of Zonnebeke and reinforcements which had been pushed up north of Ypres. That was the gap the 11th Brigade had to fill. We did not leave our billets till the morning of the 24th. We marched to the station and entrained. Detrained a few miles west of Ypres in the afternoon and sat in a field, finally getting shelter of sorts in some farms for the night, wherein we were lucky as it rained hard.

Sunday 25th we marched at 6 and rested all day in a village a few miles further on, which we destroyed by shells shortly afterward. Sunday evening we marched off again. Our orders came to relieve the Canadians, not knowing that at the time the Canadians, presses beyond endurance, had given up their trenches and were falling right back. We passed the blazing ruins of the city on our right where the great 17" shells were still crashing and destroying everything. Three beyond Ypres we learned of the Canadian's withdrawal and learned too that we could get no guides to take us out to the line. The Hampshire's were leading the Brigade. It was a horrid situation; there was a great gap, we were to fill it in and nobody knew where our ends of the gap were or where were the enemy.

The 10th Brigade, which had preceded us by 24 hours, had attacked on a line north of Ypres on the east of the canal. Their right had to prolonged, but the roads beyond their right were in possession of the Germans and it was impossible to cover the five miles across country to the far side of the gap and dig in before daylight. So Brigadier-General Hasler ordered the Hampshire's to march on Zonnebeke and get in touch with our troops there and extend westwards to meet the rest of the 11th Brigade. It was a race with dawn, for to be caught by daylight, not entrenched, meant annihilation. After reaching Zonnebeke more difficulties arose in the confusion consequent on the retirement of the Canadians. The battalion on the extreme left of the regular division there had lost touch and we could find no one to guide us to its trenches and had to trust to the map over strange country.

At 2.25 a.m. on the 26th we reached the top of a slight ridge: we knew we must be near the Royal Fusiliers and there was only an hour of darkness left. There was no time to lose and we started to dig. The men were tired out. They dug like bricks. Most of them knew that their lives depended on their being underground by dawn. Luckily for us we found some old trenches, some French, some perhaps support trenches for the Canadians, facing all ways, and more lucky still, the morning was misty, so we were able to go on digging for another couple of hours which made all the difference. But before this we had met the enemy in our centre, opposite Captain Beckett and C. Coy. A large party of advanced through the misty moonlight shouting "Ve vos de Royal Fusiliers". One of our patrols was caught sheeplike, but Captain Beckett was not so simple and quickly disposed of these Royal Fusiliers, who withdrew below the ridge. On the left, where A Coy., under Captain Sandeman, had occupied a few houses, we were not so fortunate. A surprise attack in the mist drove out the party holding the houses who pressed into the half finished trench and caused some confusion. Captain Sandeman, Captain Chapman and others were killed, but sergeant Lay and a few others gallantly formed a line across the trench and stopped the enemy's rush. When the mist lifted at 7 we were holding a curved line, C. Coy. on the right facing north-east, with a gap of some 400 yards between them and a small wood on their right front, held by the Royal Fusiliers, with whom by now Lt. Stevens and a patrol had got in touch. In the centre D Coy. on the crest of the ridge, faced nearly north and on the left A Coy. faced nearly west with their left thrown back. B.Coy. was in a second trench a little way back partly behind the crest and the Headquarters in the right end of the same trench and their left still more thrown back.

With the lifting of the mist the German guns opened. It is hopeless to attempt to describe it. Owing to our being at the extreme point of the salient we had guns almost all round of and owing to the shape of the ground the Germans holding ridges north and east, which commanded every yard of the Ypres enclave, these guns could be laid with deadly accuracy. For 8 days and nights their guns never ceased. At times shells were falling on our trenches at the rate of 50 a minute. We had three batteries of howitzers playing on us at once from different directions, sending bouquets of 12 H.E. shells at once. The marvel was that was that anyone was left alive, or any trench existing. All there is to be said is that we hung on from daylight on the 26th till darkness on the 3rd and not only did we not give away a yard, but we pushed our trenches forward on the right towards the Royal Fusiliers and extended them on the left till we eventually joined onto the Rifle Brigade and at the end of our line was intact and not a man was left behind except our hundred dead.

The 26th was our worst day. 2/Lieutenant Walford was the first officer to be killed boy a sniper. Just as the fog lifted Captain Fidler was leading back his platoon into the trenches, after he had been out to clear up the situation on our left rear, when he was hit by a bullet as he was standing on the parapet, urging his men to hurry and get down into the trench. He was a great loss to the regiment as no one had done more gallant work throughout the war. Over 100 casualties occurred this day. In the evening the shelling got worse and worse and many pieces of trench were blown in. Headquarters had a narrow escape. The C.O., Adjutant and three orderlies being buried by a shell pitching just on the parapet, and blowing in the side. Luckily the soil was light and dry and they were all dug out unharmed. Next night was a strenuous one. Trenches had to be improved, water, rations, and ammunition to be fetched, wounded to be dresses and carried three miles back on stretchers, for owing to the perpetual shelling on this narrow salient, no vehicles could get nearer than 3 miles even at night. This story grows lengthy and no words can describe the passing of those eight days, for sixteen hours of daylight we crouched in the bottom of the trenches listening to the bursting and shrieking of the shells. For eight hours of darkness we toiled at repairing and extending our lines. Some slept peacefully most of the day in spite of the noise and cramped position. Some hardly slept at all and grew more and more exhausted, but none went sick. On the 27th and 28th the shelling was less violent and our trenches safer, but B. Coy. suffered rather heavily. Captain Unwin being killed by a splinter of shell. On the night of the 27th/28th we were reinforced by two companies of the 8th Durham Light Infantry (T), who had arrived from England only in time to enter one of the worst battles of the war. Lieutenant Johnston also rejoined from sick leave and a big draft who brought into the trenches at once, replaced most of our casualties. With these reinforcements we were able to extend to the left and close the gap, linking up with the 1st R.B. of our own 11th Brigade. And so our line was complete again. On May 1st and 2nd the shelling was very heavy again and the enemy's trenches in front of us were being reinforced. We retorted by starting a sap on our right towards the Buffs wood, -The Buffs had relieved the Royal Fusiliers- and putting out a more forward post on our right. But it was evident now that our position was untenable. The French efforts to recover the ground they had lost north of us had failed and we were warned to prepare plans for withdrawal to a new line shortening the salient. Only it seemed very doubtful whether we should be able to effect the withdrawal without hard fighting. On may 3rd the German artillery surpassed itself. They poured tons of metal on our trenches and all the ground behind and this went on till after 3, when they made their first attack on the Buffs wood. In spite of the terrific bombardment they had undergone, the Buffs drove it back supported by rifle and machine-gun fire from our trenches. Again the Germans concentrated their gunfire on the Buffs wood and hardly a tree was left standing. The remainder of the Buffs drifted away to their support trench. By 5 0'clock the enemy had gained the wood and turned their main attention on us. On the right and left they were reported closing up and even the dreaded gas apparatus was seen being set up. Perhaps the wind was wrong, anyway the gas failed to appear and the attack when it did come was feeble in the extreme. It was met by C and D Coys. with ease and driven back decisively and not repeated. But Captain Twining was killed and our casualties this day was heavy.

During the afternoon we got our orders to retire and evacuate the line altogether. At 10.30 half the battalion left and Major Palk remained to cover the retirement. At midnight the rest followed, except a few picked men who stayed to bluff the enemy a little longer. Everyone got away safely. It was a fine performance. There was much crowding along the shell swept road, for this was a general retirement along a front of several miles, all confined to one road, or the fields alongside. But there was never any confusion or excitement. The machine-guns and even our tools were carried back many miles. By daylight of the 4th we were across the Yser Canal, fortunate in having escaped casualties during the retirement, though there were many narrow escapes. Heavy rain came on which prevented the Taubes and Aviatiks observing our movements. About 5 a.m. we halted in a field, very wet and very tired, some miles behind the canal, but not out of shellfire as we soon found. But there was hot tea waiting for us there – hot tea after nine days! We tried to sleep a little but French heavies in a field alongside began to fire and suddenly the air was smitten again with the horrid sound of bursting Jack Johnsons. They fell both side of a hedge along which our men were lying, but again we escaped a casualty and moved off a bit and a little later got into a large park with shady trees to hide us from aeroplanes. A glorious fine day, and all through this trying time the weather was superb, gave us a chance to clean up a bit and a thunder shower in the evening washed some of the dirt off our clothes. We moved again at night two miles further back, where so far we have escaped the shells. The fine day and warm nights with the addition of Lieutenant Cromie and another and another draft of 50 men have restored our energy and nearly brought up our numbers again, though we could do with more officers and especially some senior ones; as there are very few now with more than a few months service. Our casualties have been 6 officers killed, 5 wounded, 92 other ranks killed and 227 wounded. Unfortunately the killed include many of our best N.C.Os. who can ill be spared. Our killed were all buried near the remains of a small farm, about a mile north of Zonnebeke and the graves marked as carefully ad possible. During the last four days of the fighting the D.L.I. were replaced by the companies of the 4th East Yorks (T), who were distributed along our trenches and it is fair to say how well they behaved. They, too, came fresh from England and lost nearly half their numbers in the fighting. Their only desire was to get the enemy and square their losses. One of their officers, though twice wounded on the last day, remained with his company and marched them back to safety. The gallant deeds performed by the men of the regiment will fill pages. Few can be mentioned but we may well be filled with pride for the hundreds of unnamed officers and men who did their duty so nobly and the stretcher bearers were beyond praise. By day, crawling along or even out of the trenches to attend to the wounded; by night carrying them from dusk to dawn. They deserve the highest place in the roll of honour. Young officers of 18 (and some under) commanding platoons through such a week of terror and keeping control of their men, when in the ordinary course, they might have been trembling before an awe inspiring Headmaster.

The Regiment has been thanked by the G.O.C., Division, on its right for its timely aid and complimented by the Corps Commander for its gallant conduct, and though few remain who fought in 1914, the spirit of the Regiment remains as fine as ever.

Report of the German attack of the 13th May, 1915 (Ypres)

Dispositions 13th May – 12 noon
1.   Firing Line 11th Brigade (Right to Left)
London Rifle Brigade (2 Companies)
East Lancashires
Rifle Brigade
1st Hampshire's
Somerset Light Infantry
Division Support Line
        London Rifle Brigade (2 Companies)
        2nd Essex (12th Brigade)

        La Brique
        Ist Kings Own (12th Brigade)

Canal Bank
        2nd Monmouths
        5th South Lancashires
10th Brigade in Divisional Reserve near Vlamertinghe.
Lancashire Fusiliers 3 miles west suffering from effects of gas from 2nd May.

At Dawn the Germans attack in progress after very heavy shelling. About midday 2 attacks on Hants and Som L.I. driven back by our fire.

The bombardment very severe – continued until 3:00pm. At one time there appeared to be 3 batteries firing heavy shells into trenches around Shelltrap Farm. One officer counted 117 shells fired into his units trenches in one minute. As soon, however, as the shelling ceased, our men stood up and jeered at the Germans, hoping to goad them on to advancing; but in this they failed for the German infantry did not dare to face them.

On the right of the line near Wieltje village, Sergt. Belcher of the London Rifle Brigade was in charge of a small post of eight men, which formed the junction between 4th Division and the Cavalry Division lines. The post was practically unrecognisable, through having been blown about by shells, but by dint of continuous work and using shell holes in the neighbourhood for cover, Sergt. Belcher and his party continued to hold on throughout the day. Sergt. Belcher himself was slightly hit, three men of the original eight were wounded, and one killed.

It was undoubtedly owing to the bold front shown by this small party that the flank of the 4th Division remained intact throughout the day.

The O.C. Essex Regiment who was in support of the right of our line showed exceptional initiative and power of decision. Hearing that the line on his front was broken, he led his battalion forward without a moments hesitation, informing his brigadier that he had done so. Collecting all stragglers as he went forward, he searched out the broken portions of the line, including some that were away to a flank and filled and held them. During the approach, the battalion moved in lines of section of column in single file across about a mile of shell swept country. The Rifle Brigade and other units in the front line, who saw this advance, broke into cheers as the Essex approached. One of their companies continued its advance across the original trenches and cleared out the enemy in front with the bayonet.

On the afternoon of the 13th, the East Lancs. Regt. organised an attack on Shelltrap Farm, which had been neutral ground during the last hours of daylight, and into which the Germans attempted to get, at dusk. The first rush was made by Capt. Leake[399] with two platoons. Capt. Leake was killed, and the rush was checked at the entrance of the farm. Lieut. Lane[400] then brought up the supporting platoon and carried the farm. He was himself killed. Another platoon was then put in, passing right through the farm buildings, and re-occupying the trenches in front.

Since the night of the 13th/14th the Germans have been quiet, and little has occurred.

---

[399] *Captain George Dalton Leake, 1st Battalion, East Lancashire Regiment, aged 35 years was killed in action in the attack on Shell Trap Farm. He was the son of Colonel G.D.N. Leake, Porchester Terrace, London. He is buried in the New Irish Farm Cemetery.*

[400] *Lieutenant Hector Allan Lane, 1 Battalion East Lancashire Regiment, aged 25 years, was killed in the same action as Captain Leake, at Shell Trap Farm. He was the son of John Lane, Parkstone, Dorsetshire. His body was never recovered and is remembered on the Menin Gate Memorial.*

12th Brigade Action 24th May, 1915

NARRATIVE OF OPERATIONS 12TH BRIGADE 24TH MAY, 1915

Line of 12th Brigade was held as follows:-

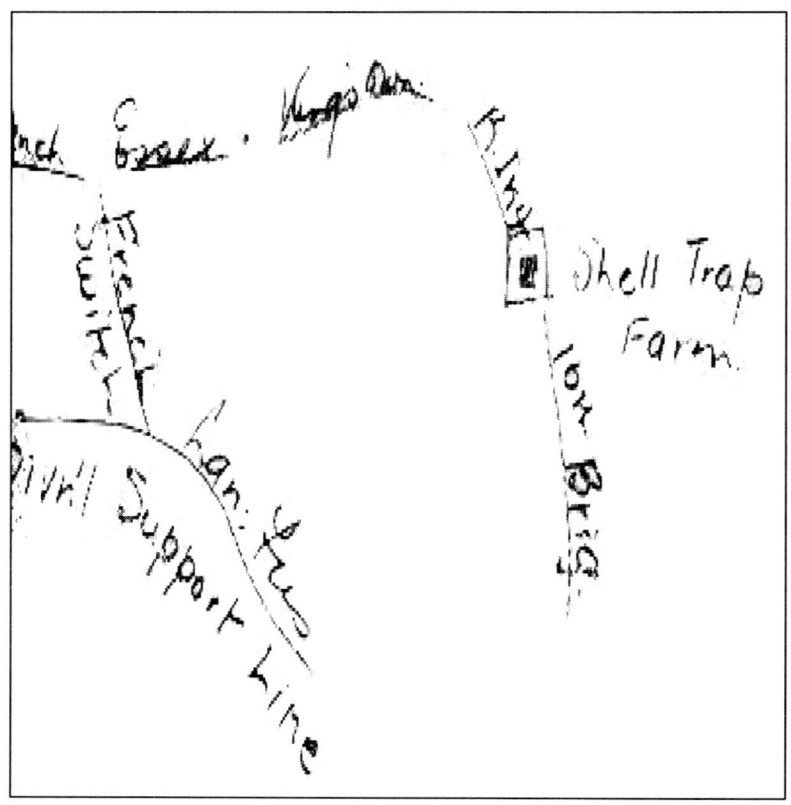

At about 2-50.a.m. the line was heavily shelled and gas was observed coming down on the trenches held by the Brigade.

Shortly after this the Officer Commanding the Lancashire Fusiliers, who was in the supporting line, saw large numbers of men of the Royal Irish Regiment and of a Regiment of the 10th Brigade which had been holding Shell Trap Farm and the trenches south of it, falling back without their rifles.

In the hopes of stopping the retirement the Head Quarter party of the Lancashire Fusiliers opened fire on theses men, but this had no effect.

Colonel Griffin Commanding the Lancashire Fusiliers at once ordered two companies forward to occupy the trenches vacated by the Royal Irish.

A Sergeant of the Royal Irish at this moment came to Colonel Griffith and reported that three companies of the Royal Irish were still holding their trenches. On this information only one company was ordered forward.

This company 120 strong pushed forward under a heavy fire of Maxims which had already been established in Shell trap Farm by the Germans. The Captain and 30 men reached the right end of the King's Own Line, the casualties in the company being about 80 men.

It now became apparent that the Germans now occupied the whole of the Royal Irish trenches and had many maxims there.

After consultation with General Officer Commanding the 10th Brigade a combined attack by the remaining companies of the Lancashire Fusiliers and the Warwickshire Regiment from the 10th Brigade was arranged.

After artillery bombardment the attack started at 10-20.a.m. but came under so heavy a fire that the Officers Commanding these Battalions decided that more artillery preparation would be necessary before the attack could hope to succeed.

It was decided that a second attempt should be made at 2.p.m.
At about 1-10.p.m. the situation was altered by the retirement of other units of the 10th Brigade who were holding the line South East of Shell Trap Farm.

This left the right flank of the 12th Brigade entirely in the air and it was considered that the Brigade must remain on the defensive pending the arrival of reinforcements.

In the meantime the line of the Essex and King's Own was heavily bombarded and attacked by Infantry. The attack was driven back. The position of the King's Own being extremely difficult as in addition to the attack in front they were fired at from their right and their right rear and they were also attacked by bombing parties working up from the Royal Irish trenches, but their own bombing parties drove the Germans back. Unfortunately the supply of bombs ran short after midday and reinforcing bombing parties were unable to reach them across the open.

As the position of the Essex and King's Own was considered precarious the French Switch was occupied at 2-15.p.m by the South Lancashire Regt., who got in touch with the right of the French line.

At 6.p.m. the Officer Commanding King's Own reported that the pressure on his front, his right flank and his right rear was increasing.

At 8.p.m. orders were received that the 12th Brigade was to fall back to the French Switch and the Divisional Supporting Line.

This movement was commenced at 8-30.p.m.; the King's Own retiring first and then the Essex. Snipers and bombing parties engaged the Germans and covered the retirement which was steadily carried out. The last Company of the Essex Regt. withdrawing at 1-30.a.m. All wounded were brought in.

Throughout the whole day the Brigade was suffering much from the effects of the gassing they had received in the morning. In addition to the gas from cylinders the Germans used an immense number of gas shells.

It was noticed that the Germans were bolder and seemed better trained than those we had been against lately.

In their attack they come on almost directly behind the gases and were extremely quick in establishing a large number of maxim guns I our vacated trenches.

I can give no reason for the hasty retirement of the Royal Irish as none of the Officers of the regiment who were in the front trench are now here. The Battalion had only recently joined the 12th Brigade.

Brigadier General,
27-5-1915.   Commanding 12th Infantry Brigade.

G.O.C, 4th Division, Report on gas attack of the 24th May, 1915

4th. Div. No. A/945
5th. Corps.

Reference your V.A.566 of 29th. inst regarding the question as to whether all men who have suffered from the effects of gas should be shewn as wounded, I am of the opinion that no man that finds his own way without orders to any of the Field Ambulance Dressing Stations should be shewn as wounded, even if he is suffering appreciably from the effects of gas.

During the last attack by means of gas, a very large number of men came into our Dressing Stations without arms or equipment and reported themselves as gassed. Some of these men were suffering appreciably from the gas, but it was in my opinion largely due to their being seized with panic and running away with the gas cloud, whereas if they had remained with their Officers and stouter-hearted comrades they would have suffered little, if as all.

Many of these men are now shewn in the 'Roll of Honour' as wounded, a distinction they have no right to.

I think men who are carried in should be shewn as wounded.

(Sd) H.F.M. Wilson,

Maj-General,
30/5/15.   Commanding 4th. Division.

Report of Raid by Seaforth's 4th July, 1915

Brig. Maj. 10th. Inf. Brigade.

With reference operations July 4th and report submitted same evening.

The assault on the German sap-head was accomplished with ease and without casualties owing to very thorough Artillery preparations.

From information gathered from N.C.O.'s and men who took part in the attack the trenches inside the sap-head appear to run roughly according to the attached rough sketch.

The following notes may be taken to be fairly accurate: -
The sap-head was found to have been destroyed by our artillery fire where marked //////

The barbed wire defences XXX at the sap-head were close up to the trenches and were not greatly damaged by our shell fire. The barbed wire formed a serious obstacle as the trestles were close up to the edge of the parapet.

The German Machine Gun X was found smashed to pieces by our shells.

In the German sap-head at A and B 6 men report that the saw two square boarded galleries 4' X 3'. This is not confirmed by the sappers whose duty it was to find mine shafts if such existed. No report from R.E. has reached me.

Both entrances (whether dug-outs or mine galleries) were badly damaged by our shell fire.

At C two large cylinders 7' X 3' were observed. Red and black wires ran from these cylinders on both directions.

At D dug-outs were observed.

At E there was a hand pump.

There must have been a strong party of the enemy in the sap-head at the time of the bombardment, as a large number of rifles, packs and water bottles were lying about.

German helmet (quite new) was brought in,

Colour German Field Grey.

Eagle and spike painted dark grey.

Rosette Right hand side (Red-white-black).

" Left hand side (Black-white-black).

Khaki cover with No.239 in green.

One helmet with brass eagle bearing No. 237 was not brought in.

One of the enemy was dressed in khaki trousers and shirt.

A lot of the dead were seen to wearing leggings as well as boots.

Some of the dead had had shoulder straps with gold bars.

A rifle with H.O.N. marked on butt was not brought in.

Several saw-edged bayonets were seen but not brought in.

The storming party found that the enemy had two organised bomb parties ready to meet the attack.

Owing to the confusion in the saphead – the barbed wire – the damage done by our artillery – and the fact that the officer in command of the storming party was wounded, our bomb parties did not press sufficiently forward. This permitted the enemy to get within range of the main body of the storming party, and cause more casualties than would otherwise have occurred.

The storming party was ordered to withdraw when it was found that there was nothing for the sappers to destroy.

The supporting party should have been sent forward as soon as the saphead was captured.

The operation orders stated that the storming party should withdraw when the sappers had carried out their work. As it was impossible to foresee what would happen, the storming party should not have been tied down in operation orders.

I consider that the successful assault was due: - To the accurate fire of the 4th. Siege Battery under the most capable observation of Capt. Heslop, who directed the fire.

To the accurate covering fire of the 14th Brigade, R.F.A.

To all orders being strictly carried out by all concerned.

2/lieut. G.R. Rawstorne who was in command of the storming party acted in the most cool and efficient manner. This Officer has only recently joined and has but little experience. He carried out his orders in the most capable manner.

The names of N.C.O's and men who acted in the most gallant manner in bringing in the wounded will be forwarded under separate cover.

July 6th. 1915.

(Sd.) R. Vandeleur,
Lt.Col.
Comdg. 2/Seaforth High.

Operations 6th-10th July, 1915 Operation Order No.1 Brig.-Gen. Prowse

By Brig-Genl. C. B. Prowse, Comdg. 11th Infantry Bde.

The line of German trenches from the southern saphead c 7 c 4.4 to the point where the trenches turn North at he bend of the road C 7 c 2.8 will be assaulted. Date and hour will be notified later. The line of the road C 7 c 4.7 to C.7 c 2.8 will be occupied and entrenched.

The enemy's trenches will be bombarded for an hour, according to instructions issued to all concerned. All troops well under cover during this phase.

The dispositions of the Infantry is shown in Appendix A. The assault will be delivered by the 1st Rifle Brigade, supported by the 1st Somerset Light Infantry, both under the command of Lt. Col. W.W. SEYMOUR.

(a) Appendix B shows:-
Positions of Dressing station and aid posts.
Positions of bridges and of R.E. for repairing the bridges.

(b) Appendix C shows: -
Positions of Headquarters of Artillery and Infantry Brigades and Battalions.

Signal communications.

The assaulting troops will carry flags for showing the limits of their advance. These flags will be red, about eighteen inches square.

The West Lancs Field Company R.E. who are responsible for the repairing of the bridges will be notified at once by telephone if any of the bridges are damaged. As the phases of the bombardment and the hour of the assault will be worked by time, the synchronising of all watches is of the utmost importance. Watches will be set at the 11th Infantry Brigade Headquarters. Date and time will be notified later. Adjutants of Artillery and Infantry will bring at least two watches each.

Reports to MORDACQ FARM B.17 c.d. south.
3.7.15   W.G. Charles
Brigade Major, 11th Infantry Bde.

Operation Order No. 1 – Lt.-Col Seymour

by
Lt-Col. W.W. Seymour
Commdg. 1st Rifle Brigade
Ref. Boesinghe 1/10,000

The intention is to attack that portion of the German trenches which lies between the southern point of the German saphead in the International Trench C.7.c.4.4, and the point where the German trench turns north at C.7.c.2.8.

Previous to the attack the 1st Battalion RIFLE BRIGADE will be distributed as follows: -
C Company will have its right at a point 25 yards east of the International Trench, and its left at point where our trench turns north. The communications trench running south from the International Trench will also be available for this company as far as the new support trench.

B Company will extend from the left of C. Company with the left of the Company on present Company Headquarters.

A Company will occupy the new support trench on the west side of the communications trench which runs south of the International.

I Company will occupy the Engineer trench which runs immediately in rear and parallel to the left Company's trench.

Companies of the Somerset L.I. will be distributed as follows: -
One Company from the left of EAST LANCS. to the right of C. Company R.B. One Company in support trench on east side of communications trench which runs south of International.

One Company from B. Company R.B. Headquarters to left of F.33.

3.   ASSAULT
At the appointed hour C. Company will assault the German saphead with one platoon, followed after a short interval by a second platoon.

This half Company will occupy the International up to the point where it is intersected by the line of iron palings. B. Company will assault the German trench at the elbow of the road.

Eight bombing parties consisting of ten men each will accompany the assaulting Companies. Three of these parties will accompany the half company of C. Company, three will accompany B. Company and the remaining two parties will work up the hedge which runs from the south end of the ditch C.12.d. – northeast corner, and will turn outwards when the reach the German trenches. Each of these parties will carry a red and yellow flag which will be planted in the ground to denote the furthest point reached. Detailed instructions will be issued to each party. Directly the German trench is occupied two platoons of I. Company will rush straight through as far as the road and proceed to dig themselves in on the line of the road. Each man of this party will carry a shovel. As the trenches are vacated these spaces will be at once filled by Companies in rear.

4.   MACHINE GUNS
Four Machine Guns will be distributed as follows:-   One   Gun will accompany the assaulting half Company of C. Company and will select a position commanding German trench running east. Two guns will advance to the left flank o B. Company and will take up positions, one to command the German trench running North, the other to open fire on Ferme 14. One gun will advance in the centre of B. Company, and take up a central position in the captured trench.

Communication trenches will be dug immediately after the assault as follows: -   The R.E. party will join up the gap in the International Trench. 30 men SOM. LI. will prolong up to the German trench the present communications trench, which runs from the point where our trench turns north.

30 men SOM L.I. will dig from the point where our present trench turns west and runs down to the Canal bank and join up with the German trench.

40 men Som. L.I. will dig a fire trench along the line of the hedge running from the south end of the ditch C.12/d. northeast corner. This trench will be continued up to the German trench.

6.   CARRYING PARTIES, To take up reserve ammunition, filled sandbags, spare grenades and wire will be provided by the SOM. L.I.
DRESS. Marching order without packs. Every man will carry two unfilled sandbags.
7.   RATIONS. The unexpended part of the current day's rations and the iron rations will be carried. Battalion Headquarters will be at the present RIFLE BRIGADE Headquarters.
2-7-15.
(Sd.) O.C. Downes,
Captain for the Adjt.
1/RIF. BRIG.

Reference procedures of 18 pr. Q.F. Gun in trenches.

4th Division,
Rest Camp,
Watou.
10th. July, 1915.
From
 2/Lieut. W.P.A. Robinson
 135th Battery R.F.A.

To.
 Officer Commanding,
 135th Battery R.F.A.

Sir,
I have the honour to report on the method of procedure of the detached sub-section of an 18 pr. Gun under my command in the trenches in the attack at 5 a.m. on the morning of the 6th. July 1915. I was detailed for this work on the afternoon of the 27th. June. On the evening of that day, Major Hawkesly took me to reconnoitre positions. Three positions were chosen as the best at 4 a.m. next morning, 28th. June 1915, by Major Hawkesly R.F.A. and myself.

On the 29th June, I took the measurement of the trench at this position and on that day (29th) and the next (30th) I had an exact facsimile of the trench, as it then stood, dug in the 135th Battery wagon line.

On the 30th June – after the facsimile had been completed, Lieut. Withington R.E. and myself inspected the trench in the wagon line and decided what alterations should be made to allow of an 18 pr. Gun firing from it.

We came to the conclusion that a hollow wooden box should be placed in the parapet which would allow the muzzle of the gun to protrude through it and yet resemble the parapet until the moment of opening fire.

This box was made by the R.E.'s under the supervision of Lieut. Withington and on the following day the trench in the wagon line was altered into a gun epaulment and the box placed in the parapet.

On the 1st. July, the epaulment in the wagon line was finished and the gun taken to it, as much in the manner as I intended taking into the actual trench as was possible.

Meanwhile Major Hawkesly, R.F.A., Lieut. Withington R.E. and myself had considered the steps necessary to take, in order to get the gun into position, and had mapped out a schedule spreading the work to be done over the nights July 1st. till July 5th.

On the night July 1st/2nd., the bridge over the stream on the British side of the canal was begun and the ramp up the British side of the canal was started.

On the day of July 2nd., I had gun drill in the epaulment at the wagon line, giving practice to three different layers and leaders and 2 observers, besides myself in case of casualties.

On the night of the 2nd. /3rd. July the bridge over the stream on the British side of the canal was finished and the ramp up that side of the canal was finished also, and the ramp up the German side of the canal was begun.

On the day of the 3rd, I had Gun drill in the wagon line.

On the night of 3rd./4th. July, the ramp on the German side of the canal bank was finished, and with a working party of 25 West Yorks (T.F.) Regt., a path was cut through two fields up from the ramp on the German side of the canal bank to the position of the gun in the trenches, cutting the grass short, and filling in all shell holes.

There were three communications trenches in the way, but these were not filled, as they were considered to be useful to the infantry in the attack.

On the day July 4th, I had gun drill at the wagon line in the morning.

In the afternoon, I took the Sergeant and first layer to the position to make them thoroughly acquainted with the gun position and target.
I also took the angle between the target and a back aiming point so I could have the gun laid on the target with the No. 7 Dial-sight before the parapet was knocked down.

The Gun and Sights were tested by the Battery Artificer, and all ammunition tested in the bore in case of jams.

In the evening the box was taken out of the parapet in the wagon line preparatory to being put in the parapet of the trench itself and the gun was taken out of the epaulment in the wagon lines.

On the night of the 4th./5th. July, I took the gun from the wagon line and ammunition (50% Trotyl).

The harness was muffled.
I took the detachment of gunners who had been picked from volunteers from the Battery.

We went by road to TUGELA FARM, the observation station of our battery (135th.); from there we went to the canal bank at a walk, the drivers bending right down over their horses necks and halting when flares went up.

When we go to the stream on the British side of the Canal bank, the teams were halted, the gun unlimbered and the ammunition dumped.

The Gun was manhandled across the bridge across the stream aided by a carrying party of 30 West Yorks and manhandled up the ramp on the British side of the Canal bank.

The gun was there handed over to Lieut. Eithington R.E., who had prepared a pontoon raft.

The digging of the epaulment was then started by a party of 10 West Yorks.

On this night we were greatly hindered by the firing of gas shells by the enemy. We had to work in smoke helmets for 1½ hours.

We were also hindered by the fact that the Somerset L.I. were relieving the Rifle Brigade.

On this night 4th./5th. July, there were also a second working party of 10 West Yorks who dug wheel tracks one foot deep for the last 30 yards of the way, that is to say from the bridge to the trench, so as to sink the Gun one foot lower for that part of the journey The detachment's dug-outs were then chosen and strengthened by sappers.

On the night of the 4th./5th. July, a 7' gap was cut in the hedge we had to cross.

On the morning of the 5th. July then this was the state of affairs.

The Gun was resting on the German side of the Canal bank covered with a tarpaulin, branches and barbed wire transoms to cover it from aerial observation.

The ammunition was just by the Gun similarly concealed.

The road from the canal to the position was made, sunk one foot for the last 30 yards of the journey.

A gap had cut in the hedge to go through.
The communications trenches had been left unbridged to enable the infantry to pass.

They had only been half dug because of the enemy's gas shell. The parapet was still intact. On the day of the epaulment was sapped out from the inside by three sappers and a sapper N.C.O., and finished.

A wooden framework for the gun was made by the sappers under Lieut. Withington R.E. to be covered with canvas and bushes in order to hide the gun when bringing up.

On the night of the 5th./6th. July the moon got up at 11.23 p.m., two things were done simultaneously:-

The box was put in the parapet. The box was 4' square with a detachable sloping front, which could be covered in sandbags and earth and resemble the trench. To put this in, it was necessary to pull down the parapet on a front of 5 feet. To do this a screen of parti-coloured canvas on a frame 10ft. X 4ft. was put over the parapet, so that the enemy should not see a gap in our parapet. Under cover of the screen, the parapet was pulled and the box put in.

The gun was taken from its resting place on the German side of the canal bank, and with a carrying party of 30 West Yorks was hauled up the ramp, across the fields through the hedge, and into position.

The Gun was covered with the screen of canvass and branches. Whenever a flare went up the men on the drag-ropes at once fell flat and remained lying down until it was dark again.

The communication trenches were bridged one by one as we came to them by wood supplied to us by the R.E. When the Gun was in position, cubby holes were dug for ammunition, one for shrapnel, and one for Trotyl. The ammunition was then brought up and put into the cubby holes. We then made back cover for ourselves with sandbags.

The detachment then rested till 3.45 a.m., when all ammunition was again tested to avoid breech jams and the fuzes were set, all Trotyl at percussion, and shrapnel 60% at percussion and 40% at Fuze 0.

At 5 a.m. covered by a salvo from the 26th. Battery Trench Mortars, we opened fire.

The saphead appeared to be demolished by the 50 rounds of Trotyl at 70 yards range. After having demolished the saphead, the gun was turned on to the wire on the left side of the sap-head facing the enemy which appeared also to be extensively piled up and out.

Our 100 rounds were fired in nine minutes, after which the detachment retired into dug-outs for half-an- hour, and then back to the battery. There was only one casualty, and this did not take place in the actual firing of the Gun, but afterwards.

The Gun was taken out of the trenches in the same manner as it was got in.

I have the honour to be,
Sir,
Your obedient Servant,
(Sd.) W.P.A. Robinson, 2/Lt., R.F.A.

Narrative of Operations, 6ᵗʰ - 10ᵗʰ July 1915

July 6ᵗʰ

The bombardment of the German positions to be attacked commenced 5am. Weather fine, but foggy, and the observers were at first unable to see the result of their fire, which was however very effective. It was reported that the first shell from the 9.s Howitzer was a direct hit on the parapet, and blew a large portion of it into the air, the sandbags bursting and showers of dust coming down.

At 6.0am the 1ˢᵗ Battalion RIFLE BRIGADE assaulted the head of the International sap, (which had been destroyed by Lt. Robinson and his 18 pounder gun of the 135ᵗʰ Battery R.F.A. firing from a distance of 60 yards, and also the main German trench facing West.

The assault was entirely successful and the wire was well cut, the Infantry being able to charge straight into the German positions, preceded by the bombing parties who blocked the communication trenches and fire trenches leading East, and the digging parties were started entrenching at once along the line of the road, covered by the bombers and a screen of riflemen.

The SOMERSET L.I., who supported the assault, at once dug communications trenches leading from the captured position back to the original lines.

The RIFLE BRIGADE found a large number of the enemy hiding in dugouts, and most of these were bayoneted, as were others who were cut off by the bombers in the communications trenches.

The position was being consolidated by 7-0am. And arrangements to meet any counter attacks were well in hand. The 32ⁿᵈ Brigade R.F.A. and the observers from all the artillery units kept a sharp and never ceasing lookout on and behind the enemy's lines, and by so doing were able to inform me and forestall every counter attack as soon as the enemy endeavoured to press it home.

To the close co-operation of the Artillery and Infantry the whole success of the operation is due, and this touch was maintained by day and night, during the latter guns being laid on all approaches to our position, and on likely places where the enemy could collect.

I cannot speak too highly of the splendid support given me by all the Artillery, and especially the success obtained by the gun of the 135th Battery R.F.A. which was taken over a high canal bank, rafted over under fire, pulled up a bank at a slope of nearly 45 degrees, then over three trenches and a skyline in full view of the enemy, who was using flares and searchlights, and finally placed in a gun pit previously dug. Within 60 yards of the enemy, without losing a man. The fire of this gun at such close range at once destroyed the strong post at the end of the enemy's saphead, and enabled the Infantry to walk in without loss.

Three counter attacks were repulsed on the 6th instant.

July 7th - 10th
From 5-30am on the 6th to the afternoon of the 8th the enemy's shell fire never ceased day or night, and our casualties were heavy. Six counter attacks were repulsed with heavy loss to the enemy, and his Infantry showed little keenness in coming to close quarters.

On one occasion he displayed a white flag near FARM 14 which was at once fired on, and after raising it six times he gave it up.

Report of Patrol Action, 13ᵗʰ August, 1915

7ᵗʰ Corps.

Reference my GG.73 of this morning.

The Following of copy of report by O.C. Company from which the patrol went out.

"This patrol under Lieut. Warnock went out to patrol the front from left to right at about 10 p.m.

" The patrol started off from No. 1 on left of line and went out right handed. They returned to the same place having seen nothing,

They then proceeded along our barbed wire to the point 2. Here they left the wire to make another right handed loop. I told them I should await them at the listening post 3, and in order to give them the direction would send up flares in the direction of B. I had been there about 20 minutes when Lieut. Low joined me. Soon after a volley was fired in the direction of X and we heard excited talking. General sniping began in that part of the German line. About 3 minutes later a party of about 6 men were seen walking up to our wire at point A. Our sentry, knowing our patrol was about, challenged twice in a very loud voice. The party began to scatter so he opened rapid fire on them, as did the sentry with him.

"Nothing more was heard until about 2-30 a.m. when news was brought me that one of the patrol had been brought in badly wounded on the right of our line." As far as I could gather from his version of the affair, the patrol was suddenly confronted by about 8 Germans who at once opened fire on them. Warnock shot one and Corpl. Murray two. Of our patrol all were hit but none were killed. Lieut. Warnock was incapable of crawling or running, whilst Corpl. Stevenson, as Corpl. Murray put it "seemed to go mad', and ran straight into the Germans. As the Germans advanced on them Corpl. Murray crawled away. He doesn't know how he got to the place he was eventually picked up at. " I think that the Germans who came up at the point A must have been searching for Corpl. Murray."

Sd. H.A. MacMullan, Capt.

O.C. "C" Company R.Irish Fusiliers."

13/8/15.   Gen. Staff,

4ᵗʰ Division.

Appendix VI –1916 – Orders and Reports

Report of Patrol Action - 11th Brigade 8th January, 1916.

A patrol from centre section consisting of a N.C.O. and 3 men, went out at 5.10pm to reconnoitre enemy's front. On reaching the foot of the bank at Q.16.a.6.8 they were fired on and the N.C.O. was wounded and one man slightly wounded. This man with another immediately retired. The third man placed the N.C.O. under cover and also retired and reported on reaching our trench. At 7.10pm he guided another patrol of an officer and 7 men and reached the bottom of the bank. Heavy rifle fire was opened by the Germans and 2 bombs were thrown. Two men were wounded and sent back. Another hostile patrol of about six men was observed trying to close in on the left flank. Out patrol fired 10 rounds rapid and withdrew to be reformed. At 12.30am two listening patrols were sent out with instructions to work forward gradually to about 30 yards in front of our wire and send back a report at 2am and await further orders. Both patrols reporting all quiet, an N.C.O. and 1 man were sent out at 2.30am with orders to creep out and try to recover the wounded man. This they did but the man was dead being riddled with bullets.

Report of an Attempted Raid on Trench 65. Night 21st/22nd March 1916.

- : -: -

The Adjt.,
        1/Som.L.I.
- - - - - - - - - - - - - -

What appeared to be a prearranged raid was made on the sap in T.65 between 3.45 am and 4 am.

This sap which is about 80 yards long looks down the HAN-NESCAMPS-ESSARTS Road. It is held by a double sentry and a flying sentry who patrols from the sap to the trench.

At 3.50 am the sentries in the sap saw four Germans get up about 10 yards away, and rush towards them. They immediately fired and one man was seen to fall. Simultaneously bombs were thrown by the enemy, wounding both sentries.

The flying sentry hearing this went up the sap, but seeing two Germans in between himself and the sap-head immediately went back and roused the occupants of the nearest dug-out. The Officer on watch Lieut. TURNER with Pte. GREY rushed up the sap, and threw six bombs with apparent success.

A few seconds after this a horn was blown and two green lights went up from a point E.18.a which were followed at once by 20 field gun shells fired on Trench 65. Rifle and machine gun fire was opened by the whole company and shortly after this a German was heard shouting "Kamerade, my leg." He was brought in at once, but expired after a few minutes.

A patrol which went out in front of our wire could see no trace of any more of the enemy, but blood and a cap was found, marking a place where a third man was apparently hit. A German rifle, revolver, bayonet and pair of wire cutters were found. Also about 15 hand bombs.

The sap was held by Pte. DAVEY and Pte. HAWKINS.

(Sgd.) R.J.R. LEACROFT, Capt.,
O/C "A" Company

Attempted raid on Trench 65 - 22/3/16. - 1st Somerset Light Infantry Hdqrs.,

11th Infantry Brigade.

- - - - - - - - - - -

I have to report as follows on points raised by G.S. 796 of 23/3/16 (VII Corps) -

It is thought that the first man hit got straight away.

It is certain that he was neither killed nor captured. Pte Davey who was wounded, and is now dead, was the only person who saw a man fall when fire was opened.

The Germans did not get into the sap in rear of the saphead. They entered from the sap-head and over the two wounded sentries. The Germans got to within 10 yards of the Sap head unperceived because the night was dark and foggy, and there were only four strands of wire to stop them. The wire had been put out earlier the same evening. It has since been strengthened. Previously the little there was lying on the ground and could be walked over easily. As far as it is possible to discover in the absence of the two sentries (both evacuated and one since dead), what actually happened was -

Four Germans were seen (by the sentries only) within ten yards of the saphead.

Both sentries fired - one German fell.

Enemy threw bombs and wounded both sentries.

Three Germans came onto the saphead.

The sentries though wounded, stopped and killed one German.

The other two Germans ran down the sap - it was these the flying sentry saw. When they got about half-way they heard Lt. Turner and Pte Grey approach and jumped over the side. It was one of these two Germans who was subsequently found dead in the wire.

(Sgd.)   J.A. THICKNESSE. Lt-Col.,
26/3/16.   Comdg 1/Somerset Light Infantry.

Timetable for the raid of 1ˢᵗ King's Own - 12ᵗʰ April, 1916.

Date: 12/4/16

Time:
2-10 a.m. Artillery open slow fire on sap 7and on front line

2-12 a.m.   Fire on sap ceases. Slow fire continues on front line. Wire cutting party (8 men) move out from listening post 12 and place 2 Bangalore Torpedoes under wire at N.W. end of saphead, and return to our wire.

2-41a.m. Torpedoes fired. Artillery fire on sap and increase rate on front line trenches and communications trenches.

Howitzers fire on Pt W.18.d.4.7. and W.18.a.3.4.

Wire cutting party (1 Offr and 8 men) move forward to clear gaps made by torpedoes, followed by assaulting party (2 Officers and 50 men) who enter sap and divide into two parties (each 1 Offr and 10 men). One party move around right and the other left, the party arriving first at entrance to communications trench moves up about 40 yards towards enemy's front line, leaving a stop at entrance.

The other party clears saphead of enemy etc.

Covering party. Follow assaulting party dividing into three parties.

2-51 a.m. Artillery drops to slow rate of fire.

2-58 a.m. Claxon Horn sounds for assaulting party to retire if they have not already returned.

Covering party cover the withdrawal

Result:
Enemy completely surprised. The Torpedoes cleared all wire except about 5 feet. This was cut by the wiring party in the assault.
1ˢᵗ Assaulting party led by 2/Lieut. McWalters, entered trench trough gap in wire without mishap and proceeded and proceeded to move around saphead.

2ⁿᵈ Assaulting party led by Lieut. Mason, did not fare so well as the enemy threw a bomb out of a dugout at them and wounded Lieut. Mason and 4 men.

The parties then tried to entice the enemy out of their dugouts but failed so they bombed two deep dugouts with 20 bombs and think they killed 6 Germans.

2/Lieut. McWalters then ordered the wounded to be taken back to our trenches and withdrew his party, bringing away a rifle, smoke helmet and some bombs.

Report of Raid by 1st King's Own - 12th April, 1916.

A raid on a German advanced post in a sap at Point W.24.a.4.8. was carried out at 2 a.m. on the 12th Instant by a party from the 1st Battalion King's Own Regiment. The post was believed to be held by about 20 men and a machine gun, but no trace of the latter was found. The operation was carried out in accordance with the attached Time Table which was closely adhered to. As the wire surrounding the post was very formidable, two Bangalore Torpedoes - 21 feet long - were used to cut through it. These torpedoes were exploded electrically, and answered extremely well, leaving very little wire to be taken on by wire cutters.

The artillery co-operation, provided by the 123rd Bde. R.F.A. 126th and 128th Batteries and 12/1 Trench Mortar Battery was excellent, and kept down all hostile fire from the trenches: and the scheme, which was drawn up by Captain Matthews, Commanding 1st Bn. King's Own Regt, worked without a hitch. A platoon commanded by 2/Lieut: MacWalter, to which was attached Lieut: J.I. Mason, carried out their part with great dash, and it is certain that 6 Germans were killed. In was not possible to take prisoners, as the Germans ran into their deep mine dug-outs. As they could not be got out they were bombed. It would be an advantage if raiding parties of this nature were provided with some form of stupefying bomb which could be thrown into the dug-outs and thus enable the assaulting party to bring out prisoners. Our casualties were - 1 Officer (Lieut: J.I.Mason) and four men wounded by bombs. All wounds were slight. 2/Lieut: Hayes, 154th Coy R.E. accompanied the party placing the torpedoes under the enemy's wire, and fixed the detonators into position. The German trench was about 12 feet deep with hardly any revetment. It was muddy and had a good deal of water in some places. The expenditure of Artillery ammunition was: -

450 - 19Pdr shells.
84 - 45" How shells.
50 - Stokes 3" T.M. shells.

The raiding party brought back 1 Smoke Helmet, I Mauser rifle and two German grenades.

Sd/ W. LAMBTON. Maj.-Genl,
12/4/16.
Commanding 4th Division

Patrol Report – Somerset Light Infantry – 16th April, 1916

A party of two officers and 20 men left trench 76 at E.17.c.2.9 at 8pm. A Lewis gun and bombs were taken, with the object of rounding up and fighting any enemy patrols encountered by the 1/East Lancashires, and to meet any large patrols moving down the ravine.

The night was extremely light and it possible that the enemy may have seen our patrol taking up its position in the old trenches in E.17.c.9.9.

In any case no hostile opposition was met with, no hostile reconnoitring patrols were seen.

Patrol report – 1/East Lancs. (2/Lt. Vincent)

On the night of the 15th I took out a patrol towards the Poplar Tree arriving there at 8.50p.m. I was reinforced here by another patrol. The two patrols took up positions about 50 yards in front of poplar. I made a personal reconnaissance of the poplar and found the enemy covering party slightly in front of it. At 9.30 acting on pre-arranged signals I opened fire with rifle grenades on point of Z, sap to the left of Z and point where enemy were wiring. At same time Lewis gun fire was opened from S. Fortin. The enemy ceased working, and their M.G. and covering party opened fire on my patrols who were slowly withdrawing. At 9.35 I again made a personal reconnaissance and found that the enemy had resumed work. I threw two bombs into their covering party and returned. At 9.40 and 10.30 I sent up white rockets as signals to the artillery that the enemy was working. At 10p.m. I sent out a patrol to work in conjunction Som.L.I. No hostile patrols were, however, encountered, nor observed.

Time Table for the Raid by 10th Brigade

-: -: -: -: -: -: -: -: -: -

3:50 p.m.   6" Hows. Commence slow rate of fire on German trench at point W.29.a.85.13.

3.55 p.m.   29th Brigade R.F.A., 127th How. Bde. R.F.A. commence firing on German 1st and 2nd line trenches, and barrage on fire and communication trenches on flanks and in rear.
Also point W.29.b.45.75 (enemy machine gun)
Also point W.23.d.90.57 (enemy machine gun)

3.55 p.m.   Wire will be cut at points of entry by above Artillery and X4. and Z4. T.M. Batteries.

4.0 p.m.   Wire cutting and firing on German 1st and 2nd line trenches between points of entry and a margin on each flank ceases.

Guns join in barrage on flanks and rear.
Trench Mortars cease firing.

4.0 p.m.   Raiding parties leave points of exit from our trenches.

4.12 p.m.   Signal for return of raiding parties given on Claxon horn.

4.25 p.m.   Artillery cease fire provided that return of all raiding parties has been reported.

If this has not been reported Artillery will continue to fire until ordered to stop by G.O.C., 29th Bde. R.F.A.

4.45 p.m.   Artillery fire 3 rounds gun fire on German front line trenches.

Preliminary Report on Raid Carried Out by 10TH Infantry Brigade on 17th April, 1916.

Ref. Trench Map 1/10,000
SCHEME.

Under cover of Artillery barrage -

two raiding parties 1st R. Warwickshire Regt. to enter German trenches at point W.29.c.27.47.
two raiding parties 1st R. Irish Fusiliers to enter German trenches at point W.29.a.85.13

OBJECTS OF RAID.
1ST R. Irish Fus.
To locate and destroy suspected mine shaft at point W.29.a.88.10.

For this purpose a party of 9th Field Coy. R.E. with explosives was attached to the raiding party.

To capture machine gun suspected at point 8513.
1st R. Warwick Regt.
     To capture two machine guns suspect at point 2747.
To kill Germans, bring away prisoners, specimens of equipment and clothing for identification.

STRENGTH OF RAIDING PARTIES.
1st R. Warwickshire Regt.
     Party A under Lieut. J.L. SHUTE.
     1 Officer, 1 N.C.O. and 10 men.
     Party B under 2/Lieut. R.W. GORTON.
     1 Officer, 1 N.C.O. and 10 men followed by small blocking party.
1st R. Irish Fus.
     Party A under Lieut. N. RUSSEL,
     1 Officer, 1 N.C.O. and 10 men.
     Party B under 2/Lieut. W.H. CROTTY,
     1 Officer, 1 N.C.O. and 10 men.
     Party C. 4 sappers 9th Field Coy R.E. under
     Lieut. H.C.C. Walker, R.E. followed by a small blocking party.
OPERATIONS.

Artillery bombardment and wire cutting by both gunners and trench mortars was most effective and all parties left our trenches and entered German trenches without opposition.

1st R. Warwick Regt.

Parties carried out pre-arranged programme.
Party A turned to their left and went down German trench.
Party B turned to their right and went down German trench. No opposition was met with. Seven deep dug-outs were bombed, sixty grenades being thrown. From noise heard they were all occupied. A few rifle shots and one grenade were fired from dugouts at our parties. No machine gun emplacements were found at the suspected points. A blocking party was left at point of entry with ladders to facilitate return of party.

At 4.9p.m. the 1st party returned, sending message to the 2nd party who then followed. One man slightly wounded.

1st R. Irish Fus.
Party A carried out pre-arranged programme. Located machine gun emplacement at 8513 (no machine gun) and worked down German front line to their right.
Party B was to work down German Service trench 25 yards in rear of front trench but communications to this were so obliterated by our artillery fire that party was unable to get into it and joined in with party A.

Party C. (R.E.) located a shaft at suspected locality of mine. It had a windlass and a rope but it was not certain that it was a mine shaft. It may have been a deep dug-out in the making.
This shaft and machine gun emplacement, which was a wood revetted one, were both destroyed by explosives.

Parties A and B on entering the trench heard a bell clang and Germans started to come out of their dug-outs. They were bombed and fired at by our men. Lieut. RUSSEL reports that 2 German officers and 13 men were counted dead in the trench. Ten dug-outs were bombed all of which contained Germans.

At 4.12 p.m. parties returned; no casualties. Party was fired at whilst in the German trench and on way back but shooting was very wild.

A blocking party was left at point of entry with ladders to facilitate return of parties.

A smoke helmet, belt and side-arms with N.C.O's Tassle and automatic pistol were brought back.

Time-table which was exactly adhered to is attached.

Sd/ C.A. Wilding, Brigadier General,
18/4/16.   Commanding 10th Infantry Brigade.

12TH Infantry Brigade Operation Order No. 8

28th April 1916.

The Brigade will hand over part of the line held by the 2/Essex Regt. from Trench 133 inclusive to Trench 140 inclusive to the 166th Infantry Brigade on the night of the 29th/30th.
On relief by Battalion of the 166th Brigade the 2/Essex (Less 1 Coy) will billet in BAILLEULVAL.

All details of relief will be arranged mutually between O.C. Battalions concerned.

The Company of 2/Esex holding trenches 128 to 132 will remain in the line and will come under the orders of O.C. Lan. Fus. to Tactical purposes.

The Vickers Machine Gun off LIMERICK LANE will remain in the line until further orders.

All trench stores less those in charge of the Company left in the line will be handed over by O.C. 2/Essex Regt. to the Relieving Battalion and Receipts obtained.

Representatives of the Relieving Battalion (1/5 North Lancs.) of 166th Infantry Brigade will visit the line tomorrow morning at 9.30 am. O.C. Essex will arrange to show them the line. In case of an attack by the enemy after 9 pm. 29th inst, the Company of the BAILLEULVAL Battalion (Duke of Wellington's) detailed to hold the CHINESE WALL (as per Defence Scheme) will move to the RAVINE with Battalion Headquarters and be in reserve.

The 2/Essex Regt. (less one Company) will remain in BAILLEULVAL in Reserve.

The 2 guns of Brigade machine Gun company which at present move to the emplacements near the CHINESE WALL will move to the RAVINE with the Brigade Machine Gun Company Reserve guns.

Completion of Relief will be reported to Brigade Headquarters.

Operation Order No. 38

SECRET

4th DIVISION – OPERATION ORDER NO: 38

Reference   (1/20,000 Map Sheets 57 D.N.E & S.E.
      (1/10,000 Trench Map "   "   "
                (HEBUTERNE & BEAUMONT)

18TH JUNE 1916.

CORPS OBJECTIVE   1
In conjunction with the offensive to carried out by the 4th Army the VIIIth Corps will attack the enemy on the line Q.17.b.1.4. to K.23.d.8.1 on a date to be notified later. This day will be known as "Z" day and the hour of assault as "Zero" throughout these orders. The final objective of the VIIIth Corps is the line R.8.b.5.7 –cross roads L.26.c.5.6. with a defensive flank facing N.N.E. from the above cross roads to out present front line at JOHN COPSE.

DISTRIBUTION OF DIVISIONS   2.   The attack of the VIIIth Corps will be carried out simultaneously 29th, 4th & 31st Divns which will be disposed in that order from South to North. The 48th Division (less 1 Infantry Bde and Divisional Artillery) will be in Corps Reserve.

The fronts to be assaulted are as follows: -
29th Division ... Q.17.b.15.40 – Q.5.c.2.8 (exclusive)

4th Division ... Q.5.a.3.0 (inclusive) – K.35.a.3.0 (exclusive)

31st Division ... K.35.a.9.8 (exclusive) – K.23.d.8.1.

4th DIVISION OBJECTIVES   3   The objectives of the 4th Division are: -
(a)   German trenches on the line Q.5.a.9.1. (Point 91) – K.35.c.9.4 (Point 94) – K.36.a..0.5 (Point 05)
(b)   German second line from Q.6.o.5.3 (Point 53) – K.36.a.8.2

(c)   German third line trenches on GRANDCOURT-SERRE RIDGE along the line R.2.b.3.0 (Point 20) – Point 26 – Point 90 – L.26.c.7.6.

Where as in the case of MUNICH and PUISIEUX Trenches, a second line of German trenches has recently been dig the Infantry will make the second line their objective, and not the original line.

29ᵗʰ DIVISION OBJECTIVES   4   The objectives of the 29ᵗʰ Division are:-

(a)   German front line system of trenches from Q.17.b.15.40 (Point 03) to Q.5.c.2.8 (Point 27).   Including the village of BEAUMONT HAMEL.

(b)   German second line trenches from R.7.c.94 to Q.6.d.40 (Point 41.)

(c)   German third line trenches from R.8.b.82 and Point 09 to R.2.b.40. (Point 20.).

OBJECTIVES 31ˢᵀ DIVISION   5.   The objectives of the 31ˢᵗ division are: -

(a) German trench from K.36.a.1.8 (Point 18) to K.36.a.1.8 (Point 18) to K.30.a.3.7 (Point37).

(b) Point 36 exclusive – Point 73 – Eastern perimeter of SERRE to K.30.b.2.9. (Point 29).

From Point 93 along PENDANT Trench to Point 84 and thence to corner of Orchard at L.25.a.26.

Trenches from L.26.c.3$^{1/2}$ .5 – L.26.c.47 (Point 47) and thence N.W. to Point 84.

ARTILLERY   BOMBARDMENT   6.   The   preliminary bombardment will cover a period of five days commencing on a date to be notified later. These five days will be known respectively by the letters U.V.W.X.Y.

GAS & SMOKE   7.
(a)   If the wind is favourable gas and smoke will be used during the "Y" artillery bombardment; further instructions on this subject will be issued.
(b)   Smoke barrages will be formed on the Northern and Southern flanks of the VIIIᵗʰ Corps front.

PREPARING WIRE   8.   The 11ᵗʰ Infantry Brigade will be for cutting the wire in front of our lines and as far back as the line TENDERLOIN – MOUNTJOY TRENCH – VALADE – CHEAPSIDE, all inclusive.

The 10th and 12th Infantry Brigades will be responsible for cutting all wire to enable them to reach their positions for assembly and for further movement up to the above line allotted to the 11th Infantry Brigade.
Lanes will be cut diagonally in all wire and this will be carried out during X/Y and Y/Z nights.

ENEMY'S WIRE   9.   The Infantry Brigade in occupation of the line during the preliminary bombardment will be responsible for keeping gaps in the enemy's wire open by burst of rifle and machine gun fire.

The artillery will cut the whole of the wire of the enemy front line, and the wire Q.5.a.8.1 –Q.5.a.40.35. and will make a5 yard path every 20 yards in all other wire.

During the preliminary bombardment, G.O.C. 11th Infantry Brigade will detail Infantry Officers to be present at the O.P's of wire cutting batteries. These Officers will reconnoitre the enemy's wire by night and report on the results of the artillery fire.

For this purpose, there will be artillery fire on the enemy's front line between the hours named below: -

2nd night….. 11p.m. to 12 midnight
3rd night….. 10-30p.m. to 11.30p.m.
4th night….. 12 midnight to 12.30am.
5th night….. 11.30p.m. to 12.30p.m.

PRELIMINARY MOVES   10.   The 11th Infantry Brigade will take over line from the 10th Infantry Brigade on X/W night. After this relief the dispositions of the Infantry will be as follows:-

11thInfantryBrigade…..MAILLY MAILLET
(less portion in trenches) (2Bns-BEAUSSART
10th Infantry Brigade…. (H.Qrs & 2 Bns – (
BERTRANCOURT

12th Infantry Brigade…. (BERTRANCOURT.
POSITIONS OF ASSEMBLY   11.   On   Y/Z   night, troops will take up positions of assembly in accordance with instructions already issued. G.O's.C. Infantry Brigades will report to Divisional H.Qrs when all troops under their command are in position.

ARTILLERY LIFTS. 12. The artillery will lift off the German front line at "zero" hour at which hour the Infantry will assault.

The attached map marked "A" shows the subsequent artillery lifts and the times of arrival of Infantry on their respective objectives.
There will be no artillery fire West of the lines marked on the map after the hour marked on them.

The times marked are for Divisional Artillery. Heavy Artillery will lift in all cases 5 minutes beforehand.

At the commencement of each Infantry attack, Divisional Artillery will lift 100 yards and continue lifting at rate of 50 yards a minute to the objective, firing three rounds of gun fire at each step. The Heavy Artillery will lift straight on to the objective.

Infantry must not arrive at the successive objectives before the time shown on the map but must make their pace conform to the artillery lifts.

If the Infantry are checked by our own barrage they must halt and wait till the barrage moves forward.

Attention is drawn to the programme of artillery lifts which will be issued in detail to Inf. Brigades.

CONTACT AEROPLANE PATROLS 13. During the attack two aeroplanes will be employed as contact patrols on the Corps front.

These aeroplanes will pick up the position of Brigade and Battalion Headquarters and the position of the front lines and will receive signals from the above Headquarters.

For this purpose Brigade and Battalion Headquarters will take forward one ground sheet for signalling to aeroplanes and 4 flares will be carried by each officer and N.C.O.
Signalling to be in accordance with "Fourth Army Tactical Notes May 1916".

ATTACK OF 4TH DIVISION 14. The attack will be carried out by the 4th Division in two phases.

The 11th Inf. Brigade will capture and consolidate the first and second objectives allotted to the Division vide paragraph 3 (a) and (b) above.

The 10th and 12th Inf. Brigades will advance through the 11th Inf. Brigade to capture and consolidate the 3rd objective of the Division.

ATTACK BY 11TH INF. BRIGADE   15.   (a)   The 11th Inf. Brigade with two battalions 48th Division attached will advance to the assault in bounds as below.

At 'zero' the leading infantry must be formed up in NO MANS LAND parallel to the objective.

The 11th Inf. Brigade will leave a net of men in our original trench to guard against counter-attack and to stop stragglers. Strength of net about 1 man to every 10 yards. These men will be taken from the 10% reinforcements kept back from all units (vide para.29)

First Bound.
Three battalions, 1st E. Lanc. R., 1st Rif. Brig. and 6th R. War. R., in that order from right to left will capture and consolidate the line Q.5.a.9.1 (Point 91) – K.35.c.9.4 (Point 94) – K.36.a.0.5 (Point 05). The above objective will be reached by 0.15 to 0.20 (vide map 'A').

Special parties will be detailed to bomb down trenches leading to Points 27, 59 and 88 to join hands with the 29th Division and similar parties on the left flank will bomb down the trenches leading towards Points 61 and 18 to join hands with the 31st Division.
Strong points will be constructed at or near points 91, 86, 94, 49, 81 and 05.

Second bound
Three battalions 1st Hamps. R., 1st Som. L. I. And 8th R.War.R. in that order from right to left will pass through the leading battalions and will capture and consolidate the German second line trenches from Q.6.c.5.3 (Point 53) to K.36.a.8.2. The above objective will be reached by 0.45.

Special parties will be detailed to bomb down trenches leading to points 04 and 41 to join hands with the 29th Division.
Strong points will be constructed at or near Points 66, 53, 78, 39, 15 and at K.36.a.8.2.

The G.O.C. 11th Inf. Brigade will detail a special party to capture any hostile guns in Q.6.b and Q.6.d immediately East of the BEAU-COURT – SERRE Road. This attack will be attack will be carried out at 1.30 at which hour the artillery will lift off these guns.

At 1.30 special patrols of the 11th Inf. Brigade will be pushed forward to cut the wire running North and South between the BEAUCOURT – SERRE and PUISIEUX Roads. None of our artillery fire will be west of this line of wire after 1.35.

Patrols will also be sent forward at the same hour to the track running Northwards from Point 45 towards PENDANT COPSE, to gain touch with the 31st Division.

(b)   During the advance of the 11th Inf. Brigade dividing lines between Divisions will be:-
Between 4th and 29th Divisions.
Q.5.a.3.0 – Point 66 – Point 53.

Between 4th and 31st Divisions.
        Point 87 and along TEN TREE ALLEY inclusive to 4th Division.

As soon as the 11th Inf. Brigade has gained its objective such units of the Brigade as are not require for consolidating the position will be organized and held in readiness as Divisional Reserve.

ATTACK ON 3RD OBJECTIVE BY 10TH AND 12TH INF. BRIGADES 10.   At 1.30 the 10th and 12th Inf. Brigades will advance to attack the 3rd Objective, 10th Brig. on the right, 12th Brig. on the left.
The dividing line between Brigades is the line K.34.c.0.5 – K.35.c.5.5 – track and communication trench running Eastward to L.31.d.2.6, all inclusive to 10th Inf. Brigade.

Dividing line between 29th Division and 10th Brigade – communication trench between Points 53 and 75 – Point 69 – R.2.b.3.0 (Point 20), all inclusive to 10th Inf. Brigade.

Dividing line between the 4th Division and 31st Division – K.35.a.9.8 – K.36.a.6.3 – southern corner of PENDANT COPSE – L.26.c.3^{1/2}.5^{1/2}; but during the advance to the final objective the left of the 12th Brigade will be directed along the line Point 87 – Point 79 – Point 93 – L.26.c.3^{1/2}.5^{1/2,} all exclusive.

The advance will be made in the following stages: -
At 1.15 the 10th and 12th Inf. Brigades will push forward strong reconnoitring patrols to reconnoitre the lines of advance East of the 11th Brigade Objective.

At 1.30 the two leading battalions of each Brigade will advance from positions of readiness West of the 2nd Objective, where they will be formed up by 2 p.m. ready to advance on the final objective. At the same time the two rear battalions of those Brigade will move forward "overland" to our front line trenches.

At 2.30 the Divisional Artillery will lift from the line of wire running North and South through Points 1 and 45 by short stops to the PUISIEUX ROAD and the Infantry will follow as closely as possible and arrive on the line of the PUISIEUX ROAD – PENDANT COPSE at 2.40.

On reaching the 3rd objective the 10th and 12th Bdes will carry forward during the advance a supply of red rockets. These will be used to give the "S.O.S" signal in the event of a counter attack either by day or night.

The signal will be five red rockets in quick succession, on which the artillery will put a barrage in front of the leading infantry.
FORWARD MOVES OF ARTILLERY 17.   (a) Two batteries of the 32nd Brigade R.F.A will move onto "NO MANS LAND" BEAUMONT HAMEL as soon as the rear lines of the 10th and 12th Infantry Bdes have cleared this area in the advance to the 3rd objective.

These two batteries will advance by the SERRE road and WATLING STREET and by track from SUNKEN road through Q.4.a. and will be reinforced as soon as possible by the remaining two batteries of the Brigade which will advance by the same routes.
The C.R.E. will mark these roads with blue flags and stake out a return route for horses.

Brigades will be placed over the German trenches in Q.5.a. and Q.5.b. by Special R.E. parties to admit of the passage of the 29th Brigade R.F.A. to position in Q.5.b. which will be occupied under orders from Divnl, H. Qrs.

The artillery will arrange for the construction of all trench bridges for any further moves.

Map "A" shows the times at which the 29th Division and 31st Division arrive at their respective objectives:-

ATTACK OF 29th DIVISION   (a)   The assault on the 1st and 2nd objectives will   be delivered by the 86th and 87th Infantry Brigades, 86th Brigade on the left. Troops for the attack of the 2nd Objective will form up on the STATION ROAD.

(b)   The 86th Brigade will detail parties to bomb up trenches leading Northwards from Points 27, 39, 88, 04, and 41 to join hands with the 11th Brigade. At 1.30 strong patrols will be sent forward to cut the wire running North and South through R.7.a.5.2. and Point 14.

As soon as the 2nd objective has been captured the 88th Infantry Brigade will move forward to the PUISIEUX Road where it will reform and at 3.10 will advance to the assault of the 3rd objective.

ATTACK OF   31st DIVISION 19.   (a)   The attack of all four objectives will be made by the 93rd and 94th Infantry Brigades, 93rd Brigade on the right. The hour of start and lines from which battalions of the 93rd Infantry Brigade will advance to attack each objective are shown below: -

2ND OBJECTIVE.   15TH W.York.R. start from assembly trenches behind our front line at 0.20.

3RD OBJECTIVE.   16th W.York.R. start from line K.36.a.8.7. – Southern corner of SERRE village at 1.30.

A stong point will be formed at PENDANT COPSE.

4TH OBJECTIVE.   18th W.York.R. start from assembly trenches east of our front line at 3.0 and move to position of assembly in rear of PENDANT TRENCH, whence at 3.10 the advance will be resumed and the 4th Objective will be assaulted at 3.30.

During the advance of the 31st Division the 93rd Infantry Brigade will bomb down trenches leading Southward towards points 55, 05 and 63 to join hands with the 11th Infantry Brigade.

TRENCH MORTAR BATTERIES 20. The medium Trench Mortar Batteries will take part in the preliminary bombardment and wire cutting under the orders of the G.O.C.R.A.

11/2) Batteries will be in position in MAXIM Street whence they will take part in the preliminary bombardment, their target being the German trenches of RIDGE REDOUBT.

As soon as the infantry assault takes place these batteries will be prepared to move forward with the 11th Infantry Brigade under orders to be issued by the G.O.C., 11th Brigade.

(c)   12/2) Batteries to be in position in WOLF Trench whence they will take part in the preliminary bombardment, their target being German trenches in the neighbourhood of QUADRILATERAL.
As soon as the Infantry assault has taken place these batteries will come under the orders of the G.O.C., 12th Infantry Brigade.

(d)   10/2) Batteries will be held in a position of readiness in TENDERLOIN Street to accompany the 10th Infantry Brigade in its advance through G.O.C., 10th Brigade in case of urgent necessity.

(e)   All Stokes Mortar Batteries taking part in the preliminary bombardment will reserve their maximum rate of fire until tem minutes before "zero" when they will commence a hurricane bombardment of the enemy's front line trenches which will continue until the infantry moves forward to the assault.

DISTIBUTION OF R.E. 21. Field Companies will be disposed as follows:
9TH FIELD COMPANY.
H.Q. and 2 sections in TENDERLOIN Street for the construction and maintenance of artillery roads and bridges both in our own and the German lines.

2 sections at BEAUSSART. After the 10th Bde have left the position of assembly these sections will be ordered forward to TENDERLOIN STREET. On arrival one section will come under the orders of the G.O.C. 10th Infantry Brigade, the remaining section will be at the disposal of the O.C. Company.

(b)   1/DURHAM FIELD COMPANY
The company (less 1 section) at BERTRANCOURT for work on communication and water supply. 1 section at 11th Brigade Headquarters and to be under the orders of G.O.C. 11th Infantry Brigade.

(c)   1/1 RENFREW FIELD COMPANY
H.Q. of Company at R.E. Divisional Store on MAILLY-COLINCAMPS Road.

Three sections at BEAUSSART. These sections will move forward to trenches in Q.1.a and b (as soon as they are vacated by the 12th Brigade) for work on roads and train lines under instructions of C.R.E.

One section will be under the orders of G.O.C. 12th Brigade and assemble at Brigade H.Q. in the trenches.

The sections placed at disposals of G.O's.C. Infantry Brigades are not to be sent forward in the attack with the fighting troops but are only to be brought up when the respective objectives have been gained.

TRAFFIC IN COMMUNICATION TRENCHES. 22.   From 2 a.m. on "Z" day communication   trenches are allotted as follows: -

All up traffic will proceed by one or other of the following routes: -
3RD AVENUE – MINDEN TRENCH (up to 1.30 'Z' day)
4TH AVENUE – PITT STREET
CHEEROH AVENUE – WOLF TRENCH
CHEEROH AVENUE – BURROW TRENCH
NEWGATE STREET – DELAUNAY AVENUE (if completed).
All down traffic by one or other of the following routes: -

FOX STREET – TOURNAI – 5TH AVENUE
EGG STREET – VALLADE CORNER – 6TH AVENUE
BORDON AVENUE – 6TH AVENUE.

The C.R.E. will arrange to mark all entrances to communication trenches and trench junctions with arrow heads to show the direction in which traffic may move.
3rd AVENUE is allotted to the 29th Division as an evacuation trench from 1.30 on Z day.

TUNNELS AND FORWARD COMMUNICATION 23.
        Four tunnels (in pairs) have been constructed towards the German lines, two from BESS STREET and one each from CAT STREET and BEET STREET.

These tunnels will be broken out by the 252nd Tunnelling Company on morning of assault.

The Northern tunnel of each pair will be used for up traffic only, the Southern one of each pair for down traffic only.

These tunnels will not be used as communication trenches but will be used only by runners and for getting telephone wires forward.

Parties from the W. Yorkshire Regt. (Pioneer Bn.) will connect the Eastern end of the tunnels to the German front line by communication trenches.

Communication trenches will also be constructed as follows by the 21st W. Yorkshire Regt. (Pioneers) –
From junction of BORDEN AVENUE with our front line to German front line about K.35.a.3.0.

From a point clear of and just South of the Redan to German front line about Q.5.a.3.6.
Work on communication trenches from the tunnels and between the two front lines will begin as soon as the 1st Objective has been gained.

SIGNAL COMMUNICATIONS. 24. (I)   A divisional observation post with central telephone and visual station has been established at q.2.b.4.5$^{1/2}$. Buried cables radiate from this station – forward to Infantry Brigade report centres, battalions in front line and Artillery Brigades, and back to Divisional H.Q. and to the Divisions on either flank.

This post will be manned throughout the bombardment and during the attack by a Divisional Staff Officer.

Visual signalling stations will be established as follows: -
At Q.2.b.4.5$^{1/2)}$ Personnel of Div. Sig. Coy. ELLES SQUARE)
(I)   The above stations are for the purpose of transmitting to the rear messages which they have received from the front.
The following stations will be established as soon as the 2nd objective is gained: -

Near K.35.b.6.4)

Near Q.6.a.2.2) By 11th Infantry Brigade.
Near K.35.d.7.9)

Near Q.6.a.2.7.) By Divisional Artillery

The above stations will be marked with small screens, blue and white side facing rear, khaki facing the front.

Authorised messages handed in to these stations will be signalled to the rear.

The method to be adopted by visual signallers working from the front will be as follows: -

The call up signal will be 20 V's in succession. The message will then be sent through four times without any answering signal being received.

When the 3rd Objective has gained the 10th and 12th Brigades will establish similar visual signalling stations at suitable points.
(iii)   O.C. Divisional Signal Coy. will arrange for telephone wires to be run out with Infantry Brigade H.Q. as they move forward.

(iv)   Two lines of D.1 cable will be taken forward with each battalion in the advance.
To supplement the above runners will be utilised for communications for communications within battalions and Brigade H.Q. They will wear a blue band with narrow white stripe on the arm above the elbow, and will be equipped with rifle and one bandolier of ammunition only.

(vi)   O.C. Divisional Signal Coy. will detail pigeon men with baskets of carrier pigeons to accompany Brigade H.Q. and H.Q. of supporting battalions.
MEDICAL ARRANGEMENTS 25.
     (a) Collecting posts will be established
     at the following points: -

On the line of evacuation via 5th AVENUE at: -

TENDERLOIN STREET.

Junction of 5th AVENUE and SUNKEN Road.

Western exit of 5th AVENUE.

On the line of evacuation via 6th AVENUE at: -

Near HYDE PARK CORNER.
Off ROMAN ROAD

Cellars at Cross roads K.33.c.2.6.
                    Q.2.a.3.3.

Casualties will be brought from the Regimental Aid Posts to the most advanced of the above Collecting Posts whence they will be carried back by relays.

(b)   An Advanced Dressing Station will be established at Q.1.d.3.2. to which casualties from both the above lines of evacuation will be taken.

(c)   A Dressing Station will be established in MAILLY MAILLET at P.12.d.8.7 and another at H.Q. 12th Field Ambce. in BERTRAN-COURT at J.33.a.7.2.

Slightly wounded cases will be directed to the Divisional Collecting Station at BEAUSSART P.5.c.6.6

The junction of BORDEN AVENUE and FOX STREET with front line trench will be marked by a red and white chequered flag to denote the points at which stretcher bearers will enter evacuation trenches. These flags will be placed in position by 12th Field Ambulance.

FORWARD ROUTE 26.
The forward route allotted to the Division for vehicular traffic runs as follows: -

MAILLY MAILLET – SERRE road as far as its junction with German trenches at K.35.a.8.7. and thence by track running from K.35.b.1.9 to K.36.a.6.3 – K.36.a.7.9. – L.31.c. central.

The return route from L.31.c central runs through K.36.c.1.5 and thence by track to be constructed to our front line at junction with EGG STREET. The further route runs parallel to the SERRE – MAILLY MAILLET road striking the SUNKEN Road at its junction with 6th AVENUE.

Bridges have been constructed on the above routes inside our trench system.

BATTLE POLICE 27.
Battle Police, for the collection of stragglers and control of traffic in communication trenches, will be established as under.

By 10th Inf. Brigade. At the points where 3rd, 4th and 5th AVENUES meet TENDERLOIN STREET and where 6th AVENUE joins the ROMAN ROAD.

<u>(b) By 12th Inf. Brigade.</u> At a point where BORDEN AVENUE crosses VALLADE TRENCH at HYDE PARK CORNER and at Point where NEWGATE STREET (if completed) crosses GREEN TRENCH.

Each of the above posts will consist of 1 N.C.O. and 6 men who are to be selected personnel of infantry units.

Special orders will be given by Infantry Brigades to N.C.Os. in charge.
A second line of posts to be detailed by and under control of the A.P.M. will be established along the eastern perimeter of MAILLY MAILLET and on the road thence to COLINCAMPS near railway crossing.
The duties of these post will be to collect stragglers who may have evaded the first line of posts and send them under escort to the Divisional Collecting Station for stragglers which will be established at P.12.a.2.6.

A Medical Officer to be detailed by the A.D.M.S. will be at the Collecting Station. All stragglers will be retained there until an opportunity id offered of sending them back to their units.

PRISONERS OF WAR 28.
A collecting station for prisoners of war will be established at P.5.d.1.4. One Officer, 4 N.C.Os. and 30 other ranks will be detailed for this station. The officer will receive instructions from the A.P.M as to the disposal of the prisoners.

The 11th Inf. Brigade will establish brigade collecting stations in VALLADE TRENCH and TENDERLOIN STREET from whence prisoners will be sent under escort to the Divnl. Collecting Station.

The 10th and 12th Inf. Brigades will hand over all prisoners to the 11th Inf. Brigade as follows: -
10th Brigade at or near Point 65 and the 12th Brigade at or near Point 63.

11th Inf. Brigade will be responsible for sending prisoners taken by both these brigades to the Divisional Collecting Station.
All escorts will return to their units or to brigade collecting stations as the case may be.

REINFORCEMENTS. 29.   Not more than 22 Officers per battalion will accompany units in the attack. The remaining Officers together with 10% of the rank and file of each unit (reduced as shown in para. 15 for the 11th Brigade) will be left behind as reinforcements.

These parties will be marched from billets at 6 p.m. Y day to point J.33.c.0.4 on the BERTRANCOURT – LOUVENCOURT road where the officers in charge will report to Captain KOSTER, D.A.A. & Q.M.G. 4th Division.

EQUIPMENT. 30.   (a) Packs and greatcoats will not be carried. Arrangements will be made for storing them in billets.

Every Infantryman will carry:-
Rifle and equipment (less pack)
One bandolier of S.A.A. (making 170 rounds in all).
2 Mills Grenades (to be carried by officers also).
One iron ration.) in Haversack
One day's ration complete)
        Waterproof sheet
        Cardigan Jacket.
        2 sandbags (in belt)
        Smoke helmets.

In addition to the above, all Infantrymen in assaulting lines, except Lewis and Machine Gunners, and bombers, will carry a pick and shovel, which will be carried underneath the equipment braces.

The haversack will be carried on the back.
Bombers will carry equipment ammunition only
Selected men per platoon will carry wire cutters: these will be attached to the person by a coloured lanyard.

Care must be taken to collect wire cutters from casualties.
One man per platoon throughout the Division will carry and Infantry marking fan.

The colour arrangements adopted for Divisions for these fans are as follows: -
29th Division   4th Division   31st Division
Every officer and N.C.O. will carry four flares.

VERY Pistols and lights will be carried under instructions to be issued by Infantry Brigades.

SYSTEM OF SUPPLY 31.   The normal system of supply will be continued as long as possible. If this method is found impossible, a system of dumps, from which stores will be drawn, will be established as follows: -

      <u>BRIGADE DUMPS.</u> (See map "B").
      10th Brigade....TENDERLOIN STREET
      11th Brigade....VALLADE TRENCH
      12th Brigade.... HYDE PARK CORNER
      These dumps contain rations, S.A.A., Grenades, R.E.Stores, the detail of which has already been notified to all concerned.
The dumps will be under the control of Infantry Brigade H.Q. who will organise carrying parties to take forward stores as found necessary.

500 carriers per Brigade (750 in the case of the 11th Brigade) will be distributed as follows: -

At 10th and 12th Brigade Dumps – 6 officers & 300 men) per Brigade

At 11th Brigade Dump   - 8 Officers & 450 men

(b) In trenches Q.1.d and) 7 officers and 300 men

Q.7.b South of the) from the 11th Brigade
MAILLY – SUCRERIE road) 7 officers and 300 men – 10th & 12th Inf. Brigs.

Parties at (a) will proceed to the Brigade ration dump on the afternoon of Y day under orders to be issued by G.Os.C. Brigades.

Parties at (b) will remain in billets until 1 a.m. Z day at which hour they will be marched to the trenches in Q.1.d. and Q.7.b. Separate portions of these trenches have been allotted to each Infantry brigade party and will be reconnoitred beforehand by the Officers i/c of each party.

In addition to the above, a Divisional dump as been formed in OR-CHARD at Q.1.d.8.5 whence Brigade Dumps will be kept supplied.
Each Brigade will detail 50 men under an Officer to work at this dump.
R.E. STORES 32.   The following R.E. stores will be placed in proximity to each Brigade ration dump: -
300 Pickets
75 coils barbed wire.
20 coils French wire.
2 coils plain wire.
10000 sandbags
12 mauls.

Trench ladders and bridges have been provided for issuing from and crossing our own trenches and will be placed in position under orders to be issued by G.Os.C. Infantry Brigades.

DISTINGUISHING MARKS. 33. (a) The troops taking part in the attack will carry triangular pieces of tin (length of side about 9") fastened on to their backs between the shoulders.

In addition to the above Divisions will wear the following distinguishing marks:-

29th Division. Red triangular badge on both arms.

4th Division. All steel helmets will be covered with sacking which will have distinctive patches, of the colours shown below, sewn onto the sides to coincide with junction of the brim and crown.

> 10th Inf. Brigade – GREEN
> 11th Inf. Brigade – YELLOW
> 12th Inf. Brigade – RED

31st Division. The men detailed for the various attacking waves will wear a piece of ribbon of a distinctive colours tied on to their right shoulder straps – colours as below.

> First Wave – GREEN.
> Second   " - RED.
> Third   " - BROWN.
> Fourth " - BLUE.

MAPS AND PAPERS. 34.   The only maps to be referred to in all orders and messages and to be carried in the attack are:-

> 1/20,000 Map Sheet 57 D N.E. and S.E.
> 1/10,000 Trench Map   "   :   : (HEBUTERNE AND BEAUMONT).

No map showing our own trenches will be taken.

Officers and N.C.Os. will carry notebooks, but no other papers will be taken.

SYNCHRONISING   35.   The O.C. Divnl. Signal Coy. will arrange for a special "clear the line time signal" to be sent out from the Divnl. H.Q. at 2 p.m. on Y day. G.Os.C. Inf. Brigades, Div. Arty., C.R.E. and A.D.M.S. will ensure that the watches of all officers under their command are synchronised with Divisional time.

DIVISIONAL 36.   Divisional Hd. Qrs. will be at BERTRAN-COURT wither all reports will be sent.

W.H. BARTHOLOMEW
Lieut. Colonel,
General Staff, 4th Division.

12th Infantry Brigade Operation Order No. 8 for Assault on the 1st July, 1916.

Secret.

References:-
>   1/20,000 Sheets 57.d.NE & SE,
>   1/10,000 Trench Maps 57.d.NE & SE,
>   (HEBUTERNE & BEAUMONT).

12th Infantry Brigade Order No.18.
- -

21st June, 1916.
- - - - - - - - - - -

1.   The VIII Corps will take part in an Assault on the German Lines on a date to be notified later.
This date will be known as Z day, and the Hour of the Assault will known as Zero Hour, in these orders.

2.   The 4th Division will attack in the Centre, the 31st Division on the left, and the 29th Division on the right.

The 48th Division will be in Corps Reserve.

The Object of the Attack is to seize the Enemy's Trenches on The GRANDCOURT -PUISIEUX RIDGE from Pt. R.8.b.5.7. to L.26.c.5.6. and form a Defensive Flank from the latter Point to our present Front Line at JOHN COPSE.

The Final Objective of the 4th Division is the Enemy's Trenches running from Pt.R.22.b.3.0. (exclusive) to Pt.L.26.c.7.6. (inclusive).

The Attack of the 4th Division on their Final Objective will be simultaneous with that of the 29th and 31st Divisions.
5. THE ATTACK OF THE 31ST DIVISION.-
OBJECTIVES:-

German Trench from Pt.18 to Pt.37.
Pt.63 (exclusive) - Pt.73 - Eastern Perimeter of SERRE to Pt.29.
Pt.93 along PENDANT TRENCH   to Pt.94, and thence the Corner of OCHARD at L.25.a.2.6.

Trenches from L.26.c.31/2.5. - Pt.47, and thence NW. to Pt.84.
The Attack on all four Objectives will be made by the 93rd & 94th Inf. Brigades, the 93rd Bde. being on the Right.

The Hour of Start and Lines from which Bns. of the 93rd Bde will attack each Objective are shown below.

SECOND OBJECTIVE : 15th W. York Regt. leave our Front Line at 0.20.
THIRD OBJECTIVE   : 16TH W. York Regt. start from Line K.36.a.8.7. - S. Corner of SERRE Village at 1.30. A Strong Point will be formed at PENDANT COPSE.

FOURTH OBJECTIVE : 18TH W. York Regt. start from Assembly Trenches West of our Front Line at 2.0 and move to Position of Assembly in rear of PENDANT TRENCH, whence at 3.10 the Advance will be resumed, and the Fourth Objective will be assaulted at 3.30.

During the Advance of the 31st Division the 93rd Inf. Bde will bomb down trenches leading Southwards towards Pts.55, 05,63, to join hands with the 11th Bde.

6. OBJECTIVES OF THE 4TH DIVISION.-

FIRST OBJECTIVE   : The Enemy's System from the Line Pt.91 - Pt.94 - Pt.05.

SECOND OBJECTIVE: The Enemy's Trenches from Pt.53 - K.36.a.8.2.

FINAL OBJECTIVE : Pt.R.2.b.3.0 - Pt.26 - Pt.90 to Pt.L.26.c.7.6.

7.PHASES OF THE ATTACK.-
1st PHASE : Five days bombardment of the Enemy's trenches, commencing on U day, and GAS Attack.

2nd PHASE : Intensive Bombardment with Artillery & Mortars.
3rd PHASE : 11th Inf. Bde. assault & capture the 1st and 2nd Objectives & consolidate them.
4th PHASE : Artillery bombard Final Objective.

5th PHASE : 10th & 12th Inf. Bdes attack & seize Final Objective & consolidate it.

During the latter Phase the 10th Inf. Bde will be on the right and the 12th Inf. Bde on the left.

The Dividing Line between the 10th & 12th Inf. Bdes is the Line K.34.c.0.5. - K.35.c.5.5. - K.36.c.0.5. - Track and Communications Trench running E. to L.31.c.4.5. - L.32.b.2.6. (all inclusive to 10th Bde.).

The Dividing Line between the 12th Bde. & the 31st Division is the Line K.35.a.81/2.71/2/ - K.36.a.6.3. (inclusive to the 12th Bde) - S. Corner of PENDANT COPSE - L.26.c.3.5.

PRELIMINARY MOVES.-
The 11th Bde will take over the Line now held by the 10th Bde on W/X night. After this Relief the disposition of the Bdes will be as follows:-
11th Inf. Bde at Mailly Maillet (less portion in trenches)
10th Inf. Bde - 2 Bns. At BEAUSSART, HQ & 2Bns. at BERTRAN-COURT.
12th Inf. Bde at BERTRANCOURT.

9. THE 12TH INF. BRIGADE WILL ASSEMBLE for the Attack in the prepared Assembly Places on Y/Z night as under:- Orders for March to Assembly Places will be issued later:-

Unit.		Assembly Places.
Bde H.Q. (Pt.K.34.a.2.1.)		Junc. of ROMAN RD.& WATLING ST.
Balance of Signal Section,	)	
1 Section Renfrew Fd. Co. RE.) In STIRLING TRENCH S. of SERRE Rd.		
1/Kings Own,	)	LYCEUM.
6 Guns Bde M.G.Coy.	)	
2/Essex,		
4 Guns Bde M.G.Coy.	)	ELLES SQUARE.
2/Duke of Wellington's,		SUCRERIE,
2/Lancashire Fusiliers,		Q.1.a.
Bde M.G.Coy HQ & remaining 6 Guns,		FORT HOYSTED
12th T.M. Battery,		In action WOLF TRENCH
Bde Carriers		VALLADE near HYDE PARK CORNER.

10. ACTION OF ARTILLERY.-

The Artillery will lift off the German Front Line at Zero hour, at which hour the Infantry will assault. There will be no Artillery fire W. of Lines as under:-

1st Objective after 0.20.

2nd Objective after 0.45.

Wire on line running N. through Pt.14 - Pt.45 after 2.30.

PUISIEUX Road (Line C.) after 2.40.

Final Objective after 3.30

300 yards East of Observation line after 4.40.

Cease fire - 4.40.

The heavy Artillery will lift in all cases five minutes before each of the above lifts.

At the commencement of each Infantry attack the Divnl. Artillery will lift 100 yds. and continue lifting at the rate of 100 yds. in two minutes to the Objective, firing three rounds of gunfire at each step.

The Heavy Artillery will lift straight on to the objective.

Infantry must not arrive on the successive Objectives before the times shown under above lifts, but must make their pace according to the above lifts.

If the Infantry are checked by our own barrage they will halt and wait till the barrage moves forward.

ATTACK OF THE 12TH BRIGADE.-

The attack of the 12th Brigade will be carried out as follows:-

Objective Enemy's trenches from Pt.L.32.d.2.6. (Pt.26) (exclusive) to Pt.L.26.c.7.6.

Disposition of troops during the Attack:-

Firing Line & Supports.		Objective.
Left Bn. Kings Own,		From Pt.L.32.b.0.6 to
	2 Guns Bde M.G. Coy	L.26.c.7.6. (both inclusive)

1 Section 12th T.M. Battery.

Right Bn.	Essex Regt.	From Pt.L.32.d.2.6 (Pt 26)
4 Guns Bde M.G.		to L.32.b.0.6. (both exclusive).

Reserve:-

Left Reserve Bn.   2/Duke of Wellington's Regt.

Right Reserve Bn.   2/Lan Fus.
6 Guns Bde M.G. Coy
1 Section 12th T.M. Battery,
1 Section Renfrew Fd. Co. RE.

Special Mission.-

4 Gun Bde M.G.Coy.

(c) For Time Table of Moves for Advance & Assault see Appendix A.

INSTRUCTIONS FOR THE ATTACK BY 12TH BRIGADE.-

ACTION OF PATROLS.-

Strong Patrols consisting of 1 officer and 5 groups of 6 NCO's & men and 2 Lewis Guns from each of the leading Bns. will advance according to Time Table and will push through the 11th Bde., advancing when the Artillery lifts.

Their Objective will be :-
to secure the advance of the Main Attack against surprise.
To locate the Enemy's Machine Guns and report their positions.
To cut gaps in any wire likely to hold the Advance up, marking these gaps with distinguishing discs. At least 8 gaps will be cut per Bn. to allow each platoon to go through.
Lewis guns will assist Patrols in getting forward and gaining information.

ACTION OF FIRING LINE & SUPPORTS.-

The Attacking Bns. will advance in Artillery formation (column of sections) from their assembly Positions, each on a frontage of 400 yds., having 8 platoons leading and 8 platoons in support.

The distance between lines of sections of the leading platoons will be: 100 yds. between 1st & 2nd and 50 yds. between the remaining lines.

The distance between leading and supporting platoons 200 yds.
The distance between lines of sections of supporting platoons will be 50 yds. (see Appendix B.)

After passing the 11th Bde Final Objective they will open out to frontage of 500 yds., remaining in column of sections unless forced by fire to extend.

The Dividing line between Bns. will be the line K.34.a.9.21/2 9Distinguishing mark Whit Diamond) - K.34.b.8.21/2 - (Distinguishing marl white post) - N. Flank of the QUADRILATERAL - Pt.K.35.a.6.3. - Pt.50 yds. S. of Pendant Copse - Pt.L.32.b.0.6.

When the leading line of sections arrive on Line C. (PUISIEUX ROAD to PENDANT TRENCH) the whole Brigade will halt, and Strong Patrols will be pushed forward to get as close the Objective as our Barrage will allow.

At 3.15 the Advance will be resumed under cover of the Artillery and in the same formation (column of sections) and will assault with the utmost vigour when within 40 yds. of the Objective.

On capturing the Enemy's First Line the leading 1/2 Bns will push forward and seize the Enemy's Support Line and send out strong patrols and Lewis guns as far as Line L.32.d.6.7. - L.32.b.6.5. - L.26.c.9.6. to cover the supporting half Bans, while they consolidate the captured position. These strong patrols will dig in on above line, which will be the line of Observation.

Fighting Patrols, consisting of an officer and 25 Other ranks from each Bn., will also to capture and put out of action any guns in squares L.27.C & D and L.33.A & B and NW. corner of C, King's Own taking squares L.27.c & D and Essex L.33.A, B, & C, advancing under cover of Artillery Barrage.

Bombing Parties will be organised to hold up communication trenches running from Pts.90,12,& L.26.c.71/2.61/2.

The consolidation of the position will consist of making five STRONG POINTS as under:-

NAME & POSITION OF STRONG POINTS & UNITS RESPONSIBLE FOR MAKING THEM.

Name.	Position.	Unit Making.
A.	L.26.c.3.3 (Pt.33)	Kings Own
B.	L.26.c.9.0. (Pt.90)	Kings Own
C.	L.32.b.1.2. (Pt.12)	Essex
D.	L.32.a.1.91/2	Lan Fus.
E.	L.32.a.3.1.	Lan Fus.

These Strong Points will be constructed as per Appendix C. to hold I Platoon each, 2 Machine Guns and a stokes mortar.

The Strong Points will eventually be joined up by a continuous Fire Trench if not already existing, and a Support Trench about 150 yds. in rear will be made if the existing trench is not suitable.

Trenches leading forward from the captured line will be filled in for a distance of 50 yds. if not required as listening posts.

Wire entanglements will be put all along the Front, using the German wire as far as possible, which will be dragged across the captured trenches in lengths of about 10 yds.

Communications trenches will be made to join the front and support line at intervals of about 200 yards.

The Essex Regt. will dig forward a communicating trench to the Observation Post on the BAILLESCOURT ROAD.

WORKING PARTY SHEDULE - see appendix D.

ACTION OF RESERVE BATTALIONS.-
The Reserve will advance in Artillery formation according to Appendix A, moving in Echelon, the right Bn. (Lancashire Fusiliers) leading and following the Essex at 400 yds. distant, the left Bn. (Duke of Welling-

ton's) keeping a distance of 400 yds. from the leading line of the right Bn. (Lan Fus).

On the Final Objective being captured, the reserve Bn. On the right (Lan Fus) will at once send all RE Material forward to the Strong Points A, B, & C, also working parties for Strong Points D & E, these parties having previously been detailed.

The Reserve Bn. On the left (Duke of Wellington's) will dig in on the PENDANT COPSE Line, selecting sites & constructing 2 Strong Points South of the PENDANT COPSE near Pts..l31.a.9.4. & L.31.a.91/2.2. Each post to hold a platoon (see Appendix c). These posts will be joined up by continuous trench when labour is available.

Should the Attacking Bns. use up all their supports & still require help, the OC. Lan Fus. will place not more than one coy. at the disposal of either Bn. without orders of the Bde.

Should the OC attacking Bns. find they have not enough men to hold the captured lines and consolidate them, the OC Lan Fus will send up further parties to help in the making of the Strong Points A, B, & C. These parties will have been previously provisionally detailed.

Should the OC Lan Fus send up reinforcements he will notify Bde Hd. Qrs.

All spare men will be used to make cover for Reserve on a Line joining PENDANT TRENCH (93rd Bde) with a Reserve Line to be dug by the 10th Bde.

This Reserve Trench will approximately pass through the following points :- L.32.b.8.5 - L.32.a.3.1.

The order for the Left Reserve bn. to move forward from the PEN-DANT COPSE Line will be given by the Brigade commander.

ACTION OF THE MACHINE GUN COMPANY.-
6 Guns will accompany the leading Bn., 2 guns on the left flank of 4th Line of Kings Own, 2 guns on each flank of the 4th Line of Essex, and on the Final Objective being captured they will be disposed as follows:-
            2 to Strong Point A,
            2 to Strong Point B,
            2 to Strong point C.

SPECIAL MISSION GUNS.-

4 Guns take up positions in captured Enemy's position near Pt.K.36.c.3.6. and cover the advance of the Bde to the Final Objective.

After 3.15 they will not fire on the Final Objective, but will remain about the same position to watch the left flank in case of counterattack.

They will also - whenever possible - assist the 10th Brigade Advance.

HD. QRS. 7 6 RESERVE GUNS.-

Hd, Qrs. 76 Reserve Guns move to position of readiness near Pt. K.36.a.7.3., moving from their Assembly place in rear of the last line of duke of Wellington's.
The OC. Will report to bde. Hd. qrs. and remain with the bde Commander.

If the assault on the Final Objective is successful, the Reserve Guns will be distributed as follows:-
> 2 to each of the Strong pts. Made by Left reserve Bn.
> 2 remain in position of readiness near Pt. K.36.a.8.2.

ACTION OF STOKES MORTAR BATTERY.-

The 12th T.M. Battery will be in position in WOLF TRENCH and will take part in the preliminary bombardment under orders of the GOC 11th Bde until the 12th Brigade move, their target being the German trenches in the neighbourhood of the QUADRILATERAL. They will reserve their maximum rate of fire until ten minute before the 11th Bde assault.

On the 12th Bde advancing, the battery will advance as follows:-
1 section follow in rear of last line of Kings Own right flank,
1section follow in rear of last line of Lan Fus on left flank.
Should the O.C. either of the leading Bns. require their assistance during the advance, they will call upon the O.C. the section, sending a guide to lead them to the place they require them.

After the Final Assault, the O.C. leading section will distribute his mortars in Strong Points as follows : 2 in A and 2 in C.
The O.C. reserve Section will remain in reserve in strong Pts on the PENDANT COPSE Line.

ACTION OF SECTION RENFREW FIELD CO. RE.-

The section will advance with the Bde Hd. Qrs. to road at Pt.36.a.5.3.

When the position has been captured, the OC Section RE will go forward and lay out communications trenches from the captured line to the PUISIEUX ROAD. These 2 communicating trenches will be dug by parties from the Duke of Wellington's and Lan Fus, each party being 100 men.

Parties to commence work on the East End of the Trench.
The position of these communicating trenches will be:
1 running from Pt.L.32.a.8.5. to Pt.L.32.c.2.6. to the PUISIEUX Road at pt. L.31.d.5.6.
The former will be made by the Duke of Wellington's, the latter by the Lan Fus.

The remainder of the Section will repair damaged roads and make communications good to the Front Line.

ACTION OF THE BRIGADE HD. QRS.-

Bde Hd. Qrs. Will move forward to the line MUNICH TRENCH, moving along the line dividing the Battalions during the Advance.

ATTACK OF THE 11TH BRIGADE.-

The 11th Bde., with two Bns. of the 48th Division, will advance to the Assault in two Bounds. At zero hour the leading Infantry will be formed up in NO MANS LAND parallel to the Objective.

FIST BOUND: Three Bns will capture and consolidate the line of the 1st Objective, reaching it at 0.15 and 0.20. Strong Points will be constructed near Pt.91, Pt.86, Pt.94, Pt.49, Pt.81, Pt.05.

SECOND BOUND:- Three Bns. will pass through the leading Bns. and will capture and consolidate the second Objective. This Objective will be reached by 0.45. Strong points will be constructed at or near Points 63,53.78,39,15, and K.36.a.8.2.

The 11th Inf. Bde will send out a special party to capture any hostile guns in Q.6.d. & Q.6.b. immediately East of BEAUCORT -SERRE & PUISIEUX ROAD.

Patrols will also be sent forward at the same hour to the track running N.& S. between the BEAUCORT-SERRE & PUISIEUX ROAD.

Patrols will also be sent forward at the same hour to the track running N. from Pt.45 towards PENDANT COPSE to gain touch with the 31st Division.

Report on Operations on "U" Night

"DRESDEN" was discharged from our trenches by Lieut. JONES and special Brigade at 10.7 p.m., the wind at the time was light and blowing from W. The discharge left our trenches and very slowly went over the German trenches. At about 10.30p.m. one of the cylinders leaked, owing to having been hit by a piece of shell. At about 10.45 p.m. the wind dropped completely and the a very light breeze from E.S.E. came up and brought the gas back. The trench was also filled with gas from the leaking cylinder.

The 3 left Companies all had to put on Smoke Helmets shortly after the discharge commenced. The Special Brigade under Lieut. JONES were badly gassed and all worked well as long as they could. As soon as the wind changed Lieut. JONES tuned off the gas and reported the same to me. It was turned off at about 11 p.m. The front lines were re-occupied by the Left and Left Centre Companies at 2 a.m. They could not be occupied earlier owing to the presence of gas.

About 10 minutes after the discharge commenced the Germans sent up Red Rockets and sounded sirens, opened Machine Gun fire but no rifle fire and sent up white "Very" lights along their front. The German Artillery at once opened fire and a "BARRAGE" in front of the front line, and between the front line and the support line. It was most intense by BURROW- FREDDY – VALLADE. They slackened down about 11.30 p.m. but did not cease till about 12.15 a.m.

Trench Mortars were fired during the BARRAGE about BESS ST and DELAUNEY Avenue. The German guns used were Field Guns. Shrapnel, 4.2" and 5.9"s.The front line trenches were damaged considerably especially K4 to 9 – and BESS ST – DELAUNEY – FREDDY, and BURROW to certain extent.

Brigadier-General
25/6/16
Commanding, 19th Infantry Brigade

Division Casualty List for 1ˢᵗ July, 1916

	Killed	Wounded	Missing	Total
10th Brigade		Officers		
1st Warwicks	-	2	-	2
2nd Seaforth's	12	10	2	24
1st R. I. Fus.	-	5		5
2nd R. Dub. Fus.	2	12		14
10th Bde. M.G. Coy.	1	1	2	4
10th T. M. Batty.	-	-	-	-
Total	15	30	4	49
		Other Ranks		
1st Warwicks	15	57	3	75
2nd Seaforth's	56	218	100	374
1st R. I. Fus.	14	111	11	136
2nd R. Dub. Fus.	52	222	40	314
10th Bde. M.G. Coy.	2	15	7	24
10th T. M. Batty.	2			2
Total	141	623	161	925
11th Brigade		Officers		
Somerset L. I.	4	9	13	26
1st East Lancs.	3	6	8	17
1st Hants.	10	16 *	-	26
1st Rifle Bde.	7	7 *	6	20
1/6th R. Warwicks	5	11	6	22
1/8th R. Warwicks	6	16	3	25
11th Bde. M. G. Coy.	1	2 *	1	4
11th T. M. Batty.	1	4	-	5
Total	37	71	37	145
		Other Ranks		
Somerset L. I.	47	171	232	450
1st East Lancs.	65	251	169	485
1st Hants.	113	249	197	559
1st Rifle Bde.	52	239	163	454
1/6th R. Warwicks	43	173	234	450
1/8th R. Warwicks	52	238	273	563
11th Bde. M. G. Coy.	3	54	8	65
11th T. M. Btty.	5	17	12	34
Total	380	1392	1288	3060
12th Brigade		Officers		
1st Kings Own.	6	13	3	22
2nd Lancs Fus.	5	12	2	19

2nd Essex	5	13 *	4	22
2nd West Riding	3	17	-	20
12th Bde M. G. Coy	1	3	-	4
12th T. M. Btty.	-	2	-	2
Total	20	60	9	89

Other Ranks

1st Kings Own.	37	209	177	423
2nd Lancs Fus.	21	241	101	363
2nd Essex	43	167	205	415
2nd West Riding	21	292	61	374
12th Bde M. G. Coy	8	47	6	374
12th T. M. Btty.	3	21	26	50
Total	133	977	576	1686
Total (all ranks)	**726**	**3153**	**2075**	**5954**

* Includes 1 Died of Wounds in each case

Report on the Attack of the 11th Infantry Brigade

ON THE GERMAN POSITIONS S.W. OF LE TRANSLOY ON
THE 18TH OCTOBER, 1916.

----oOo----

OBJECTIVE: The objectives of the attack were FROSTY - HAZY -
DEWDROP and RAINY TRENCHES together with NORTHERN
and SOUTHERN GUN PITS and the Strong Point in T.5.a.

The 12th Brigade assisting the attack on DEWDROP by a bombing
attack from the flank. At the conclusion of the operation FROSTY
TRENCH remained in our hands.

FORMATIONS FOR ATTACK: The 1st Battn. The Rifle Bri-
gade assembled for the attack on the frontage BURNABY TRENCH
T.4.b.8.6. - GERMAN TRENCH three companies in line attacking in
depth.
  "C" Company   Objective trenches in T.5.B & D.
  "I" Company   "   FROSTY & HAZY TRENCHES
  "B" Company   "   GUN PITS & STRONG POINT
  "A" Company supported "I" and "B" Companies.

All companies attacked in four waves, "II" Company of the 1st Battn.
Somerset Light Infantry in reserve under the orders of O.C. The 1st
Rifle Brigade.

The 1st Battn. East Lancashire Regiment assembled on the frontage of
BURNABY TRENCH making junction with the 1st Rifle Brigade at
T.4.b. 85 - 53. The attack was made by three companies in line in
depth, the 4th company being in reserve. The objective was DEW-
DROP TRENCH and the establishment of a line of posts 150 yards
N.E. of it.

NOTES ON ASSEMBLY TRENCHES: Neither the front trenches
nor the trenches in rear lent themselves to the to the assembling of the
various waves and the trenches themselves were badly damaged by hostile shelling. The men did know the trenches and only took up their
positions a few hours before the actual attack.

Compass bearing were taken by company officers before dark and tapes
laid out to ensure as far as possible the advance taking place in the right
direction. As a general rule the waves started in the right direction but
the right company of the East Lancs. swung off somewhat to its right.

The leading wave of this company when getting into position apparently assembled in FOGGY TRENCH and 40 minutes before ZERO moved in file to the left to its position in BURNABY.

This manoeuvre does not appear to have been seen by the enemy who at any rate, took no notice of it at the time. Owing to the attack taking place at night I gave orders for the succeeding waves to follow each other at a distance of 25 to 30 paces instead of the usual intervals and the waves we lined in shell holes where trench accommodation did not exist. The O.C. The 1st Rifle Brigade, placed his reserve company (1st Somerset Light Inf.) in SHAMROCK with orders to send inward two platoons to hold the front line after the attack started. These two platoons did not find the front line and continuing on, took part in the attack.

NOTES ON ACTION: Prior to ZERO there was a noticeable decrease in the amount of our artillery fire. Five or sic minutes before ZERO I saw the enemy send up two red rockets. I should say those rockets were sent up somewhat to the North of LESBOEUFS but could not check the direction at the time. Fire was opened accurately at ZERO and the barrage was considered very good. Earlier in the evening I asked that all barrages should remain on the enemy's trenches for 30 seconds longer than originally arranged on account of the heavy which had set in making the ground very slippery. This was arranged.

It was very dark, so observation of the attack was practically impossible.

The waves appear to have got off to time but were somewhat delayed by the state of the ground. The leading waves appear to have reached our barrage about the time that it lifted.

The O.C. The 1st Rifle Brigade that a heavy shell and shrapnel barrage was put down in front of the gun pits three seconds after our barrage opened. The hostile guns must therefore have opened the moment the flashes of our guns were seen, (The flashes from our guns unmistakably indicated an attack to any observer and is one of the serious objections to a night attack) This barrage inflicted severe loss on the supports to the company attacking the gun pits especially as the men converged on the gun pits as they came in sight of them over the slight rise BURNABY corner.

The remnants of this company were unable to make any further effort and fell back into BURNABY and FOGGY TRENCHES. "C" Company were unable to make any headway owing to M.G. fire which opened at ZERO and continued throughout our barrage.

"I" Company bore somewhat to left to start with the to the right eventually swinging right round left handed after striking a sunk lane and came back towards own lines from <u>behind</u> the gun pits. A line of shell holes partially joined up was encountered and rushed and some 20 prisoners taken. A German machine gun was then destroyed a little in advance by a patrol sent forward. Another advance was made and another machine gun captured. The company with the prisoners in front apparently came on the strong point and gun pits. A German Officer came out probably taking the prisoners as reinforcements. After he was shot considerable hand -t0-hand fighting occurred and the survivors, some fifty in number, reached our front line in BURNABY.

The 1st East Lancashire Regt. Say they reached DEWDROP TRENCH but were subjected to an intense machine gun fire <u>during the time our barrage was on the trench</u> and after they reached it. All the Officers and most senior N.C.O's are missing so that the account of their action is difficult to obtain. They further say DEWDROP was not occupied but that the machine gun fire came from beyond the trench.

I consider that the cause of failure was primarily due to the slippery state of the ground and darkness of the night. The men did not reach their objectives in a fit state to fight. If the night had been fine like the preceding nights portions of the objectives would probably have been held. The state of the ground caused great disorganisation, and disorganisation especially at night with indifferently trained Officers, N.C.O's and men, makes the consolidation of such a position very difficult.

Secondly there is no real objective to go for. All the enemy trenches were practically destroyed - in most places unrecognisable as such. The Germans probably have fifteen to twenty machine guns chiefly in shell holes placed irregularly so that at no time does our creeping or stationary barrage silence the whole lot.

The whole position lies in a hollow much like a saucer and is difficult to observe; this was probably the cause of the initial failure to take these works. Since then all the works have been subjected to such a fire as to drive the enemy out of them and he now occupies the large shell holes, represented by the overs of the heavy howitzers, in comparative safety.
Brigadier-General
Commanding 11th Infantry Brigade.

Appendix VII -1917 - Orders and Reports

Extracts from Third Army Instructions No.G.S. 1/30 Dated 25-2-17

The operation, of breaking through the enemy's system of defences, will be carried out by the VII, VI and XVII Corps. This operation is to be carried out in 4 phases, and the whole operation is to be completed in 12 hours.

The first phase is the capture of the enemy's front line system up to the black line on the map.
The second phase is the capture of the second line system - the blue line on the map.

The third phase is the capture of portions of the enemy's third line system, as shown by the brown line on the map.

The fourth phase is the occupation of certain tactical points as indicated generally by the green line.

The Artillery preparation is to begin at once. Strong points are to be destroyed. Wire is to broken, and gun positions are to be dealt with, as considered necessary.

This artillery preparation is to be arranged in such a way, that the large number of guns, which are already in the Army area, is not disclosed.

In addition to this preparation, Corps will carry out such tests as they consider necessary, with a view to ascertaining how much they can damage the wire and works in the German second and third line systems.

The actual bombardment will begin at Zero minus 48 hours. This bombardment will be maintained will be maintained continuously on the whole of the enemy's works and on his artillery positions, until each in turn is reached by our Infantry under the barrage fire.

FIRST PHASE.
Corps will advance simultaneously at Zero to the assault of the first line system. The barrage, should at first move rapidly, in order to enable to a sufficient number of waves to reach the German trenches before the German guns can begin a barrage on our front line system After a sufficient distance has been reached by our barrage, the barrage should move slowly, in order to give time for our leading waves to force their way through the tangle of trenches and obstacles compromised in the first line system.

It is estimated that the black line will be reached about Zero plus 20 minutes. Should any points hold out, these must not be allowed to delay the rate of our advance. They must be dealt with by troops advancing in support of the leading waves.

Tanks will not be used for the assault.

Arrangements must be made between the VI and XVII Corps for mutual co-operation in the Valley of the SCARPE.

On the left flank of the XVII Corps, detailed arrangements have been made with the First Army to secure co-operation at the point where the ARRAS - LENS road crosses the front line system.

Note:- The timing in the XVII Corps is Zero plus 34 minutes.

SECOND PHASE.
A PAUSE UNTIL Zero plus 2 hours will be made on the black line, in order to bring up fresh troops and prepare for the further advance.

The German second line system, including the various defended villages and strong points, is the most difficult part of the attack. Corps will satisfy themselves that sufficient shells are allotted for the purpose of destroying these works, and that all possible adjuncts, such as Gas Projectors, are made available for this phase.

It is estimated that the blur line should be reached at Zero plus 2 hours and 40 minutes. Tanks have been detailed to take part in this operation of the attack.

Co-operation will be arranged between the VII and VI Corps, to ensure mutual support in the operations about THE HARP.

Similarly, co-operation between the VI and XVII Corps will be arranged in such a way that whichever Corps reaches the blue line first, may be able to bring enfilade fire to assist the advance of the neighbouring Corps. In this advance, also, strong points and villages must not be allowed to delay the rate of the general advance. These places must be dealt with by supporting troops at a later period.

THIRD PHASE
A pause until Zero plus 6 hours and 40 minutes will be made on the blue line, in order to bombard the third line, and to bring up artillery and fresh troops. During this pause, outposts should be pushed out beyond the general line to overlook all ground between the blue line and the brown line. The greater part of the enemy's artillery is situated between these two lines. It is important that these guns should be kept continuously under machine gun fire, until the advance from the blue line begins.

It is estimated that the advance from the blue line to the brown line will occupy between one and two hours. Tanks, other those detailed for the capture of the blue line, may assist in this advance which should, at all points, be made as rapidly as possible.

FOURTH PHASE.
It is the intentions of the Army Commander to gain the green line, at all points, about three hour before darkness on Zero day.

The VII Corps will press Southwards and secure the village of MERCATEL.

The VI Corps will, as rapidly as possible, pass the brown line and secure ORANGE HILL and the high ground East of FEUCHY CHAPEL, and will then secure the high ground about MONCHY Le PREUX.

After securing the high ground about that place, the VI Corps will move North-Eastwards and, making full use of the Corps Mounted Troops, will secure the passages over the Canal and the RIVER SCARPE, between ETAING and the point reached by the right of the XVII Corps.

The XVII Corps will also pass beyond the brown line, and will secure the village of FAMPOUX, HYDERABAD REDOUBT, and such points in advance of LE POINT DE JOUR as will give observation over the plains of DOUAI.

FIFTH PHASE.

The VII Corps will then push forward to the CHAT MAIGER. At the same time, the left flank of the VII Corps will secure the high ground North-West of HENINEL, and will swing round its left and occupy the German switch line between HENINEL and FONTAINE LEZ CROISELLES.

Meanwhile, on receiving information that the blur line has been captured, the leading brigades of the Cavalry Divisions will move up to the West entrances of Arras, and the remainder of the Corps will close up. The Infantry Division attached must, at the same time, be ready to move in two columns from the line DUISANS - WAGNONLIEU - DAINEVILLE, through, or round, ARRAS, following the rear Cavalry Division.

When it receives the order to advance, the Cavalry Corps will advance and secure the line of the COJEUL RIVER, between HENINEL and ETAING, and subsequently, the line of the SENSEE RIVER, between FONTAINE LEZ CROISILLES and ETAING.

The XVII Corps must gradually close up on the two main roads West of ARRAS, so that the heads of its columns are ready to follow the Infantry Division attached to the Cavalry Corps, through, or round, ARRAS.

Consequently, on the morning of Zero plus 1 day, it is intended that the situation should be as follows:-

The VII Corps in occupation of MERCATEL, NEUVILLE-VITASSE, HENINEL, and German trenches between HENINEL and FONTAINE LEZ CROISILLES.

The Cavalry Corps in occupation of the line of the SENSEE RIVER from FONTAINE LEZ CROISILLES to ETAING.

The VI Corps facing North and East, and holding the passages of the Canal and SCARPE RIVER between ETAING and about FAMPOUX.

The XVII Corps holding the high ground North-East of FAMPOUX, and connecting with the First Army at a point between BAILLEUL - SIRE- BERTHOULT and THELUS.

When it is ascertained that these positions have been gained, the XVIII Corps will be ordered to advance, and to concentrate, facing south, on the line HENINEL - CHERISY. As soon as this concentration is completed - which, it is estimated, will be at Zero plus 48 hours - the XVIII Corps will advance Southwards to the line ST. LEGER - BULLECOURT.

The Cavalry Corps will cover the left of the XVIII Corps.

Certain variations may become necessary in the fifth phase of the operation. Two of these possible variations are to be considered, and to be prepared for:-

The first of these is that situation that would arise, should it not be possible to gain ground quickly further East than MONCHY LE PREUX.

In this case the general ides of a rapid advance Southwards will be maintained, but this Southward move will be restricted to a more westerly area.

Under these circumstances, it would become necessary to throw our weight against the line FICHEAUX, HAMELINCOURT, widening our base as we advance Southwards.

If this situation arises, the Cavalry Corps will hold the front HENINSIR-COJEUL, MONCHY LE PREUX.

The XVIII Corps, advancing from the line TELEGRAPH HILL, WANCOURT, will aim at securing the line BOIRY-ST. MARTIN, HAMELINCOURT, making a defensive flank between HENIN-SUR-COJEUIL and HAMELINCOURT.

The VII Corps, conforming to the advance of the XVIII Corps, will press South-West to the line FICHEAUX, BOIRY-ST. MARTIN.

The second variation is the situation which would arise, should the advance towards MONCHY LE PREUX be delayed at, or about, the line TILLOY-LEZ-MAFFAINES, FEUCHY, the operations North of the SCARPE move rapidly, and advance to the line PLOUVAIN, GAVRELLE, BAILLEUL-SIRE-BERTHOULT, appears practicable

Should this operation appear advisable, with a view to securing MONCH LES PREUX from the North and then continuing the general plan of an advance Southward, or with a view to changing the general plan to one having as its object an advance North-Eastward into the DOUAI - LENS area, it will be necessary to divert our reserves to the North of the SCARPE.

In this case, dependant on the situation, the Cavalry Corps, or the XVIII Corps, or both, may be directed in two columns on the roads:-
Northern outskirts of ARRAS, ST. LAURENT, BLANGY, ATHIES, FAMPOUX.

ANZIN, ST. AUBIN, ST. NICHLAS, BAILLEUL-SUR-BERTHOULT.

With reference to para 15 of the above instructions, the 34th and 51st Divisions will arrange to reach the green Line on the afternoon of Z day by pushing outposts past the Brown Line as soon as possible after reaching the latter. The actual line to be consolidated by the Divisions is that which gives the best observation over the eastern slopes of VIMY RIDGE. This modifies the instructions given in G.S.32 para 6 (iii) (last four lines) and sub-para (vi) (last 6 lines). Any field guns which cannot, from their original positions, support the Green Line as shown on the map, must move up during the night Z/Z plus 1 day so as to establish as early as possible a proper protective barrage.

H.Q., XVII Corps
Brigadier-General,
4th March, 1917.
General Staff.

Preliminary Instructions No, 2.

Part 1 - Operations.

Reference - 1/10,000 Trench Map.

1. INTENTION
The 4th Division will, with the 9th, 34th and 51st Divisions, form part of the XVII Corps and take part in the operations of the Third Army. The primary object of the operation of the XVII Corps is

to capture the German 3rd System of trenches which runs from the River SCARPE, East of ATHIES, through LE POINT DU JOUR - MAISON DE LA COTE - COMMANDANT'S HOUSE (Brown Line on Map A)

When this line has been captured a further advance will be made South of LE POINT DU JOUR to capture the southern portion of VIMY RIDGE, the 4th System of the trenches West of Fampoux, and the village of Fampoux (Green Line on Map A)

(b)   The VI Corps will be operating on the right of the XVII Corps.
The Boundary between XVII and VI Corps throughout is the River SCARPE.

The Canadian Corps will be operating on the left of the XVII Corps.

The German 3rd System of Trenches (Brown Line) on the front of the XVII Corps will be captured by the 9th, 34th and 51st Divisions (from right to left in the order given), the 4th Division being in Reserve in rear of the 9th Division.

The 4th Division will pass through the 9th Division, capture the 4th German Trench system, and the village of FAMPOUX, and establish itself on the Green Line (vide Map A).

Starting from ZERO, the 9th Division will capture the Black, Blue and Brown Lines successively according to the Time Table in APPENDIX (A).

2. PRELIMINARY DISPOSITIONS.
Prior to Z day, on a date to be notified later, the Division will be disposed as follows:-

4th Div. H.Q. - VILLERS CHATEL.

10th Inf. Brig. - X Huts about 1000^x S. of ECOIVRES

11TH Inf. Brig. - MAROEUIL AND MAROEUVIL WOOD
12th Inf. Brig. - Y Huts about 1000x West of ETRUN
on the St. POL - ARRAS Road.

4th Signal Coy. - With Divisional Headquarters.

(b)   R.E. and PIONEERS.
The following will be attached to Brigades and will be accommodated in Brigade Areas

11th Inf. Brig. - 526th (Durham) Fd. Co.R.E.

12th Inf. Brig. - 9th Fd. Co. R.E.

The 2 Field Coys, will be at the disposal of the C.R.E., who will detach 2 sectns. to each Bde. for work.

The 21st West Yorkshires (Pioneers) and 406th (Renfrew) Fd. Co. R.E. have been placed at the disposal of the XVII Corps from ZERO.

(c)   On the morning of Z day the above troops will move off as to reach their respective assembly areas (Map A) at scheduled time.

11th Inf. Brig. Group. from Z Huts via St. AUBIN - ANZIN St. AU-BIN to positions North of the road in G.8.d.

12th Inf. Brig, Group. from Y Huts via St. POL - ARRAS Road to cross roads L.10.c.2.0 - Cross roads L.10.d.8.9 - St. VAAST Bridge - track South of the CHAUSSE BRUNEHAUT to G.14.b.7.9 - thence to assembly area in G.14.b west of St. CATHERINE and via track to G.15.d.West of St. NICHOLAS.

10th Inf. Brig. Group. from X Huts follows the 11th Inf. Brig. Group to assembly area N.E. of ANZIN St. AUBIN.
(d) Brigade will halt at their assembly areas in accordance with Time Table (APPENDIX A). During this period they will be given a hot meal.

The 11th and 12th Inf. Brigs. advance to the Blue and Brown Lines in accordance with Time Table (APPENDIX A).

The 10th Inf. Brig, will follow the 11th and 12th Inf. Brigs. Using both routes, according to Time Table (APPENDIX A).

First Line Transport -

(i)   A Echelon consisting of pack animals, cookers and water carts will be left at assembly areas.
The remainder will remain in X,Y and Z Camps.

The following come under the orders of the G.O.C. 4th Division at the hour at which his leading troops pass the Brown Line.

All the Field Artillery supporting the attack.
CRE and CRA 9th Division.

1 Pioneer Battalion of the 9th Division.

2 Field Cos. R.E.   "   "   "   "

1 Signal Company "   "   "   "

3.   OBJECTIVES OF THE ATTACK.

The attack divides itself into 2 stages :-

The capture of the 4th German Trench System running North from the SCARPE, West of FAMPOUX to H.11.b.0.4.

Capture of the village of FAMPOUX and HYDERABAD REDOUBT and the establishment of a defensive line from the Railway Bridge (H.18.d.3.2) - HYDERABAD REDOUBT, connecting up with the 34th Division on our left at H.4.c.2.0 (Green Line on Map A). Strong patrols will be pushed to capture any artillery in the area and to maintain touch with the enemy.
Touch will also be obtained with the VI Corps operating South of the River SCARPE.

4.   BOUNDRIES BETWEEN BRIGADES. (Map A).

Boundaries between 11th and 12th Inf. Brigs. During the advance to the Brown Line and in the subsequent attacks will be:

12th Inf. Brig.

Right Boundary. River SCARPE.

Left Boundary. G.16.central - G.17.central - N. corner of Cemetery in G.18.b central - bridge over Railway cutting on "BLUE LINE" at H.8.c.0.0 (to Left Brigade) - thence a line due East along grid cutting the "BROWN LINE" South of the Trench junction at H.9.c.6.0 and the 4th German Trench System at H.10.d.7.0 - thence along the Communication Trench (inclusive to 12th Inf. Brig. To road junction H.17.a.8.9 (to 11th Inf. Brig.) - thence a straight line to the Green Line at H.12.c.4.8

11th Inf. Brig.

Right Boundary. As Above.

Left Boundary.

Bridge over Railway S. of the BOIS DE LA MAISON BLANCHE at H.1.d 3.0 - thence Eastwards to point where the German Trench meets the GAVRELLE Road at H.3.d 2.1 - thence a straight line to the N.E. corner of HYDERABAD REDOUBT at H.12.a 1.0.

PREPARATIONS FOR THE ATTACK BY THE ARTILLERY.

Lanes will be cut in the wire in front of the 4th German Trench System during the latter part of the bombardment on X and Y days, and from daylight on Z day. During the 2 hours that elapses between the capture of the Brown Line by the 9th Division and the advance of the 4th Division, every available Medium and Heavy Howitzer will bombard the German Fourth System.

PLAN OF ATTACK.
4th SYSTEM.

The troops detailed for the assault of the 4th German Trench System will be formed up in the German 3rd Trench System West of the Brown Line, on their respective Brigade fronts, ready to cross Brown Line at schedule time.

At the same time the standing barrage 300 yards in front of the Brown Line will wait for five minutes to enable the infantry to get close to it and will then advance at the rate of 100 yards in 2 minutes North of the Road. South of the road it will commence to move forward 10 minutes later, and the barrage will then advance parallel throughout its whole length tot he 4th German Trench System and at the rate of 100yards in 2 minutes.

The assaulting Infantry will follow the barrage as closely as possible.

The <u>Right Brigade</u> (12th Inf. Brig.) will attack with 3 Battalions in line, followed by the 4th Battalion in support.

The <u>Left Brigade</u> (11th Inf. Brig.) will attack, 2 Battalions in line, with a 3rd Battalion following in support.

The 4th Battalion will establish a double chain of posts along the Green Line from H.11.a.6.4 to H.4.c.2.0 to cover the left flank.
As soon as the trenches are captured posts will also be pushed out to the Western outskirts of FAMPOUX and to the SUNKEN Road, H.17.a.9.0 to H.11.a.6.0. Blocks will also be established in the trenches about H.11.b.2.5 and 2.2.

(b)   FAMPOUX - HYDERABAD REDOUBT.
Half an hour's halt will be made on the 4th Trench System to enable the rear Battalions to close up and pass through for the attack on FAMPOUX and HYDERABAD REDOUBT.

4 minutes after the hour fixed for the advance a special Howitzer barrage will commence to move through FAMPOUX at the rate of 100 yards in 4 minutes, reaching the Eastern edge 32 minutes later.
This barrage will be followed up by Infantry through he village, whilst others passing rapidly along the Northern edge get into positions from which to enter it from the N. and E. as soon as the barrage lifts.

(c)   Green Line.
As soon as the Green Line is in our possession, patrols will be pushed out and the organisation of a defensive line will be commenced.

Touch will also be obtained with the VI Corps operating S. of the Scarpe.

(d)   The Right Brigade will be prepared to assist the VI Corps by sweeping the slopes S. of the river with machine gun fire should favourable targets present themselves.

The 10th Inf. Brig. Will be in Divisional Reserve. It will reach the Brown Lines at schedule time and will take over from the 9th Division the work of consolidating the German 3rd Trench System.

In the event of ant portion of the advance being temporarily held up, troops on the flanks will press on and endeavour to turn the obstacle.

7.   ARTILLERY BARRAGES
(1)   The timings of the Artillery "Creeping" and "Protective barrages are given in APPENDIX B.
A salvo of shrapnel will be fired from all 18 pdrs. to mark the start of each stage of the infantry attack. Otherwise the ammunition to be employed will be 50% shrapnel and 50% H.E.

These barrages will work on the following principles:-
Up to the Brown Line the rate of advance for the first 300 yards will be at 50 yards in 11/2 Minutes, afterwards at 100 yards in 4 minutes.

The protective barrage will be placed 300 yards in front of the line held. From the Brown Line to the German 4th German System the creeping barrage will advance at 100 yards in 2 minutes. The times of starting being calculated to allow the infantry to get within 50 yds. of it.

The barrage will lift off each line of Trenches simultaneously along its whole length.

Beyond the 4th German System there will be no creeping barrage but fire will be concentrated on selected points, lifting when the infantry, advancing at 100 yards in to minutes, is within 400 - 500 yards.

A special Howitzer barrage will move through FAMPOUX at the rate of 100 yards in 4 minutes, thus giving the infantry passing along the Northern face time to get beyond and round it before the barrage lifts from the Village.

A protective gun barrage will be placed along the Western edge of FAMPOUX. It will remain until 5 minutes after the hour fixed for the advance of the Infantry to cover the latter whilst in the Village.

8.   POINTS REQUIRING SPECIAL ATTENTION.

During and after the advance to the Green Line, in order to provide for a possible counter-attack from the direction of GAVRELLE, machine guns will be placed near LE POINT DU JOUR to sweep the GAV-RELLE Road and the slopes to the south of it.

Strong Points will be formed along the Green Line both on the forward and rear slopes of the POINT DU JOUR - FAMPOUX spur (vide para. 9), and as soon as possible machine guns will be placed in the 4th Trench System to sweep the Southern slopes of the GAVRELLE spur.

9.   CONSOLIDATION

The lines to be consolidated will be :-

(i)   The "Brown Line".

The 4th German Trench System.

A defensive line on the "German Line", giving observation over the country in front.

The work of consolidation must be undertaken by the Infantry, and should be commenced immediately by the troops detailed to halt on the lines in question, (in the case of the "Brown Line", the work will have been partially carried out by the 9th Division and will be completed by 10th Inf. Brig,)

The sections of R.E. attached to each Brigade, with special Infantry working parties, will be used for constructing Strong Points behind the Green Line including the placing of HYDERABAD REDOUBT in a state of defence.

The exact sites of these Strong Points will be settled after reconnaissance on the ground, but the approximates positions will be as follows:-

12th Inf. Brig, Area

 H.18.d 2.2

H.18.c 8.8

H.18.a 5.5

H.12.c 5.1

11th Inf. Brig, Area

H.11.c 8.5

H.11.c 1.8

H.10.d 4.8

H.10.a 9.0

H.10.a 3.3

H.9.b 9.7

A Communication Trench to be dug on the second day or night from about H.9.d 6.9 to H.10.d 6.8 which will be T headed to form a rear line of defence to the strong Points, with which it will be connected up as soon as possible.

10. COMMUNICATION TRENCHES.

(a) The 9th Division intend to carry out work on communication trenches in advance of our present front line trenches as follows:-

(i) FEBRUARY AVENUE to be joined South of the St. NICHOLAS - St. LAURENT BLANGY Road to the German trench opposite.

This will be continued by the main German trench through St. LAURENT BLANGY along the main road to H.14.a 0.3.

(ii) Old sap from Trench 90 (G.12.c 20.45) to be joined up with MANGFALL Trench and MINDEL Trench to H.8.c 0.0

Sap immediately East of CUTHBERT CRATER to be joined up with ALZ Trench at G.12.a 7.2. This will continued by the German support line SALZBACH GRABEN and HELFER GRABEN H.1.d 3.0.

11. SIGNAL COMMUNICATIONS.

(a) Cables.

On Z day an advanced Divisional Signal office will be established at the Malterie at St. CATHERINE, G.15.a.4.4 from Zero hour. Communications between Infantry Brigades, while in their assembly areas in the neighbourhood of St. CATHERINE, and Divisional Headquarters will be maintained through this office.

When the Infantry Brigade Headquarters of the 4th Division move to Inf. Brig. Headquarters of the 9th Division communications with the Division will be maintained through those Headquarters.

A plan showing system of buried cable which is being completed in 9th Division Sector is attached (Plan C).

During the advance of the 9th Division, the three main cable routes will be carried forward as follows:-

(i) Along LECH Trench as far Eastward as H.13.a 60.35 thence North into MINDEL to about H.13.b 80.90

Along MANGFALL and AMBER to about Point H.7.d 70.25.

Along ALZ Trench to about H.7.b 60.00

These cable routes will be extended -

(i) From Point H.13.b 4.5 along communications trench South of the St. LAURENT BLANGY - FAMPOUX Road to ATHIES, AND EVENTUALLY TO FAMPOUX.

From Point H.7.b 60.00 along ATHIES GRABEN to junction with St. LAURENT BLANGY - GAVRELLE Road, thence along trench through Points H.8.b 3.1 - H.9.c 5.1 to H.9.b 1.2, and eventually to 4th Line German System.

(b)   Trench Wireless sets, Amplifiers and Power Buzzers.
The 9th Division are allotting Trench Wireless Sets as follows:-
1 Trench Wireless Set to 27th Inf. Brig. Which will be established about G.17.a 2.8

1 Trench Wireless Set to 1st South African Brig. To be kept in readiness to move forwards, and be erected when a new Brig. Hd. Qrs. Is established beyond our present front line.
Above sets will remain in position when the 9th Division is withdrawn.

Trench Wireless Sets, Amplifiers and Buzzers of 4th Division will be allotted as follows:-
1 Trench Wireless Set to 12th Inf. Brig. to be sent forward and to be erected in 3rd German system of trenches at H.14.b 6.4 (approx.)

1 Trench Wireless Set to 11th Inf. Brig. to be kept in reserve at Brig. Hd, Qrs. In BLUE LINE.

1 Amplifier to 12th Inf. Brig. to be sent forward and to be erected in proximity to Trench Wireless Set in 3rd German System.

1 Amplifier to 11th Inf. Brig. to be sent forward and to be erected in BROWN Line at H.9.b 1.2 (approx.)

2 Power Buzzers to 12th Inf. Brig.   ) One to be attached to a leading
Battn and   ) one to be attached to a rear Bn. of each
2 Power Buzzers to 11th Inf. Brig.   ) Brig.
2 Power Buzzers to 10th Inf. Brig.

(c)   Pigeons.

Pigeons will be issued to each Battalion of 11th and 12th Inf. Brigs.

(d)   Contact Aeroplanes.

Contact aeroplanes will be employed to receive signals from Brigade and Battalion Headquarters by means of:-

(i)   Ground signal panels.
Lamps.
and from attacking Infantry by means of flares.

(e)   Light Signals.

Light Signals will be used for communications from the front line to Batteries through ant intermediate station which it may be found necessary to establish.

Light Signals will be used according to the following code :-

Succession of Green Lights ... OPEN FIRE.

"   " White   " ... LENGTHEN RANGE

Signals will be continued until the required response is made by the Artillery.

The increment by which the range will be increased or decreased will be 100 yards.

(f)   VISUAL SIGNALLING.

A main receiving station will be established near G.23.c 5.2

This will be manned day and night in conjunction with the 9th Division.

Prior to the offensive it will be pointed out to all signallers.

The 11th Inf. Brig. will establish a station on the BLUE Line near Brig. Hd. Qrs. On spur about H.8.a central which will be relieved by the 10th Inf. Brig. when it arrives.

The 12th Inf. Brig. will establish a station on the Blue Line as near as possible to Brig. Hd. Qrs. about H.7.d 9.0.

These stations will maintain communications with the central receiving station.

Brigades and Battalions will arrange to maintain communications with one or other of these stations at different stages of the advance.

As the advance proceeds intermediate stations will be established to maintain communications between Bns. And the Brig. Hd. Qrs. stations in para. 2.

Suitable points appear to be

On the POINT DU JOUR - FAMPOUX Spur about H.16.c 5.9

H.16.c 9.1 or higher up the spur if necessary to clear the trees.

(5)   All stations should keep watch on the central receiving station and be prepared to send direct to it.

12.   MOVES OF THE 4TH DIVISIONAL AND INF. BRIG'. HD.QRS.

On Y/Z day Headquarters will be located as follows:-

4th Division   ...   VILLERS CHATEL

10TH Inf. Brig. ...   X Camp.

11th Inf. Brig. ...   Z Camp.

12th Inf. Brig. ... Y Camp.

On Z day -

(i)   Divisional Headquarters at ZERO hour will be established at ETRUN alongside 9th Divisional Headquarters and will move later to dugouts at G.17.a 23.48

12th Inf. Brig. Headquarters at ZERO hour will be established at G.14.b 9.5 (approx.) They will be established alongside 26th Inf. Brig. (9th Div.) Headquarters at G.17.a 70.45 before the Brigade crosses the original British front line and will move later to the BLUE Line at H.13.b.8.9.

11th Inf. Brig. Headquarters at ZERO hour will be established at G.8.d 7.0 (approx.) They will be established alongside the 27th Inf. Brig. (9th Div.) Headquarters at G.17.a 28.80 before the Brigade crosses the original British front line and will move later to the BLUE Line at H.7.b 6.0) approx.)

10th Inf. Brig. Headquarters at ZERO hour will be established at G.8.c 8.7 (approx.) They will be established alongside the 1st South African Brig. (9th Div.) Headquarters at G.17.a 23.48 before the Brigade crosses the original British front line trench, and will move later to FORRES-TIER REDOUBT at G.17.a 70.45, when Divnl. Headquarters moves forward.

10, 11th and 12th Inf. Brigs. Will each detail an officer of their Brigade Staff to be at Hd, Qrs. of 1st South African, 27th and 26th Inf. Brigs. Respectively from ZERO hour, so as to follow the course of operations closely. T he position of the Hd.Qrs. of adjacent units and of higher formations are given in App. C.

13.   PRISONERS OF WAR.

11th and 12th Inf. Brigs. will be responsible for conducting prisoners of War as far as L'ABBATETTE.

(b)   10th Inf. Brig. will detail a party of 1 officer and 50 men to be at the disposal of the A.P.M. to conduct the prisoners from L'AB-BEYETTE to a joint Divnl. Cage - G.15.b 5.1.

1/2 troop of Cavalry and 24 P.B. men will be placed under the orders of the A.P.M. to conduct the prisoners of War from the Divisional Cage to the Corps Cage at ETRUN Sq. (L.2.d 3.1).

Colonel,

20th March, 1917.

General Staff, 4th Division

General Remarks on the attack 4th Division 11th April, 1917

GENERAL REMARKS

The troops attacked with the utmost gallantry, pressing forward until practically annihilated by the enemy's machine guns and rifle fire. The 2nd Seaforth Highlanders alone lost 12 officers and 363 other ranks out of a total of 12 officers and 420 other ranks, whilst the losses of the 1st Royal Irish Fusiliers were on a similar scale.

The preliminary bombardment was insufficient to knock out the enemy machine guns, the position of which were only vaguely known, and these latter opened fire through the creeping barrage directly the troops left the trenches. The front on which the battalions were attacking was a very broad one and the Field Artillery supporting the attack was not sufficiently strong.

The only chance of success under these conditions from the statements of prisoners, however, lay in a possible want of determination on the part of the enemy. From the statements of prisoners, it appears that the enemy on the morning of the 9th, rushed forward fresh troops with a large proportion of machine guns with the intention of delaying the advance by all possible means.

These troops fought with determination and counter-attacked boldly. When at 2.50 p.m. it was clear that the original attack had failed, Brigades were ordered to organise a second attack in direct communications with the artillery with a view to capturing the 1st Objective at all costs (4th Div. G.58).

This message only reached the units concerned at 4 p.m. by which time the troops were digging themselves in, casualties had been severe and the units were mixed up and disorganised.

Under these circumstances, the Brigadier General Commanding the 10th Brigade did not consider it possible to carry out the order and in the light of subsequent events there is no doubt that his decision was a wise one.

11th Brigade Account of Operations of the 11th April

SECRET
11TH Inf. Bde. No.BM 4/194
4th Division on "G".

Reference your G.671 of the 20th instant. The following is an account of the operations of the 11th April, 1917:-
Early in the morning of the 11th inst., orders were received that the 4th Division was to advance and take up a line PLOUVAIN - GREEN-LAND HILL - INN I.7.a.2.8. - HYDERABAD REDOUBT. The order of Brigades from North to South was 11th, 10th and 12th.

The objectives were as follows :-
1st OBJECTIVE.   ROEUX - GAVRELLE Road as far North as the INN at I.7.a.2.6, with a defensive flank from the INN to HYDER-ABAD REDOUBT.

2ND OBJECTIVE.   FLAVAIN - GREENLAND HILL, with a defensive flank from I.7.b.2.8. to the INN.

The role of the 11th Brigade was to support the left flank of the 4th Division, forming a defensive flank in the first objective from the INN at I.7.a.2.8. to HYDERABAD REDOUBT, and in the second objective from I.7.b.2.8. to the INN.

The boundary between the 11th and 12th Brigades was a line HYDER-ABAD REDOUBT (inclusive to the 11th Brigade) to Cross Roads I.7.a.4.3. - I.7.b.2.0.

The 1st Somerset Light Infantry were detailed to support the attack of the 10th and 12th Brigades and to form the defensive flank from HY-DERABAD REDOUBT to the INN at I.7.a.2.8. later to I.7.b.2.8. Their attack was to be covered by machine gun fire from the 11th Machine Gun Coy., which was mainly directed against the ground in H.6.d. and I.1.c. , where machine guns had been located on the previous day.

Their attack was also to be supported by Lewis Gun and rifle fire by the 1st Hampshire Regiment from HAZARD TRENCH.

Zero Hour was fixed at 12 noon. For the operation, 11th Brigade Battle Head Quarters were established in the dugouts in the SUNKEN ROAD at H.11.c.8.3., while the Head Quarters of the 1st Somerset

Light Infantry were established in HYDERABAD REDOUBT. From both places good observation of the of the operations was obtained.

The attack started at 12 noon. Our artillery barrage appeared to be fairly thick but was not so dense as that on the 12th instant.

The enemy at once opened a heavy machine gunfire and after the lapse of a few minutes put down an Artillery barrage, (1) on or about our Font Line through HYDERABAD REDOUBT. (2) on the SUNKEN ROAD in H.11.c.

From the SUNKEN ROAD, the movement of the 10th and 11th Brigades could be seen as they advanced for about 200 or 300 yards suffering heavy casualties. On the South in H.18.a. and b., they may have advanced some 500 to 600 yards but the smoke made accurate observation difficult. Beyond this point the troops appeared unable to get forward and the leading lines were mown down. (Afterwards, when the smoke cleared, the dead of the 2nd Seaforth's could be observed lying in rows in front of the German line). In particular a strong point about H.12.d.9.9. was strongly held by Germans and many of our dead could be seen lying 200 -300 yards to the west of it.

The 1st Somerset Light Infantry attacked on a one-Company front and they report that they had difficulty moving out of HYDERABAD REDOUBT owing to the depth of the trenches and the fact that they were crowded out by the 10th Brigade. They do not appear to have got beyond a N. & S. line through H.12.c.7.8. They could not advance beyond this line owing to the heavy machine gun fire. Some of them got into the communications trench which runs Eastward from HYDERABAD REDOUBT and attempted to bomb towards the enemy who were stopped by machine gun fire as the trench was shallow.

They dug in on this line making a block in the communications trench running East from the REDOUBT about H.12.c.7.8. and also dug in posts East of HYDERABAD REDOUBT to about H.12.a.0.4.
There was no question of them coming back from any objective as they never got beyond a line 200 - 300 yards West of the German trench.

As far as could be observed, the 10th Brigade did not reach the German trench which ran parallel to and about 3000 yards West of the Gavrelle - Roeux Road.

Brigadier General.
21/4/17
Commanding 11th Infantry Brigade.

4th Division – Operation Order No. 31

SECRET.
Reference - Trench Map 51 B.N.W.
    2nd May, 1917.

INTENTION.
The XVII Corps forming part of the Third Army is to take part in a general attack on the enemy's positions covering FRESNES - LES-MONTAUBAN - PLOUVAIN.

The VI Corps is attacking South of the River Scarpe whilst the XIII Corps is attacking to the north of XVII Corps.

BOUNDARIES.
The 4th Division will attack on the right of the XVII and the 9th Division on the left. The boundary between the Divisions being HYDER-ABAD REDOUBT - CLYDE - CUT (all to the 9th Division), thence a straight line from junction of CUBA and CASH Trenches to the wood in I.8.d (to 9th Divn.) From this the Railway (inclusive to 9th Division) is the boundary.

The Southern boundary of the 4th Division id the River SCARPE.
The 17th Division will be in Corps Reserve.

(b)   The 4th Division will attack with two Brigades in the line, the 10th Inf. Brig. (plus one battalion 11th Inf. Brig.) on the right and the 12th Inf. Brig. on the left, dividing line between the Brigades, cross roads H.18.d. 55.10 CHEMICAL WORKS (to 12th Inf. Brig.), thence a straight line the Southern edge of PLOUVAIN at I.16.a.0.0.
The 11th Inf. Brig. (less one battalion) will be in Divisional Reserve.
OBJECTIVES.
The objectives will be :- (vide map).
BLACK Line.
BLUE Line.
RED Line.

4.   PLAN OF ATTACK.
The advance will be made simultaneously along the whole front (with the exception of three village of ROEUX) behind a creeping barrage.
The battalions of the 12th Brigade advancing North of the Railway will conform to the movements of the right Brigade of the 9th Division and will form a defensive flank, facing South, along the Southern bank of

the Railway Cutting, from its junction with CUPID Trench to the Copse in H.d. (excl.)

A battalion will be detailed to attack ROEUX after a special bombardment, details of which will be issued separately.

ACTION OF THE 11TH BRIGADE.
The 11th Inf. Brig. (less one battalion under the orders of the B.G.C. 10th Inf. Brig.) will be in Divisional Reserve and will assemble in the 4th German System and the trenches to the east of it. As the assembly trenches are vacated by the assaulting battalions it will gradually close up and occupy our present from line. Its rôle will be :-

To support the assaulting Brigades.

In case the Objectives South of the Railway are not attained, form a defensive flank along CORONA Trench and Railway Cutting, connecting up with the 9th Division at COPSE in I.8.d 8.0
In case -

(a)   One battalion is placed at the call of the 12th Inf. Brig.; this battalion will be in assembly trenches North of the Railway at ZERO +30.
In case -

Necessary orders will be issued from Divisional H.Q.

ARTILLERY.
Map showing timings of barrage lifts is attached. Copies will be issued later down to Platoon Commanders.
(b)   At the commencement of each advance a salvo of Smoke will be fired from all guns. This signal will also be used in subsequent operations involving a new artillery programme.
(c)
TRENCH MORTARS.
Brigades will carry out an intense bombardment from 3 inch Stokes Mortars commencing at ZERO and covering the advance up to their limit of range.
4 inch Stokes Mortars will discharge Thermite -
(i)   from ZERO to ZERO + 1 on to buildings near STATION.

(ii)   from ZERO to ZERO +10 on the Woods West of Roeux.
GAS.

Gas will be discharged from LIVENS Projectors after dark on Y day against the village of ROEUX if the wind is favourable.

CONTACT PATROLS.
Hour of Contact Patrols will be notified later.

The following will be carried out in accordance with Instructions already issued.

Consolidation.

Machine Gun barrage.

ZERO day and hour will be notified later.

ACKNOWLEDGE.

Colonel,
General Staff, 4th Division.

4th Division Operation Order No. 34

SECRET
10TH May, 1917.

XVII Corps will resume the offensive with the object of gaining the line ROEUX CEMETERY - CORONA - CUPID - CURLY - CHARLIE - WISH Trenches to our present front line about I.1.b.7.0.

The attack will be carried out in two phases on 11th and 12th May

On 11th May the 4th Division will attack and capture ROEUX CEMETERY - CHATEAU - CHEMICAL WORKS and Buildings North of Railway, establishing the line shewn on attached sketch map A (BLACK Line).

On the 12th May the 4th and 17th Divisions will attack simultaneously and secure the final objective (Map B - BLUE Line).

As this is contingent on the success of operations of the 11th, definite orders will be issued regarding the continuance of operations on the 12th May.

3.   (a)   The attack of the 11th inst. will be carried out by the 10th and 11th Infantry brigades. 2 Companies of 50th Inf. Bge. 17th Division, will be placed at the disposal of the 11th Inf. Brig. to assist in this attack, reverting to the command of the 50th Inf. Brig, at ZERO + 1 1/2 hours.

On the 12th inst the attack of the 4th Division will be carried out by the 11th Inf. Brig.

(b)   The 12th Inf. Brigade will place one Battalion at the (disposal) of each of the 10th and 11th Inf. Brigades.

The remainder of the 12th Infantry Brigade is placed at the disposal of the 11th Inf. Bde. from midnight 11th/12th inst, at which hour it will be in the 4th German Trench System.

Two battalions of 152nd Inf. Bde., 51st Division, in Divisional Reserve will move forward so as to reach LUE Line on morning of 12th inst at 9 a.m.

(e)   The attack on both days will be carried out in accordance with Instructions already issued.

Sketch maps shewing timings of Artillery barrages are attached -

- Z + 1day.
Troops will be prepared to light flares (Green) when called for by Contact Aeroplanes at following hours :- Z day-8.15 p.m.
All troops will be in their assembly positions before daylight on the 11th inst.

An officer from Divisional H.Q. will be at 10th Inf. Brig. H.Q. at 6 p.m. and at 11th Inf. Brig. H.Q. at 6.30 p.m. 10th inst. To synchronise watches.

<u>DOCUMENTS</u>.   Special care will be taken to ensure that no document or map referring to the attack on Z + 1 day is taken into action on Z day.
Zero hour on 11th inst. will be 7.30 p.m.

Zero hour on 12th inst. will be 6.30 a.m.
ACKNOWLEDGE.

(Sgd)   W. Kirke, Colonel
General Staff, 4th Division.

Report by G.O.C. 12ᵗʰ Brigade on Raid of 9ᵗʰ August

12ᵗʰ Infantry Brigade No. G.R. 1898
4ᵗʰ Division "G".

I have the honour to submit my remarks on the attempted Raid carried out by this Brigade on 9ᵗʰ August at 7.45.p.m.

The chief causes of failure were, in the first place, the fact that the raid was attempted in broad daylight. The troops had to cross about 200 yards of open ground in full view of the enemy and there was practically no chance of this being done in daylight.

Heavy Machine Gun fire was brought to bear on the troops as soon as they were seen, and we suffered very heavy casualties as the men still tried to go on and a few did reach the German wire and were killed there.

In the second place, our Artillery barrage and the preliminary bombardment on our front was very weak and much of the ground North of our point of entry was not shelled at all.

The work of the R.F.C. was certainly not satisfactory from the Infantry point of view. Before Zero there was over 20 of our 'planes up and 5 E.A. Our machines did very well at first, some of them engaging the enemy with machine guns, but after 15 minutes they all drew off and allowed the E.A. to fly low over our trench.

Subsequently our machines came back, but they never attacked the E.A. with any determination. I might also suggest that during practice barrage there should be approximately the same number of 'planes up there will be during the actual attack, otherwise there is very little chance of surprising the enemy.

I cannot speak too highly of the conduct of the Officers and men taking part in the raid; they went on in spite of the heavy fire, and it was to this cause that I attribute the heavy casualties.

Brigadier General,
Commanding 12ᵗʰ Infantry Brigade

4th Division Order NO. 61

Reference - BROEMBEEK and
    LANGEMARCK. 1/10,00   27th September, 1917.

(a) It is not certain what troops are holding the line immediately opposite to us.

The 208th Division has been holding the line till the 23rd instant, but as it has suffered very heavy casualties it may have been relieved.

It seems probable that if it has been relieved the new Division is the 40th (Saxon) Division.

The normal method of holding the line is one battalion per regiment in front, the 2nd battalion with two companies in the Northern end of POELCAPELLE and two companies another 1000 yards N.E. The 3rd Battalion is in and around WESTROOSEBEEK.

(b) The 2nd and 5th Armies are continuing the attack on 'Z' Day.

The objective of the 5th Army is shown by the BLUE line on the attached map.

This objective will be captured by 18th and 14th Corps, the boundary between the two Corps being the line U.24.c.4.0 - V.13.d.5.0.

The 11th Division will be the left Division of the 19th Corps.

The objective of the 14th Corps will be captured by the 4th Division on the right and the 29th Division on the left, the boundary between the two Divisions being the line U.23.central - U.10.b.5.0

(a) The 4th Division will attack at ZERO hour with two Brigades in front line and one in Reserve.

    11th Brigade will be on the right.
    10th Brigade will be on the left.
    12th Brigade will be in Reserve.

The boundary between Brigades will be the line U.23.b.8.0 - V.13.c.0.5.

The general direction of the attack is N.E.

(b) All Brigades will be in their final positions by ZERO - 2 hours on 'Z' day.

The positions of Brigades at ZERO hour will be:-

    11th Brigade in right front area H.Q. Stray FM.   C.3.c.2.7
    10th Brigade in left front area H.Q. ADELPHI   C.3.b.2.1
    12th Brigade in Support area H.Q. Fusiliers HO. C.13.c.1.2

The 11th and 12th Brigades will each detail special parties whose duties are to keep touch with the 11th and 29th Divisions respectively. They will report the situation on arrival at the following points:-

Right Bde. KANGAROO trench Cross roads,
V.19.a.25.20
Road V.19.b.1.8

Left Bde. Road junction
U.18.d.00.55

* Issued to Brigades only.
(a) The attack will be supported by a creeping artillery barrage and by a machine gun barrage, details of which will be issued separately.

The 21st W.Yorks. R. (Pioneers) will place two Lewis gun teams, with guns, at the disposal of each of the two attacking Bdes. For anti-aircraft work in the front system.

The R.E. and Pioneers will work under the orders of the C.R.E. who will receive separate instructions.

Prisoners will be sent back to ADELPHI where they will be taken over by an escort to be provided by the 12th Brigade.

This escort will consist of one officer and 20 men and will be at ADELPHI at ZERO hour on 'Z' day.

They will take the prisoners back to the cage at CACTUS PONTOON where they will be handed over to the A.P.M. for disposal.

Medical arrangements will be issued separately.

Brigades will send in reports at least every half hour after ZERO to Divisional Headquarters whether there is anything to report or not.

ZERO hour and 'Z' day will be communicated later also the arrangements for the synchronisation of watches.

Reports to WELSH FM.
ACKNOWLEDGE
Lieut. Colonel   General Staff, 4th Division.

To All Ranks of the 4TH Division

Nobody will ever forget the part taken by the 4th Division in the Great Battle of FLANDERS 1917.

In eight days you have had three fights in the most trying conditions that any troops have had to endure, and in the words of the Army Commander "the performance was marvellous".

The demands made on the artillery have surpassed all previous records and the gallantry and determination of the Infantry have been beyond all praise.

Machine Gun Companies and Light Trench Mortar Batteries have materially assisted the Infantry and in spite of heavy losses have shown the finest spirit throughout.

As usual the gallantry of the linesman and devotion to duty of all members of the Signal Service have been splendid.

But for the unceasing energies of the R.E. and Pioneers the movement across country and the transport of material up to the front would have made the operations impossible.

Last but not least a great debt of gratitude is due to the R.A.M.C. personnel with the attached Infantry stretcher bearers for their never ceasing efforts to bring in the wounded and save them from unnecessary suffering.

Nobody could be more proud than I am of commanding such troops.

I thank and congratulate you all.

Major General,
13th October, 1917.   Commanding 4th Division

Third Army G.71/164 - XVII Corps.

At the request of the American Authorities it has been decided that American Officers attached to Army Inf. Schools will visit forward areas on the termination of the present series of courses. American Officers not at the Infantry Schools of Third, Fourth and Fifth Armies will visit Divisions in the line on the front of Third Army. They will proceed to those Divisions with students returning from the course at the school.

Where possible it has been arranged for American Officers to be conducted by British Officers who have been attending the same School of Instruction. The American Officers will leave the bulk of their kits at the Infantry Schools where they have attended courses, during their visit to the forward area, and will return to Infantry Schools on conclusion of their visit in order to collect kits. They will not be accompanied by servants.

On conclusion of their visit to forward areas, the American Officers will proceed via the Infantry School concerned to report to H.Q., 1st American Division for duty, the Senior Officer of each party will report to H.Q. A.E.F. en route. The Commandants of the Infantry Schools will provide them with the necessary movement orders.

Arrangements for the return of American Officers to the Infantry Schools from Division to which they have been attached will be made between Corps and Schools concerned.

Each party of American Officers should be divided into smaller groups of two or three and be attached to different Brigades. It is not necessary that they should be attached to the particular units who have had officer students at the present course; these Officer students should conduct them to the H.Q. of Divisions to which they will be attached, and they should then be sent on under Divisional arrangements.

American Officers will be detailed in parties by the Commandants of the Schools to which they are at present attached.

Sgd. G. Thorpe. Lt.Colonel,
29th October, 1917.   for Major General, 3rd Army.

Instructions No.4 to 10th Infantry Brigade Operation Order No.80

SECRET
DUSAINS

In order to prolong the front of attack during the raid by the 10th Infantry Brigade and to draw fire off the point to be raided, two attacks will be made by dummies.

One attack just north of the CAMBRAI Road consisting of 44 dummies.

One attack north of CANNISTER AVENUE consisting of 44 dummies, which will be assisted by a creeping barrage.

The dummies will be raised directly the barrage begins and will be and will be kept up till Zero plus 7 minutes when they will be lowered.

The dummies will be placed in position during the night preceding the raid and will be taken in during the night after the raid.

Attack (a) will be manned by the Household Battalion,
Attack (b) by the 12th Infantry Brigade.

Captain, B.A.
14th November 1917.   10th Infantry Brigade.

Appendix VIII – 1918 – Orders and Reports

Report on the crossing of the River Ecaillon – 24th October 1918

DESCRIPTION OF RIVER ECAILLON

All previous information with regard to this stream proved to be unreliable. No photos could be obtained beforehand owing to weather conditions. The width of approximately 25 ft from bank to bank, and width of water 15ft. Depth 4 –6 ft.

Orders for assistance for Civilians 11th November 1918

10th Infantry Brigade
11th Infantry Brigade
12th Infantry Brigade
4th Division Arty.
4th Division Engrs.
4th Bn, M.G.Corps
A.D.M.S.

Every endeavour will be made to help repatriated civilians to put their house, gardens, etc, in order. To assist in this work, a certain number of men may be excused parade, if necessary, at the discretion of unit commanders.

Lieut Colonel
General Staff, 4th Division.
11/11/18.

Orders about disorderly conduct 11th November 1918

11th Inf, Bde. No. BM 115.

Somerset Light Inf. The B.G.C. wishes to call attention top the tendency to a certain amount of disorderly conduct amongst the troops and wishes effective measures taken at once to prevent a continuation of this.

Hampshire Regt.
Rifle Brigade.
11th T.M. Battery

The firing of Very Lights etc. apart from being bad discipline, is liable to cause considerable damage to property.

Every effort is to be made to maintain the best relationship with the civilian inhabitants.

Captain.
A/Brigade Major,
11th Infantry Brigade.
11/11/18.

Demobilization and Reconstruction

A Lecture delivered at G.H.Q. on 12-10-1918, by
MAJOR D. BORDEN-TURNER.

The object of this lecture is the communication of the principles upon which the Government has decided to carry out demobilization.

Lest the announcement of this subject should cause some alarm, I hasten to assure you that this lecture is not to be taken as any indication that the end is in sight. As a matter fact, the Government decided long ago that it was not going to be caught napping by peace as it was found unprepared for war. It is no less than two years since the plans for Demobilization were put in hand, and these have been worked at ever since – six months ago the pamphlet which I have in my hand, and which forms the basis of what I say, was issued was issued by the War Office as a guide to lecturers on the subject – for the authorities desired and do desire to take the soldier into their confidence in regard to these plans and made aquainted with the reasons for taking certain measures, they will give their willing co-operation and make every effort of their own free will to ensure the smooth and rapid working of the system to be followed.

It may as well be stated, at the very beginning, in order to remove some grave fears that are widely entertained, that the men who stayed at home, either of choice or necessity, either in military service or war production, are not going to be given priority in the matter of resettlement. Simply because they are on the spot. The man in France will have and equal chance with the man at home in getting settled comfortably and happily into civil life.

In general, the principal on which the Government has decided to carry out Demobilization is " Demobilization by individuals in accordance with Trade requirements, and not by units in accordance with Military requirements," in other words it is not primarily the convenience of the War Office that will be consulted, but the economic future of the individual soldier.

After former wars, men were disbanded according to military convenience with little regard to what was going to happen to them, with, in very many cases, the most distressing consequences. They were thrown on to the Labour Market without any considerations as to the ability of the Labour Market to absorb them. The nation is determined that, after this war, not only will the discharged soldier be given a fair chance, but he will be given every chance of satisfactory resettlement.

Mr. Roberts, the Minister foe Labour, speaking in France the other day, said that he would rather keep men in the Army in France for an extended period then have them go home only to create a large army of unemployed.

I have said that the plan of demobilization is not designed to meet the convenience of the War Office. I do not wish to imply that the War Office is opposed to it – far from it. The War Office is well aware that, if, after conducting this war to a glorious conclusion, it succeeds in restoring to the country the men it has taken, in a happy and contented spirit, fit to reap individually the fruits of a victorious peace, it will add a golden spray to its laurel wreath and it will build itself a monument more lasting than brass.

The release then of men from the army will be governed largely by the ability of industry to absorb them. And here a very pertinent question arises. " Will industry be able to absorb us all? And will the process be very slow?" WE know something about the slowness of leave allotments. Is there any hope of industry reviving quickly, or must we envisage the prospect of inflicting ourselves for an indefinite period on the long-suffering French. I shall refer in a moment to certain considerations which will delay demobilization. I have, however, the authority of the Minster of Labour for saying that there is every prospect of a speedy and marked boom in industry which will continue for a number of years. The Labour Minister has been advised in this respect by a committee of expert economists, who have made a careful study of the main industries of the country, and have come to the conclusion, that there will be such a rise in the volume of trade soon after the cessation of hostilities, that not only will there be work for all the men in the country and the men in the armies, but that it will be possible to absorb also those of the women of the country, who have entered the field of industry under the normal conditions of the war, and who desire to continue in it.

It must not be supposed however, that we are all going home within ten days or a month; even if there was a channel tunnel, and we could run trains through without stopping night and day, it would take months before the men and especially the material accumulated out here during these years could be taken home.

Demobilisation will necessarily be a slow process and there are four considerations will militate against any great rapidity in the operation:- The transformation of factories, etc., from war to peace conditions. This will inevitably take time, but I do not want you to imagine that plans for this are being left until the necessity actually arises/ It is all being arranged and thought out now, and I have excellent authority for saying that the process in most cases is not going to be nearly so slow as many people fear – but of course it is not going to be accomplished over the week end.

The removal from France to England of an immense quantity of material which has been borrowed from the industry of the country, and which will have to go back before the normal life of the country can be resumed. There are many locomotives and hundreds of miles of railway track which will have to be taken back before the necessary transport services of the country are restored.

There is a great scarcity of raw material. We have made havoc of the world's stocks of all kinds of raw material, and these raw materials must be secured before industry can get into full swing. The Government is engaged on the problem of seeking out all available sources of supply and securing control over them, but this is undoubtedly one of the most serious problems which has to be met.

The lack of transport. This will be acute at first, but will improve as the months pass. It is transport for goods that will be the difficulty; there will be enough transport to take us home as fast as the country id ready to receive us.

Subject to these considerations the process of demobilization will be carried through as quickly as possible. It is all to the interest of the Government to have no delay for it will be costing the Government money to keep us in France, and the country will be losing our productive effort.

The Government too is quite alive to the fact that The Germans have a very much easier task than we have to get their troops demobilized: in fact they may very likely all be in their own country when that moment arrives, and we are not anxious in the very least to let the Germans have any sort of start in restoring the normal industrial life.

In what order shall we go? This is the question that interests us all. This I can tell you for certain, that you will not go in the order of the inscribed in you A.B. 64, so that those who are registered Group1,2,3,4,5 may at once cease to cherish the belief that they are for home by the first or second boat. We shall, as we can be spared, and as we are required, and no one can at the present moment forecast with any accuracy what these requirements are going to be.

The first men to be released from their units, and this release will probably take effect as soon as peace is in sight and before general demobilisation actually commences will be:-
Those who are required in their military or civilian capacity for the actual work of demobilization. It is quite clear that a machine must be created and that men will be required to run it.

Regular soldiers with more that two years unexpired colour service to form the nucleus of a new regular army. Part of the new army will be required to take as soon as possible the places of the units serving in India and other places who must themselves be released. It has not been decided what the size of the new army will be, but it will certainly not be smaller than the "contemptible little army" of 1914. Nor have the conditions of service been laid down, but it is quite certain that they will be considerably more attractive than those which obtained in the old army. The army has come into its own during this war and the status of the soldier will be a very different thing in future, not only as regards pay, but as position on the social scale. Every household in the land knows now what the soldier is - –is calling has gained the respect and honour to which it is always entitled but which it did not always receive.

I can think of no more attractive career for a man whose future is not clearly laid out for him, than service in the new regular army.

Those known as "pivotal" men – that is, the key men in the various trades and industries- the men without whom the rest of the workers cannot be employed. These three classes being disposed of, there remains the question of the way in which priority will be applied to the rest of us.

There will be two categories of priority:-
of Industries.
of Individuals.

No priority list of Industries has been made yet, nor is it possible to make one at present. Even when such a list is drawn up it will not remain fixed but will change according to the industrial situation. The trade that is at the head of the list one day may be sixth or seventh on the a few days later. As a matter of fact the whole of industry hangs together and all trades must go forward at the same time.

Priority will be accorded to individuals for these three reasons:-
For long service. 10% of those who go from France will be chosen on account of long service and for no other reason.

For assured employment. Immediately hostilities have ceased, or possibly before, every man in the Army will be required to fill up a form showing, amongst other things, whether he has a promise of re-employment and from whom, or where he should like to be employed. In the former case the statements will be verified; in the latter case every endeavour will be made to secure employment, and, a soon as employment is guaranteed to any man, a release slip will be made in his favour and forwarded to his Officer Commanding. This will secure him priority.

Priority will also be given to married men other things being equal.

When the actual work of Demobilizing the B.E.F. commences, the Minister of Labour, who has been charged by the Government with the carrying out of arrangements, will have before him two returns on which he will base his demands.

A return showing the total numbers of men in the B.E.F. according (a) to their industrial groups, and (b) according to the districts of Great Britain and Ireland to which they wish to go.

A return from the employment exchanges throughout the country showing the estimated demand for labour in each district in different trades.

We will suppose that at the outset the maximum rate of dispersal from France will be 15,000 men per diem, and that of this total, the Liverpool district can absorb 12% i.e. 1,250 men each day.

G.H.Q. will therefore receive from the War Office a daily allotment of 1,250 men for this district, and at the same time a priority list of industrial groups as determined by the Ministry of Labour.

We will suppose that the first three goups are those of Butchers, Bakers and Candlestick Makers in that order.

Vacancies for dispersal in the Liverpool area are sub-allotted down the chain of formations from G.H.Q. downwards to units, until the O.C. 1st Rutlands receives an allotment of 20 men, and at the same time is told the priority list- Butchers, Bakers and Candlestick Makers.

He turns up his roll of men going to the Liverpool district and is guided by four considerations in choosing the men from the list to make that days draft.

He chooses first 10% i.e., the two men with the longest service irrespective of their trades or anything else.

He next chooses every man for whom he has a release slip, again irrespective of their trades. Let us suppose there are 13 of these. Five vacancies are left.

He then calls for the Butchers as Butchers stand first on Priority list. Three butchers are found and are put down for the draft.

He proceeds to call for the Bakers. There happen to be none. He then looks up the Candlestick Makers and finds there are four.

He only has two places and so he selects the married men; there are three of these and he chooses the two with the longest military service.

Simultaneously with the return home of individuals in this way, there will go on the process of returning units. Generally speaking, a unit will not leave the country until it has been reduced to what is called cadre strength, i.e., that strength which is necessary for the care of its arms, equipment and stores. Most units of the regular army will go home early and will take with them all men with two years unexpired colour service to run, whether they are "old regulars" or men who have enlisted on regular attestations out here.

Let me now trace the history of the man from the time he leaves his unit in France. He will proceed by rail or motor lorry or march route through a series of camps on the direct line towards the port of embarkation, where he will be put into a draft proceeding directly to the dispersal station in Great Britain nearest to his home. There he will hand in his arms and equipment and he will receive:

A railway warrant to his destination.

The War Gratuity.

An allowance for civilian clothes.

A certificate entitling him to draw pay and allowances including separation allowance for 28 days, in other words, 28 days leave.

An Unemployment Donation Policy valid for a year.

During his first four weeks leave he will be expected to get himself re-settled in civil life. If he has an appointment waiting for him so much the better, but if not he will have the assistance of the local employment exchange. In case of any difficulty in either getting back his old employment or in finding a new job, he can appeal tot he Local Advisory Committee of his district. These committees made up of equal numbers of employers and work-people have been set up all over the country by the Ministry of Labour and make their business to see that the discharged soldier id satisfactorily settled. They have already dealt with large numbers of discharged men and experience has shown that not only can employers be relied upon to keep loyally the promises of re-employment given to their men but that these committees are willing to take an infinity of trouble in finding suitable situations for the discharged soldiers. In one case no less than 48 positions were found for one man. The soldier therefore can be sure that on his release from the army, if he is in need of advice or assistance he ma go, not to an official body hampered by regulations, but to a tribunal of his fellow citizens who are prepared to give not only sympathy but active and generous help.

And now gentlemen I have told you what the country is prepared to do for you. May I say a word or two about what you can do for the country.

In the first place, it is one thing for the Government to get us back to work in civil life, it will be another and entirely different thing to insure that we will all be able to pick up our work again. Many of us are going to find it extraordinarily difficult to do so – we have so completely lost touch with the old life that it will seem exceedingly hard and possibly very irksome to resume it. Few out here are doing the same sort of work they were doing at home and whatever their work was, they have lost the knack of it to a greater or lesser degree. The army has taught us many things but has not necessarily made us any better at own job. This is a loss not ourselves only but to the whole nation. More than ever after the war the country will need efficient men. There is going to be a great economic struggle after the war with our present enemies, and industrial race-a friendly one no doubt, but a contest all the same, with our allies, and the firing of the last gun will be the signal for the start. We should be getting ready to get off the mark. Every hour of study devoted towards his future career that a man can put in before he goes home is going to help him, and not only him, but the whole country.

In the second place: we have as an army a great reputation to sustain. You remember the message sent by Lord Kitchener to the troops who first came to France. The expectation of the message has been more than abundantly fulfilled. The patience and the good temper, the kindly courtesy and cheerful self- sacrifice of the men in France have been beyond all praise. It is a great record and one which must not be spoiled. Some of us are going to be kept here till near the end, some of us to the very end, either because we are too useful, or useless, or through sheer bad luck, and we are going to sit and watch the others going home. It is going to be hard. With the removal of the tremendous discipline of battle self-discipline is going to be more difficult, but it is our duty to carry ourselves that we all do, finally leave the country, our hospitable allies as will have absolutely nothing to regret but our departure, so to comport ourselves that not one stain shall fall on the bright shield of honour that our men have carried so gallantly these four long years.

In the third place: the government has carried out in the last three years several great measures of reform. They are contemplating other measures designed to secure a better country in the future for us all, but all these measures will be unavailing unless the spirit of the nation keeps pace with the legislation. Were a social system perfect in every detail to come down to us from above I would be entirely futile unless it were quickened by the breath of life. It is to the men from France that the country is looking for the incoming of that spirit, the spirit of good sense and good humour and courage and discipline and broadmindedness which has so marvellously characterized the army in France. Consider what a wonderful enlargement of mind has come to us during these four years. We have been taken up from our small circles, swept out of our narrow grooves and brought out to live in this country amongst people foreign in language, customs and ideas. We have learnt to appreciate the many great qualities of our allies but we have not learnt to love our own country any the less. We have for the first time in our history come into intimate contact with the men of the dominions, we have seen them and lived with them and we have fought with these magnificent men from Australia, Canada, Newfoundland,

South Africa, New Zealand, and we have felt proud to belong to the same empire and the same race.

More than that we have come to know our own people as never before – men from walk and class of life have been ground together in the mill of battle, stirred together in this great melting pot, from every corner of our island, John O'Groats to Lands' End from Killarney to the Norfolk Broads, English, Scotch, Welch, Irish, we have all got to know one another. Add that enlargement of mind the sense of the value of discipline and of imperious necessity of leadership, which we have learned by the bitterest of all experience in the hardest of all schools. If we can but gather this all up together in one great spiritual dynamic, we shall send back to our country after the war a body of men capable of an intelligent and high minded participation in the affairs of the country such as no nation has ever dreamed of possessing.

At no time in our history has there ever been vouchsafed to the men of the nation such an opportunity as will come to each one of us to take determining part in the working out of the destiny of our race. Whether we will or no, that power will rest with us – whether we realise it or not - we shall go back with a tremendous influence to wield for evil or for good. "We are beginning," says a recent writer, " to wonder whether we can introduce into our civil ways of life some of the influences which have clothed the men on the field of battle with imperishable spiritual splendour." The country is looking anxiously, eagerly, expectantly, for us to supply that spiritual momentum which is the county's greatest need. We are a great citizen army: so long as we live we shall be proud of the fact that we served as soldiers in the great war. Should we be any less proud of the fact that we are citizens of an empire which, when this war is over, will be more than ever incontestably the greatest empire that the world has ever seen. The day will come when most of us will have to take off these uniforms we wear. Are we simply going to discard them, and with them, all that this khaki has brought us, all that this khaki has taught us, or are going to carry back with us into the life of the country some of the imperishable spiritual splendour and show to the world an new thing in a citizenship that will be enlightened and heroic and inspired.

Appendix IX – V.C. Awards

V.C.'s of the 4th Division

Drummer S. J. Bent -1st East Lancashire Regiment - Le Gheer -1st November 1914

Private R. Morrow -1st Royal Inniskilling Fusiliers – Messines - 12th April 1915

Private J. Lynn - 2nd Lancashire Fusiliers - St Julien - 2nd May 1915

Lance Sergeant D. W. Belcher -London Rifle Brigade – Wieltje - 13th May 1915

Drummer W. P. Ritchie -2nd Seaforth Regiment - Beaumont Hamel - 1st July 1916

Sergeant R. Downie - 2nd Royal Dublin Fusiliers – Lesboeufs - 23rd October 1916

Lieutenant D. Mackintosh - 2nd Seaforth Regiment - Fampoux - 11th April 1917

Private A. Halton -1st King's Own Royal Lancaster - Regiment Poelcappelle - 12th October 1917

2nd Lieutenant B. M. Cassidy - 2nd Lancashire Fusiliers - Arras 28th March 1918

Lance Sergeant J. E. Woodall -1st Rifle Brigade - La Pennerie - 22nd April 1918

2nd Lieutenant J. P. Huffam - 2nd Duke of Wellington's - St Servins Farm 31st August 1918

Bibliography and Recommended Reading

Essex Units in the War 1914-1919, 2nd Battalion the Essex Regiment (Vol. 2), John Wm. Burrows, F.S.A., John H. Burrows & Sons, Ltd., Southend-on-Sea (1927)

Regimental History, The Royal Hampshire Regiment (Vol. 2), C. T. Atkinson (1952), Robert Maclehose Company Ltd., The University Press, Glasgow.

Reference has also been made to the Official History, which has allowed the many gaps in the diaries to be filled with a perspective not found in the diarists' rather formal methods of recording.

Sir Douglas Haig's Despatches, J. H. Boraston, C.B., O.B.E., J. M. Dent & Sons Ltd., London.

A Brigade of the Old Army 1914, Lieutenant-General Sir Aylmer Haldane K.C.B., D.S.O., Edward Arnold, London, 1920.

The Elkington family website at www. elkingtonfamily.com.

Index

Lightning Source UK Ltd.
Milton Keynes UK
UKOW03n0829270215

246988UK00007B/54/P